THE OFFICIAL DIRECTORY OF

THE NATIONAL BED & BREAKFAST ASSOCIATION

THE BED & BREAKFAST GUIDE

For The
United States, Canada,
Bermuda, Puerto Rico
& the U.S.V.I.

Listing With Descriptions
1517
Bed & Breakfast Homes & Inns
Plus
102
Reservation Services With
Over 6000 Additional Bed & Breakfast
Accommodations

By
Phyllis Featherston
&
Barbara F. Ostler

**THE NATIONAL BED & BREAKFAST ASSOCIATION
P.O. Box 332 • Norwalk, Connecticut 06852**

Copyright ©1989 by Phyllis Featherston and Barbara F. Ostler
All rights reserved.

Library of Congress Cataloging in Publication Data

ISBN #0-9611298-3-2

Cover and Book Design: Charles Featherston/Allen Hawthorne
Typography & Graphics: Type Academy, Inc., Wilton, CT

Printed in the United States
Published by The National Bed & Breakfast Association
         P.O. Box 332, Norwalk, Connecticut 06852

Distributed by The Talman Co., N.Y., N.Y.

*This book is dedicated
to the memory of
Charles M. Featherston II,
who founded
The National Bed & Breakfast Association.*

Preface

The National Bed & Breakfast Association's fourth publication of *The Bed & Breakfast Guide* for the United States, Canada, Bermuda, Puerto Rico and the U.S.V.I., celebrates ten years of Bed & Breakfast service to the traveler. It lists 1517 individual Bed & Breakfast homes and inns with 475 pictures. Each listing is a *true* Bed & Breakfast guaranteeing either a Full or Continental breakfast with the price of a night's lodging. Through the Reservation Service section of 102 Reservation Service Specialists, the traveler will find over 6000 additional Bed & Breakfast accommodations.

Bed & Breakfasts are very popular today as they have been for centuries all over the world. Because of the hospitality and uniqueness of these establishments, there has been an increasing demand for more of them. Consequently, the Bed & Breakfast business continues to grow and afford the traveler more alternatives to the commercial hotel and motel.

We have had the pleasure of meeting some wonderful people who with great friendliness have opened their doors and welcomed the traveler in for the night. In order to continue to bring the traveler more of the very best in Bed & Breakfast service, we will continue to search out additional Bed & Breakfast homes and inns and maintain our direct contact with all those already listed in our Guide.

We welcome new Bed & Breakfast Hosts. Anyone interested in becoming a member of The National Bed & Breakfast Association should return the "Request for Membership Application" at the back of this Guide.

Contents

		Page
I.	INTRODUCTION	
	English	vii
	Francais	viii
	Espanol	ix
II.	BECOMING A BED & BREAKFAST HOST	x
III.	BED & BREAKFAST HOMES & INNS IN THE UNITED STATES	
	Alabama	1
	Alaska	3
	Arizona	6
	Arkansas	9
	California	12
	Colorado	56
	Connecticut	64
	Delaware	72
	District of Columbia	75
	Florida	76
	Georgia	85
	Hawaii	92
	Idaho	97
	Illinois	100
	Indiana	106
	Iowa	110
	Kansas	114
	Kentucky	117
	Louisiana	119
	Maine	124
	Maryland	143
	Massachusetts	153
	Michigan	183
	Minnesota	191
	Mississippi	197
	Missouri	201
	Montana	208
	Nebraska	211
	Nevada	213
	New Hampshire	215
	New Jersey	235

Contents *(continued)*

New Mexico 241
New York 247
North Carolina 274
Ohio 290
Oklahoma 295
Oregon 297
Pennsylvania 304
Rhode Island 327
South Carolina 337
South Dakota 342
Tennessee 345
Texas 350
Utah 354
Vermont 358
Virginia 383
Washington 398
West Virginia 414
Wisconsin 417
Wyoming 421

III. BED & BREAKFAST HOMES & INNS IN
CANADA, BERMUDA, PUERTO RICO & U.S.V.I.
Alberta 424
British Columbia 427
New Brunswick 433
Nova Scotia 435
Ontario 438
Prince Edward Island 446
Quebec 448
Saskatchewan 452
Bermuda, Puerto Rico, U.S.V.I. 454

IV. RESERVATION SERVICES 458

V. CRITIQUE FORMS
English 485
Francais 485
Espanol 485

VI. MEMBERSHIP FORMS 486

VII. ABOUT THE AUTHORS .... Inside Back Cover

INTRODUCTION

The Bed and Breakfast Guide of the United States and Canada is the *first* guide to compile and list ONLY those privately-owned homes and small inns which provide a night's lodging and include in their rates a full or continental breakfast.

Traveling in a more formal way, using motels or hotels, etc., is expensive and often uneventful and dull. Your personal contacts most often are with a desk clerk or an elevator operator – in most cases, not very memorable and hardly to be compared with spending an evening with a Kansas farm family or in a fisherman's ocean-front home in Nova Scotia. Having used the B and B method of travel here and abroad, we speak from personal experience. We now count many of the B and B proprietors as friends, whom we would always be glad to revisit and whose warm hospitality we will always cherish.

Not all Bed and Breakfast homes and inns are the same. Some are big, some small; some are owned and operated by an experienced innkeeper, some by an energetic housewife whose family has grown and whose home has space now that it never had in the past. If you are looking for uniformity of accommodation, you will not find it here...but, this is the beauty of our Association! Bed and Breakfast homes and inns conform in certain important respects. They must be clean, provide either a full or continental breakfast, must adhere to the listed rates in the Guide – these rates will include all taxes and surcharges.

We want you to enjoy staying at B and B's as much as we do. We do not want you, our guests, to be disappointed in any way; therefore, we suggest to you the following:

1. Call or write to confirm that a room will be available.
2. Inspect the room before you take it. The proprietor will be agreeable.
3. Verify the room rate and the provision of breakfast.
4. If children are part of the group, verify their accommodations.

WE WISH YOU HAPPY TRAVELING WHILE STAYING AT THE BED AND BREAKFAST HOMES AND INNS IN THE UNITED STATES AND CANADA!!

Sincerely,

Phyllis Featherston
Phyllis Featherston, President

Barbara F. Ostler
Barbara F. Ostler, Vice President
National Bed & Breakfast Association

INTRODUCTION

Le Guide des Pensions des États Unis et du Canada est le premier guide qui compile et enregistre seulement les maisons et les petites auberges qui fournissent le logement pour la nuit et qui comprennent dans leurs tarifs un petit déjeuner complet ou léger.

Le voyage cérémonieux, avec les motels et les hôtels, etc., coûte cher et c'est souvent monotone et ennuyeux. Vos rapports personnels sont le plus souvent avec un concierge ou un opérateur d'ascenseur – d'habitude pas très mémorable et on ne peut pas comparer ces expériences á une nuit avec une famille à une ferme dans le Kansas ou une maison d'un pêcheur au bord de la mer en Nouvelle Écosse. Nous sommes restés à ces pensions ici et à l'étranger, et nous parlons de nos expériences personnelles. Maintenant beaucoup des propriétaires des pensions sont nos amis à qui nous voulons refaire des visites et nous chérirons toujours leur hospitalité.

Toutes les pensions et les auberges ne sont les mêmes. Quelquesunes sont grandes, les autres sont petites; quelquefois il y a un hôtelier, quelquefois il y a une ménagère dont les enfants sont partis et les chambres sont libres. Si vous cherchez l'uniformité de logement, vous ne la trouverez pas ici...mais voilà la beauté de notre association! Les pensions et les auberges respectent certains règlements. Il faut être propre; fournir un petit déjeuner complet ou léger; rester fidèle aux tarifs dans le Guide – taxes et services comprises.

Nous voulons que vous aimiez le séjour en pension autant que nous: Nous ne voulons pas que vous, nos invités, soyez déçus; alor nous vous recommandons le suivant:

1. Téléphoner ou écrire pour confirmer qu'une chambre vous attend.
2. Examiner le chambre avant de la prendre; le propriètaire le veut bien.
3. Vérifier le tarif et le petit déjeuner.
4. S'il y a des enfants dans le groupe, vérifier leurs chambres.

NOUS VOUS SOUHAITONS LE BON VOYAGE PENDANT VOTRE SÉJOUR DANS LES PENSIONS ET LES AUBERGES AUX ÉTATS-UNIS ET AU CANADA!!

À beintôt

Phyllis Featherston

Phyllis Featherston, President

Barbara F. Ostler

Barbara F. Ostler, Vice President
National Bed & Breakfast Association

INTRODUCCIÓN

La Guía de Pensiones de los Estados Unidos y de Canadá es la *primera* guía que compila y cataloga solamente las casas particulares y las posadas pequeñas que proveen alojamiento e incluyen en sus precios un desayuno completo o continental.

El viajar de un modo más formal, usando moteles o hoteles, etcétera, es caro y muchas veces, exento de acontecimientos notables, y aburrido. Sus contactos personales muchas veces son con un dependiente del escritorio del hotel o con un operador del ascensor – en la mayoría de los casos, no muy memorables y casi no pueden ser comparados con pasando una noche con na familia de una finca en Kansas o en una casa de un pescador frente al océano en Nova Scotia. Como hemos usado pensiones cuando viajando aquí y en el extranjero, hablamos de una experiencia personal. Ahora contamos a muchos de los propietarios de las pensiones como amigos, a quienes siempre estarémos alegres de visitar otra vez, y cuya hospitalidad ardiente siempre la apreciamos.

No todas las pensiones son iguales. Unas son grandes, otras pequeñas; unas son propiedad de y manejados por un posadero experto, otras por una ama de casa enérgica cuya familia ha crecida y cuya casa ahora tiene el espacio que nunca lo tenía en el pasado. Si Uds., buscan la uniformidad de acomodaciones, no la encontrarán aquí... pero, iesta es la belleza de nuestra asociación! Las pensiones conforman en ciertos, respectos importantes. Deben estar limpias, proveer o un desayuno completo o un desayuno continental, deben adherirse a los precias que están en la Guía – estos precios incluirán todos los impuestos y sobrecargas.

Queremos que Uds. gozan se estancia en las pensiones tanto como nosotros. No queremos que Uds., nuestros huespedes, sean desilusionados de ninguna manera; por eso, les sugerimos lo siguiente:

1. Llamar o escribir para confirmar que habrá una habitación.
2. Inspeccionar la habitación antes de tomarla. El propietario asentirá.
3. Verificar el precio de la habitación la provisión de desayuno.
4. Si niños son parte del grupo, verificar sus acomodaciones.

¡Les deseamos un buen viaje mientras que se queden en las pensiones de los Estados Unidos y de Canadá!

Adiós

Phyllis Featherston

Phyllis Featherston, President

Barbara F. Ostler

Barbara F. Ostler, Vice President
National Bed & Breakfast Association

Becoming A Bed & Breakfast Host
(For Private Homes & Family-Run Inns)

If you have an extra bedroom or two, or more, and can set aside a bath with tub or shower for guests, you have all the overhead you need to get into the Bed & Breakfast business.

If you like meeting people, you will like being a Bed & Breakfast host, while making money at the same time.

For those of any age who are looking to add to their income without leaving their home, starting a Bed & Breakfast might be the answer.

The Requirements Are Few:

1. A friendly greeting to the traveler.
2. Allow the traveler to inspect the room in advance of engaging it.
3. The bedroom must be clean with clean sheets and blankets. All bath facilities must be clean with hot water, tub and/or shower.
4. Breakfast must be included in the price of the room.
    Either: Continental (juice, toast/roll, coffee/tea)
    Or: A full breakfast
5. What you charge for the night's lodging is strictly up to you. All B.&B.s are different in location and facilities. However, the price you charge must include any taxes.* There can be no hidden charges.
6. The bill for your services is presented at breakfast time. (Breakfast time is usually between 8:00-9:00 a.m. and generally does not go beyond 9:30 a.m.)

Before making the final decision about going into the Bed & Breakfast business, you should give thought to whether or not this will be a part time or full time business. Will the operation be a seasonal one? Will your family cooperate if they are asked to share their home with a traveler?

Once you finalize these personal questions then proceed to your local zoning board and investigate zoning requirements and regulations. If there is a Bed & Breakfast establishment already in your city or town, get in touch with them and ask their help regarding what local ordinances might be pertinent to your Bed & Breakfast business interest, such as start-up expenses, type of insurance and fire codes.

For more in-depth information about establishing your own Bed & Breakfast Home or Inn, we suggest you contact A.M. Best Company, Inc., Ambest Road, Oldwick, NJ 08858, (201) 439-2200 for their Underwriting Guide.

*State and local taxes should be verified with your city or town regulations.

Bed & Breakfast Homes & Inns in the United States of America

Alabama

The Heart of Dixie

Capital: Montgomery
Statehood: December 14, 1819; the 22nd state
State Motto: We Dare Defend Our Rights
State Song: "Alabama"
State Bird: Yellowhammer
State Flower: Camellia
State Tree: Southern Pine

At one time everything in this state relied upon King Cotton; however, with the coming of the destructive Boll Weevil in the early 1900s, the Alabama farmer had to turn to planting other crops, including the peanut, to survive. As a result, the peanut crop was so successful it revived the economy and today Alabama is often referred to as "The Peanut Capital of the World."

Along Alabama's southern shores can be found beautiful beaches and resorts. Its chief seaport, Mobile, on the Gulf of Mexico, is an exciting and bustling seaport. Its harbor is filled with ships from all over the world. The lovely old homes there reflect the style and grace of the early Spanish and French settlers.

The largest and perhaps the wealthiest city in Alabama is Birmingham, often called The Pittsburgh of the South because of its great steel mills and heavy industry. This city, however, is also known for its pioneering work in health and medical research in open heart surgery.

Among some of the most famous citizens that came from Alabama are Helen Keller, George Carver, Hugo Black and Booker T. Washington.

Alabama

Greensboro

May, Janet & Thaddeus
Box 432, R.R. #2, 36744
(205) 624-3637

Amenities: 1,2,10
Breakfast: Continental

Dbl. Oc.: $50.00
Sgl. Oc.: $40.00
Third Person: $10.00

Blue Shadows Guest House—Country setting on 320 acres, nature trail, priv. fish pond, bird sanctuary, elegant accommodations, formal garden, afternoon tea served. Nearby Antebellum homes, historical sites, antiquing. Come visit.

AMENITIES

1. No Smoking
2. No Pets
3. No Children
4. Senior Citizen Rates
5. Tennis Available
6. Golf Available
7. Swimming Available
8. Skiing Available
9. Credit Cards Accepted
10. Personal Check Accepted
11. Off Season Rates
12. Dinner Available (w/sufficient notice)

Alaska

The Last Frontier

Capital: Juneau
Statehood: January 3, 1959; the 49th state
State Motto: North to the Future
State Song: "Alaska's Flag"
State Bird: Willow Ptarmigan
State Flower: Forget-Me-Not
State Tree: Sitka Spruce

Alaska, the largest state in the United States, is a fast growing and bustling state. Purchased from Russia in 1867 by Secretary William Seward for $7,200,000, it was at that time thought to be a foolish act and was called Seward's Folly. Today, it has vast fishing and lumber industries and her new and huge pipeline brings her latest natural resource, oil, to her sister states in the Union.

Tourists find their way to Alaska by means of plane or automobile across the Alaskan Highway, or by ferryboat up from the southwest coast of Washington and Canada.

Alaska has thousands of wild and untamed wilderness acres. Fisherman and hunters hunt the salmon, tuna, brown bear and caribous. The highest mountain peaks of North America are in this state and are a constant challenge to mountain climbers.

Alaska

Anchorage

Schlehofer, Patricia & Frank
2440 Sprucewood, 99508
(907) 276-8527

Amenities: 1,2,4,5,6,7,8,9,10
Breakfast: Full
Dbl. Oc.: $49.00   **Sgl. Oc.:** $40.00
Third Person: $10.00

THE LOG HOME BED & BREAKFAST
PATT AND FRANK SCHLEHOFER
2440 SPRUCEWOOD STREET, ANCHORAGE, AK 99508
PHONE: 907-276-8527

A Log Home Bed & Breakfast—Country charm in city setting-transplanted New England hosts in antique furnished home. Walk to bike & hiking trails, theatres, & universities. Three rooms-shared bath. Enjoy our deck. Send for brochure.

Fairbanks

Horutz, Mrs. Eleanor
360 State St., 99701
(907) 452-2598

Amenities: 2,9,10,11
Breakfast: Full

Dbl. Oc.: $51.84
Sgl. Oc.: $38.88
Third Person: $10.80

Eleanor's Inn Bed & Breakfast—Walking distance to town, visitors center & stores. Clean, comfortable rooms each with TV. Children are welcome. Nice quiet neighborhood. Will pick up at train or airport with notice.

Gustavus

Unrein, Annie & Al
Box 5, 99826
(907) 697-2288

Amenities: 1,2,10,11,12
Breakfast: Full
Dbl. Oc.: $168.00   **Sgl. Oc.:** $89.00
Third Person: $49.00-$69.00

Glacier Bay Country Inn—Peaceful, storybook setting-away from the crowds. Personalized service. Fresh seafood & garden produce, homemade breads. Glacier Bay boat tours, fishing, kayaking, hiking. Transportation arranged.

Homer

Seekins, Gert & Floyd
Box 1264, 99603
(907) 235-8996

Amenities: 4,5,7,8,9,10,11
Breakfast: Continental

Dbl. Oc.: $51.00
Sgl. Oc.: $45.90
Third Person: $15.30

Homer Bed & Breakfast—Fantastic view: mountains, glaciers, beautiful Kachemak Bay. Modern cabin guest houses with complete kitchen facilities, TV, private bathrooms, outdoor wood sauna. Birds, moose, wildflowers, halibut & salmon charter tours.

AMENITIES

1. No Smoking
2. No Pets
3. No Children
4. Senior Citizen Rates
5. Tennis Available
6. Golf Available
7. Swimming Available
8. Skiing Available
9. Credit Cards Accepted
10. Personal Check Accepted
11. Off Season Rates
12. Dinner Available (w/sufficient notice)

Alaska

Juneau

Urquhart, Judy
8187 Threadneedle St., 99801
(907) 463-5886

Amenities: 8,9,10,12
Breakfast: Full

Dbl. Oc.: $65.00
Sgl. Oc.: $55.00
Third Person: $10.00

Blueberry Lodge—A rustic Alaskan experience with all amenities, only minutes away from Alaska's capital city. Handcrafted log lodge overlooking inland ocean waterway. Ski area five miles away. Complimentary shuttle.

Via Tok

Shook, Ann
MP 1260 Alaskan Hwy., 99780
(907) 778-2205

Amenities: 8,9,12
Breakfast: Full

Dbl. Oc.: $45.00
Sgl. Oc.: $35.00
Third Person: $10.00

1260 Inn—The 1st & last all service lodge on the ALCAN-4 mi. E. of Northway Jct. Decorated in Alaskan antiques, see photos, letters, & newspapers dating back to 1793. Miles of wilderness, hunting, fishing, hiking & boating. Lunch available.

AMENITIES

1. No Smoking
2. No Pets
3. No Children
4. Senior Citizen Rates
5. Tennis Available
6. Golf Available
7. Swimming Available
8. Skiing Available
9. Credit Cards Accepted
10. Personal Check Accepted
11. Off Season Rates
12. Dinner Available (w/sufficient notice)

Arizona

The Grand Canyon State

Capital: Phoenix
Statehood: February 14, 1912; the 48th state
State Motto: God Enriches
State Song: "Arizona"
State Bird: Cactus Wren
State Flower: Saguaro
State Tree: Paloverde

Arizona is a vacation land of wonder and beauty. It has one of the oldest communities in the country, going back to the 1100's. Inhabited then by the Hopi Indians, it still is a home for many American Indians today.

No other state has as many national monuments as this state. It not only boasts of the Grand Canyon, one of the natural wonders of the world, but also giant dams such as Coolidge, Glen Canyon, Hoover, Parker and Roosevelt.

Hundreds of visitors and vacationers come here every year. Many remain and make it their second home. Its warm and easy climate make it a haven for senior citizens.

Arizona

Chandler

Cone, Beverly & Howard
2804 W. Warner, 85224
(602) 839-0369

Amenities: 5,6,7
Breakfast: Continental

Dbl. Oc.: $30.00
Sgl. Oc.: $30.00

Cone's Tourist Home—Beautiful contemporary home situated on two acres, 12 miles southwest of the airport. Howard & Beverly offer private phone & TV in guest room, Arizona room, large parlor, kitchen & barbecue facilities.

Flagstaff

Dierker, Dorothy
423 W. Cherry, 86001
(602) 774-3249

Amenities: 1,2,8,10
Breakfast: Full

Dbl. Oc.: $40.00
Sgl. Oc.: $26.00
Third Person: $10.00

Dierker House—Spacious & charming old house with airy comfortable rooms, king size beds, privacy, quiet, & many extra amenities. Conveniently located in old part of city near restaurants, university, & Lowell Observatory.

Phoenix

Curran, Brian & Darrell Trapp
P.O. Box 41624, 85080
(602) 582-3868

Amenities: 4,5,6,7,9,10,11,12
Breakfast: Full
Dbl. Oc.: From $78.00
Sgl. Oc.: From $66.00
Third Person: $10.00

Westways—A deluxe private resort with a southwestern atmosphere. A place in the sun offering beauty, hospitality and a sense of paradise. Casual western comfort with a touch of class! Our guests rate us 5 stars plus.

Phoenix

Talbott, Mrs. Pauline
4702 E. Edgemont, 85008
(602) 840-3254

Amenities: 1,2,5,10
Breakfast: Continental

Dbl. Oc.: $35.00
Sgl. Oc.: $35.00

Talbot's Stop-Over is in N.E. Phoenix 5 mi. from airport, close to Scottsdale, Arizona State Univ., Indian ruins, museums, theaters, shopping, 24 Hr. restaurant. Guestroom has priv. entrance, TV, bath, fireplace & refrig.

Prescott

Faulkner, Sue & Mo
503 S. Montezuma, 86303
(602) 445-7991

Amenities: 1,2,4,5,6,7,9,10,11
Breakfast: Continental

Dbl. Oc.: $54.00-$84.00
Third Person: $12.00

The Prescott Country Inn—Old fashioned cozy comfort & charm in individual cottage. King & queen suites. 3 blks. from historic Courthouse Plaza. Surrounded by pine covered mountains, lakes & dells on scenic Rte. 89 to Grand Canyon.

AMENITIES

1. No Smoking
2. No Pets
3. No Children
4. Senior Citizen Rates
5. Tennis Available
6. Golf Available
7. Swimming Available
8. Skiing Available
9. Credit Cards Accepted
10. Personal Check Accepted
11. Off Season Rates
12. Dinner Available (w/sufficient notice)

Arizona

Prescott

Ford, Joan & Dave
212 S. Pleasant, 86303
(602) 776-1564

Amenities: 1,2,10
Breakfast: Full

Dbl. Oc.: $41.60
Sgl. Oc.: $26.00
Third Person: $10.40

Ford's Bed & Breakfast—A gracious turn-of-the-century house in Prescott's historic neighborhood. Three blocks from City Plaza, close to antique shops, restaurants, museum, Center for Fine Arts.

Prescott

Temple, Mrs. Catherine
P.O. Box 4301, 86202
(602) 778-9573

Amenities: 1,7,9,10,11,12
Breakfast: Full

Dbl. Oc.: $88.40
Sgl. Oc.: $72.80
Third Person: $10.00

Lynx Creek Farm—Secluded country elegance on 20 acre farm. 7 miles to historic Prescott. Gourmet breakfast, antique-filled guest rooms. Large heated spa. Perfect for children!

Sedona

Garland, Mary & Gary
P.O. Box 152, 86336
(602) 282-3343

Amenities: 5,6,7,9,10,12
Breakfast: Full

Dbl. Oc.: $180.00
Third Person: $40.00

Garland's Oak Creek Lodge—"Same time next year" conjurs up the warm & elegant ambiance of this historic lodge. 15 individual log cabins, apple orchards, scenery. We encourage week-day visitors. The food is fresh and fabulous.

Tucson

Bryant, M/M Charles
1640 N. Campbell Ave., 85719
(602) 795-3840

Amenities: 1,2,3,9,10,11
Breakfast: Continental

Dbl. Oc.: $75.00-$95.00
Sgl. Oc.: $81.75-$103.55

La Posada Del Valle—An elegant 1920's Inn nestled among orange trees & flower gardens; patios for sunning, 5 antique filled rooms w/private baths, gourmet breakfast, afternoon tea, close to Univ. of Arizona. Full breakfast served on weekends.

Tucson

Ford, Sheila & Tom
1202 N. Avenida Marlene, 85715
(602) 885-1202

Amenities: 1,2,3
Breakfast: Continental

Dbl. Oc.: $40.00
Sgl. Oc.: $30.00
Third Person: $30.00

Ford's Eastside Bed and Breakfast—Warm welcome at our private home B. & B. Two bedrooms, double & twin beds, private bath, entrance and sitting room.

AMENITIES

1. No Smoking
2. No Pets
3. No Children
4. Senior Citizen Rates
5. Tennis Available
6. Golf Available
7. Swimming Available
8. Skiing Available
9. Credit Cards Accepted
10. Personal Check Accepted
11. Off Season Rates
12. Dinner Available (w/sufficient notice)

Arkansas

Land of Opportunity

Capital: Little Rock
Statehood: January 15, 1836; the 25th state
State Motto: The People Rule
State Song: "Arkansas"
State Bird: Mockingbird
State Flower: Apple Blossom
State Tree: Pine

    Arkansas is a southern state with comfortable weather, warm enough to make the visitor feel unhurried and relaxed. There are beautiful rugged mountains and the Ozark Valley, where hot and cold springs invite tourists to come and soothe their aches and pains. The Buffalo National River flows across the northern boundary of Arkansas and through the Ozark Plateau. Here one can swim, canoe, fish and shoot the rapids. Here, too, the Ozark Folk Center at Mountain View has preserved the ingenuity of the country people of this state and their mountain music, crafts and folklore. Twenty-five million tourists each year come here to see and enjoy this center.
    There are two large cities in Arkansas, Little Rock and Fort Smith. Perhaps one of the most unique towns in all of the U.S. is Texarkana, built just across from the state of Texas, yet on the border of both states. One half of the town is in Texas and the other in Arkansas.
    Arkansas' national hero is Gen. Douglas MacArthur. He was born in Little Rock in 1880.

Arkansas

Brinkley

Prince, Stanley
127 W. Cedar
(501) 734-4955

Amenities: 1,2,9,10
Breakfast: Full
Dbl. Oc.: $42.40   **Sgl. Oc.:** $38.16

The Great Southern Hotel offers true southern hospitality. Restored Victorian rooms, fine, serene dining; lunch, dinner, full breakfast brought to your room. I-40 Exit 216, 1.3 miles turn on Cedar Street left.

Great Southern Hotel
Brinkley, Arkansas
72021

Clarksville

Harris, M/M Phillip
101 Railroad, 72830
(501) 754-6851

Amenities: 1,2,4,9,10,12
Breakfast: Continental
Dbl. Oc.: $44.20   **Sgl. Oc.:** $39.00
Third Person: $5.00

The May House, historic restored Victorian. Spacious bedrooms, private baths, fine linens, special touches. Just off I-40 near Ozark Nat'l Forest. Small town. Mountain views, hiking trails.

Eureka Springs

Simantel, M/M Bill
35 Kingshighway, 72632
(501) 253-8916

Amenities: 2,9,10,11
Breakfast: Full

Dbl. Oc.: $55.00-$81.00
Sgl. Oc.: $50.00-$75.00
Third Person: $12.00

Hearthstone Inn And Cottages—Well known turn-of-the-century inn in historic district of famous Victorian town. Great passion play, country music shows, antique shops, fine dining all nearby. Breakfast served. On trolley route.

Helena

Heidelberger, Martha
317 S. Biscoe, 72342
(501) 338-9155

Amenities: 4,9,10
Breakfast: Continental

Dbl. Oc.: $53.00-$62.54
Sgl. Oc.: $46.64-$53.00
Third Person: $10.60

Edwardian Inn—A turn-of-the-century national register mansion with 12 rooms & private baths. Interior architectural features attest to its being among the most elaborate homes of its time in the south.

AMENITIES

1. No Smoking
2. No Pets
3. No Children
4. Senior Citizen Rates
5. Tennis Available
6. Golf Available
7. Swimming Available
8. Skiing Available
9. Credit Cards Accepted
10. Personal Check Accepted
11. Off Season Rates
12. Dinner Available (w/sufficient notice)

Arkansas

Kingston

Sullivan, Mary Jo
HCR 30, Box 198, 72742
(501) 665-2986

Amenities: 1,3,4,9,10,11
Breakfast: Full
Dbl. Oc.: $60.00   **Sgl. Oc.:** $35.00
Third Person: $15.00

Fools Cove Ranch—A rustic setting high in the Ozark Mountains, with fine accommodations, great food. Family farm with a beautiful view, natural trails. Short drive to area attractions. Corrals available, pets welcome.

AMENITIES

1. No Smoking	**4.** Senior Citizen Rates	**7.** Swimming Available	**10.** Personal Check Accepted
2. No Pets	**5.** Tennis Available	**8.** Skiing Available	**11.** Off Season Rates
3. No Children	**6.** Golf Available	**9.** Credit Cards Accepted	**12.** Dinner Available (w/sufficient notice)

California

The Golden State

Capital: Sacramento
Statehood: September 9, 1850; the 31st state
State Motto: Eureka (I Have Found It)
State Song: "I Love You, California"
State Bird: California Valley Quail
State Flower: Golden Poppy
State Tree: California Redwood

The gold rush of 1848 started millions of people moving to California. Today more people live in the state than any other state in the union.

Farmers here have created some of the largest and most productive farms in all of our country. Their fruits, vegetables and nuts are shipped all over the U.S. California has the distinction of having the highest farm income in the nation.

Visitors visit California by the thousands every year. The wonderful climate and diversified beauty of this state, from the majestic redwood forest of the north and the giant sequoias of the Sierra Nevadas to the beautiful beaches and deserts in the south, make it a favorite vacation land.

The movie industry, located around Los Angeles, has brought excitement and glamour here as well as entertainment for the entire country since the early 1900's.

One of the most famous events of the year is perhaps the Tournament of Roses Parade in Pasadena on New Year's Day.

Our 37th President, Richard M. Nixon, is a native Californian, born in Yorbe Linda.

California

Alameda

Gladden, M/M Royce
900 Union, 94501
(415) 521-4779

Amenities: 1,2,5,6,7,9,10
Breakfast: Full

Dbl. Oc.: $65.00-$80.00
Third Person: $10.00

Garratt Mansion—10 miles from San Francisco or Berkeley. On the tranquil island of Alameda, we provide the convenience of home with the service of a 5 star hotel. An oasis for the mind and body.

Albion

Brazil, Frances & Scott
33810 Navarro Ridge Rd.,
P.O. Box 99, 95410
(707) 937-4041

Amenities: 1,2,3,6,9,10,11
Breakfast: Full

Dbl. Oc.: $86.40-$135.00
Sgl. Oc.: $81.00-$129.60
Third Person: $16.20

Fensalden Inn—A quietly beautiful inn on the Mendocino Coast. Located on 20 pastoral acres overlooking the Pacific Ocean. Originally an 1860's stagecoach stop, now a cozy seven bedroom and two common room retreat.

Angwin (Napa Valley)

Fisher, Mrs. Jacqueline
P.O. Box 302, 570 Aptos Creek Rd., 95001
(408) 688-7982

Amenities: 4,5,6,7,9,10
Breakfast: Full
Dbl. Oc.: $91.68-$107.00
Third Person: $15.00

Mangels House—Built in 1886. We are situated on 4 acres of lawn & orchard & bounded by Redwood State Park. Close to beaches, golf & many good restaurants. Mangels House is an ideal retreat from the city.

Arroyo Grande

Stalker, Jude & Don
407 El Camino Real, 93420
(805) 489-5926

Amenities: 1,2,9,10,11,12
Breakfast: Full
Dbl. Oc.: $68.90-$90.10
Sgl. Oc.: $58.30
Third Person: $10.60

The Village Inn

The Village Inn—Located in the heart of Calif. central coast. 7 spacious guest rooms, all private baths, queen beds. Decorated with old-fashioned country charm. Close to Hearst Castle, beach, & wineries. AAA approved.

AMENITIES

1. No Smoking
2. No Pets
3. No Children
4. Senior Citizen Rates
5. Tennis Available
6. Golf Available
7. Swimming Available
8. Skiing Available
9. Credit Cards Accepted
10. Personal Check Accepted
11. Off Season Rates
12. Dinner Available (w/sufficient notice)

California

Auburn

Maggenti, Mrs. Lois
13740 Dry Creek Rd., 95603
(916) 878-0885

Amenities: 1,2,5,6,7,10
Breakfast: Full

Dbl. Oc.: $60.00-$70.00
Sgl. Oc.: $55.00-$65.00

Dry Creek Inn is on four wooded acres with wild stream and birdsong. Two superior accommodations only. Memorable breakfasts. Located in heart of Gold Country. Historical sights and antiques galore.

Auburn

Sanderson, Mrs. Doreen
164 Cleveland Ave., 95603
(916) 885-1166

Amenities: 1,2,4,5,6,8,9,10
Breakfast: Full

Dbl. Oc.: $68.25-$157.70
Sgl. Oc.: $68.25-$78.75
Third Person: $78.75

Power's Mansion Inn—An elegant bed and breakfast. Century old Victorian with 13 gorgeous rooms each with private bath. Antiques and history in this restored gold-mining mansion where hospitality and comfort abound.

Avalon
(Santa Catalina Island)

Michalis, Hattie & Bob
344 Whittley Ave.,
P.O. Box 1381, 90704
(213) 510-2547

Amenities: 2,3,4,7,11
Breakfast: Continental

Dbl. Oc.: $90.00-$135.00
Sgl. Oc.: $90.00-$135.00

Gull House—Whether you're discovering the romance of Santa Catalina Island for the first time or returning, you'll find hosts Hattie & Bob offering a "touch of class!" Avalon is a square mile. Brochure avail. send #10 SASE

Avalon

Olsens, The
125 Calressa, 90704
(213) 510-0356

Amenities: 1,2,3,5,6,7,9,10,11
Breakfast: Continental
Dbl. Oc.: $135.00-$240.00
Sgl. Oc.: $135.00-$240.00

Originally Built in 1927

Garden House Inn—Steps from beach. Ocean views, priv. bath, TV, queen beds, priv. terraces, comfortable living room w/fireplace. Lge. courtyard & garden. Afternoon hors d'oeuvres, evening snack, large breakfast. Walk to all entertainment.

AMENITIES

1. No Smoking
2. No Pets
3. No Children
4. Senior Citizen Rates
5. Tennis Available
6. Golf Available
7. Swimming Available
8. Skiing Available
9. Credit Cards Accepted
10. Personal Check Accepted
11. Off Season Rates
12. Dinner Available (w/sufficient notice)

California

Ben Lomond

Feely, Frank
245 Fairview Ave., 95005
(408) 336-3355

Amenities: 1,2,3,5,6,7,9,10
Breakfast: Full

Dbl. Oc.: $89.00
Sgl. Oc.: $89.00

Fairview Manor—A charming bed and breakfast inn on three beautifully landscaped acres on the river in the Santa Cruz Mountains. Five guest rooms all with private bath. Redwood country home.

Big Bear City

Knight, Phyllis
869 S. Knickerbocker Rd., 92315
(714) 866-8221

Amenities: 1,2,5,6,7,8,10
Breakfast: Full
Dbl. Oc.: $80.10-$116.60
Sgl. Oc.: $68.90-$80.10
Third Person: $21.20

Knickerbocker Mansion—A historic 10 room log home & carriage house on 2 acres of rolling lawn surrounded by national forest. Walking distance to village & restaurants. A peaceful retreat with old world charm.

Big Bear City

Montgomery, Lynn
1117 Anita,
P.O. Box 2027, 92314
(714) 585-6997

Amenities: 1,4,5,6,7,8,10,11
Breakfast: Full

Dbl. Oc.: $75.00-$150.00
Sgl. Oc.: 70.00-$135.00
Third Person: $20.00

Gold Mountain Manor Historic Bed & Breakfast—Lavish historic log mansion; 8 spectacular fireplaces. "Breakfast is a feast." Pamper yourself with luxury! 7,000 Ft. high in Blue Sky Mountains! Pristine lake, great skiing. Reservations essential.

Bishop

Robidart, Ms. Nanette
1313 Rowan Ln., 93514
(619) 873-3133

Amenities: 1,2,3,6,8,10,11
Breakfast: Full

Dbl. Oc.: $55.00-$75.00
Sgl. Oc.: $55.00-$75.00

The Matlick House—Historic ranch house build in 1906. Five rooms, private baths, nestled at the base of the Sierra Nevadas. Winter recreational areas, spring and summer fishing & hiking.

AMENITIES

1. No Smoking
2. No Pets
3. No Children
4. Senior Citizen Rates
5. Tennis Available
6. Golf Available
7. Swimming Available
8. Skiing Available
9. Credit Cards Accepted
10. Personal Check Accepted
11. Off Season Rates
12. Dinner Available (w/sufficient notice)

California

Burbank

Bell, Harry
941 N. Frederic St., 91505
(818) 848-9227

Amenities: 2,10
Breakfast: Full

Dbl. Oc.: $35.00
Sgl. Oc.: $25.00
Third Person: $10.00

Belair—Comfortable home in residential Burbank near Universal and NBC Studios, 10 miles from LA, 5 miles from Hollywood. Host teacher, musician, world traveler, adventurer, collector of exotic art.

Burlingame

Fernandez, Elnora & Joe
1021 Balboa Ave., 94010
(415) 344-5815

Amenities: 5,6,7,10
Breakfast: Continental

Dbl. Oc.: $40.00
Sgl. Oc.: $30.00
Third Person: $10.00

Burlingame Bed & Breakfast—Private upstairs bedroom, king size bed, a priv. bathroom. Separate eating area looks out on a creek. Color TV, alarm clock radio. Public transportation one block away. 101 Hwy., 6 blocks east. Quiet.

Calistoga

Dwyer, Ms. Scarlett
3918 Silverado Tr. N., 94515
(707) 942-6669

Amenities: 2,5,6,7,8,9,10
Breakfast: Continental

Dbl. Oc.: $81.30-$102.90
Sgl. Oc.: $69.90-$86.70
Third Person: $15.00

Scarlette's Country Inn—Three exquisitely appointed suites set in the quiet mood of green lawns and tall pines overlooking the vineyards. Queen beds, private baths, secluded woodland and swimming pool. Close to wineries and spas.

Calistoga

Fouts, M/M George
3400 Mtn. Home Ranch Rd., 94515
(707) 942-6616

Amenities: 2,5,7,9,10
Breakfast: Full

Dbl. Oc.: $65.00
Sgl. Oc.: $43.00
Third Person: $12.00

Mountain Home Ranch—Warm and rural family inn, minutes from Wine Country. Lake fishing, trails in Redwood Canyon. Summer rates include full dinner and breakfast. Brochure.

Calistoga

Rogers, Philip
1250 Lincoln Ave., 94515
(707) 942-4101

Amenities: 5,6,7,9,10,12
Breakfast: Continental

Dbl. Oc.: $44.00
Sgl. Oc.: $38.50

Calistoga Inn & Pub-Brewery— "The locals choice" offering the friendliest pub in the valley. Charming inexpensive rooms, fresh seafood, fresh beer. The complete & perfect getaway.

AMENITIES

1. No Smoking
2. No Pets
3. No Children
4. Senior Citizen Rates
5. Tennis Available
6. Golf Available
7. Swimming Available
8. Skiing Available
9. Credit Cards Accepted
10. Personal Check Accepted
11. Off Season Rates
12. Dinner Available (w/sufficient notice)

California

Calistoga

Sofie, Jan & Scott
109 Wapoo Ave., 94515
(707) 942-4200

Amenities: 5,6,7,9,10,11,12
Breakfast: Full
Dbl. Oc.: $110.00-$115.50
Sgl. Oc.: $95.00-$100.50
Third Person: $15.00

Brannan Cottage Inn—In heart of Napa Valley Wine Country, part of 1860 Hot Springs Resort and on Nat'l. Registry. Original stencils, Victorian cottage decor. 4 rooms, 2 suites, all private baths and entrances.

Calistoga

Swiers, Mrs. Alma
4455 No. St. Helena Hwy., 94515
(707) 942-0316

Amenities: 1,2,3,5,6,7,9,10
Breakfast: Full

Dbl. Oc.: $98.00-$108.00
Sgl. Oc.: $81.00-$97.00
Third Person: $15.00

Quail Mountain B&B—is a secluded luxury 3 guest room B. & B. located on 26 wooded acres near tourist activities. King size beds, down comforters, private baths and decks, complimentary wine & hospitality are featured.

Calistoga

Wheatley, M/M
1805 Foothill Blvd., 94515
(707) 942-4535

Amenities: 1,2,7,10,11
Breakfast: Full

Dbl. Oc.: $93.50-$104.50
Third Person: $20.00

"Culvers" A Country Inn—completely restored 1875 Victorian Inn. Comfortable elegant atmosphere, with lovely antiques. Full breakfast, sauna, spa, pool, porch, air conditioning, warm British hospitality.

Cambria

Kilpatrick, Valarie & Ken
2476 Main St., 93428
(805) 927-3222

Amenities: 1,2,3,4,5,7,9,10
Breakfast: Continental

Dbl. Oc.: $75.00-$95.00

Olallieberry Inn—Registered historical home built in 1873, newly renovated. 6 guest rooms, private baths. Antique furnishings. Walk to village. Near Hearst Castle, beaches, wineries, fine bicycling area.

AMENITIES

1. No Smoking
2. No Pets
3. No Children
4. Senior Citizen Rates
5. Tennis Available
6. Golf Available
7. Swimming Available
8. Skiing Available
9. Credit Cards Accepted
10. Personal Check Accepted
11. Off Season Rates
12. Dinner Available (w/sufficient notice)

California

Cambria

Larsen, Anna
2555 MacLeod Way, 93428
(805) 927-8619

Amenities: 2,5,6,7,9,11
Breakfast: Full

Dbl. Oc.: $68.90-$95.40
Sgl. Oc.: $68.90-$95.30
Third Person: $15.00

Pickford House—Charming silent film era decor. Priv. baths & showers. 1869 bar from Buffalo Hilton in antique filled parlor where breakfast is served by a cozy fire. 10 min. to Hearst Castle. AAA rating. Surf-fishing, sun bathing.

Carlsbad

Hale, Mrs. Celeste
320 Walnut Ave., 92008
(619) 434-5995

Amenities: 2,3,4,5,6,7,9,10
Breakfast: Full
Dbl. Oc.: $85.00-$140
Sgl. Oc.: $75.00-$130.00
Third Person: $10.00

Pelican Cove Inn—A very special bed and breakfast; feather beds, fireplaces, private baths and entries, walk to beach, restaurants, village shops, gift certificates, Amtrack pickup.

Carmel

Black, Ruth & Dieter
P.O. Box 782,
Camino Real at 7th Ave., 93921
(408) 624-6267

Amenities: 1,2,3,10
Breakfast: Full

Dbl. Oc.: $93.50
Sgl. Oc.: $88.00
Third Person: $10.00

Holiday House—Shingled 1905 house on hillside amidst colorful garden. Rooms with slanted ceilings and dormer windows. Ocean View. Central location in quiet residential area. 3 blks to beach, 1 blk to restaurants, shops.

Carmel-By-The-Sea

Jones, Honey
Dolores & 4th, 93921
(408) 624-7738

Amenities: 3,5,6,9,10,11
Breakfast: Continental
Dbl. Oc.: $88.00-$132.00
Sgl. Oc.: $88.00-$132,00
Third Person: $20.00

Vagabond's House Inn—11 unique rooms with fireplaces surround a courtyard dominated by large Oak trees where Camelias, Rhodedendrons, hanging plants, ferns and flowers abound. Near shops, restaurants and art galleries.

AMENITIES

1. No Smoking
2. No Pets
3. No Children
4. Senior Citizen Rates
5. Tennis Available
6. Golf Available
7. Swimming Available
8. Skiing Available
9. Credit Cards Accepted
10. Personal Check Accepted
11. Off Season Rates
12. Dinner Available (w/sufficient notice)

California

Carpinteria

Schroeder, Bev. & Don
1825 Cravens Lane, 93013
(805) 684-1579

Amenities: 1,2,5,6,7,10
Breakfast: Full
Dbl. Oc.: $60.00-$65.00
Sgl. Oc.: $60.00
Third Person: $20.00

D. & B. Schroeder Ranch—Ocean view semi-tropical fruit ranch. Guest suite has TV, fridge, deck & spa in garden. Carpinteria has a good beach, surfing, shops & food. 11 miles south of Santa Barbara. Also beach condo available nightly.

Clio

Miller, Karen & Don, Vanella, Linda & Tom
Box 136, 96106
(916) 836-2387

Amenities: 1,2,5,6,7,9,10
Breakfast: Full
Dbl. Oc.: 75.00-$140.00
Sgl. Oc.: $75.00-$140.00
Third Person: $15.00

White Sulphur Springs Ranch Bed & Breakfast—For a unique journey into the past... come stay with us. An atmosphere of comfort, with elegance. Relax by the warm mineral pool, or walk among the pine trees. 50 miles from Lake Tahoe or Reno.

Cloverdale

Sauder, Ina & Allen
2955 River Rd., 95425
(707) 894-5956

Amenities: 2,5,6,9,10
Breakfast: Full

Dbl. Oc.: $80.80-$91.60

Ye Old Shelford House—Circa 1885. Stately Victorian with wrap-around porch overlooking vineyards. Bicycles, hot tub. Surrey rides to local wineries ($55.00 per couple). Crisp & clean, light & airy inn.

AMENITIES

1. No Smoking
2. No Pets
3. No Children
4. Senior Citizen Rates
5. Tennis Available
6. Golf Available
7. Swimming Available
8. Skiing Available
9. Credit Cards Accepted
10. Personal Check Accepted
11. Off Season Rates
12. Dinner Available (w/sufficient notice)

California

Davenport

McDougal, M/M
31 Davenport Ave., 95017
(408) 425-1818

Amenities: 1,2,7,8,9,10,12
Breakfast: Full
Dbl. Oc.: $58.58-$111.82
Third Person: $10.65

New Davenport Bed & Breakfast — An ocean-view hideaway halfway between Carmel/Monterey and San Francisco. Twelve rooms, private baths. Ocean access, restaurant, gallery, whale-watching, surfing, hiking.

Del Mar

Hauser, M/M Thomas
410 15th St., 92014
(619) 481-3764

Amenities: 1,2,3,5,6,7,9,10,11
Breakfast: Continental

Dbl. Oc.: $81.00-$145.80
Sgl. Oc.: $81.00-$145.80

Rock Haua—Romantic getaway to quaint seaside village. 10 rooms, 4 with private baths, 1 with fireplace, most have ocean view, down comforters. Stroll to beach, restaurants, Amtrak.

El Granada

Hayward, Susan
89 Ave. Portola
Box 1402, 94018
(415) 726-3690

Amenities: 1,2,9
Breakfast: Full
Dbl. Oc.: $81.00   **Sgl. Oc.:** $81.00
Third Person: $10.00

The Village Green Inn—An authentic English inn, family-run with ocean view suites. Located one block from the beach and harbor in a small village, 4 miles north of Half Moon Bay and 20 miles south of San Francisco.

AMENITIES

1. No Smoking
2. No Pets
3. No Children
4. Senior Citizen Rates
5. Tennis Available
6. Golf Available
7. Swimming Available
8. Skiing Available
9. Credit Cards Accepted
10. Personal Check Accepted
11. Off Season Rates
12. Dinner Available (w/sufficient notice)

California

Elk

Triebess, Miss Hildrum-Uta
6300 S. Highway 1,
Box 367, 95432
(707) 877-3321

Amenities: 1,2,5,6,7,9,10,11,12
Breakfast: Full
Dbl. Oc.: $105.44-$127.04
Sgl. Oc.: $95.04-$111.04

Elk Cove Inn overlooks the dramatic natural beauty of the Mendocino Coast. Gourmet meals either French or German. Guest rooms attractively furnished in antique fashion. Romantic rural setting perfect for hiking, biking, whale & bird watching. Dinner $21.20/person.

Eureka

Carter, Christi & Mark
1033 3rd St., 95501
(707) 445-1390

Amenities: 1,2,3,4,9,10,11,12
Breakfast: Full
Dbl. Oc.: $75.00   **Sgl. Oc.:** $58.00
Third Person: $10.00

Carter House Bed & Breakfast Inn—This spectacular inn was chosen as "Inn of the Year" for 1986. Each morning a gourmet breakfast is served in three courses. California Magazine calls this breakfast the "Best breakfast in California."

Eureka

Vieyra, Doug
17687 Kneeland Rd., 95549
(707) 443-6512 or 444-3144

Amenities: 1,2,3,7,10,11,12
Breakfast: Full
Dbl. Oc.: $105.00

Chalet de France—Exquisite carve & folk-painted Swiss Chalet on 3000' mountain top overlooking 40 mile views & Pacific Ocean peace, quiet & luxury surrounded by 1000 square miles of wilderness; 20 mi. from nearest town.

AMENITIES

1. No Smoking
2. No Pets
3. No Children
4. Senior Citizen Rates
5. Tennis Available
6. Golf Available
7. Swimming Available
8. Skiing Available
9. Credit Cards Accepted
10. Personal Check Accepted
11. Off Season Rates
12. Dinner Available (w/sufficient notice)

California

Ferndale

Thoma, Cara & Jeff
619 Main St., 95536
(707) 786-4307

Amenities: 1,2,3,9,10,11
Breakfast: Continental
Dbl. Oc.: $47.70-$84.80
Sgl. Oc.: $37.10-$47.70

Ferndale Inn—A classic Victorian home built in 1859. Five guest rooms include two private suites. Afternoon tea or wine, bicycles available and a delicious and filling breakfast. Just off 101 in Victorian Ferndale.

Fort Bragg

Bailey, Colette & John
615 N. Main St., 95437
(707) 964-0640

Amenities: 1,2,3,5,6,7,9,11
Breakfast: Full
Dbl. Oc.: $64.80-$135.00
Sgl. Oc.: $48.60-$97.20
Third Person: $21.60-$27.00

Grey Whale Inn—Premier inn on Mendocino Coast. 14 spacious rooms w/priv. baths. Each rm. has special amenity: ocean, garden, or hills view, fireplace, deck, wheel chair access., whirlpool tub, or patio. Walk to beach, skunk train.

Fort Bragg

Gunderson, M/M Eugene
700 N. Main St., 95437
(707) 964-9529

Amenities: 1,2,5,7,9,10,11
Breakfast: Full

Dbl. Oc.: $55.00-$85.00
Sgl. Oc.: $45.00-$75.00
Third Person: $10.00

Pudding Creek Inn—Two 1884 Victorian homes connected by an enclosed garden court. Ten rooms with private baths. Some have fireplaces. Restaurants, beaches and shops within walking distance.

Fort Bragg

Miller, Helen & Don
632 North Main St., 95437
(707) 964-3737

Amenities: 1,2,3,4,5,6,9,10,11
Breakfast: Continental

Dbl. Oc.: $65.00-$105.00
Sgl. Oc.: $58.00-$95.00

Country Inn—Historic charm, brass & iron beds, fireplaces, private baths on Mendocino Coast. Home baked nut and fruit muffins and complimentary wine. One block to Redwood train, dining, theatre and shops.

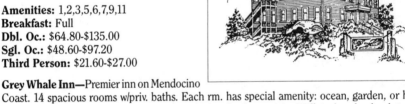

AMENITIES

1. No Smoking
2. No Pets
3. No Children
4. Senior Citizen Rates
5. Tennis Available
6. Golf Available
7. Swimming Available
8. Skiing Available
9. Credit Cards Accepted
10. Personal Check Accepted
11. Off Season Rates
12. Dinner Available (w/sufficient notice)

California

Freestone

Hoffman, Rosemary & Roger
520 Bohemian Hwy., 95472
(707) 874-2526

Amenities: 1,2,3,9,10
Breakfast: Full

Dbl. Oc.: $72.00
Sgl. Oc.: $72.00

Green Apple Inn—New England style farmhouse in a sunny meadow backed by Redwoods. Located in a designated historic village near Bodega Bay and wine country. 80 minutes north of San Francisco.

Fremont

Medeiros, Ann & Keith
43344 Mission Blvd., 94539
(415) 490-0520

Amenities: 9,10
Breakfast: Continental

Dbl. Oc.: $58.58
Sgl. Oc.: $58.58

Lord Bradley's Inn, adjacent to the historical Mission of San Jose offers 8 guest rooms with private baths, decorated in Victorian. Nearby is the Weibel Winery for touring and Mission Peak for hiking. Join us for a special occasion.

Georgetown (Gold Country)

Collin, Will
P.O. Box 43, 95634
(916) 333-4499

Amenities: 6,7,9,10
Breakfast: Full

Dbl. Oc.: $66.00-$85.00
Third Person: $15.00

American River Inn—A restored miners hotel now an exquisite B. & B. Pool w/jacuzzi, bikes, games & serenity of the gardens. Dove aviary & elegant antiques. From Auburn I-80S. Placerville I-50N to Hwy. 193.

Geysersville

Campbell, Mary Jane & Jerry
1475 Canyon Rd., 95441
(707) 857-3476

Amenities: 1,2,5,7,9,10
Breakfast: Full

Dbl. Oc.: $86.40-$108.00
Sgl. Oc.: $75.60-$97.20
Third Person: $20.00

The Campbell Ranch Inn, is located 1.6 miles off Route 101 in the heart of Sonoma County Wine Country. 35 acres, spectacular view, pool, tennis court, spa, bikes. Full breakfast, evening dessert homemade pie.

Glen Ellen

Waterman, M/M
12841 Dunbar Rd., 95442
(707) 996-8106

Amenities: 1,2,6,7,10
Breakfast: Full

Dbl. Oc.: $91.80
Third Person: $26.50

The Waterman's—Guest cottage on award winning restoration of early California winery. Perfect location, weekly rates, pool and hot tub. Brochure. Advance reservation required.

AMENITIES

1. No Smoking
2. No Pets
3. No Children
4. Senior Citizen Rates
5. Tennis Available
6. Golf Available
7. Swimming Available
8. Skiing Available
9. Credit Cards Accepted
10. Personal Check Accepted
11. Off Season Rates
12. Dinner Available (w/sufficient notice)

California

Grass Valley

Kiddy, Mrs. Pat
415 W. Main St., 95945
(916) 272-2418

Amenities: 1,2,4,5,6,7,8,9,10,11
Breakfast: Full

Dbl. Oc.: $59.60-$91.80
Sgl. Oc.: $43.20-$81.00
Third Person: $10.00

Annie Horan's Bed & Breakfast, 1874 Victorian tastefully refurbished and elegantly decorated in the heart of California's richest gold mining town. Four rooms all private baths. Hearty breakfast served on the deck.

Gualala

Flanagan, Nancy & Loren
34591 S. Highway 1, 95445
(707) 884-4537

Amenities: 1,2,3,5,6,7,9,10,11
Breakfast: Full
Dbl. Oc.: $92.00-$125.00
Sgl. Oc.: $$92.00-$125.00

North Coast Country Inn—Rustic Redwood buildings on a forrested hillside overlooking the ocean. Four large guest rooms, all with fireplace, antiques, private bath and deck. Hot tub. Ocean view.

Half Moon Bay

Baldwin, Eve & Terry
615 Mill St., 94019
(415) 726-9794

Amenities: 1,2,3,4,5,6,7,8,9,10,11
Breakfast: Full

Dbl. Oc.: $125.00-$195.00
Sgl. Oc.: $95.00-$195.00

Mill Rose Inn—Enjoy the ultimate in intimacy, romance & comfort. Walk to beach, shops, and restaurants. Fireplaces, private baths, European antiques, spas. 1/2 hour south of San Francisco.

Half Moon Bay

Lowings, M/M Simon
779 Main St., 94019
(415) 726-1616

Amenities: 5,6,9,10
Breakfast: Continental

Dbl. Oc.: $54.00-$113.40
Sgl. Oc.: $48.60-$108.00
Third Person: $15.00

Old Tyme Inn—Friendly quiet family run restored 1899 Victorian. Some private baths with double size whirlpool tubs. Fireplaces. Herb garden with over 50 varieties. Close to beaches and seafood restaurants.

Healdsburg

Baitinger, Alan & Foster, Beth
10630 Wholer Rd., 95448
(707) 887-9573

Amenities: 2,5,6,9,10
Breakfast: Full

Dbl. Oc.: $54.00-$80.00
Sgl. Oc.: $54.00-$80.00

The Raford House—Victorian farmhouse sits among the vineyards in a country setting. 7 guest rooms; fireplaces; breakfast included; historical landmark. 8 miles west of Santa Rosa.

AMENITIES

1. No Smoking
2. No Pets
3. No Children
4. Senior Citizen Rates
5. Tennis Available
6. Golf Available
7. Swimming Available
8. Skiing Available
9. Credit Cards Accepted
10. Personal Check Accepted
11. Off Season Rates
12. Dinner Available (w/sufficient notice)

California

Inverness

Brayton, Ms. Susan
105 Vision Rd.,
P.O. Box 644, 94937
(415) 669-7218

Amenities: 1,5,7,10
Breakfast: Continental

Dbl. Oc.: $60.00-$75.00
Sgl. Oc.: $60.00-$75.00
Third Person: $15.00

Alder House—A comfortable guest home; easy walk to village; in the heart of Point Reyes National Seashore; close to ocean beaches; an hour from San Francisco & two hours from SFO.

Inverness

Davies, Mary
10 Inverness Way, 94937
(415) 669-1648

Amenities: 1,2,7,9,10
Breakfast: Full
Dbl. Oc.: $110.00
Sgl. Oc.: $100.00
Third Person: $20.00

Ten Inverness Way—LA Times calls it "one of the niftiest inns in No. California." Hearty breakfasts, private baths, ebullient garden, stone fireplace. 1904 haven for hikers and rainy day readers. Don't miss it!

Inverness

Wigert, Mrs. Susan Hemphill
266 Vallejo Ave., 94937
(415) 663-8621

Amenities: 2,3,4,9,10,11
Breakfast: Full
Dbl. Oc.: $105.00-$175.00
Sgl. Oc.: $90.00-$160.00

Described by Sunset Magazine as a "Carpenter's Fantasy." The Blackthorne Inn resembles a giant treehouse. Located an hour northwest of San Francisco & adjacent to the Point Reyes National Seashore.

Inverness

Storch, Ms. Suzanne
75 Balboa Ave.
P.O. Box 619, 94937
(415) 663-9338

Amenities: 10,11
Breakfast: Full

Dbl. Oc.: $85.00-$95.00
Sgl. Oc.: $80.00-$90.00
Third Person: $15.00

Rosemary Cottage—Romantic french-country cottage. Separate unit. Handcrafted details, wood-burning stove, full kitchen, deck. Families welcome. Close to trails & beaches in Pt. Reyes Seashore.

AMENITIES

1. No Smoking
2. No Pets
3. No Children
4. Senior Citizen Rates
5. Tennis Available
6. Golf Available
7. Swimming Available
8. Skiing Available
9. Credit Cards Accepted
10. Personal Check Accepted
11. Off Season Rates
12. Dinner Available (w/sufficient notice)

California

Ione

Hubbs, Melisande
214 Shakeley Ln.,
P.O. Box 322, 95640
(209) 274-4468

Amenities: 2,3,10
Breakfast: Full

Dbl. Oc.: $50.00-$85.00
Sgl. Oc.: $45.00-$80.00
Third Person: $15.00

The Heirloom Bed & Breakfast—in the historic gold country. 1863 colonial Antebellum; fireplaces; balconies; spacious private garden retreat. Wineries, antiques, lakes, rivers, hills. Gracious hospitality.

Jackson

Beltz, Jeannine & Vic
11941 Narcissus Rd., 95642-9600
(209) 296-4300

Amenities: 1,2,3,9,10
Breakfast: Full
Dbl. Oc.: $60.00-$95.00
Sgl. Oc.: $45.00-$80.00
Third Person: $15.00

The Wedgewood Inn—Charming replica Victorian lavishly furnished with antiques; tucked away on 5 wooded acres, near excellent dining and tourist areas. Four guest rooms, all with private baths. Gourmet breakfast. Quiet.

Jamestown

Willey, Stephen
P.O. Box 502, Main St., 95327
(209) 984-3446

Amenities: 2,3,9,10,11,12
Breakfast: Continental

Dbl. Oc.: $49.00-$59.40
Third Person: $8.10

Historic National Hotel—B&B is an eleven room Gold Rush hotel (1859) fully restored, with an outstanding restaurant & the original saloon. Classic cuisine & gracious service are only part of our charm.

Jenner

Murphy, Mrs. Sheldon
10400 Coast Hwy. 1
Box 69, 95459
(707) 865-2377

Amenities: 1,2,7,9,10
Breakfast: Continental

Dbl. Oc.: $85.00
Sgl. Oc.: $80.00
Third Person: $15.00

Murphy's Jenner Inn—Rustic retreat inn, 8 rooms, antiques, 3 w/kitchens & fireplaces, ocean & river views, hot tub, restaurant, pristine ocean beaches, wineries, hiking, canoeing, fishing.

AMENITIES

1. No Smoking
2. No Pets
3. No Children
4. Senior Citizen Rates
5. Tennis Available
6. Golf Available
7. Swimming Available
8. Skiing Available
9. Credit Cards Accepted
10. Personal Check Accepted
11. Off Season Rates
12. Dinner Available (w/sufficient notice)

California

Laguna Beach

Brady, Rebecca & Charles
865 Quivera St., 92651
(714) 499-2756

Amenities: 5,11
Breakfast: Full

Dbl. Oc.: $65.00
Sgl. Oc.: $55.00

We have a 4,000 sq. foot house overlooking the ocean. City view and coastline. 6 to 8 guests, 5 bedrooms, 4 baths, close to beach and city.

Laguna Beach

Taylor, Dee
1322 Catalina St., 92651
(714) 494-8945

Amenities: 6,7,10
Breakfast: Continental

Dbl. Oc.: $81.00-$118.80
Sgl. Oc.: $81.00-$118.80
Third Person: $20.00

The Carriage House—A charming New Orleans style inn, 2 blocks from the blue Pacific. All rooms surround secluded courtyard filled with plants & flowers. Each suite has sitting room & separate bedroom & bath. Breakfast served family style.

Laguna Beach

Wirtz, Hank
741 S. Coast Hwy., 92651
(714) 494-3004

Amenities: 5,6,7,9,10
Breakfast: Full

Dbl. Oc.: $108.00-$162.00
Sgl. Oc.: $102.60-$156.60
Third Person: $10.80

Eiler's Inn—Twelve individually furnished rooms, private baths, courtyard with fountain, sundeck, parlor, fireplace. An oasis of rest and experience in European hospitality.

La Jolla

Albee, Betty
7753 Draper Ave., 92037
(619) 456-2066

Amenities: 2,3,5,7,9,10
Breakfast: Continental

Dbl. Oc.: $70.00-$175.00
Third Person: $20.00

The Bed & Breakfast Inn at La Jolla—Our elegant inn is one block from the ocean, features views, fireplaces, tennis, near galleries, restaurants, shops. We serve wine and cheese from 4-6 p.m. A lovely library/sitting room/deck for everyone.

Lake Arrowhead

Peiffer, Lila & Rick
263 S. St. Hwy. #173
P. O. Box 2177, 92352
(714) 336-3292

Amenities: 1,2,3,4,7,8,10,11
Breakfast: Full

Dbl. Oc.: $65.00-95.00
Sgl. Oc.: $65.00-$95.00
Third Person: $10.00

Bluebelle House Bed & Breakfast—Country English living room, fireplace, elegant but cozy. Five distinctive rooms, themes from European holidays. "Little Switzerland" resort area, 2 hours from Los Angeles. Walk to lake, village, shops, restaurants.

AMENITIES

1. No Smoking
2. No Pets
3. No Children
4. Senior Citizen Rates
5. Tennis Available
6. Golf Available
7. Swimming Available
8. Skiing Available
9. Credit Cards Accepted
10. Personal Check Accepted
11. Off Season Rates
12. Dinner Available (w/sufficient notice)

California

Lindsay

Braaton, Roni & Rick
229 N. Gale Hill, 93247
(209) 562-2003

Amenities: 2,6,7,8,10
Breakfast: Full

Dbl. Oc.: $59.40-$64.80
Sgl. Oc.: $59.40-$64.80

Moonlight and Roses emanates romance & homey comfort in our 1902 Victorian home. Stroll thru antiques shops and Indian trading post. We're only minutes from fishing at Lake Success and Sequoia Nat'l. Park.

Little River

deVries, Janet & Jan
8221 N. Hwy. One, 95456
(707) 937-0083

Amenities: 1,2,3,5,6,10,11
Breakfast: Continental
Dbl. Oc.: $75.60-$145.80
Sgl. Oc.: $59.40-$129.60
Third Person: $16.20

Glendeven—A warm and charming inn, 1 1/2 miles south of historic town of Mendocino. Fireplaces, antiques, lovely views and gardens. Private baths, relax and enjoy a very special experience celebrating 10 years of T.L.C.

Little River

Molnar, Carole & George
7001 North Highway One
P.O. Box 357, 95456
(707) 937-0697

Amenities: 1,2,9,10,11
Breakfast: Continental

Dbl. Oc.: $81.00-$97.20
Sgl. Oc.: $81.00-$97.20
Third Person: $15.00

Victorian Farmhouse built in 1877. Country setting, flower gardens, ten rooms, private baths, views, fireplaces, breakfast served in rooms. Two miles from Mendocino. Walking distance to ocean and parks.

Los Angeles

Burns, Murray
1442 Kellam Ave., 90026
(213) 250-1620

Amenities: 1,2,3,4,5,6,7,9,10
Breakfast: Full

Dbl. Oc.: $62.00-$102.00
Sgl. Oc.: $51.00-$102.00
Third Person: $15.00

Eastlake Victorian Inn—Ever wonder what L.A. was like in its glory days, before freeways and malls; meticulously restored Victorian in historic area "incomparably romantic" L.A. Times Best. Central location. Complimentary champagne.

AMENITIES

1. No Smoking
2. No Pets
3. No Children
4. Senior Citizen Rates
5. Tennis Available
6. Golf Available
7. Swimming Available
8. Skiing Available
9. Credit Cards Accepted
10. Personal Check Accepted
11. Off Season Rates
12. Dinner Available (w/sufficient notice)

California

Los Angeles

Moultout, Mrs. Suzanne
449 North Detroit St., 90036
(213) 938-4794

Amenities: 1,2
Breakfast: Continental

Dbl. Oc.: $50.00
Sgl. Oc.: $40.00
Third Person: $5.00

Paris Cottage—Spanish style house on quiet street close to W. Hollywood. Shady yard with fruit trees, close to CBS Studios & beaches. Convenient area with bus stop around the corner. Airport pick-up. No facilities for invalid people. Min. 2 night stay.

Los Osos

Ondang, Gerarda
1056 Bay Oaks Dr., 93402
(805) 528-3973

Amenities: 5,6,10
Breakfast: Full

Dbl. Oc.: $42.00-$49.00
Sgl. Oc.: $25.00
Third Person: $10.00

Gerarda's Bed & Breakfast—Close to Morro Bay, Hearst Castle, San Luis Obispo. Two rooms with view, one w/priv. bath. Hostess speaks Dutch, Indonisian, some Japanese, German & French. Dutch hospitality.

Malibu

Larronde, Charlou & James
P.O. Box 86, 90265
(213) 456-9333

Amenities: 7
Breakfast: Full

Dbl. Oc.: $75.00
Sgl. Oc.: $65.00
Third Person: $15.00

Casa Larronde—is 4,000 sq. ft. home on a private beach 1 mile from fishing pier & surfers beach & close to Getty Museum. Ocean suite has a 40' floor to ceiling glass, fireplace, ceiling fan, kitchenette, TV.

Mariposa

Foster, Gwendolyn & Dick
3871 Hwys. 49 So., 95338
(209) 966-2832

Amenities: 1,5,7,10
Breakfast: Full

Dbl. Oc.: $35.00
Sgl. Oc.: $30.00
Third Person: $7.00

The Pelennor, Bed & Breakfast at Bootjack was created for the traveler seeking economical lodging. An hour to Yosemite a bit further to skiing. Bagpipes and Scottish Lore. Hot tub & lap pool. 6 rooms. Honeymoon suite coming soon.

Mendocino

Allen, Sue & Tom
44800 Main,
P.O. Box 626, 95460
(707) 937-0246

Amenities: 1,2,3,5,6,7,9,10
Breakfast:

Dbl. Oc.: $59.40-$118.80
Sgl. Oc.: $59.40-$118.80
Third Person: $5.40

Mendocino Village Inn—Hummingbirds, Picassos, 1882 Victorian, French-roast coffee, Fuchsias, fireplaces, Vivaldi, country breakfasts, Pacific surf, Bokharas, fresh blackberries, four-poster beds, migrating whales, Chardonnay.

AMENITIES

1. No Smoking
2. No Pets
3. No Children
4. Senior Citizen Rates
5. Tennis Available
6. Golf Available
7. Swimming Available
8. Skiing Available
9. Credit Cards Accepted
10. Personal Check Accepted
11. Off Season Rates
12. Dinner Available (w/sufficient notice)

California

Mendocino

Patton, Ms. Patricia
499 Howard St.,
P.O. Box 150, 95460
(707) 937-4892

Amenities: 1,2,3,10
Breakfast: Full

Dbl. Oc.: $70.20-$108.00
Third Person: 15.00

Whitegate Inn—1880 Victorian in the heart of the village. Antique filled rooms, fireplaces, private baths. Hiking, whale watching, unique shops & galleries, beaches, award winning intimate restaurants, evening wine. Mid-week rates.

Mendocino

Reding, Melanie & Joe
P.O. Box 206, 95460
(707) 937-0289

Amenities: 2,4,5,6,9,10,11,12
Breakfast: Continental

Dbl. Oc.: $48.60-$145.80
Sgl. Oc.: $48.60-$145.80

Mac Callum House is located in the center of the village of Mendocino. Besides the main house, there are unique cottages on the grounds. There is an award winning restaurant and bar on the premises.

Mendocino

Stanford, Joan & Jeff
P.O. Box 487, Hwy. 1 &
Comptche Ukiah Rd., 95460
(707) 937-5615

Amenities: 5,6,7,9,10
Breakfast: Continental
Dbl. Oc.: $115.00-$135.00
Sgl. Oc.: $115.00-$135.00
Third Person: $15.00

The Stanford Inn By The Sea—an elegant inn on beautifully landscaped grounds hosting swans, llamas, & horses. Woodburning fireplaces, antiques & views of the ocean and village grace each room. Bicycles & canoes available.

Mendocino

Welter, Ed
P.O. Box 207, 95460
(707) 937-0811

Amenities: 5,6,7,10
Breakfast: Continental

Dbl. Oc.: $37.80-$70.20
Sgl. Oc.: $32.40-$70.20
Third Person: $5.40

Ames Lodge is a rustic Redwood inn east of Mendocino in the forest. Seven guest rooms, large main room with fireplace and library. Hiking trails. Breakfast 9-10 a.m. Families welcome. Call ahead.

AMENITIES

1. No Smoking
2. No Pets
3. No Children
4. Senior Citizen Rates
5. Tennis Available
6. Golf Available
7. Swimming Available
8. Skiing Available
9. Credit Cards Accepted
10. Personal Check Accepted
11. Off Season Rates
12. Dinner Available (w/sufficient notice)

California

Montara

Bechtell, M/M Bill
1125 Tamarind St., 94037
(415) 728-3946

Amenities: 1,2,3,6,9,10
Breakfast: Full
Dbl. Oc.: $65.00
Sgl. Oc.: $55.00

Just 20 mi. south of San Francisco on the scenic California coast! Semi-rural area with nearby hiking, beaches, and horseback riding. Private entrance, private bath, fireplace, ocean view, phone, and TV.

Murphys

Costa, M/M Robert
271 Jones St.,
P.O. Box 1375, 95247
(209) 728-2897

Amenities: 1,2,3,5,6,7,8,9,10,11
Breakfast: Full

Dbl. Oc.: $60.00-$70.00
Sgl. Oc.: $55.00-$65.00
Third Person: $10.00

Dunbar House, 1880—Lovely Italianate style home comfortably decorated with antiques, lace, down comforters & pillows. Full breakfast served in room, dining room or gardens. Murphys, Queen of the Sierra, quaint gold rush town.

Napa

Bowen, M/M Art
1225 Division St., 94558
(707) 257-1166

Amenities: 1,2,3,5,6,7,9,10
Breakfast: Continental
Dbl. Oc.: $55.00-$75.00
Sgl. Oc.: $55.00-$75.00

The Goodman House—One of Napa's old homes with a prestigious past. Art & June Bowen invite you to enjoy their home preserving a century of Napa Valley hospitality. Minutes from world famous wineries, walk to fine restaurants.

Napa

Campbell, Pearl
720 Seminary St., 94559
(707) 257-0789

Amenities: 1,2,6,7,9,10
Breakfast: Continental

Dbl. Oc.: $85.00-$105.00
Sgl. Oc.: $83.00-$105.00

Coombs Residence Inn on The Park—Victorian splendor, a home with a personality of its own. Down comforters and pillows, terry robes, afternoon wine and cheese, port sherry and lots of T.L.C. Weekend and weekly rates available.

AMENITIES

1. No Smoking
2. No Pets
3. No Children
4. Senior Citizen Rates
5. Tennis Available
6. Golf Available
7. Swimming Available
8. Skiing Available
9. Credit Cards Accepted
10. Personal Check Accepted
11. Off Season Rates
12. Dinner Available (w/sufficient notice)

California

Napa

Page, Mary & Jeff
5444 St. Helena Hwy., 94558
(707) 255-5907

Amenities: 9,10
Breakfast: Continental

Dbl. Oc.: $91.80-$102.60
Sgl. Oc.: $91.80-$102.60

The Trubody Ranch B&B has two beautiful rooms in a restored Victorian watertower beside our 1872 farmhouse, surrounded by 127 acres of our own vineyard land. Enjoy our flower gardens & vineyard walks.

Napa

Pitner, Robert
1727 Main St., 94559
(707) 226-3774

Amenities: 1,2,3,5,6,7,9,10,11,12
Breakfast: Full
Dbl. Oc.: $95.00-$135.00
Sgl. Oc.: $95.00-$135.00

Hennessey House Bed & Breakfast Inn— Queen Anne Victorian featuring feather beds, fireplaces, spas, sauna. Part of the historical Joseph Mathews Winery complex featuring wine tasting and the famous Sherry Oven Restaurant and Cafe.

Napa Valley

Lambeth, Dr. Harold & Corlene
415 Cold Spring Rd., Angwin 94508
(707) 965-3538

Amenities: 1,2,3,5,7,9,10,11
Breakfast: Continental
Dbl. Oc.: $124.20-$189.00
Third Person: $20.00

Forest Manor—Majestic secluded 20 acre English Tudor estate nestled among the forests and vineyards above Napa Valley. Fireplaces, decks, private baths, pool, spas, refrigerators, deluxe suites—one with private jacuzzi.

AMENITIES

1. No Smoking
2. No Pets
3. No Children
4. Senior Citizen Rates
5. Tennis Available
6. Golf Available
7. Swimming Available
8. Skiing Available
9. Credit Cards Accepted
10. Personal Check Accepted
11. Off Season Rates
12. Dinner Available (w/sufficient notice)

California

Nevada City

Meade, Ms. Annette
449 Broad St., 95959
(916) 265-4660

Amenities: 1,2,9,10
Breakfast: Full
Dbl. Oc.: $91.80-$135.00
Sgl. Oc.: $91.80-$135.00
Third Person: $20.00

Grandmere's Inn—A warm French country atmosphere on beautiful grounds. Listed on the National Register of Historical Places. Located right above downtown Nevada City. Offering homemade gourmet breakfasts in a relaxed decor.

Nevada City

Palley, Meg
12766 Nevada City Hwy., 95959
(916) 265-5427

Amenities: 1,2,6,7,8,10
Breakfast: Continental

Dbl. Oc.: $60.00
Sgl. Oc.: $30.00
Third Person: $30.00

Palley Place is located in the Sierra Foothills with a view of the mountains. Rooms are furnished with handweaving & guests may see loom & spinning work. Ski, pan for gold or enjoy cultural events. Charming town.

Nevada City

Weaver, Mary Louise & Conely
109 Prospect St., 95959
(916) 265-5135

Amenities: 1,2,3,5,6,7,8,9,10,12
Breakfast: Full
Dbl. Oc.: $70.20-$102.60
Sgl. Oc.: $64.80-$95.40
Third Person: $20.00

The Red Castle Inn—Overlooks the queen city of the northern gold mines. Strains of Mozart echo through lofty hallways, chandeliers sparkle, the aura of another time prevails. 4 story 1857 landmark; 8 rooms; private baths.

AMENITIES

1. No Smoking
2. No Pets
3. No Children
4. Senior Citizen Rates
5. Tennis Available
6. Golf Available
7. Swimming Available
8. Skiing Available
9. Credit Cards Accepted
10. Personal Check Accepted
11. Off Season Rates
12. Dinner Available (w/sufficient notice)

California

Nevada City

Wright, Mrs. Miriam M.
517 W. Broad St., 95959
(916) 265-2815

Amenities: 1,2,3,4,5,6,7,8,9,10,11
Breakfast: Full
Dbl. Oc.: $64.80-$86.40
Sgl. Oc.: $64.80-$86.40

Downey House Bed & Breakfast Inn—Circa 1869. Light, comfy, view, rooms w/pvt. bath. Lush garden w/waterfall, sunroom, porch and parlor. Generous buffet breakfast. Near fine shops, restaurants, galleries, museums and theatre.

Newport Beach

Lawrence, Jeannie & Rick
2102 West Oceanfront, 92663
(714) 675-7300

Amenities: 5,6,7,9,10
Breakfast: Continental

Dbl. Oc.: $130.00-$275.00
Sgl. Oc.: $130.00-$275.00

Romance, Luxury, And Resounding Elegance, this 10 room bed & breakfast offering 10 private fireplaces and sunken marble bathtubs. Truly an inspired expression of world class grandeur and gracious living.

Newport Beach

Sorrell, Michael
2102 W. Oceanfront, 92663
(714) 675-7300

Amenities: 4,5,6,7,9,10,12
Breakfast: Full

Dbl. Oc.: $135.00-$275.00
Third Person: $20.00

Romantic Luxury and resounding elegance await you. Enjoy any of our ten oceanfront rooms all with exquisite Victorian design, fireplaces, and imported Italian marble bathrooms, sunken tubs, breakfast in bed.

Newport

Ottens, Dick
2306 West Oceanfront, 92663
(714) 673-7030

Amenities: 2,5,6,7,9,11,12
Breakfast: Continental

Dbl. Oc.: $85.00-$210.00
Sgl. Oc.: $85.00-$210.00

Portofino Beach Hotel—Directly on the sand at Newport. Sparkling European style bed and breakfast reminiscent of the Italian Riveria. Decorated in fine period antiques. Some rooms include in room jacuzzi, patio and daybed.

AMENITIES

1. No Smoking
2. No Pets
3. No Children
4. Senior Citizen Rates
5. Tennis Available
6. Golf Available
7. Swimming Available
8. Skiing Available
9. Credit Cards Accepted
10. Personal Check Accepted
11. Off Season Rates
12. Dinner Available (w/sufficient notice)

California

Nipton

Lang, Ms. Roxanne
72 Nipton Rd., HCR #1
Box 357, 92364
(619) 856-2335

Amenities: 2,9,
Breakfast: Continental

Dbl. Oc.: $44.94
Sgl. Oc.: $44.94
Third Person: $10.70

Hotel Nipton—1904 restored hotel. In east Mojave national scenic area, 65 miles S.W. of Las Vegas. Clara Bow room; jaccuzi outside for star gazing. Perfect getaway from it all place. Only 4 rooms.

Ojai

Nelson, Ms. Mary
210 E. Matilija, 93023
(805) 646-0961

Amenities: 1,3,5,6,7,9,10
Breakfast: Continental

Dbl. Oc.: $81.00
Sgl. Oc.: $75.60

Originally A Little Brick Schoolhouse and now Ojai's oldest building. The hotel is centrally located in a lovely park-like surroundings. Six guest rooms share three baths.

Ojai

Willner, Mrs. Tiba
921 Patricia Ct., 93023
(805) 646-8337

Amenities: 5,6,7,10
Breakfast: Full

Dbl. Oc.: $70.00

Ojai B. & B.—Beautiful Ojai California. Rooms overlook Los Podres Mountains. Homecooked full breakfast; fresh orange juice from my own orchard. Enclosed rose garden and patio; antique furniture; beautiful art throughout home; quiet.

Oroville (City of Gold)

Pratt, Mrs. Jean
1124 Middlehoff Lane, 95965
(916) 533-1413

Amenities: 1,2,3,5,6,7,9,10
Breakfast: Full

Dbl. Oc.: $45.00-$65.00

Jean Pratt's Riverside Bed & Breakfast—5 acres; wooded waterfront on Feather River. Fish, swim, canoe or goldpan on premises. Historical sites; shopping; bird watching; or relax. Minutes from state highways and excellent restaurants.

Pacific Grove

Browncroft, The Family
557 Ocean View Blvd., 93950
(408) 373-7673

Amenities: 1,2,3,4,5,6,7,10
Breakfast: Full

Dbl. Oc.: $104.14-$203.14
Sgl. Oc.: $93.32-$203.14

Roserox Country Inn By-The-Sea—This intimate historic mansion, on the Pacific shore of the Monterey Peninsula, with breathtaking ocean views from each individually decorated room awaits your arrival.

AMENITIES

1. No Smoking
2. No Pets
3. No Children
4. Senior Citizen Rates
5. Tennis Available
6. Golf Available
7. Swimming Available
8. Skiing Available
9. Credit Cards Accepted
10. Personal Check Accepted
11. Off Season Rates
12. Dinner Available (w/sufficient notice)

California

Pacific Grove

The Flatley Family
555 Ocean View Blvd., 93950
(408)372-4341

Amenities: 1,2,10
Breakfast: Continental

Dbl. Oc.: $93.50-$181.50
Sgl. Oc.: Same

Seven Gables Inn built in 1886 is a victorian mansion right on Monterey Bay, furnished elegantly with fine antiques. All ocean view rooms with private baths. Close to all scenic spots. Family fun.

Pacific Grove

Martine, Marion
255 Oceanview Blvd.
(408) 373-3388

Amenities: 5,6,7,9,10,11
Breakfast: Full
Dbl. Oc.: $103.30-$191.30
Sgl. Oc.: $103.30-$191.30

This Ocean Front Palace built in the 1890's has 19 guest rooms, each with private bath. Authentic museum quality antiques in every room. Breakfast is served on old Sheffield silver & Victorian china. Oceanviews & fireplaces in some rooms.

Palo Alto

Dumond, J-Paul
1520 Bryant St., 94301
(707) 942-9581

Amenities: 1,2,3,7,9,10,11
Breakfast: Continental
Dbl. Oc.: $88.00-$176.00
Sgl. Oc.: $88.00-$176.00

The Silver Rose Inn—Experience the quiet elegance and the feeling of your own wine country estate situated on a beautifully landscaped knoll in Napa Valley with outstanding views of surrounding hills and vineyards.

AMENITIES

1. No Smoking
2. No Pets
3. No Children
4. Senior Citizen Rates
5. Tennis Available
6. Golf Available
7. Swimming Available
8. Skiing Available
9. Credit Cards Accepted
10. Personal Check Accepted
11. Off Season Rates
12. Dinner Available (w/sufficient notice)

California

Palo Alto

Hall, Susan & Maxwell
555 Lytton Ave., 94301
(415) 322-8555

Amenities: 1,2,3,9,10
Breakfast: Continental
Dbl. Oc.: $99.00-$148.50
Sgl. Oc.: $99.00-$148.50

The Victorian On Lytton offers a combination of forgotten elegance with a touch of European grace. All 10 rooms have sitting parlors & private bath. Fine restaurants & shops are 1 block away.

Palo Alto

Young, M/M Allen
P.O. Box 4528,
Stanford, 94309
(415) 321-5195

Amenities: 1,2,3,5,6,7,9,10
Breakfast: Full

Dbl. Oc.: $95.00
Third Person: $20.00

A Tyrolean Villa mini estate offers peace & tranquility in a park-like setting, 5 min. to Stanford & 25 min. to San Francisco. 5 guest rooms with private baths. Electronic security gates. Solar pool. No children under 12.

Pasadena

Woods, Jane
119 N. Meridith, 91106
(818) 440-0066

Amenities: 1,2,4,10
Breakfast: Continental

Dbl. Oc.: $66.00-$82.50
Sgl. Oc.: $55.00-$65.00
Third Person: $20.00

Donnymac Irish Inn—Turn-of-the-century 2 story craftsman. Country Irish decor, quiet residential area close to L.A. & Hollywood, museums, Rose Bowl, & race tack. Hot tub & spa; flowers, fruit and sherry in all rooms. Weekly rates.

Placerville

Irvin, Mrs. Dorothy
P.O. Box 827, 95667
(916) 622-7640

Amenities: 6,7,10
Breakfast: Full

Dbl. Oc.: $62.00-$72.00

River Rock Inn—Enjoy the quiet beauty of this inn on the bank of the American River. Fish; pan for gold in the front yard; hike along the same trail as the gold seeking 49ers; relax on the 140 foot deck or in the hot tub.

AMENITIES

1. No Smoking	**4.** Senior Citizen Rates	**7.** Swimming Available	**10.** Personal Check Accepted
2. No Pets	**5.** Tennis Available	**8.** Skiing Available	**11.** Off Season Rates
3. No Children	**6.** Golf Available	**9.** Credit Cards Accepted	**12.** Dinner Available (w/sufficient notice)

California

Placerville

Thompson, Patsy & Richard
2985 Clay St., 95667
(916) 626-6136

Amenities: 1,2,3,9,10,11
Breakfast: Full

Dbl. Oc.: $48.60-$78.60
Sgl. Oc.: $43.60-$73.60
Third Person: $10.00

The James Blair House is a 1901 Queen Anne Victorian. Rooms are furnished with an eclectic collection of antiques. Breakfast is a homecooked gourmet delight. Guests can walk to nearby Old Hangtown.

Pleasanton

Cordtz, Mrs. Joan
262 W. Angela, 94566
(415) 846-3013

Amenities: 1,2,9,10
Breakfast: Continental
Dbl. Oc.: $85.00
Sgl. Oc.: $85.00

The Plum Tree Inn is a lovely warm Victorian Inn located in quiet downtown Pleasanton, CA. Fine restaurants, shops, wineries and golf close by. Private baths and complimentary wine. Reservation deposit required.

Point Reyes Station

Bartlett, Ms. Julia
39 Cypress, Box 176, 94956
(415) 663-1709

Amenities: 1,2,3,10
Breakfast: Full
Dbl. Oc.: $81.00-$92.00
Sgl. Oc.: $75.60
Third Person: $16.00

Thirty-Nine Cypress is on a bluff with a spectacular view of Pt. Reyes National Seashore. Country gardens; all Redwood; antiques; oriental rugs; art collection. Horseback riding by arrangement.

AMENITIES

1. No Smoking
2. No Pets
3. No Children
4. Senior Citizen Rates
5. Tennis Available
6. Golf Available
7. Swimming Available
8. Skiing Available
9. Credit Cards Accepted
10. Personal Check Accepted
11. Off Season Rates
12. Dinner Available (w/sufficient notice)

California

Point Reyes Station

Gray, Karen
11561 Route #1, 94956
(415) 663-1166

Amenities: 1,10,11
Breakfast: Full
Dbl. Oc.: $104.50
Sgl. Oc.: $104.50
Third Person: $15.00

Jasmine Cottage is tucked in a quiet country garden; lovely view and romantic seclusion; charming interior with full kitchen; garden room; library; woodstove; ideal for families; sleeps 4 plus crib.

Rancho Cucamonga

Isley, Janice
9240 Archibald Ave., 91730
(714) 980-6450

Amenities: 1,2,3,5,6,7,8,9,10,12
Breakfast: Full

Dbl. Oc.: $60.50-$121.10

Christmas House Bed & Breakfast Inn—1904 Queen Anne Victorian mansion newly renovated in period elegance. 35 miles east of Los Angeles and 2 miles from Ontario International Airport. Gracious turn-of-the-century hospitality welcomes you.

Rancho Palos Verdes

Exley, Mrs. Ruth
4273 Palos Verdes Dr., So.
90274
(213) 377-2113

Amenities: 1,4,5,6,7,8,10,12
Breakfast: Full

Dbl. Oc.: $50.00
Sgl. Oc.: $35.00
Third Person: $10.00

The Exley House By-The-Sea is a cozy home in suburban Los Angeles. Friendly atmosphere; ocean front; private beach; many tourist attractions; restaurants; beautiful views; quiet.

Sacramento

Richardson, Ms. Jane
1315 22nd St., 95816
(916) 444-8085

Amenities: 1,2,3,9,10
Breakfast: Full

Dbl. Oc.: $77.00-$137.50
Sgl. Oc.: $77.00-$137.50
Third Person: $10.00

Amber House—This 1905 Craftsman style mansion is just a 7 block walk to the state capitol; elegant antique decor; private baths; telephones; TV available; full gourmet breakfast, complimentary wine; walk to restaurants.

AMENITIES

1. No Smoking
2. No Pets
3. No Children
4. Senior Citizen Rates
5. Tennis Available
6. Golf Available
7. Swimming Available
8. Skiing Available
9. Credit Cards Accepted
10. Personal Check Accepted
11. Off Season Rates
12. Dinner Available (w/sufficient notice)

California

St. Helena

Bartels, Ms. Jaymie
1200 Conn Valley Rd., 94574
(707) 963-4001

Amenities: 2,4,5,6,7,9,10,11
Breakfast: Continental

Dbl. Oc.: $105.00-$165.00
Sgl. Oc.: $105.00-$165.00
Third Person: $20.00

Bartel's Ranch Country Inn—Internationally acclaimed 100 acre estate setting in world famous wine country; romantic, secluded, with 10,000 acre view; game room, library, bicycles, pool, vineyard view; 3 miles from St. Helena; private, peaceful.

St. Helena

Clark, Mrs. Lois
1575 St. Helena Hwy., 94574
(707) 963-3890

Amenities: 1,2,3,5,6,10
Breakfast: Continental

Dbl. Oc.: $75.00-$95.00
Sgl. Oc.: $75.00-$95.00
Third Person: $20.00

The Ink House, built by T.H. Ink in 1884, is situated in the heart of the wine country. Sherry in the parlor or in the observatory; antiques and private baths; fine restaurants and shops close by.

St. Helena

Cunningham, Erika
285 Fawn Park, 94574
(707) 963-2887

Amenities: 5,6,7,10
Breakfast: Continental

Dbl. Oc.: $65.00-$150.00
Sgl. Oc.: $55.00
Third Person: $15.00

Erika's Hillside Bed & Breakfast—Peaceful and romantic country setting with breathtaking view of vineyards & wineries. Rooms bright and airy; private entrances; deep quilted beds & antique handpainted Norwegian Rosemaling furniture.

St. Helena

Hinton, Margie
1308 Main St., 94574
(707) 963-1891

Amenities: 1,2,3,4,5,6,7,9,10,11
Breakfast: Continental

Dbl. Oc.: $62.50-$100.00
Sgl. Oc.: $62.50-$100.00
Third Person: $16.95

Cornerstone B. & B. Inn—Step back in time in this gracious Victorian B. & B. inn located in the heart of the Napa Valley. 12 spacious rooms with antiques, period furnishings & quilts; nearby: wineries, bicycling, mud baths, & ballooning.

AMENITIES

1. No Smoking
2. No Pets
3. No Children
4. Senior Citizen Rates
5. Tennis Available
6. Golf Available
7. Swimming Available
8. Skiing Available
9. Credit Cards Accepted
10. Personal Check Accepted
11. Off Season Rates
12. Dinner Available (w/sufficient notice)

California

St. Helena

Martin, Athena & Mary
1309 Main St., 94574
(707) 963-4388

Amenities: 1,2,3,9,11
Breakfast: Continental
Dbl. Oc.: $82.50-$165.00
Sgl. Oc.: $82.50-$165.00
Third Person: $10.00

Hotel St. Helena—Originally established in 1881, this charming Victorian Hotel, located in the heart of the Napa Valley, provides friendly and personable staff who go out of their way to make each guest feel comfortable.

St. Helena

Wild-Runnells, Lisa & Jon
399 Zinfandel Ln., 94574
(707) 963-1190

Amenities: 2,3,4,5,6,10,11
Breakfast: Full

Dbl. Oc.: $50.00-$120.00

Shady Oaks Country Inn, secluded on 2 acres, is the ultimate in romance & tranquility. Exceptional champagne breakfast is served; minutes to wineries; one mile south of St. Helena; one hour from San Francisco.

San Diego

Burley, M/M Ernest J.
6500 San Miguel Rd.,
Bonita, 92002
(619) 479-9838

Amenities: 2,4,5,6,7,10
Breakfast: Continental

Dbl. Oc.: $55.00
Sgl. Oc.: $45.00
Third Person: $10.00

Burley Ranch—15 min. from San Diego Airport. Historic ranch home, mountain view, country setting. Large room, king bed, private bath, pool, Sea World, Balboa Park & Zoo, Tijuana, and much more.

San Diego

Chandler, Ms. Lori
2470 Heritage Park Row, 92110
(619) 295-7088

Amenities: 1,2,3,4,9,11,12
Breakfast: Full
Dbl. Oc.: $80.20-$123.00
Sgl. Oc.: $69.50-$101.60
Third Person: $15.00

Heritage Park Bed & Breakfast Inn—San Diego's most romantic setting. Beautifully restored Queen Anne on 7 acre Victorian Park in historic Old Town. 9 antique filled guest rooms. Priv. baths. Exquisite full breakfast, romantic dinners.

AMENITIES

1. No Smoking
2. No Pets
3. No Children
4. Senior Citizen Rates
5. Tennis Available
6. Golf Available
7. Swimming Available
8. Skiing Available
9. Credit Cards Accepted
10. Personal Check Accepted
11. Off Season Rates
12. Dinner Available (w/sufficient notice)

California

San Diego

Emerick, Dr./Mrs. Robert
P.O. Box 3292, 92103
(619) 299-1564

Amenities: 2,3,4,5,6,7,8,10
Breakfast: Continental

Dbl. Oc.: $45.00-$65.00
Sgl. Oc.: $45.00-$65.00
Third Person: $10.00

The Cottage, is located one mile from San Diego Zoo and the Old Globe Theatre. It is furnished with antiques and offers a quiet retreat. There are fine restaurants, shops and bus transportation within a few blocks.

San Diego

Grady, Mrs. Jerri
P.O. Box 7695, 92107
(619) 225-9765

Amenities: 1,7,10,11
Breakfast: Full
Dbl. Oc.: $70.00
Sgl. Oc.: $95.00

Surf Manor and Cottages

Surf Manor And Cottages—Charming 1 and 2 bedroom apts. and quaint cottages furnished with antiques. Near Sea World. Refrigerator stocked for self-catered breakfast. Weekly rates only July-August. Lower weekly-monthly off-peak.

San Diego

Halbig, George
432 So. Citrus,
Escondido, 92027
(619) 745-1296

Amenities: 5,6,7,10
Breakfast: Continental

Dbl. Oc.: $30.00-$35.00
Third Person: 5.00

Halbig's Hacienda—Large adobe ranch house on acreage with family fruit trees, overlooking Valley and hills. A country atmosphere on the edge of town, near San Diego Wild Animal Park, fishing lake and new shopping mall.

San Diego

Johnson, Ms. Rosemary
1955 Edgemont St., 92109
(619) 238-1677 in S. CA (800) 822-1955

Amenities: 2,3,4,5,6,11
Breakfast: Full
Dbl. Oc.: $60.00-$95.00
Sgl. Oc.: $60.00-95.00

Edgemont Inn—3 rooms, 1 suite. Rates include: refreshments upon arrival, flowers, full "home cooking" breakfast. Two rooms with balconies; 2 patios; enclosed parking; comfortable elegance; near park.

AMENITIES

1. No Smoking
2. No Pets
3. No Children
4. Senior Citizen Rates
5. Tennis Available
6. Golf Available
7. Swimming Available
8. Skiing Available
9. Credit Cards Accepted
10. Personal Check Accepted
11. Off Season Rates
12. Dinner Available (w/sufficient notice)

California

San Diego

Martin, Ms. Duan
406 Maple St., 92103
(619) 234-2926

Amenities: 5,6,7,9,10
Breakfast: Full
Dbl. Oc.: $85.00-$100.00
Sgl. Oc.: $80.00-$100.00
Third Person: $10.00

Britt House—Victorian Bed & Breakfast inn 2 blocks from Balboa, theatres & Zoo. Ten individually decorated rooms; formal garden; fresh flowers; cookies & fruit in rooms; full breakfast and afternoon tea.

San Diego

Milbourne, Dorothy
2330 Albatross St., 92101
(619) 233-0638

Amenities: 2,10,11
Breakfast: Continental

Dbl. Oc.: $50.00-$65.00
Third Person: $10.00

Harbor Hill Guest House overlooks the harbor. 5 rooms, private baths, TV's. Each level has private entrances & kitchens. Walk to Balboa Park, Zoo, harbor, downtown. Sundeck level ideal for families. Studio, complete privacy. Children under 6 free.

San Diego

Pearn, George
2331 Second Ave., 92101
(619) 239-8585

Amenities: 1,2,3,9,10
Breakfast: Continental

Dbl. Oc.: $53.00-$65.00
Sgl. Oc.: $53.00-$65.00

The Keating House Inn—4 guest rooms share 2 baths in a historically designated Queen Ann Victorian Inn in uptown San Diego near Balboa Park, Zoo, downtown, Sea World and ocean beaches.

San Francisco

Baires, Emma
225 Arguello Blvd., 94118
(415) 752-9482

Amenities: 1,5,6,7,10
Breakfast: Continental

Dbl. Oc.: $48.00-$67.00
Sgl. Oc.: $48.00-$67.00

Casa Arguello offers comfortable rooms, in a cheerful spacious flat, 10 minutes from the center of San Francisco, in a desirable neighborhood, within walking distance to restaurants & shops; near Golden Gate Park.

AMENITIES

1. No Smoking
2. No Pets
3. No Children
4. Senior Citizen Rates
5. Tennis Available
6. Golf Available
7. Swimming Available
8. Skiing Available
9. Credit Cards Accepted
10. Personal Check Accepted
11. Off Season Rates
12. Dinner Available (w/sufficient notice)

California

San Francisco

Bard, Joan
330 Edgehill Way, 94127
(415) 564-9339

Amenities: 1,2
Breakfast: Continental
Dbl. Oc.: $65.00
Sgl. Oc.: $65.00
Third Person: $10.00

Casita Blanca is a guest cottage high on a hill not far from Golden Gate Park, a delightful hide-away nestled in the trees. Twin beds, pvt. bath & comp. kitchen, & if the fog comes in you can warm up by the fireplace.

San Francisco

Goettsche, JoAnne
1265 Guerrero St., 94115
(415) 641-8803

Amenities: 1,2,9,10
Breakfast: Continental

Dbl. Oc.: $95.00
Sgl. Oc.: $90.00
Third Person: $15.00

Comfort B&B—Charming Victorian with large elegantly furnished rooms, private baths; near good public transportation.

San Francisco

Kavanaugh, Marily & Robert
#4 Charlton Ct., 94123
(415) 921-9784

Amenities: 10
Breakfast: Continental

Rates: $68.00-$184.00

The Bed & Breakfast Inn—America's first and still the finest bed and breakfast inn. Four "pension" rooms, 6 suites, phones, TV, library. You are treated as a special person here. Public transportation nearby. Reservations.

San Francisco

McDonald, Bambi
1208 Stockton, 94133
(415) 989-3960

Amenities: 1,2,5,6,7,12
Breakfast: Full

Dbl. Oc.: $46.65
Sgl. Oc.: $38.85
Triple Oc.: $57.75

Obrero Hotel And Basque Restaurant—Small European pension with family-style dining and bright cheerful rooms w/shared baths, in Chinatown on the edge of North Beach. Very centrally located, walking distance to Union Square and Fisherman's Wharf.

San Francisco

Moffatt, Mrs. Ruth
431 Hugo St., 5th Ave., 94122
(415) 661-6210

Amenities: 2,9,10
Breakfast: Continental

Dbl. Oc.: $37.74-$59.94
Sgl. Oc.: $37.74-$54.39
Third Person: $5.55

Moffatt House is a safe and comfy 1910 Edwardian home, adjacent to major attractions of exciting Golden Gate Park. Pleasant neighborhood shopping; excellent public transit; ask about runner' discount!

AMENITIES

1. No Smoking
2. No Pets
3. No Children
4. Senior Citizen Rates
5. Tennis Available
6. Golf Available
7. Swimming Available
8. Skiing Available
9. Credit Cards Accepted
10. Personal Check Accepted
11. Off Season Rates
12. Dinner Available (w/sufficient notice)

California

San Francisco

Sunchild, Sami
1665 Haight St., 94117
(415) 864-1978

Amenities: 1,2,5,6,9,10,11
Breakfast: Continental
Dbl. Oc.: $55.50-$133.20
Sgl. Oc.: $49.95-$77.70
Third Person: $11.10

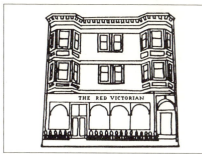

The Red Victorian—B&B, a Global Family Network Center. Flower child room; Redwood forest room; 13 more; informality fun; breakfast; afternoon tea in Peace Gallery—transformational art; near Golden Gate Park.

San Francisco

Wamsley, Helvi & George
1902 Filbert, 94123
(415) 567-1526

Amenities: 1,5,6,7,9,10
Breakfast: Continental
Dbl. Oc.: $85.00
Sgl. Oc.: $65.00
Third Person: $20.00

Art Center Bed & Breakfast—Artistic homecoming with private kitchen in posh area near everything for ideal vacations: marina, Union St., fireplaces, garden, 1, 2 & 3 room suites. 1902 Filbert at Laguna.

San Francisco

Widburg, Monica
2007 15th Ave., 94116
(415) 564-1751

Amenities: 1,3,5,6,7,10,12
Breakfast: Full

Dbl. Oc.: $50.00
Sgl. Oc.: $40.00

Located in a quiet, hilly residential area with lovely ocean views, this charming home offers one room for B. & B. Ample parking; public transportation nearby; 20 min. from airport; resident dog. Dinner $10./Person.

San Gregorio

Raynor, Lee & Bud
Rt. 1, Box 54, 94074
(415) 747-0810

Amenities: 1,2,10
Breakfast: Full

Dbl. Oc.: $70.00
Sgl. Oc.: $60.00
Third Person: 15.00

Rancho San Gregorio—15 acre mission style ranch 40 miles south of San Francisco-ocean 5 min.; creek, orchards, gardens, gazebo; 4 rooms-pvt. baths; informal, friendly; hearty country breakfast served.

AMENITIES

1. No Smoking
2. No Pets
3. No Children
4. Senior Citizen Rates
5. Tennis Available
6. Golf Available
7. Swimming Available
8. Skiing Available
9. Credit Cards Accepted
10. Personal Check Accepted
11. Off Season Rates
12. Dinner Available (w/sufficient notice)

California

San Jose

Fuhring, Cheryl & James
897 E. Jackson St., 95112
(408) 279-5999

Amenities: 1,2,5,9,10
Breakfast: Full
Dbl. Oc.: $55.00-$85.00
Sgl. Oc.: $55.00-$85.00
Third Person: $5.00

The Briar Rose—1875 Victorian restored to its former grandeur. Period furnishings; fabulously wallpapered; gardens; a pond; arbors; wrap around porch; close to historical points of interest; 10 mins. from San Jose Airport.

San Miguel

Allen, Catherine & Ed
3200 N. Mission St.,
Box 8, 93451
(805) 467-3306

Amenities: 10
Breakfast: Continental

Dbl. Oc.: $53.00-$58.30
Sgl. Oc.: $53,00-$58.30

Victorian Manor is located 1 1/4 miles north of San Miguel, where highway 101 and North Mission converge. The historic old town of San Miguel is located halfway between San Francisco and Los Angeles.

San Miguel

Van Horn, Gloria & Martin
3625 Cholame Vly. Rd., 93451
(805) 463-2320

Amenities: 1,2,7,10,12
Breakfast: Full

Dbl. Oc.: $65.00-$100.00
Sgl. Oc.: $65.00-$100.00
Third Person: $10.00

The Ranch has many acres to roam on foot or horseback; four guest rooms; priv. or shared baths; pool; hot tub; creek; ponds; quiet; complimentary wine; near: Paso Robles, wineries, Hearst Castle, & more.

San Pedro

Ginsburg, Ms. Marilyn
809 South Grand Ave., 90731
(213) 548-1240

Amenities: 1,2,3,9,12
Breakfast: Full

Dbl. Oc.: $100.80
Sgl. Oc.: $84.00
Third Person: $6.80

The Grand Cottages—Four beautifully restored California bungalow suites. Intimate hideaway with class in wharf town San Pedro. Minutes to ocean; adjoining award winning Grand House Restaurant; near shopping, sightseeing.

AMENITIES

1. No Smoking
2. No Pets
3. No Children
4. Senior Citizen Rates
5. Tennis Available
6. Golf Available
7. Swimming Available
8. Skiing Available
9. Credit Cards Accepted
10. Personal Check Accepted
11. Off Season Rates
12. Dinner Available (w/sufficient notice)

California

Santa Barbara

Canfield, Carolyn & Bill
P.O. Box 20065, 93102
(805) 966-6659

Amenities: 5,6,7,10
Breakfast: Continental

Dbl. Oc.: $45.00
Sgl. Oc.: $40.00
Third Person: $10.00

Ocean View House is 3 blocks from the ocean. Two room suite; queen size bed; private bath; den (double bed divan) with private entrance and TV. Sip on a glass of wine while viewing Channel Island. Two day minimum.

Santa Barbara

Eaton, Jeanise Suding
1908 Bath St., 93101
(805) 687-2300

Amenities: 1,2,5,6,7,9,10,11
Breakfast: Continental

Dbl. Oc.: $64.35-$99.00
Sgl. Oc.: $64.35-$99.00
Third Person: $10.00

Blue Quail Inn and Cottages—Cottages, suites and guestrooms filled with country charm; quiet and relaxing; tree shaded patios and gardens; close to town and beach; bikes; picnics; fireplace.

Santa Barbara

Eaton, Jeanise Suding
420 West Montecito St., 93101
(805) 962-8447

Amenities: 1,2,5,6,7,9,10,11
Breakfast: Full

Dbl. Oc.: $84.15-$170.50
Sgl. Oc.: $84.15-$170.50
Third Person: $10.00

The Inn By The Sea—Simply elegant accommodations in the French country manner; in-room spas; fireplaces; private baths; views.

Santa Barbara

Long, M/M Bob
317 Piedmont Rd., 93105
(805) 687-2947

Amenities: 1,2,4,10
Breakfast: Full

Dbl. Oc.: $65.00
Sgl. Oc.: $55.00

Long's Seaview Bed & Breakfast—Lovely view home near beach and all attractions. Antiques; brass 4-poster double bed; private bath; use of spa; friendly helpful hosts; wine served on arrival. Local maps and information provided.

Santa Barbara

MacDonald, Carol
1323 De La Vina St., 93101
(805) 963-2283

Amenities: 1,9,10
Breakfast: Full

Dbl. Oc.: $75.00-$145.00
Sgl. Oc.: $75.00-$145.00

Tiffany Inn—A romantic place to relax among oak antiques and French country decorating. Walking distance to shops, restaurants, theaters, and only 13 blocks from the beach. Come visit California's most favorite city.

AMENITIES

1. No Smoking
2. No Pets
3. No Children
4. Senior Citizen Rates
5. Tennis Available
6. Golf Available
7. Swimming Available
8. Skiing Available
9. Credit Cards Accepted
10. Personal Check Accepted
11. Off Season Rates
12. Dinner Available (w/sufficient notice)

California

Santa Barbara

Miller, Ms. Marie
435 E. Pedregosa, 93103
(805) 569-1914

Amenities: 1,2,10
Breakfast: Contnental

Dbl. Oc.: $45.00
Sgl. Oc.: $45.00
Third Person: $10.00

The Old Mission House was built in 1895 and is located 2 blocks from the Santa Barbara Mission within walking distance of shops, parks, and museums. The spacious rooms are furnished with antiques and have fireplaces.

Santa Barbara

Morgan, Ms. Pat
1327 Bath, 93101
(805) 966-0589

Amenities: 1,2,3,5,6,7,9,10,11
Breakfast: Continental

Dbl. Oc.: $71.24-$164.40
Sgl. Oc.: $65.76-$158.92
Third Person: $10.00

Glenborough Inn—A romantic respite; private garden hot tub; breakfast in bed or garden; easy walk to: shops, restaurants, & galleries. Bike to: beach, museum, & Mission. Drinks & snacktime; fireplace suites; antiques.

Santa Barbara

Van Tuyl, Florence
780 Mission Canyon Rd., 93105
(805) 687-6933

Amenities: 1,2,3,5,6,7,10
Breakfast: Full
Dbl. Oc.: $95.00-$125.00
Sgl. Oc.: $85.00-$115.00
Third Person: $40.00

Villa D'Italia—Splendiferous villa; marvelous gardens; massive fireplace; 20 foot ceilings; wonderful antiques; grand piano; giant projection TV; be treated like royalty. 3 course gourmet breakfast; entire wing for guest's use.

Santa Barbara

Wilson, Gillean
121 E. Arrellaga St., 93101
(805) 963-7067

Amenities: 1,2,3,9,10,11
Breakfast: Full

Dbl. Oc.: $75.00-$150.00
Sgl. Oc.: $75.00-$150.00
Third Person: $15.00

Simpson House Inn—1874 Victorian home secluded on an acre of English gardens, 5 min. walk to downtown. 6 elegant rooms with lace, oriental rugs, original art. Spacious common areas open onto porches where breakfast is served.

AMENITIES

1. No Smoking
2. No Pets
3. No Children
4. Senior Citizen Rates
5. Tennis Available
6. Golf Available
7. Swimming Available
8. Skiing Available
9. Credit Cards Accepted
10. Personal Check Accepted
11. Off Season Rates
12. Dinner Available (w/sufficient notice)

California

Santa Clara

Wigginton, Mrs. Ralph
1390 Madison St., 95050
(408) 249-5541

Amenities: 1,2,4,5,6,7,9,10,11,12
Breakfast: Full
Dbl. Oc.: $65.00
Sgl. Oc.: $55.00
Third Person: $10.00

Madison Street Inn—Just 10 mins. from San Jose Airport, is an elegant Victorian inn with landscaped gardens that will meet both business and personal needs. Only 1 hr. from San Francisco and 1 1/4 hrs. from Monterey; antiques decorated rooms.

Santa Cruz

Benjamin, Alice-June & Franz
118 1st. St., 95060
(408) 458-9458

Amenities: 1,2,3,5,6,7,9,10
Breakfast: Continental

Dbl. Oc.: $98.00-$131.00

Chateau Victorian—Built in the 1880's, has been totally renovated. Each room has a private bath, fireplace & queen bed. The inn is located 1 block from the beach, close to the boardwalk amusement park & Fisherman's Pier.

Santa Cruz

King, Helen & Tom
1025 Laurel St., 95060
(408) 427-2437

Amenities: 1,2,5,6,9,10
Breakfast: Full

Dbl. Oc.: $95.00-$140.00
Sgl. Oc.: $95.00-$140.00
Third Person: $17.00

Babbling Brook Inn—Cascading waterfalls, meandering creek, pines, Redwoods surround this secluded 1909 inn built over a 1790's flour mill. 12 rooms with private bath, telephone, fireplace or deep tub; walk to ocean, & shops.

Santa Cruz

Taylor, Sharon & Bruce
407 Cliff St., 95060
(408) 427-2609

Amenities: 1,2,3,4,9,10
Breakfast: Full

Dbl. Oc.: $81.00-$140.40

Cliff Crest Bed And Breakfast Inn—5 bedroom 1887 Queen Anne Victorian, 1 1/2 blocks from beach & boardwalk. Lush grounds; gardens; off-street parking; private bathrooms; queen or king beds; fine restaurants, shops close by.

AMENITIES

1. No Smoking
2. No Pets
3. No Children
4. Senior Citizen Rates
5. Tennis Available
6. Golf Available
7. Swimming Available
8. Skiing Available
9. Credit Cards Accepted
10. Personal Check Accepted
11. Off Season Rates
12. Dinner Available (w/sufficient notice)

California

Santa Cruz

Young, M/M Allen
P.O. Box 66593,
(Scotts Valley) 95066
(415) 321-5195

Amenities: 1,2,3,6,7,9,10
Breakfast: Full

Dbl. Oc.: $95.00
Sgl. Oc.: $95.00

Valley View Inn—Romantic hideaway; 2 bedrooms, 2 bath, Frank Lloyd Wright glass home. Magnificent view, complete privacy to one couple or group at a time. Hot spa on deck & we'll leave you the key if you prefer to be alone!

Santa Monica

Zolla, Susan
219 W. Channel Rd., 90402
(213) 459-1920

Amenities: 1,2,3,5,9,10
Breakfast: Continental

Dbl. Oc.: $90.00-$150.00

Channel Road Inn—An historic landmark house one block from the beach. Each of the 14 rooms is uniquely decorated and each has a private bath. Most rooms have ocean views. Wine and cheese served every afternoon.

Santa Rosa

Cheatham, William
4257 Petaluma Hill Rd., 95404
(707) 585-7777

Amenities: 1,2,3,9
Breakfast: Full

Dbl. Oc.: $80.00
Sgl. Oc.: $80.00
Third Person: $20.00

The Gables—A cozy retreat. An historic landmark in Sonoma County, gateway to California wine country; fireplaces; sundeck; country setting.

Santa Rosa

Gevarter, Annette & Bill
9550 St. Helena Rd., 95404
(707) 944-0880

Amenities: 1,2,3,6,10,11
Breakfast: Continental
Dbl. Oc.: $85.00
Sgl. Oc.: $75.00
Third Person: $15.00

Hilltop House Bed And Breakfast—A secluded mountain hideaway in a romantic setting on 135 acres of unspoiled wilderness. Hilltop House gives a hang glider's view of the Mayacamus Mountains; only 12 minutes from St. Helena and Rte. 29.

AMENITIES

1. No Smoking
2. No Pets
3. No Children
4. Senior Citizen Rates
5. Tennis Available
6. Golf Available
7. Swimming Available
8. Skiing Available
9. Credit Cards Accepted
10. Personal Check Accepted
11. Off Season Rates
12. Dinner Available (w/sufficient notice)

California

Sausalito

MacDonald, Liz
16 El Portal, 94965
(415) 332-4155

Amenities: 5,6,9,10
Breakfast: Continental

Shared Bath: $70.20-$81.00
Priv. Bath: $91.80-$151.20

The Sausalito Hotel is a lovely and romantic inn, decorated in Victorian antiques, located in the heart of Sausalito adjacent to the San Francisco Ferry. A truly unique place to visit.

Seal Beach

Bettenhausen, Mrs. Marjorie
212 5th St., 92683
(213) 493-2416

Amenities: 2,4,5,6,7,8,9,10
Breakfast: Full
Dbl. Oc.: $96.00-$158.00
Sgl. Oc.: $53.00-$158.00
Third Person: $10.00

The Seal Beach Inn & Gardens—This classic country inn is located near all So. California attractions. 22 romantic suites with private baths; lavish gardens, library and pool; one block from beach, near restaurants, marina and shops.

Seal Beach

Brendel, Dr. Michelle
204 Ocean Ave., 90740
(213) 594-0397

Amenities: 1,2,5,6,7
Breakfast: Full

Dbl. Oc.: $125.00
Sgl. Oc.: $100.00
Third Person: $15.00

Villa Pacifica—Spanish home on the water. Walk past greenhouses and grape arbor down winding walk out private rear gate to last sand dunes; private indoor jacuzzi. Seal Beach exit from 405 Freeway and south to ocean.

Skyforest

Wolley, Kathleen & John
28717 Highway 18, P.O. Box 362, 92385
(714) 336-1482

Amenities: 1,2,3,4,5,6,7,8,9,10,11
Breakfast: Full
Dbl. Oc.: $79.00-$135.00
Sgl. Oc.: $79.00-$135.00
Third Person: $25.00

Storybook Inn—9 elegantly decorated rooms all w/baths. Rustic 3 bedroom cabin; spectacular 100-mile view; full home-cooked breakfast; complimentary wines & hors d'oeuvres; attentive service; conference room; weddings.

AMENITIES

1. No Smoking
2. No Pets
3. No Children
4. Senior Citizen Rates
5. Tennis Available
6. Golf Available
7. Swimming Available
8. Skiing Available
9. Credit Cards Accepted
10. Personal Check Accepted
11. Off Season Rates
12. Dinner Available (w/sufficient notice)

California

Sonoma

Lewis, Donna
316 E. Napa St., 95476
(707) 996-5339

Amenities: 9
Breakfast: Continental

Dbl. Oc.: $73.14-$116.60

Beautiful Gardens & winding paths surround the swimming pool of this lovely & historic farm house. Private entrances & baths; gourmet continental breakfast served; concierge srevices provided.

Sonoma

Musilli, Mrs. Dorene
110 West Spain St., 95476
(707) 996-2996

Amenities: 2,9,10,12
Breakfast: Continental
Dbl. Oc.: $61.48-$103.88
Sgl. Oc.: $61.48-$103.88
Third Person: $15.00

The Sonoma Hotel is close to the city but a hundred years away. Furnished with polished antiques, each room has its own unique character. Within walking distance of many of Sonoma's historic landmarks.

Sonora

Birdsall, Jean & Virgil
22157 Feather River Dr., 95370
(415) 532-1248

Amenities: 1,2,3,5,6,7,8,10
Breakfast: Full

Dbl. Oc.: $48.50-$64.70
Sgl. Oc.: $37.50-$48.50

Jameson's-Gold Country Retreat built on four acres over a creek by a waterfall. Glass doors open to decks and giant oaks and cedars. Four guest rooms, mirrored game room, fireplace, and gracious service await.

Sonora

Hoffman, Mrs. Nancy
153 S. Shepherd, 95370
(209) 533-3445

Amenities: 1,2,3,4,5,6,7,8,9,10,11
Breakfast: Full

Dbl. Oc.: $70.06
Sgl. Oc.: $64.67

Ryan House is a small ninteenth century home, furnished with antiques and Victorian reproductions. Parlor has wood-burning stove. Afternoon tea and treats; breakfast served in dining room.

Sutter Creek

Brahmst, Nancy & Bob
55 Eureka St., P.O. Box 386, 95685
(209) 267-0342

Amenities: 9,10
Breakfast: Full

Dbl. Oc.: $90.10
Sgl. Oc.: $84.80

Nancy & Bob's Eureka Street Inn is a California Bungalow built in 1916. Our five spacious guest rooms, individually decorated in the mode of the past, have queen-size beds, private baths, and are air-conditioned. A full breakfast awaits.

AMENITIES

1. No Smoking
2. No Pets
3. No Children
4. Senior Citizen Rates
5. Tennis Available
6. Golf Available
7. Swimming Available
8. Skiing Available
9. Credit Cards Accepted
10. Personal Check Accepted
11. Off Season Rates
12. Dinner Available (w/sufficient notice)

California

Tahoe City

Kaye, Janie
236 Grove St.
Box 5999, 95730
(916) 583-1001

Amenities: 2,5,6,7,8,9,10,11
Breakfast: Full

Dbl. Oc.: $70.20-$108.00
Third Person: $15.00

Mayfield Inn—A snug and cozy six-room inn within walking distance of shops and fine restaurants. Restful and quiet, near beach and major ski resorts. Guests receive calls at 583-9743. Fresh juice and fruit pastries.

Tomales

Randall, Byron
25 Valley St., 94971
(707) 878-9992

Amenities: 2,3,10
Breakfast: Continental

Dbl. Oc.: $55.00-$70.00
Sgl. Oc.: $55.00-$70.00
Third Person: $20.00

A Very Special Place—Located between Bodega & Pt. Reyes on Calif. Coast Hwy. 1, Byron Randall's famous Victorian Guesthouse and Art Gallery is a lovely and tranquil retreat, secluded by trees & garden. No children under 10.

Truckee

Huebner, Mary Lou
10154 High St., 95734
(916) 587-5388

Amenities: 2,3,4,5,6,7,8,9,10,11
Breakfast: Full
Dbl. Oc.: $75.60
Sgl. Oc.: $75.60
Third Person: $16.20

Richardson House—Authentic Victorian in historic preservation district. Walking distance to dining, shopping, and historical sites. Skiing, fishing, swimming, hiking, golf etc. in and around Lake Tahoe, in the High Sierras.

Twain Harte

Pantaleoni, Mr. El
18864 Manzanita Dr., 95383
(209) 586-3111

Amenities: 2,4,5,6,7,8,9,10,11
Breakfast: Full

Dbl. Oc.: $45.00-$70.00
Sgl. Oc.: $40.00-$50.00
Third Person: $5.00

Twain Harte's Bed & Breakfast invites you to relax and enjoy the comfort of our hospitality in the romantic atmosphere of a wooded Sierra setting; beautifully restored and tastefully furnished; easy walk to downtown Twain Harte.

AMENITIES

1. No Smoking
2. No Pets
3. No Children
4. Senior Citizen Rates
5. Tennis Available
6. Golf Available
7. Swimming Available
8. Skiing Available
9. Credit Cards Accepted
10. Personal Check Accepted
11. Off Season Rates
12. Dinner Available (w/sufficient notice)

California

Ukiah

Wadley, Mrs. Shirley
858 Sanel Dr., Box 412
95482
(707) 468-5646

Amenities: 1,2,3
Breakfast: Full

Dbl. Oc.: $54.00
Sgl. Oc.: $48.60

Oak Knoll Bed & Breakfast—A home with city elegance and rustic charm with spectacular views, easy access to coast, Redwoods and wine country. A large deck with solar spa and jacuzzi. Hwy. 101 close by.

Ventura

Baida, Gisela
411 Poli St., 93001
(805) 643-3600

Amenities: 1,2,3,9,10
Breakfast: Full
Dbl. Oc.: $80.00-$115.00
Sgl. Oc.: $75.00-$110.00
Third Person: $20.00

La Mer—Hillside Victorian house with ocean view. All five rooms have private baths and private entrances. Short walk to beach and Old Town. Famous Bavarian breakfast; complimentary wine; authentic European style.

Walnut Creek

Martin, Mrs. Lois
2113 Blackstone Dr., 94598
(415) 934-8119

Amenities: 1,2,4,5,6,7,10
Breakfast: Full

Dbl. Oc.: $60.00
Sgl. Oc.: $50.00
Third Person: $10.00

Gasthaus Zum Bären offers luxury accommodations with poolside breakfasts, country charm and old world "Gemütlichkeit," just 40 minutes from downtown San Francisco. German, Spanish, Italian spoken.

West Covina

Hendrick, Mary & George
2124 E. Merced Ave., 91791
(818) 919-2125

Amenities: 2,5,6,7,10,12
Breakfast: Full
Dbl. Oc.: $30.00-$40.00
Sgl. Oc.: $25.00-$35.00

The Hendricks' Home—A real taste of California lifestyle. Gorgeous deck area w/swimming pool, jacuzzi, plenty of space to relax. Centrally located for Disneyland, L.A., mountains, & desert. Genial hosts will direct you to special undiscovered spots or to the more popular attractions.

AMENITIES

1. No Smoking
2. No Pets
3. No Children
4. Senior Citizen Rates
5. Tennis Available
6. Golf Available
7. Swimming Available
8. Skiing Available
9. Credit Cards Accepted
10. Personal Check Accepted
11. Off Season Rates
12. Dinner Available (w/sufficient notice)

California

Westport

Grigg, M/M Charles
40501 N. Hwy. One
P.O. Box 121, 95488
(707) 964-6725

Amenities: 2,10,11
Breakfast: Full

Dbl. Oc.: $54.00-$91.80
Sgl. Oc.: $54.00-$91.80
Third Person: $15.00

Howard Creek Ranch—1867 rural ocean-front ranch, 20 acres; magnificent views; beach; mountains; creeks, sauna; pool; hot tub; fireplace; antiques; flower garden; cabins; parlor with piano; near Redwoods.

Whittier

Davis, Coleen
11715 S. Circle Dr., 90601
(213) 699-8427

Amenities: 2,5,6,10,12
Breakfast: Full

Dbl. Oc.: $50.00
Sgl. Oc.: $40.00
Third Person: $15

Colleen's California Casa—3 rooms with private bath; beach view; parking; private entrance; complimentary beverage; full breakfast; lunch; dinner; no credit cards; children ok; open year round; near Disneyland & Knott's Berry; beach view.

Yountville

Back, Ruth & Dieter
6711 Washington St., 94599
(707) 944-0889

Amenities: 1,2,3,10
Breakfast: Full

Dbl. Oc.: $110.00
Sgl. Oc.: $99.00
Third Person: $11.00

Burgundy House Inn—French country stone structure built 1870, originally a brandy distillery now a B. & B. with 5 cozy guest rooms. Rustic masonary accentuated by antique country furniture. Ideal location at entrance of famous Napa Valley.

AMENITIES

1. No Smoking
2. No Pets
3. No Children
4. Senior Citizen Rates
5. Tennis Available
6. Golf Available
7. Swimming Available
8. Skiing Available
9. Credit Cards Accepted
10. Personal Check Accepted
11. Off Season Rates
12. Dinner Available (w/sufficient notice)

Colorado

The Centennial State

Capital: Denver
Statehood: August 1, 1876; the 38th state
State Motto: Nothing Without Providence
State Song: "Where the Columbines Grow"
State Bird: Lark Bunting
State Flower: Rocky Mountain Columbine
State Tree: Blue Spruce

Colorado, with its majestic rocky mountains and its cool refreshing climate, is a state tourists love to visit. It has unusual natural beauty, historic mining towns and old Indian cliff dwellings. It also is the home for the U.S. Air Force Academy.

Skiing is the big winter attraction. At Vale, Aspen and other well known areas, millions of dollars a year are spent on this sport by vacationers.

Tourists can still ride the old-time locomotive between Durango and Silverton, and the Cliff Palaces of the Indians such as Mesa Verde are a constant source of pleasure for those who enjoy Indian history.

Buffalo Bill's grave lies atop Lookout Mountain near Denver.

Colorado

Aspen

Precival, Anthony
520 West Main St., 81611
(303) 925-7696

Amenities: 2,7,8,9,10,11
Breakfast: Full

Dbl. Oc.: $46.00-$80.00
Sgl. Oc.: $40.00-$80.00
Third Person: $8-$10

Ullr Lodge—Small European style lodge family owned and operated, located in the residential west end of town. Close to music tent & Aspen Institute, ten minute walk to town. Heated pool, whirlpool sauna.

Aspen

Prodinger, Ms. Irma
134 E. Hyman, 81611
(303) 925-7632

Amenities: 2,4,7,12
Breakfast: Full

Dbl. Oc.: $134.00-$188.00
Sgl. Oc.: $134.00-$158.00
Third Person: $30.00

Hearthstone House—Distinctive lodge offering hospitality and services in the finest tradition of European luxury inns. Full breakfast & afternoon tea served daily with compliments. Excellent library in elegant living room.

Aspen

Stapleton, M/M Sam
Owl Creek Rd.
P.O. Box 98, 81612
(303) 925-7322

Amenities: 1,2,8,9,10,11
Breakfast: Continental

Dbl. Oc.: $69.03
Sgl. Oc.: $69.03
Third Person: $10-$20

Stapleton Spurr is a working cattle ranch located in the majestic Rocky Mts. between Aspen & Snowmass Village. The family settled here in 1881. The inn is a modern home with scenic views & quietness.

Basalt

Waterman, Mrs. Martha
6878 Hwy. 82
P.O. Box 875, 81621
(303) 927-3309

Amenities: 1,2,7,8
Breakfast: Full

Dbl. Oc.: $50.00
Sgl. Oc.: $40.00
Third Person: $10.00

Altamira Ranch Bed & Breakfast—Relax in a quiet, peaceful ranch atmosphere midway between Aspen, world renowned resort and Glenwood Springs with its famous hot springs pool. Gold Metal trout stream within walking distance.

Breckenridge

Wells, Jean & Jack
P.O. Box 2252, 80424
(303) 453-6456

Amenities: 2,5,6,7,8,9,10,11
Breakfast: Full

Dbl. Oc.: $33.00-$59.00
Sgl. Oc.: $26.00-$56.00
Third Person: $10.00

The Fireside Inn is 1/2 mile from ski lifts, on shuttle bus route, and 14 miles from Copper Mt. and Keystone, 2 blocks from downtown with its many shops, restaurants and lounges. Located in National Historic Zone.

AMENITIES

1. No Smoking
2. No Pets
3. No Children
4. Senior Citizen Rates
5. Tennis Available
6. Golf Available
7. Swimming Available
8. Skiing Available
9. Credit Cards Accepted
10. Personal Check Accepted
11. Off Season Rates
12. Dinner Available (w/sufficient notice)

Colorado

Colorado Springs

Clark, Sallie & Welling
1102 W. Pikes Peak Ave.
80904
(719) 471-3980

Amenities: 1,2,3,5,6,7,8,9,10
Breakfast: Full

Dbl. Oc.: $50.00-$55.00
Sgl. Oc.: $50.00-$55.00

"Holden House, 1902"—Spacious Victorian home filled with antiques, near historic district of "Old Colorado City" & 1/2 mile west of I-25. No smoking, children or pets; friendly resident cat "Mingtoy"; lodging in Victorian elegance.

Cortez

Carriker, Kristie & Rodney
14663 Co Rd. G, 81321
(303) 565-3125 or 882-4943

Amenities: 2,3,8,10
Breakfast: Full

Dbl. Oc.: $38.00
Sgl. Oc.: $30.00
Third Person: $7.00

Kelly Place—Draft Horse Covered Wagon trips; tours to major Indian ruins & trading posts; participate in ongoing excavation of Anasazil Ruins, Navajo weaving & pottery workshops; complete accommodations.

Del Norte

Wicks, Bernadette & John
605 Grande, P.O. Box 762
81132
(214) 657-2668

Amenities: 2,3,8,10
Breakfast: Full

Dbl. Oc.: $45.00-$55.00
Third Person: $10.00

Windsor Hotel Bed & Breakfast Inn—Built in 1872, the Windsor is the oldest hotel in Colorado. Many shops on lower level include antiques and collectables. Antique furniture and handmade quilts adorn turn-of-the-century hotel rooms.

Denver

Hillestad, Ann & Charles
2147 Tremont Pl., 80205
(303) 296-6666

Amenities: 1,2,3,9,10,12
Breakfast: Continental
Dbl. Oc.: $135.00
Sgl. Oc.: $125.00
Third Person: $15.00

Queen Anne Inn—Elegantly restored & furnished Victorian located in downtown Historic District. named by the press as "Best B&B in Town, one of America's top 10" wedding night sites & "The choice" for urban romantics.

AMENITIES

1. No Smoking
2. No Pets
3. No Children
4. Senior Citizen Rates
5. Tennis Available
6. Golf Available
7. Swimming Available
8. Skiing Available
9. Credit Cards Accepted
10. Personal Check Accepted
11. Off Season Rates
12. Dinner Available (w/sufficient notice)

Colorado

Dolores

Wagner, M/M
13980 Co. Rd. 29, 81323
(303) 565-8721

Amenities: 9,10
Breakfast: Full

Dbl. Oc.: $35.00
Sgl. Oc.: $35.00
Third Person: $5.00

Simon Draw Guest House—A charming private cottage in the woods. Kitchen, living room, bedroom, bath; sleeps 2-5. Large deck overlooking mini canyon, stream & trails. Near Mesa Verde Nat'l. Park. Open April-Oct.

Estes Park

Cotten, Kathleen & Ron
Box 1208, 80517
(303) 586-5104

Amenities: 2,5,6,7,8,10,11
Breakfast: Full

Dbl. Oc.: $59.00
Sgl. Oc.: $50.00
Third Person: $9.00

Cottenwood House—Enjoy old-fashioned hospitality in this immaculate circa 1928 home, just minutes from the heart of Estes Park and Rocky Mountain National Park. Full country breakfast served on sunny porch with flowers.

Estes Park

Wanek, Pat & Jim
560 Ponderosa Dr.,
P.O. Box 898, 80517
(303) 586-5851

Amenities: 1,2,3,5,6,7,8,10,12
Breakfast: Continental

Dbl. Oc.: $40.74-$46.10
Sgl. Oc.: $33.23-$36.45
Third Person: $7.50-$9.65

Wanek's Lodge At Estes—Modern mountain inn on a Ponderosa Pine covered hillside, just a few miles from Rocky Mt. Nat'l. Park. Wood beams, stone fireplace, plants, & beautiful scenery provide a comfortable and relaxed atmosphere.

Fort Collins

Clark, Mrs. Sheryl
202 E. Elizabeth, 80524
(303) 493-2337

Amenities: 1,2,5,6,7,8,10
Breakfast: Full

Dbl. Oc.: $45.00
Sgl. Oc.: $35.00
Third Person: 10.00

Elizabeth Street Guest House—One block from Colorado State University. Warm old-fashioned hospitality await you in this beautifully restored historic brick home filled with antiques & folk art. Gourmet full breakfast—home baking.

AMENITIES

1. No Smoking
2. No Pets
3. No Children
4. Senior Citizen Rates
5. Tennis Available
6. Golf Available
7. Swimming Available
8. Skiing Available
9. Credit Cards Accepted
10. Personal Check Accepted
11. Off Season Rates
12. Dinner Available (w/sufficient notice)

Colorado

Golden

Lund, Alice & George
279 Gardenia Ct., 80401
(303) 279-7137

Amenities: 1,5,7,8
Breakfast: Continental
Dbl. Oc.: $43.00
Sgl. Oc.: $35.00

Foothills Bed & Breakfast is located 1 1/2 miles to I-70. Close to all Denver attractions. 45 min. to skiing. Hosts enjoys music, skiing & hiking. Brfts. in sunny oak D.R., fresh fruit & hot breads. Two rms. avail. Quiet culdesac.

Golden

Sims, Jean and Ken
711 14th Street
(303) 278-2209

Amenities: 1,2,9
Breakfast: Full
Dbl. Oc.: $46.77
Sgl. Oc.: $41.46
Third Person: $5.00

The Dove Inn is a charming Victorian inn with 6 rms., private baths nr. Coors Tours, skiing, Rocky Mt. Nat'l. Pk. Close to Denver, yet in the foothills of Golden. The Dove Inn offers guests the best of both worlds.

Green Mountain Falls

Novicke, Barbara & Marty Hudson
P.O. Box 267, 80819
(719) 684-9062

Amenities: 5,7,8,9,11,12
Breakfast: Continental

Dbl. Oc.: $45.00
Sgl. Oc.: $35.00
Third Person: $5.00

Historic Columbine Lodge is located in the Rocky Mountains in view of Pikes Peak. Enjoy a cozy fireside dinner or a romantic moment in a hot tub under the stars. Quaint and "country" where "welcome" is always felt. A four season delight!!!

Green Mountain Falls

Ramsey, M/M Rodney
6975 Howard St., 80819
(719) 684-2303

Amenities: 1,2,5,7,9,10
Breakfast: Continental

Dbl. Oc.: $43.00
Sgl. Oc.: $38.00

Outlook Lodge—A restored Victorian (1889) set at the foot of Pike's Peak surrounded by pines on property fronted by a creek located just a block away from a lake, pool, tennis, stables, shops and restaurants.

AMENITIES

1. No Smoking
2. No Pets
3. No Children
4. Senior Citizen Rates
5. Tennis Available
6. Golf Available
7. Swimming Available
8. Skiing Available
9. Credit Cards Accepted
10. Personal Check Accepted
11. Off Season Rates
12. Dinner Available (w/sufficient notice)

Colorado

Hesperus

Alford, Lucretia & Davie
16919 Hwy. 140, 81326
(303) 385-4537

Amenities: 1,2,7,9,10
Breakfast: Full
Dbl. Oc.: $72.25-$134.38
Sgl. Oc.: $59.13-$102.13

Blue Lake Ranch is 20 minutes from Durango & 40 minutes from Mesa Verde. Elegantly rennovated Victorian farmhouse with gardens to delight the epicure and flower lover. Spectacular views; hot tub; babies in arms only.

Mesa

Tuttle, Carolyn & Jim
865 Highway 65, 81643
(303) 268-5864

Amenities: 1,8,12
Breakfast: Full

Dbl. Oc.: $35.00-$40.00
Sgl. Oc.: $30.00-$32.00
Third Person: $5.00

JJCC Tuttle Ranch Bed And Breakfast—48-acre newer comfortable home, with trout pond and stream, located on the Grand Mesa with 200 lakes. 4 miles to Powder Horn Ski Resort, 34 miles to Grand Junction Hunter's Paradise. All season recreation.

Redstone

Johnson, Rose Marie & Ken
0058 Redstone Blvd., 81623
(303) 963-3463

Amenities: 5,6,8,9,10
Breakfast: Continental

Dbl. Oc.: $69.00-$159.30
Sgl. Oc.: $69.00-$159.30
Third Person: $10.00

The Redstone Castle—35 miles from Aspen. 16 bedrooms, restored 1898 Manor House. Peaceful Rocky Mountain setting. Breathtaking views. Listed on the national historic register.

Salida

Hostetler, Dottie & Herb
8495 CR 160, 81201
(719) 539-3818

Amenities: 1,3,5,6,7,8,9,10
Breakfast: Full

Dbl. Oc.: $39.00-$49.00
Sgl. Oc.: $29.00 (Winter)
Third Person: $10.00-$15.00

The Poor Farm Country Inn—Historical Victorian home decorated in antiques and surrounded by beautiful mountains on the Arkansas River. 5 rooms, cozy atmosphere! Excellent fishing just steps away, rafting, skiing and many more.

AMENITIES

1. No Smoking
2. No Pets
3. No Children
4. Senior Citizen Rates
5. Tennis Available
6. Golf Available
7. Swimming Available
8. Skiing Available
9. Credit Cards Accepted
10. Personal Check Accepted
11. Off Season Rates
12. Dinner Available (w/sufficient notice)

Colorado

Silver Plume

Joss, Ms. Mary P.
246 Main St.
P.O. Box 473, 80476
(303) 674-5565

Amenities: 9,10
Breakfast: Continental
Dbl. Oc.: $42.84
Sgl. Oc.: $37.48
Third Person: $5.36

The Brewery Inn offers mountain retreat and opportunities to relive Colorado history. Famous Narrow Gauge R.R. in town. 1 hour from Denver and close to 10 ski areas. I-70 exit 226.

Silverton

Wallace, Ann Marie
1069 Snowden, 81433
(303) 387-5879

Amenities: 1,2,3,4,5,6,7,8,9,10,11,12
Breakfast: Full
Dbl. Oc.: $55.00-$70.00
Sgl. Oc.: $35.00
Third Person: $10.00

Fool's Gold Inn—This spacious and prominent 1883 Victorian home overlooking the historic mountain mining town of Silverton. Train packages available. "Come as a guest leave as a friend." Hearty breakfast.

Vail

Rude, Beverly
145 N. Main St., (Minturn)
P.O. Box 100, 81645
(303) 827-5761

Amenities: 1,2,3,4,5,6,8,9,10,11
Breakfast: Continental

Dbl. Oc.: $63.85-$135.25
Sgl. Oc.: $53.00-$124.45

Eagle River Inn—Quiet mountain retreat just 5 minutes from Vail. 12 rooms, southwest style, private bath, gourmet continental breakfast, evening wine & cheese.

AMENITIES

1. No Smoking
2. No Pets
3. No Children
4. Senior Citizen Rates
5. Tennis Available
6. Golf Available
7. Swimming Available
8. Skiing Available
9. Credit Cards Accepted
10. Personal Check Accepted
11. Off Season Rates
12. Dinner Available (w/sufficient notice)

Colorado

Woodland Park

Stoddard, Timothy
236 Pinecrest Rd.
Box 5760, 80866

Amenities: 1,2,3,8,9,10
Breakfast: Full
Dbl. Oc.: $57.31-$67.73
Sgl. Oc.: $57.31-$67.73
Third Person: $12.50

Pike's Peak Paradise—Romantic, peaceful, private, luxurious accommodations. Full gourmet breakfast. Each room includes: incredible view, private entrance, complimentary beverages and snacks. One-of-a-kind theatre pipe organ.

Connecticut

The Constitution State

Capital: Hartford
Statehood: January 9, 1788; the 5th state
State Motto: He Who Transplanted Still Sustains
State Song: "Yankee Doodle"
State Bird: Robin
State Flower: Mountain Laurel
State Tree: White Oak

It was the early Indians that named this state after the long tidal river of Connecticut that flowed through the state into Long Island Sound.

This New England state is proud of its history and goes back to 1639 when as a colony it adopted The Fundamental Orders of Connecticut.

Yale University is the 3rd oldest institution for higher learning and was established in New Haven in 1701. In 1748, the first American Law School was established in Litchfield, Connecticut.

Connecticut is known as the gadget state and its Yankee Peddlers traveled all over selling the craftsmanship of its citizens in clocks, brasswear, buttons, firearms, pins and combs.

Today, visitors can stroll the cobbled streets of the restored Mystic Seaport and visit the old stores, sea captains' homes and museums. The whaling ships, The Joseph Conrad and The Charles Morgan are a visitor's delight. In Groton, Connecticut, the submarine capitol of today's naval world, the first nuclear submarine, the Nautilus, was built.

Connecticut

Bolton

Smith, Cinde & Jeff
25 Hebron Rd., 06043
(203) 643-8538

Amenities: 2,5,6,7,8,10
Breakfast: Full

Dbl. Oc.: $55.00-$65.00
Sgl. Oc.: $40.00-$50.00
Third Person: $10.00

Jared Cone House offers colonial hospitality with queen-size beds, fireplaces and scenic views of the countryside. Homemade maple syrup offered. Fine cuisine nearby. 5 minutes to lake, canoe and bikes provided.

Bristol

Cimadamore, M/M Dante
5 Founders Dr., 06010
(203) 582-4219

Amenities: 2,4,5,8,9
Breakfast: Full
Dbl. Oc.: $88.00
Sgl. Oc.: $77.00
Third Person: $10.75

Chimney Crest Manor—Elegant English Tudor mansion, centrally located near Hartford, Waterbury, & Litchfield. Suites with fireplace or kitchen. Historical Federal Hill area. Long term rates available.

Greenwich

Pearson, Mr. Tog
76 Maple Ave., 06830
(203) 869-2110

Amenities: 2,4,7,9
Breakfast: Continental
Dbl. Oc.: $77.40-$107.50
Sgl. Oc.: $69.88-$107.50
Third Person: $7.00

The Stanton House Inn located in a park-like setting, 30 miles from New York City. A restored mansion designed by Stanford White. It boasts ambiance and the charm of yesterday with 20th century conveniences. Antiques.

Groton Long Point

Ellison, Helen
54 E. Shore Rd., 06340
(203) 536-1180

Amenities: 2,5,7,9,10
Breakfast: Continental

Dbl. Oc.: $50.00-$60.00

Shore Inne—Unique location in residential area. Scenic views, private beaches, fishing, & tennis. Near Mystic Seaport, Aquarium, Coast Guard Academy, Conn. college, A friendly B. & B. with 7 bedrooms, 5 baths.

AMENITIES

1. No Smoking
2. No Pets
3. No Children
4. Senior Citizen Rates
5. Tennis Available
6. Golf Available
7. Swimming Available
8. Skiing Available
9. Credit Cards Accepted
10. Personal Check Accepted
11. Off Season Rates
12. Dinner Available (w/sufficient notice)

Connecticut

Ledyard

Betz, Frankie & Tom
528 Col. Ledyard Hwy., 06339
(203) 536-2022

Amenities: 5,6,7,9,10
Breakfast: Full
Dbl. Oc.: $69.88-$102,13
Third Person: $26.88

Applewood Farm Inn, an 1826 center chimney Colonial on the national register of historic places. On a farm setting, 6 rooms, 4 with working fireplaces. 5 min. from Mystic attractions, Rt. I-95, and fine dining. Open year round.

Middlebury

Cebelenski, Mrs. Susan
96 Tucker Hill Rd., 06762
(203) 758-8334

Amenities: 5,6,7,8,10
Breakfast: Full

Dbl. Oc.: $60.00-$70.00
Third Person: $10.00

Tucker Hill Inn—A large center hall Colonial, just down from the village green, with large and spacious period rooms.

Mystic

Adams, Maureen & Ron
382 Cow Hill Rd., 06355
(203) 572-9551

Amenities: 1,2,3,7,9
Breakfast: Continental

Dbl. Oc.: $55.00
Sgl. Oc.: $55.00
Suite: $95.00

The Adams House—Charming 1790 home with 3 fireplaces, located 1 1/2 miles from downtown Mystic drawbridge. 4 bedrooms in main house. Also country suite with sauna and private entrance which accommodates up to 4 people. In-ground swimming pool.

Mystic

Comolli, Mrs. Dorothy
36 Bruggeman Pl., 06355
(203) 536-8723

Amenities: 1,2,3,10,11
Breakfast: Continental

Dbl. Oc.: $75.00
Sgl. Oc.: $65.00

Comolli's Guest House—Private, family home on quiet hill overlooking Mystic Seaport. Exit 90 off I-95, south to Bruggeman Pl. 1 mile from all attractions in Mystic. Phone for current rates. 2 rooms.

AMENITIES

1. No Smoking
2. No Pets
3. No Children
4. Senior Citizen Rates
5. Tennis Available
6. Golf Available
7. Swimming Available
8. Skiing Available
9. Credit Cards Accepted
10. Personal Check Accepted
11. Off Season Rates
12. Dinner Available (w/sufficient notice)

Connecticut

Mystic

Cornish, Patricia W.
25 Church Street, Noank, 06340
(203) 572-9000

Amenities: 1,2,3,5,6,7,9,10
Breakfast: Continental
Dbl. Oc.: $97.00-$172.00
Sgl. Oc.: $97.00-$172.00
Third Person: $25.00

The Palmer Inn—Two miles to Mystic. Historic turn-of-the-century mansion. An inn of gracious elegance and quiet charm by the sea. Children 16 yrs. and older; no pets or smoking. Open year round.

Mystic

Lucas, Kay & Ted
180 Cow Hill Rd., 06355
(203) 536-3033

Amenities: 1,2,4,10,11
Breakfast: Full

Dbl. Oc.: $65.00-$110.00
Sgl. Oc.: $60.00-$100.00
Third Person: $10.00

Brigadoon—A touch of Scotland in the heart of Mystic. Restored Victorian farmhouse 1.4 miles from Mystic Center. Relaxed, friendly atmosphere on 1 acre of lovely landscaped grounds.

New London

Beatty, Captain Morgan
265 Williams St.
P.O. Box 647, 06320
(203) 447-2600

Amenities: 1,2,3,4,5,6,7,9,11
Breakfast: Full
Dbl. Oc.: $86.00
Sgl. Oc.: $81.00
Third Person: $10.00

Queen Anne Inn in historic Mystic-Groton-New London resort area. Enjoy full breakfast and fireside afternoon tea in Victorian elegance. Private baths, fireplaces. Free health and racquet club.

New Milford

Hammer, Peggy & Rolf
5 Elm St., 06776
(203) 354-4080

Amenities: 9,10
Breakfast: Continental

Dbl. Oc.: $70.95
Sgl. Oc.: $60.20
Third Person: $6.45-10.75

The Holmstead Inn—An historic Victorian with eight guest rooms in the village center. Short walks to restaurants, shops, churches, and antiques. Private baths; open all year; year round recreation.

AMENITIES

1. No Smoking
2. No Pets
3. No Children
4. Senior Citizen Rates
5. Tennis Available
6. Golf Available
7. Swimming Available
8. Skiing Available
9. Credit Cards Accepted
10. Personal Check Accepted
11. Off Season Rates
12. Dinner Available (w/sufficient notice)

Connecticut

Norfolk

Sloan, Michele & Alan
Rt. 272
P.O. Box 467, 06058
(203) 542-5595

Amenities: 4,5,6,7,8,9,10,11,12
Breakfast: Continental

Dbl. Oc.: $91.38
Sgl. Oc.: $91.38
Third Person: $10.75

Mountain View Inn—11-room inn & restaurant in Victorian mansion. Located in the foothills of the Berkshire Mts. Seasonal activities available year round. Off-season & midweek pkgs. Children welcomed. Private baths available.

Norfolk

Zuckerman, Kim & Robert
Rte. 44, 06058
(203) 542-5100

Amenities: 2,5,7,8,9,10,12
Breakfast: Continental
Dbl. Oc.: $65.00-$125.00
Sgl. Oc.: $65.00-$125.00
Third Person: $10.00

Blackberry River Inn—A quaint 225 yr.-old country inn. 17 rooms, some with fireplaces. Fine country dining, lunch and dinner served Wed.-Sun. X-country skiing on premises, rental available.

Norwalk

Tishler, Mrs. Sheila
11 Brenner Rd., 06851
(203) 227-6330

Amenities: 1,2,5,6,7,8,12
Breakfast: Continental

Dbl. Oc.: $55.00
Sgl. Oc.: $40.00

Sheila & Irv's Place—Immaculate country home on Westport-Wilton line. Convenient to I-95, CT 15, beaches, museums, town. Area pretty for walks, foliage drives, fine restaurants. Train to New York City nearby. Hosts helpful. Modern quiet facility.

Old Lyme

Atwood, Ms. Diana Field
85 Lyme St., 06371
(203) 434-2600

Amenities: 5,6,7,8,9,10,12
Breakfast: Continental

Dbl. Oc.: $102.13-$123.63
Sgl. Oc.: $91.39-$112.88
Third Person: $30.00

The Old Lyme Inn is an elegant 1850's home with 13 guest rooms in the Victorian and Empire manner located in the historic district. Private baths, phones, classical dining room, Victorian grillroom, raw bar.

AMENITIES

1. No Smoking
2. No Pets
3. No Children
4. Senior Citizen Rates
5. Tennis Available
6. Golf Available
7. Swimming Available
8. Skiing Available
9. Credit Cards Accepted
10. Personal Check Accepted
11. Off Season Rates
12. Dinner Available (w/sufficient notice)

Connecticut

Old Lyme

Janse, Helen & Donald
11 Flat Rock Hill Rd., 06371
(203) 434-7269

Amenities: 2,3,4,5,7,10
Breakfast: Full

Dbl. Oc.: $60.00
Sgl. Oc.: $55.00
Third Person: $10.00

Janse Bed And Breakfast—Charm, hospitality. Custom Saltbox, Williamsburg interior. Gracious large room, antiques. Pvt. bath. AC, TV. On park-like yard, stone walls, country road. Near fine restaurants, historic sites, Mystic, shops, beaches.

Old Mystic

Jump, Mrs. Sandra
58 Main St., 06372
(203) 572-9422

Amenities: 1,2,9,10,11
Breakfast: Continental
Dbl. Oc.: $95.00-$110.00
Sgl. Oc.: $95.00-110.00
Third Person: $30.00

The Old Mystic Inn—Lovely 1800's Colonial home & carriage house. 8 rooms, all with private bath. 3 working fireplaces. Minutes to Mystic Seaport. Complimentary breakfast & afternoon tea served. Relax in country comfort. Full breakfast served on weekends.

Salisbury

Alexander, Doris & Dick
Route 44 East, 06068
(203) 435-9539

Amenities: 1,2,5,6,7,8,9,10
Breakfast: Full
Dbl. Oc.: $65.00-$70.00
Third Person: $22.00

Yesterday's Yankee Bed And Breakfast— A restored 1744 home in an old New England village offers: cozy rooms, home baking, warm hospitality, sports car track, Music Mountain, Appalachian Trail, independent schools, antiques, boating.

AMENITIES

1. No Smoking
2. No Pets
3. No Children
4. Senior Citizen Rates
5. Tennis Available
6. Golf Available
7. Swimming Available
8. Skiing Available
9. Credit Cards Accepted
10. Personal Check Accepted
11. Off Season Rates
12. Dinner Available (w/sufficient notice)

Connecticut

Somersville

Lumb, M/M Phyllis & Ralph
63 Maple St., 06072
(203) 763-1473

Amenities: 1,2,3,10
Breakfast: Continental
Dbl. Oc.: $55.00
Sgl. Oc.: $55.00
Third Person: $15.00

The Old Mill Inn—Just 5 miles east of I-91, exit 47. Gracious 14 room home in the middle of Tobacco Valley, with a beautiful dining room overlooking lawn surrounded by trees, shrubs, flowers. Sitting rooms, cable TV, fireplace.

Southington

Chaffee, M/M Milton
28 Reussner Rd., 06489
(203) 628-2750

Amenities: 1,2,5,6,10
Breakfast: Full

Dbl. Oc.: $55.00
Sgl. Oc.: $45.00

The Chaffee's B&B—1 twin bedroom with private full bath near I-84. Convenient to Waterbury and Hartford; near Lake Compounce Amusement Park in Bristol.

Stafford Springs

Judd, Dr./Mrs. Kirby
Beffa Rd., 06076
(203) 684-2124

Amenities: 1,2,6,7,8,10
Breakfast: Full
Dbl. Oc.: $37.63-$43.00
Sgl. Oc.: $37.63
Third Person: $5.38

Winterbrook Farm is a restored 1770 house furnished with antiques on a working farm. 3 rooms, shared baths. Ten miles to Old Sturbridge Village, & Brimfield flea market. Swim, X/C skiing, sugaring, lambs, berry picking, fishing.

Storrs

Kollet, Elaine & Bill
418 Gurleyville Rd., 06268
(203) 429-1400

Amenities: 2,5,6,7,8,10,12
Breakfast: Full

Dbl. Oc.: $55.00 & up
Sgl. Oc.: $25.00 & up
Third Person: $15.00

Farmhouse On The Hill Above Gurleyville—An elegant farmhouse, fresh food, comfortable beds, excellent basic accommodations. Close to many recreational, historic & interesting spots. Walking distance to the University of Conn. campus.

AMENITIES

1. No Smoking
2. No Pets
3. No Children
4. Senior Citizen Rates
5. Tennis Available
6. Golf Available
7. Swimming Available
8. Skiing Available
9. Credit Cards Accepted
10. Personal Check Accepted
11. Off Season Rates
12. Dinner Available (w/sufficient notice)

Connecticut

Tolland

Beeching, Susan Geddes
63 Tolland Green, 06084-0717
(203) 872-0800

Amenities: 1,2,3,5,6,9,10
Breakfast: Continental
Dbl. Oc.: $43.00-$53.75
Sgl. Oc.: $32.25-$43.00
Third Person: $10.00

The Tolland Inn—1800 Colonial on village green. Midway from NYC to Boston off I-84, 7 miles from Univ. of CT. Wicker sunporch, kitchen fireplace, antique and custom furniture. No children under 10.

Waterbury

Baysinger, Mrs. Lonetta
18 Hewlett St., 06710
(203) 574-2855

Amenities: 1,2,4,5,9,10
Breakfast: Full

Dbl. Oc.: $60.00-$70.00
Sgl. Oc.: $50.00-$60.00
Third Person: $12.00

The Parsonage Bed And Breakfast—5 minutes from I-84. 15 room Victorian home, former church rectory located in quiet historic area. Period decor, warm hospitality, sumptuous home cooking. Great area for antique shopping. 2 hrs. from N.Y.C.

Westbrook

Grandmaison, Elaine & Ray
138 S. Main St., 06498
(203) 399-7565

Amenities: 1,2,4,5,6,7,8,9,10,11
Breakfast: Continental

Dbl. Oc.: $81.00-$162.00
Sgl. Oc.: $65.00
Third Person: $21.50

The Captain Stannard House—Quiet and convenient. Midway between New York and Boston. Half mile to I-95. Short walk to beach or short drive to tourist attractions. Antique furnishings with today's comforts. Free brochure on request.

Woodbury

Hardisty, Trudy & Chet
506 Main St., 06798
(203) 263-2101

Amenities: 2,5,6,7,8,9,10,12
Breakfast: Continental

Dbl. Oc.: $37.63-$80.63
Sgl. Oc.: $32.25-$64.50
Third Person: $10.75

Curtis House—Connecticut's oldest inn located in beautiful Woodbury, noted for antique shops. Serving luncheon and dinner every day, regional American fare, canopied beds, air-conditioned, cable TV.

AMENITIES

1. No Smoking
2. No Pets
3. No Children
4. Senior Citizen Rates
5. Tennis Available
6. Golf Available
7. Swimming Available
8. Skiing Available
9. Credit Cards Accepted
10. Personal Check Accepted
11. Off Season Rates
12. Dinner Available (w/sufficient notice)

Delaware

The First State

Capital: Dover
Statehood: December 7, 1787; the 1st state
State Motto: Liberty and Independence
State Song: "Our Delaware"
State Bird: Blue Hen Chicken
State Flower: Peach Blossom
State Tree: American Holly

Delaware is called the first state because it was the first to ratify the Constitution of the United States. It is the second smallest state; however, it has so much diversification in industry and economy that it is thought of as a big state. Factories boom in the north and beautiful farmlands grace the southern part of Delaware. Rivers, bays and oceans are all part of this state. If a pollster wants to get a reading on anything, he usually comes here first. In this state there is a cross section of Americans and American industry.

DuPont, the largest chemical company in the world, has its headquarters here and its research division.

Delaware also has its pleasure side, too. The beaches along the Atlantic coast around Rehoboth and Bethany are great favorites with the tourists.

Delaware

Bethany Beach

Duvall, Dale
773-C Salt Pond Circle,
P.O. Box 62, 19930
(302) 539-3354

Amenities: 2,3,5,7,10
Breakfast: Full

Dbl. Oc.: $65.00
Sgl. Oc.: $60.00

Sea Vista Villa—Luxurious villa among the pines on Salt Pond. Six blocks to superb beach, tennis, pool. canoe, & crabbing. Enjoy happy hour and sunsets—delightful! Near state parks and wildlife park.

Bethany Beach

Gravatte, M/M Leroy T, III
99 Ocean View Pkwy.,
Box 275, 19930
(302) 539-3707, (703) 354-8500

Amenities: 2
Breakfast: Continental
Dbl. Oc.: $85.00-$95.00
Third Person: $10.00

THE ADDY SEA
Bethany Beach, DE

The Addy Sea—Circa 1905 three-story Victorian mansion with ocean view, comes complete with fourteen bedrooms, large living room, parlor, dining room, & outside a lovely ocean front porch & veranda.

New Castle

Burwell, M/M Richard
206 Delaware St., 19720
(302) 328-7736

Amenities: 1,2,10
Breakfast: Continental

Dbl. Oc.: $35.00-$70.00
Sgl. Oc.: $35.00-$70.00

William Penn Guest House—A lovely historical home, circa 1682, located across from the Court House on the Square. The house is decorated in antiques, four cheerful guest rooms, shared baths, one room with twin beds has priv. bath.

New Castle

Rosenthal, Dr. Melvin
The Strand at the Wharf, 19720
(302) 322-8944 or 323-0999

Amenities: 2,10,11,12
Breakfast: Full
Dbl. Oc.: $65.00
Sgl. Oc.: $65.00
Third Person: $10.00

THE JEFFERSON HOUSE

The Jefferson House B&B—Charming 200 yr. old river front hotel next to the park in the historic district. Complimentary wine at affiliated restaurant. Off 295 near Philadelphia. William Penn landed here.

AMENITIES

1. No Smoking
2. No Pets
3. No Children
4. Senior Citizen Rates
5. Tennis Available
6. Golf Available
7. Swimming Available
8. Skiing Available
9. Credit Cards Accepted
10. Personal Check Accepted
11. Off Season Rates
12. Dinner Available (w/sufficient notice)

Delaware

Wilmington

Brill, M/M Art
P.O. Box 25254, 19899
(302) 764-0789

Amenities: 1,2,3,7,9,12
Breakfast: Full
Dbl. Oc.: $45.00
Sgl. Oc.: $55.00
Third Person: $20.00

Small Wonder B&B—Near I-95 & duPont Chateau Country. Gracious suburban home. Two guest rooms, pool, hot tub, A/C. Award winning landscaping. $5.00 surcharge for private bath or one night. Convenient to all attractions.

AMENITIES

1. No Smoking	**4.** Senior Citizen Rates	**7.** Swimming Available	**10.** Personal Check Accepted
2. No Pets	**5.** Tennis Available	**8.** Skiing Available	**11.** Off Season Rates
3. No Children	**6.** Golf Available	**9.** Credit Cards Accepted	**12.** Dinner Available (w/sufficient notice)

To list your
Bed & Breakfast
in our next
updated Guide,
send your request to

The National Bed & Breakfast Association
P.O. Box 332
Norwalk, CT 06852

District of Columbia

Washington, D.C.

Founded: Site chosen — 1791
          Became capital — 1800

Washington, D.C. is the capital of the United States. It lies between Maryland and Virginia and it is the only American city or town that is not a part of a state.

The District is mainly made up of government buildings and monuments. Millions of people are employed here for the government, but they live outside the District.

Visitors flock here year round, but especially in the springtime when the cherry blossoms along the Potomac River Basin are in bloom. They come because it is a beautiful city, but mainly to see their government in action.

Some of the most popular attractions are the Capital Building, the House of Congress and Senate, The White House, Lincoln's and Jefferson's Memorial and the Washington Monument. There are also the Smithsonian buildings, Ford's Theatre, the J.F.K. Center for the Performing Arts and many, many other government buildings and museums to visit. Guided tours are available and through your Congressman or Senator, admission passes can be obtained to watch Congress and the Senate when they are in session.

District of Columbia

District of Columbia

Fenstemaker, Rick
1854 Mintwood Pl., NW, 20009
(202) 667-6369

Amenities: 2,4,9,10,11
Breakfast: Continental

Dbl. Oc.: $45.00-$85.00
Sgl. Oc.: $40.00-$80.00

The Kalorama Guest House—Relish the charm of our European-style bed and breakfast. Victorian townhouse offering downtown convenience and old-fashioned hospitality. Walk to metro, busses, fine restaurants and shops.

District of Columbia

Fenstemaker, Rick
2700 Cathedral Ave., NW, 20008
(202) 328-0860

Amenities: 2,4,9,10,11
Breakfast: Continental

Dbl. Oc.: $45.00-$85.00
Sgl. Oc.: $40.00-$80.00

The Kalorama Guest House At Woodley Park—Relish the charm of our European-style bed & breakfast Victorian townhouse offering downtown convenience and old-fashioned hospitality. Walk to Metro, busses, fine restaurants and shops.

District of Columbia

Reed, Mrs. Jacqueline
P.O. Box 12011, 20005
(202) 328-3510

Amenities: 2,5,7,9,10,11
Breakfast: Continental

Dbl. Oc.: $67.00-$78.00
Sgl. Oc.: $56.00-$67.00

The Reeds—Beautifully restored Vistorian townhouse 10 blocks northeast of the Whitehouse. Furnished with antiques, fireplaces, lovely gardens, convenient to public restaurants. Swimming & tennis two blocks away at the school.

District of Columbia

Thompson, M/M Eugene
1744 Lanier Pl., NW, 20009
(202) 745-3600

Amenities: 1,2,9,10
Breakfast: Continental
Dbl. Oc.: $45.00-$61.50
Sgl. Oc.: $39.50-$56.00
Third Person: $5.50

ADAMS INN

Adams Inn—Homestyle convenience in international restaurant area, south of zoo. Air-conditioned. 10-minute walk to subway to government buildings, museums, etc.

AMENITIES

1. No Smoking
2. No Pets
3. No Children
4. Senior Citizen Rates
5. Tennis Available
6. Golf Available
7. Swimming Available
8. Skiing Available
9. Credit Cards Accepted
10. Personal Check Accepted
11. Off Season Rates
12. Dinner Available (w/sufficient notice)

Florida

The Sunshine State

Capital: Tallahassee
Statehood: March 3, 1845; the 27th state
State Motto: In God We Trust
State Song: "Swanee River"
State Flower: Orange Blossom
State Tree: Sabal Palm

Florida is one of the best known states for vacationing and retirement. Its sunny climate beckons thousands of tourists and retirees every year. Its beautiful beaches, orange and grapefruit groves, palm and coconut trees blend to make it a vacationers paradise.

Walt Disney built his Disney World here and Cape Canaveral boasts of Apollo II's lift-off on its way to man's first landing on the moon.

St. Augustine, founded by a Spanish explorer in 1565, is the oldest city in the United States.

Many of Florida's cities are located on canals or waterways, making pleasure boating a way of life. Florida is often referred to as the Venice of the U.S.

Florida

Amelia Island

Grable, Gary
584 S. Fletcher, 32034
(904) 261-5878

Amenities: 2,4,5,6,7,9,10
Breakfast: Continental
Dbl. Oc.: $68.90
Sgl. Oc.: $58.30
Third Person: $10.60

The 1735 House is directly on the beach & near the historic seaport of Fernandina Beach. The guest rooms are suite size with A/C. There is also a two bedroom lighthouse available. Open year round.

Bradenton

Nielsen, Ms. Kay
2717 6th Ave., West, 34205
(813) 747-3541

Amenities: 5,6,7
Breakfast: Full

Dbl. Oc.: $45.00
Sgl. Oc.: $40.00

Nielsen Bed & Breakfast—8 miles from Gulf of Mexico beaches. Off Manatee Avenue leading to Ann Maria Island, Longboat Key & Sarasota. Open Jan.-May.

Cedar Key

Rogers, Ms. Marcia
Main St., Box 460, 32625
(904) 543-5111

Amenities: 1,2,5,7,10
Breakfast: Full
Dbl. Oc.: $77.91
Third Person: $5.00

Historic Island Hotel—Gourmet dining: antiques, relaxing island and location, birds, weddings facilitated with romance and care/stressfree trips with gourmet picnic basket available. TLC throughout the inn. Cafe European style.

Clearwater

Grimm, Vivian & David
3234 Tern Way, 34622
(813) 573-5825

Amenities: 2,6,7,10
Breakfast: Full

Dbl. Oc.: $45.00
Sgl. Oc.: $35.00
Third Person: $10.00

Bed & Breakfast Of Tampa Bay—Lovely home with pool & Oriental flair ideally located on Suncoast. 65 miles to Disney World, Epcot, & Sea World. Dali Museum & Gulf Coast beaches are 10 miles away. Fine restaurant.

AMENITIES

1. No Smoking
2. No Pets
3. No Children
4. Senior Citizen Rates
5. Tennis Available
6. Golf Available
7. Swimming Available
8. Skiing Available
9. Credit Cards Accepted
10. Personal Check Accepted
11. Off Season Rates
12. Dinner Available (w/sufficient notice)

Florida

Daytona Beach

Carlucci, Ms. Anne
509 Seabreeze Blvd., 32018
(904) 252-8743

Amenities: 7,8,9,11,12
Breakfast: Continental
Dbl. Oc.: $92.65
Sgl. Oc.: $81.75
Third Person: $16.35

St. Regis Hotel—Located in the heart of Daytona Beach and built in 1886 this quaint bed and breakfast inn offers excellent continental cuisine and true southern hospitality, a block from the ocean.

Flagler Beach

Hanchar, Mrs. Elizabeth
8119 SW Blue Run Dr., 32630
(904) 489-5362 or 489-5735

Amenities: 1,2,6,7,10
Breakfast: Full

Dbl. Oc.: $55.00
Sgl. Oc.: $40.00
Third Person: $3.00

Beach Lovers' Paradise—200 feet from ocean. Rt. A1A near St. Augustine, Dayton restaurants, shopping. 3 bedroom, 2 bath. Social drinking permitted. Open Dec. thru May.

Florida City

Newton, Mrs. Mildred
40 NW 5th Ave., 33034
(305) 247-4413

Amenities: 4,5,6,7,11
Breakfast: Full

Dbl. Oc.: $50.00
Sgl. Oc.: $45.00
Third Person: $5.00

Grandma Newton's B&B—Deep south hospitality and the relaxed country atmosphere that sets the appetite for the huge country breakfast. Gateway to the Keys and minutes to the National Parks, and 6 blocks from the turnpike.

Key West

Beres, Joe & Czaplicki, Ed
525 Simonton St., 33040
(305) 294-6712

Amenities: 2,3,7,9,11
Breakfast: Continental
Dbl. Oc.: $115.00-$258.00
Sgl. Oc.: $115.00-$258.00
Third Person: $10.00

The Watson House—Circa 1860, a small award-winning inn with distinctively furnished guest suites in a lush tropical garden setting. A relaxed atmosphere in the historic preservation district. Adults only.

AMENITIES

1. No Smoking
2. No Pets
3. No Children
4. Senior Citizen Rates
5. Tennis Available
6. Golf Available
7. Swimming Available
8. Skiing Available
9. Credit Cards Accepted
10. Personal Check Accepted
11. Off Season Rates
12. Dinner Available (w/sufficient notice)

Florida

Key West

Curtis, Libby & Mark
913 Duval St., 33040
(305) 296-4275

Amenities: 1,2,5,6,7,9,10,11
Breakfast: Continental

Dbl. Oc.: $59.95-$81.75
Sgl. Oc.: $49.05-$70.85
Third Person: $10.00

Wicker Guesthouse—Restored home, ideally located in Old Town; fully equipped kitchen; tropical garden; color cable TV: jacuzzi; barbecue; 41 foot sailboat for snorkelling/fishing; massage therapy.

Key West

Geibelt, Fred
512 Simonton St., 33040
(305) 294-9227

Amenities: 2,3,7,9,11
Breakfast: Continental
Dbl. Oc.: $47.70-$111.30
Sgl. Oc.: $47.70-$111.30
Third Person: $10.00

Heron House—Most central location in historic district. Three blocks from beach. Spacious sundecks and tropical gardens offer quiet, privacy.

Key West

Tempel, Denison
511 Eaton St., 33040
(305) 294-3800

Amenities: 2,5,6,7,9,10,11
Breakfast: Continental

Dbl. Oc.: $70.85-$207.10
Sgl. Oc.: $59.95-$119.90
Third Person: $16.35

Eaton Lodge—A handsome 1880's residence in the centre of historic district. All rooms are furnished with antiques and each has its own patio or veranda. Lush tropical gardens with coral rock whirlpool.

Key West

Zurbrigen, Robert
815 Duval St., 33040
(305) 294-1666

Amenities: 2,3,5,6,7,9,11
Breakfast: Continental

Rates: $50.00-$120.00
Third Person: $15.00

Duval House—A charming Victorian guesthouse offering rooms appointed with wicker and antiques, tropical gardens, pool, sundecks and balconies. Walk to the Gulf of Mexico and the Atlantic Ocean.

Lake Butler

Schretzmann, M/M Joseph
Rt. 3, Box 276, Providence
32054
(904) 755-0211

Amenities: 1,2,12
Breakfast: Full

Dbl. Oc.: $35.00
Sgl. Oc.: $30.00
Third Person: $5.00

Rolling Ridge Ranch—4 miles off I-75 in N. FL area noted for springs & rivers with swimming, scuba, tubing & canoeing. Our warm friendly modern ranch home offers a full breakfast with fresh fuit.

AMENITIES

1. No Smoking
2. No Pets
3. No Children
4. Senior Citizen Rates
5. Tennis Available
6. Golf Available
7. Swimming Available
8. Skiing Available
9. Credit Cards Accepted
10. Personal Check Accepted
11. Off Season Rates
12. Dinner Available (w/sufficient notice)

Florida

Lake Wales

Hinshaw, Vita & Carl
US 27 & Country Rd. 17A
P.O. Drawer AC, 33859-9003
(813) 676-6011

Amenities: 5,6,7,9,10,11,12
Breakfast: Continental
Dbl. Oc.: $81.00-$156.60
Sgl. Oc.: $70.20-$137.50
Third Person: $6.48

Chalet Suzanne Country Inn & Restaurant—Discover Europe in the heart of Florida. Historic country inn located on 70 acres surrounded by orange groves. 30 charming guest rooms w/private baths. Award-winning dining overlooking Lake Suzanne.

Marathon

Hoop, Mrs. Joan E.
5 Man-O-War Dr., 33050
(305) 743-4118

Amenities: 2,5,6,7,9,11
Breakfast: Full

Dbl. Oc.: $45.00-$110.00
Sgl. Oc.: $40.00-$75.00

Hopp Inn Guest House is located in Marathon, heart of the Florida Keys. 5 rooms, all with an ocean view or ocean front. Each room has a private bath, and private entrance. Tropical setting, quiet area.

Ocala

Barkley, Mrs. Joni
1205 E. Silver Springs Blvd., 32670
(904) 867-7700

Amenities: 4,6,7,9,10
Breakfast: Continental

Dbl. Oc.: $59.00-$81.00
Sgl. Oc.: $59.00-$81.00
Third Person: $7.00

The Ritz—Ocala's historic inn built in 1925 as a luxury apartment complex, now is a luxury all suite inn listed on the national register of historic places. 1 1/2 hours from Disney World. We offer luxury at affordable prices.

Orlando

Allen Esther
2411 Virginia Dr., 32803
(407) 896-9916

Amenities: 1,2,3,6,7
Breakfast: Continental

Dbl. Oc.: $47.70
Sgl. Oc.: $37.10
Third Person: $10.60

Esther's B&B is located near Epcot. Breakfast is homemade coffee cake, muffins, cheese, fruit & beverage. Enjoy a glass of sherry or homemade ice cream in the atmosphere of needlepoints of old masters.

AMENITIES

1. No Smoking
2. No Pets
3. No Children
4. Senior Citizen Rates
5. Tennis Available
6. Golf Available
7. Swimming Available
8. Skiing Available
9. Credit Cards Accepted
10. Personal Check Accepted
11. Off Season Rates
12. Dinner Available (w/sufficient notice)

Florida

Orlando

Freudenburg, Mrs. Delores
532 Pinar Dr., 32825
(407) 277-4903

Amenities: 1,2,10
Breakfast: Full

Dbl. Oc.: $43.60
Sgl. Oc.: $38.16
3 People: $49.05

Rio Pinar House—A ground level 9-room home on the RP golf course, near the East-West Expressway's Chickasaw Exit. Disney/Epcot, the airport, Church Street, and many fine restaurants are nearby.

Orlando

Schattauer, Eunice & Neal
313 Spencer St., 32809
(407) 855-5603

Amenities: 1,2,7,10
Breakfast: Continental

Dbl. Oc.: $43.60-$54.50
Sgl. Oc.: $43.60-$54.50
Third Person: $5.00

The Spencer Home Bed & Breakfast offers a suite for 2 to 5 people or a single bedroom. TV, private entrance, ideal location to everything, generous cont. breakfast with seasonal fruit and lots of home-loving hospitality.

Ormond Beach

Pinney, Barbara & John
34 Surfside Dr., 32074
(904) 441-8800

Amenities: 1,2,4,5,6,7
Breakfast: Full

Dbl. Oc.: $55.00
Sgl. Oc.: $50.00
Crib: $25.00

Dancing Palms Bed And Breakfast—Short walk from quiet ocean beach. Antique room or bed-sitting room, private pool, guest bath, VCR. Near Daytona and all central Florida attractions. Bikes available.

Palmetto

Kriessler, Bette & Chet
1102 Riverside Dr., 34221
(813) 723-1236

Amenities: 1,2,3,7,9,10,11
Breakfast: Full

Dbl. Oc.: $59.00-$102.00
Third Person: $10.00

Five Oaks Inn—A luxurious southern mansion located between Sarasota & St. Petersburg. Breakfast served overlooking Manatee River. Quiet, romantic, centrally located. Business travelers welcome. Fishing, beach, marina, shops.

Pensacola

Anderson, M/M Arden
600 South Palafox St., 32501
(904) 432-4111

Amenities: 2,4,9,10,12
Breakfast: Full

Dbl. Oc.: $85.02
Sgl. Oc.: $74.12
Third Person: $10.90

New World Inn—Pensacola's historic inn, charming and exclusive, furnished with waterfront district. Special weekend rates available.

AMENITIES

1. No Smoking
2. No Pets
3. No Children
4. Senior Citizen Rates
5. Tennis Available
6. Golf Available
7. Swimming Available
8. Skiing Available
9. Credit Cards Accepted
10. Personal Check Accepted
11. Off Season Rates
12. Dinner Available (w/sufficient notice)

Florida

Pompano Beach

Horsnell, M/M Chris
1070 NE 27 Ave., 33062
(305) 946-6784

Amenities: 2,4,5,6,7,11,12
Breakfast: Full

Dbl. Oc.: $55.00
Sgl. Oc.: $55.00
Third Person: $10.00

Waterside Bed And Breakfast—Watch the boats. Located on deepwater 1 block from the Intercoastal Waterway. Fine shops, restaurants & beach within walking distance. Solar heated pool. English hosts assure your comfortable stay.

St. Augustine

Burkley, Ms. Karen
70 Cuna St., 32084
(904) 829-2467

Amenities: 5,6,7,9,10
Breakfast: Continental

Dbl. Oc.: $52.50-$94.50
Sgl. Oc.: $52.50-$94.50

Restored 1883 Victorian Home in historic district. Compliments include: breakfast, bicycles, open bar, and dessert is served on weekends. Atmosphere is leisurely and casual.

St. Augustine

Constant, Kerrianne, Caitlin, & Mark
38 Marine St., 32084
(904) 824-2116

Amenities: 2,3,5,6,7,9,10
Breakfast: Continental
Dbl. Oc.: $55.00-$75.00
Sgl. Oc.: $45.00
Third Person: $10.00

Since 1886

The Kenwood Inn—For over a century this lovely old Victorian building has received visitors to St. Augustine. It now does so with the warmth and friendliness of a traditional "country inn."

St. Augustine

Erminelli, Ruth
146 Avenida Menendez, 32084
(904) 824-4301

Amenities: 2,4,9,10
Breakfast: Continental

Dbl. Oc.: $70.20-$145.80
Sgl. Oc.: $70.20-$145.80

Westcott House in historical district near beach on Matanzas Bay, furnished with antiques, king beds, cable TV, air conditioned, complimentary wine, chocolate on pillows, snifters of brandy, terry cloth robes, romantic.

AMENITIES

1. No Smoking
2. No Pets
3. No Children
4. Senior Citizen Rates
5. Tennis Available
6. Golf Available
7. Swimming Available
8. Skiing Available
9. Credit Cards Accepted
10. Personal Check Accepted
11. Off Season Rates
12. Dinner Available (w/sufficient notice)

Florida

St. Augustine

Finnegan, Joseph
279 St. George St., 32084
(904) 824-6068

Amenities: 2,7,9,10
Breakfast: Continental
Dbl. Oc.: $55.00
Sgl. Oc.: $55.00
Third Person: $8.00

The St. Francis Inn located in the historic district, has long been noted for its hospitality. It offers a variety of accommodations & is a classic example of old-world architecture.

St. Augustine

Morden, Daisy
11 Cadiz, 32084
(904) 824-5214

Amenities: 9,10
Breakfast: Continental

Dbl. Oc.: $50.00-$75.00
Sgl. Oc.: $45.00-$65.00
Third Person: $5.00

Victorian House Bed & Breakfast—Restored Victorian in the heart of the historic district. Walk & explore the charm of historic St. Augustine or rock on the front porch & enjoy the sea breezes.

St. Augustine

Stafford, Brenda & Harry
22 Avenida Menendez, 32084
(904) 829-2915

Amenities: 1,2,5,6,7,9,10
Breakfast: Continental
Dbl. Oc.: $85.00-$165.00
Sgl. Oc.: $80.00-$150.00
Third Person: $17.00

Casa De La Paz Bed & Breakfast Inn—On the bayfront in the historic district. Elegant lodging includes: single rooms & suites, private baths, antiques, sherry, chocolates, bayview, courtyard, mediterranean breakfast. Walk to all sites.

AMENITIES

1. No Smoking
2. No Pets
3. No Children
4. Senior Citizen Rates
5. Tennis Available
6. Golf Available
7. Swimming Available
8. Skiing Available
9. Credit Cards Accepted
10. Personal Check Accepted
11. Off Season Rates
12. Dinner Available (w/sufficient notice)

Florida

St. Petersburg

Powers, Antonia & Gordon
1719 Beach Dr., SE, 33701
(813) 823-4955

Amenities: 1,2,3,7,9,10
Breakfast: Continental
Dbl. Oc.: $55.00-$60.00
Sgl. Oc.: $50.00-$55.00

Bayboro House on Old Tampa Bay offers the best B&B accommodations in Florida with old-fashioned hospitality as gracious as the old south. Relax on the verandah porch swing or sink your feet in the sand and stay awhile.

Summerland Key

Pontin, M/M H.T.
1509 W. Indies Dr.,
P.O. Box 151, 33042
(305) 872-2246

Amenities: 1,2,3,5,6,7,8
Breakfast: Full

Dbl. Oc.: $81.75

Knightswood—Overlooks one of the loviest views in the Keys. Guest accommodations are: bed & bath, kitchen, rec. room, screened porch w/barbecue, snorkeling, fishing from priv. dock, fresh water pool & spa.

Tarpon Springs

Morrick, Mrs. Cher
32 West Tarpon Ave., 34689
(813) 938-9333

Amenities: 1,2,3,10
Breakfast: Continental

Dbl. Oc.: $48.60-$70.20
Sgl. Oc.: $43.20-$64.80
Third Person: $10.80

Spring Bayou Inn—Elegant in-town Victorian with modern conveniences. Walk to shops, bayou, restaurants. Sponge docks, golf, tennis, beaches and fishing nearby. No smoking, children or pets.

Venice

McCormick, Susan & Chuck
519 South Harbor Dr., 34285
(813) 484-1385

Amenities: 3,7,10,11
Breakfast: Continental

Dbl. Oc.: $37.10-$63.60
Sgl. Oc.: $37.10-$63.60
Third Person: $10.00

Banyon House—Historic Mediterranean-style home built in 1926. Enormous Banyantree shades courtyard, pool & spa. Centrally located to shopping, restaurants, beaches, & golfing.

AMENITIES

1. No Smoking
2. No Pets
3. No Children
4. Senior Citizen Rates
5. Tennis Available
6. Golf Available
7. Swimming Available
8. Skiing Available
9. Credit Cards Accepted
10. Personal Check Accepted
11. Off Season Rates
12. Dinner Available (w/sufficient notice)

Georgia

The Empire State of the South

Capital: Atlanta
Statehood: January 2, 1788; the 4th state
State Motto: Wisdom, Justice and Moderation
State Song: "Georgia On My Mind"
State Bird: Brown Thrasher
State Flower: Cherokee Rose
State Tree: Live Oak

The state of Georgia is known for its natural beauty and it has many vacation resorts attracting visitors from all over the world. The climate is mild most of the time, but in the summer it tends to get quite warm and humid.

It is the largest state east of the Mississippi and one of the leading growers of peaches. It is often called The Peach State.

The first Girl Scout troop in America was organized here by Juliette Low in 1912 and the first painless surgery was performed by Dr. Long in 1842, when he operated on a patient using ether as an anesthetic for the first time.

The capital, Atlanta, represents the modern south. Almost two million people live here. It also was the home of Dr. Martin Luther King, and he is buried here today.

Jimmy Carter, our 39th president, was born here.

Georgia

Acworth

Pettys, Jan & Bill
4965 North Main St., 30101
(404) 974-9485

Amenities: 2,12
Breakfast: Full

Dbl. Oc.: $70.00
Sgl. Oc.: $58.00
Third Person: $15.00

Jesse Lemon Bed & Breakfast—Restored 1880 historic house, 32 mi. from Atlanta, 5 bedrooms, furnished with period antiques; jacuzzi. Located on Old Dixie Highway, 1 mi. from I-75, Exit 121, near W & A RR, site of Great Locomotive Chase.

Atlanta

Schofield, Ruthanna
1234 Bellaire Dr., 30319
(404) 262-1173, 237-5456

Amenities: 10
Breakfast: Continental

Dbl. Oc.: $60.00
Sgl. Oc.: $50.00
Third Person: $10.00

Bellaire House—Rooms for guests in a private home in the desirable Buckhead area. Located near Lenox Square and Phipps Plaza for the best shopping in Atlanta. Convenient to fine restaurants and Marta Rapid Transit.

Blairsville

Deen, Mrs. Frank
Box 77886, Town Creek Rd.
Rt. 7, 30512
(404) 745-4786

Amenities: 1,2,3,5,6,7,9,10,11
Breakfast: Continental

Dbl. Oc.: $100.00
Sgl. Oc.: $100.00

1880 Victorian Inn—Antique-filled home on 5 acres in beautiful mountain location. October foliage. Near recreation, shopping, dining. 100 miles north of Atlanta. Some French & Spanish spoken.

Clayton

Thornwell, Susan & English
U.S. Highway 76, East, 30525
(404) 782-5780

Amenities: 4,5,6,7,8,9,10,11,12
Breakfast: Continental
Dbl. Oc.: $69.55
Sgl. Oc.: $60.99
Third Person: $8.00

English Manor Inns & St. Moritz Lodge—
7 luxurious inns—with fully modern kitchens, 60 rms. w/bath, 25 FP., groups, reunions, special events, forest or lake inns. Cable TV, fantastic food here or nearby! Elegance.

AMENITIES

1. No Smoking
2. No Pets
3. No Children
4. Senior Citizen Rates
5. Tennis Available
6. Golf Available
7. Swimming Available
8. Skiing Available
9. Credit Cards Accepted
10. Personal Check Accepted
11. Off Season Rates
12. Dinner Available (w/sufficient notice)

Georgia

Columbus

Crawford, Mrs. Kristine
812 Broadway, 31901
(404) 324-1144

Amenities: 2,6,9,10,12
Breakfast: Continental

Dbl. Oc.: $57.20-$65.52
Sgl. Oc.: $49.96-$52.00
Third Person: $8.32

The Deloffre House—1863 restored town house in city's historic district. 5 guest rooms furnished in Victorian antiques; private bath, phone, TV. Candlelight continental breakfast with homemade breads.

Dahlongea

Francis, Mrs. Mitzi
410 W. Main St., 30533
(404) 864-7002

Amenities: 9,10,11
Breakfast: Full
Dbl. Oc.: $65.00
Sgl. Oc.: $60.00
Third Person: $10.00

Worley Homestead Inn—1845 former family home. 7 bedrooms, private baths. Staff in period dress. Antique filled; fireplaces; gazebo. Only 2 blocks to historic town square. Step back into time.

Helen

Tysor, Ms. Frankie
Chattahoochee, P.O. Box 154,
30545
(404) 878-2388

Amenities: 5,6,7,10
Breakfast: Full

Dbl. Oc.: $55.00
Sgl. Oc.: $35.00
Third Person: $10.00

Hilltop Haus Bed And Breakfast—Located .04 mi. from Alpine Helen. 5 rooms, small apt. with fireplace. Special events: Mayfest, Oktoberfest, fishing and ballooning. Appalachian Trail nearby.

Marietta

McDaniel, Mrs. Katherine
192 Church St., 30060
(404) 426-1887

Amenities: 2,4,9,10
Breakfast: Full

Dbl. Oc.: $59.00
Sgl. Oc.: $49.00
Third Person: $29.50

Two Blocks From The Inn is Marietta Square with its restaurants, art shows, antique shops, and theater. Restored Victorian bed & breakfast furnished with antiques & with big comfortable bedrooms.

AMENITIES

1. No Smoking
2. No Pets
3. No Children
4. Senior Citizen Rates
5. Tennis Available
6. Golf Available
7. Swimming Available
8. Skiing Available
9. Credit Cards Accepted
10. Personal Check Accepted
11. Off Season Rates
12. Dinner Available (w/sufficient notice)

Georgia

Mountain City

Smith, Phyllis & Jimmy
P.O. Box 126, 30562
(404) 746-2068

Amenities: 1,2,5,6,7,8,9,10,11
Breakfast: Continental
Dbl. Oc.: $58.85
Sgl. Oc.: $53.50
Third Person: $5.35

The York House—The perfect romantic getaway, offering 13 guest rooms each with a private bath. Start with breakfast in bed served to you on a silver tray. Enjoy hiking, rafting or just rocking on our wrap-around veranda. Children 6 & under no charge.

Perry

Deibert, Melinda & Gary
1204 Swift St., 31069
(912) 987-3428

Amenities: 2,9,10
Breakfast: Continental
Dbl. Oc.: $69.55-$90.95
Sgl. Oc.: $58.85-$80.25
Third Person: $10.00

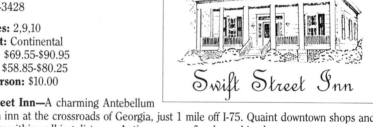

Swift Street Inn—A charming Antebellum family-run inn at the crossroads of Georgia, just 1 mile off I-75. Quaint downtown shops and restaurants within walking distance. Antiques, some fireplaces, bicycles.

Sautee

Schwartz, M/M Hamilton
Rt. 1, Box 152, 30571
(404) 878-3355

Amenities: 2,10,12
Breakfast: Continental

Dbl. Oc.: $68.75
Sgl. Oc.: $38.50
Third Person: $11.00

The Stovall House—Relax in an attentively restored 1837 farm house on 28 acres in the mountains near Helen. 5 guest rooms with private bath, period antiques, handmade curtains and stenciling. Award-winning restaurant. Dinner $15.00.

Sautee

Wunderlich, Ginger & Van
Rt. #1, Box 39, 30571
(404) 878-2580

Amenities: 1,2,10,11
Breakfast: Continental

Dbl. Oc.: $45.00-$60.00

Woodhaven Chalet Bed & Breakfast—Short drive from Alpine Village of Helen. Quaint shops & dining. Hiking & horseback riding. 1 cooking unit, all rooms have air-conditioning.

AMENITIES

1. No Smoking
2. No Pets
3. No Children
4. Senior Citizen Rates
5. Tennis Available
6. Golf Available
7. Swimming Available
8. Skiing Available
9. Credit Cards Accepted
10. Personal Check Accepted
11. Off Season Rates
12. Dinner Available (w/sufficient notice)

Georgia

Savannah

Barnett, Mrs. Anne
106 West Jones St., 31401
(912) 234-6928

Amenities: 2,3,5,6,7,10
Breakfast: Continental
Dbl. Oc.: $66.00
Sgl. Oc.: $66.00
Third Person: $22.00

Remshart-Brooks House—Enjoy the hospitality of this historic home featuring a terrace-garden suite with bedroom, living room, bath, kitchen. Home baked delicacies enhance the continental breakfast.

Savannah

Crawford, Howard
209 West Jones St., 31401
(912) 236-1774

Amenities: 5,6,7,10
Breakfast: Continental

Dbl. Oc.: $82.50
Sgl. Oc.: $77.00
Third Person: $16.50

The Jesse Mount House—1854 Greek Revival town house. Elegant & spacious three bedroom suites w/gas log fireplaces. Rare antiques; gilded harps & grand piano. For one to six persons in a party. Breakfast served in formal dining room, walled garden.

Savannah

Fort, Alan
417 E. Charlton St., 31401
(912) 233-6380

Amenities: 5,6,7,10
Breakfast: Continental

Dbl. Oc.: $88.00
Family (4 persons): $165.00

The Haslam/Fort House—Private 2 bedroom suite; living room, kitch., bath & patio. Ideal for 2-4 persons. OK for handicapped. Enclosed garden for kids & pets. Deutsch/Norsk/Espanol spoken. By advanced reservation. Children under 10 free.

Savannah

Harris, Mrs. Janie
128 W. Liberty St., 31401
(912) 233-1007, (800) 637-1007

Amenities: 2,4,5,6,7,9,10,11
Breakfast: Continental
Dbl. Oc.: $104.50
3 Room Suite: $165.00
Add'l. Couple: $11.00

Liberty Inn—Historic district. Near house museums, waterfront & restaurants. Luxury 2 & 3 room suites, queen size beds; family room, kitchenette, phone, TV & VCR. Garden, spa, grill, & parking.

AMENITIES

1. No Smoking
2. No Pets
3. No Children
4. Senior Citizen Rates
5. Tennis Available
6. Golf Available
7. Swimming Available
8. Skiing Available
9. Credit Cards Accepted
10. Personal Check Accepted
11. Off Season Rates
12. Dinner Available (w/sufficient notice)

Georgia

Savannah

McAlister, Mr. Robert
117 W. Gordon St., 31401
(912) 238-0518

Amenities: 9,10
Breakfast: Full

Dbl. Oc.: $38.00-$65.00
Sgl. Oc.: $30.00-$55.00
Third Person: $10.00

Bed & Breakfast Inn—Elegant 1853 town house on historic square w/charming garden, poster bed, rare porcelain, oriental carpets, books, original art, antiques. Quiet, convenient, residential neighborhood.

Savannah

Smith, M/M J.B.
203 W. Charlton St., 31401
(912) 232-8055, (800) 227-0650

Amenities: 5,6,7,9,10
Breakfast: Continental

Dbl. Oc.: $51.84
Sgl. Oc.: $51.84
Suites: $82.50-$193.60
(3-8 Adults)
Third Person: $5.00

Fully Equipped Kitchen And Bath—Queen size four poster beds. Furnished with antiques, oriental rugs, working fireplaces, & crystal chandeliers. Bathrooms beautifully decorated with gold-plated fixtures.

Savannah

Smith, Ms. Mary Ann
117 West Perry St., 31401
(912) 234-4088

Amenities: 5,6,10
Breakfast: Continental

Rates: $64.80-$93.60

Morel House is located in historic district. Garden-level apartment, large living room with fireplace, kitchen with eating space. Off-street parking. Completely furnished.

Savannah

Steinhauser, Susan
14 W. Hull St., 31401
(912) 232-6622

Amenities: 4,9
Breakfast: Continental
Dbl. Oc.: $181.50
Sgl. Oc.: $170.50
Third Person: $10.00

Foley House Inn—Built in 1896, the Foley House Inn is a renewal of a rich and genteel past. Each room is an individual masterpiece, with fireplaces, antique furniture, oriental rugs, VCR's and jacuzzi tubs all for you.

AMENITIES

1. No Smoking
2. No Pets
3. No Children
4. Senior Citizen Rates
5. Tennis Available
6. Golf Available
7. Swimming Available
8. Skiing Available
9. Credit Cards Accepted
10. Personal Check Accepted
11. Off Season Rates
12. Dinner Available (w/sufficient notice)

Georgia

Savannah

Sullivan, Hal
102 West Hall St., 31401
(912) 233-6800

Amenities: 2,5,9
Breakfast: Continental

Dbl. Oc.: $97.20
Sgl. Oc.: $81.00
Third Person: $10.80

The Forsyth Park Inn—An elegantly restored Victorian mansion in the historic district. Rooms feature fireplaces, wet bars, and whirlpool tubs. Evening cordials served around the grand piano beneath the majestic staircase.

Statesboro

Frondorf, M/M William A.
106 S. Main St., 30458
(912) 489-8628

Amenities: 2,4,6,9,10
Breakfast: Full

Dbl. Oc.: $56.00-$77.00
Sgl. Oc.: $48.00-$68.00
Third Person: $7.00

Statesboro Inn Bed & Breakfast—Award-winning restored 9 room country inn. All rooms with private bath, air conditioning, phone, TV, antique furnishings. Conveniently located to Hwy. 301 in center of town. Georgia's best kept secret!

Thomasville

Hoopes, Mrs. Betty
Rt. 5, 31792
(912) 228-4876

Amenities: 5,6,7,10
Breakfast: Continental

Dbl. Oc.: $45.00-$55.00
Sgl. Oc.: $45.00-$55.00
Third Person: $10.00

MANGNOLIA—100-year-old house on 20 acres, across from the country club. Completely modernized, three bedrooms, private baths, sitting room, televisions. Charming atmosphere.

AMENITIES

1. No Smoking
2. No Pets
3. No Children
4. Senior Citizen Rates
5. Tennis Available
6. Golf Available
7. Swimming Available
8. Skiing Available
9. Credit Cards Accepted
10. Personal Check Accepted
11. Off Season Rates
12. Dinner Available (w/sufficient notice)

Hawaii

The Aloha State

Capital: Honolulu
Statehood: August 21, 1959; the 50th state
State Motto: The Life of the Land is Perpetuated in Righteousness
State Song: "Hawaii Ponoi"
State Bird: Nene (Hawaiian Goose)
State Flower: Hibiscus
State Tree: Kukui

Hawaii is the only state that is completely set apart from the rest of the United States in North America. It consists of 132 beautiful islands, some larger than others, about 2,400 miles west of the United States.

These islands were first discovered by Captain Cook in 1778 and called the Sandwich Islands after the Earl of Sandwich. Inhabited then by only natives, the first white settlers were missionaries that came here in 1820. The Chinese and Japanese arrived later as laborers and workers for the plantations, but gradually entered the political and economic world here and today we have a happy mixture of many different peoples living and working together.

Hawaii's mild and beautiful climate beckons tourists from all over the world. Beautiful beaches have made swimming and surfing a way of life here.

Tourism and the pineapple and sugar industries form the leading source of income for this state.

Hawaii

Anahola (Kauai)

Matlock, Dale
Box 699, 96703
(808) 822-9451

Amenities: 3,7
Breakfast: Continental
Dbl. Oc.: $55.00-$75.00
Sgl. Oc.: $45.00-$65.00

Mahina Kai—Unique environment for discerning travelers. Asian-Pacific resort villa across from secluded beach. Guest wing with ethnic art, private lanais, exotic garden grounds, and guest kitchenette. Brochure.

Anahola

Walker, Charles
P.O. Box 562, 96703
(800) ANAHOLA

Amenities: 5,6,7,9,10,12
Breakfast: Full

Dbl. Oc.: $81.75
Sgl. Oc.: $65.40

Anahola Beach Club—Beachfront home on an acre of tropical grounds. Swim & relax on magnificent white sand beach. Anahola affords seclusion, yet is centrally located for sightseeing, activities, shopping and dining.

Haiku (Maui)

Champing, Denise & Clark
69 Haiku Rd., 96708
(808) 575-2890

Amenities: 10
Breakfast: Continental
Dbl. Oc.: $55.00
Sgl. Oc.: $45.00

Haikuleana—The true Hawaiian life— waterfalls, beach, & quiet relaxation. Far from the crowds yet close to fine dining & shopping. Built 130 years ago amidst pineapple fields, pine trees, & pastures. Serenity.

AMENITIES

1. No Smoking
2. No Pets
3. No Children
4. Senior Citizen Rates
5. Tennis Available
6. Golf Available
7. Swimming Available
8. Skiing Available
9. Credit Cards Accepted
10. Personal Check Accepted
11. Off Season Rates
12. Dinner Available (w/sufficient notice)

Hawaii

Holualoa

Twigg-Smith, Mr. & Mrs.
Mamalahoa Hwy., Box 222-N, 96725
(808) 324-1121

Amenities: 2,3,5,6,7,9,10
Breakfast: Continental
Dbl. Oc.: $92.65
Sgl. Oc.: $54.50
Third Person: $15.00

Holualoa Inn—A luxury B&B mansion set amongst lush surroundings on private estate, features a stunning coastline view. Within a ten minute drive: beaches, superb dining, shopping, great fishing.

Honolulu

Schultz, Marianne
2001 Vancouver Dr., 96822
(808) 947-6019, (800) 634-5115

Amenities: 1,2,3,9,10
Breakfast: Continental
Dbl. Oc.: $104.00
Sgl. Oc.: $104.00
Third Person: $11.00

MANOA VALLEY INN
Hawaii's Country Inn

Manoa Valley Inn, an intimate country inn located in lush Manoa Valley, two miles from Waikiki. Furnished with antiques, each room is decorated to enhance its own charm and personality.

Kapaa

Barker, Kay
P.O. Box 740, 96746
(808) 822-3073

Amenities: 5,6,7,10
Breakfast: Continental

Dbl. Oc.: $32.70-$43.60
Sgl. Oc.: $27.25-$43.60
Third Person: $10.90

Kay Barker's Bed & Breakfast has 4 bedrooms, each with private bath, in a country setting with miles of pasture and mountain views. 10 minutes from beaches, golf, tennis, restaurants and shopping.

AMENITIES

1. No Smoking
2. No Pets
3. No Children
4. Senior Citizen Rates
5. Tennis Available
6. Golf Available
7. Swimming Available
8. Skiing Available
9. Credit Cards Accepted
10. Personal Check Accepted
11. Off Season Rates
12. Dinner Available (w/sufficient notice)

Hawaii

Kaloa (Kauai)

Cichon, Ms. Dottie
2720 Hoonani Rd., RR1,
Box 308B, 96756
(808) 742-1146

Amenities: 2,4,5,6,7,9,10,11
Breakfast: Continental
Dbl. Oc.: $85.00
Sgl. Oc.: $80.00
Third Person: $10.00

Poipu Bed & Breakfast Inn—One block from beach in sunny Poipu restored plantation house furnished with white wicker, pine antiques & carousel horses. All rooms have private baths, color TV's, & refrigerators. Children welcome.

Lahaina

Patterson, Jim
174 Lahainaluna Rd., 96761
(808) 667-9225 or (800) 433-6815

Amenities: 2,5,6,7,9,10,12
Breakfast: Full
Dbl. Oc.: $103.96
Sgl. Oc.: $85.36
Third Person: $16.41

The Plantation Inn is an elegant 10 room inn, in historic Lahaina town. Old world luxury is combined with first class amenities. Pool, spa, TV's, VCR's, refrigerators, A/C, and a first class restaurant, Gerard's.

Lawai (Kauai)

Seymour, Ms. Edee
P.O. Box 930, 96765
(808) 332-9300

Amenities: 1,2,3,5,6,7,11
Breakfast: Continental
Dbl. Oc.: $55.00-$66.00
Sgl. Oc.: $44.00-$55.00
Third Person: $11.00

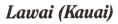

Victoria Place—Spacious and skylit with jungle and ocean view. All bedrooms open onto pool. Near beaches, boutiques, golf, botanical garden. We pamper: flowers, chocolate, homemade muffins and aloha.

AMENITIES

1. No Smoking
2. No Pets
3. No Children
4. Senior Citizen Rates
5. Tennis Available
6. Golf Available
7. Swimming Available
8. Skiing Available
9. Credit Cards Accepted
10. Personal Check Accepted
11. Off Season Rates
12. Dinner Available (w/sufficient notice)

Hawaii

Napili

Vee, Cindi
181 Hui Road F, 96761
(800) 669-5712 or (800) 367-8006

Amenities: 5,6,7,10
Breakfast: Continental
Dbl. Oc.: $82.07-$136.79
Sgl. Oc.: $82.07-$103.96
Third Person: $7.50

The Coconut Inn

The Coconut Inn is located in Napili, just north of Kaanapali. Amenities include a heated spa, free-form pool and daily maid service. All rooms are nicely furnished and have fully-equipped kitchens.

Pahoa (Hawaii)

Hanson, Margo
15 2700 Kala St., 96778
(808) 965-9132

Amenities: 3,4,11
Breakfast: Continental

Dbl. Oc.: $54.00
Sgl. Oc.: $48.00
Third Person: $40.00

Pahoa—Country near Black Sands Beach, Kala-Pana Lava Flow, and quaint Pahoa Town. Many scenic points, lush tranquil area, home-baked goodies, antiques, refrigerator, Newfoundland show dogs. Hostess 28-yr. Isle resident.

AMENITIES

1. No Smoking
2. No Pets
3. No Children
4. Senior Citizen Rates
5. Tennis Available
6. Golf Available
7. Swimming Available
8. Skiing Available
9. Credit Cards Accepted
10. Personal Check Accepted
11. Off Season Rates
12. Dinner Available (w/sufficient notice)

Idaho

The Gem State

Capital: Boise
Statehood: July 3, 1890; the 43rd state
State Motto: It Is Forever
State Song: "Here We Have Idaho"
State Bird: Mountain Bluebird
State Flower: Syringa (Mock Orange)
State Tree: Western White Pine

    Idaho is located in the Rocky Mountains with exciting scenery and enormous resources. Its natural wonders, such as Hells Canyon and the Craters of the Moon National Monument, thrill visitors to this state every year.
    Idaho is also a skier's paradise where ski areas and ski trails are considered among the best in the world.
    This state is a leading producer of silver and phosphate. The Snake River and its many dams have made for rich farmlands. The Idaho potato is its No. 1 farm product. More potatoes are grown here than in any other state in the union.

Idaho

Ashton

Jessen, Nieca C.
Highway #20, Box 11, 83420
(208) 652-3356

Amenities: 1,2,6,7,8,9,10
Breakfast: Full
Dbl. Oc.: $35.00
Third Person: $10.00

Jessen's Bed & Breakfast is 1 1/2 miles south of Ashton on Highway U.S. 20 with Yellowstone National Park to the north, Jackson Hole to the east. Our home is comfortable & hospitable.

Coeur d'Alene

Biner, Mrs. Jeanne
1521 Lakeside Ave., 83814
(208) 664-6926

Amenities: 5,6,7,9,10
Breakfast: Full

Dbl. Oc.: $37.75-$57.75
Sgl. Oc.: $26.25-$47.25
Third Person: $10.50

Cricket-On-The-Hearth—B&B is located in a resort town on a beautiful lake set amidst mountains. Restaurants, downtown, lake activities within walking distance. Winter sports nearby. Send for brochure.

Coeur d'Alene

McIlvenna, Mrs. Kristin
315 Wallace St., 83814
(208) 667-9660

Amenities: 1,2,4,5,6,7,8,9,10,11
Breakfast: Full

Dbl. Oc.: $35.00-$54.00
Sgl. Oc.: $35.00-$49.00
Third Person: $10.00

Greenbriar Inn Bed & Breakfast—4 blocks from downtown and lake, public beach, park, college and theatre all within an easy walk. The inn is nationally registered. Elegant with excellent cuisine and lots of creature comforts. Open year round.

Kooskia

Shuck, Yvette & Jerry
HCR 75, Box 32, 83539
(208) 926-0855

Amenities: 9,12
Breakfast: Full

Dbl. Oc.: $41.01
Sgl. Oc.: $36.38
Third Person: $9.63

Looking Glass Guest Ranch—Located 10 mi. east of Kooskia on Hwy. 12. Rural, wild & scenic river setting. Hiking, fishing, hunting, swimming available in season. Clean comfortable rooms, queen beds, private baths, recreation room available.

AMENITIES

1. No Smoking
2. No Pets
3. No Children
4. Senior Citizen Rates
5. Tennis Available
6. Golf Available
7. Swimming Available
8. Skiing Available
9. Credit Cards Accepted
10. Personal Check Accepted
11. Off Season Rates
12. Dinner Available (w/sufficient notice)

Idaho

Laclede

Robertson, Dale
P.O. Box 608, 83841
(208) 263-3705

Amenities: 1,2,3,7,8,9,12
Breakfast: Full

Dbl. Oc.: $47.00
Sgl. Oc.: $47.00
Third Person: $20.00

River Birch Farm—We are located on Lake Pend Oreille only 15 min. from Sandpont, where seasonal activities include boating, skiing, hiking, fishing, hunting. Scenic serenity and special hospitality of North Idaho.

S. Maries

Hedlund, Vicki & Gene
P.O. Box 572, 83861
(208) 245-4137

Amenities: 1,4,7,9,10,11,12
Breakfast: Full
Dbl. Oc.: $65.00
Sgl. Oc.: $58.00
Third Person: $7.00

Knoll Hus B&B—Cabin nestled on a wooded hillside overlooking road, lake and the shadowy St. Joe River. A unique experience. Quiet secluded retreat. Canoe & bicycles. Migratory bird sanctuary.

Sun Valley

Van Doren, Virginia
P.O. Box 182, 83353
(208) 726-3611

Amenities: 4-12
Breakfast: Full

Dbl. Oc.: $103.55-$147.15
Sgl. Oc.: $93.55-$137.15
Third Person: $16.35

River Street Inn—Each parlor suite has a view, queen bed, Japanese-style soaking tub, walk in shower, TV, phone, & small refrigerator. Large breakfast featuring fresh pastries. On a quiet street central to all area activities.

Wallace

Calkins, Kay
304 6th St., 83873
(208) 556-1554

Amenities: 6,7,9,10
Breakfast: Continental

Dbl. Oc.: $35.50
Sgl. Oc.: $32.50

Jameson Bed & Breakfast—Turn-of-the-century accommodations. Beautiful rooms with antique furniture. Wallace historic district. Historic Jameson Restaurant. Northern Pacific Depot & museum are across the street.

AMENITIES

1. No Smoking
2. No Pets
3. No Children
4. Senior Citizen Rates
5. Tennis Available
6. Golf Available
7. Swimming Available
8. Skiing Available
9. Credit Cards Accepted
10. Personal Check Accepted
11. Off Season Rates
12. Dinner Available (w/sufficient notice)

Illinois

The Land of Lincoln

Capital: Springfield
Statehood: December 3, 1818; the 21st state
State Motto: State Sovereignty, National Union
State Song: "Illinois"
State Bird: Cardinal
State Flower: Native Violet
State Tree: White Oak

Illinois boasts of having more people than any other state in the midwest, and the second largest city in the United States, Chicago. Its deep and rich soil has made for large-scale farming and its mighty deposits of coal have brought great prosperity.

The steel frames necessary for the building of sky scrapers were invented here. It resulted in the erection of some of the tallest buildings in the world, including Chicago's own Sears Towers.

Chicago is the crossroads of the country. Trains and barges leave here with the products of the midwest farms and take them from one coast to another, either by rail or waterways.

Historically, Illinois first won national attention when Abraham Lincoln debated Stephen Douglas on the subject of slavery. Although not born in the state, Lincoln's burial place in Springfield is a national shrine. Ulysses S. Grant's home in Galena is maintained as it was when he lived there. Built in 1856, it has been a state memorial since 1932.

Although our 40th President, Ronald Wilson Reagan, spent most of his life in California he was also born in this state in Tampico on 2/6/11.

The first successful railroad sleeping car was invented by George Pullman at Bloomington, Illinois in 1859. It pioneered a new way of travel for Americans.

Illinois

Belle River

Blackwell, Carollyn & W. Loyd
RR #1, Box 78, 62810
(618) 736-2647

Amenities: 2,4,7,10,12
Breakfast: Continental

Dbl. Oc.: $45.00
Sgl. Oc.: $40.00

Enchanted Crest—3-story Victorian, on national list of historical places, near beautiful lakes and woods. Unqiue barn, 2 acre park, herb gardens, 30 handmade quilts, nature walks, 10 miles from I-57 & 64.

Bishop Hill

Holden, Linda & Steve
Box 95, E. Main St., 61419
(309) 927-3500

Amenities: 2,9,10,11,12
Breakfast: Continental
Dbl. Oc.: $50.00-$65.00
Sgl. Oc.: $45.00
Third Person: $20.00

Holden's Guest House—1870, 8-room farm house adjacent to hosts on 1 1/2 acres. 2 baths, full kitchen. Nat'l historic landmark. A restored 1846 communal society offers museums, tea rooms & shops. Truly "A utopia on the prairie."

Champaign

Gold, Rita & Bob
R.R. 3, Box 69, 61821
(217) 586-4345

Amenities: 1
Breakfast: Continental
Dbl. Oc.: $40.00
Sgl. Oc.: $35.00
Third Person: $5.00

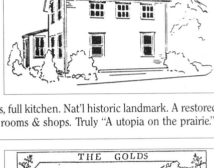

The Golds—One-half mile to I-74, 6 miles to Champaign, home of Univ. of Ill. Antique furnishings in country setting. 1820 cradle for baby, 1870 barn for your horse. 2 miles to lake, golf, & antiquing.

Chicago

Custer, Mrs. Irene
5210 So. Kenwood Ave., 60615
(312) 363-4595

Amenities: 10
Breakfast: Continental

Dbl. Oc.: $40.00
Sgl. Oc.: $40.00

Hyde Park House—Charming, spacious, Victorian home, near Lake Michigan, parks, museum, Univ. of Chicago., Museum of Science and Industry, and 20 minutes by express bus along the lake to downtown Chicago Loop.

AMENITIES

1. No Smoking
2. No Pets
3. No Children
4. Senior Citizen Rates
5. Tennis Available
6. Golf Available
7. Swimming Available
8. Skiing Available
9. Credit Cards Accepted
10. Personal Check Accepted
11. Off Season Rates
12. Dinner Available (w/sufficient notice)

Illinois

Dallas City

Massie, Virginia & Fred
R.R. 1, Box 267, 62330
(217) 852-3652 or 755-4327

Amenities: 2,3,7,10
Breakfast: Full
Dbl. Oc.: $58.00
Sgl. Oc.: $48.00
Third Person: $10.00

1850's Guest House—On 4 acres. Large comfortable rooms, 70 ft. porch, gift shop, stone with interesting history & architecture. Tri-state area on Mississippi & Great River Rd., Routes 9 & 96. Conducted tour of the 4 levels of the house.

Du Quoin

Morgan, Mrs. Francie
104 South Line, 62832
(618) 542-6686

Amenities: 2,9,10
Breakfast: Full

Dbl. Oc.: $50.00-$75.00
Sgl. Oc.: $50.00-$75.00
Third Person: $10.00

Francie's—A turn-of-the-century children's home restored to a five bedroom inn. Lunch and tea served to the public Tuesday-Saturday. 20 miles west of Illinois Interstate 57.

Galena

Bielenda, M/M Michael
515 Mars Ave., 61036
(815) 777-3880

Amenities: 2,3,4,6,7,8,9,10,11
Breakfast: Continental
Dbl. Oc.: $50.00-$55.00

The Mars Ave. Guest Home—Charming, country style, fireplaces; close to quaint antique shops & fine restaurants. Come share with us the beauty of historic Galena.

Galena

Anthony, Mrs. Sharon
2690 Blackjack Rd, 61036
(815) 777-2322

Amenities: 4,5,6,7,8,9,10
Breakfast: Continental

Dbl. Oc.: $60.00
Sgl. Oc.: $60.00
Third Person: $5.00

Country Valley Guest Home & Petting Farm—Relaxed country living on 6 1/2 acres, just 1 mile from ski lodge & 10 minutes from historic Galena; fully A/C; picnic by the streams, petting farm with registered animals, open all year.

AMENITIES

1. No Smoking
2. No Pets
3. No Children
4. Senior Citizen Rates
5. Tennis Available
6. Golf Available
7. Swimming Available
8. Skiing Available
9. Credit Cards Accepted
10. Personal Check Accepted
11. Off Season Rates
12. Dinner Available (w/sufficient notice)

Illinois

Galena

Fach, M/M Charles
418 Spring St., 61036
(815) 777-0354

Amenities: 1,2,3,6,7,8,9,10
Breakfast: Full

Dbl. Oc.: $65.35-$87.15
Third Person: $10.00

Spring St. Guest House—Two suites both featuring king-size beds, sitting rooms, color TV, private baths, central air, wood stove. Built in 1876 as an ice house for city brewery. Artistically furnished.

Galena

Lozeau, M/M William
513 Bouthillier, 61036
(815) 777-0557

Amenities: 2,3,5,6,7,8,9,10,12
Breakfast: Continental
Dbl. Oc.: $55.00-$85.00
Sgl. Oc.: $55.00-$85.00
Third Person: $10.00

Stillman's Country Inn—1858 Victorian mansion adjacent to General Grant's home, featuring fine dining & weekend nightclub. All guest rooms have private baths.

Galena

Pluyn, M/M Ken B.
Rt. 20W, 61036
(815) 777-2043

Amenities: 2,5,6,7,10
Breakfast: Continental
Dbl. Oc.: $75.11

Ryan Mansion Inn—1876 Victorian B&B Elegant rooms furnished in antiques with private bath, color TV, A/C, set in park-like settting 1 mile from historic Galena. Indoor whirlpool, outdoor pool, hiking trails, mini lake.

AMENITIES

1. No Smoking
2. No Pets
3. No Children
4. Senior Citizen Rates
5. Tennis Available
6. Golf Available
7. Swimming Available
8. Skiing Available
9. Credit Cards Accepted
10. Personal Check Accepted
11. Off Season Rates
12. Dinner Available (w/sufficient notice)

Illinois

Grant Park

Van Hook, Charlotte & Sam
302 W. Taylor, 60940
(815) 465-6025

Amenities: 1,2,3,9,10,12
Breakfast: Continental

Dbl. Oc.: $50.00-$75.00

The Bennett-Curtis House Bed & Breakfast is located 50 miles from the Chicago Loop. We are in a nice quiet residential area with good antiquing within driving distance.

Historic Elsah

Taetz, Mrs. Patricia
12 Selma, Box 156, 62028
(618) 374-1684

Amenities: 1,2,3,5,7,8,9,10,12
Breakfast: Full
Dbl. Oc.: $55.00
Sgl. Oc.: $55.00
Third Person: $35.00

Maple Leaf Cottage Inn—Established 1949. A romantic decore of linen & lace. The private grounds cover one village block with 4 buildings joined by a winding brick path and surrounded by an English garden. Open all year. Charming.

Lanark

Aschenbrenner, Ms. Maggie
540 West Carroll St., 61046
(815) 493-2307

Amenities: 1,2,3,9,10
Breakfast: Full
Dbl. Oc.: $50.00-$65.00
Sgl. Oc.: $50.00-$65.00

Standish House—Adventure in early American history (1620). English and Early American antiques with modern conveniences such as air conditioning. Walking distance to shops and restaurants. About 120 miles west of Chicago.

Naperville

Konrad, Mrs. Molly
9S265 Rt. 59, 60565
(312) 355-0835

Amenities: 6.10
Breakfast: Full

Dbl. Oc.: $50.00
Sgl. Oc.: $45.00

Die Blaue Gans—A Bed & Breakfast Guesthouse is 45 minutes from Chicago's Loop. A country setting, candlelight gourmet breakfast, old world, gazebo, charming home on 1 acre.

AMENITIES

1. No Smoking
2. No Pets
3. No Children
4. Senior Citizen Rates
5. Tennis Available
6. Golf Available
7. Swimming Available
8. Skiing Available
9. Credit Cards Accepted
10. Personal Check Accepted
11. Off Season Rates
12. Dinner Available (w/sufficient notice)

Illinois

Okland

Coon, Caroline & Max
3 Montgomery, 61943
(217) 346-2289 or 2653

Amenities: 2,6,7,9,10
Breakfast: Full

Dbl. Oc.: $48.15
Sgl. Oc.: $42.80
Third Person: $10.00

Inn-On-The-Square—Colonial inn with lovely tea room, antiques, craft, and gift shops. Close to large Amish area and Lincolnland historical sites. Three rooms with private baths.

Polo

Trotter, Nancy & Darrel
410 W. Mason St., 61064
(815) 946-2607

Amenities: 1,2,3,10
Breakfast: Full

Dbl. Oc.: $50.00-$75.00
Sgl. Oc.: $50.00-$75.00
Third Person: $10.00

Barber House Inn—Elegant 1891 mansion, hand-painted ceilings, antique furnishings. Nearby historic and recreational areas. Small, quiet town. Available for small functions, luncheons or weddings.

Rock Island

Pheiffer, M/M Gary
1906 7 Ave., 61201
(309) 788-1906

Amenities: 1,2,5,6,7,10
Breakfast: Continental
Rates: $25.00-$50.00 Per room
Third Person: $5.00

The Potter House Bed & Breakfast—Restored historic landmark, circa 1907. Near Mississippi River attractions, dinner theatre and fine restaurants. Professionally decorated with antiques and nostalgic furniture.

Springfield

Daniels, Mrs. Rhonda
718 So. 8th St., 62703
(217) 523-3714

Amenities: 4,6,10
Breakfast: Continental

Dbl. Oc.: $40.00
Sgl. Oc.: $30.00
Third Person: $10.00

Mischler House—Just two blocks from Lincoln's home, this 100 year-old home is comfortably furnished with antiques and the owner's own folk art. Children are welcome.

AMENITIES

1. No Smoking
2. No Pets
3. No Children
4. Senior Citizen Rates
5. Tennis Available
6. Golf Available
7. Swimming Available
8. Skiing Available
9. Credit Cards Accepted
10. Personal Check Accepted
11. Off Season Rates
12. Dinner Available (w/sufficient notice)

Indiana

The Hoosier State

Capital: Indianapolis
Statehood: December 11, 1816; the 9th state
State Motto: Crossroads of America
State Song: "On the Banks of the Wabash"
State Bird: Cardinal
State Flower: Peony
State Tree: Tulip Tree

    Indiana is a great steel producing state. Gary is its major industrial city, close to Lake Michigan. It produces steel products for the automobile industry. Indiana has always had a penchant for cars and their capacity for speed. This goes back to the late 1800's and the beginning of the Indianapolis races. These races continue even today, bringing thousands of racing enthusiasts here every Memorial Day to once again experience the thrill of the powerful racing machine.
    Yet, Indiana has another side. In the southern hills of this state are those who live on quiet farms independent of everyone, content to do what strikes their fancy, from beekeeping to arts and crafts. This is a state that is very much Americana.
    The Indianian likes to celebrate holidays, loves parades and picnics. He is neighborly and invites tourists to come and enjoy his state with him.
    The weather most of the year is warm and enjoyable. Winter months get their share of the snow and cold.

Indiana

Chesterton

Wilk, Timothy
350 Indian Bndry Rd., 46304
(219) 926-5781

Amenities: 1,2,3,4,5,6,7,8,9,10,11
Breakfast: Full
Dbl. Oc.: $60.00-$75.00
Sgl. Oc.: $57.00-$72.00
Third Person: $10.00

Gray Goose Inn—Amid the splendor of Dunes Country. Charming English country home. 90 wooded acres, overlooking Lake Palomara. Some rooms with fireplaces. Bikes, boats, trails. Near I-94, I-80, & 90.

Columbus

Staubin, Paul
445 Fifth St., 47201
(812) 378-4289

Amenities: 1,2,4,5,6,7,8,9,10,12
Breakfast: Full
Dbl. Oc.: $79.00-$250.00
Sgl. Oc.: $72.00-$245.00
Third Person: $15.00

The Columbus Inn—Victorian elegance in former city hall of 1895. 34 rooms & suites, private baths. In the heart of America's architectural showplace, near I-65. Tours, antiques, & more. Color brochure available.

Goshen

Graff, Chris
62644 CR. 37, 46526
(219) 642-4445

Amenities: 1,2,5,6,7,8,9,10,11,12
Breakfast: Continental

Dbl. Oc.: $96.60-$120.75
Sgl. Oc.: $71.40-$89,25
Third Person: $26.25

Checkerberry Inn—European atmosphere, French country cuisine restaurant, twelve tastefully decorated rooms with spectacular views of Amish countryside, expansive porch overlooks the 100-acre estate.

AMENITIES

1. No Smoking
2. No Pets
3. No Children
4. Senior Citizen Rates
5. Tennis Available
6. Golf Available
7. Swimming Available
8. Skiing Available
9. Credit Cards Accepted
10. Personal Check Accepted
11. Off Season Rates
12. Dinner Available (w/sufficient notice)

Indiana

Hagerstown

Warmoth, M/M Jack
300 West Main St., 47346
(317) 489-4422

Amenities: 2,6,9,10
Breakfast: Full
Dbl. Oc.: $60.50
Sgl. Oc.: $55.00
Third Person: $11.00

The Teetor House—Super accommodations in elegant home on 10-acre estate. Private baths, air-conditioned, children welcome. In eastern Indiana, 5 miles north of I-70, State Road 1 to Road 38, left about one mile.

Indianapolis

Muller, Susan
6054 Hollingsworth Rd., 46254
(317) 299-6700

Amenities: 2,3,9,10
Breakfast: Continental

Dbl. Oc.: $82.50
Suites: $104.50

Hollingsworth House Inn—An 1854 Greek revival farm house on 4 acres of land surrounded by 120 acres of undeveloped park land. House is filled with antiques, beautiful china & crystal. Two night minimum on weekends May-Sept.

Indianapolis

Stewart, Ms. Eileen
612 East 13th St., 46202
(317) 634-1711

Amenities: 2,9,10
Breakfast: Continental
Dbl. Oc.: $52.50-$105.00
Sgl. Oc.: $52.50-$105.00
Third Person: $10.00

Stewart Manor—Italianate style Victorian brick mansion. Oak woodwork, gaslight chandeliers, pocket doors. Located in downtown Indy. historic district near public transportation and downtown events.

Middlebury

Zook, Mrs. Maxine
11748 C.R. 2, 46540
(219) 825-2417

Amenities: 1,2,6,7,9,10,12
Breakfast: Continental

Dbl. Oc.: $52.00-$57.70
Sgl. Oc.: $41.95

Patchwork Quilt Country Inn—Large white farmhouse on Centennial Farm. 3 lovely bedrooms with patchwork quilts. Amish backroad tours; 5-course dinners from $9.95.

AMENITIES

1. No Smoking
2. No Pets
3. No Children
4. Senior Citizen Rates
5. Tennis Available
6. Golf Available
7. Swimming Available
8. Skiing Available
9. Credit Cards Accepted
10. Personal Check Accepted
11. Off Season Rates
12. Dinner Available (w/sufficient notice)

Indiana

Nappanee

Leksich, Kris & Robert
302 E. Market, 46550
(219) 773-4383

Amenities: 4,6,8,9,10
Breakfast: Continental
Dbl. Oc.: $40.00-$60.00
Third Person: $7.00

Victorian Guest House—A warm welcome awaits you as you enter this 100-year-old Victorian home nestled amongst the Amish countryside. Yet 30 min. from South Bend and Elkhart on Rt. 6. "Come stay with us."

Shipshewana

Miller, Ruth & Paul
R 2, Box 592, 46565
(219) 768-4221

Amenities: 1,2,9
Breakfast: Continental

Dbl. Oc.: $42.00
Sgl. Oc.: $21.00

Green Meadow Ranch is two miles from Shipshewana Amish country. Large flea market near ranch has miniature horses, donkeys, & antique quilts. Quiet place. "A Bucolle" two miles north. Closed Jan. & Feb.

Valparaiso

Johnson, Vera & Earle
238 W. Joliet Rd., 46383
(219) 462-0781

Amenities: 1,2,3,5,6,7,8,10,12
Breakfast: Continental
Dbl. Oc.: $47.00-$57.00
Sgl. Oc.: $32.00
Third Person: $15.00

The Embassy Bed And Breakfast is just two miles west of city center, it is located on 11.6 acres. Grass, trees, pond, and paths, quiet, beautiful, close to many activities. Amtrak service to N.Y. & Chicago.

AMENITIES

1. No Smoking
2. No Pets
3. No Children
4. Senior Citizen Rates
5. Tennis Available
6. Golf Available
7. Swimming Available
8. Skiing Available
9. Credit Cards Accepted
10. Personal Check Accepted
11. Off Season Rates
12. Dinner Available (w/sufficient notice)

Iowa

The Hawkeye State

Capital: Des Moines
Statehood: December 28, 1846; the 29th state
State Motto: Our Liberties We Prize and
              Our Rights We Will Maintain
State Song: "The Song of Iowa"
State Bird: Eastern Goldfinch
State Flower: Wild Rose
State Tree: Oak

    Iowa is one of the greatest farming states in the United States, sometimes called the "Corn State", or "The Land Where The Tall Corn Grows". Back in the mid-1800's, many young people heeded the advice of Horace Greeley to "Go west, young man, go west", and they did. It was the beginning of a great love affair between man and the soil. Some of the most productive corn farms are here, and some of the best-fed livestock.
    Iowa has many lakes and streams that offer fine fishing and swimming, but the greatest excitement of the year is the annual Iowa State Fair. Farmers from all over Iowa gather together to show their personal farm prizes, from hogs to preserves, each one competing for the coveted Blue Ribbon.
    Herbert Hoover, our 31st president, was born in West Branch, Iowa.

Iowa

Adel

Briley, Dr. & Mrs. Dale
RR 1, Box 30, 50003
(515) 987-1567 or 987-1338

Amenities: 5,6,7,10
Breakfast: Full

Dbl. Oc.: $45.00
Sgl. Oc.: $35.00
Third Person: $10.00

Walden Acres is near Des Moines. The former home of pitcher Bob Feller, is set on 40 acres of wooded land. Spacious home, grounds include antique shop. Stables & veterinary clinic available to board your pets.

Brandon

Andorf, M/M Michael
RR 1, 52210
(319) 938-2635 or 474-2456

Amenities: 2,3,10
Breakfast: Full

Dbl. Oc.: $48.00
Sgl. Oc.: $38.00

Willow Creek Bed & Breakfast is located in a peaceful country setting next to the 52-mile long Cedar Valley Nature Trail. Enjoy hiking & biking the beautiful trail and relaxing in our country home.

Davenport

Pohl, Mary Jo
1234 E. River Dr., 52803
(319) 326-2629

Amenities: 2,4,9,10,11
Breakfast: Full

Dbl. Oc.: $45.00-$60.00
Sgl. Oc.: $30.00-$40.00
Third Person: $10.00

River Oaks Inn—Elegance on the Mississippi. This 1858 home retains many original features: gazebo, leaded glass, fireplace, carriage drive. 4 guest rooms, 3 with private bath. Breakfast in the dining room or spacious deck.

Dubuque

Griesinger, Deborah
1105 Locust, 52001
(319) 582-1894

Amenities: 9,10
Breakfast: Continental
Dbl. Oc.: $87.20
Sgl. Oc.: $87.20
Third Person: $10.00

The Stout House—Built in 1890 by a wealthy lumberman. The Stout House now serves as a 6-room bed and breakfast. Open year round. Furnished in antiques, color TV's and phones in each room; large public spaces.

AMENITIES

1. No Smoking
2. No Pets
3. No Children
4. Senior Citizen Rates
5. Tennis Available
6. Golf Available
7. Swimming Available
8. Skiing Available
9. Credit Cards Accepted
10. Personal Check Accepted
11. Off Season Rates
12. Dinner Available (w/sufficient notice)

Iowa

Dubuque

Griesinger, Miss Debbie
504 Bluff, 52001
(319) 582-1894

Amenities: 2,9,10
Breakfast: Continental
Dbl. Oc.: $109.00-$163.50
Sgl. Oc.: $98.10-$143.70
Third Person: $10.90

The Redstone Inn—Built in 1894 by A.A. Cooper as a wedding present for his daughter, now is fully restored as a 15-room historic inn. 5 suites with whirlpools, champagne and breakfast.

Homestead

Janda, Sheila & Don
Main St., Amana Colonies, 52236
(319) 622-3937

Amenities: 9,10,11
Breakfast: Continental
Dbl. Oc.: $40.00-$55.00
Sgl. Oc.: $30.00
Third Person: $5.00

Die Heimat Country Inn—Built in 1854, this charming inn is decorated with handmade walnut and cherry furniture, homemade quilts and many antiques. The inn is located in Homestead, one of the famous Amana Colonies.

Marengo

Walker, Loy & Robert
RR #1, Box 82, 52301
(319) 642-7787

Amenities: 1,5,6,7,10
Breakfast: Full

Dbl. Oc.: $45.00
Sgl. Oc.: $30.00
Third Person: $5.00-$15.00

Loy's Bed & Breakfast—Modern contemporary farm house. Large grain and hog farm. Recreation room and yard. Farm tour. Tourist attractions: Amana Colonies, Kalona, Herbert Hoover Memorial. Iowa City, Univ., Cedar Rapids.

McGregor

Jamesen, Chris & Bud
Box 195, 126 Main St., 52157
(319) 873-3670

Amenities: 6,7,8,9,10,11
Breakfast: Full

Dbl. Oc.: $60.00
Sgl. Oc.: $45.00
Third Person: $10.00

The Little Switzerland Inn—Overlooks the Mississippi River from a building constructed in 1862. It is furnished with turn-of-the-century furniture & accessories. The newest addition is an authentic log cabin w/large jacuzzi & fireplace.

AMENITIES

1. No Smoking
2. No Pets
3. No Children
4. Senior Citizen Rates
5. Tennis Available
6. Golf Available
7. Swimming Available
8. Skiing Available
9. Credit Cards Accepted
10. Personal Check Accepted
11. Off Season Rates
12. Dinner Available (w/sufficient notice)

Iowa

Middle Amana

Hahn, Lynn & Brad
Box 124, 52307
(319) 622-3029

Amenities: 2,9,10
Breakfast: Continental

Dbl. Oc.: $41.42
Sgl. Oc.: $38.15
Third Person: $2.00

Dusk To Dawn Bed & Breakfast—Located in the historical Amana Colonies. Just 5 minutes away from 30 unique shops and 5 major restaurants. Amana decor accented with a modern greenhouse, deck, & jacuzzi.

Missouri Valley

Strub, Electa & John
RR 3, Box 129, 51555
(712) 642-2418

Amenities: 1,2,6,7,8,9,10,12
Breakfast: Full

Dbl. Oc.: $35.00
Sgl. Oc.: $29.50
Third Person: $7.50

Comfortable Quiet Country Home—1930's decor, 26-acre apple orchard in the Loess Hills. Plenty of room for walking and relaxing; jacuzzi; antiques & museum nearby; country cuisine; by reservations.

South Amana

Kessler, Marilyn & Tom
R 1, Box 66, 52334
(319) 662-4381

Amenities: 2,3,5,6,7
Breakfast: Continental

Dbl. Oc.: $43.60
Sgl. Oc.: $32.70
Suites: $54.50

Babi's Bed & Breakfast—A mini retreat, 10 wooded acres on Highway 6, near Amana Colonies. Open year round. Large deck, wood-burning stove, piano. Amish settlement & Univ. of Iowa 30 minutes away.

Tipton

Gelms, Christine
508 E. 4th St., 52765
(319) 886-2633

Amenities: 5,6,7,9,10,12
Breakfast: Full
Dbl. Oc.: $55.00
Sgl. Oc.: $35.00-$45.00
Third Person: $10.00

Victorian House Of Tipton—1885 Eastlake mansion completely restored, near Interstate 80, Iowa City. Herbert Hoover Library; 3 hours from Chicago. Bicycles available, tennis, swimming, & gourmet food.

AMENITIES

1. No Smoking
2. No Pets
3. No Children
4. Senior Citizen Rates
5. Tennis Available
6. Golf Available
7. Swimming Available
8. Skiing Available
9. Credit Cards Accepted
10. Personal Check Accepted
11. Off Season Rates
12. Dinner Available (w/sufficient notice)

Kansas

The Sunflower State

Capital: Topeka
Statehood: January 29, 1861; the 34th state
State Motto: To The Stars Through Difficulties
State Song: "Home On The Range"
State Bird: Western Meadow Lark
State Flower: Sunflower
State Tree: Cottonwood

Kansas is known as The Wheat State and The Breadbasket of America. It leads all other states in the production of wheat. The farmer is cowboy and rancher who grows cattle and grain at the same time. The wheat at harvest time stands so tall that it makes the land look like a huge sea of gold. It is a beautiful sight to see. In Kansas, wheat harvesting is the biggest part of farming. Machines roll through the fields, cutting and producing bushels of grain every minute.

Kansas is also nicknamed Cowboy Capitol of the World, suggesting Kansas' background as a cattle country. One of its most famous cities is Dodge. Visitors can see ruts made by wagons on the Santa Fe Trail. They can visit Pony Express stations and frontier forts, which were built to protect settlers from the Indians. Kansas is proud of its history and tries to keep a bit of it for all to enjoy.

Dwight D. Eisenhower's boyhood home is preserved at Abilene.

Kansas

Great Bend

Nitzel, Mrs. R. Dale
Rt. 5, Box 153, 67530
(316) 793-7527

Amenities: 1,5,6,7
Breakfas0t: Full

Dbl. Oc.: $20.0
Sgl. Oc.: $15.00
Third Person: $10.00

Peaceful Acres Bed & Breakfast is located 5 miles from Great Bend, KS. on 10 acres. Rambling farm house, goats, chickens, quineas, sheep, windmill. Close to historical sites, & Santa Fe Trail.

Haven

Schroek, M/M Robert E.
67543

Amenities: 1,2,10
Breakfast: Full

Dbl. Oc.: $40.00
Sgl. Oc.: $35.00
Third Person: $10.00

The Dauddy Haus—A nice Amish home with nice assortment of different animals. Small harness shop on premises. Buggy rides if requested. No air-conditioning. Refrigerator & apartment-size gas stove available. Child under 12 free. Dbl. Oc. with continental breakfast-$35.00.

Junction City

Thorp, Mrs. Rebecca
R3, Box 35, 66441
(913) 238-3406

Amenities: 1,2,5,6,7,10
Breakfast: Continental

Dbl. Oc.: $35.00
Sgl. Oc.: $30.00
Third Person: $10.00

Nestle Inn—Your friendly country home away from home. Just off I-70, exit 295 and Highway 77 west of Junction City. Only minutes from city, swimming, golf, tennis & beautiful Milford Lake.

Marion

Thompson, Alice & Don
Rt. 1, Box 120A, 66861
(316) 382-2286

Amenities: 1,4,6,7,8,12
Breakfast: Full

Dbl. Oc.: $46.25
Sgl. Oc.: $37.80
Third Person: $6.30

Haven Of Rest Bed & Breakfast Place—Just one half mile from beautiful Marion Lake. Lovely home on 3 acres. Quiet and restful. Historic sights closeby. Four bedrooms. Five miles east of Hillsboro KS. on Highway 56.

Tonganoxie

Tinberg, Almeda & Richard
220 South Main, 66086
(913) 845-2295

Amenities: 2,6,7,10
Breakfast: Continental

Dbl. Oc.: $33.00
Sgl. Oc.: $27.00
Third Person: $6.50

Almeda's Bed And Breakfast Inn—A historical site close to Kansas City, Kansas and Lawrence Kansas. No pets. Decorated with Almeda antiques.

AMENITIES

1. No Smoking
2. No Pets
3. No Children
4. Senior Citizen Rates
5. Tennis Available
6. Golf Available
7. Swimming Available
8. Skiing Available
9. Credit Cards Accepted
10. Personal Check Accepted
11. Off Season Rates
12. Dinner Available (w/sufficient notice)

Kansas

Valley Falls

Ryan, Marcella & Tom
R.R. 2, Box 87, 66088
(913) 945-3303

Amenities: 1,2,5,6,7,10,12
Breakfast: Full
Dbl. Oc.: $56.70
Sgl. Oc.: $48.30
Third Person: $8.00

The Barn B&B Inn—Located in the rolling hills of N.E. Kansas, 2 miles south of Valley Falls, Hwy. 4 & Mile Post 354. 100-year-old barn close to Perry Lake. Relax, good food, free supper.

Wakefield

Nuttall, Phyllis & Dick
201 Dogwood, Box 342, 67487
(913) 461-5732

Amenities: 5,7,10,12
Breakfast: Continental

Dbl. Oc.: $35.00-$45.00
Sgl. Oc.: $30.00-$40.00
Third Person: $10.00

The Rock House Bed & Breakfast—Oak warmth, built in 1918. Choice of 1 or 2 bedrooms w/full bath. 3 blocks thru park to Milford Lake. Across the street from public swimming pool open June-Aug. Fenced patio. Brochure. Teens ok.

Wakefield

Thurlow, Mrs. Pearl
Rt. 1, Box 297, 67487
(913) 461-5596

Amenities: 5,7
Breakfast: Full

Dbl. Oc.: $30.00
Sgl. Oc.: $20.00
Third Person: $5.00

Bed'n Breakfast, Country—Population 700. Friendly people, 23 mi. long lake, 75-acre park. My original prize-winning whole wheat pancakes and recipe, other good food nearby. Newly remodeled home with good beds. Farm 2 miles away.

Wichita

Eaton, Jill & Roberta
3910 East Kellogg, 67218
(316) 689-8101

Amenities: 2,5,6,7,9,10
Breakfast: Continental
Dbl. Oc.: $66.00-$115.50
Sgl. Oc.: $55.00-$104.50
Third Person: $11.00

The Max Paul's rooms have antiques, featherbeds, cable/HBO & private baths. Executive suites have fireplaces. Exercise/jacuzzi room opens to gardens, deck & pond. Close to park, shops, restaurants & airport.

AMENITIES

1. No Smoking
2. No Pets
3. No Children
4. Senior Citizen Rates
5. Tennis Available
6. Golf Available
7. Swimming Available
8. Skiing Available
9. Credit Cards Accepted
10. Personal Check Accepted
11. Off Season Rates
12. Dinner Available (w/sufficient notice)

Kentucky

The Blue Grass State

Capital: Frankfort
Statehood: January 1, 1792; the 15th state
State Motto: United We Stand, Divided We Fall
State Song: "My Old Kentucky Home"
State Bird: Cardinal
State Flower: Goldenrod
State Tree: Kentucky Coffee Tree

Kentucky is a beautiful and diverse state. Lexington, the home of thoroughbred horses and horse farms, provides hundreds of people with work. Churchill Downes is one of Kentucky's biggest tourist attractions. During the horse racing season, people come from all over the world just for the thrill of seeing these beautiful horses compete against each other. This is Old Kentucky at its best!

Southwest Kentucky is an area of caves formed by huge underground deposits of limestone. One of the caves often visited by tourists is The Mammoth. It streaches out and runs underground like a suburban city's subway.

The eastern part of Kentucky is Appalachia, named for the Appalachian Mts. Here people exist differently. Their employment depends almost entirely upon the mining of coal. This is the most important commodity in this region, and it brings good times and bad.

Tobacco growing and bourbon whiskey are also big business.

Kentucky has a steady influx of tourists because it is such a pretty and interesting state. It also claims to have mild and comfortable weather most of the time.

Kentucky

Bowling Green

Hunter, Dr./Mrs. Norman
659 East 14th Ave., 42101
(502) 781-3861

Amenities: 1,2,3,5,6,10,12
Breakfast: Continental

Dbl. Oc.: $45.00
Sgl. Oc.: $35.00
Third Person: $10.00

Bowling Green Bed & Breakfast—This comfortable 50-yr.-old home is situated on a wooded lot. Watch TV, use library, play organ or picnic in garden. Near restored town square. Western Kentucky Univ.-where your hosts teach, I-65. Mammoth Cave or Opryland close drive.

Carrollton

Gants, Judy & Bill
406 Highland Ave., 41008
(502) 732-4210

Amenities: 4,5,6,7,8,9,10
Breakfast: Full

Dbl. Oc.: $52.50
Sgl. Oc.: $47.25
Third Person: $5.25

P.T. Baker House—Beautifully restored century-old Victorian home with private baths in the historic district. Easy walk to craft & antique shops. 2 miles to state park, midway between Cincinnati & Louisville in historic district. Ideal getaway.

Georgetown

McKnight, M/M Clay
350 N. Broadway, 40324
(502) 863-3514

Amenities: 10
Breakfast: Continental

Dbl. Oc.: $60.00
Sgl. Oc.: $60.00
Third Person: $10.00

Log Cabin Bed & Breakfast—Enjoy this Kentucky log cabin (circa 1809), shake roof and chinked logs. Completely private. 2 bedrooms, fireplace, fully-equipped kitchen. 5 miles to Kentucky Horse Park. 12 miles north of Lexington. Children welcomed.

Louisville

Roosa, Nan-Ellen & Stephen
1132 South First St., 40203
(502) 581-1914

Amenities: 5
Breakfast: Continental
Dbl. Oc.: $58.00
Sgl. Oc.: $53.00
Third Person: $10.00

Victorian Secret Bed & Breakfast—A stately 14 room Queen Anne mansion with 11 fireplaces, original woodwork, restored to original elegance. Period furnishings grace spacious rooms. One mile south of city center.

AMENITIES

1. No Smoking
2. No Pets
3. No Children
4. Senior Citizen Rates
5. Tennis Available
6. Golf Available
7. Swimming Available
8. Skiing Available
9. Credit Cards Accepted
10. Personal Check Accepted
11. Off Season Rates
12. Dinner Available (w/sufficient notice)

Louisiana

The Pelican State

Capital: Baton Rouge
Statehood: April 30, 1812; the 18th state
State Motto: Union, Justice and Confidence
State Song: "Song of Louisiana"
State Bird: Brown Pelican
State Flower: Magnolia
State Tree: Bald Cypress

    In 1803, the state of Louisiana was part of the Louisiana Purchase from France. The $15,000,000 sale doubled the size of the United States.
    French and Spanish speaking people came and settled in New Orleans. Their descendants are referred to as Creoles. Later settlers arrived from Nova Scotia. Henry Wadsworth Longfellow wrote of this journey in his poem, Evangeline. The Acadians settled in Lafayette City and retained most of their old customs. As a result of this mixture of nationalities and customs, Louisiana and especially the city of New Orleans, is a most colorful and interesting place to visit. Over 4,000,000 tourists come here each year.
    The main attraction is the Mardi Gras in New Orleans and the French Quarter. The merrymaking of Carnival commences on Twelfth Night, approximately two weeks before the start of Lent, and it continues until Mardi Gras, the day before Lent starts.
    Louisiana is located along the beautiful Gulf of Mexico, with the Mississippi River flowing along its eastern border and through the state to Baton Rouge and New Orleans.

Louisiana

Baton Rouge

Dease, M/M Jack
8151 Highland Rd., 70808
(504) 766-8600

Amenities: 1,2,10
Breakfast: Full

Dbl. Oc.: $80.15

Mt. Hope Plantation—Home on National Register of Historical Sights. Inside city limits. Gift shop, museum, 4 1/2 acres.

Jackson

Harvey, M/M LeRoy
102 Bank St.
P.O. Box 1000, 70748
(504) 634-5901

Amenities: 4,9,10,12
Breakfast: Full

Dbl. Oc.: $70.00-$81.00
Sgl. Oc.: $65.00-$76.00
Third Person: $15.00

Milbank Massive Romantic Antebellum Mansion built in 1803 as a bank. Completely restored and refurnished with period antiques. All rooms in main house. The state's finest restoration available to stay in.

Napoleonville

Marshall, Millie & Keith
Rte. 2, Box 478, 70390
(504) 524-1988 or 369-7151

Amenities: 1,10,12
Breakfast: Continental-Full
Dbl. Oc.: $85.00-$150.00
Sgl. Oc.: $85.00-$125.00
Third Person: $10.00-$40.00

Madewood Plantation House—National historic landmark. Return to gracious living with dinner by candellight, canopied beds, antiques, oak trees. 75 miles to downtown New Orleans. Featured in Vogue & other magazines.

New Orleans

Chauppette, Ms. Carol
329 Dauphine, 70112
(504) 522-1331

Amenities: 2,7,9
Breakfast: Continental

Dbl. Oc.: $167.00
Sgl. Oc.: $104.00
Third Person: $10.00

Grenoble House—Restored 19th-century townhouse in heart of French Quarter. 17 spacious & elegantly-furnished suites with fully equipped kitchens. Covered bar-b-que, patio, pool, jacuzzi, concierge service, weekly rates available.

AMENITIES

1. No Smoking
2. No Pets
3. No Children
4. Senior Citizen Rates
5. Tennis Available
6. Golf Available
7. Swimming Available
8. Skiing Available
9. Credit Cards Accepted
10. Personal Check Accepted
11. Off Season Rates
12. Dinner Available (w/sufficient notice)

Louisiana

New Orleans

Dazet, Ms. Sherri
1006 Royal St., 70116
(504) 524-2222

Amenities: 4,5,6,9,11
Breakfast: Continental
Dbl. Oc.: $72.15
Sgl. Oc.: $61.05
Third Person: $3.00

The Noble Arms Inn is a truly unique way to experience the French Quarter. Private courtyard available to guests only. Enjoy shopping Royal Street by day and by night famous Bourbon Street.

New Orleans

Eager, Ms. Caryl
2448 Gladiolus, 70122
(800) 225-6667 or
(504) 947-3137

Amenities: 4,5,6,7,9,12
Breakfast: Continental

Dbl. Oc.: $29.00-$150.00
Sgl. Oc.: $25.00-$90.00
Third Person: $15.00

"Eager Arms"—Victorian charm! Antiques, chandeliers, king-size beds, private baths. 5 min. from French Quarter, Mardi Gras, Dome, Convention center, Univ., luxurious suites: $150. Airport transportation available.

New Orleans

Hilton, Joanne & Dennis
1748 Prytania Street, 70130
(504) 523-6556

Amenities: 5,6,7,8
Breakfast: Continental

Dbl. Oc.: $47.00
Sgl. Oc.: $40.00
Third Person: $10.00

St. Charles Guest House—Simple, cozy and affordable. In historic area on trolley line. Minutes to Quarter, Dome & Convention area. Best restaurants nearby. Pool, patio, and banana trees. Interesting guests!

New Orleans

Jensen, Shirley, Joni & Bruce
1631 7th St., 70115
(504) 897-1895

Amenities: 2,10
Breakfast: Continental

Dbl. Oc.: $45.00
Sgl. Oc.: $40.00
Third Person: $5.00

Jensen House—Located across from the Garden District, an area of lovely homes. St. Charles Trolley 1 block away, 15 minutes to French Quarter or uptown. 100-yr.-old Victorian home, shared bath, many lovely antiques.

AMENITIES

1. No Smoking
2. No Pets
3. No Children
4. Senior Citizen Rates
5. Tennis Available
6. Golf Available
7. Swimming Available
8. Skiing Available
9. Credit Cards Accepted
10. Personal Check Accepted
11. Off Season Rates
12. Dinner Available (w/sufficient notice)

Louisiana

New Orleans
Soubie, Mark, Jr.
417 Frenchman St., 70116
(504) 948-2166 or
(800) 831-1781

Amenities: 3,4,7,9,10,12
Breakfast: Full

Dbl. Oc.: $71.54-$110.39
Sgl. Oc.: $71.54-$110.39
Third Person: $19.37

A Hotel, The Frenchman—25 rms. 1860 creole townhouse located at the French Quarter. Parking, private bath, period furniture, TV, tropical patio, friendly 24 hr. staff, Le Petit Cafe for lunch & dinner, walk to all the attractions.

New Orleans
Spencer, Debbie & David
915 Royal St., 70116
(504) 523-1515

Amenities: 2,7,9
Breakfast: Continental

Dbl. Oc.: $83.25 & up
Sgl. Oc.: $72.15 & up

The Cornstalk Hotel—A small but elegant national register hotel in the heart of the French Quarter. Antique furnishings, breakfast and newspaper to room or balcony. Parking on grounds, 24-hour staff and southern hospitality.

New Orleans
Twohey, Patrick
1003 B. Bourbon St., 70116
(504) 581-2678 or
(800) 331-7971

Amenities: 2,9,11
Breakfast: Continental

Dbl. Oc.: $72.15-$127.65
Sgl. Oc.: $61.05-$116.55
Third Person: $17.15

Lafitte Guest House—Beautifully restored 1849 French manor house. This guest house is considered the place to stay in New Orleans. Patrick's staff will make you feel at home among the antique decor of this fine old home.

New Roads
Armstrong, Rev./Mrs. Miller
605 East Main St., 70760
(504) 638-6254

Amenities: 10
Breakfast: Full

Dbl. Oc.: $45.00
Sgl. Oc.: $40.00
Third Person: $5.00

Pointe Coupee Bed & Breakfast—Accommodations in three historic homes in downtown New Roads near False River and the Mississippi. Cajun food, historic tours, a step back in time. Follow L.A. Hwy. 1 north of Baton Rouge.

St. Francisville
Dittloff, Mr. Lyle
524 Royal St.
P.O. Box 1461, 70775
(504) 635-4791

Amenities: 2,10,12
Breakfast: Full

Dbl. Oc.: $60.50
Sgl. Oc.: $44.00
Third Person: $8.80

Barrow House—Circa 1809. Located on historic Royal St. in a quiet neighborhood of antebellum homes. Rooms have period antiques. Walking and plantation tours. Wicker rockers and gourmet cuisine.

AMENITIES

1. No Smoking
2. No Pets
3. No Children
4. Senior Citizen Rates
5. Tennis Available
6. Golf Available
7. Swimming Available
8. Skiing Available
9. Credit Cards Accepted
10. Personal Check Accepted
11. Off Season Rates
12. Dinner Available (w/sufficient notice)

Louisiana

St. Francisville

Fillet, M/M Richard
Box 1369, 70775
(504) 635-6502

Amenities: 9,11,12
Breakfast: Continental

Dbl. Oc.: $45.00-$55.00
Sgl. Oc.: $35.00-$45.00
Third Person: $8.00

1880 Victorian Gothic on edge of historic district. Louisiana Plantation country, spectacular ceiling medallion with Mardi Gras masks. Rooms open onto New Orleans-style courtyard. Lunch & dinner restaurant.

Vinton

Cooper, Danny
1335 Horridge St., 70668
(318) 589-2903

Amenities: 12
Breakfast: Full

Dbl. Oc.: $40.00
Sgl. Oc.: $30.00

Old Lyons House—Make this national register Queen Anne Victorian your home away from home. Antique furnishings, cozy rooms, crackling fireplaces, southern hospitality all combine to make your stay one to remember!

White Castle

Hidalgo, Cindy
Mississippi River Rd.
70788-0160
(504) 545-2409

Amenities: 2,5,7,9,10,12
Breakfast: Full

Dbl. Oc.: $122.28
Sgl. Oc.: $95.70
Third Person: $37.21

Nottoway Plantation Home—The south's largest plantation has 13 overnight rooms with private baths, sherry, fresh flowers, & guilded tours. Restaurant serves lunch & dinner daily. On Hwy. 1, 21 mi. south of Baton Rouge. Dinner approx. $20/person.

AMENITIES

1. No Smoking
2. No Pets
3. No Children
4. Senior Citizen Rates
5. Tennis Available
6. Golf Available
7. Swimming Available
8. Skiing Available
9. Credit Cards Accepted
10. Personal Check Accepted
11. Off Season Rates
12. Dinner Available (w/sufficient notice)

Maine

The Pine Tree State

Capital: Augusta
Statehood: March 15, 1820; the 23rd state
State Motto: I Direct or I Guide
State Song: "State of Maine Song"
State Bird: Chickadee
State Flower: White Pine Cone and Tassel
State Tree: White Pine

Of all the New England states, Maine is perhaps the largest and best known for its beautiful Atlantic coastline. Traveling along the rugged coast of Maine, a visitor can see and visit many lighthouses, fishing villages and beautiful sandy beaches.

For hundreds of years, the forest of Maine was the mainstay of its economy, and it remains that way today. However, with the modernization of machinery, the business of logging has become much safer. Paper and paper products are Maine's big business.

Maine is also known for growing potatoes. It supplies 8% of the nation's harvest.

Visitors to Maine can enjoy real clambakes. The lobsters and clams for these clambakes are found right in the Maine waters.

Maine's weather for the most part is cool. This kind of weather attracts vacationers in the summer and skiers in the winter. It has become a big vacation area.

Maine

Bar Harbor

Burns, Marian
69 Mt. Desert St., 04609
(207) 288-4263

Amenities: 2,5,6,7,9,10,11
Breakfast: Continental

Dbl. Oc.: $70.00-$125.00
Sgl. Oc.: $70.00-$125.00
Third Person: $10.00

Mira Monte Inn—A gracious 18-room Victorian estate on 1 acre, landscaped grounds; 5 min. walk to shops, waterfront. King/queen beds. Priv. baths, fireplaces, balconies, library, piano. Open May to Oct. 20

Bar Harbor

Chester, Dorothy & Mike
74 Mount Desert St., 04609
(207) 288-4970

Amenities: 1,2,3,5,6,7,9,10,11
Breakfast: Continental
Dbl. Oc.: $80.25-$96.30

Holbrook House—A beautifully decorated 1876 Victorian cottage on the town's historic corridor minutes to shops, restaurants, ocean. Library, porch, sunroom parlor, 10 bright & airy bedrooms all w/priv. baths.

Bar Harbor

Demao, Darlene & William
40 Holland Ave., 04609
(207) 288-3044

Amenities: 1,2,3,5,6,7,9,10,11
Breakfast: Full
Dbl. Oc.: $55.00-$90.00
Sgl. Oc.: $50.00-$80.00
Third Person: $10.00

Graycote Inn—Gracious hospitality, charming accommodations, quiet in-town elegance—all await your pleasure. King and queen canopy beds, fireplaces and balconies. Hearty breakfast, afternoon refreshments.

AMENITIES

1. No Smoking
2. No Pets
3. No Children
4. Senior Citizen Rates
5. Tennis Available
6. Golf Available
7. Swimming Available
8. Skiing Available
9. Credit Cards Accepted
10. Personal Check Accepted
11. Off Season Rates
12. Dinner Available (w/sufficient notice)

Maine

Bar Harbor

O'Connell/O'Brien
Box 727, Holland Ave., 04609
(207) 288-4563

Amenities: 5,6,9
Breakfast: Continental

Dbl. Oc.: $58.58
Sgl. Oc.: $58.58
Third Person: $10.00

Castlemaine Inn—Circa 1865. Refurbished inn with relaxing parlor, porches, fireplaces, AC, private baths and queen-size beds. On a quiet side street, a short walk to shops and restaurants. Sprinkler system.

Bar Harbor

Schwartz, Susan & Barry
7 High Street, 04609
(207)288-4533

Amenities: 1,2,3,9,10,11
Breakfast: Continental

Dbl. Oc.: $64.20-$96.30
Sgl. Oc.: $64.20-$96.30
Third Person: $10.00

Hearthside Inn—Small, friendly inn on a quiet side street in Bar Harbor. Restaurants, shops, harbor just a short walk. 5-minute car ride to Acadia National Park.

Bar Harbor

Suydam, Mrs. Michele
16 Roberts Ave., 04609
(207) 288-3443

Amenities: 1,2,3,5,6,7,9,10
Breakfast: Continental

Dbl. Oc.: $57.75-$80.25
Sgl. Oc.: $57.75-$80.25

The Maples—A Victorian inn, 2 blocks from the ocean, 5 minutes from Acadia National Park and the Nova Scotia Ferry. Private and shared bath. Reservations please.

Bath

Lansky, Mrs. Gladys
60 Pearl St., 04530
(207) 443-1191

Amenities: 1,2,3,6,7,10,12
Breakfast: Continental

Dbl. Oc.: $40.00-$45.00
Sgl. Oc.: $40.00-$45.00

Glad II—Nicholas, my four-legged concierge and I welcome you to our 1851 Victorian home. We want to pamper you with a good night's sleep, a tasty breakfast and an introduction to our beautiful city of ships.

Bath

Messler, M/M Vincent
45 Pearl St., 04530
(207) 443-6069

Amenities: 2,3,5,6,7,10,11
Breakfast: Full

Dbl. Oc.: $64.20-$80.25
Third Person: $15.00

Packard House—A 1790 Georgian home in Historic District, belonged to Benjamin F. Packard, a famous shipwright. Period furnishings; 3 guest rooms; museums, shops, beaches, theater, galleries nearby.

AMENITIES

1. No Smoking
2. No Pets
3. No Children
4. Senior Citizen Rates
5. Tennis Available
6. Golf Available
7. Swimming Available
8. Skiing Available
9. Credit Cards Accepted
10. Personal Check Accepted
11. Off Season Rates
12. Dinner Available (w/sufficient notice)

Maine

Bath

Pollard, M/M George
N. Bath Rd., 04530
RR 2, Box 85
(207) 443-4391

Amenities: 6,7,8,10,11
Breakfast: Full

Dbl. Oc.: $55.00-$65.00
Sgl. Oc.: $45.00
Third Person: $10.00

The Fairhaven Inn—Classic, comfortable and quiet country inn on 27 acres. Nestled into a hillside and overlooking the Kennebec River. A perfect base from which to enjoy all that Maine's coast offers.

Belfast

Chapnick, Dini & Bernie
Route One, 04915
(207) 338-5320

Amenities: 9,10,11,12
Breakfast: Continental
Dbl. Oc.: $63.13-$95.25
Third Person: $5.35

Penobscot Meadows Inn—A charming country inn, conveniently located for day trips, overlooking Penobscot Bay with a 4-star rated restaurant, outdoor dining, an extensive wine list. Private baths for every room. AAA - Mobil.

Bethel

Douglass, Mrs. Dana
Star Rte., Box 90, 04217
(207) 824-2229

Amenities: 5,6,7,8,10
Breakfast: Continental

Dbl. Oc.: $53.50
Sgl. Oc.: $42.80
Third Person: $16.50

The Douglass Place—5 guest rooms, 2 1/2 baths, skiing, hiking, leaf picking, village 1 mile Rt. 2, N.E.

Bethel

Fain, Natalie & Dick
Rt. 2, Rumford Rd., 04217
(207) 824-2002

Amenities: 1,2,3,4,8,9,10
Breakfast: Full

Dbl. Oc.: $50.00
Sgl. Oc.: $40.00
Dec.-Apr. (slightly higher)

Norseman Inn—A 200-year-old Federal farmstead offering family-style hospitality. Quiet, over four acres of grounds, 1 mile from Bethel scenic views. Fieldstone fireplaces in living & dining rooms.

AMENITIES

1. No Smoking
2. No Pets
3. No Children
4. Senior Citizen Rates
5. Tennis Available
6. Golf Available
7. Swimming Available
8. Skiing Available
9. Credit Cards Accepted
10. Personal Check Accepted
11. Off Season Rates
12. Dinner Available (w/sufficient notice)

Maine

Bethel

Zinchuk, Robin & Douglas
Corners Broad & Church
Box 206
(207) 824-2657

Amenities: 7,8,9,10,11
Breakfast: Full

Dbl. Oc.: $58.85
Sgl. Oc.: $48.15
Third Person: $10.00

Facing Village Green in national historic district. Spacious, sunny rooms. Delicious healthy breakfast. 2 private saunas. Cable, color TV. Warm, homelike atmosphere. Efficiencies available.

Bingham

Gibson, Mrs. Frances
Meadow St., 04920-0389
(207) 672-4034

Amenities: 5,8,10,11,12
Breakfast: Continental

Dbl. Oc.: $48.00
Sgl. Oc.: $24.00
Third Person: $24.00

Mrs. G's Bed & Breakfast—Four bedroom old Victorian home, walking distance to shopping, church and white water rafting on the Kennebec River. Quiet, warm homelike atmosphere. Ten beds in the loft, dormitory style.

Blue Hill

Schatz, Marcia & James
Box 437, 04614
(207) 374-5126

Amenities: 1,2,3,10,11,12
Breakfast: Continental
Dbl. Oc.: $55.85-$69.55
Sgl. Oc.: $48.15-$55.85
Third Person: $10.00

Old Farm—Rooms overlooking field, duck pond and 48 acres of woods. Nearby coast provides scenes of natural beauty and historical significance. Close to Bar Harbor and Arcadia National Park.

Boothbay

Morissette, Ellen
P.O. Box 125, 04537
(207) 633-2159

Amenities: 1,2,3,5,6,9,10,11
Breakfast: Full

Dbl. Oc.: $60.00-$80.00

The Kenniston Hill Inn—Romantic and restful B&B Rt. 27. Mid-coast Maine, one mile from Boothbay Harbor. Paul & Ellen Morissette chef/owner.

AMENITIES

1. No Smoking
2. No Pets
3. No Children
4. Senior Citizen Rates
5. Tennis Available
6. Golf Available
7. Swimming Available
8. Skiing Available
9. Credit Cards Accepted
10. Personal Check Accepted
11. Off Season Rates
12. Dinner Available (w/sufficient notice)

Maine

Boothbay

Mason, M/M David
36 McKown St., 04538
(207) 633-3431

Amenities: 4,5,6,7,9,10,11
Breakfast: Continental

Dbl. Oc.: $49.00 & up

The Welch House Inn is an early 1880's Sea Captains house with most commanding view of harbor. Most rooms with private bath. Free parking and 2-minute walk to all harbor activities, theater and restaurant.

Boothbay Harbor

Savory, Georgia
44 McKown Hill, 04538
(207) 633-2941 or 633-3839

Amenities: 5,6,7,10,12
Breakfast: Continental

Dbl. Oc.: $30.00-$40.00
Third Person: $6.00

Hilltop Guest House is located overlooking town and harbor. Three minute walk all activities: boating, shops, dinner, theatres. Nearby beach, small state park. Coffee & muffins included. Ample parking. Send for brochure.

Bridgton

Starets, Jane & Dick
37 Highland Rd., 04009
(207) 647-3733

Amenities: 1,2,5,6,7,8,10
Breakfast: Full
Dbl. Oc.: $58.85-80.25
Sgl. Oc.: $48.15-58.85
Third Person: $20.00

The Noble House—Stately manor on scenic Highland Lake. Private lake frontage w/BBQ, hammock, and canoe. Romantic restaurants, summer theatre, antiques, skiing nearby. Family suites, some with whirlpool baths.

Brunswick

Rose, Guenter
7 South St., 04011
(207) 729-6959

Amenities: 2,5,6,7,9,10
Breakfast: Continental

Dbl. Oc.: $48.15-$58.85
Sgl. Oc.: $37.45-$48.15
Third Person: $10.70

Samuel Newman House—An 1821 Federal-style house adjoining Bowdoin College. Seven comfortable rooms with antique furnishings & collectables. Breakfast features homemade breads & pastry. Near ocean, Freeport and Portland. No pets.

AMENITIES

1. No Smoking
2. No Pets
3. No Children
4. Senior Citizen Rates
5. Tennis Available
6. Golf Available
7. Swimming Available
8. Skiing Available
9. Credit Cards Accepted
10. Personal Check Accepted
11. Off Season Rates
12. Dinner Available (w/sufficient notice)

Maine

Bucksport

Stone, Audrey
210 Main St.
Box 1657, 04416-1657
(207) 469-3783

Amenities: 1,3,6,7,8,10,11,12
Breakfast: Full

Dbl. Oc.: $48.15
Sgl. Oc.: $42.80
Third Person: $10.70

The River Inn—On Hwy. 15; 1 hour to Acadia; 20 miles to Bangor. Spacious old colonial on the river. Queen, double or twin beds, shared full bath. 4 seasons area. Antiquing, fine restaurants, sports, shopping.

Camden

Doudera, Vicki & Ed
82 Elm St., 04843
(207) 236-6060

Amenities: 1,5,6,7,8,9,10,11
Breakfast: Full

Dbl. Oc.: $74.90-$85.60
Sgl. Oc.: $64.90-$78.60
Third Person: $16.05

Blackberry Inn—Stroll into town from a vintage "Painted Lady" Victorian. This elegant yet friendly B&B has lots of warmth and charm plus scrumptious full breakfast. Call or write for our brochure.

Camden

Goodspeed, Linda & Don
60 (N) Mountain St., 04843
(207) 236-8077

Amenities: 5,6,7,10
Breakfast: Continental

Dbl. Oc.: $65.25
Sgl. Oc.: $48.15
Third Person: $10.00

Goodspeed's Guest House—A 1879 farmhouse; 8 restored guest rooms, antique clocks & furniture throughout. Enjoy breakfast on the sundeck. Quiet location, spacious grounds, just 5 blocks from the village harbor.

Camden

Staub, Pauline & Brad
9 High St., 04843
(207) 236-8842

Amenities: 2,5,6,7,8,9,10,11
Breakfast: Full

Dbl. Oc.: $69.55-$214.00

Hawthorn Inn—Gracious Victorian bed & breakfast. Afternoon tea. Walk through our back garden to shops and restaurants. Carriage house apartments with private jacuzzis. Lovely harbor views. Open year round.

Camden

Tierney, Sally & Bob
22 High St., 04843
(207) 236-9636

Amenities: 2,5,6,7,8,9,10,11
Breakfast: Full

Dbl. Oc.: $69.55
Sgl. Oc.: $42.80
Third Person: $15.00

Maine Stay Bed & Breakfast—A comfortable bed and substantial breakfast served in the warmth of new-found friends and the hospitality of a treasured colonial home. A short walk to the harbor and shops. Open year round.

AMENITIES

1. No Smoking
2. No Pets
3. No Children
4. Senior Citizen Rates
5. Tennis Available
6. Golf Available
7. Swimming Available
8. Skiing Available
9. Credit Cards Accepted
10. Personal Check Accepted
11. Off Season Rates
12. Dinner Available (w/sufficient notice)

Maine

Capitol Island

Peckham, M/M Robert L.
04538
(207) 633-2521

Amenities: 1,2,5,6,7,10,11
Breakfast: Continental
Dbl. Oc.: $58.85-$69.55
Sgl. Oc.: $42.80

The Albonegon Inn sits on the water's edge in the Boothbay Harbor region. The view is spectacular, the ambiance simple, warm and welcoming. On a quiet island, it is near the amenities of town.

Center Lovell

Mosca, Susie & Bil
Rt. 5, 04016
(207) 925-1575

Amenities: 2,5,6,7,8,9,10,11
Breakfast: Full
Dbl. Oc.: $67.30
Sgl. Oc.: $50.15
Third Person: $15.50

Center Lovell Inn—1805 country farmhouse overlooking panorama of White Mts., & nearby Lake Kezar. Fully licensed, porch or fireside dining with northern Italian cuisine from family recipes. Featured in *Architectural Digest*.

Chamberlain

Hahler, M/M John J.
Box 105, Rt. 32, 04541
(207) 677-2386

Amenities: 2,3,10
Breakfast: Continental

Dbl. Oc.: $50.00
Sgl. Oc.: $40.00
Third Person: $10.00

Ocean Reefs On Long Cove—4 rooms each with private bath, 2 cabins. Watch waves break over the reef. Lobster men hauling traps or nature in its environment between tides. Children over 14 considered.

Clark Island
(Spruce Head)

Smith, Terry & Norman
Clark Island Rd., 04859
(207) 594-7644

Amenities: 5,6,7,8,9,10,11,12
Breakfast: Full

Dbl. Oc.: $63.00
Sgl. Oc.: $44.00
Third Person: $11.70

Craignair Inn—Built to house stonecutters in 1929 and now a charming family run inn. Overlooks well tended gardens and the Atlantic Ocean, ten miles south of Rockland off Route 73. Call for directions.

AMENITIES

1. No Smoking
2. No Pets
3. No Children
4. Senior Citizen Rates
5. Tennis Available
6. Golf Available
7. Swimming Available
8. Skiing Available
9. Credit Cards Accepted
10. Personal Check Accepted
11. Off Season Rates
12. Dinner Available (w/sufficient notice)

Maine

Damariscotta

Bates, Mrs. Elizabeth
Bristol Rd.
Box 004, 04543
(207) 563-1919

Amenities: 1,2,3,5,6,7,10,11
Breakfast: Full

Dbl. Oc.: $45.00
Sgl. Oc.: $40.00
Third Person: $10.00

Elizabeth's Bed & Breakfast—Charming home furnished with country antiques, overlooking Tidal Damariscotta River. Resident Herons, Terns, and Eagles. Walk to antique shops and seafood restaurants. Warm, personal attention.

Damariscotta

Hovance, Jeanne & Joseph R.
Rt. 129
HCR 64, Box 045F, 04543
(207) 563-5941

Amenities: 1,2,9,10,11
Breakfast: Continental

Dbl. Oc.: $48.15-$58.85
Sgl. Oc.: $42.80-$53.50
Third Person: $10.70

Brannon-Bunker Inn—Warm country setting, river view, 7 rooms decorated with antiques. 10 minutes to lighthouse, historic fort, golf, sandy beach, antique shops, Audubon Center, & beautiful seacoast.

Dennysville

Haggerty, Mary & Jerry
Routes 1 & 86, 04628
(207) 726-3953

Amenities: 2,5,6,7,8,9,10,11,12
Breakfast: Full

Dbl. Oc.: $144.00
Sgl. Oc.: $72.00

Lincoln House Country Inn—The centerpiece of northeastern coastal ME. Full service inn on 95 acres: a choice spot for nature lovers. Outstanding food and drink. National Register. Internationally acclaimed. Rates include dinner.

Dexter

Beal, Mary Ellen
Caswell, Roberta
37 Zions Hill, 04930
(207) 924-3130

Amenities: 1,2,9,10
Breakfast: Full

Dbl. Oc.: $48.15-$69.55
Sgl. Oc.: $37.45-$58.85
Third Person: $21.40

Brewster Inn—Gracious 19 room historic mansion formerly owned by Sen. R. Brewster. Each bedroom has priv. bath. Guests enjoy porches and gardens in a quiet area. Warm & friendly hospitality. Open all year.

Eastport

McInnis, Mrs.
Todd's Head, 04631
(207) 853-2328

Amenities: 10
Breakfast: Continental

Dbl. Oc.: $42.80
Sgl. Oc.: $26.75
Third Person: $10.70

Todd House—Step into the past in our Revolutionary era Cape with a wide panorama of Passamaquoddy Bay. Breakfast in common room before huge fireplace. Barbecue facilities. Children welcome.

AMENITIES

1. No Smoking
2. No Pets
3. No Children
4. Senior Citizen Rates
5. Tennis Available
6. Golf Available
7. Swimming Available
8. Skiing Available
9. Credit Cards Accepted
10. Personal Check Accepted
11. Off Season Rates
12. Dinner Available (w/sufficient notice)

Maine

Eliot

Raymond, Mrs. Elaine
Route 101, 03903
(207) 439-0590

Amenities: 5,6,7,10
Breakfast: Continental

Dbl. Oc.: $50.00-$60.00

Highland Meadows—1740 Colonial house in rural setting located 6 miles from historic Portsmouth, NH. Relaxed country ambiance but minutes to fine dining, factory outlet discount stores, and Maine seacoast.

Freeport

Bradley, Loretta & Alan
188 Main St., 04032
(207) 865-3289

Amenities: 2,6,9,10,11
Breakfast: Full
Dbl. Oc.: $58.85-$69.55
Sgl. Oc.: $48.15-$58.85
Third Person: $10.70

Capt. Josiah Mitchell House—5 minute walk to L.L. Bean. Historical sea captain's home. Decorated in velvets & satins of Victorian era. Oriental rugs, chandeliers, canopy beds, oil paintings. True elegance.

Freeport

Friedlander, M/M James
Independence Dr., 04032
(207) 865-9295

Amenities: 10,11
Breakfast: Full
Dbl. Oc.: $80.00-$90.00
Sgl. Oc.: $70.00-$80.00
Third Person: $15.00

The Isaac Randall House—An elegant country inn within walking distance of downtown Freeport, L.L. Bean & world famous shops. Featuring sumptuous breakfasts, antique furniture, oriental rugs & especially—warm hospitality.

Freeport

Hassett, Ed & Cates David
181 Main St., 04032
(207) 865-1226

Amenities: 2,4,7,8,9,10,11
Breakfast: Full

Dbl. Oc.: $85.60
Sgl. Oc.: $74.90
Third Person: $10.00

181 Main St.—1840 Cape, country elegance, antiques and appointments true to period. 7 guest rooms, all private baths. Intown, minutes walk from L.L. Bean and luxury outlets. Ample parking; pool; quiet.

AMENITIES

1. No Smoking	**4.** Senior Citizen Rates	**7.** Swimming Available	**10.** Personal Check Accepted
2. No Pets	**5.** Tennis Available	**8.** Skiing Available	**11.** Off Season Rates
3. No Children	**6.** Golf Available	**9.** Credit Cards Accepted	**12.** Dinner Available (w/sufficient notice)

Maine

Harrison

Fennell, M/M John
Island Pond Rd.,
Rt. 117, 04040
(207) 583-2544

Amenities: 1,2,5,7,8,9,10
Breakfast: Full

Dbl. Oc.: $42.80
Sgl. Oc.: $29.96
Third Person: $8.56

Snowbird Lodge Bed And Breakfast—An unpretentious year-round family-run lodge. Snowbird offers canoes, tennis, skiing, and golf nearby. Relax by the island pond's private beach. After a homecooked breakfast enjoy our huge fieldstone fireplace.

Kennebunk

Bachelder, Mark
P.O. Box 1129, 04043
(207) 985-3770

Amenities: 1,2,10
Breakfast: Full
Dbl. Oc.: $65.00
Sgl. Oc.: $65.00
Third Person: $20.00

Arundel Meadows Inn—1820's farmhouse filled with art and antiques. Rooms individually decorated—all private baths, fireplaces, gourmet breakfasts and teas. Open year round. Rt. 1, Arundel ME—minutes from Kennebunkport.

Kennebunkport

Downs, Eva & Jacques
P.O. Box 478A, 04046
(207) 967-5151

Amenities: 1,2,6,7,8,10,11
Breakfast: Full

Dbl. Oc.: $90.95
Third Person: $21.40

Enjoy Comfortable Elegance—In this 19th-century home beautifully appointed rooms, antiques, fireplace, fresh flowers, resident historian. Close to: ocean, river, shops and restaurants quiet area.

Kennebunkport

Gagnon, Carol & Jacques
Box 500A, Maine St., 04046
(207) 967-2117

Amenities: 5,6,7,9,10
Breakfast: Continental
Dbl. Oc.: $92.02
Sgl. Oc.: $92.02
Third Person: $5.35-$12.70

Maine Stay Inn & Cottages—Elegant B&B rooms; 10 delightful efficiency cottages; located in historical district; easy walk to harbor: shops, galleries, & restaurants. Open April-mid Dec. Children welcome.

AMENITIES

1. No Smoking
2. No Pets
3. No Children
4. Senior Citizen Rates
5. Tennis Available
6. Golf Available
7. Swimming Available
8. Skiing Available
9. Credit Cards Accepted
10. Personal Check Accepted
11. Off Season Rates
12. Dinner Available (w/sufficient notice)

Maine

Kennebunkport

Kyle, Mary & Bill
South South St.
P.O. Box 1333, 04046
(207) 967-2780

Amenities: 2,9,10,11
Breakfast: Full

Dbl. Oc.: $60.00-$70.00
Sgl. Oc.: $55.00-$76.00
Third Person: $20.00

Kylemere House, 1818—Come and become part of Kylemere House's warmth and charm. From each room's lovely details, to the most creative breakfast cuisine! Fine restaurants, shops and ocean within walking distance. Quiet area.

Kennebunkport

Ledda, Pat & Sal
Locke St.
Box 646A, 04046
(207) 967-5632

Amenities: 2,3,6,7,9,10,11
Breakfast: Full

Dbl. Oc.: $85.00-$106.00
Third Person: $32.10

1802 House B&B Inn—Walking distance to town; located on golf course; fireplace rooms available; one mile from ocean. A pleasant cozy interlude you will remember.

Kennebunkport

Litchfield, Rick, Davis, Bev
P.O. Box 800, 04046
(207) 967-3141

Amenities: 1,2,3,5,6,7,9,10,11
Breakfast: Full
Dbl. Oc.: $175.00
Sgl. Oc.: $100.00
Third Person: $25.00

The Captain Lord Mansion—An intimate Maine coast inn with 18 luxuriously queen bedded rooms, working fireplaces, warm hospitality, afternoon tea, goodies and delicious homemade breakfasts. Open year round.

AMENITIES

1. No Smoking
2. No Pets
3. No Children
4. Senior Citizen Rates
5. Tennis Available
6. Golf Available
7. Swimming Available
8. Skiing Available
9. Credit Cards Accepted
10. Personal Check Accepted
11. Off Season Rates
12. Dinner Available (w/sufficient notice)

Maine

Kennebunkport

Morphy, Francis
Box 1367, Corner of Spring & Maine, 04046
(207) 967-3728

Amenities: 2,9,11
Breakfast: Continental
Dbl. Oc.: $133.75
Sgl. Oc.: $104.86
Third Person: $26.75

Port Gallery Inn—Village center location, historic Victorian mansion offering gracious accommodations with private bath, queen size beds, color TV. We feature marine art gallery. Open year round.

Kennebunkport

Panzenhagen, Bart
RR 1, Box 656, School St., 04046
(207) 967-4169

Amenities: 2,3,5,6,7,10,11
Breakfast: Continental
Dbl. Oc.: $64.20
Sgl. Oc.: $59.20

The Farm House B&B is a gracious intimate inn. We have only 2 rooms and offer personalized service. 5 minutes to historic Dock Square, lovely beaches close by & galleries, shops & restaurants galore. Come & see us.

Kennebunkport

Severance, Sandy & Mike
Gooch's Beach
Box 631, 04046
(207) 967-4282

Amenities: 2,3,5,6,7,10,11
Breakfast: Continental

Dbl. Oc.: $78.00-$139.00
Sgl. Oc.: $76.00-$137.00
Third Person: $10.00

The Seaside 1756 Inn—Located directly on our private beach; has private baths and spacious rooms. On Rt. 9A just 1/2 mile from Dock Square and fine restaurants. 17 acre grounds. Family innkeepers for travelers since 1667.

AMENITIES

1. No Smoking
2. No Pets
3. No Children
4. Senior Citizen Rates
5. Tennis Available
6. Golf Available
7. Swimming Available
8. Skiing Available
9. Credit Cards Accepted
10. Personal Check Accepted
11. Off Season Rates
12. Dinner Available (w/sufficient notice)

Maine

Kennebunkport

Shoby, Bernice & Frank
Temple St.
P.O. Box 1123, 04046
(207) 967-5773

Amenities: 2,5,6,7,8,9,10,11
Breakfast: Full

Dbl. Oc.: $79.00-$85.00
Sgl. Oc.: $70.00
Third Person: $30.00

The Dock Square Inn—Gracious Victorian B&B country inn. Former ship builder's home located in the heart of historical Kennebunkport Village. Warm congenial atmosphere. Full breakfast, comfortable rooms, private baths, color cable TV.

Kennebunkport

Sutter, Joan & Dave
Pier Rd.
RR 2, Box 1180, 04046
(207) 967-5564

Amenities: 1,2,3,7,9,10,11
Breakfast: Full

Dbl. Oc.: $103.00
Sgl. Oc.: $93.00
Third Person: $30.00

The Inn At Harbor Head—At the water's edge on rocky ocean inlet. We have a gentle romantic air, private baths, a floating dock & hammock for two. Offering four bedrooms, elegant gourmet breakfasts, on the quiet side of town.

Kittery Point

Cane, Mrs. Claire
365 Wilson Rd., 03904
(207) 439-0302

Amenities: 2,4,10,11
Breakfast: Full

Dbl. Oc.: $55.00-$70.00
Sgl. Oc.: $55.00
Third Person: $25.00

Melfair Farm—Enjoy country charm in our 1871 Colonial home. Nearby outlet malls, beaches, historic Portsmouth—the dining capitol of New England; ambiance, elegance, fun! Lots to see and do! Call for reservations.

Kittery Point

Craig, Marian
Follett Lane, 03905
(207) 439-3242

Amenities: 1,2,3,10
Breakfast: Continental

Dbl. Oc.: $50.00
Sgl. Oc.: $50.00
Third Person: $10.00

Harbour Watch—Quiet 11 room Colonial that has been in same family for 180 years. On the water, 2 miles from I-95. Near fine seafood restaurants, theaters, discount shopping, boat trips, beaches. 50 miles from Boston or Portland, ME.

Lincolnville Beach

Curren, Lori
The Other Rd., Box 75, 04849
(207) 236-3785

Amenities: 2,3,6,7,8,10,11
Breakfast: Full

Dbl. Oc.: $42.80-$74.90
Sgl. Oc.: $35.80-$67.90
Third Person: $10.00

Longville At Lincolnville—Century-old Victorian mansion restored to original charm. Quiet atmosphere overlooking Penobscot Bay. Do something you haven't done in years—relax and be pampered. Open year round.

AMENITIES

1. No Smoking
2. No Pets
3. No Children
4. Senior Citizen Rates
5. Tennis Available
6. Golf Available
7. Swimming Available
8. Skiing Available
9. Credit Cards Accepted
10. Personal Check Accepted
11. Off Season Rates
12. Dinner Available (w/sufficient notice)

Maine

Little Deer Isle

Broadhead, Sophie
RFD 1, Box 324, 04650
(207) 348-2540

Amenities: 5,6,7,10
Breakfast: Full
Dbl. Oc.: $50.00-$60.00
Sgl. Oc.: $45.00
Third Person: $10.00

Eggemoggin Inn—A small coastal inn located right on the water with view of sailing on Eggemoggin Beach. Lobster, a Maine treat, and home cooking to be enjoyed in the area. Come and relax.

New Castle

Miller, Mrs. Doris
Glidden St.
R.R. 1, Box 740, 04553
(207) 563-1859

Amenities: 2,4,5,6,8,10,11
Breakfast: Full

Dbl. Oc.: $37.50-$58.50

Glidden House—Charming Victorian overlooking the river. Secluded garden, fine restaurants, galleries, antique auctions, historic sites; comfortable rooms, private baths, hearty breakfasts. Small apartment available.

Newcastle

Whear, Sherry & Robert
RFD 1, Box 245, 04553
(207) 563-8014

Amenities: 2,5,6,7,8,10,11
Breakfast: Full

Dbl. Oc.: $51.36-$60.99
Third Person: $15.00

Mill Pond Inn—Ambiance plus! On pond connecting to Dariscotta Lake. Cozy rooms, pretty views. Canoeing, fishing, and swimming on premises. Hearty breakfast facing pond; private baths.

Norridgewock

Whitmore, Nancy & Floyd
Upper Main St., 04957
(207) 634-3470

Amenities: 2,7,8,10
Breakfast: Full

Dbl. Oc.: $42.80-$53.50
Sgl. Oc.: $37.45
Third Person: $10.00

Norridgewock Colonial Inn is located at the junction of Rte. 2 & 8; 13 miles from Colby College; within 1 hour of Sugarloaf USA. Warmly decorated room with private bath; near lakes & mountains, quiet and restful.

AMENITIES

1. No Smoking
2. No Pets
3. No Children
4. Senior Citizen Rates
5. Tennis Available
6. Golf Available
7. Swimming Available
8. Skiing Available
9. Credit Cards Accepted
10. Personal Check Accepted
11. Off Season Rates
12. Dinner Available (w/sufficient notice)

Maine

Ogunquit

Hartwell, Trisha & James
116 Shore Rd.
Box 393, 03907
(207) 646-7210

Amenities: 2,3,5,6,7,9,10,11
Breakfast: Continental

Dbl. Oc.: $95.00-$175.00

The Hartwell House offers its guests the serenity of Maine country life on the seacoast in the midst of Ogunquit's thriving summer resort. All accommodations with private bath/shower & A/C.

Ogunquit

Sachon, Mrs. Eeta
5 Bovine Ln.
Box 1940, 03907
(207) 646-3891

Amenities: 2,3,9,10,11
Breakfast: Continental

Dbl. Oc.: $70.00-$90.00

The Morning Dove Bed & Breakfast—An elegant farmhouse furnished w/antiques & European accents. Quiet location & spectacular gardens. Near beaches, Perkins Cove, Ogunquit Playhouse. Greeting wine & chocolates on pillow.

Ogunquit

Siegel, Kaye & Lois
46 N. Main St., 03907
(207) 646-9735 or 646-9492

Amenities: 5,6,7,9,11
Breakfast: Continental

Dbl. Oc.: $40.00-$95.00
Sgl. Oc.: $40.00-$95.00
Third Person: $10.00

Clipper Ship—1820 inn decorated with antiques. Each room is unique. Private & shared baths; A/C & TV, best location; short walk to beach.

Otisfield

Ronalder, Mrs. Claire
Oxford, Box B
Rt. 121, 04270
(207) 539-2352

Amenities: 2,3,10
Breakfast: Full

Dbl. Oc.: $48.15
Sgl. Oc.: $42.80
Third Person: $9.85

Claiberns Bed & Breakfast—2 rooms, 1 king-size bed or brass beds, both cozy & private w/large breakfast to last past lunch, in quaint Cape Cod w/friendly owners in quiet lake area 38 mi. from Portland, 1 hour to N. Conway, NH.

Southwest Harbor

Brower, M/M Gardiner
Clark Pt. Rd., 04679
(207) 244-5335

Amenities: 2,5,6,7,8,10,11
Breakfast: Full

Dbl. Oc.: $49.00-$86.00
Third Person: $10.00

Lindenwood Inn—A warm, friendly inn on the quiet side of Mt. Desert Island near Acadia Nat'l. Park. Sightseeing, boating, shops, and restaurants nearby. Children over 12 welcome. Open all year.

AMENITIES

1. No Smoking
2. No Pets
3. No Children
4. Senior Citizen Rates
5. Tennis Available
6. Golf Available
7. Swimming Available
8. Skiing Available
9. Credit Cards Accepted
10. Personal Check Accepted
11. Off Season Rates
12. Dinner Available (w/sufficient notice)

Maine

Southwest Harbor

Combs, Dr. & Mrs. Theodore
Main St.
P.O. Box 583, 04679
(207) 244-3835

Amenities: 2,10,11
Breakfast: Full

Dbl. Oc.: $48.00-$95.00
Third Person: $10.00

The Inn At Southwest—This charming Victorian inn, which overlooks the harbor, is centrally located, and is minutes away from picturesque Acadia National Park, fine shops, restaurants and entertainment.

Southwest Harbor

Gill, Ms. Ann R.
Box 1006, 04679
(207) 244-5180

Amenities: 1,2,6,7,10
Breakfast: Full

Dbl. Oc.: $48.15-$64.20
Sgl. Oc.: $37.45-$42.80
Third Person: $16.05-$21.40

The Island House Bed & Breakfast—Quiet country style home on the harbor, established in 1850 as the first hotel on the island. Pleasant 1/2 mile walk to village center. Acadia National Park is a 5 minute drive away.

Southwest Harbor

King, Kathleen & James
100 Main St., Box 1426, 04679
(207) 244-5302

Amenities: 2,10,11
Breakfast: Full
Dbl. Oc.: $55.00-$75.00
Sgl. Oc.: $55.00-$75.00
Third Person: $15.00

The Kingsleigh Inn—A cozy romantic inn elegantly restored and steeped in atmosphere. Antique furnishings, private baths and harbor views from our wicker-filled wrap-a-round porch. Just a stroll to dining, shops and harbor.

Southwest Harbor

Lazareth, Ms. Dorothy
Box 829, 04679
(207) 244-9627

Amenities: 2,3,6,7,10
Breakfast: Continental

Dbl. Oc.: $64.20

Two Seasons—Dine on a lobster pier or walk to four other restaurants. Breakfast of fresh fruits and muffins in our sunroom overlooking the harbor. Colorful rooms with private baths & harbor views—that's Maine.

AMENITIES

1. No Smoking
2. No Pets
3. No Children
4. Senior Citizen Rates
5. Tennis Available
6. Golf Available
7. Swimming Available
8. Skiing Available
9. Credit Cards Accepted
10. Personal Check Accepted
11. Off Season Rates
12. Dinner Available (w/sufficient notice)

Maine

Southwest Harbor

Strong, Grechen & Toby
Main St., Box 68, 04679
(207) 244-7102

Amenities: 2,6,7,8,10,11
Breakfast: Full

Dbl. Oc.: $48.15
Sgl. Oc.: $39.59

Penury Hall—Six guests share scrumptous breakfasts, convivial atmosphere, sauna, daysailor, canoe, and our interest in art, antiques and gardening. Open all year. On the quiet side of Acadia National Park.

Stratton

Hopson, Mary & Jerry
P.O. Box 150, 04982
(207) 246-6910

Amenities: 1,2,6,8,10,11,12
Breakfast: Full

Dbl. Oc.: $47.00
Sgl. Oc.: $44.90
Third Person: $21.36

The Widow's Walk—In the heart of Maine's Western Mountains, 10 minutes from Sugarloaf ski area, stressing friendliness and comfort rather than elegance. In downtown Stratton at intersection of Routes 27 and 16.

York Beach

Jennings, Genie & Stan
44 Freeman St.
P.O. Box 1216, 03910
(207) 363-4087, 748-0916

Amenities: 9,10
Breakfast: Continental

Dbl. Oc.: $58.85
Sgl. Oc.: $48.15
Third Person: $5.35-$10.70

The Candleshop Inn—A visit to The Candleshop Inn is like a visit to Grandma's house with all the aunts and uncles and cousins... if Grandma lives near the beach in a quaint New England village. If she doesn't...join us!!

Waldboro

Hills, M/M Victor
P.O. Box 787, 04572
(207) 832-7776

Amenities: 3
Breakfast: Continental

Dbl. Oc.: $35.00
Sgl. Oc.: $25.00

Country Bed & Breakfast—Country home in rural setting. Two miles from town, musuem nearby. Reservations needed.

Waterville

Weisser, Barb & Art
184 Silver St., 04901
(207) 873-7724

Amenities: 1,2,10,11
Breakfast: Continental

Dbl. Oc.: $65.00
Sgl. Oc.: $48.00
Third Person: $18.00

The Inn At Silver Grove—Just 2 miles from I-95, exit 33. Near Colby & Thomas Colleges. Enjoy the comfort, beauty and charm of our home.

AMENITIES

1. No Smoking
2. No Pets
3. No Children
4. Senior Citizen Rates
5. Tennis Available
6. Golf Available
7. Swimming Available
8. Skiing Available
9. Credit Cards Accepted
10. Personal Check Accepted
11. Off Season Rates
12. Dinner Available (w/sufficient notice)

Maine

Weld

Strunk, Marti
Rt. 142, Webb Lake, 04285
(207) 585-2243 or 778-4306

Amenities: 1,2,5,7,10,11
Breakfast: Continental

Dbl. Oc.: $44.94-$49.94
Sgl. Oc.: $39.59
Third Person: $10.00

Kawan Hee Inn Lakeside—10 rooms, camp like atmosphere, Western ME., Mts., hiking, swimming, sandy beach, canoe rental, restaurant/bar serves 2 meals a day. On lake, screened porch, beautiful sunsets, game room, pool table, ping pong.

Wells

Simard, Patricia
213 Webhannet Dr.
RR 1, 04090
(207) 646-9260

Amenities: 2,5,6,7,8,9,11
Breakfast: Continental

Dbl. Oc.: $45.00 & up
Sgl. Oc.: $40.00 & up
Third Person: $10.00

Bayview Inn Bed & Breakfast—A restored 1890 carriage house with a fantastic view of the Atlantic Ocean & located next to a lobster pound. Hiking, tennis, golf, shops, antiquing, dining all nearby. Come relax in our warm friendly atmosphere.

AMENITIES

1. No Smoking
2. No Pets
3. No Children
4. Senior Citizen Rates
5. Tennis Available
6. Golf Available
7. Swimming Available
8. Skiing Available
9. Credit Cards Accepted
10. Personal Check Accepted
11. Off Season Rates
12. Dinner Available (w/sufficient notice)

Maryland

The Old Line State

Capital: Annapolis
Statehood: April 28, 1788, the 7th state
State Motto: Manly Deeds, Womanly Words
State Song: "Maryland, My Maryland"
State Bird: Baltimore Oriole
State Flower: Black-Eyed Susan
State Tree: White Oak (Wye Oak)

Maryland was founded in 1634 by an Englishman named Calvert, who named it for Queen Henrietta Marie of England.

Francis Scott Keye wrote The Star Spangled Banner while watching the British bombard Fort McHenry during the War of 1812. He was inspired by the rockets and glare from the guns, and his inspiration became the National Anthem.

Today, Maryland is the bedroom for hundreds of government workers in Washington, D.C. The Baltimore harbor is one of the busiest on the eastern seaboard. Much of our imports from Europe come through here.

The Chesapeake Bay divides Maryland almost in half. In 1952, the world's first all-steel bridge over salt water was erected. Before this time, the people of each section of Maryland led entirely different lives, the country folk vs. the city folk.

Fishermen have wonderful fishing in the Chesapeake Bay. They are known all over the world for their oysters and clams.

The United States Naval Academy was established in Annapolis in 1845. It is a tourist attraction for hundreds of people every year.

Maryland

Annapolis

Dodwell, Susan & Jim
74 Charles St., 21401
(301) 268-1451

Amenities: 5,6,7,10
Breakfast: Continental
Dbl. Oc.: $60.00
Sgl. Oc.: $60.00

The Charles Inn in historic Annapolis offers antiques, lace, flowers, gourmet fare, & off-street parking. Come enjoy our unique town on the Chesapeake Bay.

Annapolis

Evans, Mary & Ted
2654 Ogleton Rd., 21403
(301) 268-0781

Amenities: 1,2,3,6,7,10,12
Breakfast: Continental

Dbl. Oc.: $55.00
Sgl. Oc.: $50.00

Bay View B&B—Contemporary home in lovely wooded community, with water views. Access to golf course and private beach. Minutes from historic Annapolis and the Chesapeake Bay. Enjoy English hospitality. Open April-Nov.

Annapolis

Fitzgerald, Eileen
110 Prince George St., 21401
(301) 268-5555

Amenities: 2,3,9,10
Breakfast: Continental
Dbl. Oc.: $72.15-$133.20
Sgl. Oc.: $61.05-$122.10
Third Person: $11.10

Gibson's Lodgings—Two homes, one 18th century Georgian, one 19th century stucco and the new conference annex offer 20 guest rooms and suites, parlors, dining and meeting rooms all furnished with antiques.

Annapolis

Groverman, M/M Bill
232 Prince George St., 21401
(301) 263-6418

Amenities: 2,3,4,5,6,7,10
Breakfast: Continental

Dbl. Oc.: $68.25
Sgl. Oc.: $52.50

Prince George Inn located in the heart of historic city near Naval Academy, shops and restaurants. Victorian townhouse with many antiques. Shared bath. Brochure available. Open all year.

AMENITIES

1. No Smoking
2. No Pets
3. No Children
4. Senior Citizen Rates
5. Tennis Available
6. Golf Available
7. Swimming Available
8. Skiing Available
9. Credit Cards Accepted
10. Personal Check Accepted
11. Off Season Rates
12. Dinner Available (w/sufficient notice)

Maryland

Annapolis

Page, Greg
8 Martin St., 21401
(301) 626-1506

Amenities: 1,2,3,10
Breakfast: Continental

Dbl. Oc.: $70.00-$120.00

William Page Inn, Bed & Breakfast is located in the center of the historic district, within minutes of the city docks and Naval Academy. It is furnished in authentic antiques & provides off-street parking.

Baltimore

Fisher, Ms. Deb
1125 N. Calvert St., 21202
(301) 752-7722

Amenities: 2,9,10
Breakfast: Continental
Dbl. Oc.: $99.90-$122.10
Sgl. Oc.: $99.90

Society Hill, Government House, Society Hill's guests are visually treated to chandeliers, ornate wallpaper and unusual wall decor which are tasteful blandishments of Victorian Baltimore. Each guest room provides an individual view.

Baltimore

Fritz, Ms. Jo-Ann
3404 St. Paul St., 21218
(301) 235-8600

Amenities: 2,9,10
Breakfast: Continental
Dbl. Oc.: $99.90-$122.10
Sgl. Oc.: $99.90

Society Hill-Hopkins, built during the 1920's, this little charming historic inn is filled with antiques and original art. A visual tapestry of period decorating styles enhance every room with its own personal view.

Baltimore

Hopkins, Ms. Kate
58 W. Biddle St., 21201
(301) 837-3630

Amenities: 2,9,10,12
Breakfast: Continental

Dbl. Oc.: $77.70-$122.10
Sgl. Oc.: $77.70-$99.90

Society Hill Hotel—This fifteen room inn offers the exciting combination of a bed & breakfast and an American country inn. The hotel's bar & restaurant enjoys the distinctive honor of creating new culinary adventure.

AMENITIES

1. No Smoking
2. No Pets
3. No Children
4. Senior Citizen Rates
5. Tennis Available
6. Golf Available
7. Swimming Available
8. Skiing Available
9. Credit Cards Accepted
10. Personal Check Accepted
11. Off Season Rates
12. Dinner Available (w/sufficient notice)

Maryland

Baltimore

Grater, Betsey
1428 Park Ave., 21217
(301) 383-1274

Amenities: 2,7,8,9,10
Breakfast: Full
Dbl. Oc.: $65.00
Sgl. Oc.: $60.00
Third Person: $25.00

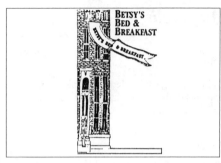

Betsey's B&B—Elegant 4 story townhouse downtown. 7 mins. from Inner Harbor, walking distance to cultural center, antiques, subway trolley. Historic area, off-street parking, large spacious rooms, 12 ft. ceilings, restaurants nearby.

Baltimore

Groff, Kelly
888 South Broadway, 21231
(301) 522-7377

Amenities: 1,2,6,9,10,11,12
Breakfast: Continental

Dbl. Oc.: $122.10
Sgl. Oc.: $99.90
Third Person: $10.00

Admiral Fell Inn—Historic inn located on the waterfront in the historic neighborhood of Baltimore called Fells Point. Each room decorated in Federal period antiques. Restaurant and pub located on premises.

Baltimore

Paulus, Mrs. Lucie
2406 Kentucky Ave., 21213
(301) 467-1688

Amenities: 1,2,4,5,6,10
Breakfast: Full
Dbl. Oc.: $55.00
Sgl. Oc.: $50.00
Third Person: $10.00

The Paulus Gasthaus, located in a lovely residential area 3 miles from Inner Harbor and all downtown attractions. We offer quality accommodations and Gemütlichkeit. Hostess speaks fluent German & some French.

Baltimore

Steininger, Ellen
205 W. Madison St., 21201
(301) 728-6550

Amenities: 2,4,9,10,11
Breakfast: Continental

Dbl. Oc.: $65.00-$85.00
Sgl. Oc.: $55.00-$75.00
Third Person: $10.00

The Shirley Madison Inn—A Victorian mansion decorated with the elegance of a by-gone era. Short walk to Inner Harbor and city's cultural corridor. Landscaped courtyard. English antiques. Complimentary evening sherry.

AMENITIES

1. No Smoking
2. No Pets
3. No Children
4. Senior Citizen Rates
5. Tennis Available
6. Golf Available
7. Swimming Available
8. Skiing Available
9. Credit Cards Accepted
10. Personal Check Accepted
11. Off Season Rates
12. Dinner Available (w/sufficient notice)

Maryland

Baltimore

Vaughan, Gwen & Bob
308 Morris Ave., Lutherville, 21093
(301) 252-3131

Amenities: 1,2,3,4
Breakfast: Full
Dbl. Oc.: $65.00
Sgl. Oc.: $60.00

Twin Gates Bed & Breakfast—Victorian mansion with queen-size beds in large rooms. Located in a serene village just fifteen minutes from Harborplace, National Aquarium, and free winery tours. Be sure to ask to see the secret room.

Bel Air

Fox, Dorothy & Howard
Tudor Hall, 21014
(301) 838-0466

Amenities: 2,7,10
Breakfast: Continental

Dbl. Oc.: $50.00
Sgl. Oc.: $50.00

Home Of The Maryland Booths—18th-century Gothic Revival cottage built as a country retreat by Junius Brutus Booth (1796-1852).

Berlin

Jacques, Pamela & Stephen
2 N. Main St., 21811
(301) 641-0189

Amenities: 2,6,9,12
Breakfast: Continental

Dbl. Oc.: $60.00 & up
Sgl. Oc.: $60.00 & up
Third Person: $60.00 & up

Atlantic Hotel—Built in 1895, this restored Victorian hotel is located in the heart of Berlin, Maryland's historic district. Numerous antique shops within walking distance and 8 miles from Ocean City.

Betterton

Washburn, M/M Kenneth
115 Ericsson Ave., 21610
(301) 348-5809

Amenities: 3,5,7,9,10
Breakfast: Full

Dbl. Oc.: $52.50
Sgl. Oc.: $42.00

Lantern Inn—A 1904 eastern shore inn on the Chesapeake Bay. Air conditioned & tastefully furnished rooms just 1 1/2 blocks from a sand beach. Historic Chestertown, wildlife refuges, crabbing & fine restaurants nearby.

AMENITIES

1. No Smoking
2. No Pets
3. No Children
4. Senior Citizen Rates
5. Tennis Available
6. Golf Available
7. Swimming Available
8. Skiing Available
9. Credit Cards Accepted
10. Personal Check Accepted
11. Off Season Rates
12. Dinner Available (w/sufficient notice)

Maryland

Cambridge

Brannock, Shirley & Earl
215 Glenburn Ave., 21613
(301) 228-6938

Amenities: 2,9,10
Breakfast: Continental

Dbl. Oc.: $69.00-$79.00
Sgl. Oc.: $69.00-$79.00
Third Person: $10.50

Commodores Cottage—2 cottage suites in 3 acre garden setting. Full kitchen, A/C, TV, complete privacy, quiet. Near river, historic area, fishing villages, wildlife refuge, maritime museum, antiques, seafood.

Chesapeake City

Sunkler, Gunter
26 Bank St., 21915
(301) 885-2201

Amenities: 1,2,6,9,12
Breakfast: Full

2 Couples: $262.50
1 Couple: $157.50

The McNulty House—Accommodations for 1 or 2 couples. Lovely restored Victorian home overlooking the C. & D. Canal with a view of ocean going vessels. Breakfast is included each morning and a complimentary bottle of champagne.

Chestertown

Brook, Mrs. Marge
R. 3, Box 360, 21620
(301) 778-5540

Amenities: 1,2,3,10
Breakfast: Full

Dbl. Oc.: $63.00
Sgl. Oc.: $57.75
Third Person: $10.00

Radcliffe Cross—A pre-revolutionary (circa 1725) brick house with many original features. We invite you to enjoy a delightful night's lodging and breakfast amid the colonial charm of yesteryear.

Chestertown

Maisel, Mary Susan
231 High St., 21620
(301) 778-2300

Amenities: 2,6,7,10
Breakfast: Continental

Dbl. Oc.: $78-75-$105.00
Sgl. Oc.: $78.75-$105.00
Third Person: $25.00

White Swan Tavern—Built 1730, beautifully restored, located in 18th century Chestertown on Maryland's eastern shore. Each guest receives complimentary wine and fruit.

Denton

Lyons, Thelma & John
R. 3, Box 7-B, 21629
(301) 479-4321

Amenities: 7,10
Breakfast: Full

Dbl. Oc.: $36.75
Sgl. Oc.: $36.75
Third Person: $5.00

Sophie Kerr House—Centrally located on Maryland's eastern shore, 1 1/2 hours from Washington, C.D. and Baltimore, 40 minutes from ocean resorts, St. Michael, and Oxford. Nearby four star French restaurant.

AMENITIES

1. No Smoking
2. No Pets
3. No Children
4. Senior Citizen Rates
5. Tennis Available
6. Golf Available
7. Swimming Available
8. Skiing Available
9. Credit Cards Accepted
10. Personal Check Accepted
11. Off Season Rates
12. Dinner Available (w/sufficient notice)

Maryland

Frederick

Compton, Beverly & Ray
7945 Worman's Mill Rd., 21701
(301) 694-0440

Amenities: 1,2,3,10
Breakfast: Continental
Dbl. Oc.: $75.00-$85.00
Sgl. Oc.: $65.00-$75.00
Third Person: $15.00

Spring Bank—On national register of historical places, formerly home to a gentleman farmer/banker. Original 1880 details, period furnishings. On 10 acres, 3 miles north of Frederick's historical district. Fine dining nearby.

Gaithersburg

Danilowicz, Suzanne & Joe
18908 Chimney Pl., 20879
(301) 977-7377

Amenities: 1,5,6,7,10,12
Breakfast: Full

Dbl. Oc.: $47.00
Sgl. Oc.: $37.00
Third Person: $10.00

Gaithersburg Hospitality B&B—is near fine restaurants and shops. A luxury private home with all amenities close to Washington, D.C., metro system & 17 miles south of historic Frederick, MD. Home cooking.

Georgetown

Fernandes, Carlos, A.
Rt. 213, 21930
(301) 648-5777

Amenities: 1,2,4,5,6,7,9,10,11,12
Breakfast: Full
Dbl. Oc.: $50.00-$90.00
Sgl. Oc.: $50.00-$90.00
Third Person: $15.00

Kitty Knight House C. 1775—Historic inn & restaurant. An intimate country inn on the upper eastern shore of Maryland. Set high on a hill overlooking the Sassafras River & Georgetown harbor. 1 1/2 hours from Philadelphia & Baltimore.

AMENITIES

1. No Smoking
2. No Pets
3. No Children
4. Senior Citizen Rates
5. Tennis Available
6. Golf Available
7. Swimming Available
8. Skiing Available
9. Credit Cards Accepted
10. Personal Check Accepted
11. Off Season Rates
12. Dinner Available (w/sufficient notice)

Maryland

Havre De Grace

Rothwell, Charles
301 South Union Ave., 21078
(301) 939-5200

Amenities: 2,3,5,6,7,8,9,10,12
Breakfast: Full
Dbl. Oc.: $99.00-$129.00
Sgl. Oc.: $89.00-$118.00

Vandiver Inn—Journey back to the heyday of gracious Maryland living, Chesapeak Bay style, turn-of-the-century charm, Victorian hospitality, and unforgettable dining await the visitor at the historic Vandiver Inn.

New Market

Rimel, M/M Thomas
9-11 W. Main St.
P.O. Box 299, 21774
(301) 865-5055

Amenities: 2,5,6,9,10,12
Breakfast: Continental

Dbl. Oc.: $90.00
Sgl. Oc.: $52.25

National Pike Inn B&B—is located in historic New Market, antique capitol of Maryland. Diverse shopping, excellent dining make this a special retreat 1 hour from Washington, D.C. & Baltimore. Ext. 62, I-70.

North East

Demond, M/M
12 Mill Lane, 21901
(301) 287-3532

Amenities: 1,2,9
Breakfast: Full

Dbl. Oc.: $55.00
Sgl. Oc.: $50.00

The Mill House—Circa 1710 completely furnished in antiques with 3 acres of grounds that include mill ruins on a tidal creek. 2 miles south of I-95 exit & less that an hour to points of interest in a tri-state area.

Oakland

Umbel, Ms. Ruth M.
Rt. 5, Box 268, 21550
(301) 387-6606

Amenities: 2,5,7,8,9,10
Breakfast: Continental

Dbl. Oc.: $75.00
Sgl. Oc.: $35.00
Third Person: $10.00

Red Run Inn—Top of a big old barn, bar/restaurant below overlooking a lake. Entertainment. 6 rooms; 3 suites, 3 economy rooms. 180 miles west of Washington, D.C.

AMENITIES

1. No Smoking
2. No Pets
3. No Children
4. Senior Citizen Rates
5. Tennis Available
6. Golf Available
7. Swimming Available
8. Skiing Available
9. Credit Cards Accepted
10. Personal Check Accepted
11. Off Season Rates
12. Dinner Available (w/sufficient notice)

Maryland

Oxford

Clark, Eleanor & Jerry
110 North Morris St.
Box 658, 21654
(301) 226-5496

Amenities: 2,3,5,6,7,10
Breakfast: Continental

Dbl. Oc.: $70.20-$81.00
Sgl. Oc.: $70.20-$81.00
Third Person: $16.20

The 1876 House—A elegantly restored 19th-century Victorian home with three guest rooms furnished in Queen Anne reproductions, oriental carpets, & wide plank pine floors. A retreat back in time. Open Jan. 2-Dec. 23.

Princess Anne

Monick, Mrs. Helen
P.O. Box 220, 21853
(301) 651-1066

Amenities: 1,2,9,10,12
Breakfast: Full

Dbl. Oc.: $84.00-$104.45
Sgl. Oc.: $73.50-$91.85

Elmwood Circ. 1770—An air of timeless tranquillity clings to Elmwood, a manor house dating from the 17th century. Its commanding site on the Manokin River, its fields, woods, and water compose an eastern shore prospect.

Rock Hall

Peacock, Mrs. Eleanor
Rt. 20, Gratitude, 21661
(301) 639-7468

Amenities: 10
Breakfast: Continental

Dbl. Oc.: $45.00-$50.00
Sgl. Oc.: $45.00
Third Person: $25.00

The Strawberry Factory is on the eastern shore of Maryland on the Chesapeake Bay 12 miles south of Chestertown. Guests enjoy water view & local seafood at several restaurants. Sailing, swimming, fishing, crabbing in season.

Sharpsburg

Reed, Paula & Doug
Rt. 65, 21782
Antietam National Battlefield
(301) 797-1862

Amenities: 1,2,3,9,10
Breakfast: Continental

Dbl. Oc.: $51.45-$72.45

Piper House Bed & Breakfast Inn—Restored historic farmhouse that served as a Civil War headquarters during Battle of Antietam, near Bloody Lane. Four guest rooms each with private bath, period antiques, parlors, A/C, serenity & comfort.

Sharpsburg

Fairbourn, Mrs. Betty
220 East Main St., 21782
(301) 432-6601

Amenities: 5,6,7,9,10
Breakfast: Continental

Dbl. Oc.: $55.00-$85.00
Sgl. Oc.: $42.50
Third Person: $15.00

The Inn At Antietam, located 60 miles from Wash., D.C., Baltimore, MD. or Harrisburg, PA on battlefield. Beautiful restored Victorian. Historic area of fine antique shops and restaurants.

AMENITIES

1. No Smoking
2. No Pets
3. No Children
4. Senior Citizen Rates
5. Tennis Available
6. Golf Available
7. Swimming Available
8. Skiing Available
9. Credit Cards Accepted
10. Personal Check Accepted
11. Off Season Rates
12. Dinner Available (w/sufficient notice)

Maryland

Vienna

Altergott, Elsie & Harvey
111 Water St.
P.O. Box 98, 21869
(301) 376-3347

Amenities: 2,3,5,9,10
Breakfast: Full

Dbl. Oc.: $55.00 & up
Sgl. Oc.: $50.00 & up

The Tavern House—Authentic Colonial tavern on Nanticoke River. Great for relaxing, biking, exploring small towns, observing wildlife and birds of the Bay, rivers and marshes. Blackwater Refuge nearby.

AMENITIES

1. No Smoking
2. No Pets
3. No Children
4. Senior Citizen Rates
5. Tennis Available
6. Golf Available
7. Swimming Available
8. Skiing Available
9. Credit Cards Accepted
10. Personal Check Accepted
11. Off Season Rates
12. Dinner Available (w/sufficient notice)

Massachusetts

The Bay State

Capital: Boston
Statehood: February 6, 1788; the 6th state
State Motto: By The Sword We Seek Peace,
　　　　　　But Peace Only Under Liberty
State Song: "All Hail To Massachusetts"
State Bird: Chickadee
State Flower: Mayflower
State Tree: American Elm

Much of the history of our country began in this state. The Pilgrims landed in Plymouth in 1620 and the Boston Tea Party took place in Boston Harbor on Dec. 16, 1773. The historic ride of Paul Revere on April 19, 1775 is still reenacted each year, and the battlefields of Lexington and Concord remain a great tourist attraction.

Massachusetts, a champion of education, boasts of having the oldest college in our country. Harvard College was established in 1636 in Cambridge, and the first public library was started here when John Harvard gave his collection of books to the college. Today, in this state, there are over 75 fine colleges and higher institutions of learning.

The vacationer will find beautiful beaches from Newburyport on the north shore to Cape Cod on the south shore. The lovely Berkshire Hills in the western part of the state provide the stage for the Annual Berkshire Music Festival. Downtown Boston, and especially Quincy Market, is a haven of entertainment, gourmet restaurants and lovely shops. The Boston skyline, with its new buildings, reflect the Bostonian's initiative for progress set forth by their forefathers. Throughout the state, large industrial and technological companies are springing up because of the proximity to the educational facilities that are here.

The people of Massachusetts are very proud of their colonial heritage and often express it in their style of home and decor.

Presidents John Adams, John Quincy Adams, John F. Kennedy and George Herbert Walker Bush, our 41st President, were all born here.

Massachusetts

Ashfield

Alessi, Stacy & Scott
P.O. Box 129, 01330
(413) 628-4571

Amenities: 2,4,5,6,7,8,9,10,11
Breakfast: Continental
Dbl. Oc.: $80.00
Sgl. Oc.: $60.00
Third Person: $10.00

The Ashfield Inn is a stately Georgian mansion situated on 9 acres overlooking Ashfield Lake. Fine restaurants and shops in surrounding area. Just minutes from historic Deerfield. Come stay with us.

Auburn

O'Toole, M/M Jack
609 Oxford St., So., 01501
(617) 832-5282

Amenities: 1,2,7,9,10,12
Breakfast: Full
Dbl. Oc.: $65.00
Sgl. Oc.: $48.00
Third Person: $18.00

Capt. Samuel Eddy House B&B Inn—Historic 1765 homestead restored to its original charm & era. Sturbridge fireplaces, beehive oven, bed chambers adorned with herbs & antiques, queen-size beds w/canopies. Herb gardens & country shop.

Barnstable

Bain, Fay & Donald
Box 856, 3660 Rte. 6A, 02630
(617) 362-8044

Amenities: 2,3,5,6,7,9,10
Breakfast: Full
Dbl. Oc.: $109.70-$159.07
Sgl. Oc.: $109.70-$159.07
Third Person: $60.00

Ashley Manor—A very special place. Secluded 1699 mansion in Cape Cod's historic area. Gracious, romantic & comfortable. Oriental rugs, antiques. Beautiful rooms & suites with private baths, fireplaces. HMMMM!

Barnstable

Chester, Ms. Evelyn
Powder Hill Rd., 02630
(617) 362-9356

Amenities: 2,3,5,6,7,10,12
Breakfast: Full
Dbl. Oc.: $141.90-$163.90
Sgl. Oc.: $141.90-$163.90

Cobb's Cove—Secluded on a 1643 historic site offers couples spacious rooms, private baths, whirlpool tubs, water views, superb breakfasts on the garden patio. Truly a tonic in all seasons.

AMENITIES

1. No Smoking
2. No Pets
3. No Children
4. Senior Citizen Rates
5. Tennis Available
6. Golf Available
7. Swimming Available
8. Skiing Available
9. Credit Cards Accepted
10. Personal Check Accepted
11. Off Season Rates
12. Dinner Available (w/sufficient notice)

Massachusetts

Barnstable

Eddy, Mrs. Eleanor
2701 Route 6A, 02630
(508) 362-6379

Amenities: 2,7,9,11
Breakfast: Full
Dbl. Oc.: $85.00
Sgl. Oc.: $85.00
Third Person: $15.00

Thomas Huckins House—Experience the charm of old Cape Cod. Sleep in canopy beds next to working fireplaces, breakfast in antique-filled keeping room. Walk to ocean & village. All rooms have private baths. 2-Br. suite available.

Barnstable

Gedrim, Genny
61 Pine Lane, 02630
(508) 362-8559

Amenities: 1,2,3,5,6,7,10
Breakfast: Continental

Dbl. Oc.: $65.00
Sgl. Oc.: $60.00
Third Person: $10.00

The Goss House Bed & Breakfast is located on the quiet northside of mid Cape Cod. Three rooms with private baths. No children under 12, please. Open May 15 through October 31.

Barnstable

Livermore, Anne & Bob
2839 Main St., (6A), 02630
(508) 362-6618

Amenities: 2,5,6,7,9,10
Breakfast: Full

Dbl. Oc.: $98.30-$137.13
Third Person: $15.00

Beechwoo—A romantic Victorian inn authentically restored & furnished with elegant period antiques; private baths, fireplaces, water views located on Cape Cod's unspoiled north shore in historic district.

Brewster (Cape Cod)

Geisler, Marge & Jim
74 Locust Lane, Rt. 2, 02631
(617) 255-7045

Amenities: 1,2,3,6,7,10
Breakfast: Full
Dbl. Oc.: $60.00-$85.00
Sgl. Oc.: $50.00-$85.00

Ocean Gold—Lovely 2 story gambrel home situated in a pine tree wooded private area next to a state park and bike trails. Peaceful, quiet. Jim loves to talk and garden, Marge is active in crafts.

AMENITIES

1. No Smoking
2. No Pets
3. No Children
4. Senior Citizen Rates
5. Tennis Available
6. Golf Available
7. Swimming Available
8. Skiing Available
9. Credit Cards Accepted
10. Personal Check Accepted
11. Off Season Rates
12. Dinner Available (w/sufficient notice)

Massachusetts

Brewster (Cape Cod)

Manchester, Sugar & Doug
1861 Main St.
P.O. Box 839, 02631
(508) 896-3149

Amenities: 2,5,6,7,9,10,11
Breakfast: Continental

Dbl. Oc.: $88.00-$98.00
Sgl. Oc.: $88.00-$98.00
Third Person: $25.00

The Old Manse Inn is a beautiful antique sea captain's home. There are 9 charming guest rooms all with private baths. Gourmet dining by candlelight on the sunporch. Wines & liquor. Dinner $30 & up P.P.

Brewster

Rowan, Michele & Stephen
2553 Main St., 02631
(617) 896-6114

Amenities: 2,3,9,10,11,12
Breakfast: Full

Dbl. Oc.: $39.49-$82.29
Sgl. Oc.: $39.49-$82.29
Third Person: $16.45

Old Sea Pines Inn—Charming turn-of-the-century mansion. Near Bayside beaches, bicycle trail, golf and tennis. Rooms with fireplaces. 3 1/2 acres of privacy. Furnished with antiques. Warm, personal service excellent dining.

Boston

Travtlein, John & Linda Thompson
P.O. Box 93
(617) 353-1111

Amenities: 1,2,9
Breakfast: Full
Dbl. Oc.: $75.00-$125.00
Sgl. Oc.: $75.00-$125.00
Third Person: $15.00

Joshua Bennet House—1830 townhouse in the loviest historic district of Boston. Rooms with priv. baths, fireplaces, A/C. Afternoon tea in parlor & breakfast delights served daily. Short walk to shops, museums, & fine dining.

Centerville

Diehl, Joyce
497 Main St., 02632
(508) 771-5488

Amenities: 2,3,5,6,7,9,10,11
Breakfast: Full

Dbl. Oc.: $82.27
Sgl. Oc.: $82.27

Copper Beech Inn—Capt. Hillman Crosby's home built in 1830 is a short walk from the beach. Situated among tall trees in an inviting setting, the inside features include private baths, full breakfasts and warm hospitality.

AMENITIES

1. No Smoking
2. No Pets
3. No Children
4. Senior Citizen Rates
5. Tennis Available
6. Golf Available
7. Swimming Available
8. Skiing Available
9. Credit Cards Accepted
10. Personal Check Accepted
11. Off Season Rates
12. Dinner Available (w/sufficient notice)

Massachusetts

Chatham

DeHan, Ms. Peggy
364 Old Harbor Rd.
Box 468, S. Chatham, 02633
(508) 945-5859

Amenities: 2,3,9,10,11
Breakfast: Continental

Dbl. Oc.: $95.00
Third Person: $15.00

The Ship Inn At Chatham—Delightful, restored antique home, centrally located. Walk to dining, shopping and beaches. Tastefully furnished guestroom, all with private bath. Continental breakfast is served.

Concord

Anderson, Charlotte
154 Fitchburg Tpk., Rt. 117
(508) 369-3756

Amenities: 2,4,9,10
Breakfast: Continental
Dbl. Oc.: $80.00
Sgl. Oc.: $70.00
Third Person: $10.00

Anderson Wheeler Homestead—A charming Victorian family homestead built in 1890 with wrap-around veranda. Tastefully decorated with antiques accentuated with fireplaces. Rural yet convenient to historic area..

Concord

Williams, Kate
1694 Main St., 01742
(617) 369-9119

Amenities: 1,2,3,5,6,8,9,10,11
Breakfast: Continental

Dbl. Oc.: $75.00-$85.00
Sgl. Oc.: $66.00-$77.00
Third Person: $12.00

Colonel Roger Brown House—Small, friendly B&B inn. Historic home of Concord Minuteman; Colonial charm with private baths and A/C. Full use of adjacent fitness center. Trains to Boston & Cambridge.

Cotuit

Allen, Ellen & James W.
60 Nickerson La.
P.O. Box 222, 02635
(617) 428-5702

Amenities: 5,6,7,10
Breakfast: Full

Dbl. Oc.: $50.00-$55.00
Sgl. Oc.: $25.00-$27.00
Third Person: $10.00-$15.00

Allen's Bed And Breakfast—Victorian home with large porch in quiet village just 10 miles to Hyannis, Falmouth, & Sandwich. Beaches, playground, tennis, golf, boat launch within walking distance. TV in rooms, bikes & beach towels provided.

AMENITIES

1. No Smoking
2. No Pets
3. No Children
4. Senior Citizen Rates
5. Tennis Available
6. Golf Available
7. Swimming Available
8. Skiing Available
9. Credit Cards Accepted
10. Personal Check Accepted
11. Off Season Rates
12. Dinner Available (w/sufficient notice)

Massachusetts

Cummington

McColgan, Mary & Ed
RR 1, Rte. 112
Box 110, 01026
(413) 634-5529

Amenities: 1,2,5,7,8,10
Breakfast: Full

Dbl. Oc.: $55.00
Sgl. Oc.: $40.00
Third Person: $10.00

Cumworth Farm—200-year-old farmhouse raising sheep, producing berries & maple syrup. Close to cross country ski trails, hiking nearby. 45 minutes to Tanglewood located on scenic Rte. 112 between Cummington and Worthington.

Cummington

Westwood, Carolyn & Arnold
RR #1, Box 170, 01026
(413) 684-3786

Amenities: 2,10
Breakfast: Full

Dbl. Oc.: $50.00
Sgl. Oc.: $40.00
Third Person: $10.00

Windfields Farm—Secluded, spacious 1810 Berkshire Hills homestead. Hiking & ski trails, pond, blueberry pasture, organic gardens, eggs, maple syrup. Guest entrance & living rooms. Near concerts & drama. Closed March-Apr.

Dennis

Brophy, Mrs. Marie
152 Whig St., 02638
(617) 385-9928

Amenities: 1,2,5,6,7,9,10,11
Breakfast: Continental
Dbl. Oc.: $50.50-$83.00
Sgl. Oc.: $47.00-$71.50
Third Person: $12.00

The Isaiah Hall House B&B Inn—Relax and enjoy a lovely country retreat quietly located within walking distance of the beach, village shops and restaurants. Private baths, balconies and fireplace available.

Dennis

Robinson, Diane
946 Main St., Rte. 6A, 02638
(508) 385-6317

Amenities: 2,5,6,7,9,10,11
Breakfast: Continental

Dbl. Oc.: $45.00-$85.00
Third Person: $15.00

The Four Chimneys Inn—A comfortable 1881 Victorian home with lovely gardens located on historic Route 6A. 9 guest rooms, 7 with private baths. Fireplaced living room, large bright rooms, walk to beach, lake, playhouse, restaurants, & shops.

AMENITIES

1. No Smoking
2. No Pets
3. No Children
4. Senior Citizen Rates
5. Tennis Available
6. Golf Available
7. Swimming Available
8. Skiing Available
9. Credit Cards Accepted
10. Personal Check Accepted
11. Off Season Rates
12. Dinner Available (w/sufficient notice)

Massachusetts

East Gloucester

Balestraci, Mrs. Barbara
28 Eastern Point Rd., 01930
(617) 281-1953

Amenities: 2,9,11
Breakfast: Continental

Dbl. Oc.: $45.00-$65.00
Sgl. Oc.: $45.00
Third Person: $10.00

Colonial Inn—The inn is two miles from town. Public transportation is available. We are within walking distance to beaches and restaurants.

East Orleans

Anderson, Donna & Butcher, Peter
Beach Rd., Box 756, 02643
(617) 255-1312

Amenities: 2,3,5,7,10,11
Breakfast: Continental
Dbl. Oc.: $47.00-$93.00
Sgl. Oc.: $47.00-$93.00
Third Person: $15.00

The Ship's Knees Inn is a restored sea captain's house that offers an intimate setting that's only a short walk to scenic Nauset Beach. Enjoy our swimming pool & tennis court in our country setting.

East Orleans

Shand, Chris & Lloyd
202 Main St., 02643
Box 1016, 02643
(508) 255-8217

Amenities: 2,9,10,11
Breakfast: Continental

Dbl. Oc.: $45.00-$60.00
Sgl. Oc.: $45.00
Third Person: $10.00

The Parsonage—1770 Cape home with 6 antique furnished rooms. Friendly & comfortable. Close to Nauset Beach, walk to restaurants, great biking. Freshly-baked breakfast served on the patio or in your room.

East Sandwich

Loring, Richard
11 Wing Blvd., 02537
(617) 888-0534

Amenities: 5,6,7,9,10,12
Breakfast: Full

Dbl. Oc.: $115.00-$150.00
Sgl. Oc.: $95.00 & up
Third Person: $50 & up

Wingscorton Farm Inn—1785 antique farm house and working farm. All rooms have working fireplaces and private baths. Antique carriage house with balcony & fireplace. Private beach in back of farm. Eight acres with animals and fields. Dinner $25.00

AMENITIES

1. No Smoking
2. No Pets
3. No Children
4. Senior Citizen Rates
5. Tennis Available
6. Golf Available
7. Swimming Available
8. Skiing Available
9. Credit Cards Accepted
10. Personal Check Accepted
11. Off Season Rates
12. Dinner Available (w/sufficient notice)

Massachusetts

Edgartown (Marth's Vineyard)

del Real, M/M Jaun
Pease's Point Way, 02539
(508) 627-3797

Amenities: 2,3,7,9,10,11
Breakfast: Continental
Dbl. Oc.: $135.00-$185.00
Sgl. Oc.: $115.00-$165.00
Third Person: $25.00

The Shiverick Inn—An exquisitely restored 19th-century inn offering charming suites and guestrooms with fireplaces, private baths, a picturesque garden room and historic Edgartown at your doorstep.

Edgartown

Hall, Peggy
222 Upper Main St., 02539
(508) 627-8137

Amenities: 2,3,9,10,11
Breakfast: Continental
Dbl. Oc.: $82.28-$104.22
Sgl. Oc.: $82.28-$104.22

The Arbor—This turn-of-the-century Victorian cottage is delightfully New England. Relax in the garden, have tea in the parlor, stroll to the enchanting village of Edgartown and the harbor. Be our guest at the Arbor.

Edgartown

O'Connor, Daniel
59 N. Water, St.
Box 1333, 02539
(617) 627-4600

Amenities: 2,9,10,11
Breakfast: Full

Dbl. Oc.: $98.73-$137.12
Sgl. Oc.: $60.33-$137.12
Third Person: $12.00

The Dagget House—A pre-revolutionary war inn overlooking Edgartown harbor. Spacious lawn, parking and TV room. Two blocks from main street shops and restaurants.

Edgartown

Radford, Earle
56 N. Water St., 02539
(508) 627-4794

Amenities: 2,5,6,7,10,11
Breakfast: Full

Dbl. Oc.: $80.00-$125.00
Third Person: $10.00

The Edgartown Inn—Historic New England inn. Early guests were Daniel Webster, Nathaniel Hawthorne, later John Kennedy. In town near restaurants, shops, & beaches. Famous for breakfasts with homemade bread, cakes and pancakes.

AMENITIES

1. No Smoking
2. No Pets
3. No Children
4. Senior Citizen Rates
5. Tennis Available
6. Golf Available
7. Swimming Available
8. Skiing Available
9. Credit Cards Accepted
10. Personal Check Accepted
11. Off Season Rates
12. Dinner Available (w/sufficient notice)

Massachusetts

Edgartown

Smith, Linda & Ben
104 Main St., 02539
(508) 627-8633

Amenities: 2,9,10,11
Breakfast: Continental

Dbl. Oc.: $120.00-$200.00
Sgl. Oc.: $108.00-$180.00
Third Person: $20.00

Point Way Inn—Located on the island of Martha's Vineyard. Open year round. Fifteen rooms, ten with fireplaces. Enjoy playing croquet in the summertime or reading a good book by the fire in the winter. Make reservations early.

Fairhaven

Reed, Kathy
2 Oxford St., 02719
(508) 997-5512

Amenities: 2,10
Breakfast: Continental
Dbl. Oc.: $45.00-$70.00
Sgl. Oc.: $35.00-$60.00
Third Person: $10.00

Edgewater—A gracious waterfront house, overlooking New Bedford harbor. 5 rooms, each with private bath, 2 with fireplaces, sitting rooms. Close to historic areas, beaches, outlets, 5 minutes from I-95.

Falmouth

Bazur, Almary
75 Clinton Ave., 02540
(508) 548-2229

Amenities: 7,10,11
Breakfast: Continental

Dbl. Oc.: $50.00-$70.00
Sgl. Oc.: $50.00-$70.00
Third Person: $10.00

Cox Pond Guest House—Old family residence on 4 acres. Pond with pedal boat, canoe, and private beach on Vineyard Sound. Many fine shops and restaurants within easy walking distance.

Falmouth

Lloyd, Caroline & James
27 Main St., 02540
(508) 548-3786

Amenities: 1,2,3,4,5,6,7,10,11
Breakfast: Full
Dbl. Oc.: $90.00-$110.00
Sgl. Oc.: $75.00-$95.00
Third Person: $20.00

Mostly Hall Bed & Breakfast Inn—This 1849 southern plantation-style house is located in the historic district near beaches and island ferries. Six large corner rooms with private bath and queen size beds. Gourmet breakfast. Bicycles.

AMENITIES

1. No Smoking
2. No Pets
3. No Children
4. Senior Citizen Rates
5. Tennis Available
6. Golf Available
7. Swimming Available
8. Skiing Available
9. Credit Cards Accepted
10. Personal Check Accepted
11. Off Season Rates
12. Dinner Available (w/sufficient notice)

Massachusetts

Falmouth

Long, Linda & Don
40 W. Main St., 02540
(508) 548-5621

Amenities: 1,2,3,10,11
Breakfast: Full
Dbl. Oc.: $80.00-$95.00
Sgl. Oc.: $70.00-$85.00
Third Person: $15.00

Village Green Inn—Graciously decorated rooms in lovely old Victorian. Ideally located on historic village green. Walk or bike to fine shops, restaurants, and beach. Relax amidst 19th century charm and warm hospitality.

Falmouth

Peacock, Phyllis
81 Palmer Ave., 02540
(508) 548-1230

Amenities: 2,3,5,6,7,9,10,11
Breakfast: Full
Dbl. Oc.: $81.00-$87.00

Palmer House Inn—An intimate Victorian B&B, located in the historic district. A romantic return to grandma's day. Full gourmet breakfast, private baths. Bicycles available to guests. Walking distance to village.

Falmouth

Railsback, Carole
718 Palmer Ave., 02540
(508) 540-7069

Amenities: 2,3,5,6,7,10,11
Breakfast: Full

Dbl. Oc.: $81.85
Sgl. Oc.: $93.25
Third Person: $25.00-$29.22

Wyndemere House At Sippewissett—Charming English country inn. Modern private baths, antique furnishings, five minutes to beaches, restaurants, shops, ferry to islands. Afternoon tea on terrace. Quiet idyllic setting. Biking & riding nearby.

AMENITIES

1. No Smoking
2. No Pets
3. No Children
4. Senior Citizen Rates
5. Tennis Available
6. Golf Available
7. Swimming Available
8. Skiing Available
9. Credit Cards Accepted
10. Personal Check Accepted
11. Off Season Rates
12. Dinner Available (w/sufficient notice)

Massachusetts

Falmouth

Sabo-Feller, Mrs. Barbara
75 Locust St., 02540
(508) 540-1445

Amenities: 1,2,3,4,5,6,7,9,10,11
Breakfast: Full
Dbl. Oc.: $90.00
Sgl. Oc.: $60.00
Third Person: $20.00

Capt. Tom Lawrence House—1861 whaling captain's residence close to downtown, beach, bikeway & ferries. Cozy fireplace, Steinway, firm beds. Homemade foods from organic grains such as Belgian waffles. Explore entire Cape & islands by day trips.

Gloucester

Swinson, Ginny & Hal
83 Riverview, 01930
(617) 281-1826

Amenities: 2,4,5,6,7,10
Breakfast: Continental

Dbl. Oc.: $55.00-$65.00
Sgl. Oc.: $50.00-$60.00
Third Person: $10.00

Riverview B&B—In historic Cape Ann on the Annisquam, a busy waterway. Enjoy boat traffic from this lovely Victorian home. Great beaches, antiques, restaurants, whale watching nearby.

Great Barrington

Littlejohn, Herbert, Jr.
1 Newsboy Monument Lane
01230
(413) 528-2882

Amenities: 2,3,5,6,7,8,10,11
Breakfast: Full

Dbl. Oc.: $63.42-$79.28
Sgl. Oc.: $58.14-$73.99

Littlejohn Manor—Victorian charm is recaptured in this uniquely personable turn-of-the-century home dedicated to your comfort. Near Tanglewood, Jacobs Pillow, theatres, museums, Butternut & Catamount ski areas.

Great Barrington

Thorne, Mrs. Terry
453 Stockbridge Rd., 01230
(413) 528-3828

Amenities: 1,2,3,5,6-12
Breakfast: Full

Dbl. Oc.: $75.00-$125.00
Sgl. Oc.: $55.00-$75.00
Third Person: $15.00

An Intimate Family-Run Inn—Close to all attractions year round. Lovely full breakfast served in our warm dining room. The feeling of country elegance is enhanced by the antique furniture.

AMENITIES

1. No Smoking
2. No Pets
3. No Children
4. Senior Citizen Rates
5. Tennis Available
6. Golf Available
7. Swimming Available
8. Skiing Available
9. Credit Cards Accepted
10. Personal Check Accepted
11. Off Season Rates
12. Dinner Available (w/sufficient notice)

Massachusetts

Harwich Port

Ayer, Mrs. Calvin
74 Sisson Rd., 02646
(508) 432-9452

Amenities: 2,3,5,6,7,9,10
Breakfast: Continental

Dbl. Oc.: $65.00
Sgl. Oc.: $65.00

The Coach House—Quiet, comfortable, elegance, king or queen beds, private baths, ideally located for day trips to the Islands. National Seashore or whale waching. Open May-Oct. 2 night minimum requested.

Harwich Port

Cunningham, Alyce & Wally
24 Pilgrim Road, 02646
(508) 432-0810

Amenities: 5,6,7,8,9,10,11
Breakfast: Continental
Dbl. Oc.: $77.00-$125.00
Sgl. Oc.: $77.00-$125.00

Dunscroft Inn—300 feet from beautiful private beach on Nantucket Sound. Romantic Bed & Breakfast inn. Private baths, large, sunny rooms of eyelet ruffles & lace. Walk to shops & restaurants. 2 efficiency apartments & cottage also on premises.

Harwich Port

Girard, Dottie
3 Sea St., 02646
(508) 432-3837

Amenities: 2,5,6,7,10,11
Breakfast: Continental

Dbl. Oc.: $90.00
Sgl. Oc.: $90.00

The Shoals Guesthouse is located right on the sandy shores of Nantucket Sound in a quiet residential area. Each room has a private bath and is very clean. A short walk to restaurants, shops, stores.

Harwich Port

Silverio, Mrs. Janet
88 Bank St., 02646
(508) 432-3206

Amenities: 2,5,6,7,9,10,11
Breakfast: Continental

Dbl. Oc.: $71.31
Sgl. Oc.: $65.82
Third Person: $15.00

The Inn On Bank Street—A Bed & Breakfast located in the center of Harwich Port on Cape Cod is just a five minute walk to the ocean. Six rooms with private baths. Enjoy breakfast on the sunporch.

AMENITIES

1. No Smoking
2. No Pets
3. No Children
4. Senior Citizen Rates
5. Tennis Available
6. Golf Available
7. Swimming Available
8. Skiing Available
9. Credit Cards Accepted
10. Personal Check Accepted
11. Off Season Rates
12. Dinner Available (w/sufficient notice)

Massachusetts

Harwich Port

Van Gelder, Kathleen & David
85 Bank St., 02646
(508) 432-0337 or
(800) 992-6550 (outside MA)

Amenities: 2,3,5,6,7,9,10,11
Breakfast: Continental
Dbl. Oc.: $60.00-$85.00
Sgl. Oc.: $60.00-$85.00

Captain's Quarters—An 1850 Victorian with a large wrap around porch, has 5 fine guest rooms with queen size brass beds, private baths. Separate cottage also grounds. Walk to beach and shops. Perfect for honeymooners.

Harwich Port

Van Gelder, Kathleen & David
326 Lower County Rd., 02646
(508) 432-0377 or
(800) 992-6550 (outside MA)

Amenities: 2,5,6,7,9,10,11
Breakfast: Continental
Dbl. Oc.: $60.00-$85.00
Sgl. Oc.: $60.00-$85.00
Third Person: $12.50

Harbor Breeze—Across the road from picturesque Allen Harbor, has 9 lovely rooms & family suites around a garden courtyard. TVs & swimming pool. Short walk to a fine beach, shops, restaurants and theater.

Harwich Port

Van Gelder, Kathleen & David
255 Lower County Rd., 02646
(508) 432-0337 or
(800) 992-6550 (outside MA)

Amenities: 5,6,7,9,10,11
Breakfast: Continental

Dbl. Oc.: $60.00-$110.00
Sgl. Oc.: $60.00-$110.00
Third Person: $12.50

Bayberry Shores—A walk-to-beach Cape Cod home with 2 spacious guest rooms and 2 room suite with private baths and color TVs. Charming country common room and a brick terrace shaded with lilacs and pines. Fine location.

AMENITIES

1. No Smoking
2. No Pets
3. No Children
4. Senior Citizen Rates
5. Tennis Available
6. Golf Available
7. Swimming Available
8. Skiing Available
9. Credit Cards Accepted
10. Personal Check Accepted
11. Off Season Rates
12. Dinner Available (w/sufficient notice)

Massachusetts

Hyannis

Battle, Mrs. Patricia
397 Sea St., 02601
(508) 771-2549 or 771-7213

Amenities: 2,5,6,7,9,11
Breakfast: Continental

Dbl. Oc.: $60.34-$76.79
Sgl. Oc.: $60.34-$76.79
Third Person: $10.00

Sea Breeze Inn—A warm hospitable family-run inn only a 3 min. walk to beach, close to restaurants and shopping, also close to boats for Martha's Vineyard and Nantucket. All rooms have private baths and some with ocean views.

Hyannis

Krajewski, Ms.
156 Main St., 02601
(508) 775-5611

Amenities: 2,7,9,11
Breakfast: Continental
Dbl. Oc.: $80.00
Sgl. Oc.: $80.00
Third Person: $15.00

Captain Sylvester Baxter House—High ceilinged rooms in former sea captain's home, circa 1850. Short walk to harbor, beaches and shops. Private bath, A/C, pool, cottages. Families welcome.

Hyannis

Nelson, Mrs. Lois
358 Sea St., 02601
(508) 775-8030

Amenities: 1,2,3,5,6,7,9,10
Breakfast: Full
Dbl. Oc.: $60.34-$87.76
Sgl. Oc.: $60.34-$87.76
Third Person: $15.00

Inn On Sea Street—An elegant Victorian inn just steps from the beach. Canopy beds & antiques grace 5 unique guest rooms. Sterling & china compliment homebaked gourmet breakfast. Walk to all attractions. Smoking discouraged.

Hyannis

Siefken, Mrs. Barbara
Rosetta St., 02601
(508) 775-7049, (800) 992-0096

Amenities: 5,6,7
Breakfast: Full

Dbl. Oc.: $49.00
Sgl. Oc.: $49.00

Cranberry Cove—A charming Cape Cod home situated on the edge of a cranberry bog. Walking distance to island ferries, beaches, and local restaurants. A true Cap Cod experience, rustic and serene.

AMENITIES

1. No Smoking
2. No Pets
3. No Children
4. Senior Citizen Rates
5. Tennis Available
6. Golf Available
7. Swimming Available
8. Skiing Available
9. Credit Cards Accepted
10. Personal Check Accepted
11. Off Season Rates
12. Dinner Available (w/sufficient notice)

Massachusetts

Lenox

Farrelly, Joy & Scottie
25 Clifford St., 01240
(413) 637-3330

Amenities: 3,5,6,7,8,10,11
Breakfast: Continental
Dbl. Oc.: $80.00-$145.00
Sgl. Oc.: $75.00-$140.00
Third Person: $20.00

Clifford Inn— "belle epoque" mansion, 6 bedrooms with fireplace, private bath, spacious living/dining area, swimming pool, large veranda, hammocks. Tanglewood & 40 other performing groups in area. French, Italian, & Spanish spoken.

Lenox

Jacob M/M Robert
15 Hawthorne St., 01240
(413) 637-3013

Amenities: 2,5,6,7,8,9,10,11
Breakfast: Full

Dbl. Oc.: $65.00-$125.00
Sgl. Oc.: $65.00-$125.00
Third Person: $15.00

Brook Farm Inn—There is poetry here. Shaded glen, pool, private bath, full breakfast, English tea; near shops, Tanglewood, & museums; Fall foliage, fireplaces, large library, 650 volumes of poetry on tape; 12 rooms. Children 15 & over.

Lenox

Lanoue, Mrs. Marcie
76 Cliffwood St., 01240
(413) 637-0236

Amenities: 2,3,5,6,7,8,9,11
Breakfast: Continental
Dbl. Oc.: $95.00-$130.00
Third Person: $20.00

Underledge—Enjoy the romance of our country mansion. Perfect, elevated location on four acres. Charming rooms, private baths, all A.C. 26 miles of hiking and cross country skiing. 1 1/2 miles to Tanglewood.

AMENITIES

1. No Smoking
2. No Pets
3. No Children
4. Senior Citizen Rates
5. Tennis Available
6. Golf Available
7. Swimming Available
8. Skiing Available
9. Credit Cards Accepted
10. Personal Check Accepted
11. Off Season Rates
12. Dinner Available (w/sufficient notice)

Massachusetts

Lenox

Mears, M/M Richard
5 Greenwood St., 01240
(413) 637-0975

Amenities: 2,,7,8,9,10,11
Breakfast: Continental
Dbl. Oc.: $68.90-$174.90
Sgl. Oc.: $58.30-$68.90
Third Person: $25.00

Whistlers' Inn—Elegant antique-filled Tudor mansion on seven wooded acres. 11 bedrooms with new private baths; complimentary sherry & tea. 8 fireplaces, library and music room, garden-terrace. 2 blocks to Lenox town center.

Lenox

Mekinda, Lynn & Mario
141 Main St., 01240
(413) 637-0193

Amenities: 2,5,6,7,8,9,10,11
Breakfast: Continental

Dbl. Oc.: $110.00
Sgl. Oc.: $100.00
Third Person: $20.00

Garden Gables—Charming, small, restful and private inn set away from the street on 4 acres of beautiful grounds in the center of town. All rooms with private baths. Fireplaces; library; 72 ft.-long swimming pool.

Lenox

Newton, M/M Frank
103 Walker St. 01240
(413) 637-3416

Amenities: 2,3,5,7,8,9,10,11
Breakfast: Continental
Dbl. Oc.: $60.00-$125.00
Sgl. Oc.: $60.00-$125.00
Third Person: $20.00

The Gables—Former home of Edith Wharton. Built 1885, furnished in period style, fireplaces in some rooms, also special theme rooms. Walk to Tanglewood in the summer or skiing in winter.

Lexington

Halewood, Carol
2 Larchmont Lane, 02173
(617) 862-5404

Amenities: 1,2,3,5,6,7
Breakfast: Continental

Dbl. Oc.: $55.00
Sgl. Oc.: $50.00
Third Person: $10.00

Halewood House—Less than one mile from Lexington Center and historic landmarks. Lovely New England Cape home offers privacy and upstairs double rooms, custom bath, separate from hostess living area.

AMENITIES

1. No Smoking
2. No Pets
3. No Children
4. Senior Citizen Rates
5. Tennis Available
6. Golf Available
7. Swimming Available
8. Skiing Available
9. Credit Cards Accepted
10. Personal Check Accepted
11. Off Season Rates
12. Dinner Available (w/sufficient notice)

Massachusetts

Marblehead

Bacon, Margaret & Sandy
9 Gregory St., 01945
(617) 631-1890

Amenities: 1,2,4,5,7,9,10,11
Breakfast: Continental

Dbl. Oc.: $75.00
Sgl. Oc.: $65.00
Third Person: $10.00

Sea Street Bed And Breakfast—Turn-of-the-century Victorian home ideally located in historic district offers sparkling harbor views; near fine restaurants, art galleries, shops and beaches; easy access to Boston, Rte. 128 and Salem.

Marblehead

Blake, Ms. Susan
23 Gregory St., 01945
(617) 631-1032

Amenities: 1,2
Breakfast: Continental
Dbl. Oc.: $60.00
Sgl. Oc.: $45.00

Harborside House—Handsome 1830 Colonial overlooks picturesque harbor. Sunny breakfast porch; third story deck; two guest rooms; shared bath; near antique shops. gourmet restaurants, historic sites.

Marblehead

Pabich, Richard
25 Spray Ave., 01945
(508) 741-0680

Amenities: 2,9,10
Breakfast: Continental

Dbl. Oc.: $89.95-$116.27
Sgl. Oc.: $89.95-$116.27
Third Person: $10.00

Spray Cliff On The Ocean—Wonderful old English Tudor mansion 15 miles north of Boston. Spacious rooms, some overlooking the sea. Sandy beach nearby. Elegant yet affordable. Private baths. Brick terrace amidst overflowing flower gardens.

Nantucket Island

Conway, M/M Peter C.
26 North Water St., 02554
(508) 228-0720

Amenities: 2,3,5,6,7,9,10,11
Breakfast: Continental

Dbl. Oc.: $69.00-$130.00
Sgl. Oc.: $39.00-$110.00
Third Person: $15.00

Carlisle House Inn—Beautifully restored 18th Century inn. Working fireplaces, canopy beds, antiques, private baths, and the best intown location, only three hundred yards from ferry and beaches.

AMENITIES

1. No Smoking
2. No Pets
3. No Children
4. Senior Citizen Rates
5. Tennis Available
6. Golf Available
7. Swimming Available
8. Skiing Available
9. Credit Cards Accepted
10. Personal Check Accepted
11. Off Season Rates
12. Dinner Available (w/sufficient notice)

Massachusetts

Nantucket Island

Grieder, Mrs. Ruth
43 Orange St., 02554
(508) 228-1399

Amenities: 2,5,6,7,10,11
Breakfast: Continental
Dbl. Oc.: $50.00-$70.00
Sgl. Oc.: $50.00
Third Person: $12.00

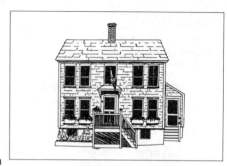

Grieder Guest House—5 minutes walk from center. Built in 1700's, spacious rooms have 4-poster twin beds, antiques, parking permit, refrigerator. Owned & operated by above since 1952. Pleasant off-street yard with chairs, picnic table, etc.

Nantucket

Hammer-Yankow, Mrs. Robin
5 Ash St., 02554
(508) 228-1987

Amenities: 2,5,6,7,10,11
Breakfast: Continental

Dbl. Oc.: $80.00-$120.00
Third Person: $20.00

Cobblestone Inn—Circa 1725, 5 rooms all priv. baths. Located on a quiet street in town, just a few blocks from the ferry/shops/restaurants/museums. Enjoy our living room/sunporch/yard. Open year round.

Nantucket

Heron-Connick, Jean & Gerry
10 Cliff Rd., 02554
(508) 228-0530

Amenities: 5,6,7,9,10,11
Breakfast: Continental
Dbl. Oc.: $85.64-$117.70
Sgl. Oc.: $69.55

The Century House—B&B Inn, serving the island traveler since mid 1800's; situated in prestigious Cliff Rd. historic district; minutes to beach, restaurants, galleries, shops, museums. Antique appointments, Laura Ashley decor.

AMENITIES

1. No Smoking
2. No Pets
3. No Children
4. Senior Citizen Rates
5. Tennis Available
6. Golf Available
7. Swimming Available
8. Skiing Available
9. Credit Cards Accepted
10. Personal Check Accepted
11. Off Season Rates
12. Dinner Available (w/sufficient notice)

Massachusetts

Nantucket

Kennan, Mary & John
18 Gardner St., 02554
(508) 228-1155

Amenities: 9,10,11
Breakfast: Continental
Dbl. Oc.: $86.67-$125.19
Sgl. Oc.: $89.93-$139.10
Third Person: $16.05

Eighteen Gardner Street is an early nineteenth century inn on the island of Nantucket. Canopy beds, fireplaces and private bathrooms. A short stroll down cobblestoned streets to shops and restaurants.

Nantucket

McIntyre, Sharon
61 Center St., 02554
(508) 228-0678

Amenities: 2,3,9,10,11
Breakfast: Continental

Dbl. Oc.: $98.73-$137.13
Sgl. Oc.: $49.37
Third Person: $10.00

Martin's Guest House—Located in historic district of Nantucket. Walk to beach, restaurants, and shops. Large, airy rooms, living room with fireplace, lovely porch to relax on. Very peaceful.

Nantucket

Parker, Matthew S.
7 Sea St., 02554
(508) 228-3577

Amenities: 1,2,5,6,7,9,10,11
Breakfast: Continental
Dbl. Oc.: $75.00-$150.00
Sgl. Oc.: $65.00-$140.00
Third Person: $15.00

Seven Sea Street—A small luxurious post & beam country inn. Distinguished by canopied beds, private baths, jacuzzi, whirlpool and a view of harbor from the widows walk. Quiet location in the historic district. We welcome you to our inn.

AMENITIES

1. No Smoking
2. No Pets
3. No Children
4. Senior Citizen Rates
5. Tennis Available
6. Golf Available
7. Swimming Available
8. Skiing Available
9. Credit Cards Accepted
10. Personal Check Accepted
11. Off Season Rates
12. Dinner Available (w/sufficient notice)

Massachusetts

Nantucket

Wasserman, Marcia
8 Chester St., 02554
(508) 228-9696

Amenities: 2,9,10,11
Breakfast: Continental
Dbl. Oc.: $133.75
Sgl. Oc.: $133.75
Third Person: $15.00

Centerboard Guest House—A Victorian guest house with quiet country elegance, lovingly renovated and restored in 1987. Known for its warm and gracious hospitality. Cobblestoned main street and white sand beaches nearby.

Nantucket

Watts, Mrs. Lynda
10 Upper Vestal St., 02554
(508) 228-3828

Amenities: 5,6,7,10,11
Breakfast: Continental

Dbl. Oc.: $60.00
Sgl. Oc.: $60.00
Third Person: $15.00

Lynda Watts Bed & Breakfast—Located on a quiet street, only a seven minute walk to town. Guest rooms equipped with TV's and refrigerators. Weather permitting, breakfast is served on the patio. A two night minimum stay is required.

Newburyport

Crumb, Judy
3 Federal St., 01950
(508) 462-3778

Amenities: 9,10
Breakfast: Full

Dbl. Oc.: $85.00
Sgl. Oc.: $79.00
Third Person: $20.00

The Windsor House—An 18th-century seaport Federal-style mansion featuring Yankee hospitality and traditional bed and breakfast. Two blocks from town center, two blocks from harbor.

North Eastham

Keith, Margaret & Bill
Box 238, Rt. 6, 02651
(508) 255-6632

Amenities: 2,3,5,6,7,9,10,11
Breakfast: Full

Dbl. Oc.: $77.00-$89.00

The Penny House—Experience the quaint charm of this 1751 ship builder's bow roof Cape. Convenient to National Seashore, Audubon Sanctuary & bicycle trails. Adults only.

AMENITIES

1. No Smoking
2. No Pets
3. No Children
4. Senior Citizen Rates
5. Tennis Available
6. Golf Available
7. Swimming Available
8. Skiing Available
9. Credit Cards Accepted
10. Personal Check Accepted
11. Off Season Rates
12. Dinner Available (w/sufficient notice)

Massachusetts

Northampton

Lesko, Mrs. Lee
230 No. Main St,, 01060
(413) 584-8164

Amenities: 1,2,3,5,6,7,10
Breakfast: Full
Dbl. Oc.: $43.08
Sgl. Oc.: $37.70

The Knoll B&B—A home of English Tudor design located in the 5 college area of Northampton. Situated well off the road on a knoll overlooking 17 acres of farm and forest. In town yet country setting.

Oak Bluffs (Martha's Vineyard)

Rosenzweig, Harry
Kennebec & Park Ave., 02557
(508) 693-0043

Amenities: 2,3,7,9,11
Breakfast: Continental

Dbl. Oc.: $52.85
Sgl. Oc.: $52.85
Third Person: $10.00

The Nashua House, 1873—Clean antique rooms, shared bath, steps to beach ferries, buses, bike rentals, movies, restaurants, historic gingerbread camp grounds, and the spiritual refreshment of ocean park by the sea. Lowest rates.

Orleans

Standish, M/M Clark D.
163 Beach Rd., 02653
(508) 255-6654

Amenities: 5,6,7,9,10
Breakfast: Continental

Dbl. Oc.: $52.00-$80.00

The Farmhouse—Walk to Nauset Beach; quiet country inn; seashore setting. Open year round.

Peru

Halvorsen, Alice & Richard
East Windsor Rd., 01235
(413) 655-8292

Amenities: 7,8,10
Breakfast: Full

Dbl. Oc.: $40.00-$45.00

Chalet d'Alicia—A Swiss chalet-style home set high in the Berkshires, offering a private casual atmosphere. Tanglewood, Jacob's Pillow, Williamstown Theatre, cross-country skiing all nearby.

AMENITIES

1. No Smoking
2. No Pets
3. No Children
4. Senior Citizen Rates
5. Tennis Available
6. Golf Available
7. Swimming Available
8. Skiing Available
9. Credit Cards Accepted
10. Personal Check Accepted
11. Off Season Rates
12. Dinner Available (w/sufficient notice)

Massachusetts

Petersham

Day, Jean & Robert
North Main St., 01366
(508) 724-8885

Amenities: 2,9,10
Breakfast: Continental
Dbl. Oc.: $84.56
Sgl. Oc.: $63.42
Third Person: $15.86

Winterwood At Petersham—An elegant revival mansion just off the town common. All rooms with private bath, most with working fireplaces. Built in 1842, Winterwood is on the national register of historic homes.

Plymouth

Reynolds, Ms. Leigh
6 Carver St., 02360
(508) 747-5767

Amenities: 1,2,7,10
Breakfast: Full

Dbl. Oc.: $60.00
Sgl. Oc.: $55.00
Third Person: $15.00

No. Six Carver St. Bed & Breakfast—Located on top of historic Coles Hill. Rooms have ocean views. Walk to Plymouth Rock, Mayflower, all historic waterfront attractions. Eat a hearty breakfast overlooking the busy harbor area.

Plymouth

Smith, M/M James
1 Morton Park Rd., 02360
(508) 747-1730

Amenities: 2,5,6,7,9,10,11
Breakfast: Continental

Dbl. Oc.: $52.00-$87.00
Sgl. Oc.: $47.00-$75.00
Third Person: $15.00

Morton Park Place is a comfortable place to relax. 10 minutes west of Plymouth center. Easy on/off access to Rte. 3 & 44.

Princeton

Plumridge, Don & Maxine
30 Mountain Rd., 01541
(508) 464-2030

Amenities: 1,2,3,5,7,8,9,10,12
Breakfast: Continental

Dbl. Oc.: $140.00
Sgl. Oc.: $140.00
Third Person: $35.00

Country Inn At Princeton—1890 late Victorian mansion. 50 mile valley view. Six spacious parlor suites for discerning adults. Striking ambiance, restful and romantic retreat. 4-star gourmet dining. Ideal place for pampered palates.

AMENITIES

1. No Smoking
2. No Pets
3. No Children
4. Senior Citizen Rates
5. Tennis Available
6. Golf Available
7. Swimming Available
8. Skiing Available
9. Credit Cards Accepted
10. Personal Check Accepted
11. Off Season Rates
12. Dinner Available (w/sufficient notice)

Massachusetts

Provincetown

Culligan, Ms. Susan
178 Bradford St., 02657
(508) 487-1616

Amenities: 5,6,7,9,10
Breakfast: Full

Dbl. Oc.: $69.00-$109.00
Sgl. Oc.: $65.00-$125.00
Third Person: $16.20

Bradford Gardens Inn is a lovely 1820 Colonial charmer, very clean & famous for gourmet breakfasts. Excellent dining & entertainment nearby. Rates include maid service, firewood (6 fireplaced rooms) & breakfast.

Provincetown

Paoletti, Leonard
156 Bradford St., 02657
(508) 487-2543

Amenities: 2,5,7,9,11
Breakfast: Continental

Dbl. Oc.: $48.60-$75.60
Third Person: $20.00

Elephant Walk is a turn-of-the-century inn, centrally located with free parking. The 8 spacious rooms are decorated with antiques & art. Each room has its own bath, cable color TV & refrigerator.

Provincetown

Schoolman, David
22 Commercial St., 02657
(508) 487-0706

Amenities: 2,3,5,7,10,11
Breakfast: Continental
Dbl. Oc.: $60.00-$100.00
Sgl. Oc.: $60.00-$100.00
Third Person: $15.00

Land's End Inn—High on hill overlooking Provincetown and Cape Cod Bay, Land's End offers comfortable, antique-filled room, large common areas and quiet surroundings. One mile from Provincetown center's shops and galleries.

Salem

Kessler, Ms. Patricia
284 Lafayette St., 01970
(508) 744-4092

Amenities: 2,9,11
Breakfast: Continental
Dbl. Oc.: $76.10
Sgl. Oc.: $76.10
Third Person: $8.46

The Coach House Inn—Cozy, comfortable rooms retain the charm of this Victorian mansion located in an historic district of Salem. One-half mile from shopping & tourist attractions. On Routes 114 and 1A. Off-street parking.

AMENITIES

1. No Smoking
2. No Pets
3. No Children
4. Senior Citizen Rates
5. Tennis Available
6. Golf Available
7. Swimming Available
8. Skiing Available
9. Credit Cards Accepted
10. Personal Check Accepted
11. Off Season Rates
12. Dinner Available (w/sufficient notice)

Massachusetts

Salem

Nash, Nadine
98 Essex St., 01970
(508) 744-5281

Amenities: 4,5,6,7,9,10,11
Breakfast: Continental

Dbl. Oc.: $72.50
Sgl. Oc.: $72.50
Third Person: $72.50

The Suzannah Flint House—Four charming rooms in historic district, one block from waterfront and four musuems. Cable TV, AC, private baths.

Salem

Pabich, Diane & Richard
7 Summer St., 01970
(508) 741-0680

Amenities: 2,9,10,12
Breakfast: Continental

Dbl. Oc.: $72.93-$95.13
Sgl. Oc.: $72.93-$95.13
Third Person: $10.58

The Salem Inn—Delight yourself with an uncommon lodging experience, in the heart of one of America's oldest cities. The Salem Inn has an uncommon place in history, and it is perfect for your relaxation and enjoyment.

Salem

Roberts, Mrs. Ada May
16 Winter St., 01970
(508) 744-8304

Amenities: 1,2,3,9
Breakfast: Continental

Dbl. Oc.: $53.00-$80.00

The Amelia Payson Guest House—An 1845 Greek Revival home where visitors enjoy restored elegance in the heart of Salem's historic district. A five minute stroll finds nearby shopping, historic houses and museums, or waterfront dining.

Sandwich

Dickson, Harry
152 Main St., 02563
(508) 888-6142

Amenities: 1,2,5,6,7,9,10,11
Breakfast: Continental
Dbl. Oc.: $48.61-$70.55

Capt. Ezra Nye House—Quiet, friendly hospitality in the heart of Sandwich, Cape Cod's oldest town. Fine restaurants, museums, antique shops, beaches and the world famous Heritage Plantation nearby. Children six and over only.

AMENITIES

1. No Smoking
2. No Pets
3. No Children
4. Senior Citizen Rates
5. Tennis Available
6. Golf Available
7. Swimming Available
8. Skiing Available
9. Credit Cards Accepted
10. Personal Check Accepted
11. Off Season Rates
12. Dinner Available (w/sufficient notice)

Massachusetts

Sheffield

Maghery, M/M Richard
2 Underermountain Rd., Rt. 41, 01257
(413) 229-2143

Amenities: 5,6,7,8,10,11
Breakfast: Continental
Dbl. Oc.: $58.00-$82.00
Third Person: $10.00

Ivanhoe Country House—In the Berkshire Hills has nine rooms, all with private bath, two with kitchenettes. Swimming pool, 25 wooded acres. Near Tanglewood, antique shops, hiking trails, ski areas. Child $10.50 in room w/parent.

Sheffield

Stendardi, Mrs. May
Rte. 41, P.O. Box 729, 01257
(413) 229-3363

Amenities: 1,2,3,5,6,7,8,11
Breakfast: Full
Dbl. Oc.: $75.00-$105.00
Sgl. Oc.: $70.00-$95.00

A Unique Bed & Breakfast Inn—Cozy and warm. A log home nestled in pines with a special touch for the discernable guest. 20 mins. Tanglewood, 10 mins. several ski areas. Fantastic restaurants, antiques.

South Egremont

Black, John
Old Sheffield Rd., 01258
(413) 528-2111

Amenities: 5,6,7,8,9,10,12
Breakfast: Full
Dbl. Oc.: $93.50-$184.80
Sgl. Oc.: $77.00-$112.00
Third Person: $20.00

The Egremont Inn—Built in 1780 as a stage coach stop inn, is a 23 room inn located in a nationally registered historic district. It is 25 minutes from Tanglewood and 10 minutes from Butternut.

AMENITIES

1. No Smoking
2. No Pets
3. No Children
4. Senior Citizen Rates
5. Tennis Available
6. Golf Available
7. Swimming Available
8. Skiing Available
9. Credit Cards Accepted
10. Personal Check Accepted
11. Off Season Rates
12. Dinner Available (w/sufficient notice)

Massachusetts

Sterling

O'Brien, Ms. Rita
285 Route 140, 01564
(508) 442-6678

Amenities: 1,7,8
Breakfast: Continental

Dbl. Oc.: $65.00
Sgl. Oc.: $60.00
Third Person: $10.00

An Irish B&B Glen Cara—Come share our friendly home and love of Irish culture. We're on 2 acres next to a brook. Great hiking and fishing! 20 minutes to Centrum. Close to 15 antique shops. Let's have tea and hot Irish bread!

Sturbridge

MacConnell, Kevin
11 Summit, 01518
(617) 347-7603

Amenities: 5,6,7,8,10,11
Breakfast: Full
Dbl. Oc.: $45.00-$55.00
Third Person: $10.00

Commonwealth Inn—16 room Victorian home in the heart of Sturbridge. 1 mile from Old Sturbridge Village. Includes: jacuzzi, private baths, player piano, 6 foot wall mural.

Sudbury

MacDonald, Irene & Stuart
5 Checkerberry Circle, 01776
(508) 443-8660

Amenities: 1,2,5,7,10
Breakfast: Full

Dbl. Oc.: $55.00-$60.00
Sgl. Oc.: $45.00-$50.00

Checkerberry Corner B&B—is located in the heart of historic Minuteman country in a quiet residential neighborhood. Savor historic New England or visit colleges and Boston. Close to many fine restaurants.

Sudbury

Somers, Nancy & Don
3 Drum Lane, 01776
(508) 443-2860

Amenities: 1,2,5,6,7,10
Breakfast: Continental

Dbl. Oc.: $50.00
Sgl. Oc.: $40.00
Third Person: $10.00

Sudbury B&B—offers friendly lodging for the New England visitor. This lovely colonial home is on a quiet tree-studded acre close to Boston, Concord, and Lexington. Children welcome.

AMENITIES

1. No Smoking
2. No Pets
3. No Children
4. Senior Citizen Rates
5. Tennis Available
6. Golf Available
7. Swimming Available
8. Skiing Available
9. Credit Cards Accepted
10. Personal Check Accepted
11. Off Season Rates
12. Dinner Available (w/sufficient notice)

Massachusetts

Truro

Parker, Ms. Jane
Rte. 6A, Box 114, 02666
(508) 349-3358

Amenities: 2,3,5,6,7,11
Breakfast: Continental

Dbl. Oc.: $55.00
Sgl. Oc.: $48.00

Parker House is an 1800 house in the least developed Cape town. 3 rooms with shared baths near beautiful beaches, the National Seashore, restaurants, galleries and shops of larger towns.

Tyringham

Rizzo, Lilja & Joe
Main Rd., 01264
(413) 243-3008

Amenities: 5,6,7,8,10
Breakfast: Full

Dbl. Oc.: $58.14-$95.13
Third Person: $10.57 (Apt.)

The Golden Goose—A warm friendly country B&B inn nestled between Stockbridge, Lenox and Becket. Antiques, fireplaces, homemade breakfast fare. 5 guest rooms plus charming studio apartment. Beautiful year-round.

Vineyard Haven

Clarke, M/M John
Owen Park, Box 1939, 02568
(508) 693-1646

Amenities: 2,7,9,10,11
Breakfast: Continental
Dbl. Oc.: $87.00-$135.00
Third Person: $15.00

Lothrop Merry House—Charming 18th century home overlooking the harbor. One block from the ferry. Beautiful views; private beach; 7 rooms some with fireplaces; private baths. Sunfish, canoe, and sailing charters available.

Vineyard Haven

Ross, Ms. Julia
100 Main St.
Box 2457, 02568
(508) 693-6564

Amenities: 2,3,9,10,11
Breakfast: Continental

Dbl. Oc.: $95.00-$140.00
Third Person: $20.00

Captain Dexter House—This 1843 sea captain's home has been meticulously restored and exquisitely furnished. Guests can walk to beach, ferry, restaurants and shops. Relax with us! A canopy bed and fireplace does wonders.

AMENITIES

1. No Smoking
2. No Pets
3. No Children
4. Senior Citizen Rates
5. Tennis Available
6. Golf Available
7. Swimming Available
8. Skiing Available
9. Credit Cards Accepted
10. Personal Check Accepted
11. Off Season Rates
12. Dinner Available (w/sufficient notice)

Massachusetts

West Barnstable

Rosenthal, Barbara & Bob
591 Main St., 02668
(508) 362-8418

Amenities: 2,3,5,6,7,9,10,11,12
Breakfast: Full
Dbl. Oc.: $95.00-$110.00
Third Person: $15.00

Honeysuckle Inn—Charming Victorian inn near Sandy Neck Beach. All private baths, feather beds, some fireplaces, afternoon tea, homemade pastries. Exit 5 off Hwy.6 to W. Barnstable, left on 6A to inn. Reservations advised.

West Falmouth

Mazzucchelli, Betty & Joe
Rte. 28A, Box 895, 02574
(508) 540-7232

Amenities: 1,2,7,10,11
Breakfast: Full

Dbl. Oc.: $81.81
Sgl. Oc.: $81.81

The Elms—A refurbished old Victorian home, built in the 1800's, features 9 double rooms, 7 with private baths, one half mile from the beach. Landscaped grounds, gazebo and herb gardens; home is furnished with antiques.

West Harwich

Connell, Eileen & Jack
77 Main St., Box 667, 02671
(508) 432-9628

Amenities: 2,3,5,6,7,9,10,12
Breakfast: Full

Dbl. Oc.: $75.00
Sgl. Oc.: $75.00
Third Person: $30.00

Cape Cod Sunny Pines B&B Inn—Irish hospitality in a Victorian ambiance. Candlelight gourmet Irish breakfast, all private suites; walk to Nantucket Sound, theater, restaurants, hiking and biking trails. A lovely day trip to Provincetown & islands.

West Harwich

Lockyer, Kathleen & Bill
186 Belmont Rd.
Box 444, 02671
(508) 432-7766

Amenities: 2,5,6,7,9,10,12
Breakfast: Full

Dbl. Oc.: $78.51-$89.48
Sgl. Oc.: $73.26-$84.23

The Lion's Head Inn—A romantic inn with a sense of history. Built as a Cape Half-House in 1800. former home of a sea captain, located close to Nantucket Sound. Golf, summer theatre, fine shopping & dining. Open year round.

AMENITIES

1. No Smoking
2. No Pets
3. No Children
4. Senior Citizen Rates
5. Tennis Available
6. Golf Available
7. Swimming Available
8. Skiing Available
9. Credit Cards Accepted
10. Personal Check Accepted
11. Off Season Rates
12. Dinner Available (w/sufficient notice)

Massachusetts

West Harwich

Myers, M/M William
91 Chase St., 02671
(617) 432-3714

Amenities: 2,5,6,7,10,11
Breakfast: Full

Dbl. Oc.: $71.31
Sgl. Oc.: $49.37
Third Person: $10.97

The Tern Inn Bed & Breakfast on Nantucket Sound. Two century old Cape Half-House with 5 rooms furnished in antiques. Near excellent restaurants, shops, bicycle trails, & National Seashore.

Williamsburg

Sylvester, Carl
9 South St., 01096
(413) 268-7283

Amenities: 5,6,7,8,10
Breakfast: Full

Dbl. Oc.: $40.00
Sgl. Oc.: $35.00
Third Person: $10.00

Carl & Lotties B&B—Our comfortable ten room home is one quarter mile from town and 8 miles from I-91. Fine restaurants and shops within walking distance, private entrance and living room for our guests. Quiet area, 3 rooms.

Williamstown

Gangemi, Mrs. J. Marvin
520 White Oaks Rd., 01267
(413) 458-3774

Amenities: 1,2,5,6,7,8,10
Breakfast: Continental

Dbl. Oc.: $55.00
Sgl. Oc.: $35.00
Third Person: $10.00

Steep Acres Farm Bed & Breakfast—Located 2 miles from Williams College. A country home in a high knoll, spectacular views. Trout & swimming pond on working 52 acre farm.

Worthington

Korzec, Ellen & Walter
HC 65, Box 96, 01098
(413) 238-5914

Amenities: 1,2,6,7,8,10,12
Breakfast: Full

Dbl. Oc.: $50.00
Sgl. Oc.: $30.00
Third Person: $10.00

The Hill Gallery is located just 2 1/2 miles from Rt. 9 in the Berkshires. An owner designed and built, multi-level contemporary with separate five room cottage and swimming pool on 23 wooded acres.

AMENITIES

1. No Smoking
2. No Pets
3. No Children
4. Senior Citizen Rates
5. Tennis Available
6. Golf Available
7. Swimming Available
8. Skiing Available
9. Credit Cards Accepted
10. Personal Check Accepted
11. Off Season Rates
12. Dinner Available (w/sufficient notice)

Massachusetts

Yarmouth Port

Graham, Gerrie & Milt
83 Main St., 02675
(508) 362-5157

Amenities: 2-11
Breakfast: Full

Dbl. Oc.: $85.00-$135.00

Wedgewood Inn—6 rooms, 2 with private screened poches & 1 with a sitting room, private baths, fireplaces. Close to whale watching, fine restaurants, antique shops and museums. Golf, tennis and bike trails nearby.

Yarmouth Port

Perna, Malcolm
277 Main St., Rte. 6A, 02675
(508) 362-4348

Amenities: 1,2,9,10,11,12
Breakfast: Continental
Dbl. Oc.: $88.00
Sgl. Oc.: $77.00
Third Person: $20.00

Colonial House Inn was an old captian's mansion & is now a lovely inn serving breakfast & dinner to our guests. All rooms w/priv. bath, furnished w/antiques. Open 7 days, year round. TV, A/C, 1/2 mile to town center, 2 miles to airport & bus.

Yarmouth Port

Tilly, Sven
101 Main St., 02675
(508) 362-4496

Amenities: 2,3,5,6,7,10,11
Breakfast: Continental

Dbl. Oc.: $65.82
Sgl. Oc.: $54.85
Third Person: $10.00

Olde Captain's Inn—On the Cape. Charming restored captain's home. Private apartments also. 20% discount weekly. Third nite free. Spring, fall & winter lower off-season rates. Walk to fine restaurants & shops.

Yarmouth Port

Wright, Stephanie & Bill
1 Centre St., 02675
(508) 362-8910

Amenities: 1,2,4,9,10,11,12
Breakfast: Full

Dbl. Oc.: $71.31
Sgl. Oc.: $65.82
Third Person: $16.46

One Center Street Has wide-board pine floors. Parlour, dining rm. & fireplaced den are furnished with old tables, hutches, antique clocks, comfortable couches & chairs. Guest rooms have antique beds, dressers & private bath.

AMENITIES

1. No Smoking
2. No Pets
3. No Children
4. Senior Citizen Rates
5. Tennis Available
6. Golf Available
7. Swimming Available
8. Skiing Available
9. Credit Cards Accepted
10. Personal Check Accepted
11. Off Season Rates
12. Dinner Available (w/sufficient notice)

Michigan

The Wolverine State

Capital: Lansing
Statehood: January 26, 1837; the 26th state
State Motto: If You Seek Pleasant Peninsula, Look About You
State Song: "Michigan, My Michigan"
State Bird: Robin
State Flower: Apple Blossom
State Tree: White Pine

Michigan is known for its long history of automobile manufacturing. Henry Ford built his first automobile here in 1896. The city of Detroit became the center of this industry and is called 'The Automobile Capital of the World.'

To get automobiles to market, it was necessary to use the waterways that are readily available here. The Soo Canals at Sault Ste. Marie are the busiest ship canals in the western hemisphere. The railroads played a big part in this new industry, too. In 1855, the first railroad in Michigan was the Erie and Kalamazoo, linking Michigan with Ohio.

The people of Michigan like to enjoy life. They are known for their delight in having tourists visit and, in fact, tourism is very big here. The residents of Michigan use more of their lands for recreation than anything else.

Michigan

Allegan

Miller, Mrs. Gail
524 Marshall St., 49010
(616) 673-3621

Amenities: 2,3,4,5,6,7,8,9,10
Breakfast: Full
Dbl. Oc.: $55.00-$95.00
Sgl. Oc.: $45.00-$85.00
Third Person: $10.00

Winchester Inn—Let us pamper you in the elegance of a by-gone era in this historic 1863 Italianate mansion. Antiquing, downhill x-country skiing, Lake Michigan beaches nearby. Murder mystery weekend pkgs.

Caseville

Deprer, Beth & Michael
5048 Conkey Rd., 48725
(517) 856-3110

Amenities: 3,6,7,8,10
Breakfast: Full

Dbl. Oc.: $55.00
Sgl. Oc.: $45.00

Country Charm Farm, Bed & Breakfast—Located one and a half miles from Sleepers State Park. We offer several different animals to discover and enjoy. Our lovely home hospitality is country all the way, with a special breakfast in the morning.

Charlevoix

Shaw, Penny & Doug
113 Michigan, 49720
(616) 547-6606

Amenities: 1,2,3,9,10,11
Breakfast: Continental

Dbl. Oc.: $64.00-$85.00
Sgl. Oc.: $59.00-$80.00
Third Person: $16.00

The Bridge Street Inn offers a step back to a gentler era. The nine guest rooms furnished with antiques and quilts. Located downtown near restaurants, shops, and beaches.

Fennville

Kennedy, Edward, X.
5975-128th Ave., 49408
(616) 561-2491

Amenities: 2,3,10
Breakfast: Full

Dbl. Oc.: $78.00-$93.60
Sgl. Oc.: $78.00-$93.60

Hidden Pond Farm rests on 28 acres of woodland. Tranquil & quiet atmosphere. 13 rooms decorated with antiques & period furniture. 2 living rooms w/fireplaces, guest rooms have decks overlooking the ravine & pond.

AMENITIES

1. No Smoking	4. Senior Citizen Rates	7. Swimming Available	10. Personal Check Accepted
2. No Pets	5. Tennis Available	8. Skiing Available	11. Off Season Rates
3. No Children	6. Golf Available	9. Credit Cards Accepted	12. Dinner Available (w/sufficient notice)

Michigan

Frankenmuth

Hodge, M/M Richard
327 Ardussi St., 48734
(517) 652-9019

Amenities: 1,10
Breakfast: Continental

Dbl. Oc.: $31.20
Sgl. Oc.: $26.00

Bed And Breakfast At The Pines has a casual atmosphere in our private ranch-style home with a secluded yard in a quiet residential area within walking distance of main tourist shops & restaurants.

Grand Haven

Gray, Carolyn
114 S. Harbor, 49417
(616) 846-0610

Amenities: 1,2,3,5,6,7,8,9,10,11
Breakfast: Continental

Dbl. Oc.: $79.50-$121.90
Third Person: $25.00

Harbor House Inn—All new construction which recaptures the splendor of yesteryear. Each room is spacious and distinctive and offers a scenic vista of the harbor. Homemade breads to toast. Convenient location to shops.

Grand Haven

Meyer, Susan
20009 Breton
Spring Lake, 49456
(616) 842-8409

Amenities: 2,5,6,7,8,9,10,11
Breakfast: Full

Dbl. Oc.: $63.60-$79.50
Sgl. Oc.: $63.60-$79.50
Third Person: $20.00

Seascape Bed & Breakfast—Nautical seashore cottage on the beautiful sands of Lake Michigan. Relax on private beach or sundeck. Scenic lake front rooms. Full breakfast served overlooking Grand Haven Harbor. Open year round.

Holland

Plaggemars, Fran & Dave
133 West 11th St., 49423
(616) 396-6601

Amenities: 1,2,3,4,5,6,8,9,10,11
Breakfast: Continental

Dbl. Oc.: $45.00-$75.00
Third Person: $10.00

Old Holland Inn—1895 Victorian inn. Original oak, brass, fireplace, & stained glass! Patio breakfasts with china and linens. Fresh flowers, chocolates. Air conditioning. Listed in national register. Dunes, Lake Michigan! Nice!

Holland

Verwys, Bonnie
6 East 24th St., 49423
(616) 396-1316

Amenities: 1,2,3,4,5,6,7,8,10,11
Breakfast: Full

Dbl. Oc.: $52.00-$72.80
Sgl. Oc.: $42.00-$62.80

The Parsonage 1908—Charming, A-1 quiet residential neighborhood. Close to Hope College, summer theatre, shopping, Saugatuck Resort, Lake Michigan, excellent dining. 3 hrs. to Chicago, Detroit, Traverce City. By plane-10 min. to airport & businesses.

AMENITIES

1. No Smoking
2. No Pets
3. No Children
4. Senior Citizen Rates
5. Tennis Available
6. Golf Available
7. Swimming Available
8. Skiing Available
9. Credit Cards Accepted
10. Personal Check Accepted
11. Off Season Rates
12. Dinner Available (w/sufficient notice)

Michigan

Ithaca

Chaffin, Mrs. Sue
3239 W. St. Charles Rd., 48847
(517) 463-4081

Amenities: 1
Breakfast: Full

Dbl. Oc.: $36.40
Sgl. Oc.: $20.80
Third Person: $10.40

Chaffin Farms Bed & Breakfast—Three bedrooms furnished with family antiques. Guests are welcome to use the parlor, garden, fireplace and bicycles. Full country breakfast served in the family kitchen. Working 600 acre cash crop farm.

Lakeside

Lawrence, Jean
15093 Lakeshore Rd., 49116
(616) 469-1416

Amenities: 2,3,5,7,8,9,10
Breakfast: Full
Dbl. Oc.: $77.00
Sgl. Oc.: $72.00
Third Person: $5.00

The Pebble House—1912 craftsman style buildings connected by wooden walkways. 7 period rooms. Like going home to Grandmas. Private baths, Scandinavian breakfast, fireplaces, decks, across from Lake Michigan.

Ludington

Schneider, Robert
2458 S. Beaune Rd., 49431
(616) 843-9768

Amenities: 1,5,6,7,8,10
Breakfast: Full

Dbl. Oc.: $33.00-$49.00
Sgl. Oc.: $26.00-$42.00
Third Person: $7.00

Bed & Breakfast At Ludington—Very private acres close to town & Lake Michigan summer beaches, salmon charter & Wisconsin Ferry. Use our 3-acre lawn picnic area, hot tub, groom XC, snow-shoe, toboggan, 5 bedrooms, 3 baths, crib.

Mackinac Island

Bacon, Dr. & Mrs. Michael, M.
Market St., 49757
(906) 847-6234 or (616) 627-2055

Amenities: 2,4,5,6,7,9,10,11
Breakfast: Continental
Dbl. Oc.: $97.76-$130.00
Sgl. Oc.: $97.76-$130.00
Third Person: $15.60

Metivier Inn—Charming country inn, located in historic downtown area. 15 rooms, two efficiencies with queen beds and private baths. Large wicker furnished front porch; cozy living room with fireplace. Open May-Oct.

AMENITIES

1. No Smoking
2. No Pets
3. No Children
4. Senior Citizen Rates
5. Tennis Available
6. Golf Available
7. Swimming Available
8. Skiing Available
9. Credit Cards Accepted
10. Personal Check Accepted
11. Off Season Rates
12. Dinner Available (w/sufficient notice)

Michigan

Mecosta

Huisgen, Elaine & Frank
9765 Blue Lake Lodge Ln.
Box 1, 49332
(616) 972-8391

Amenities: 1,2,7,10
Breakfast: Continental
Dbl. Oc.: $36.40
Sgl. Oc.: $31.20

Blue Lake Lodge—located on a beautiful lake in west central Mich. 9 bedrooms, entire lodge available. Fishing, boating, gazebo & lots of lawn furniture. Gas & charcoal grills. Open year round. Get the most for vacation dollars.

Niles

Behre, Ms. Nan
950 South Third St., 49120
(616) 683-0876

Amenities: 2,5,6,7,8,9,10
Breakfast: Full

Dbl. Oc.: $44.00-$52.00
Sgl. Oc.: $37.00-$45.00
Third Person: $10.00

Woods & Hearth B&B—Charming 10 room colonial on 9 acres of woods and lawn. Close to I-80 & 90, Notre Dame Univ., antique mall, water and winter sports, nature center and winery. Fine restaurants.

Niles

Semler, M/M Phillip
518 N. 4th, 49120
(616) 683-6079

Amenities: 1,2,9,10
Breakfast: Full

Dbl. Oc.: $47.70
Sgl. Oc.: $47.70
Third Person: $10.00

Yesterday's Inn B&B—5 unique rooms w/private bath 2 blocks from the small quaint town of Niles on St. Joe River. Located 8 miles north of Notre Dame University off I-80. Antiques & shops within walking distance. Hot tub.

Pentwater

Gunn, Ms. Janet
180 E. Lowell, Box 98, 49449
(616) 869-5909

Amenities: 2,3,5,7,8,9,10
Breakfast: Full
Dbl. Oc.: $43.68-$57.20
Sgl. Oc.: $31.20
Third Person: $10.00

The Pentwater Inn—Open all year, gift certificates available. Walk to town beach, charter boats. Six rooms, one with private bath. Tandem bike, ping pong, Victorian house built in 1880. Come for retreats, family reunions, quiet getaway.

AMENITIES

1. No Smoking
2. No Pets
3. No Children
4. Senior Citizen Rates
5. Tennis Available
6. Golf Available
7. Swimming Available
8. Skiing Available
9. Credit Cards Accepted
10. Personal Check Accepted
11. Off Season Rates
12. Dinner Available (w/sufficient notice)

Michigan

Plymouth

Lorenz, The Family
827 W. Ann Arbor Tr., 48170
(313) 453-1620

Amenities: 1,2,6,9,10,12
Breakfast: Full
Dbl. Oc.: $75.60
Sgl. Oc.: $65.10
Third Person: $10.00

Mayflower Bed & Breakfast Hotel—A 60-year-old family owned and operated inn, located in colonial downtown Plymouth. Within walking distance of 150 shops, a movie theatre and a park.

Port Austin

Babcock, Lori
8510 Lake St., 48467
(517) 738-5253

Amenities: 2,5,6,7,10,11
Breakfast: Continental
Dbl. Oc.: $50.00
Sgl. Oc.: $40.00
Third Person: $5.00

Questover Inn—Circa 1850, this 3-story Victorian inn is located within walking distance to the beach, harbor, shopping and dining in the New England style village of Port Austin. Come and experience life 'The way it was.'

Port Huron

Marinez, Sheila
1229 Seventh St., 48060
(313) 984-1437

Amenities: 2,5,7,9,10,12
Breakfast: Continental
Dbl. Oc.: $45.00-$60.00

The Victorian Inn, featuring dining and guest rooms in authentically restored elegance one hour north of Detroit where the beautiful Bluewater Bridge crosses into Canada at Lake Huron.

AMENITIES

1. No Smoking
2. No Pets
3. No Children
4. Senior Citizen Rates
5. Tennis Available
6. Golf Available
7. Swimming Available
8. Skiing Available
9. Credit Cards Accepted
10. Personal Check Accepted
11. Off Season Rates
12. Dinner Available (w/sufficient notice)

Michigan

Port Sanilac

Denison, Mrs. Shirley
111S Ridge (M-25), 48461
(313) 622-8800

Amenities: 1,2,3,6,7,10,11
Breakfast: Continental

Dbl. Oc.: $52.00
Sgl. Oc.: $52.00
Third Person: $10.40

Raymond House Inn—Gracious Victorian built in 1871 at Lake Huron by lumber merchants. Antiqued-filled 7 rooms, all private baths. Marina, charters, salmon fishing. Two hours north of Detroit.

Saline

Grossman, Mrs. Shirley
9279 Macon Rd., 48176
(313) 429-9625

Amenities: 2,3,5,6,8,9,10
Breakfast: Full

Dbl. Oc.: $47.00-$52.00
Sgl. Oc.: $27.00-$47.00
Third Person: $16.00

The Homestead B&B—1851 brick farmhouse: comfort, country, Victorian elegance; walk, relax, X/C ski, 15 minutes to Ann Arbor & Ypsilanti, 40 minutes to Detroit or Toledo. Children over 12. By reservation only.

Saugatuck

Benkert, Ronald L.
131 Griffith B-1106, 49453
(616) 857-4249

Amenities: 5,6,7,8,9,10,11,12
Breakfast: Continental

Dbl. Oc.: $75.00
Sgl. Oc.: $75.00
Third Person: $10.00

Newnham Inn—A turn-of-the-century Victorian home located downtown. Period furnishings, air-conditioning, pool, hot tub. Walk to shopping, beaches, recreational facilities. Winter sports. Open all seasons.

Saugatuck

Louis, Dr. & Mrs. Warren E.
510 Butler Street, 49453
(616) 857-1097

Amenities: 2-11
Breakfast: Continental
Rates: $65.00-$115.00

Wickwood Inn—Elegance and style near Lake Michigan shore. Featured in Brides and Glamour magazines. Antiques, Laura Ashley decor. 11 bedrooms, 11 baths. Air conditioned. Steps from great shops, restaurants, & yacht harbor.

AMENITIES

1. No Smoking
2. No Pets
3. No Children
4. Senior Citizen Rates
5. Tennis Available
6. Golf Available
7. Swimming Available
8. Skiing Available
9. Credit Cards Accepted
10. Personal Check Accepted
11. Off Season Rates
12. Dinner Available (w/sufficient notice)

Michigan

Saugatuck

Mitchell, Donald
428 Butler St., P.O. Box 1059, 49453
(616) 857-2788

Amenities: 5-12
Breakfast: Continental
Dbl. Oc.: $56.16-$139.36
Sgl. Oc.: $56.16-$139.36
Third Person: $10.40

The Maplewood Hotel—Downtown restored resort hotel. 13 rooms, private baths, some with fireplaces and double jacuzzi tubs. A/C and cable TV. Spacious lounge areas, gourmet restaurants. Open all year.

Saugatuck

Petty, Lynda
888 Holland St., 49453
(616) 857-4535

Amenities: 9,10,11
Breakfast: Continental

Dbl. Oc.: $62.40-$78.00
Sgl. Oc.: $62.40-$78.00
Third Person: $10.00

The Park House—Built in 1857, Park House is Saugatuck's oldest residence. Private rooms & a 2 bedroom suite offer the comfort of queen beds & private baths with the charm of wide plank pine floors & period antiques.

Saugatuck

Simcik, Mrs. Denise
900 Lake St., P.O. Box 881
49453
(616) 857-4346

Amenities: 2,5,6,7,8,9,10,11
Breakfast: Continental

Dbl. Oc.: $49.00-$89.00

Twin Gables Country Inn And Cottages—The state historic country inn offers warm hospitality in a charming setting overlooking the lake. Private baths, fireplace, swimming pool, indoor hot tub, also three cottages for weekly rental. Open all year.

Saugatuck

Tatsch, M/M Terry
633 Pleasant St., 49453
(616) 857-2919

Amenities: 1-11
Breakfast: Continental
Dbl. Oc.: $67.60-$98.80
Third Person: $15.00

Kemah Guest House is furnished throughout with antiques that accent the history of the house. The interior is immaculate and sports a combination of old world German flavor, art deco and south western airiness.

AMENITIES

1. No Smoking
2. No Pets
3. No Children
4. Senior Citizen Rates
5. Tennis Available
6. Golf Available
7. Swimming Available
8. Skiing Available
9. Credit Cards Accepted
10. Personal Check Accepted
11. Off Season Rates
12. Dinner Available (w/sufficient notice)

Minnesota

The Gopher State

Capital: St. Paul
Statehood: May 11, 1858; the 32nd state
State Motto: The Star of the North
State Song: "Hail! Minnesota"
State Bird: Common Loon
State Flower: Pink and White Lady's Slipper
State Tree: Norway Pine

Minnesota is the land of ten thousand lakes. Many of its cities and towns are named for lakes, falls or rapids. For every 20 acres of land, there is an acre of water. It is a popular playground for campers and canoers, with its many acres of wilderness along each lake site. Water skiing was developed here and the blue lakes attract swimmers, boaters and fishermen.

This state's million dairy cows make it a leading butter producing state. And with its flour mills it isn't hard to see how it got the name of "the bread and butter state."

The city of Duluth is its major port on Lake Superior. From here the grain and manufactured products of Minnesota are shipped to the Great Lakes cities and overseas.

The Mayo Clinic was established at Rochester in 1889 by Dr. William W. May and his two sons, William and Charles. It is one of the greatest medical research centers in the world.

Minnesota

Cannon Falls

Anderson, Denise & Karpinsky, David
615 West Hoffman St., 55009
(507) 263-5507

Amenities: 1,2,5,6,7,8,9,10,12
Breakfast: Full
Dbl. Oc.: $60.00-$105.00
Sgl. Oc.: $50.00-$95.00
Third Person: $10.00

Quill & Quilt—1897 Colonial revival home. 4 guest rooms, suite with whirlpool, A/C, all private baths; in scenic Cannon River Valley; biking, hiking, skiing, canoeing, etc. Evening social hour. 1 hour from Twin cities.

Dassel

Gabrielson, Elaine & Don
R. Rt., 1, Box 269, 55325
(612) 275-3609

Amenities: 1,2,3,4,5,8,10
Breakfast: Continental

Dbl. Oc.: $42.00
Sgl. Oc.: $37.00
Third Person: $10.00

Gabrielson's B&B—Perched on a hilltop, this 1910 white clapboard farmhouse, decorated in country style, overlooking a private lake. A paddleboat is at your use and a canoe. Wine, cheese and rolls in the frig. Hot tub to use.

Deerwood

Manly, Anne & Richard
Rt. #1, Box 193, 56444
(612) 692-4379

Amenities: 2,3,5,6,7,8,10
Breakfast: Full

Dbl. Oc.: $63.60
Sgl. Oc.: $47.70

Walden Woods Bed & Breakfast—Enjoy the natural serenity of this spacious log home beautifully furnished with antiques and collectables located on a secluded lake in the Brainerd recreational area.

Dodge Center

Chapin, Mrs. Margaret
Route 1, Box 215, 55927
(507) 527-2311

Amenities: 2,5,6,7,10,12
Breakfast: Full
Dbl. Oc.: $35.00-$45.00
Sgl. Oc.: $25.00-$35.00
Third Person: $10.00

Eden Bed & Breakfast—1898 home in country near historic Mantorville. 25 miles from Rochester Mayo Clinic. 4 rooms, antique decor; located 3 miles north of Hwy. 14 on Hwy. 56, and 1/4 mile east on County Rd. 16. Families welcome.

AMENITIES

1. No Smoking
2. No Pets
3. No Children
4. Senior Citizen Rates
5. Tennis Available
6. Golf Available
7. Swimming Available
8. Skiing Available
9. Credit Cards Accepted
10. Personal Check Accepted
11. Off Season Rates
12. Dinner Available (w/sufficient notice)

Minnesota

Garvin

Reinert, Charles P.
R.R. 1, Glenview, 56132
(507) 629-4808

Amenities: 1,8,10,12
Breakfast: Full

Dbl. Oc.: $48.76
Sgl. Oc.: $43.46
Third Person: $5.00

Glenview Bed & Breakfast—A prairie home cozy and serene located on 100 acres of private prairie land. Wooded hiking trails, nearby recreational lakes. Soak in freedom of S.W. Minnesota, pioneer history to explore. Fireplace.

Good Thunder

Christensen, Mavis
Rt. 2, Box 147, 56037
(507) 524-3813

Amenities: 10
Breakfast: Full

Dbl. Oc.: $47.70
Sgl. Oc.: $37.10
Third Person: $10.00

Cedar Knoll Farm B&B—138 acre working farm. Modern Cape Cod house; three double guest rooms; shared bath. Children welcome. Eclectic decor. Country European antiques. A "Peaceable kingdom" retreat. Brochure available.

Graceville

Walters, Joyce & Chuck
113 W. 2nd St., 56240
(612) 748-7657

Amenities: 2,5,6,7,10
Breakfast: Continental

Dbl. Oc.: $31.80
Sgl. Oc.: $26.50
Third Person: $5.30

Lakeside Bed & Breakfast—Comfortable two story home on small lake. Private baths, TV, sun room, large deck. Walking distance to park and golf course. Hunters welcome.

Grand Marais

Beattie, Mary & Scott
Box 181, Gunflint Trail, 55604
(218) 387-1276, (800) 542-1226

Amenities: 1,2,8,9,10,11
Breakfast: Full
Dbl. Oc.: $58.00-$80.00
Sgl. Oc.: $53.00-$75.00
Third Person: $16.00

Pincushion Mountain Bed & Breakfast—
3 mi. from Grand Marais Ridge overlooking north shore of Lake Superior 1000 ft. below. Four guestrooms, country decor. Great hiking, mountain biking, X-C ski trails at the doorstep. Free brochure.

AMENITIES

1. No Smoking
2. No Pets
3. No Children
4. Senior Citizen Rates
5. Tennis Available
6. Golf Available
7. Swimming Available
8. Skiing Available
9. Credit Cards Accepted
10. Personal Check Accepted
11. Off Season Rates
12. Dinner Available (w/sufficient notice)

Minnesota

Grand Marais

Kerfoot, Sue & Bruce
Gunflint Trail, Box 100, 55604
(800) 328-3325

Amenities: 7,8,9,10,12
Breakfast: Full
Dbl. Oc.: $110.00
Sgl. Oc.: $55.00
Third Person: $30.00

Gunflint Lodge—Country inn type lodge next to the boundary waters wilderness. Nature activity program, fishing, hiking, swimming, canoeing, dining room, cabins w/fireplace, cross country skiing, sauna, lit ski trails.

Hendricks

Larson, Mrs. Joan
Rt. 1, Box 141, 56136
(507) 275-3740

Amenities: 1,2,10
Breakfast: Full

Dbl. Oc.: $35.00
Sgl. Oc.: $30.00
Third Person: $5.00

Triple L Farm Bed And Breakfast, a 283-acre working family farm. Snuggle under the covers of homemade quilts. Rise to the aroma of a farm fresh breakfast. Experience the sounds and sights of nature.

Lake City

Grettenberg, Sandra & Joel
620 South St., 55041
(612) 345-2167

Amenities: 1,2,3,5,6,7,8,10
Breakfast: Continental
Dbl. Oc.: $45.00-$55.00
Sgl. Oc.: $40.00-$45.00
Third Person: $5.00

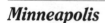

The Victorian Bed And Breakfast—1896 Victorian. Each room with a lake view. Carved wood work, stained glass, antique music boxes and furnishings; air conditioned; dinner cruises. 65 miles south of Minneapolis on Hwy. 61, 35 miles south to Mayo Clinic.

Minneapolis

Evelo, Sheryl & David
2301 Bryant Ave., S., 55405
(612) 374-9656

Amenities: 10
Breakfast: Full

Dbl. Oc.: $30.00-$35.00
Sgl. Oc.: $20.00-$25.00
Third Person: $10.00

Evelo's Bed & Breakfast—Located in the historic Lowry Hill East neighborhood. Close to downtown, Gutherie Theatre, city lakes, many restaurants, Walker Art Center and Minneapolis Institute of Art. Only 1/2 block to bus stop.

AMENITIES

1. No Smoking
2. No Pets
3. No Children
4. Senior Citizen Rates
5. Tennis Available
6. Golf Available
7. Swimming Available
8. Skiing Available
9. Credit Cards Accepted
10. Personal Check Accepted
11. Off Season Rates
12. Dinner Available (w/sufficient notice)

Minnesota

Morris

Berget, Mrs. Karen
410 E. Third St., 56267
(612) 589-4054

Amenities: 2,5,6,7,10
Breakfast: Full

Dbl. Oc.: $35.00-$40.0
Sgl. Oc.: $20.00-$35.00
Third Person: $42.00

The American House is a Victorian home decorated with antiques and country charm. Ride our tandem bike on scenic trails. Within walking distance to area restaurants and shops. Located 1 block from Univ. of Minneapolis Morris Campus.

Park Rapids

Dickson, Mrs. Helen K.
202 E. 4th St., 56470
(218) 732-8089
(800) 426-2019

Amenities: 1,2,5,9,10,11
Breakfast: Continental

Dbl. Oc.: $25.50-$34.50
Sgl. Oc.: $19.50-$28.50

Dickson Viking Huss—Cedar sided home, rock deck, living room w/vaulted ceiling, & fireplace. Close to: fun, food, & shops. King room w/private bath & electric fireplace; Queen & prince rooms w/electric heater & shared bath. A/C.

Red Wing

Whalker, Jane
706 W. 4th, 55066
(612) 388-5945

Amenities: 6,8,10,11
Breakfast: Continental

Dbl. Oc.: $69.00-$89.00
Sgl. Oc.: $65.00-$85.00
Third Person: $10.00

The Pratt-Taber Inn—A true step back in time in quaint fun filled river town. 14 room Italianate mansion; bike; Amtrack. National B&B adventure packages available, let us plan your trip via B&B.

Rochester

Van Sant, Ms. Jeffrey
723 2nd, St., SW, 55902
(507) 289-5553

Amenities: 1,2,3,5,6,7,8,9,10
Breakfast: Full

Dbl. Oc.: $71.50
Sgl. Oc.: $60.50

Canterbury Inn Bed & Breakfast—Walk to: Mayo Clinic, fine dining, antiquing. All private baths, A/C, evening hors' doeuvres & libations, fabulous breakfasts, in bed if desired. All the comforts of a fine hotel in a lovely B&B setting.

AMENITIES

1. No Smoking
2. No Pets
3. No Children
4. Senior Citizen Rates
5. Tennis Available
6. Golf Available
7. Swimming Available
8. Skiing Available
9. Credit Cards Accepted
10. Personal Check Accepted
11. Off Season Rates
12. Dinner Available (w/sufficient notice)

Minnesota

St. Paul

Gustafson, Donna
984 Ashland Ave., 55104
(612) 227-4288

Amenities: 1,2,10
Breakfast: Continental
Dbl. Oc.: $55.12-$90.10
Sgl. Oc.: $44.52-$79.50
Third Person: $8.00

Chatsworth Bed And Breakfast—Spacious, lace-curtained Victorian home in quiet, convenient neighborhood. 15 minutes from airport and downtown Minneapolis. Walk to shopping area. 2 whirlpool baths.

Spring Valley

Chase, Jeannine & Bob
508 N. Huron Ave., 55975
(507) 346-2850

Amenities: 1,2,5,6,7,8,9,10
Breakfast: Full

Dbl. Oc.: $65.00

Chase's—1879 mansion listed on national register, located in historic Bluff County. Near: Amish areas, Laura Ingalls-Wilder site, caves, bird watching, canoeing, trout & bass fishing, hiking, bike, & X-C ski trails.

AMENITIES

1. No Smoking
2. No Pets
3. No Children
4. Senior Citizen Rates
5. Tennis Available
6. Golf Available
7. Swimming Available
8. Skiing Available
9. Credit Cards Accepted
10. Personal Check Accepted
11. Off Season Rates
12. Dinner Available (w/sufficient notice)

Mississippi

The Magnolia State

Capital: Jackson
Statehood: December 10, 1817; the 20th state
State Motto: By Valor and Arms
State Song: "Go Mis-sis-sip-pi"
State Bird: Mockingbird
State Flower: Magnolia
State Tree: Magnolia

Once a land of quiet towns, Mississippi is fast becoming an urbanized state. Although the cotton growing industry is still an important industy here, more and more people are being employed in the lumber and manufacturing of wood product industries.

Because Mississippi has a warm climate with long summers and short winters, more tourists are vacationing here and finding it an enjoyable retreat. There are large, sunny beaches along the Gulf Coast and fine hotels. Costumed guides are available to show visitors through the handsome mansions and plantations. There is also excellent hunting and fishing, but most of all, genteel and wonderful southern hospitality.

Mississippi

Lorman

Hylander, Col. & Mrs. Walt
Route 552, 39096
(601) 437-4215

Amenities: 2,4,9,10,12
Breakfast: Full
Dbl. Oc.: $79.50
Sgl. Oc.: $68.90
Third Person: $26.50

Rosswood Plantation—An 1857 mansion on a real plantation near Natchez and Vickburg, offers: luxury, privacy, romance, charm and hospitality. Ideal for honeymoons. Mississippi landmark, national register, AAA approved.

Natchez

Bryne, Mayor & Mrs. Tony
712 N. Union, 39120
(601) 442-1344,
(800) 654-8859

Amenities: 2,3,7,9,10,12
Breakfast: Full

Dbl. Oc.: $81.00-$135.00
Sgl. Oc.: $70.20-$124.20
Third Person: $21.60

The Burn—One of Natchez's most historical pure Greek revival mansions. The Burn pampers overnight guests with: seated plantation breakfast, tours, & a swimming pool. Dinner parties, lunches & picnics may be arranged.

Natchez

Feltus, Jeanette
1 Linden Pl., 39120
(601) 445-5472

Amenities: 5,6,10
Breakfast: Full
Dbl. Oc.: $81.00
Sgl. Oc.: $70.20
Third Person: $21.60

Linden is situated on seven acres of park-like grounds in downtown Natchez's historic district. Furnished in 18th & 19th century antiques the inn offers a cozy atmosphere and delicious food. Four star rated.

Natchez

Hedderel, Mr.
211 Clifton Ave., 39120
(601) 446-5730

Amenities: 2,10,12
Breakfast: Continental

Dbl. Oc.: $75.00
Sgl. Oc.: $65.00
Third Person: $20.00

Riverside—Overlooking the Mississippi River, beautiful rooms with antiques in center of town. Private baths, teester beds.

AMENITIES

1. No Smoking
2. No Pets
3. No Children
4. Senior Citizen Rates
5. Tennis Available
6. Golf Available
7. Swimming Available
8. Skiing Available
9. Credit Cards Accepted
10. Personal Check Accepted
11. Off Season Rates
12. Dinner Available (w/sufficient notice)

Mississippi

Pontotoc

Walls, Danny
27 Oxford St., 38863
(601) 489-8484

Amenities: 6,9,10,11,12
Breakfast: Full

Dbl. Oc.: $50.00
Sgl. Oc.: $45.00

The Nisbet House was built in 1888. 5 bedrooms downstairs, private baths, large shaded lot, 15 miles from Tupelo, Mississippi birth place of Elvis Presley. Historic surroundings. Private reading room, quiet neighborhood.

Port Gibson

Lum, M/M William D.
1207 Church St., 39150
(601) 437-4350, 437-5300

Amenities: 1,2,5,6,7,9,20
Breakfast: Full
Dbl. Oc.: $65.00-$75.00
Sgl. Oc.: $55.00-$65.00
Third Person: $15.00

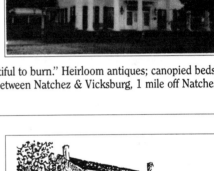

Oak Square—Antebellum mansion in the town General U.S. Grant said was "Too beautiful to burn." Heirloom antiques; canopied beds; national register. Located on U.S. Hwy. 61, between Natchez & Vicksburg, 1 mile off Natchez Trace Pkwy.

Vicksburg

Mackey, Estelle & Ted
2200 Oak St., 39180
(601) 636-1605, (800) 862-1300

Amenities: 1,2,7,9,10,11
Breakfast: Full
Dbl. Oc.: $65.00-$105.00
Sgl. Oc.: $65.00-$75.00
Third Person: $20.00

Cedar Grove—A magnificent mansion inn, circa 1840; the largest Antebellum home in Vicksburg. Romantic gasoliers throughout the house; 18 guest rooms, all with private baths and beautifully furnished; pool & spa; situated on 4 acres.

AMENITIES

1. No Smoking
2. No Pets
3. No Children
4. Senior Citizen Rates
5. Tennis Available
6. Golf Available
7. Swimming Available
8. Skiing Available
9. Credit Cards Accepted
10. Personal Check Accepted
11. Off Season Rates
12. Dinner Available (w/sufficient notice)

Mississippi

Vicksburg

Whitney, Bettye & Cliff
601 Klein St., 39180
(601) 636-7421

Amenities: 9,10,11
Breakfast: Full
Dbl. Oc.: $70.00-$90.00
Sgl. Oc.: $60.00-$80.00
Third Person: $20.00

The Corners—Mansion has original parterre gardens, sixty foot long gallery across the front with a spectacular view of the Mississippi. 7 bedrooms with private baths, TVs, & antiques. On national register; convenient location.

AMENITIES

1. No Smoking
2. No Pets
3. No Children
4. Senior Citizen Rates
5. Tennis Available
6. Golf Available
7. Swimming Available
8. Skiing Available
9. Credit Cards Accepted
10. Personal Check Accepted
11. Off Season Rates
12. Dinner Available (w/sufficient notice)

Missouri

Show Me State

Capital: Jefferson City
Statehood: August 10, 1821; the 24th state
State Motto: The Welfare Of The People Shall Be The Supreme Law
State Song: "The Missouri Waltz"
State Bird: Bluebird
State Flower: Hawthorne
State Tree: Flowering Dogwood

Missouri is a state of yesterday's history and today's progress. Lewis and Clark started their trek to the Pacific Coast in 1804 from St. Louis, then called The Gateway to the West. The Pony Express originated in St. Joseph in 1860 and traveled across the west to Sacramento, California, bringing mail for the first time from one coast to another. The ice cream cone, hot dog and iced tea were all introduced and made popular at the 1904 St. Louis World's Fair. Jesse James was born here, as well as Samuel Clemens, who grew up to write about the adventures he and his friends had along the Mississippi River, and signed his name Mark Twain.

Today, the St. Louis Gateway Arch is the nation's tallest manmade monument and remains the symbol of St. Louis, The Gateway to the West. It is an important transportation city, with buying and selling of everything from cattle to antiques.

Tourism has become a very important part of Missouri's economy, and the climate during most of the year is pleasant enough to bring visitors here and, in some cases, very often to stay.

President Truman was born here and died here.

Missouri

Arrow Rock

Borgman, Kathy & Helen
706 Van Buren, 65320
(816) 837-3350

Amenities: 1,2
Breakfast: Continental

Dbl. Oc.: $40.00
Sgl. Oc.: $30.00
Third Person: $15.00

Borgman's Bed & Breakfast—Enjoy our comfortable century old home and homebaked breakfast in this national historic town. Professional theatre, antique shops, restaurants within walking distance. Come enjoy Arrow Rock, we do!

Carthage

Brewer, Renee & Arch
R.R. 1, 64836
(417) 358-6312

Amenities: 10
Breakfast: Full

Dbl. Oc.: $40.00
Sgl. Oc.: $40.00
Third Person: $10.00

Brewer's Maple Lane B&B—National historic 22 room home, on 676 acres, furnished mostly with family heirlooms. Tours, gamerooms, 22 acre lake, hunt, fish, play & picnic area, petting animals. 2 bedroom furnished cottage.

Carthage

Scoville, Mrs. Ella
1157 S. Main St., 64836
(417) 358-6145

Amenities: 1,2,10
Breakfast: Full

Dbl. Oc.: $42.54
Sgl. Oc.: $26.60

Hill House is a 100-year-old Victorian mansion full of antiques in this historic city, site of the 1st. Civil War battle, just 7 blocks to the famous courthouse. It has 10 fireplaces, stained glass, & an antique store.

Eminence

Peters, Mrs. Lynett
HCR 1, Box 11, 65466
(314) 226-3233

Amenities: 4,7,10,11
Breakfast: Continental

Dbl. Oc.: $52.00
Third Person: $8.00

River's Edge Bed And Breakfast Resort—Each room opens to a deck with steps down to the Jack's Fork River. Firewood & inner tubs are included. Eminence offers; canoe outfitters, horseback riding, swimming, hiking, & sight seeing!

Gravois Mills

Blochberger, M/M Min
R.R. #3
P.O. Box 338-D, 65037
(314) 372-2481

Amenities: 4,5,6,7
Breakfast: Full

Dbl. Oc.: $55.00
Sgl. Oc.: $26.50
Third Person: $15.00

Lingerlong—Summer home on the lake of Ozarks. Boating & golfing is just a few yards away. Arrive by boat or car. Recreation is nearby. Delicious homemade cinnamon rolls with full breakfast.

AMENITIES

1. No Smoking
2. No Pets
3. No Children
4. Senior Citizen Rates
5. Tennis Available
6. Golf Available
7. Swimming Available
8. Skiing Available
9. Credit Cards Accepted
10. Personal Check Accepted
11. Off Season Rates
12. Dinner Available (w/sufficient notice)

Missouri

Hannibal

Andreotti, Donalene & Mike
213 South Fifth St., 63401
(314) 221-0445

Amenities: 2,10,11,12
Breakfast: Full

Dbl. Oc.: $50.00
Sgl. Oc.: $40.00
Third Person: $7.00

Fifth Street Mansion Bed & Breakfast—Built in 1865 and on the national register of historic places, this home has unusual fireplaces, stained glass, & antiques. Restaurants, shops, Mark Twain historic district are within walking distance.

Hannibal

Feinberg, Diane & Irv
RR #1, New London Gravel Rd., 63401
(314) 221-2789

Amenities: 1,2,3,5,6,7,10
Breakfast: Full

Dbl. Oc.: $66.00
Third Person: $10.50

Garth Woodside Mansion—1871 Victorian mansion unchanged. A room to come to where romance and history come together. Pampering includes full elegant breakfast, turndown service and nightshirts. A feeling as much as a place.

Hannibal

Rendlen, Mrs. Charles
303 North Sixth St., 63401
(314) 221-7244

Amenities: 5,6,10,11
Breakfast: Full

Dbl. Oc.: $45.00
Sgl. Oc.: $39.00
Third Person: $10.00

The Admiral Coontz House—Historic (1854), comfortable, spacious, peaceful. Four blocks to Mark Twain home, Mississippi Riverfront, shops. Private baths, A/C, antiques, 2 porches, special breads, teatime extras. Children welcome.

Hermann

Birk, Gloria & Elmer
700 Goethe St., 65401
(314) 486-2911

Amenities: 2-10
Breakfast: Full
Dbl. Oc.: $61.37
Sgl. Oc.: $50.69
Third Person: $13.34

Birk's Goethe Street Gasthaus—Victorian mansion built by the 3rd largest winery in the world. B&B everyday except 2 weekends a month you can be Sherlock Holmes & solve a murder mystery. Write or call for information.

AMENITIES

1. No Smoking
2. No Pets
3. No Children
4. Senior Citizen Rates
5. Tennis Available
6. Golf Available
7. Swimming Available
8. Skiing Available
9. Credit Cards Accepted
10. Personal Check Accepted
11. Off Season Rates
12. Dinner Available (w/sufficient notice)

Missouri

Independence

Harold, Ruth & Lane
1212 W. Lexington, 64050
(816) 833-2233

Amenities: 1,2,4,9,11
Breakfast: Full

Dbl. Oc.: $45.00
Sgl. Oc.: $37.50
Third Person: $5.00

Woodstock Inn—In the heart of historic Independence; eleven guest rooms all with private baths, each tastefully decorated. Private parking; handicap accessible. Free city tourist bus nearby. Warm hospitality.

Jamesport

Smith, Jayla
Box 277, 64648
(816) 684-6664

Amenities: 1,2,3,9,10,11,12
Breakfast: Full
Dbl. Oc.: $47.80
Sgl. Oc.: $47.80
Third Person: $10.62

Richardson House Bed And Breakfast—
Antique filled farmhouse in Amish community, perfect for family adventure or romantic retreat. You'll enjoy the whole house to yourselves, sleeps 8. Amish shops, antiques, fishing, babysitting, TV, A/C.

Kansas City

Litchfield, Carolyn & Edward
217 East 37th St., 64111
(816) 753-2667

Amenities: 2,5,9,10
Breakfast: Full
Dbl. Oc.: $60.00-$90.00
Sgl. Oc.: $60.00-$90.00
Third Person: $7.50

Doanleigh Wallagh Inn—Located between Crown Center and the plaza, this 1904 Georgian style home is outfitted with English and American antiques. Five guest rooms, private baths, cable TV, 4 movie channels, phones, A/C.

AMENITIES

1. No Smoking
2. No Pets
3. No Children
4. Senior Citizen Rates
5. Tennis Available
6. Golf Available
7. Swimming Available
8. Skiing Available
9. Credit Cards Accepted
10. Personal Check Accepted
11. Off Season Rates
12. Dinner Available (w/sufficient notice)

Missouri

Marthasville

Jones, M/M Jim
Rt. 3, Box 410, 63357
(314) 433-2675

Amenities: 10
Breakfast: Full
Dbl. Oc.: $45.00
Sgl. Oc.: $30.00
Third Person: $15.00

Gramma's House is a lovely old farmhouse which sits atop a hill in the peace and quiet of the country. Located just outside of Marthasville, on Hwy D. Close to shops, wineries, Daniel Boone's home and monument.

New Haven

Kliethermes, Mrs. Mary Lee
RR 1, Box 42, 63068
(314) 239-3452

Amenities: 2,6,10,12
Breakfast: Continental
Dbl. Oc.: $95.00
Sgl. Oc.: $20.00
Third Person: $20.00

Augustin River Bluff Farm Guest House— Secluded 99 acre river view estate in the heart of the wine country. 1 hour west of St. Louis—near Hermann and Augusta. We will rent to private parties of 1-8 people.

Parkville

Coons, Lola & Bill
Rt. 22, 64152
(816) 891-1018

Amenities: 4,5,6,7,8,10,12
Breakfast: Full

Dbl. Oc.: $63.74
Sgl. Oc.: $53.11
Third Person: $15.00

Down To Earth Lifestyles—Farm near attractions & points of interest. Unique spacious earthcontact home. Country antique furnishings. Each guest room has pvt. bath, radio, color TV, & phone. Indoor pool nearby, fishing, animals, & walking.

Rogersville

Atkinson, Mrs. Lazelle
Rt. 11, Box 750, 65742
(417) 753-2930

Amenities: 2,10
Breakfast: Continental

Dbl. Oc.: $40.00
Sgl. Oc.: $30.00
Third Person: $5.00

Anchor Hill Lodge—Rock farm house on 1200 acre ranch. 2 guest rooms, each with private bath. 3 miles off U.S. Highway on gravel road. Children and horses welcome.

AMENITIES

1. No Smoking
2. No Pets
3. No Children
4. Senior Citizen Rates
5. Tennis Available
6. Golf Available
7. Swimming Available
8. Skiing Available
9. Credit Cards Accepted
10. Personal Check Accepted
11. Off Season Rates
12. Dinner Available (w/sufficient notice)

Missouri

Springfield

Brown, Ms. Karol
900 E. Walnut St., 65805
(417) 864-6346

Amenities: 1,2,3,9,10,12
Breakfast: Full
Dbl. Oc.: $70.00
Third Person: $15.00

Walnut Street Bed & Breakfast—A gracious 1894 Victorian inn in the historic district. Featured as the city's showcase home, all rooms have beautiful antiques and private baths. 1 block from S.M.S.U. and the Performing Arts Center.

Ste. Genevieve

Beckerman, Rob
1021 Market St., 63670
(314) 883-5881

Amenities: 5,6,7,9
Breakfast: Full

Dbl. Oc.: $36.80-$47.50
Sgl. Oc.: $42.15-$52.80
Third Person: $10.00

Steiger Haus situated in Historic Ste. Genevieve (est. 1735) near restored French Colonial tour homes. Steiger Haus (1880) features private suites, an indoor swimming pool, and special murder mystery weekends.

St. Louis

Milligan, Sarah & Jack
2156 Lafayette Ave., 63104
(314) 772-4429

Amenities: 2,10
Breakfast: Full

Dbl. Oc.: $37.80-$48.60
Sgl. Oc.: $43.20-$64.80
Third Person: $10.00

Lafayette House is an 1876 Victorian mansion "In the center of things to do in St. Louis." Children welcome. Private & shared baths, 3rd floor suite with kitchen. Resident cats.

St. Louis

Winter, Kendall
Box 922, 63188
(314) 664-4399

Amenities: 1,2,3,5,9,10
Breakfast: Continental

Dbl. Oc.: $48.00
Sgl. Oc.: $42.00
Third Person: $10.00

The Winter House—This 1897, 10 room 2+ story home with turret, has a pressed tin ceiling in the first floor bedroom with private bath. Near Shaw's Garden, Fox Theater & Powell Symphony. 3 miles to Union Station & downtown.

AMENITIES

1. No Smoking
2. No Pets
3. No Children
4. Senior Citizen Rates
5. Tennis Available
6. Golf Available
7. Swimming Available
8. Skiing Available
9. Credit Cards Accepted
10. Personal Check Accepted
11. Off Season Rates
12. Dinner Available (w/sufficient notice)

Missouri

Washington

Davis, Charles
Box 527, #3 Lafayette, 63090
(314) 239-2417

Amenities: 1,10,11
Breakfast: Full
Dbl. Oc.: $70.00
Sgl. Oc.: $65.00

Washington House, built circa 1837. This authentically restored inn, on the Missouri River, features: river views, canopy beds, antique furnishings, complimentary wine and full breakfast. Only 50 minutes west of St. Louis.

Washington

Drewel, Sunny
#4 Lafayette, 63090
(314) 239-6499, (800) 332-5223

Amenities: 1,2,5,6,7,8,9,10
Breakfast: Full
Dbl. Oc.: $110.00
Sgl. Oc.: $95.00
Third Person: $20.00

Zachariah Foss Guest House, overlooking the Missouri River, is in the heart of the wine country. Excellent restaurants & shops within walking distance. Tandem bike, wine & juice included. This entire 7 room historic house, embellished with antiques, is "yours"!!

Washington

Lause, Mrs. Norma
438 West Front St., 63090
(314) 239-5025

Amenities: 2,9,10
Breakfast: Continental
Dbl. Oc.: $60.00
Sgl. Oc.: $50.00
Third Person: $10.00

Schwegmann House Bed And Breakfast Inn—One hour west of St. Louis. Visit historic sites, hike wilderness trails, discover unique shops, enjoy excellent cuisine, tarry along the wide Missouri's romantic valley. . .and stay in an historic home!

AMENITIES

1. No Smoking	**4.** Senior Citizen Rates	**7.** Swimming Available
2. No Pets	**5.** Tennis Available	**8.** Skiing Available
3. No Children	**6.** Golf Available	**9.** Credit Cards Accepted

10. Personal Check Accepted	
11. Off Season Rates	
12. Dinner Available (w/sufficient notice)	

Montana

The Treasure State

Capital: Helena
Statehood: November 8, 1889; the 41st state
State Motto: Gold and Silver
State Song: "Montana"
State Bird: Western Meadow Lark
State Flower: Bitterroot
State Tree: Ponderosa Pine

This is Big Sky Country, the land of mountain goats and grizzly bears. Montana is the fourth largest state in the union. The mountains, the old gold camps and the vast lonely distances still make a visitor feel close to the American frontier.

The beautiful and exciting Glacier National Park is visited by hundreds of tourists every year. Sportsman from all over the world travel here to fish, hunt and enjoy the national forest, ranches and lodges.

Montana has its share of gold and silver mines as well as the largest deposit of copper in the world.

Montana

Bigfork

Burggraf, Natalie J.
Rainbow Dr., 59911
(406) 837-4608

Amenities: 7,8,10,11,12
Breakfast: Full

Dbl. Oc.: $55.00
Sgl. Oc.: $45.00

Burggraf's Countrylane Bed & Breakfast—47 miles south of Glacier Park on Swan Lake. Country log home, private baths, color TV, king size beds, complimentary fruit, wine & cheese. Nature paths, secluded area, fishing, hiking, snowmobiling atmosphere.

Bigfork

Doohan, Margot & Tom
675 Ferndale Dr., 59911
(406) 837-6851

Amenities: 4,5,6,7,8,9,10
Breakfast: Full

Dbl. Oc.: $50.00-$65.00
Sgl. Oc.: $42.50
Third Person: $10.00

O'Dauch'ain Country Inn is a log luxury mountain-style inn on 5 acres of solitude and artistry. It is the gateway to Glacier Park, Nat'l. Bison Range, Flathead & Sean Lake, Big Mountain skiing, Jewel Basin hiking, & "Bob Marshall."

Bozeman

Hillard, Doris & Larry
11521 Axtell Gateway Rd., 59715
(406) 763-4696

Amenities: 7,8,10,12
Breakfast: Full

Dbl. Oc.: $62.40
Sgl. Oc.: $52.00
Third Person: $5.20

Hillard's Bed And Breakfast—A warm hospitable peaceful setting, located 10 miles from Bozeman. Good fishing & hunting; 75 miles to Yellowstone Park. Children welcome. 2 ski resorts within 25 miles. Major airport 12 miles aways.

Bozeman

Tonn, Ruthmary
319 So. Williams, 59715
(406) 587-0982

Amenities: 1,2,9,10
Breakfast: Full

Dbl. Oc.: $60.00-$75.00
Sgl. Oc.: $50.00-$65.00
Third Person: $12.00

Voss Inn Bed & Breakfast—Magnificent decor! 2 hours from Yellowstone National Park. Walking distance to unique shopping, restaurants, and movies. Great skiing, fishing, hiking, etc. nearby. See the Museum of the Rockies.

East Glacier Park

Schauf, Mrs. Les
Box 144, 59434
(406) 226-4482

Amenities: 9,10,12
Breakfast: Continental

Dbl. Oc.: $30.00
Sgl. Oc.: $25.00

Bison Creek Ranch is on Highway 2 and has 6 modern cabins, nestled amongst the trees. We are near Glacier National Park where there are: yacht trips, hiking, fishing, golf, sightseeing, horseback riding, etc.

AMENITIES

1. No Smoking
2. No Pets
3. No Children
4. Senior Citizen Rates
5. Tennis Available
6. Golf Available
7. Swimming Available
8. Skiing Available
9. Credit Cards Accepted
10. Personal Check Accepted
11. Off Season Rates
12. Dinner Available (w/sufficient notice)

Montana

Polson

Hunter, Mrs. Ruth
802 7th Ave., W., 59860
(406) 883-2460

Amenities: 6,7
Breakfast: Continental

Dbl. Oc.: $20.80
Sgl. Oc.: $15.60
Third Person: $5.20

Ruth's Bed And Breakfast is 1 block from the city limits on Flathead River, with a view of the mountains. There is a cottage away from main home with porta-potties. Bath & showers can be had in main home & is shared, 1 room in main home; restaurant nearby.

Sula

Bacon, Sharon
760 HC 10 S., 59871
(406) 821-3508

Amenities: 1,8,10
Breakfast: Full
Dbl. Oc.: $40.00
Sgl. Oc.: $32.00
Third Person: $10.00

Camp Creek Inn—9 miles north of Lost Trail Pass on Hwy. 93. Great hunting, fishing & skiing. Horse stables, bring your horse & ride our 50 miles of trails, stabling nightly or weekly. Children welcome. Restaurants nearby.

Stevensville

Thompson, Lisa
852 Willoughby Rd., 59870
(406) 777-3145

Amenities: 1,2,5,6,7,8,10,12
Breakfast: Full

Dbl. Oc.: $36.40
Sgl. Oc.: $31.20
Third Person: $6.24

The Country Caboose is an authentic wooden caboose set on rails in the quiet countryside of the Bitterroot Valley. It sleeps two-three & the view from your pillow is spectacular. 35 miles south of Missoula.

Whitefish

Powell, Laurel & Cloan
P.O. Box 1527, 59937
(406) 752-5122

Amenities: 1,2,3,4,5,6,7,8,10,11,12
Breakfast: Full
Dbl. Oc.: $79.00
Sgl. Oc.: $69.00

Bear Country Inn—Montana country Victorian with mountain views near gateway to Glacier Nat'l. Park. Welcome tea & fruit. Each room with down comforter on antique queen bed, private bath & spa. Homemade breads and jams.

AMENITIES

1. No Smoking
2. No Pets
3. No Children
4. Senior Citizen Rates
5. Tennis Available
6. Golf Available
7. Swimming Available
8. Skiing Available
9. Credit Cards Accepted
10. Personal Check Accepted
11. Off Season Rates
12. Dinner Available (w/sufficient notice)

Nebraska

The Cornhusker State

Capital: Lincoln
Statehood: March 1, 1867; the 37th state
State Motto: 'Equality Before The Law'
State Song: "Beautiful Nebraska"
State Bird: Western Meadow Lark
State Flower: Goldenrod
State Tree: Cottonwood

The name Nebraska comes from the Oto Indian word, "Nebrathka" meaning flat water. Nebraska was a flat area of vast land with very cold winters and extremely hot summers when the first pioneers arrived. They came to farm and evidence of their hard labor can be seen where hundreds of trees first planted for shade, still stand today. "D" Street in Lincoln is famous for the many huge Oak trees that remain a symbol of these first settlers.

Every year, thousands of visitors drive the Nebraska Hwy that follows the Oregon and Morman trails. Ruts left by the pioneer's covered wagons can be seen along the roadside. In Gothesburg the Pony Express Station stands reminding us of where fresh supplies of horses were kept for the early mail carriers.

Today Omaha is the state's largest city and the center of trade and industry for eastern Nebraska and western Iowa. The capitol long ago moved from the open prairie is at Lincoln and is the second largest city of this state.

The leading crop is corn, but during WW II Nebraska farmers produced millions of tons of corn, oat, potatoes and wheat to meet the wartime shortage.

Nebraska is very proud of its well known sons & daughters: 38th President Gerald Ford, William Jennings Bryant, Willa Cather, Father Edward Flanagan, founder of Boys' Town, and Buffalo Bill Cody whose frontier ranch home still stands at Scout Rest near North Platte.

Nebraska

Gordon

Vinton, Chris & Pat
HC 84, Box 103, 69343
(308) 282-0835

Amenities: 8,11,12
Breakfast: Full

Dbl. Oc.: $60.00
Sgl. Oc.: $40.00

Spring Lake Ranch is 18,000 acres, 30 square miles for your entertainment. Hiking, horseback riding, memorable homecooked meals, antique furnishings, library & telescope. Very private. Maximum 10 guests. Reservation required.

Omaha

Jones, Theo & Donald
1617 S. 90th St., 68124
(402) 397-0721

Amenities: 6,10
Breakfast: Continental

Dbl. Oc.: $25.00
Sgl. Oc.: $20.00
Third Person: $10.00

Large, Comfortable Home on 1 acre of land, 5 minutes from I-80, near large shopping centers and racetrack.

Pawnee City

Dalluge, M/M Duane
1041 5th St., 68420
(402) 852-3131

Amenities: 1,2,5,6,7,9
Breakfast: Full

Dbl. Oc.: $31.50-$36.75
Sgl. Oc.: $31.50-$36.75

My Blue Heaven Bed & Breakfast is located 70 miles S. of Lincoln, NE. A few blocks to shopping, 2 parks, golf course, fine museum. 3 lakes, 15 minutes away. 20's house decorated with antiques, guilts & tatting.

AMENITIES

1. No Smoking
2. No Pets
3. No Children
4. Senior Citizen Rates
5. Tennis Available
6. Golf Available
7. Swimming Available
8. Skiing Available
9. Credit Cards Accepted
10. Personal Check Accepted
11. Off Season Rates
12. Dinner Available (w/sufficient notice)

Nevada

The Silver State

Capital: Carson City
Statehood: October 31, 1864; the 36th state
State Motto: All for Our Country
State Song: "Home Means Nevada"
State Bird: Mountain Bluebird
State Flower: Sagebrush
State Tree: Single Leaf Pinon

In this state, rich deposits of silver ore were discovered in 1859. Virginia City became the site of one of the largest bonanzas of silver ore discovered by Henry Comstock. The massive strike brought hundreds of prospectors rushing to Nevada to 'strike it rich'. Some did, but many others did not. Along with mining came ranching, but in early 1869 when mining became less lucrative, gambling was legalized and the beginning of the state's largest and fastest growing industries began, tourism.

Over twenty million people visit this state each year. They enjoy the night life and gambling of Las Vegas, Reno, Lake Tahoe and Virginia City, as well as the summer and winter sports.

Hoover Dam is another tourist attraction. Man-made, and one of the highest concrete dams in the world, measuring 726 ft. from base to crest.

Nevada

Genoa

Falcke, Mrs. Hope
188 Carson, P.O. Box 77, 89411
(702) 782-2640

Amenities: 5,6,7,10
Breakfast: Full

Dbl. Oc.: $50.00
Sgl. Oc.: $40.00

Orchard House in historic Genoa, Nevada's oldest town, is close to lake Tahoe, Virginia City, Reno & Carson City. This old house offers informal, relaxed & comfortable accommodations. Children welcome.

AMENITIES

1. No Smoking
2. No Pets
3. No Children
4. Senior Citizen Rates
5. Tennis Available
6. Golf Available
7. Swimming Available
8. Skiing Available
9. Credit Cards Accepted
10. Personal Check Accepted
11. Off Season Rates
12. Dinner Available (w/sufficient notice)

New Hampshire

The Granite State

Capital: Concord
Statehood: June 21, 1788; the 9th state
State Motto: Live Free or Die
State Song: "Old New Hampshire"
State Bird: Purple Finch
State Flower: Purple Lilac
State Tree: White Birch

The White Mountains make this New England state one of the most beautiful of all. Mt. Washington, the tallest mountain in this range, is one of the most popular attractions for visitors. It brings great excitement to the winter skier, and is a summer tourist delight. The mountain can be climbed either by foot, car or cog-railroad. In any case, it is not easy, and not everyone makes it to the top.

New Hampshire was settled in 1633 and the people worked the land and quarries. Factories sprung up, but in the late '30s and early '40s, they either moved south or closed completely. People had to look elsewhere for an income. Tourism became that other income. Today, tourism is a major source of income for this state.

The taxes are very low here and the people wish to keep them this way. Because of this, more and more people are moving here.

Daniel Webster and our 14th president, Franklin Pierce, were both born in New Hampshire.

New Hampshire

Alexandria

Clarke, Peg & Dick
652 Fowler River Rd., 03222
(603) 744-6066

Amenities: 2,7,8,10
Breakfast: Full

Dbl. Oc.: $40.66
Sgl. Oc.: $26.75
Third Person: $16.05

Stone Rest Bed & Breakfast—Spectacular views of Mt. Cardigan, near Newfound Lake. Fly fishing & picnicking on grounds. River frontage. Queen-sized rooms. Private & shared baths. Newly renovated cabins.

Antrim

Beehner, Barbara & Carl
R.R. 1, Box 78, 03440
(603) 588-6772

Amenities: 2,5,6,7,8,9,10
Breakfast: Full

Dbl. Oc.: $50.00-$65.00
Sgl. Oc.: $45.00-$58.00
Third Person: $15.00

The Steele Homestead Inn—Enjoy warm, personal hospitality in beautifully restored 1810 home. Lovely decor and filled with antiques. Four spacious guest rooms, 2 with private bath & fireplace. Friendly, relaxed atmosphere.

Bethlehem

Burns, Cheryl & Bob,
Mulkigan, Linda & Moe
Main St., 03574
(603) 869-3389

Amenities: 1,2,5,6,7,8,9,10,12
Breakfast: Full
Dbl. Oc.: $69.55
Sgl. Oc.: $37.45
Third Person: $10.70

The Mulburn Inn—A sprawling summer estate built in 1913 as a family retreat, known as the Ivie Estate. Seven spacious elegant rooms all with private baths. Minutes from Franconia Notch and Mt. Washington attractions.

Bethlehem

Newman, Grace & Hall, Judith
Valley View Ln.,
P.O. Box 118A, 03574
(603) 869-3978

Amenities: 2,5,6,7,9,10
Breakfast: Continental

Dbl. Oc.: $69.00-$80.00
Sgl. Oc.: $45.00-$80.00
Third Person: $10.00

The Highlands Inn—View spectacular fall foliage on our 100-acre mountain setting. 19 charming guest rooms; spacious fireplaced common areas; hot tub & trails at the inn. Antiquing nearby. Open Sept. & Oct. only.

AMENITIES

1. No Smoking
2. No Pets
3. No Children
4. Senior Citizen Rates
5. Tennis Available
6. Golf Available
7. Swimming Available
8. Skiing Available
9. Credit Cards Accepted
10. Personal Check Accepted
11. Off Season Rates
12. Dinner Available (w/sufficient notice)

New Hampshire

Bethlehem

Sims, M/M Bill
Strawberry Hill St., 03574
(603) 869-2647

Amenities: 2,5,6,7,8,10
Breakfast: Full
Dbl. Oc.: $60.00
Sgl. Oc.: $45.00
Third Person: $15.00

The Bells—In the heart of the White Mountains. I-93, exit 40, 2 1/2 miles east on Rt. 302. In town; walk to: golf, tennis, restaurants & shops. Choose one of our 3 suites or cupola room; private baths. Open all years.

Bradford

Cotter, Mrs. Barbara **Amenities:** 2,5,6,7,8,10,11,12 **Dbl. Oc.:** $37.45
Old Center Rd., 03221 **Breakfast:** Full **Sgl. Oc.:** $37.45
(603) 938-5571   **Third Person:** $10.00

Candlelight Inn—Rt. 114 historic Victorian inn. Minutes to all activities in 4-season Sunapee area. Attractively decorated, impeccably clean. Make yourself at home.

Bradford

Fullerton, Carol & Phil
Rte. 114, 03221
(603) 938-2136

Amenities: 2,7,8,9,10,12
Breakfast: Full
Dbl. Oc.: $80.00
Sgl. Oc.: $50.00
Third Person: $18.50

Mountain Lake Inn—A classic country inn, circa 1760, nestled in the foothills of the White Mountains. Hike our unspoiled 167 acres and swim from our private sandy beach. Three major ski areas closeby.

AMENITIES

1. No Smoking
2. No Pets
3. No Children
4. Senior Citizen Rates
5. Tennis Available
6. Golf Available
7. Swimming Available
8. Skiing Available
9. Credit Cards Accepted
10. Personal Check Accepted
11. Off Season Rates
12. Dinner Available (w/sufficient notice)

New Hampshire

Bradford

Mazol, Connie & Tom
Box 40, Main St., 03221
(603) 938-5309

Amenities: 4,5,6,7,8,9,10,12
Breakfast: Full
Dbl. Oc.: $73.80-$104.55
Sgl. Oc.: $68.80-$99.55
Third Person: $18.45

The Bradford Inn is a historical hotel, circa 1898, that has been restored to its Victorian splendor. Rooms or suites all with private bath. Enjoy gracious dining & fine accommodations while exploring the S.W. region.

Bradford

Munroe, Diane & Mike
Rt. 103, 03221
(603) 938-2920

Amenities: 2,5,6,7,8,9,10,11
Breakfast: Full

Dbl. Oc.: $53.80
Sgl. Oc.: $48.15
Third Person: $16.05

A 4-Season Bed & Breakfast near Mt. Sunapee, on Lake Todd. 6 rooms w/private bath in an 1860 Victorian on 10 acres. Guest kitchen, books & board games. Nearby are shops, restaurants, and activities.

Bridgewater

Edrick, Mrs. Barbara
Star Rte. 1, Box 1066, 03222
(603) 744-9111

Amenities: 2,3,5,6,7,8,9,10,11,12
Breakfast: Full
Dbl. Oc.: $63.00
Sgl. Oc.: $77.00
Third Person: $30.00

The Pasquaney Inn On Newfound Lake—
One of the few remaining inns, built as an inn. This somewhat secret 26-room turn-of-the-century charmer recaptures a by-gone era. Private beach, French/Belgian cuisine. Open year round. Near Tenney Mt.

AMENITIES

1. No Smoking
2. No Pets
3. No Children
4. Senior Citizen Rates
5. Tennis Available
6. Golf Available
7. Swimming Available
8. Skiing Available
9. Credit Cards Accepted
10. Personal Check Accepted
11. Off Season Rates
12. Dinner Available (w/sufficient notice)

New Hampshire

Campton

Preston, Susan & Nick
Mad River Rd.,
P.O. Box 553, 03223
(603) 726-4283

Amenities: 1,2,4,5,6,7,8,9,10,12
Breakfast: Full

Dbl. Oc.: $60.00
Sgl. Oc.: $38.00
Third Person: $24.00

The Mountain Fare Inn—Charming village setting in White Mountain beauty. 9 guest rooms, private baths. 2 1/4 hrs. from Boston. Open year round. Ski lodge in winter. Rates 15% off mid-week. Welcome to adventure.

Centre Harbor

Lamprey, Peg & Bob
Rt. 25, Box 997, 03226
(603) 253-6711

Amenities: 2,5,6,7,8,10
Breakfast: Continental
Dbl. Oc.: $53.50
Sgl. Oc.: $53.50
Third Person: $10.00

Dearborn Place—Bob & Peg Lamprey, owners of this 1876 B&B welcome all guests to stop by. Feel at home with our antique atmosphere, private baths, eye-opener breakfasts, views to Lake Winnipesaukee, & much, much more!

Centre Harbor

Leavitt, Don; Miller, Rick
Rt. 25B & College Rd., 03226
(603) 279-7001

Amenities: 8,12
Breakfast: Full
Dbl. Oc.: $70.00
Sgl. Oc.: $60.00
Third Person: $15.00-$20.00

Red Hill Inn Ltd.—A lovely restored mansion, comfortable antiques, fireplaces, 50 private acres overlooking Squam Lake ("On Golden Pond") and White Mountains. Excellent country-gourmet cuisine, lounge with fireplace. Dinner $8.75-$16.95 P.P.

AMENITIES

1. No Smoking
2. No Pets
3. No Children
4. Senior Citizen Rates
5. Tennis Available
6. Golf Available
7. Swimming Available
8. Skiing Available
9. Credit Cards Accepted
10. Personal Check Accepted
11. Off Season Rates
12. Dinner Available (w/sufficient notice)

New Hampshire

Chocorua Village

Dyrenforth, Kathie & John
P.O. Box 14, Page Hill Rd., 03817
(603) 323-8707

Amenities: 2,5,6,7,8,10
Breakfast: Full
Dbl. Oc.: $60.00
Sgl. Oc.: $50.00
Third Person: $10.00-$15.00

The Farmhouse Bed & Breakfast—Country charm, gracious hospitality. Quaint N.E. village in heart of the White Mts. Nearby: lakes, hiking, skiing, summer theatre, antiques, fine dining. Farm fresh breakfast. Babysitting available.

Conway

Lein, Lynn & Robert
P.O. Box 1649, 148 Washington St., 03818
(603) 447-3988

Amenities: 1,2,7,9,10
Breakfast: Full
Dbl. Oc.: 60.00
Third Person: $15.00

Mountain Valley Manor—A restored Victorian accented with antiques. Mt. Washington and covered bridge views. 5 ski areas, golf, hiking, canoeing, snowmobiling and water slides nearby. Walk to village.

Danbury

Issa, George; Williams, April
Rte. 104, 03230
(603) 768-3318

Amenities: 1,2,6,7,8,10,12
Breakfast: Full

Dbl. Oc.: $44.95
Sgl. Oc.: $27.00
Third Person: $14.95

The Inn At Danbury is a warm and charming 19th-century farmhouse located in a quiet New England town. The inn greets travelers with pleasant, comfortable surroundings and home-cooked meals.

E. Hebron

Fortescue, M/M Peter
SR Box 114, 03232
(603) 744-2029

Amenities: 2,5,6,7,8,9,10,12
Breakfast: Full

Dbl. Oc.: $50.00
Sgl. Oc.: $40.00
Third Person: $10.00

Six Chimneys—1791 country tavern located on the quiet Newfound Lake on Rt. 3A south of Plymouth. White Mountain attractions easily accessible.

AMENITIES

1. No Smoking
2. No Pets
3. No Children
4. Senior Citizen Rates
5. Tennis Available
6. Golf Available
7. Swimming Available
8. Skiing Available
9. Credit Cards Accepted
10. Personal Check Accepted
11. Off Season Rates
12. Dinner Available (w/sufficient notice)

New Hampshire

Franconia

Kerivan, Kate
P.O. Box 15, 03580
(603) 823-7775, 949-2919

Amenities: 1-3,5-12
Breakfast: Full

Dbl. Oc.: $55.00-$75.00
Sgl. Oc.: $45.00-$55.00
Third Person: $25.00

Bungay Jar Bed & Breakfast—Six miles south of Franconia on 8 acres in White Mountains near all major attractions. House made from a century-old barn. Fireplaced living room, canopy beds, views, privacy, sauna, great food.

Franconia

Larson, The Family
Cannon Mt., 03580
(603) 823-5501

Amenities: 2,4,5,7,8,9,10,12
Breakfast: Continental

Dbl. Oc.: $75.00
Sgl. Oc.: $75.00
Third Person: $10.00

The Horse And Hound Inn located off Rt. 18. Traditional inn, pine panelled lounge & dining rooms. Recommended by Bon Appetite, Brides, & Ski Magazine. Near all Franconia Notch attractions.

Franconia

Morris, Alec & Richard
Eastern Valley Rd., 03580
(603) 823-5542

Amenities: 2,5,6,7,8,9,10,11,12
Breakfast: Full
Dbl. Oc.: $127.00
Sgl. Oc.: $100.00
Third Person: $27.00

Franconia Inn—Our inn offers its guests 4 clay tennis courts, riding stables, (sleigh rides in winter), golf priviledges, hiking, biking, waterfalls. X-C touring center. French and continental cuisine. Package plans.

Franconia

Vail, Shannon, Brenda & John
RFD 1, Box 75, 03580
(603) 823-7061

Amenities: 1,2,5,6,7,8,9,10,12
Breakfast: Full
Dbl. Oc.: $55.00
Sgl. Oc.: $35.00
Third Person: $25.00

Blanche's B&B—English-style B&B in a restored Victorian farmhouse. Rurally situated in the Easton Valley, the house looks upon the Kinsman Ridge. 6 miles from Franconia Notch and Cannon Mountain. 100% cotton sheets.

AMENITIES

1. No Smoking
2. No Pets
3. No Children
4. Senior Citizen Rates
5. Tennis Available
6. Golf Available
7. Swimming Available
8. Skiing Available
9. Credit Cards Accepted
10. Personal Check Accepted
11. Off Season Rates
12. Dinner Available (w/sufficient notice)

New Hampshire

Freedom

Daly, Marjorie & Bob
1 Maple St., Box 478, 03836
(603) 539-4815

Amenities: 1,2,5,6,7,8,9,10
Breakfast: Full

Dbl. Oc.: $40.50-$43.50
Sgl. Oc.: $29.50
Third Person: $10.00

Freedom House Bed'N Breakfast is minutes off Routes 25 & 153. Offering genuine New England charm & hospitality with a hearty country breakfast. No smoking in bedrooms or breakfast room, please. Charmingly redecorated Victorian country.

Gilford

Shortway, Mrs. Gretchen
83 Old Lakeshore Rd., 03246
(603) 528-1172

Amenities: 4,5,6,7,8,9,10,11
Breakfast: Full

Dbl. Oc.: $58.85
Sgl. Oc.: $48.15
Third Person: $10.00

Cartway House Inn located in the heart of N.H. lakes region. 1771 Colonial, a scrumptious breakfast, foreign language spoken. Skiing nearby. Dinners upon request, $15.00 P.P. Groups welcome. Children under 6 free.

Greenfield

Mangini, Barbara
Box 156, Forest Rd., 03047
(603) 547-6327

Amenities: 5,6,7,9,10
Breakfast: Full

Dbl. Oc.: $45.00-$60.00

Greenfield Inn—1½ hrs. from Boston in the valley of The Monadonck Mountains with views of all of them. Minutes to skiing & backpacking. Fine restaurants; newly restored; near State Park; honeymoon suites; catered small weddings. Free brochure.

Greenland

Engel, Priscilla & David
47 Park Ave., 03840
(603) 436-5992

Amenities: 1,4,5,6,7,10
Breakfast: Full

Dbl. Oc.: $45.00-$50.00
Sgl. Oc.: $40.00
Third Person: $10.00

Thomas Ayers House, built circa 1737, is located near historic Portsmouth, fine restaurants, shops, & many historic sites. Five miles from the ocean; private or shared baths.

Hampton

Griesmyer, M/M Donald
124 Landing Rd., 03842
(603) 926-9666

Amenities: 5,6,7,10
Breakfast: Full

Dbl. Oc.: $38.00
Sgl. Oc.: $32.00
Third Person: $7.00

Blue Heron Inn; 200-year-old family home next to Tidal Marsh. Close to: beach, playhouse, racetrack, & discount shopping. I-95 to 51 East, right at light, 1/4 mile on right.

AMENITIES

1. No Smoking
2. No Pets
3. No Children
4. Senior Citizen Rates
5. Tennis Available
6. Golf Available
7. Swimming Available
8. Skiing Available
9. Credit Cards Accepted
10. Personal Check Accepted
11. Off Season Rates
12. Dinner Available (w/sufficient notice)

New Hampshire

Hampton Beach

Windemiller, Deborah & Duane
365 Ocean Blvd., 03842
(603) 926-3542

Amenities: 1,2,5,6,7,9,11
Breakfast: Continental
Dbl. Oc.: $95.00-$125.00
Sgl. Oc.: $80.00-$120.00
Third Person: $25.00

The Oceanside—A remodeled New England inn on the ocean front. 10 tastefully decorated rooms w/private baths, many w/period antiques. Not particularly suitable for children. Central heat & A/C.

Henniker

Davis, June & Wilfred
35 Flanders Rd., 03242
(603) 428-3228

Amenities: 1,2,5,6,7,8,9,12
Breakfast: Full
Dbl. Oc.: $62.06-$94.16
Sgl. Oc.: $51.36-$64.20
Third Person: $12.84

The Meeting House Inn—Romantic getaway with your comfort in mind. Cozy rooms with attention to details. Full in bed breakfast, private hot tub & sauna. We are a full service country inn, family run, taking pride in service & quality.

Holderness

Webb, Bonnie & Bill
Rte. 3, 03245
(603) 968-7269

Amenities: 1,2,3,6,7,8,9,10
Breakfast: Full

Dbl. Oc.: $80.00
Sgl. Oc.: $60.00
Third Person: $25.00

The Inn On Golden Pond offers 9 bright and cheerful guest rooms and is surrounded by 55 wooded acres. Nearby is Squam Lake, setting for the film "On Golden Pond." Open year round.

Jackson

Crocker, Robin
Route 16A, 03846
(603) 383-6666

Amenities: 2,3,5,6,7,8,9,10,11
Breakfast: Continental

Dbl. Oc.: $60.00-$85.00
Sgl. Oc.: $50.00-$75.00
Third Person: $10.00

Village House—Country living and warm hospitality with swimming pool, tennis court, hiking, golfing, horseback riding, fine dining, shopping, and Mt. Washington Valley attractions at our doorstep. Full breakfast in winter.

AMENITIES

1. No Smoking
2. No Pets
3. No Children
4. Senior Citizen Rates
5. Tennis Available
6. Golf Available
7. Swimming Available
8. Skiing Available
9. Credit Cards Accepted
10. Personal Check Accepted
11. Off Season Rates
12. Dinner Available (w/sufficient notice)

New Hampshire

Jackson

Lubao, Barbara & Barry
Box 656, Rt. 16, 03846
(603) 383-9339

Amenities: 2,5,6,7,8,9,10,11,12
Breakfast: Full
Dbl. Oc.: $93.60-$128.70
Sgl. Oc.: $81.90-$117.00
Third Person: $23.40-$35.10

River House—Enjoy fine lodging & superb country dining in our warm & gracious turn-of-the-century farmhouse nestled in the heart of the White Mountains overlooking the spectacular Ellis River. Jacuzzi spa & homemade breads.

Jackson

Tradwell, Mrs. Lori
Thorne Hill Rd.,
Box 120, 03846
(603) 383-4321

Amenities: 5,6,8,9,10,11
Breakfast: Full

Dbl. Oc.: $78.00
Sgl. Oc.: $45.00
Third Person: $15.00

Inn At Jackson—Babbling brooks, glorious foliage, sparkling snows, a reason for every season. The joy of the White Mountains in this stately mansion overlooking the Village of Jackson.

Jackson

Zeliff, Sydna & Bill
Box CC, Rts. 16B, 03846
(603) 383-4313

Amenities: 2,5,6,7,8,9,10,11,12
Breakfast: Full

Dbl. Oc.: $68.00-$72.00
Sgl. Oc.: $53.00-$57.00
Third Person: $45.00

Christmas Farm Inn—Award-winning English-style gardens, brilliant fall foliage, winter's crystal clear air & crunchy snow. Guest rooms: cozy inn, family suites over the barn, deluxe 2 bedroom, 2 bath; living room with fireplace cottages, or large Salt Box.

Jackson Village

Burns, Tom, J.
Dinsmore Rd., 03846
(603) 383-9443

Amenities: 7,8,9,10,11
Breakfast: Full

Dbl. Oc.: $75.00-$95.00
Sgl. Oc.: $45.00
Third Person: $20.00

Nestlenook Inn—Charming country inn on 65 acres. Pool & pony rides at the farm. X/C skiing and sleigh rides in winter; hot tub; children welcome. Off Route 16A through covered bridge in Jackson Village, onto Dinsmore Rd.

AMENITIES

1. No Smoking
2. No Pets
3. No Children
4. Senior Citizen Rates
5. Tennis Available
6. Golf Available
7. Swimming Available
8. Skiing Available
9. Credit Cards Accepted
10. Personal Check Accepted
11. Off Season Rates
12. Dinner Available (w/sufficient notice)

New Hampshire

Jaffrey

Rettig, Richard
Route 124 East, 03452
(603) 532-6637

Amenities: 2,6,7,8,9,10
Breakfast: Full

Dbl. Oc.: $69.55
Sgl. Oc.: $58.85
Third Person: $26.95

Benjamin Prescott Inn is situated 2 miles from Jaffrey on Rt. 124 East. A classic Greek Revival home w/private baths, minutes from Mt. Monadnock, skiing, auctions, antiquing & lakes. Located near Franklin Pierce College & Cathedral of the Pines.

Jefferson

Brown, Greg
Rt. 2, Box 68A, 03583
(603) 586-7998

Amenities: 1,2,5,6,7,8,9,10,11
Breakfast: Full
Dbl. Oc.: $55.00
Sgl. Oc.: $50.00
Third Person: $10.00

The Jefferson Inn—1896 Victorian near Mt. Washington. Superb mountain views; huge porch; swim in pond; hike from inn; evening tea; hearty breakfast; small village setting; summer theater; golf; X-C & alpine skiing; skating in winter.

Jefferson

Leslie, Ms. Janet
Davenport Rd., 03583
(603) 586-4320

Amenities: 1,2,6,7,8,9,10
Breakfast: Full

Dbl. Oc.: $63.00
Sgl. Oc.: $53.00
Third Person: $22.00

The Davenport Inn offers you the perfect place to relax and unwind. Whether you enjoy the comforts of reading by the fire or on the porch. Peace & serenity abound in this N.H. paradise.

Keene

Hueber, Judy & Phil
Rt. 9, W. Chesterfield, 03466
(603) 256-3211

Amenities: 2,3,5,6,7,8,9,10
Breakfast: Full
Dbl. Oc.: $95.00-$145.00
Sgl. Oc.: $95.00-$145.00
Third Person: $15.00

Chesterfield Inn—Elegant 1781 country inn 2 miles from Brattleboro VT. All rooms have private bath and A/C some with jacuzzi, balcony & fireplace. Public dining by reservation.

AMENITIES

1. No Smoking
2. No Pets
3. No Children
4. Senior Citizen Rates
5. Tennis Available
6. Golf Available
7. Swimming Available
8. Skiing Available
9. Credit Cards Accepted
10. Personal Check Accepted
11. Off Season Rates
12. Dinner Available (w/sufficient notice)

New Hampshire

Laconia

Blazok, Maureen C.
1047 Union Ave., 03246
(603) 528-4185

Amenities: 7,8,9,10,11
Breakfast: Full

Dbl. Oc.: $68.00
Sgl. Oc.: $58.00
Third Person: $15.00

The Tin Whistle Inn—Enjoy gracious hospitality at a charming 1915 home. Fireplaced parlor; lead glass windows; oak woodwork. View memorable sunsets from the large veranda; close to all Lake Winnipesaukee attractions.

Laconia

Damato, Dianne & Joe
R1, Box 335, 03246
(603) 524-0087

Amenities: 1,2,5,6,7,8,10
Breakfast: Full

Dbl. Oc.: $58.85-$69.35
Sgl. Oc.: $48.15-$58.85
Third Person: $10.00

Ferry Point House—A 150-year-old country Victorian on picturesque Lake Winnisquam. Spend lazy days on our 60 ft. veranda with a great view of the lake & mountains or join in the areas many activities. Call for directions or brochure.

Lincoln

Deppe, Loretta & Bill
Box 562, Pollard Rd., 03251
(603) 745-8517

Amenities: 1,2,5,6,7,8,9,10,11
Breakfast: Full
Dbl. Oc.: $64.20
Sgl. Oc.: $40.00
Third Person: $15.00

Red Sleigh Inn Bed & Breakfast—Family run inn with mountain views from each window, just off the scenic Kancamagus Hwy. One mile to Loon Mt. ski area, Waterville & Cannon closeby too. Great summer & fall area. Shops, dining nearby.

Lisbon

Bromley, Laura & Steve
Bishop Rd., 03585
(603) 838-6118

Amenities: 1,2,5,6,7,8,9,10,11,12
Breakfast: Continental
Dbl. Oc.: $62.06-$69.55
Sgl. Oc.: $51.36-$58.85
Third Person: $10.70

The Ammonoosuc Inn is nestled in a quaint valley amongst the beautiful White Mountains of N.H. A genuine New England country inn with 9 charming guest rooms, all with private baths.

AMENITIES

1. No Smoking
2. No Pets
3. No Children
4. Senior Citizen Rates
5. Tennis Available
6. Golf Available
7. Swimming Available
8. Skiing Available
9. Credit Cards Accepted
10. Personal Check Accepted
11. Off Season Rates
12. Dinner Available (w/sufficient notice)

New Hampshire

Lisbon

Hymoff, Helene
RFD 1, Rte. 302, 03585
(603) 838-6370

Amenities: 5,6,7,8,10
Breakfast: Continental
Dbl. Oc.: $55.00
Sgl. Oc.: $45.00
Third Person: $15.00

Bridgehouse Bed & Breakfast is a charmingly restored farmhouse minutes from Franconia Notch State Park. Lovely scenic area close to major routes 91 & 93. Three hours from Boston & Montreal.

Littleton

Carver, Ann & Jim
247 West Main St., 03561
(603) 444-2661

Amenities: 5,6,7,8,9,10,11
Breakfast: Continental

Dbl. Oc.: $42.80-$96.30
Sgl. Oc.: $37.45-$53.50
Third Person: $21.40-$37.45

Beal House Inn offers warm New England hospitality. Rooms furnished with antiques give it a real country charm. Near all White Mountain attractions. Most rooms have private baths. Fireside breakfast with hot popovers.

Manchester

Dennis, Ms. Jan
503 Beech St., 03104
(603) 669-8600

Amenities: 1,2,3,4,9
Breakfast: Continental

Dbl. Oc.: $52.43
Sgl. Oc.: $47.08

Manor On The Park is an intown bed and breakfast inn located across from a lovely park, yet just minutes from downtown. The rooms are light, airy, and spotlessly clean. Open all year.

Marlborough

Gage, Marge & Cal
Thatcher Hill Rd., 03455
(603) 876-3361

Amenities: 1,2,3,5,6,7,8,9,10
Breakfast: Full
Dbl. Oc.: $58.85-$80.25
Sgl. Oc.: $53.50-$74.90

Thatcher Hill Inn—Revitalized 1794 country home. Beautiful 60 acres setting near easy to climb Mt. Monadnock. Tastefully appointed, spacious rooms, all baths private; leisurely buffet breakfasts; wheelchair access.

AMENITIES

1. No Smoking
2. No Pets
3. No Children
4. Senior Citizen Rates
5. Tennis Available
6. Golf Available
7. Swimming Available
8. Skiing Available
9. Credit Cards Accepted
10. Personal Check Accepted
11. Off Season Rates
12. Dinner Available (w/sufficient notice)

New Hampshire

New London

Rich, Margaret & Grant
Box 1030, Pleasant St., 03257
(603) 526-6271

Amenities: 2,3,5,6,7,8,9,10,12
Breakfast: Full
Dbl. Oc.: $72.00-$90.00
Sgl. Oc.: $50.00-$55.00
Third Person: $24.00

Pleasant Lake Inn—Our 5 wooded acre lake front 4 season country inn is tucked away 2 miles from main street. Its history goes back to 1790. The inn offers 13 rooms decorated with its own country personality & fabulous views.

Newport

Tatem, Judi & Dick
HCR 63, Box 3, Rt. 10, 03773
(603) 863-3583

Amenities: 2,5,6,7,8,9,10,11,12
Breakfast: Full
Dbl. Oc.: $55.00-$135.00
Sgl. Oc.: $45.00-$125.00
Third Person: $20.00

The Inn At Coit Mountain—Something more than a bed & breakfast. "Ohhh" is the best way to describe the library with its oak panelling & granite fireplace. Sheer elegance! Breakfast is country-style or gourmet, as you wish.

North Conway

Begley, Ann & Hugh
Box 3297, Surprise Rd., 03860
(603) 356-2625

Amenities: 2,5,6,7,8,9,10,11
Breakfast: Full
Dbl. Oc.: $54.00-$88.00
Sgl. Oc.: $69.00
Third Person: $17.00

The Buttonwood Inn—Tucked away on Mt. Surprise, 2 miles to village. Secluded & quiet; 9 rooms w/private & shared baths; living room w/wood stove; TV room; gameroom w/fireplace; lawn sports; pool; X-C skiing from the door.

AMENITIES

1. No Smoking
2. No Pets
3. No Children
4. Senior Citizen Rates
5. Tennis Available
6. Golf Available
7. Swimming Available
8. Skiing Available
9. Credit Cards Accepted
10. Personal Check Accepted
11. Off Season Rates
12. Dinner Available (w/sufficient notice)

New Hampshire

North Conway

Halpin, Valerie & Dave
River Rd., 03860
(603) 356-2831

Amenities: 1,2,5,6,7,8,9,10
Breakfast: Full
Dbl. Oc.: $58.85
Sgl. Oc.: $42.80
Third Person: $16.05

Nereledge, a 1787 small country inn & English pub. Warm atmosphere; quiet setting; close to: skiing, fishing, hiking, shopping and attractions. Delicious breakfast w/apple crumble; open year round.

North Conway

Helfand, Dennis
P.O. Box 1194, 03860
(603) 356-2044

Amenities: 2,5,6,7,8,9,10,11,12
Breakfast: Full
Dbl. Oc.: $65.00-$105.00
Sgl. Oc.: $55.00-$95.00
Third Person: $15.00-$27.00

Cranmore Mt. Lodge—A small country inn with big facilities. We offer quiet rooms sharing baths; "Barn loft" offers new rooms w/private baths, A/C & color TV. 40 bed dorm available for groups.

North Conway

Hurley, Judy & Jack
Rte. 16/ Main St., 03860
(603) 356-6381

Amenities: 2,5,6,7,8,9,10,11,12
Breakfast: Full
Dbl. Oc.: $107.00
Sgl. Oc.: $53.50
Third Person: $20.00

The Scottish Lion Inn—Highland hospitality with award-winning Scottish-American cuisine; cozy pub; 3 fireplaces; screened-in dining; all rooms with private bath; adjacent Scottish Lion import shop; in beautiful Mt. Washington Valley.

North Conway

Jackson, Claire
Kearsarge Rd., 03860
(603) 356-9041

Amenities: 2,5,6,7,8,9,10,11
Breakfast: Full
Dbl. Oc.: $95.00
Sgl. Oc.: $85.00
Third Person: $47.50

Peacock Inn—Recapture the romance in our intimate country inn. Enjoy our scrumptious country breakfast while overlooking the mts. Access to health club and indoor pool. Explore the quaint village of No. Conway.

AMENITIES

1. No Smoking
2. No Pets
3. No Children
4. Senior Citizen Rates
5. Tennis Available
6. Golf Available
7. Swimming Available
8. Skiing Available
9. Credit Cards Accepted
10. Personal Check Accepted
11. Off Season Rates
12. Dinner Available (w/sufficient notice)

New Hampshire

North Conway

Minnix, Ms. Tracy
Servey Street, 03860
(603) 356-6239

Amenities: 5,6,7,8,9,10
Breakfast: Full

Dbl. Oc.: $34.00-$64.00
Sgl. Oc.: $23,00-$58.00
Third Person: $16.00

Sunny Side Inn is a friendly & comfortable B&B. We are within walking distance of town or Mt. Cranmore. 11 guest rooms, some w/priv. bath. All the wonder of the White Mountains are around us. Quiet location.

North Conway

Rattay, Peter
Route 16, Box 1937, 03860
(603) 356-3271
(800) 525-9100 N.E.

Amenities: 2,5,6,7,8,9,12
Breakfast: Full

Dbl. Oc.: $83.55
Sgl. Oc.: $79.25

Stonehurst Manor—Come savor the elegance of a turn-of-the-century mansion where old oak & stained glass surround you. Gourmet dining, lounge, tennis, pool, hot tub. Mobile - 3 star, AAA - 3 diamonds. Dinner $16.05/person.

N. Woodstock

Town, Gloria & Joe
Rt. 3, S. Main St., 03262
(603) 745-2711

Amenities: 2,3,5,6,7,8,9
Breakfast: Full

Dbl. Oc.: $48.00
Sgl. Oc.: $28.00
Third Person: $23.00

Mt. Adams Inn where "hospitality abounds." 19th-century inn in the heart of the White Mountains. Famous for its informal atmosphere, excellent food & hospitality. Located at the edge of the village on the bank of the Moosilouke River.

Plymouth

Crenson, M/M William
RFD 2, Box 200 B, 03264
(603) 536-4476

Amenities: 2,3,5,6,7,8,9,10
Breakfast: Full
Dbl. Oc.: $65.00-$75.00
Sgl. Oc.: $65.00-$75.00
Third Person: $16.00

Crab Apple Inn, 1835 brick Colonial. Lovely guest rooms; fireplaces; gourmet breakfast, patio; spacious grounds with brook; gardens and wooded paths. At gateway to White Mts. near ski areas and lakes.

AMENITIES

1. No Smoking
2. No Pets
3. No Children
4. Senior Citizen Rates
5. Tennis Available
6. Golf Available
7. Swimming Available
8. Skiing Available
9. Credit Cards Accepted
10. Personal Check Accepted
11. Off Season Rates
12. Dinner Available (w/sufficient notice)

New Hampshire

Plymouth

McWilliams, Mrs. Micheline
RFD 1, U.S. Rt. 3, N., 03264
(603) 536-2838

Amenities: 7,8,10
Breakfast: Full

Dbl. Oc.: $38.50
Sgl. Oc.: $25.50
Third Person: $5.50-$10.00

Northway House—Hospitality plus awaits the traveler in this charming Colonial. Close to lakes and mountains. Gourmet breakfast; reasonable rates; children welcome.

Portsmouth

Martin Hill Inn
c/o J. & P. Harnden
404 Islington St., 03801
(603) 436-2287

Amenities: 2,3,9,10,11
Breakfast: Full

Dbl. Oc.: $75.00-$90.00

Martin Hill Inn—Portsmouth's premier bed and breakfast inn. Beautifully appointed rooms with period antiques. Elegant dining room; private bath in all rooms. Parking; air-conditioning; convenient location.

Portsmouth

Laurie, Martha
314 Court St., 03801
(603) 436-7242

Amenities: 1,2,4,5,6,7,8,9,10,11
Breakfast: Continental
Dbl. Oc.: $99.00
Sgl. Oc.: $84.00
Third Person: $10.00

The Inn At Strawbery Banke—Come stay at our cozy bed & breakfast inn that was built for Captain Holbrook at the turn of the 19th century. Experience the charm of yesteryear and the convenience of our modern facilities.

Portsmouth

Stone, Ms. Catherine
69 Richards Ave., 03801
(603) 433-2188

Amenities: 2,5,6,7,9,10,11
Breakfast: Full

Dbl. Oc.: $69.66-$80.25

Leighton Inn—An 1809 Federal home elegantly furnished in period antiques. Five guest rooms; private baths available. 6-minute walk to Market Square and Strawbery Banke. Call or write for brochure.

AMENITIES

1. No Smoking
2. No Pets
3. No Children
4. Senior Citizen Rates
5. Tennis Available
6. Golf Available
7. Swimming Available
8. Skiing Available
9. Credit Cards Accepted
10. Personal Check Accepted
11. Off Season Rates
12. Dinner Available (w/sufficient notice)

New Hampshire

Rindge

Linares, Carmen
03461
(603) 899-5166, 899-5167

Amenities: 1,2,3,5,6,7,8,10
Breakfast: Full

Dbl. Oc.: $60.00-$65.00
Sgl. Oc.: $40.00

Grassy Pond House—1831 homestead nestled among 150 forested acres, overlooking water and gardens. Convenient to main roads, restaurants, antique shops, weekly auctions, summer theater, & craft fairs. Hike Grand Monadnock.

Rindge

Nottiangham, Mrs. W.B.
Box 229, 03461
(603) 899-6646

Amenities: 1,2,3,5,6,7
Breakfast: Continental

Dbl. Oc.: $35.00-$45.00
Sgl. Oc.: $18.00-$20.00
Third Person: $18.00

The Tokfarm—150-year-old farmhouse on 100-acre Christmas tree farm, on 1,400 foot hill. Tri-state view; swimming (2 ponds); fine restaurants, Cathedral of the Pines, Mt. Monadnock; Franklin Pierce College; all summer sports nearby.

Rye

Marineau, M/M Norman
1413 Ocean Blvd.
Rt. 1A, 03870
(603) 431-1413

Amenities: 1,2,3,5,6,7,8,10
Breakfast: Full

Dbl. Oc.: $64.20
Sgl. Oc.: $58.85
Third Person: $15.00

Rock Ledge Manor—Ideally located to all New Hampshire & southern Maine seacoast activities. Excellent ocean view from all rooms. Guest rooms have private baths. Reservations are advised. Open year round.

Strafford

Garboski, Eunice & Stephen
P.O. Box 309, Bow Lake, 03884
(603) 664-2457

Amenities: 2,5,6,7,8,10
Breakfast: Full
Dbl. Oc.: $55.00
Sgl. Oc.: $55.00
Third Person: $7.00

Province Inn—A lakefront Colonial in a completely unspoiled country setting, midway between New Hampshire's seacoast and mountains. Antique hunters' paradise; a mini-resort without the crowds.

AMENITIES

1. No Smoking
2. No Pets
3. No Children
4. Senior Citizen Rates
5. Tennis Available
6. Golf Available
7. Swimming Available
8. Skiing Available
9. Credit Cards Accepted
10. Personal Check Accepted
11. Off Season Rates
12. Dinner Available (w/sufficient notice)

New Hampshire

Sugar Hill

Hern, Meri & Mike
Main Street, 03585
(603) 823-5695

Amenities: 5,6,7,8,9,10,12
Breakfast: Full

Dbl. Oc.: $53.50-$64.20
Sgl. Oc.: $42.80
Third Person: $12.85

The Hilltop Inn—Relax in our lovely Victorian inn. Enjoy: antique furnishings, cozy flannel sheets, sunset views, & large country breakfasts. Minutes from Franconia Notch for skiing & hiking. Children and pets welcome.

Tilton

Foster, Janet & Bob
308 W. Main St., 03276
(603) 286-4524

Amenities: 2,6,7,8,9,10
Breakfast: Full

Dbl. Oc.: $58.85-$69.55
Sgl. Oc.: $48.15-$58.85
Third Person: $15.00

The Black Swam Inn—The Fosters welcome you to an elegant but warm 1880 Victorian. Located on Rtes. 3 & 11 with 4 acres; 6 comfortable rooms; queen size beds & four baths; living room; music room; TV available. In lakes area.

West Springfield

Alexander, M/M Samuel
Philbrick Hill, Box 128, 03284
(603) 763-5065

Amenities: 5,6,7,8,10,12
Breakfast: Full
Dbl. Oc.: $95.00
Sgl. Oc.: $70.00
Third Person: $25.00

Wonderwell Inn—For peaceful people with pampered palates who prefer woodland seclusion; civilized plumbing in picturesque surroundings; luxurious privacy romantic views; the songs of birds & the warmth of hospitality.

Wolfboro

LeBlanc, Rose
P.O. Box 1329, 03894
(603) 569-3529

Amenities: 5,6,7,8,9,10,11
Breakfast: Full
Dbl. Oc.: $64.20
Sgl. Oc.: $53.50
Third Person: $10.70

Isaac Springfield House, just 2 miles from Lake Winnepesaukee. Summer and winter activities include: swimming, boating, hiking, bicycling, XC skiing and ice sailing. 1871 Victorian-4 guest rooms.

AMENITIES

1. No Smoking
2. No Pets
3. No Children
4. Senior Citizen Rates
5. Tennis Available
6. Golf Available
7. Swimming Available
8. Skiing Available
9. Credit Cards Accepted
10. Personal Check Accepted
11. Off Season Rates
12. Dinner Available (w/sufficient notice)

New Hampshire

Wolfboro

Limberger, Irma
68 North Main St., 03894
(603) 569-5702

Amenities: 2,4,5,6,7,8,9,10,11
Breakfast: Full

Dbl. Oc.: $72.00-$80.00
Sgl. Oc.: $72.00-$80.00
Third Person: $15.00

Tuc Me Inn—A comfortable Colonial only steps from shopping, restaurants, & Lake Winnipesaukee. Seven rooms, some with air/conditioning & private bath. Come stay a day, a weekend, awhile, and enjoy our country breakfast.

AMENITIES

1. No Smoking
2. No Pets
3. No Children
4. Senior Citizen Rates
5. Tennis Available
6. Golf Available
7. Swimming Available
8. Skiing Available
9. Credit Cards Accepted
10. Personal Check Accepted
11. Off Season Rates
12. Dinner Available (w/sufficient notice)

New Jersey

The Garden State

Capital: Trenton
Statehood: December 18, 1787; the 3rd state
State Motto: Liberty and Prosperity
State Bird: Eastern Goldfinch
State Flower: Purple Violet
State Tree: Red Oak

New Jersey is a state of hundreds of thousands of people. Most of these people live in the northern industrial area around Newark. They are hard working and are involved in just about every kind of manufacturing there is in America. Sixty of the largest companies we have in the United States have plants in New Jersey.

The New Jersey Turnpike is the busiest turnpike in the country, bringing people in and out of this state on their way either north, south, east or west.

There are many historic places to visit in New Jersey, and also some very beautiful beaches along the Atlantic coast. Vacationers love this state. Atlantic City and the boardwalk has been a tremendous tourist attraction for years.

Organized baseball was first played in Hoboken, New Jersey in 1846, and Grover Cleveland was born in Cadwell in 1837.

New Jersey

Atlantic City

Bandle, Mrs. Jeannine
10 S. Morris Ave., 08401
(609) 345-4700 or 345-4916

Amenities: 5,6,7,9
Breakfast: Continental

Dbl. Oc.: $58.00
Sgl. Oc.: $48.00

Another Time B&B—Atlantic City's oldest Victorian-style residence is now Atlantic City's newest B&B. One block from the Tropicana Casino, boardwalk, and beach parking.

Bay Head

Conover, Mrs. Beverly
646 Main Ave., 08742
(201) 892-4664

Amenities: 1,2,5,6,7,9,10,11
Breakfast: Continental

Dbl. Oc.: $65.00-$125.00
Sgl. Oc.: $60.00-$115.00
Third Person: $20.00

Conover's Bay Head Inn—N.J. shore's finest antique-filled B&B. Special touches for a memorable stay. Just a short walk to: shops, restaurants, ocean. A view from every window! Tea served in winter; full breakfast Sundays & winter.

Bayville

Turash, Mrs. Mary
217 Oak St., 08721
(201) 269-6590

Amenities: 1,2,4,5,6,7,8,11
Breakfast: Continental

Dbl. Oc.: $45.00
Sgl. Oc.: $30.00
Third Person: $15.00

The Bayville Bed And Breakfast—One mile from shopping district & public transportation to: Atlantic shore points, Atlantic City, New York, & Philadelphia. A warm hospitable family-run home; quiet area; children welcome.

Cape May

Burow, M/M Greg
609 Hughes St., 08204
(609) 884-7293

Amenities: 1,2,5,6,7,9,10,11
Breakfast: Full
Dbl. Oc.: $104.00
Sgl. Oc.: $104.00
Third Person: $15.00

The Wooden Rabbit, located on the prettiest street in Cap May; in the heart of the historic district, surrounded by Victorian cottages. Our decor is country. All rooms have private bath. 2 blocks from beach, 1 block from shops & fine food.

AMENITIES

1. No Smoking
2. No Pets
3. No Children
4. Senior Citizen Rates
5. Tennis Available
6. Golf Available
7. Swimming Available
8. Skiing Available
9. Credit Cards Accepted
10. Personal Check Accepted
11. Off Season Rates
12. Dinner Available (w/sufficient notice)

New Jersey

Cape May

Le Duc, Anne
301 Howard St., 08204
(609) 884-8409

Amenities: 1,2,5,6,7,9,10,11,12
Breakfast: Full

Dbl. Oc.: $81.00-$134.00
Sgl. Oc.: $67.00
Third Person: $30.00

Chalfonte Hotel—This Victorian country inn by the sea, Cape May's oldest hotel, offers homecooked southern fare, historic accommodations, and a porch filled with rockers. We invite you to a retreat from the everyday.

Cape May

Rein, Barry B.
1513 Beach Dr., 08204
(609) 884-2228

Amenities: 1,2,3,9,10,11
Breakfast: Full
Dbl. Oc.: $101.00-$132.50
Sgl. Oc.: $91.00-$122.50
Third Person: $25.00

Colvmns By The Sea—Fall asleep to the sounds of the surf and awake to a breathtaking view of the Atlantic. Visit our turn-of-the-century mansion filled with the charm and grace of a bygone era.

Cape May

Schmidt, Lorraine & Terry
29 Ocean St., 08204
(609) 884-4428

Amenities: 1,2,3,5,7,11
Breakfast: Full

Dbl. Oc.: $90.00-$198.00
Sgl. Oc.: $80.00-$175.00
Third Person: $20.00

The Humphrey Hughes House, nestled in the heart of Cape May's historic section, is one of her most authentically restored inns. It is perhaps the most spacious and gracious of them all with Victorian charm & elegance coupled with hospitality.

Cape May

Smith, Spurgeon
619 Hughes St., 08204
(609) 884-0613

Amenities: 1,2,7,10,11
Breakfast: Continental

Dbl. Oc.: $104.00
Sgl. Oc.: $94.00

White Dove Cottage in historic district of Victorian Cape May offers: bright sunny rooms; ocean breezes; air conditioned suites; shaded veranda and private parking. Walk to restaurants, historical sites, & entertainment. Exclusive.

AMENITIES

1. No Smoking
2. No Pets
3. No Children
4. Senior Citizen Rates
5. Tennis Available
6. Golf Available
7. Swimming Available
8. Skiing Available
9. Credit Cards Accepted
10. Personal Check Accepted
11. Off Season Rates
12. Dinner Available (w/sufficient notice)

New Jersey

Cape May

Wells, Joan & Dane
102 Ocean St., 08204
(609) 884-8702

Amenities: 1,2,5,6,7,9,10,11
Breakfast: Full
Dbl. Oc.: $55.00-$120.00
Sgl. Oc.: $44.40-$109.40
Third Person: $10.60

The Queen Victoria treats you royally; hearty breakfast, afternoon tea, bikes & evening turndown. Restored Victorian furnished with antiques & quilts. 11 rooms, 2 luxury suites. Reduced rates Sept.-May.

Cherry Hill

Balaban, Mrs. Rae
6 Willow Court, 08003
(609) 428-6206

Amenities: 1,2,3,5,6
Breakfast: Continental

Dbl. Oc.: $42.00
Sgl. Oc.: $30.00

The Balabans—Lovely suburban home; fine restaurants nearby. 10 minutes from N.J. Turnpike, Exit 4; near Rt. 295; 20 minutes from downtown Philadelphia. Children over 10 welcome. Lovely gardens, art, antiques, music. Upstairs TV room.

Denville

Bergins, M/M Alex
11 Sunset Trail, 07834
(201) 625-5129

Amenities: 2,5,7,10
Breakfast: Full

Dbl. Oc.: $45.00
Sgl. Oc.: $35.00

Lakeside B&B—1 mile from I-80, between NYC & PA. Private guest quarters with a stunning view of the bay. Double bed, family room with color TV. Swimming, boating, fishing, ice skating on the lake.

Manahawkin

Carney, Maureen
190 North Main St., 08050
(609) 597-6350

Amenities: 2,6,7,11
Breakfast: Continental

Dbl. Oc.: $66.00
Sgl. Oc.: $60.00

The Goose N. Berry Inn—(Garden State Exit 63) adjacent to Barnegat Bay, the Pine Barrens, and Long beach Island; 30 minutes to Atlantic City. A historic home furnished with country antiques.

AMENITIES

1. No Smoking
2. No Pets
3. No Children
4. Senior Citizen Rates
5. Tennis Available
6. Golf Available
7. Swimming Available
8. Skiing Available
9. Credit Cards Accepted
10. Personal Check Accepted
11. Off Season Rates
12. Dinner Available (w/sufficient notice)

New Jersey

Mays Landing

Sperlin, Dawn & Steve
320 W. Main St., 08330
(609) 625-5682

Amenities: 2,3,10,11
Breakfast: Full
Dbl. Oc.: $69.00
Sgl. Oc.: $69.00
Third Person: $21.00

Abbott House—Enjoy a restored 1845 Victorian B&B. Comfortable rooms furnished with period pieces, located on the river 1/2 block to lake; a short drive to Atlantic City. Breakfast is full course with fresh baked goods.

Ocean Grove

Chernik, Dr. Doris
26 Webb Ave.. 07756
  (201) 774-3084 or (212) 751-9577

Amenities: 2,4,7,10
Breakfast: Continental
Dbl. Oc.: $40.00
Sgl. Oc.: $30.00
Third Person: $5.00

The Cordova is located in historic Ocean Grove, a beautiful Victorian community with old world charm. One block from the beach; recently featured in New Jersey Magazine as one of the 7 best places on the New Jersey shore.

Ocean Grove

Mason, Karen
10 Main Ave., 07756
(201) 775-3264

Amenities: 1,2,3,5,6,7,9,10,11
Breakfast: Continental

Dbl. Oc.: $55.12-$90.10
Sgl. Oc.: $44.52-$84.80
Third Person: $10.00

The Pine Tree Inn is a 13-room Victorian inn, 4 houses from the ocean. Innkeepers Francis & Karen will graciously help their guests to get the most out of this quaint historic seaside haven of Victoriana. Children over 12 welcome. Bikes available.

Spring Lake

Galisch, Miss Maggie
214 Monmouth Ave., 07762
(201) 974-1882

Amenities: 1,2,9,10,11
Breakfast: Continental

Dbl. Oc.: $68.90-$100.70
Sgl. Oc.: $63.60-$95.40
Third Person: $10.60

Victoria House—Charming Victorian just 65 miles from either New York or Philadelphia. Close to: ocean, village, churches, and fine restaurants. Easily reached by car, bus or train. A perfect retreat from todays hustle.

AMENITIES

1. No Smoking
2. No Pets
3. No Children
4. Senior Citizen Rates
5. Tennis Available
6. Golf Available
7. Swimming Available
8. Skiing Available
9. Credit Cards Accepted
10. Personal Check Accepted
11. Off Season Rates
12. Dinner Available (w/sufficient notice)

New Jersey

Spring Lake

Mills, Ms. Lesley
1505 Ocean Ave., 07762
(201) 449-5327

Amenities: 4,7,10,11,12
Breakfast: Continental

Dbl. Oc.: $77.00
Sgl. Oc.: $44.00
Third Person: $13.20

The Kenilworth is an 1883 English ocean front inn. 23 pretty rooms with antiques. Seaside serenity, sun & moonrise views. Abundant breakfast BVF. Pri. beach in small, quiet town 1½ hrs. from NYC & Philadelphia. Winter 40% off.

Stockton

Salassi, David
6 Woolverton Rd., 08559
(609) 397-0802

Amenities: 2,3,5,6,7,8,9,10,12
Breakfast: Full
Dbl. Oc.: $60.00-$95.00
Third Person: $15.00

The Woolverton Inn—A 10 acre private estate with a stone Victorian manor house set amidst stately trees and formal gardens. We are minutes from the Bucks Co. tourist area and Delaware River recreation. No children under 14.

Woodbine

Thurlow, Ann & Marty
Cape May County
Rd #3, Box 298, 08270
(609) 861-5847

Amenities: 6,7,9,10,12
Breakfast: Full
Dbl. Oc.: $55.00-$75.00
Sgl. Oc.: $45.00
Third Person: $20.00

Henry Ludlam Inn is a romantic, historic home circa 1800. Rooms have fireplaces & are furnished with antiques. Gourmet breakfast is served on the porch overlooking 56 acre lake. 15 minutes from the ocean. Dinner $25/person.

AMENITIES

1. No Smoking
2. No Pets
3. No Children
4. Senior Citizen Rates
5. Tennis Available
6. Golf Available
7. Swimming Available
8. Skiing Available
9. Credit Cards Accepted
10. Personal Check Accepted
11. Off Season Rates
12. Dinner Available (w/sufficient notice)

New Mexico

The Land of Enchantment

Capital: Santa Fe
Statehood: January 6, 1912; the 47th state
State Motto: It Grows As It Goes
State Song: "O Fair New Mexico"
State Bird: Road Runner
State Flower: Yucca Flower
State Tree: Pinon or Nut Pine

New Mexico is a warm and scenic country. Its magnificent scenery attracts visitors from everywhere. The days are mild and sometimes quite warm, but the evenings are cool and delightful.

Lovers of history can visit Indian ruins, frontier forts and Spanish missions. They can see homes and shops still made from dried adobe bricks. Mexican food is still the most popular food here and fine jewelry is sold along the streets by vendors at bargain prices.

The Palace of Governors, the oldest government building in the United States, is here, as well as the most interesting Carlsbad Caverns.

New Mexico

Albuquerque

Careleno, Uta & Richard
701 Roma Ave., NW, 87102
(505) 242-8755

Amenities: 5,6,8,9,10
Breakfast: Continental

Dbl. Oc.: $60.00-$75.00
Sgl. Oc.: $55.00-$70.00
Third Person: $10.00

W.E. Mauger Estate—Centrally located, this charming historic residence accommodates 16 souls in a style reminiscent of an era when graciousness, thoughtfulness, and elegance were a way of life.

Albuquerque

Morse, Mrs. Dorothy
1011 Ortega NW, 87114
(505) 898-0654

Amenities: 1,5,6,7,8,10
Breakfast: Continental

Dbl. Oc.: $40.00-$62.00
Sgl. Oc.: $30.00-$57.00
Third Person: $5.00-$10.00

Adobe and Roses is a quietly elegant adobe hacienda in Albuquerque. Large guest suite with: fireplace, piano, patio, Mexican tiles, garden, & pool. 1 hour from Santa Fe; a truly lovely place.

Alto (Ruidoso)

Goodman, Lila & Larry
Ft. Stanton Rd.,
P.O. Box 463, 88312
(505) 336-4515

Amenities: 1,2,3,5,6,7,8,9,10
Breakfast: Full

Dbl. Oc.: $69.39

Sierra Mesa Lodge—Nestled into a wooded hillside, five elegant, luxurious guest rooms & private baths, each in a different decor. Indoor spa. Restaurants, galleries & shops nearby. Enjoy horse racing, fishing, & hiking.

Cedar Crest

Nelson, Elaine
Box 444, 87008
(505) 281-2467

Amenities: 1,2,8
Breakfast: Continental

Dbl. Oc.: $55.00-$75.00
Sgl. Oc.: $55.00-$75.00
Third Person: $10.00

Elaine's Bed & Breakfast—Romantic hideaway on historic Turquoise Trail. Minutes from Alburquerque and Santa Fe. Beautiful 3-story log home nestled in Sandia Mountains offers a blend of warmth, serenity, & mountain scenery.

Corrales

Briault, Mary
Plaza San Ysidro, 87048
(505) 897-4422

Amenities: 9,10,12
Breakfast: Full

Dbl. Oc.: $63.67
Sgl. Oc.: $52.81
Third Person: $6.00-$20.00

Corrales Inn—Six gracious rooms with bath surrounding a courtyard with fountain & hot tub. A rural oasis 12 miles north of Albuquerque. 2,000 volume library. French country dinners. French spoken.

AMENITIES

1. No Smoking
2. No Pets
3. No Children
4. Senior Citizen Rates
5. Tennis Available
6. Golf Available
7. Swimming Available
8. Skiing Available
9. Credit Cards Accepted
10. Personal Check Accepted
11. Off Season Rates
12. Dinner Available (w/sufficient notice)

New Mexico

Corrales

Montgomery, Pat & James
P.O. Box 2263, 87048
(505) 898-7027

Amenities: 5,6,7,8,9,10
Breakfast: Continental

Dbl. Oc.: $58.00
Sgl. Oc.: $58.00

"Yours Truly"—Nice contemporary adobe with fantastic views. A carafe of coffee and the morning paper await outside your door. Breakfasts in the sunlit kitchen or patio. Marvelous hot tub. Fun folks, unique place.

Hernandez

Vigil, Eileen
P.O. Box 66, US Hwy. 84,
Mile Post 270, 87537
(505) 753-6049

Amenities: 5,7,8,9,12
Breakfast: Full
Dbl. Oc.: $61.34-$71.95
Sgl. Oc.: $61.34-$71.95
Third Person: $12.50

Casa del Rio—A tiny working horse & sheep ranch nestled in the pink cliffs of northern New Mexico. Visit 8 Indian Pueblos. Equal distance to Taos & Santa Fe. Horse facilities available. Come and stay.

Las Cruces

Lundeen, Linda & Gerry
618 S. Alameda Blvd., 88005
(505) 526-3355, 526-3327

Amenities: 1,4,9,10,11
Breakfast: Continental
Dbl. Oc.: $54.31-$76.04
Sgl. Oc.: $48.88-$70.61
Third Person: $10.59

Lundeen, Inn Of The Arts is located in downtown Las Cruces. Mexican-territorial adobe. gracious hacienda, adjoining the Linda Lundeen Gallery. All 8 rooms named after American artists, private baths.

AMENITIES

1. No Smoking
2. No Pets
3. No Children
4. Senior Citizen Rates
5. Tennis Available
6. Golf Available
7. Swimming Available
8. Skiing Available
9. Credit Cards Accepted
10. Personal Check Accepted
11. Off Season Rates
12. Dinner Available (w/sufficient notice)

New Mexico

Pilar (Taos)

Thibodeau, Dick
2886 State Rte. 68,
Box 1-A, 87571
(800) 552-0070, Ext., 822

Amenities: 1,7,8,9,10
Breakfast: Continental

Dbl. Oc.: $39.50
Sgl. Oc.: $35.00
Third Person: $7.50

The Plum Tree—A country place in the Rio Grande Valley. Southwest hacienda style, lovely gardens and patios. A great area for enjoying nature. A short drive to the cultural centers of Santa Fe and Taos. Welcome.

Sandia Park

Johnston, Lois
13 Tejano Cyn Rd., Box 94, 87047
(505) 281-1384

Amenities: 2,8,9,10
Breakfast: Continental
Dbl. Oc.: $55.00-$105.00
Sgl. Oc.: $45.00
Third Person: $15.00

The Pine Cone—A unique mountain retreat for all seasons located on the scenic and historic "Turquoise Trail." 5 miles to Sandia ski area, 20 minutes ot Albuquerque city limits. Fireplace & kitchen in deluxe 2 bedroom suite.

Santa Fe

Behm, Amy & Herbert
138 W. Manhattan, 87501
(505) 984-8001

Amenities: 2,8,9,10,11
Breakfast: Continental

Dbl. Oc.: $93.18
Sgl. Oc.: $71.25
Third Person: $10.96

Pueblo Bonito Bed & Breakfast Inn—Secluded adobe compound, five minute walk to plaza. Close to skiing and opera. 14 quiet casitas, each with private bath & fireplace. Breakfast served to your room! Romantic 100-year-old estate.

Santa Fe

Bennett, Mrs. Gloria
436 Sunset, 87501
(505) 983-3523

Amenities: 5,6,7,10
Breakfast: Continental

Dbl. Oc.: $45.00-$55.00
Sgl. Oc.: $45.00-$55.00

Ideal Location 3 blocks to plaza; 14 miles to ski area; one block to sports complex. Artistic, friendly atmosphere; wonderful views of mountains and sunsets from deck.

AMENITIES

1. No Smoking
2. No Pets
3. No Children
4. Senior Citizen Rates
5. Tennis Available
6. Golf Available
7. Swimming Available
8. Skiing Available
9. Credit Cards Accepted
10. Personal Check Accepted
11. Off Season Rates
12. Dinner Available (w/sufficient notice)

New Mexico

Santa Fe

Gosse, Jean D.
2407 Camino Capitan
(505) 471-4053

Amenities: 1,2,4,5,6,7,10
Breakfast: Continental

Dbl. Oc.: $35.00
Sgl. Oc.: $30.00

Jean's Place is a quiet, modest home in a family neighborhood. Ten to 15 minutes south of Plaza. Love fills this simple home. Queen-size bed.

Santa Fe

Walter, Martin
122 Grant Ave., 87501
(505) 983-6678

Amenities: 2,8,9,10,11
Breakfast: Full
Dbl. Oc.: $50.00-$110.00
Sgl. Oc.: $45.00
Third Person: $15.00

Grand Corner Inn is a delightful bed and breakfast hotel in a restored Colonial home 2 blocks from Santa Fe's historic Plaza. Restaurant serving gourmet breakfast to the public.

Taos

Carp, M/M Douglas
East Kit Carson Rd.,
P.O. Box 2983, 87571
(505) 758-8001

Amenities: 1,2,5,6,7,8,10
Breakfast: Full

Dbl. Oc.: $55.00-$70.00
Sgl. Oc.: $50.00-$65.00
Third Person: $15.00

Gallery House West is an adobe inn on historic Kit Carson Road. Inn-side and out you will feel the mystic of Taos. Minutes walk from galleries, museums, restaurants, short drive to Pueblo, ski valley & gorge.

Taos

Otero, Kitty & George
Box 3400, Morada Ln., 87571
(505) 758-9456

Amenities: 2,8,10,12
Breakfast: Full

Dbl. Oc.: $59.00-$120.00
Sgl. Oc.: $59.00-$120.00
Third Person: $15.00

Maben Dodge Lyhan House—National historic site. Come through gates to a place where D.H. Lawrence, Georgia O'Keefe & other famous artists & writers gathered. Ten bedroom adobe resembling Taos Pueblo. Downtown, five acres.

AMENITIES

1. No Smoking
2. No Pets
3. No Children
4. Senior Citizen Rates
5. Tennis Available
6. Golf Available
7. Swimming Available
8. Skiing Available
9. Credit Cards Accepted
10. Personal Check Accepted
11. Off Season Rates
12. Dinner Available (w/sufficient notice)

New Mexico

Taos

Pelton, Carol & Randy
Box 177, 87571
(505) 758-0287

Amenities: 1,2,5,8,9,10
Breakfast: Continental

Dbl. Oc.: $50.00-$100.00
Sgl. Oc.: $39.00-$82.00
Third Person: $20.00

Hacienda del Sol—Historic 180+-year-old adobe once owned by Mabel Dodge. With a majestic view of Taos Mountain across 95,000 acres of Indian land. Most rooms have fireplaces & private baths. Jacuzzi. Only 1 miles from famous Taos Plaza.

Taos

Ripley, Patricia
Box 1C-:Pilar, 87571
(505) 758-2596

Amenities: 10
Breakfast: Full

Dbl. Oc.: $60.00
Sgl. Oc.: $50.00
Third Person: $20.00

PTR—Pilar efficiency apartment with porch overlooking Rio Grande. Easy access to: Taos/Santa Fe, hiking, fishing, rafting; rural village atmosphere.

Taos

Russell, Gail
Box 241, 87571
(505) 776-8474

Amenities: 5,10,12
Breakfast: Full

Dbl. Oc.: $52.00-$63.00
Sgl. Oc.: $32.50-$38.00
Third Person: $20.00

Mountain Light B&B—Spacious Pueblo-style adobe with: rustic architecture, fireplaces, family kitchen. The magnificent view includes the Sangre De Christo Mountains at Taos. Home of noted southwest photographer Gail Russell.

Taos

Stevens, Susan
207 Brooks St.,
P.O. Box 4954, 87571
(505) 758-1489

Amenities: 1,2,4,8,9,10
Breakfast: Continental

Dbl. Oc.: $71.50
Sgl. Oc.: $60.50
Third Person: $8.00

The Brooks Street Inn is a casual little inn with a touch of elegance. Artwork & handcrafted furniture fill our seven guest rooms. Historic plaza, galleries, shops and museums are within walking distance.

Truchas

Frank, Curtiss
P.O. Box 338, 87578
(505) 689-2374

Amenities: 10
Breakfast: Full

Dbl. Oc.: $45.00
Sgl. Oc.: $35.00
Third Person: $15.00

A Small Working Farm at the gateway to the Pecos wilderness area for those seeking a healthful retreat, outdoor recreation and a spectacular view.

AMENITIES

1. No Smoking
2. No Pets
3. No Children
4. Senior Citizen Rates
5. Tennis Available
6. Golf Available
7. Swimming Available
8. Skiing Available
9. Credit Cards Accepted
10. Personal Check Accepted
11. Off Season Rates
12. Dinner Available (w/sufficient notice)

New York

The Empire State

Capital: Albany
Statehood: July 26, 1788; the 11th state
State Motto: Ever Upward
State Song: "I Love New York"
State Bird: Bluebird
State Flower: Rose
State Tree: Sugar Maple

New York is a mecca for tourists. It offers something for everyone. Commercially, it is the greatest manufacturing state in the United States, and it far out-ranks all other states in foreign trade and wholesale and retail trade.

Besides everything else, it is the nation's center for transportation, banking and finance.

It is a farming state, as well. Some of the finest fruits and vegetables are grown here.

Tourists can find just about any kind of recreation in this state, from the quiet and beauty of its mountains and streams, to the Big Apple, New York City, the largest city in the state. New York City offers skyscrapers, the United Nations Building, Statue of Liberty, New York Stock Exchange, and numerous choices of theatres and sports.

Four presidents have been born in this state, Martin Van Buren, Millard Fillmore, Theodore Roosevelt, and Franklin D. Roosevelt.

New York

Afton

Fabricius, Ms. Patricia H.
155 East Main St., 13730
(607) 639-1842

Amenities: 6,7,8,9,10
Breakfast: Full

Dbl. Oc.: $45.00-$60.00
Sgl. Oc.: $38.00
Third Person: $10.00

Jericho Farm Inn B&B—Historic mansion; six-acre riverfront; picnic; canoe; fish; jacuzzi; TV's; hunt. Three hours to New York City. I-88, Exit 7, 30 minutes east of Binghamton. Walk to restaurants. Business travelers welcome, long or short term.

Altamont

Beckmann, Laurie & Gerd
Rte. 146, Box 18, RD 3, 12009
(518) 861-8344

Amenities: 1,2,5,6,7,8,9,10
Breakfast: Full
Dbl. Oc.: $53.50
Sgl. Oc.: $37.45
Third Person: $10.70

Appel Inn—Historic inn from 1765. Spacious rooms with fireplaces, porches, iron beds, down comforters, & wide plank floors. On 6 acres, minutes from Albany & Schenectady, 30 minutes to Saratoga. Available for weddings.

Amenia

Flaherty, James
Box 26, Leedsville Rd., 12501
(914) 373-9681

Amenities: 2,3,5,6,7,8,9,10
Breakfast: Full
Dbl. Oc.: $345.75 & up

Troutbeck—English country estate on 442 acres; indoor & outdoor pools; tennis; four star rating for cuisine. Executive retreat during the week, country inn on weekends only; beautiful weddings. Rates include 3 meals & spirits.

Ashland

Jakobleff, Billie & Bill
P.O. Box 53, 12407
1 (518) 734-3358

Amenities: 6,8
Breakfast: Continental

Dbl. Oc.: $60.00
Sgl. Oc.: $55.00

Ashland Farmhouse is a restored farmhouse and circa 1870 barn with all the comforts of modern living; hot tub by the wood stove, queen size beds and private baths. Stocked trout pond, hunting.

AMENITIES

1. No Smoking
2. No Pets
3. No Children
4. Senior Citizen Rates
5. Tennis Available
6. Golf Available
7. Swimming Available
8. Skiing Available
9. Credit Cards Accepted
10. Personal Check Accepted
11. Off Season Rates
12. Dinner Available (w/sufficient notice)

New York

Averill Park

Tomlinson, Thelma & Clyde
Rt. 3, Box 301, 12018
(518) 766-5035

Amenities: 1,2,3,8
Breakfast: Full

Dbl. Oc.: $55.00
Sgl. Oc.: $45.00

Ananas Hus Bed And Breakfast—Hillside ranch home with panoramic view of the Hudson River Valley, in west Stephentown midway between Albany and Pittsfield. Near ski areas and cultural attractions.

Bolton Landing

Richards, Anita & Charles
6883 Lakeshore Dr., 12814
(518) 644-2492

Amenities: 2,5,6,7,8,10
Breakfast: Full
Dbl. Oc.: $40.00
Sgl. Oc.: $30.00
Third Person: $10.00

Hilltop Cottage B&B is a short walk from beaches, marinas, restaurants, and shops in Bolton on Lake George. Three rooms share bath; also guest cabin; pets here; breakfast on porch; smoking limited. Brochure.

Brookfield

Tanney, Mrs. Donna
Dugway Rd., 13314
(315) 899-5837

Amenities: 10,12
Breakfast: Full
Dbl. Oc.: $47.00-$64.00
Sgl. Oc.: $50.00
Third Person: $17.50

Gates Hill Homestead—A Saltbox with a massive fireplace, stenciling & cozy hand-done interior, set in a quiet hardwood forest, offers horse-drawn sleigh or stagecoach tours & homecooked dinners by reservation. Dinner $12.50/Person.

AMENITIES

1. No Smoking
2. No Pets
3. No Children
4. Senior Citizen Rates
5. Tennis Available
6. Golf Available
7. Swimming Available
8. Skiing Available
9. Credit Cards Accepted
10. Personal Check Accepted
11. Off Season Rates
12. Dinner Available (w/sufficient notice)

New York

Buffalo

Trinidad, Virginia
440 Le Brun Rd., 14226
(716) 836-0794

Amenities: 1,2,3,6,8,10
Breakfast: Full

Dbl. Oc.: $48.60
Sgl. Oc.: $32.40

B&B Of Niagara Frontier—A well-traveled health professional welcomes you to this elegantly furnished suburban home. Proximity to: downtown, Niagara, airport, public transport, & university. Enjoy the home as you would your own.

Burdett

Schmanke, Ms. Sandra
Picnic Area Rd., 14818
(607) 546-8566

Amenities: 2,3,7,8,9,10,12
Breakfast: Full

Dbl. Oc.: $55.85
Sgl. Oc.: $37.45
Third Person: $5.35

Red House Country Inn, near Watkins Glen & Seneca Lake, in 13,000-acre national forest. 28 miles of hiking/X-C ski trails. Wineries nearby. Beautiful 1840 farmstead, antiques thru-out. Children 12+ welcome. Dinner $14.98/Person.

Canandaigua

Adams, Alicen
4510 Bristol Valley Rd.,
Rte. 64, 14424
(716) 229-5343

Amenities: 3,8,9,12
Breakfast: Full

Dbl. Oc.: $48.15
Sgl. Oc.: $37.45
Third Person: $16.05

Cricket Club Tearoom, Bed And Breakfast—English style, near lakes. Festivals, vineyards, wineries, historic homes, & musuems abound. Ski, sail, hunt, hike, golf, ride. Tour the region in the many seasons & acitivities. Rochester, 45 minutes, Canada, 2 hours away.

Canandaigua

Freese, Betty & Howard
4761 Rte. 364, Rushville, 14544
(716) 554-6973

Amenities: 1,2,5,7,8,10
Breakfast: Full

Dbl. Oc.: $45.00-$50.00
Sgl. Oc.: $35.00
Third Person: $15.00

Lakeview Farm Bed & Breakfast—Hospitality & nature at our country home on 170 acres overlooking Canadaigua Lake. Two antique furnished lake view rooms, shared bath, sitting room. Close to marina, sandy beach excellent restaurants.

Canandaigua

Scott, Dixy & Murray
5741 Bristol Valley Rd., 14424
(716) 374-5355

Amenities: 8
Breakfast: Full

Dbl. Oc.: $58.85
Sgl. Oc.: $42.80
Third Person: $10.70

Nottingham Lodge Bed & Breakfast—The view is Bristol Mountain ski center. Golf, summer theatre, grape pies and pottery in the area. Three bedrooms (canopy, four poster or brass and iron) two baths; casual elegance; ski packages.

AMENITIES

1. No Smoking
2. No Pets
3. No Children
4. Senior Citizen Rates
5. Tennis Available
6. Golf Available
7. Swimming Available
8. Skiing Available
9. Credit Cards Accepted
10. Personal Check Accepted
11. Off Season Rates
12. Dinner Available (w/sufficient notice)

New York

Canadaigua

Swartout, Miss Linda C.
5648 N. Bloomfield Rd., 14425
(716) 394-8132

Amenities: 1,2,5,6,7,8,9,10,12
Breakfast: Full

Dbl. Oc.: $65.00
Sgl. Oc.: $59.00
Third Person: $17.00

Wilder Tavern, an 1829 brick stagecoach stop, restored as a small country inn. Four charming rooms furnished with quilts, samplers, & memorabilia. 30 minutes east of Rochester in the heart of the Finger Lakes.

Canaseraga

Coombs, Renee & Robert
37 Mill St., 14822
(607) 545-6439

Amenities: 5,6,7,10
Breakfast: Full

Dbl. Oc.: $35.00
Sgl. Oc.: $20.00

The Country House—Sample the heart of New York's Southern Tier with a bed & breakfast stay at our century old Victorian home. Minutes to skiing, Letchworth State Park, Corning Glassworks, hunting, fishing, hiking & scenic solitude.

Cazenovia

Barr, H. Grey
5 Albany St., 13035
(315) 655-3431

Amenities: 2,4,6,7,8,9,10,12
Breakfast: Continental

Dbl. Oc.: $72.76
Sgl. Oc.: $62.06
Third Person: $7.00

Brae Loch Inn—A family run Scottish Inn with old world charm, located across from beautiful Cazenovia Lake. Fine dining and Scottish gift shop.

Chappaqua

Crabtree, John & Dick
11 Kittle Rd., 10514
(914) 666-8044

Amenities: 9,12
Breakfast: Continental

Dbl. Oc.: $81.55
Sgl. Oc.: $73.95
Third Person: $10.00

Crabtree's Kittle House—Gourmet restaurant set in gracious country surrounding, yet easy access to New York City or myriad antique shops.

Chestertown

Caesteckea, Alison
Friends Lake, 12817
(518) 494-2828

Amenities: 2,7,8,9,10,12
Breakfast: Full

Dbl. Oc.: $103.15
Sgl. Oc.: $81.00
Third Person: $10.00

The Balsam House—An elegant country inn and restaurant, serving the finest in country French cuisine. 20 charming, guest rooms, no one like another. Located on beautiful Friends Lake. Open year round.

AMENITIES

1. No Smoking
2. No Pets
3. No Children
4. Senior Citizen Rates
5. Tennis Available
6. Golf Available
7. Swimming Available
8. Skiing Available
9. Credit Cards Accepted
10. Personal Check Accepted
11. Off Season Rates
12. Dinner Available (w/sufficient notice)

New York

Clinton

Van Deusen, Carolyn & Wayne
46 Williams St., 13323
(315) 853-8389

Amenities: 1,2,3,10
Breakfast: Full

Dbl. Oc.: $56.00
Sgl. Oc.: $46.00
Third Person: $10.00

The Victorian Carriage House is in the historic district of the village, within walking distance of restaurants and shops. Decorated with antiques and family heirlooms, the rooms are warm and charming.

Cold Spring

Sawyer, Ms. Mary Pat
2 Main St., 10516
(914) 265-9355

Amenities: 5,6,7,8,9,10,11,12
Breakfast: Continental
Dbl. Oc.: $85.00
Sgl. Oc.: $75.00
Third Person: $45.00

Hudson House, A Country Inn—A restored 1832 historic landmark on the banks of the Hudson River. Antique-filled guest rooms with private baths. Full restaurants & American country menu. Antique shops, historic restorations nearby.

Conesus

Esse, Ginny & Dale
2388 East Lake Rd., 14435
(716) 346-6526

Amenities: 1,2,7,9,11
Breakfast: Full
Dbl. Oc.: $60.00
Sgl. Oc.: $50.00
Third Person: $8.00

Conesus Lake Bed & Breakfast—Overnite docking, private beach and picnic facilities available. Two attractive rooms share a bath with double whirlpool tub. Reservations suggested. Open year round.

AMENITIES

1. No Smoking
2. No Pets
3. No Children
4. Senior Citizen Rates
5. Tennis Available
6. Golf Available
7. Swimming Available
8. Skiing Available
9. Credit Cards Accepted
10. Personal Check Accepted
11. Off Season Rates
12. Dinner Available (w/sufficient notice)

New York

Cooperstown

Bohlman, Joyce
63 Chestnut St., 13326
(607) 547-2633

Amenities: 1,2,3,4,5,6,7,8,9,10
Breakfast: Full
Dbl. Oc.: $53.00-$68.90
Sgl. Oc.: $53.00-$68.90

The J.P. Sill House is a marvelously restored 1864 Italianate Victorian home, featured in Victorian Homes Magazine, with marble fireplaces, down comforters, & firm queen beds. A short walk to Baseball Hall of Fame, Lake Ostego, dining & more...

Cooperstown

Dann, Mrs. Jacqueline, A.
Box 614, RD 3, Rte. 166, 13326
(607) 286-7056

Amenities: 7,8
Breakfast: Full

Dbl. Oc.: $48.00
Sgl. Oc.: $38.00

Middlefield Guest House—Panoramic views from each window of this 1823 restored Hop Picker house nestled at the foot of the Catskills, 6 miles from Cooperstown. Clean comfortable rooms, with a delicious breakfasts.

Cooperstown

Grimes, Joan & Jack
RD #2, Box 514, 13326
(607) 547-9700

Amenities: 1,2,5,6,7,8,10
Breakfast: Full

Dbl. Oc.: $55.00
Sgl. Oc.: $45.00
Third Person: $10.00

The Inn At Brook Willow Farm—Listed as one of the 100 best B&B's in America. The inn is furnished with antiques and warm hospitality. Choose a room in the re-born barn or main house. A slice of serenity on 14 acres.

Corning

DePumpo, Mrs. Mary
188 Delevan Ave., 14830
(607) 962-2347

Amenities: 1,6,8,10
Breakfast: Full

Dbl. Oc.: $65.40
Sgl. Oc.: $54.50
Third Person: $10.90

Delevan House—Southern Colonial home on hill overlooking Corning. Quiet surroundings; shared and private bath accommodations; warm hospitality; very private; full breakfast. We also invite you to relax on sun porch.

AMENITIES

1. No Smoking
2. No Pets
3. No Children
4. Senior Citizen Rates
5. Tennis Available
6. Golf Available
7. Swimming Available
8. Skiing Available
9. Credit Cards Accepted
10. Personal Check Accepted
11. Off Season Rates
12. Dinner Available (w/sufficient notice)

New York

Corning

Gehl, Lois & Fran
69 E. First St., 14830
(607) 962-6355

Amenities: 2,9,10
Breakfast: Continental
Dbl. Oc.: $71.00
Sgl. Oc.: $50.00
Third Person: $11.00

"1865" White Birch Bed & Breakfast—
Each room is uniquely decorated to give you that "visiting grandma" feeling. We're located within a few blocks of everything Corning has to offer. The Finger Lakes are just a short drive away.

Corning

Peer, Winifred & Dick
134 East First St., 14830
(607) 962-3253

Amenities: 9,10
Breakfast: Continental

Dbl. Oc.: $66.00-$104.00
Sgl. Oc.: $55.00-$83.00
Third Person: $20.00

Rosewood Inn—Step back into a time of Victorian elegance. Enjoy antique-filled guest rooms with private baths, some with fireplaces. Walk to nearby restored Market Street or Corning's noted glass center, museums & fine dining.

Corning

Walsh, G. Lauriston, Jr.
402A Hornby Rd., 14830
(607) 962-3979

Amenities: 5,6,7,8,9,10,12
Breakfast: Full
Dbl. Oc.: $75.00
Sgl. Oc.: $55.00
Third Person: $20.00

West Wind Farm—A beautiful secluded setting just ten minutes from Corning attractions. 120 acres; X/C skiing; horseback riding; archery; jacuzzi; sauna; volleyball; badmitton; etc. Boarding kennel and stables available.

AMENITIES

1. No Smoking
2. No Pets
3. No Children
4. Senior Citizen Rates
5. Tennis Available
6. Golf Available
7. Swimming Available
8. Skiing Available
9. Credit Cards Accepted
10. Personal Check Accepted
11. Off Season Rates
12. Dinner Available (w/sufficient notice)

New York

Davenport

Hodge, William B.
Main St., 13750
(607) 278-5068

Amenities: 2,6,7,8,9,10,12
Breakfast: Continental
Dbl. Oc.: $35.56-$47.85
Sgl. Oc.: $19.76-$35.56
Third Person: $8.32

The Davenport Inn is a historic tavern built in 1819. It is close to Cooperstown and Oneonta. Our dining room features corn fritters! Private & shared baths available. Five rooms. Reservations please!!

Dolgeville

Naizby, Mrs. Adrianna
44 Stewart St., 13329
(315) 429-3249

Amenities: 5,6,7,8,10
Breakfast: Full

Dbl. Oc.: $37.45
Sgl. Oc.: $32.10
Third Person: $15.00

Adrianna is located just off the New York State Thruway's exit 29A, amid glorious views of the Adirondeck foothills & short rides to Saratoga, greater Utica & Syracuse areas. Open year round.

Dryden

Brownell, Margaret Thacher
9 James St., Box 119, 13053
(607) 844-8052

Amenities: 1,2,10
Breakfast: Continental

Dbl. Oc.: $40.00
Sgl. Oc.: $35.00
Third Person: $10.00

Margaret Thacher's Spruce Haven Bed & Breakfast—Log home surrounded by Spruce trees. Warm & friendly; 2 rooms, shared bath. Upstate New York within 12 miles: Ithaca, Cortland, lakes, skiing, colleges, & museums. 1 night's deposit to hold reservation.

Dundee

Kidd, Mrs. Wm. James
4798 Dundee-Himrod Rd., 14837
(607) 243-8628

Amenities: 1,2,10
Breakfast: Full
Dbl. Oc.: $55.00
Sgl. Oc.: $45.00
Third Person: $25.00

Country Manor Bed & Breakfast—1830's Italianate farmhouse on 7 wildlife acres. Three double bedrooms, 2 shared baths. Homemade jams and delicacies. Library; parlor; TV room; garden swing; open all year; near wineries, museums, & races.

AMENITIES

1. No Smoking
2. No Pets
3. No Children
4. Senior Citizen Rates
5. Tennis Available
6. Golf Available
7. Swimming Available
8. Skiing Available
9. Credit Cards Accepted
10. Personal Check Accepted
11. Off Season Rates
12. Dinner Available (w/sufficient notice)

New York

Dundee

Patnoe, Chris & George
660 E. Wanet Lake Rd.,
Box 197, RD #1, 14837
(607) 292-6606

Amenities: 3,7,9,10
Breakfast: Continental

Dbl. Oc.: $48.15
Sgl. Oc.: $43.87

Lakeside Terrace—Air conditioned bedrooms in a comfortable rustic home located on Waneta Lake. Enjoy swimming, fishing, rafting, small sail boat and a canoe or just relax on the beach. Central to Finger Lakes attractions.

Dundee

Wilgus, M/M John
N. Glenora Rd., 65, 14837
(607) 243-7686

Amenities: 2,3,6,7,9,10
Breakfast: Full
Dbl. Oc.: $50.00
Sgl. Oc.: $35.00

Glenora Bed & Breakfast—Enjoy quiet comfort on lovely Seneca, heart of the Finger Lakes. Near: wineries, Corning Glass Center, and other attractions. Beautiful view..

Eagle Bay

Bennett, Bonnie & Douglas
On Big Moose Lake, 13331
(315) 357-2042

Amenities: 2,5,7,8,9,12
Breakfast: Continental

Dbl. Oc.: $39.00-$60.00
Sgl. Oc.: $32.00-$55.00
Third Person: $5.00-$10.00

Big Moose Inn on Big Moose Lake—our 20th year. Cozy Adirondack rooms; lakeside dining; cocktail lounge; guest lounge with fireplace; neighboring marina. Enjoy outdoor activities or just relax.

East Hampton

Chancey, Harry
13 Woods Lane, 11937
(516) 324-9414

Amenities: 1,2,3,9
Breakfast: Full
Dbl. Oc.: $161.25
Sgl. Oc.: $161.25

Centennial House—Historic estate district home between ocean & village. Marble bathrooms adjoin elegant bedrooms. Generous buffet breakfast served in Georgian dining room. Formal parlor matching crystal chandeliers.

AMENITIES

1. No Smoking
2. No Pets
3. No Children
4. Senior Citizen Rates
5. Tennis Available
6. Golf Available
7. Swimming Available
8. Skiing Available
9. Credit Cards Accepted
10. Personal Check Accepted
11. Off Season Rates
12. Dinner Available (w/sufficient notice)

New York

Elizabethtown

Pushee, Beki & Bruce
136 River St., 12932
(518) 873-2294

Amenities: 2,5,6,7,8,10,11
Breakfast: Full
Dbl. Oc.: $32.00-$38.00
Sgl. Oc.: $25.00-$32.00
Third Person: $20.00

Old Mill Studio—Located in a small Adirondack village, 25 miles east of Lake Placid and minutes west of Lake Champlain. The mill has a long and enchanting history, from Millwright to artist.

Falconer

Viramontes, Debra & Frank
Gerry Levant Rd.,
RD 1, Box 633, 14733
(716) 665-2352

Amenities: 2,4,10
Breakfast: Full

Dbl. Oc.: $55.00-$65.00
Sgl. Oc.: $40.00-$50.00
Third Person: $5.00

Mansard Inn—1857 Victorian country villa surrounded by ornamental trees and flower gardens is decorated to re-create the Victorian era. Nearby skiing, antique shops, the Chautauqua Institute. Located 1 mile off Rt. 17.

Glens Falls

Crislip, M/M Ned
Box 57, RD #1, Ridge Rd.,
12801
(518) 793-6869

Amenities: 1,6,8,9,10,11
Breakfast: Full

Dbl. Oc.: $60.00
Sgl. Oc.: $50.00
Third Person: $5.00

Crislip's Bed & Breakfast, located in Adirondack resort area, is a historic home featuring spacious antique-filled rooms with private baths. Recreational & cultural sights nearby at Lake George & Saratoga. Off I-87. Winter, ski West Mountain.

Gowanda

Lay, Mrs. Phyllis
RD #1, Box 543, 14070
(716) 532-2168

Amenities: 2,5,6,7,8,10
Breakfast: Full

Dbl. Oc.: $35.00
Sgl. Oc.: $30.00
Third Person: $10.00

The Tepee—A bed and breakfast establishment on the Cattaraugus Indian Reservation. Light, bright rooms; Seneca Indians artifacts; tours of reservation and Amish country. Send or call for brochure.

AMENITIES

1. No Smoking
2. No Pets
3. No Children
4. Senior Citizen Rates
5. Tennis Available
6. Golf Available
7. Swimming Available
8. Skiing Available
9. Credit Cards Accepted
10. Personal Check Accepted
11. Off Season Rates
12. Dinner Available (w/sufficient notice)

New York

Gowanda

Mansfield, Jane & Fox
Jamestown, US Rt. 62, 14070
(716) 532-4252

Amenities: 2,4,5,6,8,10,12
Breakfast: Continental

Dbl. Oc.: $35.00
Sgl. Oc.: $30.00
Third Person: $10.00

The Fox's Den—Gracious 100+year home with spacious rooms. Near: skiing, hiking, hunting, fishing, boating, rafting, fossil hunting, Amish community (quilts), & Seneca Indian reservation. Good food, pleasant hospitality.

Groton

Gere, Jessie & Donald
217 So. Main St., 13073
(607) 898-4127

Amenities: 5,6,7,8,10
Breakfast: Full

Dbl. Oc.: $48.15
Sgl. Oc.: $48.15

Whispering Pines, built around 1890, has 3 guestrooms for guests. Located 7.5 miles from Ithaca, close to Ithaca College, Cornell, state parks, Greek Peak and fine dining. A beautiful place to visit.

Groton

Gleason, Irene, M.
307 Old Stage Rd., 13073
(607) 898-4676

Amenities: 1
Breakfast: Full

Dbl. Oc.: $35.00
Sgl. Oc.: $35.00

Gleason's Bed & Breakfast—an 1840 farmhouse 15 minutes from Cornell & Cortland. Less than an hour from Syracuse, Binghamton & Auburn. Fine restaurants nearby.

Hammondsport

Bowman, Manita & Jack
61 Lake St., P.O. Box 586, 14840
(607) 569-2516

Amenities: 1,2,3,10,11
Breakfast: Continental
Dbl. Oc.: $70.85
Sgl. Oc.: $65.40

The Bowman House, A Bed And Breakfast—Quiet comfort in picturesque Hammondsport Village. Spacious 1800's home with comfortable bedrooms & sitting rooms. 4 rooms; 2 private, 2 semi-private baths. Visit lakes, museums, & wineries; ideal vacation.

AMENITIES

1. No Smoking
2. No Pets
3. No Children
4. Senior Citizen Rates
5. Tennis Available
6. Golf Available
7. Swimming Available
8. Skiing Available
9. Credit Cards Accepted
10. Personal Check Accepted
11. Off Season Rates
12. Dinner Available (w/sufficient notice)

New York

Hammondsport

Laufersweiler, Mrs. Ellen
11 William St., 14840
(607) 569-3402

Amenities: 1,2,7,10
Breakfast: Full

Dbl. Oc.: $60.00
Sgl. Oc.: $55.00
Third Person: $15.00

The Laufersweiler's Blushing Rose' Inn, located in historic Hammondsport. Museum, shops and lake within walking distance. Wineries nearby. Four generous bedrooms all with private baths. Quiet and cozy.

Hampton Bays

Ute, Hostess
Box 106, Hampton Bays, 11946
(516) 728-3560

Amenities: 2,3,5,6,7,10,11
Breakfast: Full
Dbl. Oc.: $60.00-$80.00
Sgl. Oc.: $50.00-$70.00
Third Person: $20.00

House On The Water—80 miles east New York City, 7 miles to Southampton, 2 miles to ocean beaches. 2 acres on bay; garden; terrace; lounges; kitchen privileges; TV; bicycles; boats; windsurfers. Rooms w/priv. bath & entrance, waterview. Great breakfast.

Homer

Stone, Mrs. Connie
80 S. Main St., 13077
(607) 749-3548

Amenities: 1,2,5,6,7,8,10
Breakfast: Full

Dbl. Oc.: $32.00-$45.00
Sgl. Oc.: $28.00-$36.00
Third Person: $5.00

The David Harum House is just four tenths of a mile off exit 12 on Interstate 81. It is a well known historic house built in 1815 with a beautiful spiral staircase & antique furniture; two guest rooms.

Hancock

Toth, Adele & James
RD 1, Box 232B, Walton, 13856
(607) 865-7254

Amenities: 1,4,6,8
Breakfast: Continental

Dbl. Oc.: $35.36
Sgl. Oc.: $30.16
Third Person: $10.40

Sunrise Inn B&B—A 19th century farmhouse with 2 cozy guest rooms & a woodstove, garden gazebo, antique shop, and trout creek for guests to enjoy in a peaceful country setting. 135 miles NW of New York City. Fine local dining.

AMENITIES

1. No Smoking
2. No Pets
3. No Children
4. Senior Citizen Rates
5. Tennis Available
6. Golf Available
7. Swimming Available
8. Skiing Available
9. Credit Cards Accepted
10. Personal Check Accepted
11. Off Season Rates
12. Dinner Available (w/sufficient notice)

New York

Hopewell Junction

Benich, Roy
Rt. 52, Carpenter Rd., 12533
(914) 221-1941

Amenities: 2,3,5,7,9,10,12
Breakfast: Continental
Dbl. Oc.: $94.73
Sgl. Oc.: $84.46
Third Person: $15.78

Le Chambord Restaurant & Inn—1863 Georgian estate. 4 star rated. Nine beautiful rooms with private baths, phones, continental breakfast, fine paintings & antiques; historic sites, wineries, antique shops. Open year round. Elegance on 10 acres.

Ithaca

Grunberg, Mrs. Wanda
P.O. Box 581, 14851
(607) 589-4771

Amenities: 8,9,10,12
Breakfast: Full

Dbl. Oc.: $53.00
Sgl. Oc.: $42.00
Third Person: $10.00

Log Country Inn—Rustic charm of log house at edge of 7,000 acre state forest. 15 minutes to Ithaca. Modern accommodation provided in the spirit of international hospitality; 3 rooms, home atmosphere. Call for reservations.

Ithaca

Rumsey, Margie
110 E. Buttermilk Falls Rd., 14850
(607) 273-3947 or 272-6767

Amenities: 1,2,4,7,8,9,10,11
Breakfast: Full
Dbl. Oc.: $54.50-$103.55
Sgl. Oc.: $43.60-$87.20
Third Person: $21.80-$32.70

Buttermilk Falls Bed And Breakfast—Built 1814 at the foot of the waterfalls just off Rte. 13, south edge of Ithaca, 3 1/2 miles to Cornell & Cayuga Lake. Six heritage-filled rooms, four baths. Spectacular wooded gorge, trails, & hiking. Five generation home.

AMENITIES

1. No Smoking
2. No Pets
3. No Children
4. Senior Citizen Rates
5. Tennis Available
6. Golf Available
7. Swimming Available
8. Skiing Available
9. Credit Cards Accepted
10. Personal Check Accepted
11. Off Season Rates
12. Dinner Available (w/sufficient notice)

New York

Ithaca

Tomlinson, Ms. Jeanne Marie
224 Bostwick Rd., 14850
(607) 272-8756

Amenities: 4,5,6,7,8,9,10,11
Breakfast: Full

Dbl. Oc.: $88.75
Sgl. Oc.: $70.85
Third Person: $21.80

Glendale Farm Bed And Breakfast—Our home built in 1865 is large & comfortable. Furnished with antiques, oriental carpets & a beamed ceiling in the living room. Six rooms are available for our guests in single, double or family accommodations.

Johnson

Scott, Elaine
Box 27, 10933
(914) 355-8811

Amenities: 1,6
Breakfast: Full

Rates: $15.00/Person

On Route 284, 10 miles from I-84.—Beautiful old home with antique shop on premises, 20 minutes from the Delaware River. Children & pets ok. Country atmosphere; open since 1980. Cribs free.

Keene

Wilson, Mr. Joe-Pete
Alstead Hill Rd., 12942
(518) 576-2221

Amenities: 5,6,7,9,10
Breakfast: Full
Dbl. Oc.: $93.60
Sgl. Oc.: $46.80
Third Person: $12.60-$25.20

The Bark Eater, a true country inn, located on a spacious farm minutes from the Olympic Village of Lake Placid. Spectacular sightseeing; country-style gourmet food. Featured in "Country Inn & Back Roads." Dinner-$24.00.

Keene Valley

Champagne, Sherry & Norman
Rte. 73, P.O. Box 701, 12943
(518) 576-2003

Amenities: 1,2,8,9,10,11,12
Breakfast: Full

Dbl. Oc.: $58.85-$74.90
Sgl. Oc.: $37.45
Third Person: $16.05

Champagne's High Peaks Inn—Cozy B&B inn quality meals general hospitality & comfortable lodging scenic wrap-around porch, large stone fireplace in living room. Endless outdoor activities close to Lake Placid and Olympic sites. In the Adirondacks.

AMENITIES

1. No Smoking
2. No Pets
3. No Children
4. Senior Citizen Rates
5. Tennis Available
6. Golf Available
7. Swimming Available
8. Skiing Available
9. Credit Cards Accepted
10. Personal Check Accepted
11. Off Season Rates
12. Dinner Available (w/sufficient notice)

New York

Kent

Ward, Bonnie & Ashley
14846 Roosevelt Hwy., 14477
(716) 682-3037

Amenities: 2,6,10
Breakfast: Continental

Dbl. Oc.: $42.00
Sgl. Oc.: $21.00

Ward's Farm House—35 minutes west of Rochester; 45 minutes east of Niagara Falls. 5 minutes to Oak Orchard River, center of sport fishing for King & Coho Salmon, Rainbow, Lake & Brown Trout. Charter information available.

Kingston

Calcavecchio, Adele & Ralph
88 W. Chester, 12401
(914) 331-2369

Amenities: 5,7,10
Breakfast: Full
Dbl. Oc.: $58.85
Sgl. Oc.: $42.80
Third Person: $10.70

Rondout Bed & Breakfast—Close to Hudson River cruises, theatres, antiquing, restaurants, & historic sites. Spacious & gracious 1905 mansion on two acres, two hours from New York City via Thruway, near Woodstock.

Lake Placid

Blair, Mrs. Mary
338 Old Military Rd., 12946
(518) 523-1114

Amenities: 10,11
Breakfast: Full

Dbl. Oc.: $50.00-$60.00
Sgl. Oc.: $50.00-$60.00
Third Person: $6.00

Mountain Hearth Inn—A 19th century renovated farmhouse with wonderful mountain views. One mile from center of town. Charming country decor in three comfortable rooms. Common room with fireplace; shared baths.

Lake Placid

Blazer, Cathy & Teddy
3 Highland Place, 12946
(518) 523-2377

Amenities: 2,5,6,7,8,9,10,11
Breakfast: Full

Dbl. Oc.: $55.00
Sgl. Oc.: $45.00
Third Person: $15.00

Highland House Inn—Centrally located in the village. Each room is uniquely appealing. In summer enjoy dining on the enclosed garden porch. Blueberry pancakes, a year round specialty!

AMENITIES

1. No Smoking
2. No Pets
3. No Children
4. Senior Citizen Rates
5. Tennis Available
6. Golf Available
7. Swimming Available
8. Skiing Available
9. Credit Cards Accepted
10. Personal Check Accepted
11. Off Season Rates
12. Dinner Available (w/sufficient notice)

New York

Lake Placid

Billerman, Gail & Bill
59 Sentinel Rd., 12946
(518) 523-3419

Amenities: 8,10,11
Breakfast: Full

Dbl. Oc.: $40.00-$60.00
Sgl. Oc.: $30.00
Third Person: $10.00

The Blackberry Inn is a large Colonial home situated one mile from the center of town close to all recreational & sightseeing activities. Newly redecorated rooms & a home baked breakfast await our guests.

Lake Placid

Eldridge, Betty
Cascade Rd., 12946
(518) 523-9369

Amenities: 2,5,6,7,8,10,12
Breakfast: Full

Dbl. Oc.: $44.00-$50.00
Sgl. Oc.: $22.00
Third Person: $10.00

South Meadow Farm & Lodge—Small working farm, adjacent to Olympic X/C trails. Free pass, sauna, hot cider, lessons & baby sitting available. Trails to high peaks from back door; family atmosphere. 7 miles east of Lake Placid on Rt. 73.

Lake Placid

Hoffman, Carol
31 Sentinel Rd., 12946
(518) 523-9350

Amenities: 1,2,9,10,11
Breakfast: Continental

Dbl. Oc.: $37.45
Third Person: $5.35

Spruce Lodge Bed & Breakfast—A family-run lodge within a ten mile radius of all area activities such as: skiing, hiking, skating, shopping, concerts, fishing, golf, tennis, hockey or anything else you might like to do.

Lake Placid

Johnson, Carol & Roy
15 Interlaken Ave., 12946
(518) 523-3180

Amenities: 2,6,7,8,9,10,11,12
Breakfast: Full
Dbl. Oc.: $109.00-$146.00
Sgl. Oc.: $67.00
Third Person: $25.00

Interlaken Lodge & Restaurant, located on Signal Hill, 2 blocks from Main St. Charming Victorian house with twelve rooms, all with private bath. Lovely romantic dining room serving dinner and breakfast. A true 4 season area.

AMENITIES

1. No Smoking
2. No Pets
3. No Children
4. Senior Citizen Rates
5. Tennis Available
6. Golf Available
7. Swimming Available
8. Skiing Available
9. Credit Cards Accepted
10. Personal Check Accepted
11. Off Season Rates
12. Dinner Available (w/sufficient notice)

New York

Lake Pleasant

Doyle, Cathy & John
Route 8, 12108
(518) 548-6386

Amenities: 1,9
Breakfast: Full

Dbl. Oc.: $46.00
Sgl. Oc.: $40.66
Third Person: $16.05

Hummingbird Hill Bed & Breakfast—Simply country charm in a lovely natural setting. Year round vacation area in Adirondack Park. Large house; fieldstone fireplace; 40 acres. Golf, hiking, fishing, boating, hunting, skiing available nearby.

Lansing

Flinn, M/M David, G.
813 Ridge Rd., 14882-8805
(607) 533-4612

Amenities: 1,4,9,10,11
Breakfast: Full

Dbl. Oc.: $59.95-$76.30
Sgl. Oc.: $38.15
Third Person: $10.90

The Bay Horse—1876 Victorian home furnished with antiques. Afternoon tea served weekdays Nov.-Apr. First floor guest rooms, handicap accessible. 25 minutes from Cornell Univ. & Ithaca College. Central Finger Lakes region.

Leroy

Choquet, Warren
7856 Griswold Circle, 14482
(716) 768-2340

Amenities: 5,6,7,8,9,10
Breakfast: Continental

Dbl. Oc.: $45.00-$55.00
Sgl. Oc.: $40.00
Third Person: $10.00

Edson House Bed & Breakfast Inn with private baths and many nearby places to explore: museums, gardens, state parks, etc. Located on Rt. 19 at exit 47, NYS Thruway & West End I-490. Children with advance notice.

Mayville

Green Sandy & George
Chautaugua-Stedman Rd.
RD 2, Box 332, 14757
(716) 789-5309

Amenities: 1,2,3,5,6,7,8,9,10
Breakfast: Continental

Dbl. Oc.: $55.00-$65.00
Sgl. Oc.: $50.00-$60.00

Plumbush At Chautauqua—Beautifully restored circa 1865 Victorian country home with tower, surrounded by 125 acres, offers year round hospitality one mile from Chautauqua Institution. Antique furnishings; private bath.

Mayville

Rice, Molly & Nora
P.O. Box 176, (Rt. 430), 14757
(716) 753-3800

Amenities: 2,3,5,6,7,8,10
Breakfast: Full

Dbl. Oc.: $58.85-$69.55
Sgl. Oc.: $53.50

The Inn At Hobnobbin Farm is on a 200 acre working standardbred horse farm. 6 guest rooms, each with a private bath. Minutes from Chautauqua Institute. Furnished with many lovely antiques.

AMENITIES

1. No Smoking
2. No Pets
3. No Children
4. Senior Citizen Rates
5. Tennis Available
6. Golf Available
7. Swimming Available
8. Skiing Available
9. Credit Cards Accepted
10. Personal Check Accepted
11. Off Season Rates
12. Dinner Available (w/sufficient notice)

New York

Montauk

Adams, M/M Warren, F.
P.O. Box 122-Essex St., 11954
(516) 668-5013

Amenities: 2,3,5,6,7,10,11
Breakfast: Continental

Dbl. Oc.: $80.63-$96.75
Sgl. Oc.: $80.63-$96.75
Third Person: $10.00

Greenhedges Oceanside Villa—Charming brick & stucco Tudor, 3 rooms with private bath, & lovely gardens. Walk to: beach, village, restaurants, and shops. Excellent fishing nearby. Brochure available. Open March-November.

Mt. Tremper

LaScala, Peter
P.O. Box 51, 12457
(914) 688-5329

Amenities: 1,2,3,5,7,8,9,10
Breakfast: Full
Dbl. Oc.: $55.00-$85.00
Sgl. Oc.: $55.00-$85.00

Mt. Tremper Inn—Victorian hospitality & antiques await you in this 1850, 23 room mansion. Large parlor with fireplace, game/reading room, & classical music. Near Woodstock & all ski slopes.

Naples

Stanhope, Celeste
3300 Slitor Rd., 14512
(716) 544-6271

Amenities: 2,3,7,8,9,10,12
Breakfast: Continental
Dbl. Oc.: $70.00-$125.00
Sgl. Oc.: $65.00-$120.00

The Vagabond Inn—Mountainous and secluded, the ultimate in contemporary luxury. Suites, private baths, jacuzzi, swimming pool. The heart of wineries, Finger Lakes & skiing. Open all year. Truly magnificent!

North Hudson

Schoch, M/M Peter
Route 9, 12855
(518) 532-9255

Amenities: 2,5,6,7,8,10,12
Breakfast: Full

Dbl. Oc.: $48.15
Sgl. Oc.: $37.45
Third Person: $10.70

Pine Tree Inn B&B—Turn-of-the-century classic Adirondack inn. Homemade breads with full breakfast. Near tourist attractions; X-C & downhill skiing nearby. Open all year. 1/2 mile north on Rt. 9 from exit 29, I-87.

AMENITIES

1. No Smoking
2. No Pets
3. No Children
4. Senior Citizen Rates
5. Tennis Available
6. Golf Available
7. Swimming Available
8. Skiing Available
9. Credit Cards Accepted
10. Personal Check Accepted
11. Off Season Rates
12. Dinner Available (w/sufficient notice)

New York

Penfield

Whited, Mrs. Cynthia
1883 Penfield Rd., 14526
(716) 385-3266

Amenities: 2,3,5,6,7,8,9,10
Breakfast: Continental
Dbl. Oc.: $66.00
Sgl. Oc.: $55.00
Third Person: $16.50

Strawberry Castle near Rochester and The Finger Lakes wine country. Victorian landmark on three acres; fine dining in immediate area. Located on Rt. 441 east of Rochester. Brass beds and Victorian furnishings await you.

Penn Yan

Pearson, Donna & Thomas
661 East Lake Rd., 14527
(315) 536-3146

Amenities: 2,7,10
Breakfast: Continental

Dbl. Oc.: $53.50
Sgl. Oc.: $37.80
Third Person: $10.70

Finton's Landing—An original steamboat landing. Relax in a nineteenth century Victorian house nestled on the east shore of Keuka Lake. Four spacious rooms & two baths. Minutes from wineries & historic landmarks.

Penn Yan

Worth, Evie & Norm
351 Elm St., Rt. 54-A, 14527
(315) 536-4591

Amenities: 1,2,5,6,7,9,10
Breakfast: Full

Dbl. Oc.: $55.00
Sgl. Oc.: $45.00
Third Person: $10.00

Wagner Estate Bed & Breakfast—Casual elegance in a historic home (1790) on four scenic acres. Central to: New York's beautiful Finger Lakes, wineries, museums, cultural activities, car & horse racing, summer sports and antiquing.

Pittstown

Town, Mrs. Margaret E.
Box 82, RD 2,
Valley Falls, 12185
(518) 663-8369, 686-7331

Amenities: 1,10
Breakfast: Full

Dbl. Oc.: $30.00
Sgl. Oc.: $15.00
Third Person: $5.00

Maggie Towne's B&B—Lovely old Colonial; lawns & trees to welcome playing children. 20 miles to historic Bennington, 30 miles to Saratoga. Enjoy a glass of wine on the porch or by the fireplace. Free crib.

AMENITIES

1. No Smoking
2. No Pets
3. No Children
4. Senior Citizen Rates
5. Tennis Available
6. Golf Available
7. Swimming Available
8. Skiing Available
9. Credit Cards Accepted
10. Personal Check Accepted
11. Off Season Rates
12. Dinner Available (w/sufficient notice)

New York

Preble

Martin, Jeanne & Dick
1446 Masters Rd., 13141
(607) 749-7137

Amenities: 2,8,10
Breakfast: Full

Dbl. Oc.: $45.00
Sgl. Oc.: $40.00
Third Person: $10.00

The Martin House offers rural serenity, modern facilities, & homemade specialties. 30 miles south of Syracuse, NY on I-81. Exit 13 to Preble, right on Preble Rd., right on Otis Co. Valley Rd., first left to Masters Rd.

Rhinebeck

Kohler, Ms. Judy
31 Center St., 12572
(914) 876-8345

Amenities: 2,3,4,9,10,11,12
Breakfast: Full

Dbl. Oc.: $85.00-$120.00
Sgl. Oc.: $85.00-$120.00
Third Person: $40.00

Village Victorian Inn—A Victorian fantasy filled with antiques, laces, canopy beds & private baths, just 2 hours from New York City. The ambiance is quite gentle, private & romantic. Come let us pamper you.

Richfield Springs

Smith, Mrs. Lona
72 E. Main St., Box 388, 13439
(315) 858-2024

Amenities: 2,10,12
Breakfast: Full

Dbl. Oc.: $47.70-$58.30
Sgl. Oc.: $37.10-$47.70
Third Person: $10.60

Summerwood—Sunny & spacious Queen Anne Victorian, listed on national registry of historic places, near: Cooperstown, opera, theatre, museums, antique shops, & lakes. 12 miles to New York State Thruway. 3 acres of lawn & trees.

Rochester

Campo, Mrs. Joyce
189 Stoneridge Dr., 14615
(716) 865-7552

Amenities: 1,6,7,8,9,10,12
Breakfast: Full

Dbl. Oc.: $55.00
Sgl. Oc.: $44.00

Swan Walk—Oriental gardens & swans create a peaceful haven minutes from: downtown Rochester, Kodak, & great shopping. American country decor; queen beds; oversized towels; special breakfasts. Come let us pamper you.

Rock Stream

Gerth, Heidi & Al
3975 Rt. 14, 14878
(607) 535-7909

Amenities: 1,2,3,6,7,8,10,11
Breakfast: Full

Dbl. Oc.: $53.75
Sgl. Oc.: $48.15
Third Person: $10.00

Vintage View—1865 farmhouse, 3 miles north of Watkins Glen. Pool; vineyard; hiking; X/C skiing; llamas; charter fishing on Seneca Lake. Near all Finger Lake attractions; four rooms with 2 baths.

AMENITIES

1. No Smoking
2. No Pets
3. No Children
4. Senior Citizen Rates
5. Tennis Available
6. Golf Available
7. Swimming Available
8. Skiing Available
9. Credit Cards Accepted
10. Personal Check Accepted
11. Off Season Rates
12. Dinner Available (w/sufficient notice)

New York

Roscoe

Pusey, Ellen & Kevin
Old Rt. 17, 12776
(607) 498-5772

Amenities: 1,2,5,6,7,10
Breakfast: Full
Dbl. Oc.: $32.10-$53.50
Sgl. Oc.: $27.10-$45.50
Third Person: $10.00

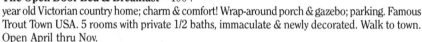

The Open Door Bed & Breakfast—"100+" year old Victorian country home; charm & comfort! Wrap-around porch & gazebo; parking. Famous Trout Town USA. 5 rooms with private 1/2 baths, immaculate & newly decorated. Walk to town. Open April thru Nov.

St. James

Vitale, Pat & Joe
133 Valley Path, 11780
(516) 862-8159

Amenities: 2,3,7,10,11,12
Breakfast: Continental

Dbl. Oc.: $60.00
Sgl. Oc.: $50.00

PJ's Bed & Breakfast—A Colonial home in a small community situated on the north shore of Long Island. A country setting, offering comfort and seclusion. A short distance from: the beaches, Stony Brook Univ., museums, antique shops, etc.

Saratoga Springs

Melvin, Stephanie & Bob
102 Lincoln Ave., 12866
(518) 587-7613

Amenities: 1,2,4,5,6,7,8,10,11
Breakfast: Continental
Dbl. Oc.: $54.00-$81.00
Sgl. Oc.: $54.00-$81.00

The Westchester House—Gracious guest accommodations in the Victorian tradition. This 1885 Queen Anne Victorian is furnished with antiques. All the charm and excitement of historic Saratoga Springs is at our doorstep.

Saugerties

Richards, Pat & Tad
7480 Fite Rd., 12477
(914) 246-8584

Amenities: 2,5,7,8,10,12
Breakfast: Full

Dbl. Oc.: $75.00
Sgl. Oc.: $60.00
Third Person: $25.00

The House On The Quarry—Two hour drive from New York City will guarantee you peace & quiet in a setting of woods & sculpture. Enjoy beautiful walking trails & unlimited tennis. Perfect for a weekend getaway.

AMENITIES

1. No Smoking	**4.** Senior Citizen Rates	**7.** Swimming Available
2. No Pets	**5.** Tennis Available	**8.** Skiing Available
3. No Children	**6.** Golf Available	**9.** Credit Cards Accepted

10. Personal Check Accepted
11. Off Season Rates
12. Dinner Available (w/sufficient notice)

New York

Severance

Wildman, Helen
P.O. Box 125, 12872
(518) 532-7734

Amenities: 1-12
Breakfast: Full

Dbl. Oc.: $60.00
Sgl. Oc.: $30.00
Third Person: $15.00
Dinner: $15.00

Helen Wildman's B&B is 1 mile off 87 on 74; 16 miles from Ticonderoga. Charming 150-year-old Adirondack house on outlet of Paradox Lake. Closed December to May. Four miles from Schroon Lake Village.

Southold

Mooney-Getoff, Ms. Mary
1475 Waterview Dr., 11971
(516) 765-3356

Amenities: 1,2,4,5,6
Breakfast: Full
Dbl. Oc.: $65.00
Sgl. Oc.: $45.00
Third Person: $20.00 (Child only)

Goose Creek Guesthouse is a spacious pre-- Civil War farmhouse on the creek surrounded by six wooded acres. We are a resort area near ferries to Montauk via Shelter Island and the ferry to New London.

Spencer

Carlisle, Ruth & Chuck
31 Harrison St., Box 351, 14883
(607) 589-4754

Amenities: 1,7,10
Breakfast: Full
Dbl. Oc.: $37.45
Sgl. Oc.: $21.40
Third Person: $10.70

Haven Of Rest—Large Colonial-style home with spacious rooms & a homey atmosphere, on a quiet village side street, within walking distance of a small shopping area. 15 minutes south of Ithaca (Cornell University).

Stone Ridge

Baker, Douglas & Delgado, Linda
RD 2, Box 80, 12484
(914) 687-9795

Amenities: 1,2,3,5,6,7,8,9,10
Breakfast: Full

Dbl. Oc.: $68.00-$85.00
Third Peson: $20.00

The Brick House—Welcome to our historic 1815 Brick House furnished with antiques amidst a wonderful setting. Enjoy fireplaces, private baths & a gourmet breakfast.

AMENITIES

1. No Smoking
2. No Pets
3. No Children
4. Senior Citizen Rates
5. Tennis Available
6. Golf Available
7. Swimming Available
8. Skiing Available
9. Credit Cards Accepted
10. Personal Check Accepted
11. Off Season Rates
12. Dinner Available (w/sufficient notice)

New York

Stone Ridge

Delgado, Linda & Baker, Douglas
RD 2, Box 80, 12484
(914) 687-9795

Amenities: 1,2,3,5,6,7,8,9,10
Breakfast: Full

Dbl. Oc.: $68.00-$85.00
Third Person: $20.00

Baker's Bed & Breakfast—Welcome to our restored 1780 stone farmhouse in an exquisite mountain setting with private baths, fireplaces, & hot tub. Gourmet breakfast served.

Stone Ridge

Johnnes, Abby
RD 2, Box 144, 12484
(914) 687-0723

Amenities: 2,6,7,8,10,11,12
Breakfast: Full
Dbl. Oc.: $62.00-$72.00
Sgl. Oc.: $41.00
Third Person: $15.00

Fruit in season
orange juice
fruit filled Swedish pancakes
eggs mollet fines herbes
chicken liver kebobs marinated
in soy sauce and honey
bread with home made jellies
coffee from freshly ground
coffee beans or tea.

Kripplebush Bed And Breakfast—Come stay at a former stagecoach stop. Enjoy our large rooms with down quilts and antiques; hot pots with makings for coffee, tea or chocolate. Ski, hike or grape stomp in our beautiful Hudson Valley.

Syracuse

Samuels, Miss Elaine
145 Didama St., 13224
(315) 446-4199

Amenities: 1,3,5,6,7,8,10
Breakfast: Continental

Dbl. Oc.: $44.94
Sgl. Oc.: $34.24
Third Person: $10.70

Ivy Chimney is a cozy white Colonial with wide porch, well furnished cheerful bedrooms, & shared 1 1/2 baths. Very convenient location, handy to restaurants, university, shopping, & city bus. Reservations.

Tannersville

Abramczyk, Julie & Abe
County Rd. 16, 12485
(518) 589-5363

Amenities: 2,5,6,7,8,9,10,11,12
Breakfast: Full

Dbl. Oc.: $80.25-$90.95
Sgl. Oc.: $64.20
Third Person: $21.40

The Eggery Inn—19th century country inn; spectacular vistas; charming rooms; private bath; cable TV's, antiques; player piano; dining room faces mountain range; Hunter; skiing; miles of hiking trails; near Woodstock. Weekend rates higher.

AMENITIES

1. No Smoking
2. No Pets
3. No Children
4. Senior Citizen Rates
5. Tennis Available
6. Golf Available
7. Swimming Available
8. Skiing Available
9. Credit Cards Accepted
10. Personal Check Accepted
11. Off Season Rates
12. Dinner Available (w/sufficient notice)

New York

Trumansburg

Norris, Dorry
112 E. Main, Box 121, 14886
(607) 387-6449

Amenities: 1,2,10
Breakfast: Full

Dbl. Oc.: $39.00-$45.00
Sgl. Oc.: $34.00-$41.00
Third Person: $10.00

Sage Cottage—Comfortably elegant, lovingly rejuvinated, Gothic Revival home. Herb gardens, cooking classes; close to: lakes, wineries, biking, swimming, hiking; Ithaca 10 miles. Great restaurants in all directions.

Turin

Abbey, Ann & Roger
Rt. 26 & West Rd., 13473
(315) 348-8122

Amenities: 2,5,6,7,8,9,10,11,12
Breakfast: Full
Dbl. Oc.: $110.00
Sgl. Oc.: $61.00
Third Person: $30.00

The Towpath Inn—A stagecoach stop in the 1800's, it is now the only on-site lodging at this ski area in the Adirondack north country. There is also a 18 hole golf course across the road.

Union Springs

Ludwig, Jean & George
Box 453, 13160
(315) 889-5940

Amenities: 2,7
Breakfast: Full
Dbl. Oc.: $59.00
Sgl. Oc.: $49.00
Third Person: $15.00

Ludwig's B&B—2 large rooms with 2 double beds, on the lake. Dock, boating, swimming, fishing, cable TV; rooms have microwaves, refrigerators, fans, fiberglass showers; movies on VCR in community room; beach fires at night.

Vernon

Doring, Lyn
Route 1, Box 325, 13476
(315) 829-2440

Amenities: 2,6,7,8,10,11,12
Breakfast: Full

Dbl. Oc.: $64.20
Sgl. Oc.: $48.15
Third Person: $16.05

Lavender Inn—New York State Route 15. 1799 restored Federal homestead in historic Mohawk Valley. 1 hr. to Cooperstown; 13 miles to Utica; 35 miles to Syracuse. Boating; fishing; Oneida Lake; trout streams; antique outlets; harness track.

AMENITIES

1. No Smoking
2. No Pets
3. No Children
4. Senior Citizen Rates
5. Tennis Available
6. Golf Available
7. Swimming Available
8. Skiing Available
9. Credit Cards Accepted
10. Personal Check Accepted
11. Off Season Rates
12. Dinner Available (w/sufficient notice)

New York

Warrensburg

Carrington, The Family
2 Hudson St., 12885
(518) 623-2449

Amenities: 2,3,5,6,7,8,9,12
Breakfast: Full
Dbl. Oc.: $115.00
Sgl. Oc.: $100.00

The Merrill Magee House—Historic house in the heart of this Adirondack village known for antiquing & year round outdoor recreation. Luxurious rooms; fine dining; cozy pub; secluded garden; outdoor pool; jacuzzi.

Waterloo

Cohen, Mrs. Leonard
115 East Main St., 13165
(315) 539-3032

Amenities: 1,2,3,9,10,12
Breakfast: Full

Dbl. Oc.: $240.75
Sgl. Oc.: $240.75

The Historic James Russell Webster Mansion Inn—Finger Lakes, Rts. 5 & 20, between Geneva & Seneca Falls. 1845 Greek Revival mansion; private; romantic; palatial; museum suites; marble bathrooms & fireplaces; haute cuisine dining; cat figurine museum.

Watertown

Brown, Mrs. Marsha
253 Clinton St., 13601
(315) 788-7324

Amenities: 2,5,6,7,8,9,10
Breakfast: Full
Dbl. Oc.: $69.55-$80.25
Sgl. Oc.: $58.85
Third Person: $10.00

Starbuck House Bed And Breakfast Inn—Gracious, warm hospitality awaits you at this historic 1869 mansion, two blocks from downtown. The city is the gateway to the Thousand Islands, Adirondacks, & Canada. Children over 10 welcome. Handicap accessible.

AMENITIES

1. No Smoking
2. No Pets
3. No Children
4. Senior Citizen Rates
5. Tennis Available
6. Golf Available
7. Swimming Available
8. Skiing Available
9. Credit Cards Accepted
10. Personal Check Accepted
11. Off Season Rates
12. Dinner Available (w/sufficient notice)

New York

Westhampton

Collins, Mrs. Elsie
2 Seafield La., 11978
(516) 288-1559

Amenities: 1,2,3,5,6,7,10,11
Breakfast: Full
Dbl. Oc.: $75.00-$150.00
Third Person: $35.00

Seafield House—90 minutes from Manhattan; a perfect romantic hideaway. 100-year-old antique-filled & lovely preserved home. Aromas of freshly brewing coffee & muffins baking in the oven are likely to awaken our guests.

AMENITIES

1. No Smoking
2. No Pets
3. No Children
4. Senior Citizen Rates
5. Tennis Available
6. Golf Available
7. Swimming Available
8. Skiing Available
9. Credit Cards Accepted
10. Personal Check Accepted
11. Off Season Rates
12. Dinner Available (w/sufficient notice)

North Carolina

The Tar Heel State

Capital: Raleigh
Statehood: November 21, 1789; the 12th state
State Motto: To Be, Rather Than To Seem
State Song: "The Old North State"
State Bird: Cardinal
State Flower: Flowering Dogwood
State Tree: Pine

The brown gold of the ripe tobacco leaf has made North Carolina prosperous and the leading grower of tobacco in our country. Nothing is more exciting to the tobacco farmer than to take his product to town and listen to the auctioneer chanting his tobacco prices.

Another prosperous industry in the state is furniture. From the early settlers' own pine trees and pioneering style, came perfect pieces of furniture and the beginning of what became another prosperous industry for North Carolina.

Situated along the Atlantic seacoast, tourists can enjoy swimming as well as visiting the beautiful gardens, historical battlefields and gracious southern mansions.

The first airplane flight by the Wright Brothers took place at Kitty Hawk, and both presidents Andrew Johnson and James Polk were born in this state.

North Carolina

Asheville

Curtis, Alice & Will
83 Hillside, 28801
(704) 252-0106

Amenities: 10
Breakfast: Continental

Dbl. Oc.: $42.00-$52.00
Sgl. Oc.: $32.00-$42.00
Third Person: $5.00

The Ray House Bed & Breakfast—The Curtis's welcome you to their charming 1891 home hidden among spruces & native trees, which provide privacy in a park-like setting. Interior features include windows of unusual design, beamed ceilings & lovely woodwork.

Asheville

Faber, M/M Fred
100 Reynolds Heights, 28804
(704) 254-0496

Amenities: 5,6,7,10
Breakfast: Continental
Dbl. Oc.: $40.00-$65.00
Sgl. Oc.: $32.00-$59.00
Third Person: $10.00

The Old Reynolds Mansion—An Ante-bellum mansion listed on the historical registry. A country setting amidst acres of trees. Mountain views from all rooms; woodburning fireplaces; two story verandas; pool.

Asheville

Halton, Carol & Fred
30 Lookout Rd., 28804
(704) 252-0035

Amenities: 2,9,10
Breakfast: Full
Dbl. Oc.: $55.00-$95.00
Sgl. Oc.: $55.00-$95.00
Third Person: $10.00

The Bridle Path Inn on mountain overlooking city. All rooms have private baths, TV, elegant full breakfast included. Secluded but close to all attractions.

AMENITIES

1. No Smoking
2. No Pets
3. No Children
4. Senior Citizen Rates
5. Tennis Available
6. Golf Available
7. Swimming Available
8. Skiing Available
9. Credit Cards Accepted
10. Personal Check Accepted
11. Off Season Rates
12. Dinner Available (w/sufficient notice)

North Carolina

Asheville

LoPresti, Linda & Jim
62 Cumberland Circle, 28801
(704) 254-2244

Amenities: 1,2,5,9,10,11
Breakfast: Full
Dbl. Oc.: $65.00-$75.00
Sgl. Oc.: $60.00
Third Person: $10.00

Applewood Manor—A fine old Colonial manor located on two acres in Asheville's historic district. Antiques, collectibles, and fine linen & lace help to recreate the ambiance of the early 1900's. Come romance yourselves.

Asheville

McEwan, Barbara & M. Jack
674 Biltmore Ave., 28803
(704) 252-1389

Amenities: 1,2,3,9,10
Breakfast: Continental
Dbl. Oc.: $65.00-$97.00
Sgl. Oc.: $60.00-$92.00
Third Person: $15.00

Cedar Crest Victorian Inn, located 1/4 mile from the Biltmore Estate, this 1891 Queen Anne mansion is listed on the national historic register. Decorated with Victorian antiques, the house boasts lavish carved woodwork throughout.

Asheville

Mellin, Mrs. Rosina
86 Edgemont Rd., 28801
(704) 255-0027

Amenities: 1,2,3,5,6,7,8,9,10
Breakfast: Full

Dbl. Oc.: $52.92-$74.52
Sgl. Oc.: $50.76-$72.36
Third Person: $6.48

The Albemarle Inn—In the national historic register, Albermarle provides spacious and gracious accommodations in a turn-of-the-century environment. Relax in the cool mountains; enjoy a rich and colorful cultural experience.

Asheville

Spradley, Mrs. Karen
53 St. Dunstans Rd., 28803
(704) 253-3525

Amenities: 1,2,4,9,10,11,12
Breakfast: Full

Dbl. Oc.: $63.00
Sgl. Oc.: $52.50
Third Person: $15.75

Corner Oak Manor is a lovely English Tudor home located just one third mile from the Biltmore Estate. Full breakfast is served daily. Decorated with oak antiques and handmade items; outdoor jacuzzi.

AMENITIES

1. No Smoking
2. No Pets
3. No Children
4. Senior Citizen Rates
5. Tennis Available
6. Golf Available
7. Swimming Available
8. Skiing Available
9. Credit Cards Accepted
10. Personal Check Accepted
11. Off Season Rates
12. Dinner Available (w/sufficient notice)

North Carolina

Asheville

Vogel, Lynne, Marion & Rick
116 Flint St., 28801
(704) 253-6723

Amenities: 2,3,9,10
Breakfast: Full
Dbl. Oc.: $70.00
Sgl. Oc.: $50.00
Third Person: $10.00

The Flint Street Inns—Two lovely old family homes offering the best in bed & breakfast accommodations. They are within a comfortable walking distance to shops and restaurants. Full southern-style breakfast is served.

Asheville

Willard, Linnda & Ross
64 Linden Ave., 28801
(704) 254-9336

Amenities: 2,3,5,6,7,8,9,10
Breakfast: Full

Dbl. Oc.: $40.00-$60.00
Sgl. Oc.: $35.00-$55.00
Third Person: $10.00

Heritage Hill—1909 comfortable country-style inn with wrap-around porch, private baths & fireplaces. An acre of lovely old trees provide privacy and quiet. close to downtown. 6 cozy rooms; air conditioning available. Welcome.

Belhaven

Smith, Mr. Axson, Jr.
600 E. Main St., 27810
(919) 943-2151

Amenities: 2,5,9,12
Breakfast: Full

Dbl. Oc.: $45.00-$75.00
Third Person: $10.00

River Forest Manor—Elegant Victorian mansion located on the ICW. It has a marina, restaurant, tennis court, and hot tub/jacuzzi. Relaxed atmosphere; southern hospitality; historic area. Seasonal opening.

Black Mountain

Miller, Mrs. Barbara Dehaan
P.O. Box 965, 28711
(704) 669-8303

Amenities: 2,10,11
Breakfast: Continental

Dbl. Oc.: $48.60-$54.00
Sgl. Oc.: $43.20
Third Person: $10.00

The Blackberry Inn is a red brick Colonial set on a secluded hilltop surrounded by oaks and evergreens. The inn has private baths and s suite with TV & VCR. Just 15 minutes from Asheville.

AMENITIES

1. No Smoking
2. No Pets
3. No Children
4. Senior Citizen Rates
5. Tennis Available
6. Golf Available
7. Swimming Available
8. Skiing Available
9. Credit Cards Accepted
10. Personal Check Accepted
11. Off Season Rates
12. Dinner Available (w/sufficient notice)

North Carolina

Blowing Rock

Latham, Marilyn & Ray
Box 1120, Sunset Dr., 28605
(704) 295-3331

Amenities: 2,5,6,7,8,9,10,11
Breakfast: Continental

Dbl. Oc.: $70.20
Sgl. Oc.: $54.00
Third Person: $5.00

Maple Lodge is located 1/2 block from center of the village. It is an extremely comfortable B&B with 2 parlors, TV room, & guest rooms w/private baths. Guests are encouraged to use the house & feel "at home."

Blowing Rock

Milner, Mrs. Jane
6148 Gideon Ridge,
Box 1929, 28605
(704) 295-3644

Amenities: 2,3,5,6,8,9,10,11,12
Breakfast: Full

Dbl. Oc.: $97.20-$118.80

Gideon Ridge Inn—A stately stone house high on a ridge with a glorious view. 8 guest rooms with antique furnishings on 5 acres. 3 1/2 miles south of Blue Ridge Pky.; 1/4 mile west of US 321.

Blowing Rock

Villani, Joyce & Joe
Box 1927, Sunset Dr., 28605
(704) 295-9703

Amenities: 2,5,6,7,8,9,10,11,12
Breakfast: Continental

Dbl. Oc.: $48.60-$91.80
Sgl. Oc.: $43.20-$91.80
Third Person: $10.00

Beautiful Bark Covered eighty year old former summer estate. Fantastic candlelit restaurant featuring continental cuisine. 1/2 block from town park & varied shops. Beautiful rooms appointed with good art.

Boone

Probinsky, Dr. Jean
209 Meadow View Dr., 28607
(704) 262-3670

Amenities: 4,5,6,7,8
Breakfast: Continental

Dbl. Oc.: $35.00
Sgl. Oc.: $22.00
Third Person: $10.00

Grandma Jean's Bed & Breakfast—Hook a trout, sit a spell, ride a horse, climb a mountain, hike a trail, ski a slope, play 18 holes, buy some folk art. Charming 60 year old country home in the heart of the Blue Ridge Mtns. near Grandfather Mtn.

Brevard

Ong, Lynne & Peter
412 W. Probart, 28712
(704) 884-9349

Amenities: 5,6,7,10,11
Breakfast: Full

Dbl. Oc.: $34.00-$42.00
Sgl. Oc.: $34.00-$42.00
Third Person: $8.00

The Red House, built in 1851, has been lovingly restored, furnished with family antiques and opened to the public as a bed & breakfast establishment. Come by and relax on our porch in the mountains.

AMENITIES

1. No Smoking
2. No Pets
3. No Children
4. Senior Citizen Rates
5. Tennis Available
6. Golf Available
7. Swimming Available
8. Skiing Available
9. Credit Cards Accepted
10. Personal Check Accepted
11. Off Season Rates
12. Dinner Available (w/sufficient notice)

North Carolina

Brevard

Womble, Beth & Steve
301 W. Main, 28712
(704) 884-4770

Amenities: 2,5,6,10,11
Breakfast: Continental

Dbl. Oc.: $48.60
Sgl. Oc.: $41.01
Third Person: $7.56

Womble Inn, located two blocks from town, is a small six-room inn with the personal touch. Restaurants and shopping are within walking distance; decorated in 18th & 19th-century antiques. Like home with service.

Bryson City

Brown, M/M George
Fryemont Rd.,
P.O. Box 459, 28713
(704) 488-2159

Amenities: 2,4,5,7,9,10,11,12
Breakfast: Full

Dbl. Oc.: $80.00-$107.00
Sgl. Oc.: $63.00-$70.00
Third Person: $22.00-$34.00

The Fryemont Inn overlooks the Great Smokey Mountains Nat'l. Park. Enormous stone fireplaces; dining & lodging in the atmosphere of a bygone era. Full dinner and breakfast included in room rate. Open mid-April thru Oct.

Chapel Hill

Kelly, M/M Robert
Box 267, 27514
(919) 563-5583

Amenities: 2,3,5,6,10
Breakfast: Full

Dbl. Oc.: $78.00
Sgl. Oc.: $68.00
Third Person: $15.00

The Inn At Bingham School—Restored headmaster home listed on the national register. 10 rolling acres of farm land; 12 minutes from Chapel Hill. Six bedrooms, with private baths, furnished with family antiques.

Charlotte

Dearien, Peggy & Frank
5901 Sardis Rd., 28226
(704) 365-1936

Amenities: 1,2,3,9,10
Breakfast: Full
Dbl. Oc.: $59.40-$70.20
Sgl. Oc.: $54.00-$64.80

The Homeplace—Located in southeast Charlotte on 2 1/2 acres with a garden, gazebo, and wrap-around porch. 1902 restored Victorian with 4 rooms decorated in country charm. Warm and friendly atmosphere; antiques; quilts.

AMENITIES

1. No Smoking
2. No Pets
3. No Children
4. Senior Citizen Rates
5. Tennis Available
6. Golf Available
7. Swimming Available
8. Skiing Available
9. Credit Cards Accepted
10. Personal Check Accepted
11. Off Season Rates
12. Dinner Available (w/sufficient notice)

North Carolina

Durham

Ryan, Barbara & Jerry
106 Mason Rd., 27712
(919) 477-8430

Amenities: 2,5,6,7,9,10
Breakfast: Full

Dbl. Oc.: $54.00-$91.80
Sgl. Oc.: $48.60
Third Person: $10.00

Arrowhead Inn—A 1775 manor house restored to charming and homey comfort. Four acres, trees, arbors and gardens. Near Duke; Univ. of North Carolina, & historic attractions. Homemade baked goods & preserves enhance the full breakfast.

Edenton

Edwards, M/M Arch
300 North Broad St., 27932
(919) 482-3641

Amenities: 2,5,6,7,12
Breakfast: Continental
Dbl. Oc.: $68.25
Sgl. Oc.: $47.25
Third Person: $10.00

The Lords Proprietor's Inn—Elegant accommodations in the heart of lovely historic Edenton. The inn offers twenty spacious rooms each with private bath in three wonderfully restored adjacent houses.

Edenton

Harlan, M/M Worthley
Box 370, Rt. 4, 27932
(919) 482-2282

Amenities: 2,3,9
Breakfast: Continental

Dbl. Oc.: $50.00
Sgl. Oc.: $50.00
Third Person: $10.00

The Trestle House Inn—20 acre lake on 70 acres. Immaculate accommodations, private baths, color TV, HBO, giant fireplaces, billiards, shuffleboard, excercise room, steam bath, sun deck & fishing.

Franklin

Brokaw, M/M Bill
44 McClure Mill Rd., 28734
(704) 524-5526

Amenities: 1,2,3,5,6,7,8,10,11
Breakfast: Continental
Rates: $55.00-$75.00

Olde Mill House Inn—Quiet elegant mountain retreat. 3 fireplaces; honeymoon suite; footed tubs; porches; library; player piano; horseback riding; whitewater rafting; gem mining; antique & craft shops. A little bit of yesteryear.

AMENITIES

1. No Smoking
2. No Pets
3. No Children
4. Senior Citizen Rates
5. Tennis Available
6. Golf Available
7. Swimming Available
8. Skiing Available
9. Credit Cards Accepted
10. Personal Check Accepted
11. Off Season Rates
12. Dinner Available (w/sufficient notice)

North Carolina

Franklin

Giampola, Mrs. Pat
67 Harrison Ave., 28734
(704) 524-7907

Amenities: 2,9,10
Breakfast: Continental

Dbl. Oc.: $47.52
Sgl. Oc.: $43.20

The Franklin Terrace—100-year-old Italianate with private baths, TV, wrap-around porch, & spectacular mountain views. Restaurants & shops within walking distance. Sweet shop & antiques shop on premises. Hospitality emphasized!

Glenville

Carter, M/M George
Big Ridge Rd., 28736
(704) 743-3094

Amenities: 1,2,3,5,6,7,10
Breakfast: Full
Dbl. Oc.: $33.00
Sgl. Oc.: $18.00

"Mountain High"—4,200 feet up; cool; quiet; beautiful mountain views. Resort area with lots to do; horseback riding available; excellent restaurants.

Graham

Morrow, Mrs. Carolyn
215 E. Harden St., 27253
(919) 226-5978

Amenities: 1,2,4,5,6,7,10,11
Breakfast: Full

Dbl. Oc.: $45.00
Sgl. Oc.: $35.00
Third Person: $10.00

Leftwich House—Built in the early 1920's, Leftwich House is comfortable and cozy, with high ceilings, chandeliers & ceiling fans. Located within a 10 minute drive to over 200 factory outlets.

Greensboro

Green, Jo Anne
205 N. Park Dr., 27401
(919) 274-6350

Amenities: 2,5,6,7,9,10
Breakfast: Continental

Dbl. Oc.: $37.80-$64.80
Sgl. Oc.: $32.40
Third Person: $10.80

Greenwood—1905 home on park, 3 minutes from downtown historic district. 5 guest rooms, TV room, guest kitchen & pool. Hearty continental breakfast. Living rooms with 2 working fireplaces; eclectic decor. Open all year.

AMENITIES

1. No Smoking
2. No Pets
3. No Children
4. Senior Citizen Rates
5. Tennis Available
6. Golf Available
7. Swimming Available
8. Skiing Available
9. Credit Cards Accepted
10. Personal Check Accepted
11. Off Season Rates
12. Dinner Available (w/sufficient notice)

North Carolina

Henderson

Cornell, M/M Richard
Rte. 3, Box 610, 27536
(919) 438-2421

Amenities: 1,2,3,6,7,9,10
Breakfast: Full
Dbl. Oc.: $73.50
Sgl. Oc.: $73.50

La Grange Plantation Inn—Nationally registered 18th-century plantation house on Kerr Lake near the Virginia border. Five elegant rooms with private baths. 5 miles from I-85 following Nutbush Recreation area signs.

Hendersonville

Carberry, Marie & Fred
755 N. Main St., 28739
(704) 697-7778

Amenities: 2,5,9,10,11,12
Breakfast: Full
Dbl. Oc.: $48.60-$63.72
Sgl. Oc.: $37.80-$42.12
Third Person: $8.10

The Claddagh Inn is a beautifully restored country inn/bed & breakfast, located in downtown Hendersonville & nominated for the national registry. Open all year; near national forest & national parks.

Hendersonville

Sheiry, Diane & John
783 N. Main St., 28739
(800) 537-8195

Amenities: 2,5,6,7,9,10,11,12
Breakfast: Full
Dbl. Oc.: $68.00
Sgl. Oc.: $58.00
Third Person: $10.00

The Waverly Inn

The Waverly Inn built in 1898 & listed on the national register of historic places. Frequented by French counts & General MacArthur during WW II. Easy walk to town shops. Charming, warm & recently renovated.

Hendersonville

Zebos, M/M Steve
783 N. Main, 28739
(704) 693-9193

Amenities: 5,9,10,11
Breakfast: Full
Dbl. Oc.: $49.00-$55.00
Sgl. Oc.: $30.00-$35.00
Third Person: $7.00

The Waverly is 90 years old, has 20 guest rooms, a library, dining room, parlor, & large porch with rocking chairs. We are 2 blocks to antique shops, 1 block to a cafeteria. Cheery, comfortable!

AMENITIES

1. No Smoking
2. No Pets
3. No Children
4. Senior Citizen Rates
5. Tennis Available
6. Golf Available
7. Swimming Available
8. Skiing Available
9. Credit Cards Accepted
10. Personal Check Accepted
11. Off Season Rates
12. Dinner Available (w/sufficient notice)

North Carolina

Hertford

Harnisch, Mrs. Jenny
103 S. Church St., 27944
(919) 426-5809

Amenities: 2,9,10
Breakfast: Full

Dbl. Oc.: $42.00
Sgl. Oc.: $36.75

Gingerbread Inn on Bus. 17, 65 miles south of Norfolk. Restored early 1900 home with large rooms, king & queen beds, central A/C, HBO TV. Free to our guests, our famous gingerbread boy souvenir. Try our continental pastries.

Hickory

Mohney, Jane & Bill
464 7th St., SW, 28602
(704) 324-0548

Amenities: 2,5,6,7,8,10
Breakfast: Full

Dbl. Oc.: $40.00-$45.00
Sgl. Oc.: $30.00-$35.00
Third Person: $10.00

The Hickory Bed And Breakfast—Travelers, join us for friendly service. Prominent house, large lot, good parking offered. City center, restaurants, theaters, and major furniture showrooms nearby.

Highlands

Alley, Donna & Chris
Rt. 1, Hickory St.,
Box 22B, 28741
(704) 526-2060

Amenities: 1,2,9,10,11
Breakfast: Full

Dbl. Oc.: $65.00-$75.00
Sgl. Oc.: $55.00-$65.00
Third Person: $6.00

Colonial Pines Inn—Quiet country guest house on two acres with a lovely mountain view. Close to Highlands' fine shopping & dining as well as waterfalls and magnificent scenery.

Highlands

Williams, Carol
Main St., Rt. 1,
Box 55, 28741
(704) 526-2590

Amenities: 1,2,9,10,11,12
Breakfast: Full

Dbl. Oc.: $49.00
Sgl. Oc.: $39.00
Third Person: $10.00

21 Rooms With Antique furnishings and private baths in downtown Highlands. Double fireplace; homecooked family-style dinners; rocking chairs. Weekly and monthly rates.

Kill Devil Hills

Combs, Phyllis & Robert
500 N. Virginia Dare Trail
27948
(919)441-6126

Amenities: 2-11
Breakfast: Continental

Dbl. Oc.: $55.00-$65.00
Sgl. Oc.: $55.00-$65.00
Third Person: $10.00

Ye Old Cheerokee Inn on the fabulous outer banks in the Nags Head area. Relax, unwind in our big pink beach house with private baths just 500 feet from the ocean. Great restaurants.

AMENITIES

1. No Smoking
2. No Pets
3. No Children
4. Senior Citizen Rates
5. Tennis Available
6. Golf Available
7. Swimming Available
8. Skiing Available
9. Credit Cards Accepted
10. Personal Check Accepted
11. Off Season Rates
12. Dinner Available (w/sufficient notice)

North Carolina

Kill Devil Hills

Ianni, Ann
417 Helga St., 27948
(919) 441-6929

Amenities: 2,3,5,6,7,8,10,11
Breakfast: Continental

Dbl. Oc.: $65.00-$89.00
Third Person: $5.00

The Figurehead Bed And Breakfast—By the sea and sound front: nature, beaches, fishing, historical areas, bird watching, bicycling; A/C, fireplace, VCR; private baths. Free brochure; 2 day minimum.

Lake Lure

Nunn, Alan
Rt. One, Box 529A, 28746
(704) 625-2789

Amenities: 2,4,5,6,7,9,10
Breakfast: Continental

Dbl. Oc.: $61.95
Sgl. Oc.: $57.75
Third Person: $10.50

The Lodge On Lake Lure—Elegant lodge on the shore of Lake Lure with boating, fishing, & swimming; built for the Highway Patrol in 1932 in the Blue Ridge Mountains of western North Carolina; 25 miles southwest of Asheville & Biltmore.

Little Switzerland

Ulmer, Mrs. Hazel
P.O. Box 459, Rt. 226A, 28749
(704) 765-4257, (800) 654-5232

Amenities: 1,2,3,6,9,10,12
Breakfast: Full

Dbl. Oc.: $82.00
Sgl. Oc.: $70.00
Third Person: $20.00

Big Lynn Lodge—Set at an altitude of 3,200 feet, Big Lynn Lodge is an old fashioned country inn popular with older folks who return every summer to stay in a quiet homey atmosphere. Full dinner & breakfast included.

Mars Hill

Wessel, Mrs. Yvette
121 S. Main St., 28754
(704) 689-5722

Amenities: 2,5,6,8,10,11
Breakfast: Full

Dbl. Oc.: $42.00-$52.50
Third Person: $10.00

Baird House, 85 year old brick charmer. Furnished in fine antiques. Elegant yet homey. Tiny college town 18 miles north of Asheville in rural Appalachian Mountain county.

Mount Airy

Haxton, Ellen & Manford
2893 W. Pine St., 27030
(919) 789-5034

Amenities: 2,4,5,6,7,8,10,11,12
Breakfast: Continental

Dbl. Oc.: $42.00-$78.75
Sgl. Oc.: $42.00-$78.75
Third Person: $10.50

Pine Ridge Inn—1949 mansion just 2 miles east of I-77, Hwy. 89, offers: private bedroom suites with bath, swimming pool, large indoor hot tub, an exercise room, & airport transportation.

AMENITIES

1. No Smoking
2. No Pets
3. No Children
4. Senior Citizen Rates
5. Tennis Available
6. Golf Available
7. Swimming Available
8. Skiing Available
9. Credit Cards Accepted
10. Personal Check Accepted
11. Off Season Rates
12. Dinner Available (w/sufficient notice)

North Carolina

New Bern

Cleveland, Lois & Rick
509 Pollock St., 28560
(919) 636-5553

Amenities: 1,2,9,10
Breakfast: Full
Dbl. Oc.: $81.00
Sgl. Oc.: $56.16
Third Person: $21.60

The Aerie is located in the historic district, within sight of Tryon Palace and close to shops & restaurants. 7 rooms, private baths, central air, and of course, a generous country breakfast.

New Bern

Hansen, Diane & A.E.
215 Pollock St., 28560
(919) 636-3810

Amenities: 2,9,10
Breakfast: Full

Dbl. Oc.: $70.20
Sgl. Oc.: $48.60

Harmony House Inn—Comfortable elegance in the historic district. Front porch with rocking chairs, swings, back yard, nine rooms with private baths. Restaurants, shops, & Tryon Palace within walking distance.

New Bern

Parks, Diana & David
212 Pollock St., 28560
(919) 638-4409

Amenities: 5,6,7,9,10
Breakfast: Continental

Dbl. Oc.: $63.00-$65.00
Sgl. Oc.: $45.00
Third Person: $5.00

Kings Arms Inn—Enjoy late 18th-century charm in this elegantly restored inn. Each spacious room has a lovely fireplace and its own modern private bath. Located in the heart of the historic district, 3 blocks from Tryon Palace.

New Bern

Wilkins, M/M Joel
709 Broad St., 28560
(919) 636-2250

Amenities: 4,5,6,7,9,10,11
Breakfast: Full

Dbl. Oc.: $81.00
Sgl. Oc.: $54.00
Third Person: $15.00

New Berne House Bed & Breakfast offers the closest accommodation to Tryon Palace. Beautifully restored Colonial Revival home features lovely gardens, parlour & library. 6 guest rooms with private vintage baths; country breakfast.

AMENITIES

1. No Smoking
2. No Pets
3. No Children
4. Senior Citizen Rates
5. Tennis Available
6. Golf Available
7. Swimming Available
8. Skiing Available
9. Credit Cards Accepted
10. Personal Check Accepted
11. Off Season Rates
12. Dinner Available (w/sufficient notice)

North Carolina

Old Fort

Aldridge, Debbie & Chuck
W. Main St.,
P.O. Box 1116, 28762
(704) 668-9384

Amenities: 5,6,7,8,10
Breakfast: Continental

Dbl. Oc.: $38.00
Sgl. Oc.: $33.00
Third Person: $5.00

The Inn At Old Fort—1880's Victorian bed & breakfast inn furnished with antiques. Large front porch for rocking, terraced lawn, 3 1/2 acres overlooking historic Blue Ridge town. Near Asheville & the Blue Ridge Parkway.

Pittsboro

Fitch, Jenny & R.B.
Fearrington Village Ctr., 27312
(919) 542-2121

Amenities: 1,2,3,7,9,10,12
Breakfast: Continental
Dbl. Oc.: $95.00-$175.00
Sgl. Oc.: $75.00-$175.00

Fearrington House Country Inn, situated just eight miles south of Chapel Hill, has fourteen bedrooms with private baths, a garden house, & courtyard. A truly beautiful setting with interesting shops & fine dining in the heart of the countryside.

Raleigh

Newton, Ms. Diana
411 N. Bloodworth St., 27604
(919) 832-9712

Amenities: 1,2,3,9,10
Breakfast: Full

Dbl. Oc.: $70.00-$86.00
Sgl. Oc.: $59.00-$70.00

The Oakwood Inn—The elegance and serenity of the Victorian era is recalled in this 1871 inn, located in downtown historic district. 6 rooms, furnished with equisite period antiques, all with private baths.

Robbinsville

Wilson, Kathy & Roy
200 Santeetlah Rd., 28771
(704) 479-8126

Amenities: 2,9
Breakfast: Full

Dbl. Oc.: $80.00
Sgl. Oc.: $45.00
Third Person: $40.00

Blue Boar Lodge—open April- mid-October. Near Joyce Kilmer Forest & Lake Santeetlah, boat rentals & fishing. Relax in the cool mountain breezes. Family-style meals. Lodge is rustic but modern, each room has private bath, no phones or TV.

AMENITIES

1. No Smoking
2. No Pets
3. No Children
4. Senior Citizen Rates
5. Tennis Available
6. Golf Available
7. Swimming Available
8. Skiing Available
9. Credit Cards Accepted
10. Personal Check Accepted
11. Off Season Rates
12. Dinner Available (w/sufficient notice)

North Carolina

Rosman

Young, Joyce & Buddy
Star Rt., Box 200, 28772
(704) 884-6868

Amenities: 9,10,12
Breakfast: Full

Dbl. Oc.: $51.30
Sgl. Oc.: $40.00
Third Person: $7.50

Red Lion Inn And Restaurant—A warm hospitable small family-operated inn on a mountain stream. Nice getaway place to relax, enjoy nature, & excellent food. 10 miles south of Brevard on Hwy. 178, 3 1/2 miles south of Rosman, NC.

Spruce Pine

Stevens, Margaret & John P.
110 Henry Lane
(704) 765-4917

Amenities: 2,5,6,7,8,10
Breakfast: Full
Dbl. Oc.: $60.00
Sgl. Oc.: $54.00
Third Person: $10.00

The Fariway Inn—3 miles from Blue Ridge Parkway, on Hwy. 226. The inn overlooks an 18-hole golf course & there are restaurants & shops available. Come experience the joy of mountain life and true relaxation.

Sparta

Turbiville, Mrs. Maybelline
E. Whitehead St., 28675
(919) 372-8490

Amenities: 3,5,6,10,12
Breakfast: Full

Dbl. Oc.: $40.00
Sgl. Oc.: $25.00
Third Person: $10.00

Turbyvilla—We live in the rural area of Alleghany Co. in Sparta, N.C., located on a 20 acre farm with a beautiful view of the Blue Ridge Mts. The home has an acre of beautiful trees & lawn & a glassed-in porch.

Tarboro

Miller, Patsy & Tom
304 E. Park Ave., 27886
(919) 823-1314

Amenities: 2,5,9,10
Breakfast: Full

Dbl. Oc.: $57.75-$68.25
Sgl. Oc.: $50.40-$60.90
Third Person: $26.25

Little Warren B&B, established in 1760, is a large old family home that has been renovated & modernized. Located on the town common in the quiet historic district, down east along the Albermarle Trail on the Tar River in Tarboro.

AMENITIES

1. No Smoking
2. No Pets
3. No Children
4. Senior Citizen Rates
5. Tennis Available
6. Golf Available
7. Swimming Available
8. Skiing Available
9. Credit Cards Accepted
10. Personal Check Accepted
11. Off Season Rates
12. Dinner Available (w/sufficient notice)

North Carolina

Tryon

Kessler, Wm., "Chip"
P.O. Box 1251, 28782
(704) 859-6992

Amenities: 2,4,10
Breakfast: Continental

Dbl. Oc.: $48.00
Sgl. Oc.: $40.00
Third Person: $7.00

Mill Farm Inn—Enjoy: the home-like atmosphere, peace & quiet, specialty breads, continental breakfast, private baths, large sitting porch, country setting, & beautiful grounds. 2 miles off I-26 on Hwy. 108. Tryon's finest.

Wanchese

Gray, Mrs. Nancy
Old Wharf Rd.,
P.O. Box 427, 27981
(919) 473-5466

Amenities: 5,6,7,9,10
Breakfast: Full

Dbl. Oc.: $48.38
Sgl. Oc.: $48.38

C.W. Pugh's B&B—Ancestral home located in quiet fishing village. Short drive to ocean beaches, parks, tours, sailing, & fishing. South end of Roanoke Island. Private, relaxing atmosphere with warm hospitality. Children, no charge.

Washington

Hervey, Jeanne & Lawrence
400 E. Main St., 27889
(919) 946-7184

Amenities: 2,5,9,10
Breakfast: Full
Dbl. Oc.: $57.75—$68.25
Sgl. Oc.: $47.25-$57.75
Third Person: $10.00

Pamlico House—Turn-of-the-century home in historic district. Comfortable guest rooms, private baths, parlor, large wrap-around porch, full breakfast. On historic Albermarle tour route; easy drive to Carolina beaches.

Waynesville

Minick, Mr. Jeff
108 Pigeon St., 28786
(704) 456-7521

Amenities: 2,10,11
Breakfast: Full

Dbl. Oc.: $50.00
Sgl. Oc.: $35.00
Third Person: $7.00

Built before the turn of the century, The Palmer House, located within one block of Main St., is one of the last of Waynesville's once numerous tourist homes. Private baths; good food; a home away from home.

AMENITIES

1. No Smoking
2. No Pets
3. No Children
4. Senior Citizen Rates
5. Tennis Available
6. Golf Available
7. Swimming Available
8. Skiing Available
9. Credit Cards Accepted
10. Personal Check Accepted
11. Off Season Rates
12. Dinner Available (w/sufficient notice)

North Carolina

Wilmington

Meyer, Terry & Walsh, Kate
412 S. 3rd St., 28401
(919) 762-8562

Amenities: 3,10
Breakfast: Full
Dbl. Oc.: $75.00
Sgl. Oc.: $75.00

The Worth House B&B specializes in personal service. Enjoy fireside breakfast in bed, on the veranda, or in the garden. In the historic district near riverfront shops & restaurants. Door to door carriage rides available.

Wilson

Stewart, June & Doug
600 W. Nash St., 27893
(919) 243-4447

Amenities: 9,10
Breakfast: Full

Dbl. Oc.: $39.99-$59.00
Sgl. Oc.: $39.00-$59.00
Third Person: $10.00

Pilgrim's Rest B&B—Located downtown in historic district near antique shops & museum. Wilson is the world's greatest tobacco market. Located in central North Carolina on I-95.

Winston-Salem

Jones, Terri
Summit & W. 5th, 27101
(919) 777-1887

Amenities: 2,5,7,9,10
Breakfast: Continental

Dbl. Oc.: $59.40-$116.64
Sgl. Oc.: $48.60-$105.84

The Colonel Ludlow House—Nat'l. register of historic place homes in historic district. Wonderful mix of antiques & modern conveniences. Private baths, phones, stereos/tapes, 2-person w/pools, cablevision. Walk to gourmet restaurants.

AMENITIES

1. No Smoking
2. No Pets
3. No Children
4. Senior Citizen Rates
5. Tennis Available
6. Golf Available
7. Swimming Available
8. Skiing Available
9. Credit Cards Accepted
10. Personal Check Accepted
11. Off Season Rates
12. Dinner Available (w/sufficient notice)

Ohio

The Buckeye State

Capital: Columbus
Statehood: March 1, 1803; the 17th state
State Motto: With God, All Things Are Possible
State Song: "Beautiful Ohio"
State Bird: Cardinal
State Flower: Scarlet Carnation
State Tree: Buckeye

Ohio took its name from the Iroquois Indian word meaning something great. Ohio is great, and it has a mixture of great people with different living habits settled in pockets up and down this state. You can get the feeling you are in New England, West Virginia or Iowa, depending upon what section of the state you happen to be visiting.

Johnny Chapman, the original Johnny Appleseed, walked through Ohio sewing his apple seeds so that the frontier families might have fresh fruit. His orchards can still be found, but a modern Ohio has replaced his frontier land.

The state of Ohio is proud of her contribution to the space program. John Glenn, the first astronaut to orbit the world, and Neil Armstrong, the first astronaut to walk on the moon, both came from this state. Seven presidents were also born in Ohio: Grant, Hayes, Garfield, Harrison, McKinley, Taft and Harding.

Ohio

Akron

Pinnick, Jeanne & Harry
601 Copley Rd., 44320
(216) 535-1952

Amenities: 5,6,7,8,10
Breakfast: Full

Dbl. Oc.: $28.00
Sgl. Oc.: $22.00
Third Person: $6.00

The Portage House, 2 miles east of I-77, is a three story Tudor in an historic area of Akron. Delicious homemade breads and jams are specialties of the house.

Avon Lake

Williams, Mrs. Margaret
249 Vinewood, 44012
(216) 933-5089

Amenities: 1,2,3,4,7,10
Breakfast: Full

Dbl. Oc.: $40.00
Sgl. Oc.: $25.00

Williams House—20 miles west of Cleveland; 3 to 5 miles north of I-90; 1 mile from Lake Erie public beach. Quiet residential area. Private bath.

Cleveland Heights

Frisch, Mrs. Sarah
1564 S. Taylor Rd., 44118
(216) 321-5694

Amenities: 1,2,4,10,12
Breakfast: Continental

Dbl. Oc.: $40.00
Sgl. Oc.: $25.00-$30.00

The Sarah Frisch House—Comfortably furnished rooms near Cleveland's cultural and medical centers & museums. Near major universities, shopping, recreational areas and bus lines. Homelike atmosphere.

Columbus

Slavka, Ms. Gloria
180 Reinhard Ave., 43206
(614) 443-6076

Amenities: 5,7,10
Breakfast: Full

Dbl. Oc.: $50.00
Sgl. Oc.: $35.00
Third Person: $35.00

Slavka's Bed & Breakfast—Old fashioned hospitality await you at this 100 year old home on the park in German Village steps away from old world shops, & houses. Owner/artist's artwork, studio/gallery. Homebaked breads.

East Fultonham

Graham, Dawn & Jim
7320 Old Town Rd., 43735
(614) 849-2728

Amenities: 4,10,12
Breakfast: Full

Dbl. Oc.: $32.00
Sgl. Oc.: $25.00

Hill View Acres—10 miles S.W. of Zanesville off U.S. 22 W. Spacious home on 21 acres with pond. Area population for antiquing, potteries, fishing. Attractions nearby; Y-Bridge, Zane Gray Museum, Ohio Ceramic Center.

AMENITIES

1. No Smoking
2. No Pets
3. No Children
4. Senior Citizen Rates
5. Tennis Available
6. Golf Available
7. Swimming Available
8. Skiing Available
9. Credit Cards Accepted
10. Personal Check Accepted
11. Off Season Rates
12. Dinner Available (w/sufficient notice)

Ohio

Geneva-On-The-Lake

Otto, C. Joyce
5653 Lake Rd., 44041
(216) 466-8668

Amenities: 2,4,5,6,7,10,12
Breakfast: Full
Dbl. Oc.: $38.50
Sgl. Oc.: $24.00
Third Person: $7.50

The Otto Court Bed And Breakfast, on Lake Erie. Walk to amusement center, specialty shops, restaurants and state park; bicycling, recreation and picnic areas. Cottages with full kitchens also available. Newly opened marina nearby.

Granville

Orr, M/M Orville
313 E. Broadway, 43023
(614) 587-0001

Amenities: 2,5,6,7,9,10,12
Breakfast: Continental

Dbl. Oc.: $65.40-$87.20
Sgl. Oc.: $59.95-$76.30
Third Person: $10.90

Buxton Inn, built in 1812, is 30 miles east of Columbus on SR 37. Fifteen rooms are air conditioned, have color cable TV, & telephone. Breakfast, lunch & dinner served daily. Fine antique shops in walking distance.

Lexington

Hiser, Ellen & Bill
8842 Denman Rd., 44904
(419) 884-2356

Amenities: 1,5,8,10,11
Breakfast: Full

Dbl. Oc.: $62.00
Sgl. Oc.: $52.00
Third Person: $10.00

The White Fence Inn—A 97-year-old farmhouse on 73 acres of land. 7 miles S.W. of Mansfield & only 1/2 mile from the Mid-Ohio Racetrack. Enjoy country quiet & choose to stay in either the Victorian, Amish, Country or Southwestern room.

Morrow

Hughes, Mrs. Rhea
6315 Zoar Rd., 45152
(513) 899-2440

Amenities: 1,2,3,10
Breakfast: Full
Dbl. Oc.: $40.00-$50.00
Sgl. Oc.: $30.00
Third Person: $10.00

Country Manor, circa 1868. Located on 55 quiet, rolling acres just 45 minutes from Cincinnati or Dayton, Ohio. Restaurants, antique shops & Kings Island Amusement Park only 10 minutes away. Join us!

AMENITIES

1. No Smoking
2. No Pets
3. No Children
4. Senior Citizen Rates
5. Tennis Available
6. Golf Available
7. Swimming Available
8. Skiing Available
9. Credit Cards Accepted
10. Personal Check Accepted
11. Off Season Rates
12. Dinner Available (w/sufficient notice)

Ohio

Old Washington

Wade, Mrs. Ruth D.
Box 115, Main St., 43768
(614) 489-5970

Amenities: 7,10
Breakfast: Continental
Dbl. Oc.: $40.00-$60.00
Sgl. Oc.: $32.00
Third Person: $10.00

Zane Trace—1859 brick Victorian with antiques & in-ground pool. Master suite plus 2 double bedrooms; 1 full size plus 1/2 bath; A/C, large porch & antique parlor. Historical sites, quiet village. Exit 186, I-70, 8 miles from Cambridge, Ohio.

Peebles

Bagford, Marilyn & Larry
25675 State Rt. 41, 45660
(513) 587-2221

Amenities: 1,2,4,6,7,10,11
Breakfast: Full

Dbl. Oc.: $35.00
Sgl. Oc.: $25.00
Third Person: $12.00

The Bayberry Inn—1888 Victorian farmhouse. Come enjoy breakfast with homemade bread then relax on the front porch. This B&B is a hub for geological and historical discoveries. Open: May-October.

Plain City

Yoder, M/M Loyd
8144 Cemetery Pike, 43064
(614) 873-4489

Amenities: 2,12
Breakfast: Full
Dbl. Oc.: $53.00
Sgl. Oc.: $43.00

Yoders Spring Lake Bed & Breakfast—Located 3/4 mile south of Plain City. 100 acre farm; stocked 5 acre fishing lake; bicycling, jogging and walking paths; Amish restaurants and shops nearby. 30 minutes from downtwon Columbus, Ohio.

Put-In-Bay

Barnhill, Barbi & Mark
Box 283, 43456
(419) 285-6181

Amenities: 1,2,3,4,7,10
Breakfast: Full

Dbl. Oc.: $50.00-$65.00
Sgl. Oc.: $50.00
Third Person: $15.00

The Vineyard B&B—This 130-year-old farmhome, full of family antiques, offers the best of 2 worlds; 20 acres of quiet seclusion with private beach and vineyard, yet just 1 mile from the heart of this historic/scenic island.

AMENITIES

1. No Smoking
2. No Pets
3. No Children
4. Senior Citizen Rates
5. Tennis Available
6. Golf Available
7. Swimming Available
8. Skiing Available
9. Credit Cards Accepted
10. Personal Check Accepted
11. Off Season Rates
12. Dinner Available (w/sufficient notice)

Ohio

Sandusky

Ryan, M/M James R., Sr.
2501 S. Campbell St., 44870
(419) 627-6821

Amenities: 1,2,5,6,7,10
Breakfast: Continental

Dbl. Oc.: $35.00-$42.00
Sgl. Oc.: $25.00
Third Person: $8.00

The Big Oak—A warm, hospitable 14-room family-run Victorian farmhouse on large shaded grounds. Located minutes from Cedar Point, Put-In-Bay, and Kellys Island in Lake Erie vacationland.

Somerset

Murray, Mrs. Mary Lou
200 S. Columbus St., Box 308, 43783
(614) 743-2909

Amenities: 1,10
Breakfast: Full
Dbl. Oc.: $30.00
Sgl. Oc.: $25.00
Third Person: $10.00

Somer Tea Bed And Breakfast—Dick and Mary Lou invite you to their large historic home. Circa 1850's, their home offers yesterday's charm with today's conveniences. There are two guest bedrooms furnished with the old & new.

Thornville

Mechling, M/M Paul P.
5663 State Route 204NW
43076
(614)246-5450

Amenities: 10
Breakfast: Full

Dbl. Oc.: $30.00
Sgl. Oc.: $25.00
Third Person: $10.00

Wal-Mec Farm is located about 7 miles south of I-70, 4 miles east of State Route 13 on State Route 204 in the rolling hills of Perry County, Ohio.

Troy

Smith, Mrs. F. June
434 So. Market St., 45373
(513) 335-1181

Amenities: 1,2,6,9,10
Breakfast: Full
Dbl. Oc.: $63.60
Sgl. Oc.: $42.40
Third Person: $21.20

H.W. Allen Villa Bed & Breakfast—1874 Victorian mansion furnished with antiques throughout. In-room private bath, air, TV, phone, snack bar. Just north of Dayton near wineries and Air Force Museum.

AMENITIES

1. No Smoking
2. No Pets
3. No Children
4. Senior Citizen Rates
5. Tennis Available
6. Golf Available
7. Swimming Available
8. Skiing Available
9. Credit Cards Accepted
10. Personal Check Accepted
11. Off Season Rates
12. Dinner Available (w/sufficient notice)

Oklahoma

The Sooner State

Capital: Oklahoma City
Statehood: November 16, 1907; the 46th state
State Motto: Labor Conquers All Things
State Song: "Oklahoma"
State Bird: Scissor-Tailed Flycatcher
State Flower: Mistletoe
State Tree: Redbud

Oklahoma was the last of the Indian territories in America. In 1893, the U.S. Government opened it up to the white man for settlement. The name Oklahoma was derived from two Indian words: "okla" for people, and "homa" for red. Some Indians have chosen to remain in the Ozark Hills and still speak Cherokee.

With the coming of irrigation, the land is now productive. However, for years the farmers had a difficult time. During the drought of the 1930's, this state suffered from the worst dry spell in years, and those who managed to stay alive pushed on with what little they had left to live in California. John Steinbeck wrote of them in his best seller, The Grapes of Wrath.

Natural gas and oil are the largest industries today in Oklahoma. It is one of the leading states in oil production.

Oklahoma's most famous personality was Will Rogers. He was a great American humorist and had much to say about many things. On this country, he is well remembered for saying, "There ought to be a law against anybody going to Europe until they have seen the things we have here."

Oklahoma

Grove

Schoenecker, Mozetta & Ed
P.O. Box 1746, 74344
(918) 786-4116

Amenities: 1,2,3,7,10
Breakfast: Continental

Dbl. Oc.: $36.50
Sgl. Oc.: $31.25

Edgewater Bed & Breakfast—Modern home on beautiful Grand Lake in N.E. OK. Country decor, queen beds & ceiling fans. Use den with beamed ceiling, skylights & fireplace. Deck overlooking lake. Resort/retirement area. Write for brochure.

Oklahoma City

Flora, M/M Newt
2312 N.W. 46, 73112
(405) 840-3157

Amenities: 2,3,10
Breakfast: Continental

Dbl. Oc.: $35.00
Sgl. Oc.: $30.00

Flora's Bed & Breakfast—Home furnished with antiques, collectibles; library, TV & VCR. Large deck overlooks city. Close to expressway; near Cowboy hall of Fame, museum race track & zoo.

AMENITIES

1. No Smoking
2. No Pets
3. No Children
4. Senior Citizen Rates
5. Tennis Available
6. Golf Available
7. Swimming Available
8. Skiing Available
9. Credit Cards Accepted
10. Personal Check Accepted
11. Off Season Rates
12. Dinner Available (w/sufficient notice)

Oregon

The Beaver State

Capital: Salem
Statehood: February 14, 1859; the 33rd state
State Motto: The Union
State Song: "Oregon, My Oregon"
State Bird: Western Meadow Lark
State Flower: Oregon Grape
State Tree: Douglas Fir

Oregon is noted for its mountains and coastal scenery. It is our most northwestern state, and forest covers almost half of it. It receives a tremendous amount of rain, which results in these forests and the beautiful green everywhere. Oregon leads the nation in lumber and in wood products. Much of this is exported, but most is used right here at home. The freezing and packing of home-grown fruits and the vast salmon, shrimp, crab and tuna industry are the main source of income for Oregon.

Vacationers love to visit this state. Millions come here every year to visit the beautiful parks and enjoy the excitement of camping in them. Mt. Hood is Oregon's majestic mountain, and a vacationer's paradise. It is perfect for the skier, hiker and climber.

Oregon

Albany

Hill, Charlene & Ival
7070 Springhill Dr., NW, 97321
(503) 928-9089

Amenities: 4.10,12
Breakfast: Continental

Rates: Contribution Only

The Farm "Mini Barn" Guest House—One room mini barn with queen bed. Located on Silver Dome Dairy Farm, bath facilities in building close by. Light breakfast; antique, vineyard, & maps. Open April through October.

Ashland

Huntley, Barbara & Bill
1313 Clay St., 97520
(503) 488-1590

Amenities: 1,2,5,6,7,8,9,10,11
Breakfast: Full

Dbl. Oc.: $75.00-$85.00
Sgl. Oc.: $70.00-$80.00
Third Person: $20.00

Country Willows Bed & Breakfast Inn—Quiet 5 acre hideaway only minutes to Shakespearean Festival. 5 rooms with private baths; panoramic view of mountains; hiking, rafting, fishing; home-baked bread.

Ashland

Levy, Alice & Roy
514 Siskiyou Blvd., 97520
(503) 482-5623

Amenities: 1,2,10,11
Breakfast: Full

Dbl. Oc.: $45.00-$65.00
Sgl. Oc.: $38.00-$58.00
Third Person: $20.00

Royal Carter House, on the national historic registry, this beautiful 1909 Craftsman home is only 4 blocks from Ashland's famous Shakespearean theater. Private baths, AC, and decorator antiques enhance this comfortable inn.

Ashland

Savage, K. Lynn, Orell, Gaile
451 N. Main St., 97520
(503) 482-4563

Amenities: 1,2,5,6,7,8,9,10,11
Breakfast: Full
Dbl. Oc.: $79.60
Sgl. Oc.: $68.90
Third Person: $9.00

Hersey House—Gracious living in elegantly restored Victorian. Colorful English country garden; sumptuous breakfasts; short walk to Shakespearean theater and park. Queen, twin beds, private baths, A/C. Hospitality hour.

AMENITIES

1. No Smoking
2. No Pets
3. No Children
4. Senior Citizen Rates
5. Tennis Available
6. Golf Available
7. Swimming Available
8. Skiing Available
9. Credit Cards Accepted
10. Personal Check Accepted
11. Off Season Rates
12. Dinner Available (w/sufficient notice)

Oregon

Ashland

Treon, M/M Francis
1819 Colestin Rd., 97520
(503) 482-0746

Amenities: 1,2,7,8,10,11
Breakfast: Full

Dbl. Oc.: $55.00
Sgl. Oc.: $50.00
Third Person: $10.00

Treon's Country Homestay—A peaceful B&B nestled in the tall pine forest south of Ashland provides: pond for swimming & boating, hiking, inside & outdoor recreation, queen/twin rooms, guest kitchen, BBQ, & country fresh breakfasts.

Bend

Hukari, Cheryl
640 NW Congress, 97701
(503) 388-4064

Amenities: 1,2,8,9,10
Breakfast: Full

Dbl. Oc.: $58.15
Sgl. Oc.: $51.01

Lara House Bed & Breakfast—Enjoy the comfort of this historic home nestled in a wooded setting near Bend's famous Drake Park. Within walking distance of downtown; close to Mt. Bachelor. Hot tub, sauna, fireplace.

Bend

Kellum, Ms. Beryl
1054 NW Harmon Blvd., 97701
(503) 389-1680

Amenities: 2,3,5,6,7,8,10
Breakfast: Full

Dbl. Oc.: $63.00-$84.50
Sgl. Oc.: $58.25-$79.50
Third Person: $15.50

Mirror Pond House—A small inn at water's edge where wild ducks and geese glide ashore. Near downtown in a quiet area with: big beds, private baths, complimentary wine, a sunny deck, and guest canoe.

Brookings

Holmes, Mrs. Lorene
17350 Holmes Dr., 97415
(503) 469-3025

Amenities: 1,2,5,7,8,10
Breakfast: Continental

Dbl. Oc.: $57.50-$62.50
Sgl. Oc.: $52.50-$57.50
Third Person: $10.00

Holmes Sea Cove Bed & Breakfast is located 2 miles north of Brookings, nestled in the SW tip of Oregon. 3 lovely rooms, spectacular ocean view, beach and private park.

Coburg

Wheeler, Isabel & Joe
P.O. Box 8201, 97401
(503) 344-1366

Amenities: 9,10
Breakfast: Full

Dbl. Oc.: $35.00
Sgl. Oc.: $30.00
Third Person: $10.00

Wheeler's Bed & Breakfast—Located in the national historical town of Coburg, 1/2 mile off Interstate 5. Quiet country atmosphere, 7 miles north of the metropolitan city of Eugene.

AMENITIES

1. No Smoking
2. No Pets
3. No Children
4. Senior Citizen Rates
5. Tennis Available
6. Golf Available
7. Swimming Available
8. Skiing Available
9. Credit Cards Accepted
10. Personal Check Accepted
11. Off Season Rates
12. Dinner Available (w/sufficient notice)

Oregon

Depoe Bay

Schwabe, Paul
P.O. Box 56, 97341
(503) 765-2140

Amenities: 6,9,10
Breakfast: Full

Dbl. Oc.: $42.00-$147.00
Third Person: $15.00

Channel House Bed & Breakfast Inn—Cape Cod Salt Box architecture on bluff overlooking Pacific Ocean and entrance to Depoe Bay. Six of eleven rooms have private whirlpool tubs; great spot for whale watching and storm watching; a unique inn.

Elmira

McGillivray, Evelyn R.
88680 Evers Rd., 97437
(503) 935-3564

Amenities: 1,2,9,10
Breakfast: Full

Dbl. Oc.: $50.00-$60.00
Sgl. Oc.: $40.00-$50.00
Third Person: $15.00-$25.00

McGillivrays Log Home bed & Breakfast— King beds, private baths, A/C; the best of yesterday with the comforts of today. Breakfast usually prepared on the antique woodburning cookstove. 14 miles west of Eugene, OR, on way to coast.

Eugene

Kjaer, Mrs. George
814 Lorane Hwy., 97405
(503) 343-3234

Amenities: 1,2,10
Breakfast: Full

Dbl. Oc.: $55.00
Sgl. Oc.: $38.00
Third Person: $10.00

The House in The Woods offers urban convenience and suburban tranquility in 78-year-old home on quiet road. Hiking trails and bike paths nearby, easy access to downtown and university.

Gold Beach

Fass, Nicki
31780 Edson Creek Rd., 97444
(503) 247-6037

Amenities: 1,6,7,9,10,11,12
Breakfast: Full

Dbl. Oc.: $49.00
Sgl. Oc.: $47.00
Third Person: $8.00

Nicki's Country Place—Nicki's combines a love of horses and country French surroundings with the openess of a wilderness lodge. Among the trees on 11 acres its within 4 miles of the ocean, Rogue River, national forest and town.

Grants Pass

Gustafson, June & John
678 Troll View Rd., 97527
(503) 479-7998

Amenities: 1,2,5,6,7,9,10
Breakfast: Full

Dbl. Oc.: $55.00
Sgl. Oc.: $50.00
Third Person: $10.00

Mt. Baldy B&B—New ranch-style home with large deck, beautiful view. Meals on deck, weather permitting. Two guest rooms, private baths and entrance, queen size beds, quiet area.

AMENITIES

1. No Smoking
2. No Pets
3. No Children
4. Senior Citizen Rates
5. Tennis Available
6. Golf Available
7. Swimming Available
8. Skiing Available
9. Credit Cards Accepted
10. Personal Check Accepted
11. Off Season Rates
12. Dinner Available (w/sufficient notice)

Oregon

Grants Pass

Head, Barbara
1304 NW Lawnridge, 97526
(503) 479-5186

Amenities: 1,4,5,6,7,8,10,11
Breakfast: Full
Dbl. Oc.: $45.00-$65.00
Sgl. Oc.: $35.00-$55.00
Third Person: $10.00

Lawnridge House—1909 historic home. Honeymoon suite, canopy beds, private & shared baths. Antique furnishings, fireplace, mountain views, air-conditioned. Quiet location near I-5. 45 minutes to Ashland & Shakespeare Festival.

Lakeside

Sindell, Carolyn & Roy
777 Country Lane,
P.O. Box Y, 97449
(503) 759-3869

Amenities: 1,2,3,10
Breakfast: Full

Dbl. Oc.: $45.00
Sgl. Oc.: $40.00
Third Person: $10.00

Country Lane Bed & Breakfast welcomes you to our chalet-style homestead with great room/fireplace. Enjoy forest trails, hammock, BBQ, badminton. Explore dunes, Tenmile Lakes, beaches; homemade pie. Open all year.

Oakland

Pringle, M/M Jim
7th at Locust, 97462
(503) 459-5038

Amenities: 1,2,3,5,6,7,10
Breakfast: Full

Dbl. Oc.: $40.00
Sgl. Oc.: $30.00
Third Person: $10.00

The Pringle House B&B—Attractive 1893 Victorian on national register in quiet historic town. Clean, comfortable, delicious breakfast. One hour south of Eugene near I-5. Fine dining, antiques, fishing, golf and 6 wineries nearby.

Oceanside

Holloway, Kathy & Ross
1685 Maxwell Mountain Rd.
97134
(503) 842-6126

Amenities: 10
Breakfast: Full

Dbl. Oc.: $45.00-$50.00
Sgl. Oc.: $35.00-$40.00
Third Person: $10.00

Three Capes Bed & Breakfast overlooks the majestic Pacific at Oceanside, Oregon. Each room has private bath & ocean view. Private entrance & deck available. Local seafood specialties served on weekends.

AMENITIES

1. No Smoking
2. No Pets
3. No Children
4. Senior Citizen Rates
5. Tennis Available
6. Golf Available
7. Swimming Available
8. Skiing Available
9. Credit Cards Accepted
10. Personal Check Accepted
11. Off Season Rates
12. Dinner Available (w/sufficient notice)

Oregon

Portland

Hall, Ms. Lori
125 SW Hooker, 97201
(503) 222-4435

Amenities: 1,2,5,6,7,9,10
Breakfast: Continental
Dbl. Oc.: $54.50-$76.30
Sgl. Oc.: $43.60-$65.40
Third Person: $20.00

General Hooker's B&B is a casually elegant Victorian in a quiet, historical neighborhood in downtown Portland. Adult oriented with many amenities, original art, roof garden w/river view. Illustrated brochure.

Portland

Loughlin, Mrs. Milli
5758 NE Emerson, 97218-2406
(503) 282-7892

Amenities: 1,2,4,5,6,8,10,11,12
Breakfast: Full

Dbl. Oc.: $25.00-$35.00
Sgl. Oc.: $20.00-$30.00
Third Person: $10.00

Hostess House—Offers warmth and hospitality in a contemporary setting. The quiet residence is 5 minutes from Portland's airport, 10 minutes from the famous Lloyd Center, and has easy access to I-5, I-84 & I-205.

Sandy

Coburn, Mrs. Lois
23200 S.E. Green Acres Rd., 97055
(503) 668-4283

Amenities: 2,6,8,9,10
Breakfast: Full

Dbl. Oc.: $70.00
Sgl. Oc.: $30.00
Third Person: $10.00

Whispering Firs—Warm comfortable house on 10 wooded acres. Large porch for sitting, reading, or visiting. Small cabin for day use. Mt. Hood 1/2 hour away by car.

Seal Rock

Tarter, Mrs. Barbara
6576 NW Pacific Coast Hwy 101, 97376
(503) 563-2259

Amenities: 1,2,3,9,10
Breakfast: Full

Dbl. Oc.: $50.00
Sgl. Oc.: $45.00

Blackberry Inn—Small country home 12 miles south of Newport on the central Oregon coast. Hot tub; short walk to beach; trails; farm critters; private entrance; rooms have private bath. Brochure available.

AMENITIES

1. No Smoking
2. No Pets
3. No Children
4. Senior Citizen Rates
5. Tennis Available
6. Golf Available
7. Swimming Available
8. Skiing Available
9. Credit Cards Accepted
10. Personal Check Accepted
11. Off Season Rates
12. Dinner Available (w/sufficient notice)

Oregon

Wolf Creek

Gleisner, Kris
P.O. Box 124, 97497
(503) 476-8812

Amenities: 1,2,3,5,6,7,8,10,11,12
Breakfast: Continental

Dbl. Oc.: $55.00
Sgl. Oc.: $45.00
Third Person: $10.00

Valley Creek Cottage offers total privacy in a spacious creekside cabin. Hot tub, woodstove, TV/VCR, sundeck and refrigerator. Enjoy the country peace and quiet. Only 4 miles from I-5 in southern Oregon. Near the Rogue River.

AMENITIES

1. No Smoking
2. No Pets
3. No Children
4. Senior Citizen Rates
5. Tennis Available
6. Golf Available
7. Swimming Available
8. Skiing Available
9. Credit Cards Accepted
10. Personal Check Accepted
11. Off Season Rates
12. Dinner Available (w/sufficient notice)

Pennsylvania

The Keystone State

Capital: Harrisburg
Statehood: December 12, 1787; the 2nd state
State Motto: Virtue, Liberty and Independence
State Bird: Ruffed Grouse
State Flower: Mountain Laurel
State Tree: Hemlock

Pennsylvania is enjoyed by tourists because it offers such a variety of things to see and do. It is the land where liberty began, the land of chocolate candy, steel mills, and the beginning of Little League baseball.

One of the major attractions for tourists is the Liberty Bell in Philadelphia. This bell is a reminder to all Americans that here is where our Constitution was adopted and signed, giving all of us the right to private enterprise and initiative, and the right to live and worshop as we wish.

The steel mills in Pittsburgh, the beautiful Amish farms in Reading and Lancaster, the lively homes and cooking of the Pennsylvania Dutch throughout the heart of this state, is representative of what our forefathers visualized.

Pennsylvania offers scenic beauty and many historical attractions, from Valley Forge to the Gettysburg battlefields.

One of the oldest universities in our country is Pennsylvania University.

James Buchanan, our 15th president, was born here in 1791.

Pennsylvania

Airville

Hearne, Mrs. Ray
Muddy Creek Forks, 17302
(717) 927-6906

Amenities: 5,6,7,9,10
Breakfast: Full

Dbl. Oc.: $63.60 & Up
Sgl. Oc.: $53.00 & Up
Third Person: $10.00

18th Century Stone Inn—Country luxuries include featherbeds, antiques, superb breakfast, & tea on arrival. Near wineries, Lancaster & York. Woodstoves, piano and original paintings provide for a cozy visit.

Akron

Wenger, Janice & Paul
224 Bomberger Rd., 17501
(717) 859-2220

Amenities: 2,12
Breakfast: Full

Dbl. Oc.: $50.00
Sgl. Oc.: $45.00
Third Person: $10.00

"Oasis"—Quiet country setting, 4 1/2 acres adjacent to Akron Hobby Farm with sheep and horses in the heart of PA. Dutch country. Close to major Rt. 222; 20 minutes to Lancaster; 1 hour from Philadelphia & Harrisburg.

Allentown

Orth, Judith & Ollie
910 East Emmaus Ave., 18103
(215) 791-4225

Amenities: 2,3,9,10
Breakfast: Full

Dbl. Oc.: $106.00-$121.90
Sgl. Oc.: $106.00-$121.90

Salisbury House, built in 1810, is a gracious country inn surrounded by acres of lawn, garden and woodland, just 10 minutes from Bethlehem and Allentown. A full gourmet breakfast is served by candlelight.

Beach Lake

Miller, Erika
P.O. Box 144,
Main St., & Church Rd., 18405
(717) 729-8239

Amenities: 1,2,3,7,8,9,10,12
Breakfast: Full
Dbl. Oc.: $79.50
Sgl. Oc.: $79.50

Beach Lake Hotel And Country Store—
Restored Victorian inn with six rooms, private baths, & furnished with antiques. Intimate dining, cozy pub, antique/gift shop. Located in Poconos near Delaware River; all activities; perfect getaway.

AMENITIES

1. No Smoking
2. No Pets
3. No Children
4. Senior Citizen Rates
5. Tennis Available
6. Golf Available
7. Swimming Available
8. Skiing Available
9. Credit Cards Accepted
10. Personal Check Accepted
11. Off Season Rates
12. Dinner Available (w/sufficient notice)

Pennsylvania

Benton

Low, M/M Zehnder
RD 2, Box 256-B, 17814
(717) 925-2858

Amenities: 4,6,7,8,10,12
Breakfast: Full

Dbl. Oc.: $52.00
Sgl. Oc.: $38.00
Third Person: $26.00

"**The White House On North Mountain**"—Visit the past. Restored 1840 home, furnished in antiques, surrounded by 60,000 acres of gameland. Getaway weekends our specialty. Easy access from Philadelphia and NYC—45 minutes from I-80. Open year round.

Bird-In-Hand

Davis, Sally & Ed
2658 Old Philadelphia Pike,
P.O. Box 270, 17505
(717) 393-4233

Amenities: 2,4,5,6,9,10,11
Breakfast: Continental
Dbl. Oc.: $56.18 & up
Sgl. Oc.: $56.18 & up
Third Person: $10.60

Greystone Manor Bed & Breakfast is located in the heart of the Amish community on 2 grassy acres. Rooms are in a French Victorian mansion and carriage house. Private baths, TV, & quilts; craft shop on premises.

Blakeslee

Whitner, Marian & George
Box 431, Rte. 940, 18610
(717) 646-4893

Amenities: 2,4,8,10
Breakfast: Continental

Dbl. Oc.: $45.00
Sgl. Oc.: $30.00
Third Person: $6.00

Toby Valley Lodge—Pocono vacation lodge has seven rooms, all with private baths, color TV and view of adjacent woods. Enjoy breakfast in the family room with stone fireplace. Close to ski areas and Pocono Raceway.

Blue Ridge Summit

Price, Winnie
Box 280, 7214
(717) 794-8816

Amenities: 6,9,10
Breakfast: Continental

Dbl. Oc.: $53.00
Sgl. Oc.: $50.00
Third Person: $5.00

The Greystone—A charming country inn amid historic surroundings, state parks and forests. Excellent golf & hiking nearby. Gettysburg 15 miles away.

AMENITIES

1. No Smoking
2. No Pets
3. No Children
4. Senior Citizen Rates
5. Tennis Available
6. Golf Available
7. Swimming Available
8. Skiing Available
9. Credit Cards Accepted
10. Personal Check Accepted
11. Off Season Rates
12. Dinner Available (w/sufficient notice)

Pennsylvania

Brackney

Frierman, M/M Howard
Tripp Lake Rd.,
RD 1, Box 68, 18812
(717) 663-2645

Amenities: 2,6,7,8,9,11,12
Breakfast: Continental

Dbl. Oc.: $44.52
Sgl. Oc.: $37.10
Third Person: $7.42

Indian Mountain Inn/B&B, in the endless mountains of northeast PA. 10 bedrooms; dining hall; 8 baths; spa; 10 wooded acres; lake district; liquor license; very secluded; near Binghamton, Finger Lakes, & Scranton. 12 miles off Rte. 81.

Canadensis

Dornich, Charlotte & Dick
Rte. 447,
P.O. Box 275, 18325
(717) 595-2532

Amenities: 5,7,9,10
Breakfast: Full

Dbl. Oc.: $90.00
Sgl. Oc.: $75.00
Third Person: $20.00

Charming Country Inn includes: breakfast, gourmet dining, swimming, tennis, hiking. Art workshops offered through Oct. 31. Art gallery open to public. We offer charm, uniqueness, & peaceful surroundings. Dinner-$20.00

Canadensis

Robinson, Barb & Dick
RD 1, Box 630, 18325
(717) 595-3152

Amenities: 1,5,6,7,8,10
Breakfast: Full
Dbl. Oc.: $40.00-$50.00
Sgl. Oc.: $30.00
Third Person: $12.50

"Nearbrook"

'Nearbrook'—Pocono Mts., centrally located for summer and winter sightseeing and activities. It's contagious informality encourages the musician, artist and writer to come and do their thing!

Carlisle

Fitting, Mrs. Jeanne
McClures Gap Rd.,
RD 3, Box 480, 17013
(717) 249-1455

Amenities: 1,2,3,6,12
Breakfast: Full

Dbl. Oc.: $40.00
Sgl. Oc.: $32.00
Third Person: $4.25

Alwayspring Farm—Friendly 40 acre farm with chickens, geese, & horses. 10 minute drive to Carlisle, United States War College, & Dickinson College. Cozy, comfortable home, A/C.

AMENITIES

1. No Smoking
2. No Pets
3. No Children
4. Senior Citizen Rates
5. Tennis Available
6. Golf Available
7. Swimming Available
8. Skiing Available
9. Credit Cards Accepted
10. Personal Check Accepted
11. Off Season Rates
12. Dinner Available (w/sufficient notice)

Pennsylvania

Carlisle

Line, Joan & Bob
2070 Ritner Hwy., 17013
(717) 243-1281

Amenities: 1,6,10
Breakfast: Full

Dbl. Oc.: $40.00
Sgl. Oc.: $30.00
Third Person: $20.00

Line Limousin Farm House—The Farm House, part of a Limousin Beef Cattle Farm on 100 acres, has been in the family since 1778. One room with private bath, other rooms with shared bath. Located 2 miles from Exit 12 of I-81.

Christiana

Metzler, Mrs. Robert
107 Noble Rd., 17509
(215) 593-5535

Amenities: 1,2,6,7
Breakfast: Full

Rates: $38.00
Third Person: $10.00

Winding Glen is a dairy farm located in a beautiful valley in Lancaster County. Guests stay in the farmhouse. Watch the cows being milked or visit Amish craft and quilt shops nearby.

Chuchtown

Smith, M/M Stuart
Rt. 23, 17555
(215) 445-7794

Amenities: 1,2,3,4,6,7,8,9,10,12
Breakfast: Full
Dbl. Oc.: $49.00-$80.00
Sgl. Oc.: $44.00-$75.00
Third Person: $17.50

Churchtown Inn, circa 1735; heart of Pennsylvania Dutch country. Lovely 18th century home filled with charm & history minutes from: PA Tpke., tourist attractions, antique markets & outlets. Private & shared bath, A/C, TV, cozy!

Columbia

Stark, Jean & Bob
420 Chestnut St., 17512
(717) 684-3173

Amenities: 1,2,5,6,7,8,9,11
Breakfast: Continental

Dbl. Oc.: $50.00
Sgl. Oc.: $50.00
Third Person: $10.00

The Old Bridge Inn—We welcome you to our 100-year-old Victorian home in historic Columbia, on the Susquehanna River. Located bewteen Lancaster, York and Hershey. Visit the Amish, outlets and many other attractions.

AMENITIES

1. No Smoking
2. No Pets
3. No Children
4. Senior Citizen Rates
5. Tennis Available
6. Golf Available
7. Swimming Available
8. Skiing Available
9. Credit Cards Accepted
10. Personal Check Accepted
11. Off Season Rates
12. Dinner Available (w/sufficient notice)

Pennsylvania

Cooksburg

Williams, E.F.
P.O. Box 150, 16217
(814) 744-8171

Amenities: 2,6,7,8,9,11,12
Breakfast: Continental

Dbl. Oc.: $83.75
Sgl. Oc.: $83.75
Third Person: $15.00

Clarion River Lodge—Friendly romantic 20 room inn located on Clarion River beside Cook Forest Park. Private baths, A/C, TV, phones, fireplaces, full dining; 20 minutes north on I-80, exit 13. Open year round.

Cresco

Swingle, Kay
RD 2, Box 1051, 18326
(717) 676-4225

Amenities: 2,6,7,8,10
Breakfast: Continental

Dbl. Oc.: $30.00
Sgl. Oc.: $20.00
Third Person: $10.00

La Anna Guest House—Victorian house, over 100 years old, furnished in period antiques & spacious rooms. Quiet mountain village in the heart of the Poconos with waterfalls, woodland, hiking, & fine dining nearby. $10.00 deposit with reservation.

East Berlin

Spangler, Ruth
400 West King St., 17316
(717) 259-7760

Amenities: 1,2,4,5,6,8,9,10,11
Breakfast: Continental
Dbl. Oc.: $82.25-$132.50
Sgl. Oc.: $47.70-$106.00
Third Person: $20.00

The Leas-Bechtel Mansion Inn—Hospitable, restored Victorian mansion within a national historic district on the western frontier of the Pennsylvania Dutch country. Convenient to Gettysburg, York, & Lancaster County.

Ephrata

Grobengieser, Jan
318-324 N. State St., 17522
(717) 733-8696

Amenities: 2,9,10
Breakfast: Continental

Dbl. Oc.: $62.54-$137.80
Sgl. Oc.: $54.06-$127.20
Third Person: $10.00

Guesthouse At Doneckers—Country elegance; suites; fireplaces; jacuzzis; markets; antiques; folk art; stenciled decor; fashion stores; restaurant; & historic Lancaster County.

AMENITIES

1. No Smoking
2. No Pets
3. No Children
4. Senior Citizen Rates
5. Tennis Available
6. Golf Available
7. Swimming Available
8. Skiing Available
9. Credit Cards Accepted
10. Personal Check Accepted
11. Off Season Rates
12. Dinner Available (w/sufficient notice)

Pennsylvania

Euphrata

Smith, Shirley & Ray
287 Duke St., 17522
(717) 733-0263

Amenities: 2,3,5,6,7,9,10,11,12
Breakfast: Full
Dbl. Oc.: $53.00-$79.50
Sgl. Oc.: $47.70-$68.90

Gerhart House, built in 1926 by Alexander Gerhart, has 5 lovely rooms, elegant queen canopy bed, also double & twin, with private or shared baths, a Victorian parlor & sunny breakfast room. Pennsylvania Dutch country.

Gettysburg

Agard, Mrs. Mimi
44 York St., 17325
(717) 337-3423

Amenities: 1,2,5,6,7,8,9,10
Breakfast: Full
Dbl. Oc.: $65.00
Sgl. Oc.: $50.00
Third Person: $10.00

The Brafferton Inn, Gettysburg's first home, circa 1787. 8 stenciled rooms with 18th century antiques. 4 private baths, large living room, library, player piano. Breakfast amidst primitive mural. One of PA's finest restorations.

Gettysburg

Beamer, Rick
89 Steinwehr Ave., 17325
(717) 334-2100

Amenities: 1,2,5,6,7,8,9,10,11,12
Breakfast: Full

Dbl. Oc.: $66.55
Sgl. Oc.: $54.45
Third Person: $18.15

Gettystown Inn is centrally located within walking distance of the National Park Visitor's Center and most major attractions. A Civil War era home with seven rooms decorated with period furniture.

Gettysburg

Bishop, Karen & Ethan
40 Hospital Rd., 17325
(717) 334-9530

Amenities: 2,3,5,6,8,10
Breakfast: Continental

Dbl. Oc.: $80.00
Sgl. Oc.: $80.00
Third Person: $20.00

Bishop's Rocking Horse Inn—Romantic getaway. 17 formal gardens, gazebo, brick patio, tennis court; 3 guest rooms, one with private bath; historian on premises. Reservation requested. 1 1/2 miles from town. 4 acre estate.

AMENITIES

1. No Smoking
2. No Pets
3. No Children
4. Senior Citizen Rates
5. Tennis Available
6. Golf Available
7. Swimming Available
8. Skiing Available
9. Credit Cards Accepted
10. Personal Check Accepted
11. Off Season Rates
12. Dinner Available (w/sufficient notice)

Pennsylvania

Gettysburg

Martin, Mrs. Mary, Hammett, Dr/M James
96 Hickory Bridge Rd., 17353, Orrtanna
(717) 642-5261

Amenities: 9,10,11,12
Breakfast: Full
Dbl. Oc.: $68.90
Sgl. Oc.: $31.80
Third Person: $10.00

Hickory Bridge Farm—8 miles west of Gettysburg in a quiet country setting. Cottages by mountain stream; farmhouse rooms with many antiques; all private baths; fireplaces; fine country dining—Fri., Sat., & Sun. Very relaxful!

Gettysburg

Skradski, Maribeth & Frank
218 Carlisle St., 17325
(717) 337-1711

Amenities: 2,5,6,7,8,9,10
Breakfast: Full
Dbl. Oc.: $58.30-$86.92
Sgl. Oc.: $58.30-$86.92
Third Person: $10.60

The Old Appleford Inn—Described as, a "brick cottage" in 1867, Judge McCurdy's elegant 16 room mansion today features 9 guest rooms & a suite. 5 fireplaces, full breakfast, gracious common areas, & antiques provide a cozy getaway. A/C.

Gordonville (Intercourse)

Sawyer, Joy & Barry
313 Osceola Mill Rd., 17529
(717) 768-3758

Amenities: 1,2,3,10
Breakfast: Full

Dbl. Oc.: $53.00-$74.20
Sgl. Oc.: $53.00-$74.20
Third Person: $10.00

The Osceola Mill House—Circa 1776 is located in scenic Lancaster County surrounded by Amish farms in quaint historic setting. Fireplaces in keeping room and bedrooms. Near Intercourse and Lancaster.

AMENITIES

1. No Smoking
2. No Pets
3. No Children
4. Senior Citizen Rates
5. Tennis Available
6. Golf Available
7. Swimming Available
8. Skiing Available
9. Credit Cards Accepted
10. Personal Check Accepted
11. Off Season Rates
12. Dinner Available (w/sufficient notice)

Pennsylvania

Hanover

Hormel, Mrs. Monna
315 Broadway, 17331
(717) 632-3013

Amenities: 2,3,5,6,7,9,10
Breakfast: Full
Dbl. Oc.: $58.30-$90.10
Sgl. Oc.: $51.94-$83.74
Third Person: $10.60

Beechmont Inn is 13 miles from Gettysburg. Elegant 1834 Federal period inn with 7 rooms, antiques, private baths, gourmet breakfast, fireplace, & A/C. Antiquing, wineries, & a large state park with a lake are nearby.

Hawley

Lazan, Judith & Sheldon
528 Academy St., 18428
(717) 226-3430

Amenities: 5,6,7,9
Breakfast: Full
Dbl. Oc.: $70.00
Sgl. Oc.: $45.00
Third Person: $25.00

Academy Street B&B—Historic Italianate Victorian with 7 large rooms, elegant lodging, gourmet breakfast. N.E. Poconos; all lake recreational activities nearby. 3 bedroom w/private bath, 4 w/shared bath. A/C.

Hershey

Long, M/M James
50 Northeast Dr., 17033
(717) 533-2603

Amenities: 1,2,5,6,7,10,11
Breakfast: Continental

Dbl. Oc.: $47.70
Sgl. Oc.: $47.70
Third Person: $5.00

Pinehurst Inn Bed And Breakfast—A country setting adjacent to all Hershey attractions. 12 guest rooms with additional spacious rooms for casual gatherings. Handicap facilities.

AMENITIES

1. No Smoking
2. No Pets
3. No Children
4. Senior Citizen Rates
5. Tennis Available
6. Golf Available
7. Swimming Available
8. Skiing Available
9. Credit Cards Accepted
10. Personal Check Accepted
11. Off Season Rates
12. Dinner Available (w/sufficient notice)

Pennsylvania

Holicong

Rawes, Carolyn
Box 202, 18928
(215) 794-5373

Amenities: 2,3,5,6,7,8,9,10
Breakfast: Continental
Dbl. Oc.: $63.60-$74.20
Sgl. Oc.: $63.60-$74.20
Third Person: $10.00

Ash Mill Farm, an 18th century farmhouse on 10 sheep-filled acres. Adjacent to Peddler's Village and minutes from New Hope. 4 guest rooms furnished with country antiques. Full continental breakfast and afternoon tea.

Kennett Square

Hicks, Mrs. Anne
201 E. Street Rd., 19348
(215) 444-3903

Amenities: 2,5,6,7,9,10,12
Breakfast: Full
Dbl. Oc.: $45.00
Sgl. Oc.: $35.00
Third Person: $10.00

Meadow Spring Farm—Circa 1836. Enjoy a week, weekend or day on the farm. TV in each room, fresh flowers and fruit, full country breakfast served to guests. Home filled with antiques, crafts, and dolls. No pets.

Kinzer

Groff, M/M Harold
766 Brackbill Rd., 17535
(717) 442-8223

Amenities: 1,2,5,6,7,10,11
Breakfast: Continental

Dbl. Oc.: $31.80-$49.70
Sgl. Oc.: $29.68-$47.70
Third Person: $15.90

Groff Tourist Farm Home—Old stone modern farmhouse, Amish neighbors, semi-private baths, continental breakfasts, air-conditioned, spacious lawn and flower beds, 12,000 chickens, 106 veal calves, handstitched quilts on beds.

AMENITIES

1. No Smoking
2. No Pets
3. No Children
4. Senior Citizen Rates
5. Tennis Available
6. Golf Available
7. Swimming Available
8. Skiing Available
9. Credit Cards Accepted
10. Personal Check Accepted
11. Off Season Rates
12. Dinner Available (w/sufficient notice)

Pennsylvania

Lahaska (Bucks County)

Jamison, Earl
Rt. 202 & Rt. 263, Peddler's Village, 18931
(215) 794-7438

Amenities: 2,9,10
Breakfast: Full
Rates: $85.00-$150.00
Third Person: $15.00

Golden Plough Inn—Luxurious rooms, private baths, fireplaces, TV, private balconies, refrigerators; 18th century shopping village, 62 specialty shops, 5 excellent restaurants, antiques, art galleries.

Lahaska

Kearney, Mrs. Sue
Rt. 202, Box 500, 18931
(215) 794-0440

Amenities: 1,2,3,4,9,10,11,12
Breakfast: Continental
Dbl. Oc.: $85.00-$100.00
Third Person: $16.00

Lahaska Hotel—Bucks County Victorian inn; 6 rooms of individual personality with private baths. 4 miles to New Hope, across from Peddler's Village. Walk to antique shops, boutiques, galleries, restaurants. Bus from N.Y.

Lancaster

Dingeldein, Laurie & Keith
1105 E. King St., 17602
(717) 293-1723

Amenities: 1,5,6,9,10,11
Breakfast: Full

Dbl. Oc.: $53.00-$63.60
Third Person: $15.90

The Dingeldein House—A lovely restored home located close to beautiful Amish farms and other attractions. Owner/chef prepares a superb breakfast. Cozy rooms, exquisite gardens, unending hospitality.

AMENITIES

1. No Smoking
2. No Pets
3. No Children
4. Senior Citizen Rates
5. Tennis Available
6. Golf Available
7. Swimming Available
8. Skiing Available
9. Credit Cards Accepted
10. Personal Check Accepted
11. Off Season Rates
12. Dinner Available (w/sufficient notice)

Pennsylvania

Lancaster

Hartung, Mr. Brant
2014 Old Philadelphia Pike, 17602
(717) 299-5305

Amenities: 5,6,7,10
Breakfast: Continental
Dbl. Oc.: $55.00-$75.00
Sgl. Oc.: $55.00-$75.00
Third Person: $10.00

Historic 1725 Witmer's Tavern

Witmer's Tavern—Historic 1725 inn, Lancaster's only authentic pre-revolutionary inn still lodging travelers. Fireplaces, fresh flowers in rooms, romantic, Pandora's antique & quilt shop. On national register of historic places. Pennsylvania Dutch heartlands.

Lancaster

Maxcy, Mrs. Betty Lee
990 Rettew Mill Rd., 17522
(717) 733-1592

Amenities: 1,2,6,7,10,12
Breakfast: Full
Dbl. Oc.: $53.00
Sgl. Oc.: $47.70
Third Person: $15.90

Covered Bridge Inn—Beautiful 174-year-old historic home situated by a covered bridge and an old mill. 4 large sun-filled rooms furnished with antiques, flowers and herbs. Large country breakfast by the fire or on the porch.

Lancaster

Mitrani, Jacqueline & Stephen
Box 161A, RD 3, Narvon, 17555
(215) 445-6713

Amenities: 1,2,3
Breakfast: Full

Dbl. Oc.: $53.00
Sgl. Oc.: $42.40
Third Person: $10.60

The Foreman House is an elegant old home furnished with antiques & quilts. It is in a tiny village in the Amish area of Pennsylvania & surrounded by farms. Lancaster County is a wonderful area for crafts & gourmets.

AMENITIES

1. No Smoking
2. No Pets
3. No Children
4. Senior Citizen Rates
5. Tennis Available
6. Golf Available
7. Swimming Available
8. Skiing Available
9. Credit Cards Accepted
10. Personal Check Accepted
11. Off Season Rates
12. Dinner Available (w/sufficient notice)

Pennsylvania

Lancaster

Owens, Karen & Jim
1049 E. King St., 17602
(717) 397-1017

Amenities: 1,2,5,6,7,9,10,11
Breakfast: Full
Dbl. Oc.: $105.00
Sgl. Oc.: $105.00
Third Person: $16.00

The King's Cottage—Thoughtful hosts with a sumptuous regal retreat in Amish country. Award-winning Spanish mansion with designer's eye for detail & comfort. King/queen beds, private baths, afternoon tea, cordials & mints.

Lancaster

Thomas, Mrs. Leon
2336 Hollinger Rd., 17602-4728
(717) 464-3050

Amenities: 1,2,5,6,7,10,11
Breakfast: Full
Dbl. Oc.: $47.70
Sgl. Oc.: $37.10
Third Person: $15.90

Hollinger House B&B was built by a tanner in 1870. Hosted by a Mennonite family it is grand but homey. Close to Amish country, good restaurants, farmers markets, outlets & much more. Tours arranged; deposit required.

Leesport

Smith, Mary & Gene
RD 1, Box 1420, 19533
(215) 926-3217

Amenities: 2,5,6,7,8,10
Breakfast: Full

Dbl. Oc.: $47.70
Sgl. Oc.: $47.70
Third Person: $15.00

The Loom Room—A lovely 1812 log & stone farmhouse with weaving studio, herb garden, & gazebo. Rural; near major antique & outlet shops; Amish country; nature trails. 3 miles north of Reading.

Ligonier

Grant, Mrs. Marilyn
244 W. Church St., 15658
(412) 238-5135

Amenities: 1,2,3,5,6,7,8,10
Breakfast: Continental

Dbl. Oc.: $53.00
Sgl. Oc.: $50.00
Third Person: $10.00

Grant House B&B is a restored Victorian located 1 block north of the town center in Ligonier Valley. Restaurants, shops, & historic fort are within walking distance. Falling water, parks, nature trails, & white water rafting nearby.

AMENITIES

1. No Smoking
2. No Pets
3. No Children
4. Senior Citizen Rates
5. Tennis Available
6. Golf Available
7. Swimming Available
8. Skiing Available
9. Credit Cards Accepted
10. Personal Check Accepted
11. Off Season Rates
12. Dinner Available (w/sufficient notice)

Pennsylvania

Lincoln University

Hershey, Arlene & E.E.
Route 1, Box 93, 19352
(215) 932-9257

Amenities: 1,2,10
Breakfast: Continental

Dbl. Oc.: $35.00
Sgl. Oc.: $25.00
Third Person: $10.00

Hershey's Bed & Breakfast—Quiet country 5 acre wooded area; bike riding, hiking, picnic area etc. Along Pennsylvania Rt. 10, 1 miles north of Rt. 1 Bypass, 4 miles north of Oxford. 1/2 hour from Amish country, historical sites and beautiful gardens.

Lumberville

Nessler, Harry
River Rd., 18933
(215) 297-5661

Amenities: 2,3,5,6,7,10
Breakfast: Full

Dbl. Oc.: $65.00-$77.00

The 1740 House—Situated in the most charming section of Bucks County, this B&B inn offers guests 24 early-American rooms each with private bath, and either terrace or balcony overlooking the Delaware River.

Manheim

Avella, Dr./M Alfred
140 S. Charlotte St., 17545
(717) 644-4168

Amenities: 2,4,5,7,9
Breakfast: Full

Rates: $50.00-$60.00

Manheim Manor—Old historic house, Victorian decor, 7 guest rooms (each sleeps 4), 1 apartment (sleeps 8). Near fishing, sightseeing & shopping. Warm friendly atmosphere; near Hershey Park. Come & enjoy our warm hospitality.

Manheim

Herr, M/M Barry A.
RD #7, Box 587, 17545
(717) 653-9852

Amenities: 2,9,10
Breakfast: Continental

Dbl. Oc.: $68.90-$79.50
Sgl. Oc.: $68.90-$79.50
Third Person: $10.00

Herr Farmhouse Inn, 1738 restored stone farmhouse, is a perfect retreat on 26 acres of farmland. Relax amidst period furnishings, old pine floors, mouldings & 6 working fireplaces. Fine dining & Amish country nearby.

Marianna

Midla, Louise & Joe
RD 1, 15345
(412) 267-3513

Amenities:
Breakfast: Full

Dbl. Oc.: $40.00
Sgl. Oc.: $30.00
Third Person: $5.00

Flat Stone Lick Farm Bed is a short distance from I-70, 79 or Route 40 in south western Pennsylvania. A farm home with panoramic view, nearby antique shops, historic sites, restaurants, & the Monongahela River.

AMENITIES

1. No Smoking
2. No Pets
3. No Children
4. Senior Citizen Rates
5. Tennis Available
6. Golf Available
7. Swimming Available
8. Skiing Available
9. Credit Cards Accepted
10. Personal Check Accepted
11. Off Season Rates
12. Dinner Available (w/sufficient notice)

Pennsylvania

Marietta

Fogie, M/M Thomas
RD 1, Box 166, 17547
(717) 426-3992

Amenities: 1,2,4,10,12
Breakfast: Full

Dbl. Oc.: $40.00-$59.00
Sgl. Oc.: $35.00
Third Person: $5.00

Olde Fogie Farm—Old fashioned working farm, avoiding chemicals; cater to special diets; run natural food co-op. Peaceful pond; efficiency apartment & B&B rooms. Kids love it here. Near Hershey, Amish, & Gettysburg.

McElhattan

Maguire, Shirley & James
P.O. Box 241, 17748
(717) 769-6035

Amenities: 2,5,6,7,8,10
Breakfast: Full

Dbl. Oc.: $42.40
Sgl. Oc.: $37.10
Third Person: $15.90

Restless Oaks Bed And Breakfast—Come relax and enjoy our spacious white Victorian home located 5 miles north of Lock Haven on US Route 220. In the heart of the Pine Creek Valley and 3 minutes from The Woolrich Outlet Store.

Mercer

Slagle, Gala & Gene
129 South Pitt St., 16137
(412) 662-4611

Amenities: 2,5,6,7,9,10,11,12
Breakfast: Full
Dbl. Oc.: $63.60-$79.50
Sgl. Oc.: $53.00-$74.20
Third Person: $10.60

Magoffin Guest House is a historical Victorian home furnished in period antiques. Magoffin features 7 gracious rooms with private baths, cozy fireplaces, & a full breakfast with savory coffees & teas.

Mercer

Stranahan IV, M/M James
117 E. Market St., 16137
(412) 662-4516

Amenities: 1,2,6,7
Breakfast: Full

Dbl. Oc.: $50.00
Sgl. Oc.: $45.00
Third Person: $10.00

The Stranahan House—150-year-old Colonial Empire-style home furnished in antiques. Historical area; Amish country; 5 minutes from I-79 & I-80. Located in center of town just a few steps from county courthouse.

AMENITIES

1. No Smoking
2. No Pets
3. No Children
4. Senior Citizen Rates
5. Tennis Available
6. Golf Available
7. Swimming Available
8. Skiing Available
9. Credit Cards Accepted
10. Personal Check Accepted
11. Off Season Rates
12. Dinner Available (w/sufficient notice)

Pennsylvania

Mertztown

Dimick, Elsa
RD 2, Box 26, 19539
(215) 682-6197

Amenities: 2,5,6,7,8,9,10,12
Breakfast: Full

Dbl. Oc.: $63.60-$68.90
Sgl. Oc.: $53.00
Third Person: $37.10

Longswamp Bed And Breakfast, an 18th century home set in lush farmlands is minutes away from Allentown or Rutztown with excellent antiquing, reading outlet, biking, hiking & good restaurants nearby.

Milford

Schneider, Mrs. Effie
RD 2, Box 9285, 18337
(717) 296-6322

Amenities: 1,2,9,10,11
Breakfast: Full

Dbl. Oc.: $84.70
Sgl. Oc.: $84.70

A Large Secluded Estate for a small exclusive clientele. Tudor-style stone house with marble fireplace, 12 bedrooms with brass beds. 150 acres located near Delaware River.

Montoursville

Mesaris, Harold
RD 1, Box 23, 17754
(717) 433-4340

Amenities: 5,6,7,8,10
Breakfast: Continental

Rates: $47.70-$58.30

The Carriage House At Stonegate provides 1,400 square feet of privacy for guests on 2 floors with 2 bedrooms. Located in the middle of an all season recreation area, minutes north of I-80 off I-80 on a 1800's era farm.

Mt. Gretna

Cook, Bill
17064
(717) 964-3234

Amenities: 1,2,3,8
Breakfast: Continental

Dbl. Oc.: $79.50-$132.50

Mt. Gretna Inn—Magnificent mansion for relaxing. Tour Pennsylvania Dutch country, cultural events, outlet shop nearby, hiking, fall foliage and X-country skiing. Gorgeous bedrooms in antique & traditional furniture.

Mount Joy

Brubaker, Mrs. Velma
745 Pinkerton Rd., 17552
(717) 653-4866

Amenities: 1,2,3,7,10
Breakfast: Full

Dbl. Oc.: $45.00
Sgl. Oc.: $35.00

Stonebridge Farm B&B—Quiet country home 1 mile south of Mt. Joy, midway between Lancaster & Harrisburg. Original part of house built in 1730. The farm overlooks a stream & a picturesque bridge built in 1883.

AMENITIES

1. No Smoking
2. No Pets
3. No Children
4. Senior Citizen Rates
5. Tennis Available
6. Golf Available
7. Swimming Available
8. Skiing Available
9. Credit Cards Accepted
10. Personal Check Accepted
11. Off Season Rates
12. Dinner Available (w/sufficient notice)

Pennsylvania

Mount Joy

Groff, Betty & Abe
RD #1, Box 305, 17552
(717) 653-1773

Amenities: 1,2,3,5,7,9,10,11,12
Breakfast: Continental

Dbl. Oc.: $63.60-$111.30
Sgl. Oc.: $63.60-$111.30
Third Person: $10.60

Cameron Estate Inn, located 15 miles from Lancaster & Hershey, has 18 spacious rooms. It sits on 15 landscaped & wooded aacres with a stocked trout stream that flows through the property.

Mount Joy

Swarr, Gladys & Russell
305 Longenecker Rd., 17552
(717) 653-4655

Amenities: 1,2,9,10
Breakfast: Continental

Dbl. Oc.: $53.00
Sgl. Oc.: $48.00
Third Person: $15.00

Cedar Hill Farm—Restored stone farmhouse overlooks peaceful stream. All private baths, comfortably furnished air-conditioned bedrooms, private guest entrance. Near Amish country & Hershey, PA. Host born on the farm.

Muncy

Smith, Marie Louise & David
307 S. Main St., 17756
(717) 546-8949

Amenities: 1,2,5,7,8,9,10
Breakfast: Full
Dbl. Oc.: $47.70
Sgl. Oc.: $31.80
Third Person: $10.60

The Bodine House is on a tree-lined street 3 blocks from town center. It is 180 years old and has been restored and furnished with antiques. The nearby mountains offer many activities and grand scenery.

New Cumberland

Combs, Rev. & Mrs. Chad
204 Limekiln Rd., 17070
(717) 744-2683

Amenities: 1,2,3,9,10
Breakfast: Full

Dbl. Oc.: $53.00-$58.00
Sgl. Oc.: $45.00-$50.00
Third Person: $15.00

Farm Fortune—Suburban Harrisburg 1780's limestone farmhouse furnished in antiques. Antique shop; location convenient to Gettysburg, Hershey, and Lancaster County. Reservation recommended.

AMENITIES

1. No Smoking
2. No Pets
3. No Children
4. Senior Citizen Rates
5. Tennis Available
6. Golf Available
7. Swimming Available
8. Skiing Available
9. Credit Cards Accepted
10. Personal Check Accepted
11. Off Season Rates
12. Dinner Available (w/sufficient notice)

Pennsylvania

Newfoundland

Wilkinson, Judy & George
RD 1, Box 215, 18445
(717) 676-3162

Amenities: 1,5,7,9,10,12
Breakfast: Full

Dbl. Oc.: $63.00
Sgl. Oc.: $51.00
Third Person: $30.00

White Cloud Sylvan Retreat—Quiet, rural setting. Beautiful woods & meadows in the heart of the Pocono Mountains. Restaurant offers three meatless meals per day. 5 miles south of I-84, 25 miles north of I-80. Discounts available.

New Hope

Dolan, Karla
144 Old York Rd., 18938
(215) 862-9571

Amenities: 2,3,7,9,10
Breakfast: Full

Dbl. Oc.: $75.00
Sgl. Oc.: $70.00
Third Person: $20.00

Backstreet Inn is just a 10 minute stroll from center of New Hope. Full gourmet breakfast served. All rooms have A/C. Pool, croquet, private & semi-private baths, quiet, romantic setting. Gift certificates available.

New Hope

Wass, Svella & Mike
RD 2, Box 250,
Pineville Rd., 18938
(215) 598-7945

Amenities: 1,2,3,5,6,7,9,10
Breakfast: Full

Dbl. Oc.: $85.00-$120.00
Sgl. Oc.: $85.00-$120.00

The Whitehall Inn, circa 1794. Experience our four-course candlelit breakfast using period china, crystal & heirloom sterling. High tea; fireplaces; pool; tennis court; air-conditioned; dressage horses.

Orbisonia

Salvino, Mrs. Elaine
Box 116, Ridgley St., Rte. 522, 17243
(814) 447-5616

Amenities: 9,10
Breakfast: Continental
Dbl. Oc.: $31.80
Sgl. Oc.: $26.50
Third Person: $10.60

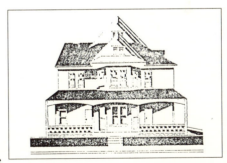

Salvino's Guest House—Old Victorian home with 5 rooms & 2 baths. Quilt shop next door. 1/2 mile from East Broad Top R.R. & Trolley museum; 1 hr. to Lake Rays Town; between Turnpike & Rt. 22. Children welcome. Available for quilt seminars.

AMENITIES

1. No Smoking
2. No Pets
3. No Children
4. Senior Citizen Rates
5. Tennis Available
6. Golf Available
7. Swimming Available
8. Skiing Available
9. Credit Cards Accepted
10. Personal Check Accepted
11. Off Season Rates
12. Dinner Available (w/sufficient notice)

Pennsylvania

Paradise

Rohrer, M/M Edwin
505 Paradise Lane, 17562
(717) 687-7479

Amenities: 1,2,6,10,11
Breakfast: Continental
Dbl. Oc.: $38.00-$48.00
Sgl. Oc.: $35.00-$45.00
Third Person: $8.00

The Maple Lane Guest House, on 200 working acres in the heart of Amish country, has 4 guest rooms with antiques, quilts, needlework & stenciling. Quiet; 40 mile view; good food and attractions nearby.

Pequea

Detwiler, Mrs. Dolores
693 Bridge Valley Rd., 17565
(717) 284-4662

Amenities: 1,2,3,10
Breakfast: Continental

Dbl. Oc.: $47.70
Sgl. Oc.: $37.10

Lake Aldred Lodge—Antiques & elegance in a rambling cottage overlooking the Susquehanna River. Comfortable accommodations located in the small, quiet village of Pequea, 13 miles south of Lancaster on Route 324.

Philadelphia

Mand, Ms. Arlene
301 Chestnut St., 19106
(215) 925-1919

Amenities: 2,9,10,12
Breakfast: Continental

Dbl. Oc.: $99.90-$122.10
Sgl. Oc.: $99.90

Society Hill Hotel—This twelve room "Urban Inn" delights its guests with small cozy rooms that echo its rich historical singificance. The hotel's restaurant and an outdoor cafe boasts of a European atmosphere.

Pittsburgh

Graf, Mrs. Mary Ann
614 Pressley St., 15212
(412) 231-3338

Amenities: 2,4,9,10
Breakfast: Continental

Dbl. Oc.: $75.00-$120.00
Sgl. Oc.: $70.00-$120.00
Third Person: $10.00

Restored Victorian Priory—Antiques; courtyard or city view; sitting room; library; fireplace; courtyard; free parking; shuttle to downtown; complimentary wine; national register district.

AMENITIES

1. No Smoking
2. No Pets
3. No Children
4. Senior Citizen Rates
5. Tennis Available
6. Golf Available
7. Swimming Available
8. Skiing Available
9. Credit Cards Accepted
10. Personal Check Accepted
11. Off Season Rates
12. Dinner Available (w/sufficient notice)

Pennsylvania

Pittsburgh

Schipper, Mrs. Teodora
5321 Butler St., 15201
(412) 781-8724

Amenities: 2,10,12
Breakfast: Full

Dbl. Oc.: $50.00
Sgl. Oc.: $35.00
Third Person: $15.00

Teddy's Restaurant—A nice garden overlooking the hills of the Allegheny River, ten minutes from downtown Pittsburgh. Clean rooms; warm atmosphere; excellent food in Teddy's restaurant La Filipiniana. Parking available.

Ronks

Rupp, Vivian & David
2574 Lincoln Hwy., East 17572
(717) 299-6005

Amenities: 1,2,5,6,9,10,11
Breakfast: Full

Dbl. Oc.: $53.00-$55.00
Sgl. Oc.: $42.40-$47.70
Third Person: $10.00

The Candlelite Inn B&B is located in the heart of the Pennsylvania Dutch Country on U.S. Rt. 30. This large country home is surrounded by acres of Amish farmland, and offers four spacious candlelit rooms.

Selinsgrove

Thomson, Marilyn F.H.
350 South Market St., 17870
(717) 374-2929

Amenities: 2,5,6,7,9,10
Breakfast: Full
Dbl. Oc.: $66.25
Sgl. Oc.: $55.65
Third Person: $10.60

The Blue Lion Inn—Elegant Greek Revival inn, circa 1849, located on Rts. 11 & 15 between Harrisburg & Williamsport. Enjoy antique furnishings, gourmet breakfasts & complimentary fruit & wine. Carriage house antique shop.

Scottdale

Horsch, Mrs. Ruth
Rt. 1, Box 634, 15683
(412) 887-5404

Amenities: 1,5,6,8,10
Breakfast: Continental

Dbl. Oc.: $45.00-$50.00
Sgl. Oc.: $35.00-$40.00
Third Person: $5.00-$20.00

Pine Wood Acres is in the Laurel Highlands. 10 miles from I-70 & the Pennsylvania Turnpike exits at New Stanton. A country home with 4 acres of woods, gardens, herbs. Near falling water & other attractions.

AMENITIES

1. No Smoking
2. No Pets
3. No Children
4. Senior Citizen Rates
5. Tennis Available
6. Golf Available
7. Swimming Available
8. Skiing Available
9. Credit Cards Accepted
10. Personal Check Accepted
11. Off Season Rates
12. Dinner Available (w/sufficient notice)

Pennsylvania

Solebury

Jay, M/M Jerry
Route 263, 18963
(215) 862-3136, (800) 722-4877

Amenities: 2,3,5,7,9
Breakfast: Full
Dbl. Oc.: $111.30-$238.50
Third Person: $25.00

Rambouillet At Hollyhedge Estate—Exclusive & elegant estate on 100 acres, catering to the discriminating traveler. 16 guest rooms, all with private baths. Refreshments any time; fireplaces. Bucks County's famous antiques, dining, shopping.

Starlight

McMahon, Judy & Jack
Box 27, 18461
(717) 798-2519

Amenities: 5,7,8,9,10,12
Breakfast: Full

Dbl. Oc.: $98.60
Sgl. Oc.: $64.65
Third Person: $33.90

The Inn At Starlight Lake, built in 1909, is a full service country inn on a beautiful quiet lake. Year round activities from swimming to skiing. 27 main house and cottage rooms. Families welcome.

Strasburg

Joy, Mrs. Deborah M.
958 Eisenberger Rd., 17579
(717) 687-8585

Amenities: 1,2,10,11
Breakfast: Full

Dbl. Oc.: $53.00
Sgl. Oc.: $53.00
Third Person: $10.60

The Decoy, a former Amish home with 4 guest rooms all with private baths. Quiet rural location, 4 miles south of Strasburg, near local sites and outlets. Open year round.

Thompson Boro

Stark, Mr. Douglas T.
RD 2, Box 36, Rt. 171, 18465
(717) 727-2625

Amenities: 6,8,10,12
Breakfast: Full

Dbl. Oc.: $25.00
Sgl. Oc.: $15.00
Third Person: $15.00

Jefferson Inn—Warm country atmosphere built in 1871 with a full menu restaurant. Enjoy one of the most reasonable inns in N.E. Pennsylvania. Rolling hills, lots of snow trails, skiing, hunting or just taking it easy.

AMENITIES

1. No Smoking
2. No Pets
3. No Children
4. Senior Citizen Rates
5. Tennis Available
6. Golf Available
7. Swimming Available
8. Skiing Available
9. Credit Cards Accepted
10. Personal Check Accepted
11. Off Season Rates
12. Dinner Available (w/sufficient notice)

Pennsylvania

Valley Forge

Williams, Mrs. Carolyn
P.O. Box 562, 19481
(215) 783-7783

Amenities: 4,6,7,8,9,10,12
Breakfast: Full

Dbl. Oc.: $63.60
Sgl. Oc.: $42.40
Third Person: $10.00

Valley Forge Mountain Home—French country home, Cal.-king bed, private bath, gourmet breakfast, A/C, 202 & Tpk. Exit 24, 18 miles NW of Philadelphia, adjacent to Valley Forge Park, near Chester City attractions, PA Dutch country & Reading.

Washington Crossing

Behun, Mrs. Donna
150 Glenwood Dr., 18977
(215) 493-1974

Amenities: 2,3,9,10
Breakfast: Continental

Dbl. Oc.: $55.00-$85.00
Sgl. Oc.: $50.00-$70.00
Third Person: $10.00

Bucks City's Most Modern Inn. 5 guest rooms, with private baths, on 10 wooded acres near New Hope & I-95. Your hosts welcome you to the comfort of their hearth & home with complimentay wine & cheese. Full breakfast on weekends & holidays.

Wellsboro

Kaltenbach, Lee
Stony Fork Rd., RD 6, Box 106A, 16901
(717) 724-4954

Amenities: 1,2,5,6,7,8,9,12
Breakfast: Full
Dbl. Oc.: $53.00-$79.50
Sgl. Oc.: $37.50
Third Person: $26.50

Kaltenbach's Bed And Breakfast, a spacious attractive home on 72 acres, is just 2 miles from Wellsboro; turn left on Stony Fork Rd. A warm hospitable small family-run inn with 10 large rooms & fireplace. Golf package.

West Chester

Rupp, Mrs. Winifred
409 S. Church St., 19382
(215) 692-4896

Amenities: 1,2,3,7,10
Breakfast: Full

Dbl. Oc.: $65.00
Sgl. Oc.: $60.00
Third Person: $10.00

The Crooked Windsor—Charming Victorian home centrally located in West Chester & completely furnished with fine antiques. Full breakfast served, tea time refreshments for those who so desire. Pool & garden in season.

AMENITIES

1. No Smoking
2. No Pets
3. No Children
4. Senior Citizen Rates
5. Tennis Available
6. Golf Available
7. Swimming Available
8. Skiing Available
9. Credit Cards Accepted
10. Personal Check Accepted
11. Off Season Rates
12. Dinner Available (w/sufficient notice)

Pennsylvania

Whitehaven

Moore, Emma & John
Box 9B, Eastside Boro, 18661
(717) 443-7186

Amenities: 6,7,8,10
Breakfast: Continental

Dbl. Oc.: $40.00
Sgl. Oc.: $20.00

The Redwood House is 10 minutes from skiing, golfing, fishing, state park & PA Turnpike Rt. 9-Exit 35 & Rt. 80. Within 40 minutes of Scranton's coal mine tour. Restaurants & Eckley Village nearby.

Wrightstown

Lenoff, Ms. Myra
677 Durham Rd.
Rt. 413, 18940
(215) 598-3100

Amenities: 1,2,3,4,9,10,11
Breakfast: Full

Dbl. Oc.: $95.40
Sgl. Oc.: $79.50

Hollileif Bed & Breakfast Estb.—If you expect a visit to Hollileif to be clean, comfortable & cozy, and with a bountiful breakfast, you won't be disappointed, it's what we do best. If you arrive as a stranger you'll leave as a friend.

Wycombe

McKissock, Mr. Bill
1073 Mill Creek Rd., 18980
(215) 598-7000

Amenities: 7,8,9,10,12
Breakfast: Full

Dbl. Oc.: $90.00
Sgl. Oc.: $45.00

A warm welcome awaits you at the Wycombe Inn in the quaint historic village of Wycombe, Bucks Co. PA. Most rooms are furnished with queen size beds, fireplaces, phones, private baths, and kitchenettes. Dinner $20.00-$30.00.

AMENITIES

1. No Smoking
2. No Pets
3. No Children
4. Senior Citizen Rates
5. Tennis Available
6. Golf Available
7. Swimming Available
8. Skiing Available
9. Credit Cards Accepted
10. Personal Check Accepted
11. Off Season Rates
12. Dinner Available (w/sufficient notice)

Rhode Island

Little Rhody

Capital: Providence
Statehood: May 29, 1790; the 13th state
State Motto: Hope
State Song: "Rhode Island"
State Bird: Rhode Island Red
State Flower: Violet
State Tree: Red Maple

Rhode Island is the smallest of the fifty states. Only 1,214 sq. miles, it lies on beautiful Narragansett Bay, just a little way out on the Atlantic Ocean.

It is quite a resort state. Thousands of visitors come here every year. The beaches afford plenty of swimming and boating.

In Newport, the tourist can take the Cliff Walk by the most beautiful mansions in the world, or see the America's Cup Sailboat Race off the coast of Newport.

Jewelry and silver seem to be the prime source of income for this state, along with tourism. The people of Rhode Island are very proud of their state, and love to have others come to see it. They make wonderful hosts.

Rhode Island

Block Island

McQueeny, Mr. & Mrs. Stephen
High Street, 02807
(401) 466-2494

Amenities: 2,3,4,7,9,10,11
Breakfast: Continental
Dbl. Oc.: $88.00-$105.00

The Sheffield House is an 1888 Victorian Home in historic district. Five minutes to the beach, shops, restaurants. Quiet rooms on beautiful island.

Block Island

Rose, Mrs. Judith
Roslyn Rd., 02807
(401) 466-2021

Amenities: 2,3,5,9
Breakfast: Continental
Dbl. Oc.: $92.00-$175.00
Third Person: $20.00

Rose Farm Inn—Sea and country setting convenient to downtown and beaches. Comfortable rooms with ocean view furnished with antiques, king or queen size bed. Breakfast served on our great stone porch. Free brochure.

Block Island

Schleimer, Mrs. Kathleen
Box 356, Water St., 02807
(401) 466-2651

Amenities: 9,10,11
Breakfast: Full
Rates: $55.00-$135.00
Third Person: $15.00

The New Shoreham Inn is a traditional Block Island Inn, open year round, built during the latter part of the 19th century. We offer rooms with one or two double beds, and we welcome families. Children free.

Bristol

Anderson, Wendy & Richard
956 Hope St., 02809
(401) 253-3282

Amenities: 1,4,9,10,11,12
Breakfast: Continental
Dbl. Oc.: $55.00-$75.00
Sgl. Oc.: $30.00
Third Person: $12.00

Joseph Reynolds House—Lafayette slept here. Circa 1693, a national landmark, the oldest 3-story 17th century building in New England. Near water, Newport, Boston, etc. 22 room Salt Box; warm hospitality; family-run; good food.

AMENITIES

1. No Smoking
2. No Pets
3. No Children
4. Senior Citizen Rates
5. Tennis Available
6. Golf Available
7. Swimming Available
8. Skiing Available
9. Credit Cards Accepted
10. Personal Check Accepted
11. Off Season Rates
12. Dinner Available (w/sufficient notice)

Rhode Island

Jamestown

Lacaille, Miss A. Lori
14 Union St., 02835
(401) 423-2641

Amenities: 4,5,6,7,9,10,11
Breakfast: Continental
Dbl. Oc.: $60.00
Sgl. Oc.: $40.00
Third Person: $10.00

The Calico Cat Guest House—Victorian home 200 feet from the Jamestown Harbour & 10 minutes away from beautiful Newport with its many shops & restaurants, fishing, sailing, swimming and mansion tours.

Jamestown

Murphy, Mrs. Mary W.
59 Walcott Ave., 02835
(401) 423-1338

Amenities: 2,5,6,7,10
Breakfast: Full

Dbl. Oc.: $55.00-$66.00
Sgl. Oc.: $44.00
Third Person: $10.00

Colonial Style Home situated on an island in Narragansett Bay connected by the bridge to Newport. 3 bedrooms, shared bath, walking distance to restaurants, shops and beach. Spacious grounds and gardens.

Middletown

Canning, Ms. Polly
349 Valley Rd., 02840
(401) 847-2160

Amenities: 1,7,10
Breakfast: Continental

Dbl. Oc.: $75.00
Sgl. Oc.: $75.00
Third Person: $25.00

Polly's Bed And Breakfast—Attractive clean comfortable rooms very convenient to Newport, also lovely apartment by the week in private setting. Near beaches and town; plenty of parking; many wild birds and plenty of fresh air..

Middletown

Duce, Mrs. Alice H.
467 Wolcott Ave., 02840
(401) 846-9376

Amenities: 2,7,11
Breakfast: Full
Dbl. Oc.: $75.00
Sgl. Oc.: $50.00

Wolcott House By The Sea, bed and breakfast. Country ocean view, ten minute walk to beach swimming; mile and half to Newport.

AMENITIES

1. No Smoking
2. No Pets
3. No Children
4. Senior Citizen Rates
5. Tennis Available
6. Golf Available
7. Swimming Available
8. Skiing Available
9. Credit Cards Accepted
10. Personal Check Accepted
11. Off Season Rates
12. Dinner Available (w/sufficient notice)

Rhode Island

Middletown

Lindsey, Anne & Dave
6 James St., 02840
(401) 846-9386

Amenities: 2,7,10,11
Breakfast: Full

Dbl. Oc.: $44.00-$55.00
Sgl. Oc.: $38.50-$44.00
Third Person: $10.00-$15.00

Lindsey's Guest House—Off street parking; 10 min. walk to beaches; restaurants; free loop bus; 2 mi. from Newport's mansions; cliff walk; Ocean Drive; harbor front wharves; boat tours; boutiques & dining. Handicapped accessible. Deck a.m.

Narragansett

Murphy, Mrs. Martha
43 South Pier Rd., 20882
(401) 789-1824

Amenities: 1,2,10
Breakfast: Full

Dbl. Oc.: $55.00-$65.00
Sgl. Oc.: $40.00-$45.00

Murphy's B&B—Comfortable 100 year old Victorian, 1 block from ocean. We offer the traveler comfort, privacy, immaculate rooms, and a delicious full breakfast. Relax at the beautiful beach; lots to see & do in the area.

Narragansett

Raggio, Ms. Chris
41 Robinson St., 02882
(401) 789-2392

Amenities: 1,2,5,6,7,10
Breakfast: Full

Dbl. Oc.: $45.00-$65.00
Sgl. Oc.: $45.00-$65.00
Third Person: $10.00

Ilverthorpe Cottage—A charming Victorian home, built in 1896, is 3 blocks from the ocean; decorated with antiques, flowers, and lace. Special touches include: complimentary wine and beside chocolates.

Narragansett

Snee, Mrs. Mildred A.
191 Ocean Rd., 02882
(401) 783-9494

Amenities: 2
Breakfast: Full

Dbl. Oc.: $53.00
Sgl. Oc.: $37.10
Third Person: $10.60

The House Of Snee—Within easy walking distance of beach, movies, restaurants, & shops. Facing the open Atlantic ocean, the house is a turn-of-the-century Dutch Colonial with a cozy porch. Newport nearby.

AMENITIES

1. No Smoking
2. No Pets
3. No Children
4. Senior Citizen Rates
5. Tennis Available
6. Golf Available
7. Swimming Available
8. Skiing Available
9. Credit Cards Accepted
10. Personal Check Accepted
11. Off Season Rates
12. Dinner Available (w/sufficient notice)

Rhode Island

Newport

Bayuk, Pam & Bruce
123 Spring St., 02840
(401) 846-0040

Amenities: 1,2,9,10,11
Breakfast: Continental
Dbl. Oc.: $83.50-$104.50
Sgl. Oc.: $83.50-$104.50
Third Person: $15.00

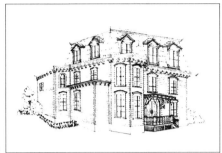

The Pilgrim House Inn is in the heart of Newport's historic hill within walking distance to waterfront shops and restaurants. Breakfast is served on the third floor deck overlooking Newport harbor.

Newport

Borsare, Marilyn
One Kyle Terrace, 02840
(401) 846-3119

Amenities: 2,3,5,11
Breakfast: Continental

Dbl. Oc.: $70.00-$85.00
Sgl. Oc.: $70.00-$85.00

Flower Garden Guests—Contemporary exterior with a warm country antique interior. Romantic ambiance; gazebo deck; near: famous mansions, beaches, & shops. Couples only. No credit cards or checks. A special place!

Newport

Droual, Margot & Louis
96 Pelham St., 02840
(401) 847-4400

Amenities: 2,10,11
Breakfast: Full

Dbl. Oc.: $55.00-$85.00
Third Person: $7.50

La Forge Cottage—Classic Victorian makes the B&B one of the most pleasant inns around. On historic hill close to beaches & downtown. Private bath, TV, phone, fridge; breakfast served to you in your room. Reservations please.

Newport

Goddin, Sally
29 Pelham St., 02840
(401) 846-3324

Amenities: 1,4,5,6,7,9,10,11
Breakfast: Continental
Dbl. Oc.: $82.50-$192.50
Sgl. Oc.: $82.50-$192.50
Third Person: $11.00

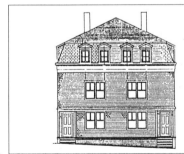

Inn Of Jonathan Bowen—An elegant inn on gaslit historic hill, 1/2 block to harbor. Renovated eclectic antique decor, luxury rooms, safe parking, walk everywhere, gourmet continental breakfast included. 8 rooms, 6 suites, private baths.

AMENITIES

1. No Smoking
2. No Pets
3. No Children
4. Senior Citizen Rates
5. Tennis Available
6. Golf Available
7. Swimming Available
8. Skiing Available
9. Credit Cards Accepted
10. Personal Check Accepted
11. Off Season Rates
12. Dinner Available (w/sufficient notice)

Rhode Island

Newport

Gallon, June & Audrey
32 Cranston Ave., 02840
(401) 847-7094

Amenities: 1,2,5,6,7,10,11
Breakfast: Full

Dbl. Oc.: $80.00
Sgl. Oc.: $80.00
Third Person: $30.00

Clover Hill Guest House—Gracious Victorian home built circa 1891. Within walking distance to wharf area with its restaurants, shops and harbor. Minutes away is Bellvue Avenue and the mansions, Cliff Walk and the ocean drive.

Newport

Grant, Suzanne & Richard
29 Pelham St., 02840
(401) 846-3324

Amenities: 2,3,9,10
Breakfast: Continental

Dbl. Oc.: $104.50-$148.50
Third Person: $11.00

The Inn Of Jonathon Bowen is a romantically elegant inn, on a gas-lit street, in the heart of historic hill. One-half block from the water and within walking distance of the mansions. A quiet getaway.

Newport

Jenkins, Mrs. Sally
206 R.I. Ave., 02840
(401) 847-6801

Amenities: 5,6,7,10
Breakfast: Continental

Dbl. Oc.: $45.00
Sgl. Oc.: $45.00
Third Person: $10.00

Dave And Sally Jenkins invite you into the friendly atmosphere of their 10 room expanded cape where they raised their 8 children. Walk to beach, mansions, harbor front, shops, and restaurants. Quiet.

Newport

Mailey, Susan
22 Channing St., 02840
(401) 846-6113

Amenities: 2,9,10,11
Breakfast: Continental

Dbl. Oc.: $75.00
Sgl. Oc.: $65.00
Third Person: $10.00

Turn-Of-The-Century Inn is a family-run B&B with two rooms. It is 1/2 mile from downtown & beaches. The atmosphere is friendly & informal but the decor is period antiques and whimsical collections.

Newport

Moy, Mariann & Ed
12 Clay St., 20840
(401) 849-6865

Amenities: 5,6,7,9,10,11,12
Breakfast: Continental

Dbl. Oc.: $80.00-$145.00
Sgl. Oc.: $80.00-$145.00
Third Person: $15.00

Ivy Lodge—Step back in time in Newport's elegant mansion area. Enjoy spacious rooms & quiet comfort. Relax on our porch with afternoon tea; walk to beach, mansions & shopping. Special gourmet continental breakfast.

AMENITIES

1. No Smoking
2. No Pets
3. No Children
4. Senior Citizen Rates
5. Tennis Available
6. Golf Available
7. Swimming Available
8. Skiing Available
9. Credit Cards Accepted
10. Personal Check Accepted
11. Off Season Rates
12. Dinner Available (w/sufficient notice)

Rhode Island

Newport

Rogers, Rita & Sam
39 Clarke St., 02840
(401) 847-0640

Amenities: 2,3,5,6,7,9,10,11
Breakfast: Continental
Dbl. Oc.: $82.50-$93.50
Sgl. Oc.: $82.50-$93.50

The Melville House—7 rooms in the heart of the historic district. One block from brick market & the wharfs. Stay at a Colonial inn built circa 1750, "Where the past is present." Off-street parking; complimentary sherry hour.

Newport

Rubeck, Nancy
82 Gibbs Ave., 02840
(401) 847-6568

Amenities: 10,11
Breakfast: Continental

Dbl. Oc.: $85.00
Sgl. Oc.: $65.00

The Yellow Cottage—Bridge tokens sent and given; stamped cards in rooms; nine blocks from town. The Yellow Cottage was built in 1900 as a summer cottage. Being a B&B is just one of the joys of my life.

Newport

Russell, Mrs. Kay
2 Seaview Ave., 02840
(401) 847-1811

Amenities: 2,3,9,10
Breakfast: Continental
Dbl. Oc.: $71.50-$93.50
Third Person: $11.00

Cliffside Inn—An elegant Victorian home in a quiet residential neighborhood, less than a 5 minute walk from the Cliff Walk and the beach. 10 gracious rooms with private baths. A romantic inn.

AMENITIES

1. No Smoking
2. No Pets
3. No Children
4. Senior Citizen Rates
5. Tennis Available
6. Golf Available
7. Swimming Available
8. Skiing Available
9. Credit Cards Accepted
10. Personal Check Accepted
11. Off Season Rates
12. Dinner Available (w/sufficient notice)

Rhode Island

Newport

Walsh, Mary & Alex
300 Gibbs Ave., 02840
(401) 847-4441

Amenities: 2,5,7,10,11
Breakfast: Continental
Dbl. Oc.: $60.00
Sgl. Oc.: $50.00
Third Person: $10.00

Hillside—A warm charming late Victorian Queen Anne mansion near downtown Newport where the Walshes raised their ten children. Pictured in Life Magazine Oct. 12, 1962 in article on families living in mansions.

Newport

Weintraub, Amy
23 Brinley St., 02840
(401) 849-7645

Amenities: 2,3,7,11
Breakfast: Continental

Dbl. Oc.: $93.50
Sgl. Oc.: $82.50
Third Person: $15.00

Brinley Victorian Inn—Antique & fresh flowers decorate each room. Attention to details, friendly & unpretentious service make this a romantic haven in the heart of Newport, 1 block off Bellevue. Walk to historic sites & beach.

Providence

Thiel, Ms. Diane M.
144 Benefit St., 02903
(401) 751-2002

Amenities: 2,3,9,10
Breakfast: Continental

Dbl. Oc.: $105.00-$160.00
Third Person: $15.00

The Old Court is located on the historic east side of Providence. Close to colleges and downtown. Ten rooms, all with private bath and telephone. Romantically furnished with antiques in several styles.

Warren

Lynch, M/M Robert
125 Water St., 02885
(401) 245-6622

Amenities: 1,2,5,6,7,8,9,10
Breakfast: Continental

Dbl. Oc.: $65.00
Sgl. Oc.: $65.00
Third Person: $15.00

Nathaniel Porter Inn—In the historic waterfront district, has 1795 stencilling, French mural wallpaper, an elegant tea room. Rooms have fireplaces and private shower-baths. Antique shops nearby.

AMENITIES

1. No Smoking
2. No Pets
3. No Children
4. Senior Citizen Rates
5. Tennis Available
6. Golf Available
7. Swimming Available
8. Skiing Available
9. Credit Cards Accepted
10. Personal Check Accepted
11. Off Season Rates
12. Dinner Available (w/sufficient notice)

Rhode Island

Westerly

Grande, Patricia
275 Shore Rd., 02891
(401) 596-6384

Amenities: 1,4,9,10,11
Breakfast: Continental
Dbl. Oc.: $66.00-$99.00
Sgl. Oc.: $58.30-$91.30
Third Person: $15.00

Grandview—Stately turn-of-the-century home with a splendid ocean view. Sit out on the magnificent wrap-around stone porch or sun yourself in a lawn chair on the spacious grounds. Walk to tennis & golf near beaches.

Westerly

Madison, Dr. Ellen L.
Woody Hill Rd., RR 3,
Box 676E, 02891
(401) 322-0452

Amenities: 1,2,5,6,7,10,11
Breakfast: Full

Dbl. Oc.: $62.70
Sgl. Oc.: $49.50
Third Person: $10.00

Woody Hill Guest House—Off Route 1, just 2 miles from superb ocean beaches, is a Colonial reproduction Gambrel-roofed home in a quiet pastoral setting. It welcomes you with antiques, quilts, and caring.

Westerly

Maiorano, Mr. Jerry
Box 257, Shore Rd., 02891
(401) 348-8637 or 596-1054

Amenities: 2,4,5,6,7,9,10
Breakfast: Continental
Dbl. Oc.: $49.00-$95.00
Sgl. Oc.: $45.00-$90.00
Third Person: $5.00-$10.00

Villa Maiorano—An attractive villa surrounded by spacious grounds, gardens, swimming pool & spa. Adjacent to Winnapaug Golf & Country Club on scenic 1-A, 1/2 mile from ocean beaches. Fine restaurants and shopping nearby; year round.

AMENITIES

1. No Smoking
2. No Pets
3. No Children
4. Senior Citizen Rates
5. Tennis Available
6. Golf Available
7. Swimming Available
8. Skiing Available
9. Credit Cards Accepted
10. Personal Check Accepted
11. Off Season Rates
12. Dinner Available (w/sufficient notice)

Rhode Island

Wyoming

Stetson, Billie & Bill
161 New London Turnpike, 02898
(401) 539-7233

Amenities: 6,7,10
Breakfast: Continental
Dbl. Oc.: $53.00
Sgl. Oc.: $53.00
Third Person: $10.00

The Way Stop—Step back in time at our 1757 farmhouse situated on 50 acres. The house overlooks a farm & pond. Beaches, Mystic, Newport & Providence are a short trip away.

AMENITIES

1. No Smoking
2. No Pets
3. No Children
4. Senior Citizen Rates
5. Tennis Available
6. Golf Available
7. Swimming Available
8. Skiing Available
9. Credit Cards Accepted
10. Personal Check Accepted
11. Off Season Rates
12. Dinner Available (w/sufficient notice)

South Carolina

The Palmetto State

Capital: Columbia
Statehood: May 23, 1788; the 8th state
State Motto: Prepared in Mind and Resources, While I Breathe, I Hope
State Song: "Carolina"
State Bird: Carolina Wren
State Flower: Carolina Jessamine
State Tree: Palmetto

South Carolina is a great state to visit, and for those who live there, it is a great place to call home. It stretches from the beautiful Appalachian foothills to the spacious and popular Atlantic Coast beaches.

It is home for more than three million energetic and resourceful people. These people share a common bond, whether they live in the larger municipalities of the Palmetto State or in its growing small towns and rural communities. That common bond is a commitment to preserving a quality of life which is their heritage and building upon it by encouraging businesses and industries to grow and prosper here.

South Carolina is a most gracious state and invites visitors to come and enjoy its beautiful beaches and flower gardens, and fish and hunt in its well-stocked fields and streams.

South Carolina

Beaufort

Harrison, Marianne & Steve
1009 Craven St., 29902
(803) 524-9030

Amenities: 2,5,6,7,9,10,12
Breakfast: Full

Dbl. Oc.: $65.00-$91.00
Third Person: $16.00

The Rhett House Inn—An authentic B&B inn that beautifully recreates the feeling of the "Old South." 8 guest rooms all with private bath, fully air-conditioned. All guest rooms have been furnished for your comfort & convenience.

Beaufort

Roe, Kathleen & Gene
601 Bay St., 29902
(803) 524-7720

Amenities: 2,5,6,7,9,10
Breakfast: Continental

Dbl. Oc.: $65.00
Sgl. Oc.: $55.00
Third Person: $15.00

Bay Street Inn—Antebellum townhouse on the water in the historic district. Featured in Antiques, NY Times, Southern Living, Colonial Homes, etc. Antiques, art, library, bikes. Between Savannah and Charleston.

Bluffton

Tuttle, Dana & Grant
Bridge St., Box 857, 29910
(803) 757-2139

Amenities: 1,2,6,7,9,10
Breakfast: Full

Dbl. Oc.: $52.00
Sgl. Oc.: $46.00
Third Person: $11.00

The Fripp House Inn, circa 1835, is a historic landmark in a quiet village on the May River. Private gardens with pool and fountains; spacious home with warm hospitality and hearty food. 5 minutes from Hilton Head Island.

Charleston

Chadman, Benjamin
30 King, 29401
(803) 577-2633

Amenities: 2,5,6,7,10
Breakfast: Continental
Dbl. Oc.: $55.00-$75.00
Third Person: $20.00

The Hayne House located in the heart of the historic residential district, one block from Battery. Walk everywhere; 1770's home with 1840's addition, furnished in antiques; lots of good books, no TV.

AMENITIES

1. No Smoking
2. No Pets
3. No Children
4. Senior Citizen Rates
5. Tennis Available
6. Golf Available
7. Swimming Available
8. Skiing Available
9. Credit Cards Accepted
10. Personal Check Accepted
11. Off Season Rates
12. Dinner Available (w/sufficient notice)

South Carolina

Charleston

Dunn, Sherri & Richard
126 Wentworth St., 29401
(803) 723-7166

Amenities: 5,9,10,11
Breakfast: Full

Dbl. Oc.: $52.43-$90.95
Sgl. Oc.: $52.43-$90.95
Third Person: $10.00-$20.00

1837 Bed & Breakfast—Enjoy a circa 1800 cotton planter's home. Walk to historic sites, cafes, and the market. Full gourmet breakfast is served in the formal dining room. Tea room serves shoe-crab soup, high tea, and desserts.

Charleston

Fox, Laura
198 King St., 29401
(803) 723-7000

Amenities: 5,6,7,9,10
Breakfast: Continental
Dbl. Oc.: $112.35
Sgl. Oc.: $85.60

Kings Courtyard Inn—Restored (1983) inn located in the heart of Charleston's historic district. Rooms feature 18th century reproduction furniture, many with fireplaces & canopy beds. Free parking, AAA 4 Diamond Rated.

Charleston

Hancock, Aubrey W.
138 Wentworth St., 29410
(803) 577-7709

Amenities: 1-3,5,6,8,9,10,11
Breakfast: Full

Dbl. Oc.: $75.00-$85.00
Sgl. Oc.: $75.00-$85.00
4 People: $110.00

Villa de La Fontaine—A classic revival porticoed mansion, built in 1838, restored and furnished with museum quality furniture. Located in the heart of the historic area. Operated by a retired interior designer. Formal gardens.

Charleston

Mulholland, Lucille & Bob
East Bay & George St., 29401
(803) 723-8691

Amenities: 1,2,5,6,9,10,11
Breakfast: Continental
Dbl. Oc.: $144.45
Sgl. Oc.: $144.45
Third Person: $10.70

Maison DuPre—"The inn of historic elegance." Fifteen rooms with honeymoon suite. Downtown in historic Anson Borough. "Low country tea party" & carriage ride. Private baths; antiques; original paintings by Lucille.

AMENITIES

1. No Smoking
2. No Pets
3. No Children
4. Senior Citizen Rates
5. Tennis Available
6. Golf Available
7. Swimming Available
8. Skiing Available
9. Credit Cards Accepted
10. Personal Check Accepted
11. Off Season Rates
12. Dinner Available (w/sufficient notice)

South Carolina

Charleston

Spell, David S.
2 Meeting St., 29401
(803) 723-7322

Amenities: 2,3,4,6,10,11
Breakfast: Continental

Dbl. Oc.: $58.85-$133.75
Third Person: $15.00

Two Meeting Street Inn is located in the historic district. Charleston's most renowned and elegant inn where guests enjoy the entire inn. No pets and children under 8. Across from Battery Park on waterfront.

Charleston

Spell, Jim
40 Rutledge Ave., 29401
(803) 722-0973

Amenities: 5,6,7,10
Breakfast: Continental
Dbl. Oc.: $85.00
Sgl. Oc.: $65.00
Third Person: $15.00

Belvedere Guest Home offers hospitable accommodations in our gracious mansion overlooking Colonial Lake, here in the historical district of downtown Charleston—corner of Rutledge Ave., and Queen Street.

Charleston

Weed, Ms. Diane Deardurff
105 Tradd St., 29401
(803) 577-0682

Amenities: 1,2,10,11
Breakfast: Continental

Dbl. Oc.: $75.00
Sgl. Oc.: $75.00
Third Person: $25.00

Country Victorian Bed And Breakfast has private entrances & baths. Rooms have antique iron & brass beds, old quilts, antique oak & wicker furniture. In historical area within walking distance of everything. Bicycles, parking & many extras.

Charleston

Widman, Richard
116 Broad Street
(803) 723-7000/800-845-6115

Amenities: 1,5,6,9
Breakfast: Full

Dbl. Oc.: $139.10
Sgl. Oc.: $101.65
Third Person: $16.05

John Rutledge House Inn located in historic district. Built in 1763 by John Rutledge. Co-author and signer of U.S. Constitution. Nightly turndown with brandy. Breakfast delivered to room. Wine & sherry in lobby.

AMENITIES

1. No Smoking
2. No Pets
3. No Children
4. Senior Citizen Rates
5. Tennis Available
6. Golf Available
7. Swimming Available
8. Skiing Available
9. Credit Cards Accepted
10. Personal Check Accepted
11. Off Season Rates
12. Dinner Available (w/sufficient notice)

South Carolina

Columbia

Vance, Dan
2003 Greene St., 29205
(803) 765-0440

Amenities: 1,2,4,7,9,10
Breakfast: Continental

Dbl. Oc.: $83.50
Sgl. Oc.: $73.00
Third Person: $10.00

Claussen's Inn At Five Points is just minutes from the capitol building in downtown Columbia. We are located next to the University of South Carolina and are within walking distance to the shops and restaurants in Five Points.

Georgetown

Shaw, Mrs. Mary
8 Cypress Court, 29440
(803) 546-9663

Amenities: 4,5,6,10
Breakfast: Full

Dbl. Oc.: $40.00
Sgl. Oc.: $40.00
Third Person: $10.00

Shaw House is a two story Colonial with a beautiful view of Willobank Marsh. Hostess is knowledgeable about antiques. Rocking chairs & cool breezes on front porch along with wine or a pot of coffee.

Johnston

Derrick, Mrs. Scott
602 Lee St., Box 486, 29832
(803) 275-3234

Amenities: 2,10
Breakfast: Continental

Dbl. Oc.: $40.00-$50.00

The Cox House Inn, located on Hwy. #121, is an attractive Victorian home offering 4 suites, each suite consists of a modern private kitchen and bath. Bed arrangements vary. Reservations.

Mayesville

Dabbs, M/M William
Rt. #1, Box 300, 29104
(803) 453-5004

Amenities: 2,6,12
Breakfast: Full

Dbl. Oc.: $45.00
Sgl. Oc.: $35.00

Windsong—Excellent location for stop-over of north/south traffic. Spacious house, large den with open fireplace, separate entrance for guests, A/C. In the midst of quiet open farm land. Children welcome; tray supper—$5.00 person.

Myrtle Beach

Ficarra, Ellen & Cos
407-71 Ave., N., 29577
(803) 449-5268

Amenities: 2,5,6,7,9,10,11
Breakfast: Continental

Dbl. Oc.: $60.00-$90.00
Third Person: $10.70

Serendipity, An Inn—Award-winning AAA mission-style inn, all rooms A/C, color TV, private baths, pool, jacuzzi; near 40 golf courses; 300 yds. to ocean beach; 60 miles to historic Wilmington, N.C., and 90 miles to Charleston, S.C.; centrally located.

AMENITIES

1. No Smoking
2. No Pets
3. No Children
4. Senior Citizen Rates
5. Tennis Available
6. Golf Available
7. Swimming Available
8. Skiing Available
9. Credit Cards Accepted
10. Personal Check Accepted
11. Off Season Rates
12. Dinner Available (w/sufficient notice)

South Dakota

The Sunshine State

Capital: Pierre
Statehood: November 2, 1889; the 40th state
State Motto: Under God The People Rule
State Song: "Hail, South Dakota"
State Bird: Ring-Necked Pheasant
State Flower: American Pasqueflower
State Tree: Black Hills Spruce

South Dakota is a land of rare beauty and unusual landscapes. It has fertile crop-growing land, canyons, the strange Badlands and the enchanting Black Hills.

The wild west look is still here. Buffaloes can be seen roaming Custer's State Park in herds.

South Dakota is visited by hundreds of tourists every year. Probably one of the most popular attractions is Mt. Rushmore. Here in 1928, Gutzon Borglum began a memorial to freedom and to the spirit of the American people. It took him and his small group of men 14 years to complete this task, but when he finished, the sculptured and carved faces of four of our greatest presidents, George Washington, Abraham Lincoln, Thomas Jefferson and Theodore Roosevelt, were enshrined here forever.

South Dakota

Brookings

Pierce, M/M Lowell
Rt. 4, Box 251, 57006
(605) 693-4375

Amenities: 1,6,7,8,10,12
Breakfast: Full

Dbl. Oc.: $35.00
Sgl. Oc.: $25.00
Third Person: $10.00

Spindel Bottom Farm—A picturesque little farm with sheep and horses, near the Big Sioux River. Just off, but parellel to I-29 south of Brookings. Baby sitting available. Choice of breakfast, but caramel rolls are a specialty.

Buffalo

Vroman, M/M Larry
HCR 4, Box 8, 57720
(605) 375-3577

Amenities: 1,10,12
Breakfast: Full

Dbl. Oc.: $30.00
Sgl. Oc.: $20.00
Third Person: $5.00

Vroman Ranch Bed & Breakfast—Visit a real working cattle ranch in the wide open spaces of northwestern South Dakota, located 2 hours north of the Black Hills, near Hwy. 85. Children & pets are welcomed.

Canova

Skoglund, Delores & Alden
Rt. #1, Box 45, 57321
(605) 247-3445

Amenities: 5,6,7,10,12
Breakfast: Full

Rates: $15.60-$26.00

Skoglund Farm, Wide open spaces; ride horses; play piano; watch: cattle, fowl, peacocks; feel at home; relax; coffee pot always on. Welcome to a working farm. Children under 5 free. Evening dinner included with rates.

Deadwood

Crosswait, Rebecca & Bruce
22 Van Buren, 57732
(605) 578-3877

Amenities: 1,2,3,5,6,7,8,9,10
Breakfast: Continental
Dbl. Oc.: $78.75
Sgl. Oc.: $73.50
Third Person: $21.00

1892 Queen Anne Victorian—Period furnishings; 4 bedrooms w/private baths. Historic Deadwood in the Black Hills—Wild Bill & Calamity Jane. Easy access to Mt. Rushmore. On national register of historic places.

AMENITIES

1. No Smoking
2. No Pets
3. No Children
4. Senior Citizen Rates
5. Tennis Available
6. Golf Available
7. Swimming Available
8. Skiing Available
9. Credit Cards Accepted
10. Personal Check Accepted
11. Off Season Rates
12. Dinner Available (w/sufficient notice)

South Dakota

Lead

LeMar, M/M Jim
HC 37, Box 1220, 57754
(605) 584-3510

Amenities: 2,6,8,9
Breakfast: Full

Dbl. Oc.: $49.00

Cheyenne Crossing Bed & Breakfast—A B&B at a true country store located in one of America's prettiest canyons. Year round outdoor recreation center. Close to Mt. Rushmore, Devils Tower, historic Deadwood & much more.

Rapid City

Kuhnhauser, Mrs. Audry
RR 8, Box 2400, 57702
(605) 342-7788

Amenities: 1,2,10
Breakfast: Full

Dbl. Oc.: $65.00
Sgl. Oc.: $60.00
Third Person: $15.00

Audrie's Cranbury Corner B&B—Located in the beautiful Black Hills, 30 miles from Mt. Rushmore. Private entrances, hot tubs, and fireplaces. Rooms furnished in lovely antiques. Complimentary appetizers; quiet; Highway 44 west.

Wall

Shearer, M/M Lavon
HCR 1, Box 9, 57790
(605) 279-2198

Amenities: 12
Breakfast: Full

Dbl. Oc.: $38.00
Sgl. Oc.: $25.00
Third Person: $5.00

Western Dakota Ranch Vacations Bed & Breakfast, 9 miles off I-90. Ranch home; private baths; patio entrance in sunken garden; deck to view wide open spaces. Rec. room, 7x14 trampoline; wagon rides; cattle drives; excellent hunting.

AMENITIES

1. No Smoking
2. No Pets
3. No Children
4. Senior Citizen Rates
5. Tennis Available
6. Golf Available
7. Swimming Available
8. Skiing Available
9. Credit Cards Accepted
10. Personal Check Accepted
11. Off Season Rates
12. Dinner Available (w/sufficient notice)

Tennessee

The Volunteer State

Capital: Nashville
Statehood: June 1, 1796; the 16th state
State Motto: Agriculture and Commerce
State Song: "Rocky Top Tennessee"
State Bird: Mockingbird
State Flower: Iris
State Tree: Tulip Poplar

Tennessee is a state of varied industries. In the east there are the coal mines; in the middle of the state, the farmers raise cattle and tobacco; and in the west there are large cotton plantations. But regardless, there is one thing everyone here enjoys, and that is Country Music, as played at the Grand Ole Opry in Nashville.

There is a lot of Civil War history here and beautiful scenic drives. However, the majority of visitors that come to Tennessee come first to see the Grand Ole Opry.

Three presidents were born and lived here: Andrew Jackson, James Polk and Andrew Johnson.

Tennessee

Clarksville

Hach, Mrs. Phila
1601 Madison St., 37043
(615) 647-4084

Amenities: 9,10,12
Breakfast: Full
Dbl. Oc.: $59.26
Sgl. Oc.: $48.48
Third Person: $10.00

Hachland Hill Inn—Tennessee's most celebrated inn is owned by renowned chef Phila Hach, a former American Airlines flight attendant and TV personality. Great recipes are served from her famous cookbooks.

Cleveland

Brown, Beverlee
215 20th St., 37311
(615) 476-8029

Amenities: 1,2,4,5,6,7,9,11
Breakfast: Full

Dbl. Oc.: $62.00
Sgl. Oc.: $52.00
Third Person: $9.00

Browns Manor—Luxury manor on 3 acres in quaint southern town off I-75 on route to Florida. Chattanooga Choo Choo 30 miles, white water rafting 10 miles, Smokey Mts. 2 hours. Privacy, pampering, & afternoon tea time.

Duck River

McEwen, M&M William
Box 97, 38454
(615) 583-2378

Amenities: 9,10,12
Breakfast: Continental

Dbl. Oc.: $91.60
Sgl. Oc.: $80.81
Third Person: $10.00

McEwen Log Cabin B&B—Spacious 1820 log cabin complete with modern facilities. Located in a beautiful rural area. Close to the Natchez Trace Parkway and the Duck River. One hour from Nashville. Canoe rental available.

Gatlinburg

Burns, Connie & John
Rt. 3, Box 384, 37738
(615) 436-5920

Amenities: 2,10
Breakfast: Continental

Dbl. Oc.: $74.00
Sgl. Oc.: $74.00
Third Person: $10.00

Mountain Oaks—Secluded wooded setting; view of the Smokey Mountains; quiet walk areas. Two suites each with private kitchen, bathroom, living & sleeping rooms. 1 1/2 miles to Greenbrier entrance of great Smokey Mountains Nat'l. Park

---

AMENITIES

1. No Smoking
2. No Pets
3. No Children
4. Senior Citizen Rates
5. Tennis Available
6. Golf Available
7. Swimming Available
8. Skiing Available
9. Credit Cards Accepted
10. Personal Check Accepted
11. Off Season Rates
12. Dinner Available (w/sufficient notice)

Tennessee

Knoxville

Rogers, Cindy & Brad
501 Mtn. Breeze Lane
37922
(615) 966-3917

Amenities: 2,10
Breakfast: Full

Dbl. Oc.: $48.15
Sgl. Oc.: $48.15
Third Person: $10.70

Mountain Breeze Bed & Breakfast—A two story Cape Cod located on a quiet cul-de-sac in a wooded setting just 2 1/2 miles from I-40 & 75. Warmly furnished with antiques & country accents. Freshly baked cookies await each guest in their rooms.

Lynchburg

Tipps, Mike
P.O. Box 34, 37352
(615) 759-7158

Amenities: 4,5,6,9
Breakfast: Continental

Dbl. Oc.: $45.36
Sgl. Oc.: $41.04
Third Person: $5.00

The Lynchburg Bed And Breakfast is within walking distance of the Jack Daniel Distillery, two blocks from the Town Square and numerous antique and gift shops. Very quiet & relaxing. Children under 12 free.

Memphis

Long, Martha
217 N. Waldran, 38105
(901) 527-7174

Amenities: 2,4,9,10
Breakfast: Continental
Dbl. Oc.: $50.00
Sgl. Oc.: $50.00
Third Person: $10.00

Lowenstein-Long House—Beautifully restored mansion near downtown, river, & all tourist attractions. Free off-street parking at 1084 Poplar Ave. Good access to bus & X-way. A peaceful retreat.

Monteagle

Teasley, Merrily
Box 365, 37356
(615) 924-2669

Amenities: 2,3,5,10
Breakfast: Continental
Dbl. Oc.: $50.00
Sgl. Oc.: $45.00
Third Person: $5.00

Edgeworth Inn—A friendly 8 room 1896 mountain top inn in national historic district near the University of The South at Sewanee. Come sit by the library fire or rock on the porch or swing in rope hammocks.

AMENITIES

1. No Smoking
2. No Pets
3. No Children
4. Senior Citizen Rates
5. Tennis Available
6. Golf Available
7. Swimming Available
8. Skiing Available
9. Credit Cards Accepted
10. Personal Check Accepted
11. Off Season Rates
12. Dinner Available (w/sufficient notice)

Tennessee

Murfresboro

Deaton, Barbara & Robert
435 E. Main St., 37130
(615) 893-6030

Amenities: 10
Breakfast: Continental
Dbl. Oc.: $35.00
Sgl. Oc.: $28.00
Third Person: $3.00

Clardy's Guest House is a 20 room, 1898 Romanesque, completely furnished in antiques. We're in the historic district, just 3 1/2 blocks from downtown. Take exit 81 or 78-B from I-24, just 30 miles S.E. of Nashville.

Rogersville

Netherland-Brown, Carl
Town Square, 37857
(615) 272-5171

Amenities: 2,5,6,7,9,12
Breakfast: Continental
Dbl. Oc.: $35.00-$65.00
Sgl. Oc.: $30.00-$60.00
Third Person: $10.00

Hale Springs Inn

Hale Springs Inn has been open since 1824. Andrew Jackson stayed here in 1837. Beautifully restored antique-filled rooms have fireplaces and canopied beds. Air conditioned. Candlelight dining.

Rugby

Stagg, Barbara
Hwy. 52, Box 8, 37733
(615) 628-2441

Amenities: 1,2,7,9,10,12
Breakfast: Full

Dbl. Oc.: $52.00-$62.00
Sgl. Oc.: $44.00-$54.00

Newbury House At Historic Rugby—Small antique furnished 1880 inn in rural national register village. Historic building tours, museum shops, river gorge trails, near Big South Fork National Park.

Sevierville

Barnhart, M/M Ray
Box 4972, 37864
(615) 428-4858

Amenities: 1,2,3,9,11
Breakfast: Full

Dbl. Oc.: $50.00-$90.00

Milk & Honey Country Hideaway—Just a few minutes from Pigeon Forge, outlet malls, Dollywood; close to the beautiful Smokies and Gatlinburg. Cozy rooms—in a quiet country setting away from it all.

AMENITIES

1. No Smoking
2. No Pets
3. No Children
4. Senior Citizen Rates
5. Tennis Available
6. Golf Available
7. Swimming Available
8. Skiing Available
9. Credit Cards Accepted
10. Personal Check Accepted
11. Off Season Rates
12. Dinner Available (w/sufficient notice)

Tennessee

Wartrace

Rigler, Norma & Bill
R 2, Box 152, 37183
(615) 455-1935, 455-2546

Amenities: 1,9,10
Breakfast: Continental
Dbl. Oc.: $60.00
Sgl. Oc.: $60.00
Third Person: $10.00

Ledford Mill—A private hideaway where you are the only guests. A cozy open suite, with kichenette. Spend the night in a 19th century grist mill listening to the waterfalls & murmuring waters of Shippmans Creek.

AMENITIES

1. No Smoking
2. No Pets
3. No Children
4. Senior Citizen Rates
5. Tennis Available
6. Golf Available
7. Swimming Available
8. Skiing Available
9. Credit Cards Accepted
10. Personal Check Accepted
11. Off Season Rates
12. Dinner Available (w/sufficient notice)

Texas

The Lone Star State

Capital: Austin
Statehood: December 29, 1845; the 28th state
State Motto: Friendship
State Song: "Texas, Our Texas"
State Bird: Mockingbird
State Flower: Bluebonnet
State Tree: Pecan

Texas is second in size to Alaska. It is so big that when it entered the union, Congress gave it the right to divide into five states, but it preferred to remain one and BIG. It is called the Lone Star State because of the one lone star on its flag.

Many colorful people from history have come from Texas, including Davy Crockett, Jim Bowie and one of our more modern-day heros, President Lyndon B. Johnson.

Texas has many millionaires because of the great oil strikes there over the years. There is also much cattle, and great cattle farms. The King Ranch is perhaps the largest cattle-raising ranch in the world.

The cities of Houston, Dallas, San Antonio and Fort Worth are exciting places for the tourist to visit.

Texas

Austin

Danley, M/M Roger
613 W. 32nd, 78705
(512) 451-6744

Amenities: 1,2,3,9,10
Breakfast: Full

Dbl. Oc.: $50.00
Sgl. Oc.: $40.00
Third Person: $10.00

The McCallum House is a lovely late Victorian home 10 blocks north of the University of Texas, 20 blocks from the Capitol & downtown. Antique furnishings, private baths. 2 rooms w/kitchens; 2 w/porches. Friendly, quiet, elegant.

Austin

Hagler, Sandy
609 W. 33rd St., 78705
(512) 459-0534

Amenities: 1,9,10
Breakfast: Continental

Dbl. Oc.: $55.00
Sgl. Oc.: $55.00
Third Person: $20.00

Brook House—1920's petit estate; quiet residential neighborhood near University of Texas and Capitol. Beautiful landscaped grounds; children welcomed; breakfast served in bed on request; close to airport and I-35.

Burton

Neinast, Jeanne & Bill
Rt. 1, Box 86-A, 77835
(409) 289-3171

Amenities: 10,12
Breakfast: Full
Dbl. Oc.: $66.60
Sgl. Oc.: $55.50
Third Person: $22.20

Long Point Inn, on a cattle ranch. Pet the cattle; traipse the woods; fish the ponds; listen to the quiet. Near: Star of the Republic Museum, miniature horse farm, antique rose emporium, Fistival Hill. Children welcome.

Fredericksburg

Bartlett, Bebe
110 E. Creek St., 78624
(512) 997-9398

Amenities: 1,3,9,10,11
Breakfast: Full
Dbl. Oc.: $84.00
Sgl. Oc.: $25.00

Barons Creek Inn—Choose from our 3 room Sunday house or one of our 4, 3 room suites, in a 1911 German house. All units have parlor, bedroom, kitchen and bath. Wide veranda on both floors; located two blocks from main street.

AMENITIES

1. No Smoking
2. No Pets
3. No Children
4. Senior Citizen Rates
5. Tennis Available
6. Golf Available
7. Swimming Available
8. Skiing Available
9. Credit Cards Accepted
10. Personal Check Accepted
11. Off Season Rates
12. Dinner Available (w/sufficient notice)

Texas

Fredericksburg

Schmidt, Dr/M Charles
Rt. 2, Box 112A3, 78624
(512) 997-3234

Amenities: 9,10
Breakfast: Full

Dbl. Oc.: $60.95
Sgl. Oc.: $51.94
Third Person: $15.90

The Schmidt Barn—125 year old barn turned guest house located next to host's home. Cover feature of 4/88 Country Living Magazine; country setting; deer and other wildlife; herb garden; only 5 minutes from town; restful.

Galveston

Hanemann, Mrs. Helen
1805 Broadway, 77550
(409) 763-0194

Amenities: 9,10
Breakfast: Full

Dbl. Oc.: $113.00-$141.25
Third Person: $22.60

The Gilded Thistle—Enter a wonderland of fanciful ambiance, down-home elegance, superb service & bountiful amenities. Enjoy the memorable experience of choosing "One of the best guest residences' Texas has to offer." Texas Monthly Press.

Galveston

Isbell, Mrs. Allen C.
1715 35th St., 77550
(409) 763-3760

Amenities: 1,2,3,9,10
Breakfast: Full

Dbl. Oc.: $90.40
Sgl. Oc.: $90.40
Third Person: $22.60

1916 Post-Victorian Red Brick Home. Large living areas, porches, spacious grounds with original fish pond and fountain. Furnished with antiques, collectibles, and original works of art. Delightful!

Goliad

Harvey, M/M Don
203 N. Commercial, 77963
(512) 645-2701

Amenities: 1,2,3,6,7,9,10
Breakfast: Full

Dbl. Oc.: $45.00-$56.00
Sgl. Oc.: $37.00

The White House Inn Bed & Breakfast Inn—A lovely old home in historic Mission Town. Lake & bay fishing; guide available. Tours arranged to view Whooping Cranes in winter.

Houston

Swanson, Marguerite
921 Heights Blvd., 77008
(713) 868-4654

Amenities: 1,2,3,9,10,12
Breakfast: Full

Dbl. Oc.: $50.00
Sgl. Oc.: $40.00

Durham House Bed & Breakfast—On national register of historical places; lovely antique furnishings; only five minutes from downtown; gazebo; tandem bicycle; screened Victorian backporch; perfect for weddings and parties.

AMENITIES

1. No Smoking
2. No Pets
3. No Children
4. Senior Citizen Rates
5. Tennis Available
6. Golf Available
7. Swimming Available
8. Skiing Available
9. Credit Cards Accepted
10. Personal Check Accepted
11. Off Season Rates
12. Dinner Available (w/sufficient notice)

Texas

San Antonio

Cross, Mrs. Steven
621 Pierce St.
Box 8059, 78208
(512) 223-9426

Amenities: 2,4,5,6,9,11
Breakfast: Continental

Dbl. Oc.: $35.03-$66.67
Sgl. Oc.: $27.12-$59.89
Third Person: $5.65

Bullis House Inn—Lovely historic Texas mansion, built in 1906-1909, only minutes from downtown. Large columns, chandeliers, fireplaces, veranda; 7 rooms; free parking. Located off I-35 next to historic Fort Sam Houston.

San Antonio

Haley, Nancy
950 E. Grayson St., 78208
(512) 271-9145

Amenities: 9,10
Breakfast: Full

Dbl. Oc.: $71.50-$82.80
Sgl. Oc.: $55.53-$65.00
Third Person: $11.30

Terrell Castle Bed & Breakfast—An authentic historic 4 story limestone Texas castle. 9 guest rooms furnished in antiques; 18 blocks from downtown; a full gourmet breakfast; an elegant Victorian experience. San Antonio is a unique city.

San Antonio

Sackett, Alice & Roger
3806 Highcliff, 78218
(512) 655-2939

Amenities: 1,10
Breakfast: Full

Dbl. Oc.: $28.00
Sgl. Oc.: $20.00

Cardinal Cliff—Comfortable home in quiet residential area overlooking wooded river valley. 20 minutes from downtown attractions. Homemade bread and jam a breakfast feature; attractive antique furnishings.

AMENITIES

1. No Smoking
2. No Pets
3. No Children
4. Senior Citizen Rates
5. Tennis Available
6. Golf Available
7. Swimming Available
8. Skiing Available
9. Credit Cards Accepted
10. Personal Check Accepted
11. Off Season Rates
12. Dinner Available (w/sufficient notice)

Utah

The Beehive State

Capital: Salt Lake City
Statehood: January 4, 1896; the 45th state
State Motto: Industry
State Song: "Utah, We Love Thee"
State Bird: Sea Gull
State Flower: Sego Lily
State Tree: Blue Spruce

Utah was settled in 1847 by the Mormon pioneers, led by Bringham Young. They were industrious people, and came to the west to live where they could express their religious beliefs as they wanted. Today most of the people of Utah live along the Wasatch Mountain area. Salt Lake City is a modern city with wide streets and tree-lined sidewalks. It has an open and very clean look. Tourists are attracted here from all over the country to hear the magnificent Mormon Chapel Singers and to see the Mormon church buildings.

Oil and copper have been the main occupation of the people of Utah for many years, but tourism has become a major source of income in the past 10 years. There are several National Parks here, including Bryce Canyon and Zion National Park.

Utah

Bluff

Goldman, Ms. Rosalie
Box 158, 84512
(801) 672-2220

Amenities: 1,7,10,11,12
Breakfast: Full

Dbl. Oc.: $50.00
Sgl. Oc.: $45.00

Frank Lloyd Wright style home nestled in huge boulders at the foot of the Red Cliffs. Located on a main highway between Mesa Verde & Grand Canyon, yet secluded on 17 private desert acres on Wild San Juan River. Close to 9 national parks.

Cedar City

Fishler, M/M Art
P.O. Box 356, 84720
(801) 682-2495

Amenities: 1,2,9,10
Breakfast: Full

Dbl. Oc.: $50.00-$60.00
Sgl. Oc.: $33.00-$43.00
Third Person: $10.00

Meadeau View Lodge—Attractive; surrounded by pines and Aspens; situated near Zion, Bryce and Cedar Breaks National Parks; hiking, fishing, X/C skiing. Children over 5—$10.00 each. Open all year; enjoy homey atmosphere.

Kanab

Barden, Aprile & Ronald
30 N. 200 West, 84741
(801) 644-5952

Amenities: 1,2,6,9
Breakfast: Full

Dbl. Oc.: $40.00
Sgl. Oc.: $40.00
Third Person: $5.00

Miss Sophie's Bed & Breakfast, is a restored 1800's home with an in-town location. Guest rooms have antiques and private baths. Kanab, hub to parks, is called "Little Hollywood," for its movie past. Nice weather; open May-Oct.

Nephi

Gliske, M/M Robert C.
110 South Main St., 84648
(801) 623-2047

Amenities: 1,2,9,12
Breakfast: Full
Dbl. Oc.: $56.00
Sgl. Oc.: $45.00
Third Person: $11.00

The Whitmore Mansion combines Victorian elegance with warm personal service, reflecting the charm of days long past. Private baths and a hearty breakfast help insure a pleasant stay.

AMENITIES

1. No Smoking
2. No Pets
3. No Children
4. Senior Citizen Rates
5. Tennis Available
6. Golf Available
7. Swimming Available
8. Skiing Available
9. Credit Cards Accepted
10. Personal Check Accepted
11. Off Season Rates
12. Dinner Available (w/sufficient notice)

Utah

Odgen

Rogers, M/M Frank
914 29th St., 84403
(801) 393-5824

Amenities: 1,2,3,4,5,6,7,8,10
Breakfast: Continental

Dbl. Oc.: $30.00
Sgl. Oc.: $25.00

Rogers Rest—Intimate, air conditioned, eclectically decorated ranch. Central to city; quiet neighborhood; 20 minutes from 3 ski resorts; X/country skiing, hiking.

Park City

Daniels, Hugh
615 Woodside Ave.,
Box 2639, 84060-2639
(801) 645-8068

Amenities: 1,2,5,6,7,8,9,10,11
Breakfast: Full

Dbl. Oc.: $44.00-$171.00
Sgl. Oc.: $39.00-$166.00
Third Person: $16.50

The Old Miners' Lodge—A B&B in the national historic district of Park City known for its magnificent skiing and golf. 30 miles east of Salt Lake City. Restricted smoking; many amenities.

St. George

Curtis, Mrs. Donna
217 No. 100 West, 84770
(801) 628-3737

Amenities: 1,5,6,7,9,10,12
Breakfast: Full

Dbl. Oc.: $38.15-$70.85
Sgl. Oc.: $27.25-$70.85
Third Person: $10.00

Seven Wives Inn is two side by side antique-filled pioneer adobes. Fifteen guest rooms, all with private bath; swimming pool and hot tub; close to Zion National Park; TV in most rooms.

Salt Lake City

Bartholome, Katie & Mike
936 E. 1700 S., 84105
(801) 485-3535

Amenities: 1,2,5,6,7,8,9,10
Breakfast: Continental

Dbl. Oc.: $51.35-$84.12
Sgl. Oc.: $51.35-$84.12
Third Person: $10.00

The National Historic Bed & Breakfast—One of Salt Lake's most significant homes. Seven minutes from downtown, The Latter Day Saints Temple, & the airport. Minutes from 7 ski resorts. 3 story Victorian inn offering fresh flowers, music & fine breakfasts.

Salt Lake City

Dutton, Lisa & Glenn
6151 South 900 East, 84121
(801) 268-8762

Amenities: 1,2,8,9,10,11
Breakfast: Continental

Dbl. Oc.: $40.00-$70.00
Sgl. Oc.: $40.00
Third Person: $10.00

The Spruces Bed And Breakfast—Set amongst 16 tall spruces on a farm. The inn has four suites all have private baths, two have kitchens, one has a hydropulse tub. Good shopping, restaurants and skiing are close.

AMENITIES

1. No Smoking
2. No Pets
3. No Children
4. Senior Citizen Rates
5. Tennis Available
6. Golf Available
7. Swimming Available
8. Skiing Available
9. Credit Cards Accepted
10. Personal Check Accepted
11. Off Season Rates
12. Dinner Available (w/sufficient notice)

Utah

Sandy

Smith, Jean
3744 E. N. Little Cottonwood Rd., 84092
(801) 942-2858

Amenities: 1,2,4,7,8,10
Breakfast: Continental
Dbl. Oc.: $48.00-$52.00
Sgl. Oc.: $40.00
Third Person: $10.00

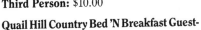

Quail Hill Country Bed 'N Breakfast Guesthouse on private drive. Little Cottonwood Canyon; 10 minutes from ski areas of Alto & Snowbird. Summer affords swimming pool & spa; continental buffet breakfast; each room different; TV; phone.

Vermont

The Green Mountain State

Capital: Montpelier
Statehood: March 4, 1791; the 14th state
State Motto: Vermont, Freedom and Unity
State Song: "Hail Vermont"
State Bird: Hermit Thrush
State Flower: Red Clover
State Tree: Sugar Maple

Vermont is called The Green Mountain State because of its beautiful and overwhelming green mountains. It is a state that receives much snow, and their longest season is winter. However, the other seasons, although shorter in length, are just as beautiful because of the colorful foliage and magnificent scenery.

Vermont is the only New England state that does not have a coastline, but its lovely lakes and recreational facilities more than make up for the lack of a seashore. Swimming and boating in the summer and the best of skiing in the winter makes Vermont a tourist paradise.

The tapping of their own maple trees brings the Vermonters the sugar to make maple sugar products for which they are so well known.

Presidents Chester A. Arthur and Calvin Coolidge were both born here.

Vermont

Arlington

Hardy, Joanne & George
RR #2, Box 2015, 05250
(802) 375-2269

Amenities: 2,4,5,6,7,8,9,10,11,12
Breakfast: Full
Dbl. Oc.: $64.00
Sgl. Oc.: $42.50
Third Person: $23.50

Hill Farm Inn—One of Vermont's original farm inns located in two renovated farmhouses built in 1790 & 1830. Quiet, comfortable, relaxed atmosphere; delicious country cooking; splendid mountain view.

Arlington

Kenny, Mrs. Mathilda
Box 2480, Rte. 1, 05250
(802) 375-2272

Amenities: 10,12
Breakfast: Full

Dbl. Oc.: $40.00-$48.00
Sgl. Oc.: $20.00-$24.00
Third Person: $20.00

The Evergreen Inn—Old fashioned country inn nestled in the Green River Valley, off the beaten path. Family owned and operated for 52 years. Beautiful scenery; home cooking and baking; casual & relaxed atmosphere.

Arlington

Kruzel, Mrs. Madeline
Historic Rte. 7A, 05250
(802) 375-6532

Amenities: 2,5,6,7,8,9,10,12
Breakfast: Continental
Dbl. Oc.: $100.00
Sgl. Oc.: $100.00
Third Person: $12.00

The Arlington Inn—Enjoy our antique-filled guest rooms in one of Vermont's finest Greek Revival homes. Sample our creative American cuisine by romantic candlelight. Winner of the 1988 Travel Holiday Award—3 star Mobil.

AMENITIES

1. No Smoking
2. No Pets
3. No Children
4. Senior Citizen Rates
5. Tennis Available
6. Golf Available
7. Swimming Available
8. Skiing Available
9. Credit Cards Accepted
10. Personal Check Accepted
11. Off Season Rates
12. Dinner Available (w/sufficient notice)

Vermont

Arlington

Wall, Peggy & Tom
RR 2, Box 2440, 05250
(802) 362-4213

Amenities: 5,6,7,9,10
Breakfast: Full
Dbl. Oc.: $80.00
Third Person: $20.00

The Inn At Sunderland is a restored Victorian farmhouse nestled at the foot of Mt. Equinox just south of Manchester. Comfortable rooms, antiques, fireplaces, porches with lovely mountain views.

Barnet

Pierce, Doris & George
Box 35, 05821
(802) 633-4100

Amenities: 2,5,6,7,8,10
Breakfast: Continental

Dbl. Oc.: $45.00
Sgl. Oc.: $25.00

The Old Homestead—A circa 1850 Colonial, off exit 18, I-91 in Barnet Village in Vermont's northeast kingdom. An inn since the turn of the century, it is convenient to all year-round recreational activities.

Barre

Somaini, Terry & Robert
13 East St., 05641
(802) 476-7745

Amenities: 1,2,3,8,10
Breakfast: Full

Dbl. Oc.: $60.00
Sgl. Oc.: $40.00
Third Person: $10.00

Woodruff House is a large Victorian on quiet park near center of town. Interior is unique, cozy, warm & inviting, like going home to grandmas. Half way between Boston and Montreal off I-89. Central Vermont's home away from home!

Belmont

Firshein, Mrs. Cynthia
Church St., 05730
(802) 259-2009

Amenities: 1,7,8,9,10
Breakfast: Full

Dbl. Oc.: $68.90-$84.80
Sgl. Oc.: $58.30
Third Person: $15.90

The Parmenter House—This stylish Victorian is of particular interest to restoration buffs. Its location in the quaint mountain hamlet of Belmont is off the beaten track but convenient to sports and tourist highlights.

AMENITIES

1. No Smoking
2. No Pets
3. No Children
4. Senior Citizen Rates
5. Tennis Available
6. Golf Available
7. Swimming Available
8. Skiing Available
9. Credit Cards Accepted
10. Personal Check Accepted
11. Off Season Rates
12. Dinner Available (w/sufficient notice)

Vermont

Bennington

Baker, Irene & Hugh
Rte. 7A, 05201
(802) 442-5619

Amenities: 6,7,8,9,10,11
Breakfast: Full

Dbl. Oc.: $45.00
Sgl. Oc.: $40.00

Bakers At Bennington B&B—Minutes to historic sites, antiquing, restaurants, theatres & ski areas. Our 1859 farm home has guest rooms with sinks; shared hall bath, living room, library, grounds for relaxation. Enjoy our mountain views.

Bennington

Gashi, Suzanne & Mark
124 Elm St., 05201
(802) 447-3839

Amenities: 1,2,3,6,7,8,9,10,11
Breakfast: Full

Dbl. Oc.: $88.00-$126.50
Third Person: $10.00

The South Shire Inn—Lovely Victorian inn styled with antiques/period pieces. Rooms are large and elegantly appointed with private baths and fireplaces. The inn has been called one of the finest in Bennington.

Bennington

Koks, Alex, Erickson, Andra
21 West Rd., 05201
(802) 447-3500

Amenities: 2,3,5,6,7,8,9,10,11,12
Breakfast: Continental
Dbl. Oc.: $132.50
Sgl. Oc.: $80.00
Third Person: $16.00

Four Chimneys Restaurant & Inn—Its park-like setting, its spacious bedrooms & meal preparation by master chef Alex Koks create an experience of elegance. The village ultimate. Call for reservation.

Bethel

Jaynes, Carmen & Bob
Combined Rts. 12 & 107
05032
(802) 234-5426

Amenities: 5,6,7,10
Breakfast: Continental

Dbl. Oc.: $35.00
Sgl. Oc.: $24.00
Third Person: $12.00

Poplar Manor, warm, hospitable, quiet, 1810 house furnished with antiques. Beautiful shops and restaurants nearby. You'll like it, as has everybody else. Near 12 south.

AMENITIES

1. No Smoking
2. No Pets
3. No Children
4. Senior Citizen Rates
5. Tennis Available
6. Golf Available
7. Swimming Available
8. Skiing Available
9. Credit Cards Accepted
10. Personal Check Accepted
11. Off Season Rates
12. Dinner Available (w/sufficient notice)

Vermont

Bethel

Wolf, Lyle
RD 2, Box 60, 05032
(802) 234-9474

Amenities: 5,6,7,8,9,10
Breakfast: Continental
Dbl. Oc.: $40.00-$80.00
Sgl. Oc.: $30.00-$70.00
Third Person: $10.00

Greenhurst Inn—National register of historical places. Victorian mansion on the White River in the center of Vermont with the elegance of another age. Rt. 107, 3 miles west of I-89 in a quiet rural setting. Midway Boston-Montreal.

Bolton Valley

McKinnis, M/M Phil
Mountain Rd., 05477
(802) 434-2126 or 2920

Amenities: 1,2,5,6,7,8,9,10,11,12
Breakfast: Full
Dbl. Oc.: $109.00
Sgl. Oc.: $99.00
Third Person: $29.00

The Black Bear Inn—24 uniquely comfortable rooms with private baths. Close to north Vermont's most popular year round attractions. Golf & ski packages; excellent cuisine. A Vermont inn with European charm.

Bradford

Carlan, J. Robert
Box 354, Main St., 05033
(802) 222-9303

Amenities: 2,3,5,6,7,8,9,10,12
Breakfast: Continental

Dbl. Oc.: $53.00
Sgl. Oc.: $37.10
Third Person: $10.00

The Village Inn of Bradford, built in 1826, this inn is a mix of several styles Federal, Victorian & Colonial decor featuring a king bed suite & guest rooms with shared & priv. baths. 23 miles to Dartmouth campus; walk to village.

Brandon

Mondlak, Mrs. Janet
25 Grove St., (Rte. 7)
(802) 247-3235

Amenities: 2,9,10
Breakfast: Full

Dbl. Oc.: $65.00
Sgl. Oc.: $65.00
Third Person: $10.00

The Gazebo Inn—Reflects the charm and friendliness of old New England. Private baths available; homemade breakfast. The ultimate in Colonial comfort.

AMENITIES

1. No Smoking
2. No Pets
3. No Children
4. Senior Citizen Rates
5. Tennis Available
6. Golf Available
7. Swimming Available
8. Skiing Available
9. Credit Cards Accepted
10. Personal Check Accepted
11. Off Season Rates
12. Dinner Available (w/sufficient notice)

Vermont

Bristol

Conway, Beverly & Michael
RD 1, Box 560, 05443
(802) 453-3233

Amenities: 2,7,8,10,12
Breakfast: Full

Dbl. Oc.: $70.00
Sgl. Oc.: $40.00

Comfortable Country Inn built in 1799 by lumberjacks in Lincoln. Wrap-around rocking chair porch overlooking trout stream. Hiking available on Long Trail. Dinner available. Meal prepared by innkeepers.

Brookfield

Simpson, Pat & Peter
P.O. Box 494, 05036
(802) 276-3412

Amenities: 1,2,6,7,8,10,12
Breakfast: Full
Dbl. Oc.: $83.00
Sgl. Oc.: $60.00
Third Person: $17.00

Green Trails Inn—By famous floating Famous Bridge. A cozy, informal country inn—"like going home to grandma's." Decorated with quilts & antiques; featured on the Today Show. "The epitome of a country inn."

Brownsville

Carriere, K.
Box 410, Rte. 44, 05037
(802) 484-7283

Amenities: 4,5,6,7,8,9,10,11
Breakfast: Full

Dbl. Oc.: $63.80
Sgl. Oc.: $40.60
Third Person: $11.40

The Mill Brook—Charming 1890 farmhouse across road from Mt. Ascutney, 15 miles from Woodstock exit 8 or off I-91. 8 guest rooms, living room, lobby, 2 sitting rooms, 1 game room; hearty afternoon tea; picnic, BBQ & dining areas.

Calais

Yankee, Joani & Glenn
RD #2, Plainfield, 05667
(802) 454-7191

Amenities: 5,6,7,10
Breakfast: Full

Dbl. Oc.: $40.00-$45.00
Sgl. Oc.: $35.00-$40.00
Third Person: $15.00-$10.00

Yankee's Northview B&B—Off quiet country road in historic/picturesque Calais. Set on a hill & surrounded by garden walls, meadows, & mountain views. Antiques/stencilled walls; excellent recreation in all seasons.

AMENITIES

1. No Smoking
2. No Pets
3. No Children
4. Senior Citizen Rates
5. Tennis Available
6. Golf Available
7. Swimming Available
8. Skiing Available
9. Credit Cards Accepted
10. Personal Check Accepted
11. Off Season Rates
12. Dinner Available (w/sufficient notice)

Vermont

Charlotte

Smith, Ms. Mary Louise
Box 1300, Mt. Philo Rd.
05445
(802) 425-3059

Amenities: 1,2,5,6,7,8,10
Breakfast: Full

Dbl. Oc.: $60.00
Sgl. Oc.: $50.00
Third Person: $10.00-$15.00

Green Meadows Bed And Breakfast—Nestled in a small valley near Lake Champlain, Green Meadows is a charmingly restored Victorian home. Small-print wallpaper, antiques, ruffled curtains abound. 4 rooms, 1 with priv. bath & jacuzzi.

Chelsea

Papa, Mary Lee & James
Main St., Rte. 110, 05038
(802) 685-3031

Amenities: 1,2,3,5,6,8,9,10,11,12
Breakfast: Full
Dbl. Oc.: $75.00
Sgl. Oc.: $75.00
Third Person: $10.00

Chelsea is Vermont's quintessential small village and we're Vermont's finest small village inn. 1832 brick Federal home; gourmet dining; 4 rooms with working fireplaces; all rooms have private baths. Scenery abound.

Chester

Bowman, Ms. Jean
Box 646, Green Mt. Tpk.
05143
(802) 875-2674

Amenities: 8,9,10,11
Breakfast: Full

Dbl. Oc.: $78.00
Sgl. Oc.: $45.00
Third Person: $15.00

Henry Farm Inn—Old time Vermont in a 1750 restored farmhouse. Private baths, fireplaces, wide pine floors; skiing, hiking, fishing. The peace and quiet of the beautiful Green Mountains.

Chester

Strohmeyer, Janet & Donald
Route 11 West, 05143
(802) 875-2525

Amenities: 5,6,7,8,9,10,11,12
Breakfast: Full

Dbl. Oc.: $52.00-$76.00
Sgl. Oc.: $44.00
Third Person: $3.00

Stone Hearth Inn—Lovely & informal 1810 country inn known for good food & hospitality. 10 lovingly restored guest rooms, library, dining room, pub & large game room. Near major ski areas & antiquing. Perfect for families.

AMENITIES

1. No Smoking
2. No Pets
3. No Children
4. Senior Citizen Rates
5. Tennis Available
6. Golf Available
7. Swimming Available
8. Skiing Available
9. Credit Cards Accepted
10. Personal Check Accepted
11. Off Season Rates
12. Dinner Available (w/sufficient notice)

Vermont

Chester

Thomas, Georgette
Box 32, Main St., 05143
(802) 875-2412

Amenities: 1,9,10
Breakfast: Full
Dbl. Oc.: $75.00-$80.00
Sgl. Oc.: $55.00-$65.00
Third Person: $10.00-$20.00

The Hugging Bear Inn & Shoppe—Classic 1850 Victorian home with 6 guest rooms, private baths, teddy bear in every bed & over 3,000 huggables in our gift shop. Hiking, ski area & antique shops nearby.

Chester

Wright, Irene & Norm
Main St., Box 708, 05143
(802) 875-2205

Amenities: 2,5,6,8,9,10
Breakfast: Full
Dbl. Oc.: $40.00-$70.00
Sgl. Oc.: $30.00-$55.00
Third Person: $10.00

The Chester House is a charming 1780 nationally registered historic home located in the quaint village of Chester. The beautifully restored inn is designed for your complete comfort and enjoyment.

Craftsbury Common

Schmitt, Penny & Michael
Main St., 05827
(802) 586-9619

Amenities: 5,6,7,8,9,10,12
Breakfast: Full
Dbl. Oc.: $160.00-$180.00
Sgl. Oc.: $100.00-$120.00

The Inn On The Common—Beautifully decorated, superb cuisine, all sports video and book libraries. Great gardens, hiking trail system, pool, lake, tennis court, & sports center. 18 lovely bedrooms all with private baths.

AMENITIES

1. No Smoking
2. No Pets
3. No Children
4. Senior Citizen Rates
5. Tennis Available
6. Golf Available
7. Swimming Available
8. Skiing Available
9. Credit Cards Accepted
10. Personal Check Accepted
11. Off Season Rates
12. Dinner Available (w/sufficient notice)

Vermont

Cuttingsville

Smith, Donna & William
Box 120, 05738
(802) 492-3367

Amenities: 2,8,10
Breakfast: Full

Dbl. Oc.: $40.00
Sgl. Oc.: $20.00
Third Person: $5.00

Maple Crest Farm located in the heart of the Green Mountains, Rutland area. 1808 farmhouse lovingly preserved for 5 generations. Downhill & x-country skiing nearby and hiking on premises. Two night minimum.

Danby

Edson, M/M Charles
Box 221, Main St., 05739
(802) 293-5099

Amenities: 2,6,7,8,9,10
Breakfast: Full

Dbl. Oc.: $47.70-$58.30
Sgl. Oc.: $37.10-$42.40
Third Person: $15.90

The Quail's Nest Bed & Breakfast Inn is nestled among the Green Mts. in a quiet Vermont village. Quiet old-fashioned country fun in a circa 1835 antique-filled inn. Skiing, hiking, swimming, fishing.

Derby Line

Moreau, Phyllis & Tom
46 Main St., 05830
(802) 873-3604

Amenities: 1,2,6,7,9,10,12
Breakfast: Full

Dbl. Oc.: $48.00-$58.50
Sgl. Oc.: $37.50
Third Person: $16.00

Derby Village Inn—Tom & Phyllis Moreau welcome you to their elegant Victorian home. Five beautifully decorated rooms with private baths. Golf, swimming, biking or just peace in a lovely village setting at Canadian border.

Dorset

Kingston, Jean & Jim
Main St., 05251
(802) 867-5747

Amenities: 2,7,8,9,10,11
Breakfast: Continental
Dbl. Oc.: $90.00
Sgl. Oc.: $85.00
Third Person: $15.00

The Dovetail Inn stands on pristine historic Dorset village green one of New England's most charming. Relax by our pool; enjoy home baked breakfast, afternoon tea. Great restaurants, summer theatre, biking, hiking nearby.

AMENITIES

1. No Smoking
2. No Pets
3. No Children
4. Senior Citizen Rates
5. Tennis Available
6. Golf Available
7. Swimming Available
8. Skiing Available
9. Credit Cards Accepted
10. Personal Check Accepted
11. Off Season Rates
12. Dinner Available (w/sufficient notice)

Vermont

East Burke

Lewin, Mrs. Beverly
RR 1, Box 81, 05832
(802) 467-3472

Amenities: 2,6,7,8,9,10
Breakfast: Continental
Dbl. Oc.: $42.40-$44.52
Sgl. Oc.: $31.80-$34.00
Third Person: $10.00

Burke Green...
A Country Guest House
in Vermont's Northeast Kingdom

"Burke Green"—A comfortable guest house in Vermont's unspoiled northeast kingdom. Spacious, comfortable remodelled farmhouse overlooking Burke Mountain, near beautiful Willoughby Lake, Families welcome, residential cat.

East Dorset

Conroy, Catherine & Dennis
Benedict Rd., 05253
(802) 362-4889

Amenities: 1,2,5,6,7,8,9,10
Breakfast: Full

Dbl. Oc.: $43.00
Sgl. Oc.: $22.00
Third Person: $10.00

Warm And Charming Home in a four season locale minutes from social activities and fine dining. We are open 11 months during the year.

Fair Haven

Soder, M/M Paul
Route 22A, South, 05743
(802) 265-8039

Amenities: 2,9
Breakfast: Continental
Dbl. Oc.: $74.20-$106.00
Sgl. Oc.: $74.20-$106.00
Third Person: $20.00

Maplewood—Beautiful 1850's Greek Revival inn with elegant period furnished rooms & suites. TV room; B.Y.O.B. tavern; parlor. One mile south of town. Lakes region, near skiing & all activities. Open all year.

Fairlee

Wright, Sharon & Scott
S. Main St., 05045
(802) 333-4326

Amenities: 2,3,5,6,7,9,10
Breakfast: Continental

Dbl. Oc.: $30.00-$48.00
Sgl. Oc.: $28.00-$46.00
Third Person: $5.00

The Silver Maple Lodge—A quaint bed & breakfast country inn located in a scenic resort area. Boating, fishing, golf, horseback riding & tennis nearby. Convenient to winter skiing. Walk to restaurant.

AMENITIES

1. No Smoking
2. No Pets
3. No Children
4. Senior Citizen Rates
5. Tennis Available
6. Golf Available
7. Swimming Available
8. Skiing Available
9. Credit Cards Accepted
10. Personal Check Accepted
11. Off Season Rates
12. Dinner Available (w/sufficient notice)

Vermont

Jay

Angliss, M/M Robert J.
Rt. 242, 05859
(802) 988-2643
(800) 227-7452 outside VT

Amenities: 2,3,5,6,7,8,9,12
Breakfast: Continental

Dbl. Oc.: $64.00
Sgl. Oc.: $64.00
Third Person: $5.00

Jay Village Inn—One of Vermont's finest inns in village location, 3 miles from Jay Peak. Fine dining & gracious service in a romantic setting. Full bar & extensive wine list. 15 guest rooms with private baths; outdoor pool.

Jericho

Milliken, Mrs. Jean
RD #2, Box 397, 05465
(802) 899-3993

Amenities: 1,2,5,8,10
Breakfast: Full

Dbl. Oc.: $37.00-$57.00
Sgl. Oc.: $30.00-$50.00
Third Person: $5.00

Milliken's—An early Victorian hosted by Rick, a hotel manager and Jean, a choreographer, Bethany, 12, and Patrick, 4. 12 miles from Burlington on Rte. 15. Breakfast on glassed-in porch. Children welcome.

Killington

McGrath, M/M Kyran
Rt. 4, P.O. Box 267, 05751
(802) 775-7181

Amenities: 2,4,7,9,10,11,12
Breakfast: Full
Dbl. Oc.: $58.00-$80.00 Summer rates
Sgl. Oc.: $46.00 Summer rates
Third Person: $18.00 Summer rates

The Inn At Long Trail—Located high in Vermont mountains alongside Appalachian Trail. Wonderful hiking, swimming, tennis, summer theater nearby; 16 cozy rooms & 6 fireplace suites. Irish pub with Guinness on tap & darts. Library.

Londonderry

Kidde, M/M Richard
RR 1, Magic Mtn. Rd.,
Box 29, 05148
(802) 824-5908

Amenities: 3,5,6,7,8,9,10,12
Breakfast: Full

Dbl. Oc.: $42.00-$127.00
Sgl. Oc.: $35.00-$96.00
Third Person: $14.00-$34.00

Blue Gentian Lodge—Small quiet inn, 14 rooms with private baths, large rooms with color TV; walk to ski lifts, outdoor pool; lounge with fireplace; B.Y.O.B., ice furnished. Fine country dining, dinner $10.00/person.

AMENITIES

1. No Smoking
2. No Pets
3. No Children
4. Senior Citizen Rates
5. Tennis Available
6. Golf Available
7. Swimming Available
8. Skiing Available
9. Credit Cards Accepted
10. Personal Check Accepted
11. Off Season Rates
12. Dinner Available (w/sufficient notice)

Vermont

Londonderry

Letch, Ms. Claire
Rt. 100, 01845
(802) 824-3019

Amenities: 2,5,7,8,9,10,11,12
Breakfast: Full

Dbl. Oc.: $81.00
Sgl. Oc.: $75.00
Third Person: $13.00

The Highland House—An 1842 country inn set on 32 peaceful acres. Unique guest rooms with private baths; large heated swimming pool and tennis court. Fine dining by candlelight. Close to sites of interest, shopping, & skiing.

Ludlow

Combes, M/M William
Box 275, RFD# 1, 05149
(802) 228-8799

Amenities: 9,10,11,12
Breakfast: Full

Dbl. Oc.: $83.50
Sgl. Oc.: $66.10
Third Person: $17.40

The Combes Family Inn—This century-old farmhouse is situated on a quiet country backroad. Set on 50 acres of woods and meadows for exploring and cross country skiing. A great spot for families. Near skiing, lakes, and hiking.

Manchester

Eichorn, Patricia & Robert
Highland Ave., Box 1754, 05255
(802) 362-4564

Amenities: 1,2,5,6,7,8,9,10,11
Breakfast: Full
Dbl. Oc.: $104.06
Sgl. Oc.: $64.13
Third Person: $24.20

Manchester Highland Inn—Turreted Queen Anne Victorian on hilltop above Manchester. Full gourmet breakfast or breakfast in bed. Relax poolside in summer, hearthside in winter. Minutes to skiing, fishing, hiking, & shops.

Manchester

Lee, M/M Lee, Jr.
West Road, Box 346, 05254
(802) 362-2761

Amenities: 2,3,5,6,7,8,9,10,12
Breakfast: Full
Dbl. Oc.: $116.16
Sgl. Oc.: $72.60
Third Person: $30.25

Birch Hill Inn—Quiet country inn, built in 1790, set away from the busy village streets. panoramic views; swimming pool; trout pond; walking trails on premises; cross-country skiing. We eat with our guests at 7:30 at a common table.

AMENITIES

1. No Smoking
2. No Pets
3. No Children
4. Senior Citizen Rates
5. Tennis Available
6. Golf Available
7. Swimming Available
8. Skiing Available
9. Credit Cards Accepted
10. Personal Check Accepted
11. Off Season Rates
12. Dinner Available (w/sufficient notice)

Vermont

Marlboro

Durkin, Janet & Tom
P.O. Box 86, Rte. 9, 05344
(802) 257-1545

Amenities: 2,3,7,8,9,10,11,12
Breakfast: Full
Dbl. Oc.: $100.00
Sgl. Oc.: $75.00
Third Person: $25.00

Longwood A Country Inn is restfull, relaxing, exceptional, charming, "New England's finest country inn," N.E. Monthly Mag. Fireplace rooms; award-winning cuisine; skiing, sleigh rides, woodsy walks, swimming. Better than home—that special inn seldom surpassed.

Mendon

Schwartz, Elliot
Woodward Rd., 05701
(802) 775-2290

Amenities: 2,5,6,7,8,9,10,11,12
Breakfast: Full

Dbl. Oc.: $65.00-$90.00
Sgl. Oc.: $60.00-$80.00
Third Person: $30.00

Red Clover Inn—Charming country inn in mountain valley. 15 beautiful rooms, library, living room, award-winning cuisine, warm and gracious hospitality, AAA & Mobil Guide; spectacular views.

Middlebury

Cole, Linda & Roger
RD #3,
Box 2460, 05753-8751
(802) 388-6429

Amenities: 1,3,4,5,10,11
Breakfast: Full

Dbl. Oc.: $53.00-$90.00
Sgl. Oc.: $53.00-$80.00

Brookside Meadows—Comfortable & attractive new home with 2 bedrooms and a 2 bedroom suite w/private entrance and private baths. Near Middlebury College, Morgan Horse Farm, & Shelburne Museum. Excellent restaurants; 2 night preferred.

Middlebury

Nelson, Andrea & John
25 Stewart Lane, 05753
(802) 388-9925

Amenities: 2,6,7,8,9,10,12
Breakfast: Full
Dbl. Oc.: $60.00-$99.00
Sgl. Oc.: $55.00-$94.00
Third Person: $10.00

Swift House Inn—Enjoy warm and gracious lodging and dining. Fireplaces in bedrooms, all private baths, some with whirlpool tubs. 3 acres of gardens; 2 blocks from excellent shopping and restaurants.

AMENITIES

1. No Smoking
2. No Pets
3. No Children
4. Senior Citizen Rates
5. Tennis Available
6. Golf Available
7. Swimming Available
8. Skiing Available
9. Credit Cards Accepted
10. Personal Check Accepted
11. Off Season Rates
12. Dinner Available (w/sufficient notice)

Vermont

Middlebury

Stevenson, Mary & William
RD 4, Box 300, 05753
(802) 462-2866

Amenities: 1,7,8,10
Breakfast: Full

Dbl. Oc.: $50.00
Sgl. Oc.: $40.00
Third Person: $10.00

Stevenson's Home—South of Middlebury on Rt. 30, 2 miles from town. Excellent shops & restaurants; Middlebury College, Morgan Horse Farm & Vermont state crafts shop. Mountains & lakes nearby. Year round area. Children welcome.

Middletown Springs

Sax, Steven
Box 1068, 05757
(802) 235-2198

Amenities: 1,2,3,8,9,10,12
Breakfast: Full

Dbl. Oc.: $80.00
Sgl. Oc.: $40.00
Third Person: $40.00

The Middletown Springs Inn—An 1879 Victorian mansion located on the green of an historic village in the foothills of the Green Mountains. Biking & hiking from the inn. Antique, craft and outlet shops nearby.

Morgan

Hunt, Mrs. Pat
RR 1, Box 570,
W. Charleston, 05872
(802) 895-4432, 334-8322

Amenities: 5,6,7,8,10
Breakfast: Full

Dbl. Oc.: $30.00
Sgl. Oc.: $20.00

Hunt's Hideaway—Modern split-level home. Two double guest rooms separate from living quarters. 100 acres of woods & fields. 20x40 in-ground pool. 2 miles west of Lake Seymour off Rt. 111, 5 miles from I-91 Exit 28.

Newfane

Rees, Mrs. Carol
Rt. 1, Box 2654, 05345
(802) 365-4656

Amenities: 1,7,8,10
Breakfast: Continental

Dbl. Oc.: $45.00-$65.00
Sgl. Oc.: $45.00
Third Person: $10.00

Redwing Farm Bed Breakfast, a 115 acre working farm in southern Vermont. Spectacular views; hike, bike, canoe, horse-drawn wagon or sleigh rides; farm animals. Ski Mount Snow or Stratton Mountain, or cross-country ski.

North Hero

Apgar, John
Rt. 2, Box 106,
Champlain Islands, 05474
(802) 372-8237

Amenities: 1,2,5,7,10,12
Breakfast: Full

Dbl. Oc.: $90.00
Third Person: $18.00

North Hero House—A beautiful island country inn with a magnificent view across Lake Champlain to Mt. Mansfield. North Hero House offers fine accommodations, gracious hospitality & delicious food in abundance.

AMENITIES

1. No Smoking
2. No Pets
3. No Children
4. Senior Citizen Rates
5. Tennis Available
6. Golf Available
7. Swimming Available
8. Skiing Available
9. Credit Cards Accepted
10. Personal Check Accepted
11. Off Season Rates
12. Dinner Available (w/sufficient notice)

Vermont

North Hero

Clark, John
Box 88, 05474
(802) 372-8822

Amenities: 3,5,6,7,10
Breakfast: Continental

Dbl. Oc.: $45.00

Charlie's Northland Lodge—Beautiful Lake Champlain beckons from the doorstep of this island lodge which offers unparalleled views of both lake and mountains. A place to go to fish, sail, canoe, play tennis or just plain relax.

North Troy

Plourde, Russell
15 Railroad St., 05859
(802) 988-2527

Amenities: 10
Breakfast: Full

Dbl. Oc.: $31.80
Sgl. Oc.: $21.20

North Troy Inn—An old home with eight guest rooms and full breakfast. Near famous Jay Peak, in sight of Canada's Owl's Head ski area. Near border, one and one half hour ride to Montreal. Open all year. Nine acres and a brook.

Orwell

Korda, Mrs. Joan
Route 22A, 05750
(802) 948-2727

Amenities: 5,6,7,10
Breakfast: Full

Dbl. Oc.: $135.00
Sgl. Oc.: $60.00
Third Person: $15.00

Historic Brookside Farms, a national registered landmark. Our 1789 farmhouse & elegant 1843 Greek revival mansion on a lush 300-acre estate. 9 room guest house is decorated in period antiques, Folk art & country collectibles.

Peru

Okun, Gary
Rte. 11, 05152
(802) 824-5533

Amenities: 1,2,3,5,6,7,8,9,10,11,12
Breakfast: Full
Dbl. Oc.: $72.60-$84.70
Sgl. Oc.: $108.90-$127.05
Third Person: $25.00

Johnny Seesaw's—Rustic log lodge on Rte. 11 next to Bromley Mtn. Cottages with fireplaces; rooms & suites in lodge; red clay tennis court; olympic size pool; great menu; licensed pub; Children's game room.

AMENITIES

1. No Smoking
2. No Pets
3. No Children
4. Senior Citizen Rates
5. Tennis Available
6. Golf Available
7. Swimming Available
8. Skiing Available
9. Credit Cards Accepted
10. Personal Check Accepted
11. Off Season Rates
12. Dinner Available (w/sufficient notice)

Vermont

Pittsfield

Yennerell, Tom
Rt. 100, Box 526, 05762
(802) 746-8943

Amenities: 2,5,6,7,8,9,12
Breakfast: Continental

Dbl. Oc.: $29.00-$39.00
Sgl. Oc.: $49.00-$69.00
Third Person: $30.00

Pittsfield Inn is an old stagecoach stop, circa 1835, on a small village green in the center of Vermont's Green Mountains. 10 rooms with private baths; furnished with antiques & period wallpapers; close to restaurants.

Plymouth

Stanford, Ann & Glen
Jct. Rts. 100 & 100A
05056
(802) 672-3748

Amenities: 1,2,3,5,6,7,8,9,10,11,12
Breakfast: Full

Dbl. Oc.: $78.00-$140.00
Sgl. Oc.: $72.00-$132.00
Third Person: $25.00

Salt Ash Inn, built in 1830 as a stagecoach stop, and also used as the town post office, general store, and dance hall! 14 rooms with private bath. English pub, cable TV room, hot tub. 5 miles to Killington ski resort!

Rochester

Harvey, M/M Donald
05767
(802) 767-4273

Amenities: 5,6,7,8,10
Breakfast: Full

Dbl. Oc.: $38.00
Sgl. Oc.: $42.00

Harvey's Mt. View Inn & Farm, small year round resort accommodating about 20 visitors. Rates include breakfast & dinner. Farm animals, heated pool and pond for fishing provide endless entertainment. One chalet rental available.

Rochester

Kennett, Elizabeth & Robert
Liberty Hill Rd, 05767
(802) 767-3926

Amenities: 2,5,6,7,8,10,12
Breakfast: Full
Dbl. Oc.: $60.00
Sgl. Oc.: $30.00

Liberty Hill Farm is a 200 yr. old working dairy farm between White River & the Green Mts. Ideal hiking, skiing, or relaxing. Family style meals, pastry specialties; children welcome; family rates; dinner.

AMENITIES

1. No Smoking
2. No Pets
3. No Children
4. Senior Citizen Rates
5. Tennis Available
6. Golf Available
7. Swimming Available
8. Skiing Available
9. Credit Cards Accepted
10. Personal Check Accepted
11. Off Season Rates
12. Dinner Available (w/sufficient notice)

Vermont

Royalton

Curley, Mrs. Gary
Rt. 14, Box 108F, 05068
(802) 763-8437

Amenities: 2,7,9
Breakfast: Full

Dbl. Oc.: $45.00
Sgl. Oc.: $27.00

Fox Sand Inn—An historic brick building built in 1818. Restaurant and tavern open to the public. Six guest rooms with shared baths. Located 1 mile off I-89. Situated on the bank of the White River.

Shoreham

Saenger, Mrs. Rene
Box 205, 05770
(802) 897-2101

Amenities: 10,12
Breakfast: Full

Dbl. Oc.: $40.00
Sgl. Oc.: $25.00
Third Person: $10.00

Cream Hill Farm dates from the 1800's. 360 degree views include Green Mountains, Adirondacks, & Lake Champlain. 1,000's of acres give you room to roam, bike, fish, ski, or experience beef & sheep farming firsthand.

Shrewsbury

Husselman, Grace & Samuel
Lincoln Hill Rd., Box 118, 05738
(802) 492-3485

Amenities: 1,2,5,6,7,8,11
Breakfast: Full
Dbl. Oc.: $37.10-$53.00
Sgl. Oc.: $31.80
Third Person: $15.00

Buckmaster Bed & Breakfast—Historic 1801 stagecoach stop in Green Mts. country village. Spacious rooms, porches, library lounge with fireplace plus family heirlooms, hiking, biking, Alpine & x-country skiing. Shopping, lovely views.

South Burlington

Perkins, Jann & Chuck
916 Shelburne Rd., 05403
(802) 862-2144

Amenities: 2,9
Breakfast: Continental

Dbl. Oc.: $50.00-$75.00

Lindenwood, a country inn. Gracious hospitality; spacious grounds; separate carriage house; chalet that sleeps 6-10; inn—rooms elaborate; near lake, colleges, & shopping. Just off I-89, exit 13.

AMENITIES

1. No Smoking
2. No Pets
3. No Children
4. Senior Citizen Rates
5. Tennis Available
6. Golf Available
7. Swimming Available
8. Skiing Available
9. Credit Cards Accepted
10. Personal Check Accepted
11. Off Season Rates
12. Dinner Available (w/sufficient notice)

Vermont

South Londonderry

Cavanagh, Jean & Jim
Rte. 100, Box 301, 05155
(802) 824-5226

Amenities: 2,5,6,7,8,10,11,12
Breakfast: Continental

Dbl. Oc.: $42.40-$73.14
Sgl. Oc.: $31.80-$73.14
Third Person: $14.84-$19.08

The Londonderry Inn—This 1826 homestead has been a country inn for 50 years. Near Bromley, Magic, Stratton ski areas, Green Mtn. Nat'l. Forest. Living room with library, billiards & game room, bar. Family accommodations.

So. Strafford

Alden, Anna & Lincoln
Rt. 132,
P.O. Box 101, 05070
(802) 765-4314

Amenities: 2,5,6,7,8,10
Breakfast: Full

Dbl. Oc.: $53.00
Sgl. Oc.: $26.50
Third Person: $10.60

Watercourse Way B&B—1850 Cape with gardens, pasture & tree farm & river. Near Hanover, Woodstock, waterfalls, hiking, & more! Enjoy breakfast by the large flagstone fireplace in a serene country setting.

So. Wallingford

Crelin, Tracy & Ed
RR 1, 400 Rte. 7, 05773
(802) 446-2611

Amenities: 7,8,9,10,11
Breakfast: Full

Dbl. Oc.: $42.40
Sgl. Oc.: $31.80
Third Person: $10.60

The Green Mt. Tea Room was built as a stagecoach stop in 1792. Our homey inn boasts nearly 200 years of hospitable history. Casual & comfortable; relax on the banks of the picturesque Otter Creek. Hiking, antiquing & shopping nearby.

Starksboro

Hill, Kathy
State Prison Hollow Rd.
05487
(802) 453-2008

Amenities: 1,2,10
Breakfast: Continental

Dbl. Oc.: $53.00
Sgl. Oc.: $13.25-$26.50

Millhouse Bed & Breakfast—Elegant and historic Vermont country home within 25 miles of ski resorts, golf courses, & Lake Champlain. Fine dining in Burlington, Waitsfield or Middlebury; much more.

AMENITIES

1. No Smoking
2. No Pets
3. No Children
4. Senior Citizen Rates
5. Tennis Available
6. Golf Available
7. Swimming Available
8. Skiing Available
9. Credit Cards Accepted
10. Personal Check Accepted
11. Off Season Rates
12. Dinner Available (w/sufficient notice)

Vermont

Starksboro

Mashburn, Kathy & Gene
Route 116, 05487
(802) 453-3911

Amenities: 1,2,3,9,12
Breakfast: Full
Dbl. Oc.: $55.00
Sgl. Oc.: $40.00

North Country Bed And Breakfast—Centrally located between Burlington & Middlebury, we are a B&B of European tradition. 2 queen size and 1 twin bedded rooms; full breakfast served family style. Reservations preferred.

Stowe

Baas, M/M John
Edson Hill, RR 1,
Box 2280, 05672
(802) 253-8376

Amenities: 2,5,6,7,8,10,11
Breakfast: Continental

Dbl. Oc.: $45.00
Sgl. Oc.: $35.00
Third Person: $8.00

Baa's Gastehaus—Member: American Bed & Breakfast. Beautiful home in pastoral setting; twin & double bedded rooms, crib. 5 minutes to Mt. Mansfield, less to best X/C skiing. 40 attractions within one hour drive. Call Dee.

Stowe

Heath, Anita & Larry
Edson Hill, RR 1, Box 2480, 05672
(802) 253-7371

Amenities: 2,4,5,6,7,8,9,10,11,12
Breakfast: Full
Dbl. Oc.: $79.00
Sgl. Oc.: $69.00
Third Person: $19.00

Edson Hill Manor—Film site of Alan Alda's Four Seasons. Heath family owned for 35 years. Rooms with private bath, fireplaces; fine dining. Year long horseback riding; summer pool & fishing; winter X/C ski, or nearby sleigh rides.

AMENITIES

1. No Smoking
2. No Pets
3. No Children
4. Senior Citizen Rates
5. Tennis Available
6. Golf Available
7. Swimming Available
8. Skiing Available
9. Credit Cards Accepted
10. Personal Check Accepted
11. Off Season Rates
12. Dinner Available (w/sufficient notice)

Vermont

Stowe

Heiss, Trude & Dietmar
RR 1, Box 1450, 05672
(802) 253-7336

Amenities: 4,5,7,8,9,11,12
Breakfast: Full
Dbl. Oc.: $54.00-$65.00
Third Person: $15.00

Andersen Lodge—A small Austrian inn, with gourmet food prepared by Austrian chef, located on Route 108, Mountain Road.

Stowe

Henzel, John M.
Mtn. Rd., Box 1360, 05672
(802) 253-7574

Amenities: 5,6,7,9,12
Breakfast: Full

Dbl. Oc.: $67.00
Sgl. Oc.: $42.00
Third Person: $8.00

Just Like Home Only Better! Located midway from village & mountain, comfortable lodging in old Vermont farmhouse. Authentic Mexican dinners, unique Sunday brunch; outdoor hot tub; 3 miles north of VT. 108, from Stowe. Dinner $15.00/person.

Stowe

Heyer, M/M Larry
Rt. 108, 05672
(802) 253-4050

Amenities: 5,6,7,8,10,12
Breakfast: Continental

Dbl. Oc.: $60.00-$90.00
Sgl. Oc.: $60.00-$90.00
Third Person: $15.00-$30.00

Ski Inn—A Vermont country inn noted for good food & good conversation plus the warmth & informality of an old fashioned ski lodge where guests enjoy themselves & each other. Next to downhill & cross country skiing. Full breakfasts-winter.

Stowe

Horman, Mrs. Christel
Mt. Road, Rt. 108, 05672
(802) 253-4846

Amenities: 2,3,5,6,7,8,9,10,11
Breakfast: Full

Dbl. Oc.: $63.60
Sgl. Oc.: $49.82
Third Person: $22.26

Guest House Christel Horman—European hospitality. 8 large double rooms with full private bathrooms & beautiful living room on one floor. Breakfast will be served outside in summer.

AMENITIES

1. No Smoking
2. No Pets
3. No Children
4. Senior Citizen Rates
5. Tennis Available
6. Golf Available
7. Swimming Available
8. Skiing Available
9. Credit Cards Accepted
10. Personal Check Accepted
11. Off Season Rates
12. Dinner Available (w/sufficient notice)

Vermont

Stowe

Hubbard, Rick & Rose Marie Matulionis
School St., Box 276, 05672
(802) 253-7351

Amenities: 1,2,5,6,7,8,9,10,11
Breakfast: Full
Dbl. Oc.: $85.00-$100.00
Sgl. Oc.: $65.00-$75.00
Third Person: $15.00

The 1860 House—Center village; national historic register; non-smokers. Exceptional accommodations: king/queen beds, all private baths, quilts, antiques, piano, classical music, friendly conversation, jacuzzi.

Stowe

Jenson, M/M Wes
Cottage Club Rd., 05672
(802) 253-7603

Amenities: 5,6,7,9,10
Breakfast: Buffet

Dbl. Oc.: $56.00-$86.00

Timberholm Inn—Gracious living room with huge stone fireplace, picture windows & game room. Valley and mountain views. Winter—complimentary homemade soups apres skiing; summer: cookies, lemonade, deck and flowers.

Stowe

Shelter, Len
R #1, P.O. Box 2290, 05672
(800) 426-6697

Amenities: 5,6,7,8,9,10,11
Breakfast: Full

Dbl. Oc.: $65.00
Sgl. Oc.: $45.00
Third Person: $15.00

Logwood Inn & Chalet is located 3 miles from Stowe Village on #108. 5 acres of trees & lawns in private setting; flower boxes on windows; large swimming pool; clay tennis court; near 18 hole golf course; hiking trails; not a B&B in winter.

Vergennes

Bring, Michelle & Ron
RD 1, Box 9, 05491
(802) 877-3337

Amenities: 1,2,5,6,7,8,9,10,11,12
Breakfast: Full
Dbl. Oc.: $68.90
Sgl. Oc.: $58.30
Third Person: $10.60

Strong House Inn—Comfortably elegant lodging in a gorgeous 1834 Greek Revival home on the national historic register. Valley setting with magnificent mountain vistas. Full country breakfast featuring homebaked delights.

AMENITIES

1. No Smoking
2. No Pets
3. No Children
4. Senior Citizen Rates
5. Tennis Available
6. Golf Available
7. Swimming Available
8. Skiing Available
9. Credit Cards Accepted
10. Personal Check Accepted
11. Off Season Rates
12. Dinner Available (w/sufficient notice)

Vermont

Waitsfield

Gorman, Mrs. Joan
RFD Box 62, 05673
(802) 496-2405

Amenities: 1,2,3,9,10,11,12
Breakfast: Full

Dbl. Oc.: $84.80-$106.00
Sgl. Oc.: $106.00-$137.80
Third Person: $37.10

Millbrook—Classic Cape-style farmhouse decorated with antiques, handmade quilts, hand stenciling. Reputation for fine dining with homemade soups, bread, desserts, pasta & fresh local ingredients; candlelit atmosphere.

Waitsfield

Pratt, Betsey
Rt. 17, 05673
(802) 496-3310

Amenities: 2,4,5,6,7,8,9,10,11,12
Breakfast: Continental

Dbl. Oc.: $58.00
Sgl. Oc.: $35.00

Mad River Barn—15 rooms; enjoy the comfort of large private rooms & baths. 8 deluxe rooms with TV & kitchenette, swimming pool, woodland trails. Child under 10 free in room with parents. Lounge and game room.

Waitsfield

Stinson, Millie, Janet & Bill
Route 100, Box 8, 05673
(802) 496-3450

Amenities: 2,5,6,7,8,9,10,11
Breakfast: Full
Dbl. Oc.: $64.00
Sgl. Oc.: $44.00
Third Person: $25.00

Valley Inn—Family hospitality. Green Mountains; historical Waitsfield Village; many local events; activities & skiing nearby; hot tub & sauna. Winter rates available.

Wallingford

Lombardo, M/M Joseph
9 North Main, Box 404, 05773
(802) 446-2849

Amenities: 5,6,7,8,9,10
Breakfast: Full
Dbl. Oc.: $74.20
Sgl. Oc.: $53.00
Third Person: $20.60

The Wallingford Inn, a charming 1876 Victorian mansion offering 10 guest rooms, antiques, polished wood floors & oak woodwork. Enjoy candlelight dining Fri. & Sat. evenings; full service bar. Located on Rt. 7.

AMENITIES

1. No Smoking
2. No Pets
3. No Children
4. Senior Citizen Rates
5. Tennis Available
6. Golf Available
7. Swimming Available
8. Skiing Available
9. Credit Cards Accepted
10. Personal Check Accepted
11. Off Season Rates
12. Dinner Available (w/sufficient notice)

Vermont

Warren

Chapman, Janice & Howard
RR Box 38, Sugarbush Access Rd., 05674
(802) 583-3211

Amenities: 2,4,5,6,7,8,9,10,11
Breakfast: Full
Dbl. Oc.: $84.00
Sgl. Oc.: $57.00
Third Person: $30.00

Sugartree Inn an intimate mountainside country inn with handmade quilts atop canopy brass and antique beds. Christmas card setting. Cool mountain evenings. All rooms with antiques and private baths.

Waterbury

Gosselin, Pam & Gary
RR #1, Box 1266, 05676
(802) 244-7529

Amenities: 6,7,8,9,10
Breakfast: Full

Dbl. Oc.: $68.00
Sgl. Oc.: $59.00
Third Person: $12.00

Inn At Blush Hill—Circa 1790 Cape Cod located midway between Stone & Sugarbush. Quiet area with fine restaurants and shops nearby. Atmosphere is warm & cozy, lots of antiques, fireplaces & spectacular mountain views.

West Arlington

Masterson, Woody
Rt. 313, 05250
(802) 375-6372

Amenities: 6,7,8,10
Breakfast: Full

Dbl. Oc.: $63.60
Sgl. Oc.: $37.10
Third Person: $10.60

Shenandoah Farm—Experience New England at its peak in this lovingly restored 1820 Colonial overlooking the Battenkill River. Wonderful Americana year round. Full "farm fresh" breakfast is served daily.

West Dover

Chabot, Liz & Ernie
HCR 63, Door Fitch Rd.,
Box 57, 05356
(802) 464-5426

Amenities: 2,5,6,7,8,10,11
Breakfast: Full

Dbl. Oc.: $40.00-$65.00
Sgl. Oc.: $18.00-$32.00

The Weathervane—Tyrolean style ski lodge; Colonial charm; antiques; fireplaced lounge & recreation room; BYOB bar. Winter: X/C skiing, snowshoeing, sledding; summer: boating, fishing, museums & the Marlboro Festival.

AMENITIES

1. No Smoking
2. No Pets
3. No Children
4. Senior Citizen Rates
5. Tennis Available
6. Golf Available
7. Swimming Available
8. Skiing Available
9. Credit Cards Accepted
10. Personal Check Accepted
11. Off Season Rates
12. Dinner Available (w/sufficient notice)

Vermont

West Dover

Collingwood, M/M John
Rt. 100, Box 938, 05356
(802) 464-2474

Amenities: 2,5,6,7,8,9,11
Breakfast: Full

Dbl. Oc.: $56.00
Sgl. Oc.: $36.00
Third Person: $22.00

The Gray Ghost Inn, located on Rte. 100 is minutes to golf, tennis and ski areas. Attractive rooms with private baths. Hearty Vermont breakfasts served. Family operated. Lounge with fireplace, game room and sauna.

Weston

Granger, Sandy & Dave
Route 100, Box 104, 05161
(802) 824-6789

Amenities: 1,2,5,6,7,8,9,10
Breakfast: Full

Dbl. Oc.: $55.00-$70.00

1830 Inn On The Green—Recognized by the national register of historic places as part of the Weston historic district. The inn sits across the green from the oldest summer theater in the state and steps from numerous shops.

Williamstown

Laveroni, Mrs. Elaine
Main St., Rt. 14,
Box 31, 05679
(802) 433-5822

Amenities: 2,4,7,8,9,10
Breakfast: Full

Dbl. Oc.: $53.00
Sgl. Oc.: $42.40
Third Person: $10.60

Rosewood Inn Bed & Breakfast—Gracious 1898 Victorian, in a charming country village, with beautiful original woodwork & spacious rooms. Centrally located for all seasonal activities. Excellent restaurants nearby.

Williston

Bryant, Sally & Roger
102 Partridge Hill,
Box 52, 05495
(802) 878-4741

Amenities: 1,2,10
Breakfast: Continental

Dbl. Oc.: $50.00
Sgl. Oc.: $25.00

Partridge Hill—Contemporary chalet on hilltop with panorama view of the Green Mountains. Located 8 miles east of Burlington in quiet wooded country.

AMENITIES

1. No Smoking
2. No Pets
3. No Children
4. Senior Citizen Rates
5. Tennis Available
6. Golf Available
7. Swimming Available
8. Skiing Available
9. Credit Cards Accepted
10. Personal Check Accepted
11. Off Season Rates
12. Dinner Available (w/sufficient notice)

Vermont

Wilmington

Bonney, Jacki & Jerry
HCR 63, Box 28, Smith Rd., 05363
(802) 464-3362

Amenities: 2,5,6,7,8,9,10,11
Breakfast: Full
Dbl. Oc.: $106.00
Sgl. Oc.: $75.00
Third Person: $25.00

The Inn at Quail Run

The Inn At Quail Run—Charming & romantic country inn nestled away on 12 acres with mountain view. Antiques, brass beds with cozy comforters & private baths. Hearty country breakfast starts each day.

Wilmington

Meadowcroft, Doris
Rt. 100, 05363
(802) 464-2631

Amenities: 5,6,7,8,9,10,11
Breakfast: Continental

Dbl. Oc.: $42.40-$68.90
Sgl. Oc.: $31.80-$47.70

Darcroft's Schoolhouse—1837 one-room schoolhouse remodelled to accommodate guests or small groups. Large living room, lounge with fireplace; 2 rooms with shared bath, 1 room with private bath; use of kitchen. Children welcome.

Wilmington

Schneider, Mafia Shaffer
Shafter St., Box 27
(802) 464-3783

Amenities: 2,3,5,6,7,8,9
Breakfast: Full

Dbl. Oc.: $63.60
Third Person: $31.80

Salom Lodge is a charming Victorian inn remodelled to a fine B&B. Nice clean guest rooms, shared bath, 1 private. Cozy lounge with Franklin fireplace, TV & HBO. 4 miles to Haystack, 8 miles to Mt. Snow. Homemade jams.

AMENITIES

1. No Smoking
2. No Pets
3. No Children
4. Senior Citizen Rates
5. Tennis Available
6. Golf Available
7. Swimming Available
8. Skiing Available
9. Credit Cards Accepted
10. Personal Check Accepted
11. Off Season Rates
12. Dinner Available (w/sufficient notice)

Virginia

The Mother Of Presidents

Capital: Richmond
Statehood: June 25, 1788; the 10th state
State Motto: Thus Always To Tyrants
State Song: "Carry Me Back To Old Virginia"
State Bird: Cardinal
State Flower: Flowering Dogwood
State Tree: Sugar Maple

Virginia is perhaps one of the most beautiful and historic states in the union. The climate is never too hot or too cold, an ideal vacation area. There is so much to see in this state, from the beautiful sandy beaches on the east coast to the rolling horse farms in the interior to the natural beauty of the Shenandoah Mountains and the breathtaking Skyline Drive.

The battlefield scars of two wars are here, along with their surrender points, Yorktown and Appomattox Court House. Historians come here to visit historic Jamestown, Colonial Williamsburg, Thomas Jefferson's home, Monticello, and his University of Virginia, as well as Mount Vernon, our first president's home.

Eight presidents of the United States were born here: George Washington, Thomas Jefferson, James Madison, James Monroe, William Harrison, Zackary Taylor, James Tyler and Woodrow Wilson.

Virginia

Basye

Seay, Mona Lesa
Rt. 263, Box 80, 22842
(703) 856-2147

Amenities: 5,6,7,8,9,10,12
Breakfast: Full

Dbl. Oc.: $75.71
Sgl. Oc.: $70.96
Third Person: $15.20

Sky Chalet Country Inn—Swiss style mountain top lodge hideaway in the Shenandoah Valley. Spectacular panoramic mountain views; scrumptious dining; comfortable lodging; relax in: hammocks, cozy pub, or by our fireplaces.

Blacksburg

Good, Vera G.
Rt. 1, Box 348, 24060
(703) 951-1808

Amenities: 1,4,5,6,10
Breakfast: Full

Dbl. Oc.: $60.00
Sgl. Oc.: $60.00
Third Person: $10.00

L'Arche Farm Bed And Breakfast—A cozy 1790 southwest Virginia farmhouse on 5 rural acres. Convenient to Virginia Tech., Radford University & the scenic & recreational attractions of the New River Valley. 2 miles on Mt. Tabor Rd.

Burke

Williams, Mrs. Luisa
6011 Liberty Bell Ct., 22015
(703) 451-1661

Amenities: 7,9,10,11,12
Breakfast: Continental

Dbl. Oc.: $58.00
Sgl. Oc.: $45.00

The Heritage House—Tastefully decorated. 20 miles to : Mt. Vernon, Old Town Alexandria, & Washington, D.C. Complimentary coffee; weekend rates available.

Cape Charles

Goffigon, Sara & Cooke
Box 97AA, 23310
(804) 331-2212

Amenities: 1,6,7,10,12
Breakfast: Full

Dbl. Oc.: $50.00
Sgl. Oc.: $40.00

Pickett's Harbor On Virginia Historic Eastern Shore—Colonial home on Chesapeake Bay & acres of private beach. Antiques, reproductions & collectables decorate the home. A rural retreat for auctions & nearby nature tours. Wild flora & fauna abounds.

Charles City

Copland, M/M Geroge F.
Rt. 1, Box 13A, 23030
(804) 829-5176

Amenities: 2,10
Breakfast: Full

Dbl. Oc.: $60.00
Sgl. Oc.: $60.00
Third Person: $15.00

North Bend Plantation Bed & Breakfast—A Virginia historic landmark, James River Plantation area. Southern hospitality abounds with one of Virginia's oldest families! Still farmed by owners.

AMENITIES

1. No Smoking
2. No Pets
3. No Children
4. Senior Citizen Rates
5. Tennis Available
6. Golf Available
7. Swimming Available
8. Skiing Available
9. Credit Cards Accepted
10. Personal Check Accepted
11. Off Season Rates
12. Dinner Available (w/sufficient notice)

Virginia

Charlottesville

Dwight, Shelley & Tim
3001 Hollymead Dr., 22901
(804) 978-4686

Amenities: 1,2,3,5,7,9,10,12
Breakfast: Continental
Dbl. Oc.: $90.53-$111.83
Sgl. Oc.: $69.23-$90.53
Third Person: $21.30

Silver Thatch Inn—7 romantic bedrooms with private baths. All rooms are decorated with country quilts and antiques. We offer fine evening dining Tuesday through Saturday. B&B open seven days a week.

Chincoteague

Bond, Carlton P.
600 S. Main St., 23336
(804) 336-3221

Amenities: 2,5,6,7,9,10,11
Breakfast: Continental

Dbl. Oc.: $65.00-$85.00
Third Person: $10.00

Year Of The Horse Inn—Waterfront rooms, private bath, color TV. Ten minutes to ocean refuge. See the wild ponies or deer and waterfowl. Private pier for crabbing. Central heat and air in all rooms. Balcony on rooms to enjoy sunsets.

Chincoteague

Stam, Dr. James, C.
113 N. Main St., 23336
(804) 336-6686

Amenities: 1,2,3,7,10,11
Breakfast: Full
Dbl. Oc.: $59.00-$95.00
Sgl. Oc.: $49.00-$85.00
Third Person: $10.00

Miss Molly's Inn—A charming Victorian inn on the Bay. All rooms air-conditioned and furnished in period antiques. Near beach and wildlife refuge. Marguerite Henry stayed here while writing Misty of Chincoteague.

AMENITIES

1. No Smoking
2. No Pets
3. No Children
4. Senior Citizen Rates
5. Tennis Available
6. Golf Available
7. Swimming Available
8. Skiing Available
9. Credit Cards Accepted
10. Personal Check Accepted
11. Off Season Rates
12. Dinner Available (w/sufficient notice)

Virginia

Culpeper

Walker, Kathi & Steve
609 S. East St., 22701
(703) 825-8200

Amenities: 2,5,6,7,8,9,10
Breakfast: Continental
Dbl. Oc.: $70.00
Sgl. Oc.: $60.00
Third Person: $10.00

Fountain Hall Bed & Breakfast Inn—Centrally located in northern Virginia. 1859 Colonial revival home 6 blocks from Amtrack with major airports nearby. Come & enjoy the charm of Culpeper's first B&B while admiring the antique decor.

Flint Hill

Irwin, Phil
Rt. 1, Box 2080, 22627
(703) 675-3693

Amenities: 1,2,3,4,5,6,7,8,9,10,12
Breakfast: Full
Dbl. Oc.: $73.15-$104.50
Third Person: $15.68

Caledonia Farm Bed & Breakfast—A working cattle farm adjacent to Shenandoah National Park. Elegant 1812 stone home has fireplaces, A/C, mountain scenery, outstanding comfort & hospitality for conference, vacation or overnight. 65 miles to DC.

Fredericksburg

Bannan, M/M Edward
1200 Princess Anne St., 22401
(703) 371-7600

Amenities: 4,9,10,12
Breakfast: Continental
Dbl. Oc.: $82.00
Sgl. Oc.: $71.00
Third Person: $10.00

Kenmore Inn Of Fredericksburg—Located in the heart of historic Old Town. This elegant 18th century inn offers superlative dining. Close to major historic sites & antique shops. 13 guest rooms, 4 with fireplaces. All private baths.

AMENITIES

1. No Smoking
2. No Pets
3. No Children
4. Senior Citizen Rates
5. Tennis Available
6. Golf Available
7. Swimming Available
8. Skiing Available
9. Credit Cards Accepted
10. Personal Check Accepted
11. Off Season Rates
12. Dinner Available (w/sufficient notice)

Virginia

Fredericksburg

Schiesser, Mrs. Michele
Rte. 3, Box 1255, 22401
(703) 898-8444

Amenities: 2,9
Breakfast: Full

Dbl. Oc.: $70.00
Sgl. Oc.: $54.00
Third Person: $11.00

La Vista Plantation—1838 Classical revival manor home with 10 acre grounds & pond. 4 room suite with private bath, kitchen, 2 fireplaces, & A.C.

Gordensville

Allison, Mrs. Beverly
Rt. 3, Box 43, 22942
(703) 832-5555

Amenities: 5,7,9,10,12
Breakfast: Full
Dbl. Oc.: $55.00-$80.00
Sgl. Oc.: $43.00-$53.00
Third Person: $15.00

Sleepy Hollow Farm Bed & Breakfast—Historic Rt. 231, lovely countryside, restored farmhouse, cottage, pond. Near Montpelier, horse trails, historic sites, fine dining. Child under 7 free dinners; lunch by arrangement.

Irvington

Taylor, Mrs. Marilyn
P.O. Box 425, 22480
(804) 438-6053

Amenities: 5,6,7,10
Breakfast: Full
Dbl. Oc.: $57.48-$62.70
Sgl. Oc.: $47.03-$52.25

King Carter Inn—A Victorian inn with nine rooms, four with private bath. Full breakfast featuring inn-baked breads, country sausage, & fresh squeezed juices. Bicycles provided; golf, tennis, & boating nearby.

Lexington

Thornber, Ms. Ellen
603 S. Main St., 24450
(703) 463-3235

Amenities: 2,4,5,6,7,8,9,10,11
Breakfast: Full

Dbl. Oc.: $60.00-$70.00
Sgl. Oc.: $45.00
Third Person: $10.00

Llewellyn Lodge—A warm and friendly atmosphere await guests to this lovely brick Colonial that is just a 10 minute walk to the historic district. Fully air conditioned, private baths. A hearty breakfast is served each day.

AMENITIES

1. No Smoking
2. No Pets
3. No Children
4. Senior Citizen Rates
5. Tennis Available
6. Golf Available
7. Swimming Available
8. Skiing Available
9. Credit Cards Accepted
10. Personal Check Accepted
11. Off Season Rates
12. Dinner Available (w/sufficient notice)

Virginia

Lexington

Tichenor, Pat & Jim
Rt. 5, Box 87, 24450
(703) 463-1013

Amenities: 1,2,3,9,10
Breakfast: Continental
Dbl. Oc.: $42.93-$69.23
Sgl. Oc.: $37.28-$63.90
Third Person: $10.00

Fassifern Bed & Breakfast—1867 brick Victorian country home, on 3 1/2 acres, 2 miles from the center of historic Lexington. Filled with antiques & several comfortable lounging areas. Warm & gracious! Many extra amenities. Friendly!

Luray

Lushpinsky, Vera
Rte. 4, Box 620, 22835
(703) 743-7855

Amenities: 2,4,5,6,7,8,9,10,11
Breakfast: Full
Dbl. Oc.: $75.00-$95.00
Sgl. Oc.: $65.00-$90.00

Elegant Bed & Breakfast
The Ruffner House
1739

The Ruffner House—Gracious, historic (1793) manor on 18 acres Arabian horse farm. Elegant period furnishings, private bath, mountain views, hearty breakfast. In Shenandoah Valley near Skyline Drive and Luray Caverns.

Luray

Lushpinsky, Vera
Rte. 4, Box 620, 22835
(703) 743-7855

Amenities: 2,4,5,6,7,8,9,10,11
Breakfast: Full

Dbl. Oc.: $55.00-$75.00
Sgl. Oc.: $45.00-$70.00

The Cottage—Charming country home on 18 acre Arabian horse farm. Cheerful, cozy. Hearty breakfast in Victorian dining room at Ruffner House. In Shenandoah Valley near Skyline Drive, Luray Caverns & antique shops.

AMENITIES

1. No Smoking
2. No Pets
3. No Children
4. Senior Citizen Rates
5. Tennis Available
6. Golf Available
7. Swimming Available
8. Skiing Available
9. Credit Cards Accepted
10. Personal Check Accepted
11. Off Season Rates
12. Dinner Available (w/sufficient notice)

Virginia

Luray

Mayes, M/M Gary
Wallace Ave., Rt. 4, Box 79, 22835
(703) 743-4701

Amenities: 2,3,5,6,7,8,9,10,11,12
Breakfast: Full
Dbl. Oc.: $75.00-$95.00
Third Person: $10.00

Spring Farm—Restored historic 1795 inn. Inviting, warm, charming & private surroundings. Nearby antique shops, breathtaking Skyline Drive & world famous Luray Caverns. Many recreational areas access Rt. 211.

Luray

Middleton, M/M Edward
147 S. Court St., 22835
(703) 743-7712

Amenities: 1,2,3,5,6,10
Breakfast: Full

Dbl. Oc.: $60.00
Sgl. Oc.: $60.00
Third Person: $15.00

Serendipity Court—A restored 1863 in-town home with a country setting & breathtaking mountain views. Located in Shenandoah Valley minutes from Skyline Drive, caverns, Civil War battlefields, national parks and forests.

Mathews

Goldreyer, Annette W.
Rt. 14 E., Box 310, 23109
(804) 725-9975

Amenities: 2,4,5,6,10
Breakfast: Full

Dbl. Oc.: $57.20-$83.20
Sgl. Oc.: $55.00-$79.00
Third Person: $20.00

Riverfront House—1840 farmhouse on 7 acres. Private dock, crabbing, biking. Walk to village shops & restaurants. Under an hour to Williamsburg & Busch Gardens & plantations. Boat trips available.

Mollusk

Smith, Pam & Walt
Rt. 354, Box 174, 22517
(804) 462-5995

Amenities: 2,3,7,10,12
Breakfast: Full
Dbl. Oc.: $63.00
Sgl. Oc.: $58.00

Greenvale Manor—Historic waterfront manor home on 13 acres. Pool, boating, beach, bicycling, private baths. Near historic sites, golf, & tennis. Lots of hospitality & tranquility. Weekly cottage rental available.

AMENITIES

1. No Smoking
2. No Pets
3. No Children
4. Senior Citizen Rates
5. Tennis Available
6. Golf Available
7. Swimming Available
8. Skiing Available
9. Credit Cards Accepted
10. Personal Check Accepted
11. Off Season Rates
12. Dinner Available (w/sufficient notice)

Virginia

Montrose

Longman, M/M Michael A.
Courthouse Square, 22520
(804) 493-9097

Amenities: 2,3,4,5,6,9,10
Breakfast: Continental
Dbl. Oc.: $67.60
Sgl. Oc.: $57.20
Third Person: $10.40

The Inn At Montrose—On site of 17th century tavern, many historic attractions nearby. Each of the inn's 6 guest rooms feature antiques, private baths, and A/C. Restaurant & English pub room on premises.

Mt. Jackson

Kip, Mrs. Rosemary
Rt. 698, Box 117, 22842
(703) 477-2400

Amenities: 4,7,8,9,10,12
Breakfast: Full

Dbl. Oc.: $50.00-$70.00
Sgl. Oc.: $45.00-$60.00
Third Person: $10.00

The Widow Kip's—1830 Shenandoah homestead. 6 bedrooms with fireplaces, antique fourposter or sleigh beds. Separate cozy cottage; gift & antique shop; overlooks mountains, near river.

Nellysford

Versluys, M/M Martin
P.O. Box 431, 22958
(804) 361-9357

Amenities: 1,2,3,5,6,7,8,9,10
Breakfast: Continental

Dbl. Oc.: $45.00

Acorn Inn is conveniently near historic Charlottesville, VA., and 10 miles from Wintergreen ski resort. Charming atmosphere with refreshing Blue Ridge Mountains & hiking trails nearby. Beautiful views.

New Market

Kasow, Dawn
9329 Congress St., 22844
(703) 740-8030

Amenities: 2,5,6,7,8,10
Breakfast: Full

Dbl. Oc.: $65.00
Sgl. Oc.: $55.00

A Touch Of Country—A warm, relaxing atmosphere in historic New Market. 1/10 of a mile from the center of town; within walking distance of restaurants and shops.

AMENITIES

1. No Smoking
2. No Pets
3. No Children
4. Senior Citizen Rates
5. Tennis Available
6. Golf Available
7. Swimming Available
8. Skiing Available
9. Credit Cards Accepted
10. Personal Check Accepted
11. Off Season Rates
12. Dinner Available (w/sufficient notice)

Virginia

Newport

Kurstedt, Dr. & Mrs. Harold
Rt. 2, Box 561-E, 24128
(703) 961-2480

Amenities: 1,2,3,4,5,8,9,10,12
Breakfast: Full
Dbl. Oc.: $75.00
Sgl. Oc.: $70.00
Third Person: $10.00

The Newport House—A country inn with new private baths, A/C. Well maintained 30 acres in southwest Virginia, 19 miles from I-81, 1 mile to Rt. 460. Comfortable, private accommodations, several common areas for guests.

Norfolk

Straddeck, Mrs. Erika
232 E. Bayview Blvd., 23503
(804) 583-5725

Amenities: 2,3,4,5,6,10,11
Breakfast: Continental

Dbl. Oc.: $35.00
Sgl. Oc.: $30.00

"Erikas"—This charming Cape Cod home is close to I-64, Colonial Williamsburg, Busch Gardens & VA Beach. Your hostess offers large private patio, in-ground pool & hot tub. Guests may use large living room, kitchen & laundry.

Orange

Ramsey, Shirley
P.O. Box 707, Rt. 15 S., 22960
(703) 672-5597

Amenities: 1,2,3,9,10,12
Breakfast: Full
Dbl. Oc.: $90.53-$101.18
Third Person: $8.53

Mayhurst Inn, an Italiante Victorian mansion, has 6 guest rooms & 1 cottage, private baths, fireplaces. An historic landmark on 36 acres of Oaks, Cedars & Magnolias. 2 hours from Washington, D.C. & Richmond.

Richmond

Abbott, Dr./Mrs. James
2304 East Broad St., 23223
(804) 780-3746

Amenities: 9,10
Breakfast: Full

Dbl. Oc.: $77.50-$92.50
Sgl. Oc.: $67.50-$82.50

The Catlin-Abbott House—Four poster beds, roaring fireplaces, sherry, bedside turn down service, breakfast in bed with freshly brewed coffee; early morning walks in historic district.

AMENITIES

1. No Smoking
2. No Pets
3. No Children
4. Senior Citizen Rates
5. Tennis Available
6. Golf Available
7. Swimming Available
8. Skiing Available
9. Credit Cards Accepted
10. Personal Check Accepted
11. Off Season Rates
12. Dinner Available (w/sufficient notice)

Virginia

Richmond

Benson, Lyn M.
2036 Monument, 23220
(804) 648-7560

Amenities: 1,2,9,10
Breakfast: Continental
Dbl. Oc.: $72.00-$95.00
Sgl. Oc.: $68.00-$85.00
Third Person: $10.00-$15.00

The Benson House—Lovely 1914 Italian Renaissance located on historic avenue, totally restored. It offers four guest rooms, each with private bath (one with jacuzzi) and two with fireplace. Furnished with antiques & traditional pieces.

Richmond

Fleming, Barbara
P.O. Box 4503
(804) 353-4656, 353-5855

Amenities: 1,2,3,4,10
Breakfast: Full

Dbl. Oc.: $55.00-$65.00
Sgl. Oc.: $40.00-$45.00
Third Person: $27.50-$32.50

Abbie Hill Bed & Breakfast—Gracious accommodations in heart of Richmond's historic Fan district/Monument Ave. area. Near museums, eateries, historic sites. Traditional breakfast includes homemade muffins, jellies, eggs & bacon. 2 1/2 miles to I-95.

Scottsville

Sushka, Mary Jae Abbitt & Peter
Rt. 4, Box 6, 24590
(804) 286-2218

Amenities: 1,4,7,8,10,12
Breakfast: Full
Dbl. Oc.: $85.00
Sgl. Oc.: $69.00
Third Person: $15.00

HIGH MEADOWS ...
A Virginia Historic Landmark

VIRGINIA'S VINEYARD INN

High Meadows—Virginia's vineyard inn. An historic landmark on the national register. On 23 acres, 7 guest rooms each with private bath, 1832/1882 period antiques, romantic setting, south of Charlottesville, VA.

AMENITIES

1. No Smoking
2. No Pets
3. No Children
4. Senior Citizen Rates
5. Tennis Available
6. Golf Available
7. Swimming Available
8. Skiing Available
9. Credit Cards Accepted
10. Personal Check Accepted
11. Off Season Rates
12. Dinner Available (w/sufficient notice)

Virginia

Smith Mt. Lake

Tucker, Mary Lynn & Lee
Rt. 1, Box 533, 24184
(703) 721-3951

Amenities: 1,2,4,5,6,7,9,10,12
Breakfast: Full
Dbl. Oc.: $53.25
Sgl. Oc.: $53.25

The Manor At Taylor's Store—Romantic elegance in historic mansion with private baths, hot tub. "Innkeepper's dinner." 1000 acre estate offering hiking, fishing, canoeing. Near Smith Mt. Lake, Blue Ridge Parkway & Roanoke, VA.

Smithsfield

Earl, Sam
1607 S. Church St., 23430
(804) 357-3176

Amenities: 2,4,6,9,10
Breakfast: Continental

Dbl. Oc.: $51.21
Sgl. Oc.: $51.21
Third Person: $8.36

Isle of Wight Inn—Luxurious bed & breakfast. 10 rooms & antique shop; private baths, 4 poster beds, fireplaces, jacuzzi; from $49.00. Near Colonial Williamsburg, Busch Gardens, and huge outlet malls.

Standardsville

Schwartz, Mrs. Eleanor
Rt. 2, Box 303, 22973
(804) 985-3782

Amenities: 1,2,10,12
Breakfast: Full

Dbl. Oc.: $65.00
Sgl. Oc.: $60.00
Third Person: $15.00

Edgewood Farm Bed & Breakfast—Restored Colonial farmhouse on 130 acres. Blue Ridge view, near wineries, Monticello, Montpelier, & National Park. A small family-run B&B, located on VA Rt. 667.

Stanley

Beers, Marley & Jetze
Rt. 2, Box 375, 22851
(703) 778-2209 or 778-2285

Amenities: 5,6,7,8,9,10,12
Breakfast: Full
Dbl. Oc.: $69.25
Sgl. Oc.: $58.85
Third Person: $10.00

Jordan Hollow Farm Inn—200 year old Colonial horse farm. 16 charming guest rooms in lodge with private bath; full service restaurant, pub; horseback riding; view of Shenandoah National Park; 6 miles south of Luray Caverns.

AMENITIES

1. No Smoking
2. No Pets
3. No Children
4. Senior Citizen Rates
5. Tennis Available
6. Golf Available
7. Swimming Available
8. Skiing Available
9. Credit Cards Accepted
10. Personal Check Accepted
11. Off Season Rates
12. Dinner Available (w/sufficient notice)

Virginia

Staunton

Fannon, Elizabeth & Daniel
Rt. 1, Box 63, Swoope, 24479
(703) 337-6929

Amenities: 1,2,10
Breakfast: Full

Dbl. Oc.: $36.58
Sgl. Oc.: $31.35

Lambsgate Bed & Breakfast—In the historic Shenandoah Valley, 6 miles west of Staunton on Rt. 254. Restored 1816 farmhouse in pastoral setting facing Allegheny Mtns. Near antiquing, hiking, & scenic attractions. Request brochure.

Staunton

Harman, Joe
18 East Frederick St., 24401
(703) 885-4220

Amenities: 1,2,4,5,6,7,8,9,10,11,12
Breakfast: Full
Dbl. Oc.: $43.00-$64.00
Sgl. Oc.: $37.00-$59.00
Third Person: $6.00-$11.00

Frederick House Historic Inn, circa 1810. Large comfortable rooms or suites with one or two bedrooms and living room, all with private bath, TV, AC, and phone. Oversized beds, antiques, ceiling fans.

Staunton

Hoaster, M/M Ray
531 Thornrose Ave., 24401
(703) 885-7026

Amenities: 1,5,6,7,8,10
Breakfast: Full

Dbl. Oc.: $50.00-$55.00
Sgl. Oc.: $40.00-$45.00
Third Person: $5.00-$10.00

Thornrose House At Gypsy Hill—Elegant Georgian B&B in park setting, with antiques & family heirlooms. Guest rooms have private baths & A/C. Huge porch for summer & fireplaces for winter. Afternoon tea & conversation. Shenandoah Valley.

Stephens City

Bitto, Mrs. Jonathan
5408 Main St., 22655
(703) 869-4149

Amenities: 7,10,12
Breakfast: Full

Dbl. Oc.: $50.00
Sgl. Oc.: $45.00
Third Person: $8.00

Newton Tavern Bed & Breakfast has offered a warm welcome and a unique experience for the visitor to the Shenandoah Valley for over 165 years. Near historic sites of the Valley, Skyline Drive. Reservations required.

AMENITIES

1. No Smoking
2. No Pets
3. No Children
4. Senior Citizen Rates
5. Tennis Available
6. Golf Available
7. Swimming Available
8. Skiing Available
9. Credit Cards Accepted
10. Personal Check Accepted
11. Off Season Rates
12. Dinner Available (w/sufficient notice)

Virginia

Virginia Beach

Yates, Mrs. Barbara
302 24th St., 23451
(804) 428-4690

Amenities: 1,4,5,6,7,11
Breakfast: Continental
Dbl. Oc.: $41.23-$56.42
Sgl. Oc.: $34.72-$47.74
Third Person: $10.00

Angie's Guest Cottage—Cute, clean and cozy beach house in the heart of the resort area, one block from beach. International atmosphere with casual and comfortable surroundings. Sundeck and cookout facilities available.

Washington

Harris, Camille; Foster, Patrick
Main St., Box 333, 22747
(703) 675-3757

Amenities: 5,9,10
Breakfast: Continental
Dbl. Oc.: $64.20
Sgl. Oc.: $53.50
Third Person: $5.35-$10.70

The Foster-Harris House is a Victorian B&B in the historic village of Washington, Va. 5-star restaurant, Skyline Drive, hiking, antiquing nearby. 65 miles west of Washington, D.C. Vacation plan special.

Waterford

Anderson, Marie & Charles
The Pink Mouse, 22190
(703) 882-3453

Amenities: 2,3,10
Breakfast: Full

Dbl. Oc.: $100.00
Sgl. Oc.: $100.00
Third Person: $10.00

The Pink House, 1795—Suites with private baths & entrance, fireplace & TV in national landmark of Waterford, settled 1732. Easy access to Washington, D.C., Dulles Airport, Civil War sites, Skyline Dr., Harpers Ferry.

Williamsburg

Cottle, Mrs. June
8691 Barhamsville Rd.,
Toano, 23168
(804) 566-0177

Amenities: 4,10,12
Breakfast: Full

Dbl. Oc.: $50.00
Sgl. Oc.: $40.00
Third Person: $15.00

Bluebird Haven is southern hospitality with gourmet food, clean comfortable rooms in an at-home atmosphere. Children welcome. Quiet area located 9 miles from Colonial Williamsburg, 4 miles from pottery.

AMENITIES

1. No Smoking
2. No Pets
3. No Children
4. Senior Citizen Rates
5. Tennis Available
6. Golf Available
7. Swimming Available
8. Skiing Available
9. Credit Cards Accepted
10. Personal Check Accepted
11. Off Season Rates
12. Dinner Available (w/sufficient notice)

Virginia

Williamsburg

Hirz, Sandi & Brad
1022 Jamestown Rd., 23185
(804) 253-1260

Amenities: 1,2,10
Breakfast: Full

Dbl. Oc.: $70.00-$95.00
Sgl. Oc.: $70.00-$95.00
Third Person: $22.00

Liberty Rose Colonial B&B offers warmth & hospitality with great antiques, charming collectibles & old-fashioned touches lavishly tucked into every niche of the house. Join us for a traditional B&B experience.

Williamsburg

Hite, Mrs. Faye
704 Monumental, 23185
(804) 229-4814

Amenities: 10
Breakfast: Continental

Dbl. Oc.: $38.00
Third Person: $5.00

Hite's Guest Home—Attractive Cape Cod, large rooms, antiques. 10 minute walk to Colonial Williamsburg, 1/2 mile to Visitor's Center. TV and phone in rooms.

Williamsburg

Hughes, Mrs. Genevieve O.
106 Newport Ave., 23185
(804) 229-3493

Amenities: 1,2,5,6,10
Breakfast: Continental

Dbl. Oc.: $45.00
Sgl. Oc.: $45.00
Third Person: $5.00

Hughes Guest Home—Located one half block from restored area. Our home is furnished with family antiques & the A/C guest rooms are ground level. Children are welcome. All seasons fun. Dining facilities within the block.

Williamsburg

Jones, Mrs. Marty
605 Richmond Rd., 23185
(804) 229-0205

Amenities: 1,2,5,6,7,9,10,11
Breakfast: Continental

Dbl. Oc.: $65.00-$90.00
Sgl. Oc.: $55.00
Third Person: $15.00

Applewood Colonial Bed & Breakfast—Elegant Colonial decor, canopy beds, fireplaces & an apple collection. Walking distance to Colonial Williamsburg & College of William & Mary. 4 rooms w/private baths, romantic & quiet with all the comforts of home.

AMENITIES

1. No Smoking
2. No Pets
3. No Children
4. Senior Citizen Rates
5. Tennis Available
6. Golf Available
7. Swimming Available
8. Skiing Available
9. Credit Cards Accepted
10. Personal Check Accepted
11. Off Season Rates
12. Dinner Available (w/sufficient notice)

Virginia

Williamsburg

Strout, Fred
616 Jamestown Rd., 23185
(804) 229-3591

Amenities: 1,10
Breakfast: Continental
Dbl. Oc.: $60.00
Sgl. Oc.: $60.00
Third Person: $5.00

The Cedars—Brick Georgian Colonial home, air conditioned, family antiques, 9 rooms, brick guest cottage with kitchen for six, just 1/4 mile from historic area directly across from William & Mary. Quiet area.

Wintergreen

Dinwiddie, M/M Edward
Wintergreen Dr., Box 280,
Nellysford, 22958
(804) 325-9126

Amenities: 5,6,7,8,9,10,12
Breakfast: Full
Dbl. Oc.: $83.20-$93.60
Sgl. Oc.: $67.60-$72.80
Third Person: $36.40

Trillum House—12 rooms, private baths, located within 10,000 acre resort of Wintergreen. 1 mile from Blue Ridge Parkway. Featured in CIBR, AAA, 3 Diamond, Mobil Guide 3 Star, and Great Inns of America. Dinner $18.72-$20.80.

AMENITIES

1. No Smoking
2. No Pets
3. No Children
4. Senior Citizen Rates
5. Tennis Available
6. Golf Available
7. Swimming Available
8. Skiing Available
9. Credit Cards Accepted
10. Personal Check Accepted
11. Off Season Rates
12. Dinner Available (w/sufficient notice)

Washington

The Evergreen State

Capital: Olympia
Statehood: November 11, 1889; the 42nd state
State Motto: Alki (Bye & Bye)
State Song: "Washington, My Home"
State Bird: Willow Goldfinch
State Flower: Coast Rhododendron
State Tree: Western Hemlock

The state of Washington receives an abundance of rain. Because of this, it has great forests and lumber is its major industry. It also is known as a great land for hunting and fishing.

Olympia, the capital, and other cities on Puget Sound are sheltered from most of the heavy rain and are able to maintain a busy harbor to send supplies north to Alaska and receive in return oil to be refined.

There are also farmlands here irrigated by means of the harnessing of the water by dams. The chief dam being the Coulee Dam, is considered to be one of the greatest pieces of engineering ever completed.

The state of Washington is also well known for her delicious Washington state apples.

Washington

Anacortes

Hasty, Melinda & T., Mikel
1312 8th St., 98221
(206) 293-5773

Amenities: 1,2,3,5,6,7,8,9,10,11
Breakfast: Full

Dbl. Oc.: $48.35-$80.25
Sgl. Oc.: $48.35-$80.25
Third Person: $15.00

Hasty Pudding House—Lovely 1913 Edwardian home. Charming, antique-filled rooms; quiet neighborhood; walk to historic downtown. Near restaurants, marina and quaint shops; a romantic retreat.

Anacortes

McIntyre, M/M Dennis
2902 Oakes Ave., 98221
(206) 293-9382

Amenities: 1,2,3,6,7,9,10,11
Breakfast: Full

Dbl. Oc.: $74.18
Sgl. Oc.: $48.38
Third Person: $10.00

The Channel House—Relax in the hot tub; bike the scenic loop road of Washington Park; ride the ferries; shop for antiques; and be welcomed home with evening cookies and tea. Four guest rooms with shared baths.

Ashford

Jenny, Ms. Susan
P.O. Box 103, 37311
SR 706 98304
(206) 569-2339

Amenities: 1,2,8,10
Breakfast: Full

Dbl. Oc.: $65.70-$87.60
Sgl. Oc.: $54.75
Third Person: $16.43

Growly Bear—Enjoy your mountain stay at a rustic 1890 homestead house. Hike in nearby Mt. Ranier National Park; dine at unique restaurants; listen to sounds of Goat Creek; indulge in pastries from Growly Bear Bakery.

Bainbridge Island

Cameron, Ms. Bunny
8490 Beck Rd. N.E., 98110
(206) 842-3926

Amenities: 1,2,5,6,7,8,9,10
Breakfast: Continental

Dbl. Oc.: $53.90-$84.08
Sgl. Oc.: $48.51-$79.08
Third Person: $10.00

The Bombay House, a spectacular 35 minute ferry ride from downtown Seattle, sits on a hillside overlooking "Rich Passage". Unstructured gardens, scenic & quiet, 1907 Victorian close to beach; excellent restaurant nearby.

Bainbridge Island

Baker, John & Trail, Marilyn
15415 Harvey Rd., 98110
(206) 842-4671

Amenities: 1,2,5,6,7,8,9,10
Breakfast: Continental

Dbl. Oc.: $40.00
Sgl. Oc.: $35.00
Third Person: $10.00

Olympic View Bed & Breakfast—Rural guest home on Puget Sound with thrilling water & mountain views. Easy access by ferry to downtown Seattle with its cultural & sports events, & shopping. Musician owner welcomes artists; drive to ocean & Canada.

AMENITIES

1. No Smoking
2. No Pets
3. No Children
4. Senior Citizen Rates
5. Tennis Available
6. Golf Available
7. Swimming Available
8. Skiing Available
9. Credit Cards Accepted
10. Personal Check Accepted
11. Off Season Rates
12. Dinner Available (w/sufficient notice)

Washington

Bellevue

Garnett, Carol & Cy
830-100 Ave. S.E., 98004
(206) 453-1048

Amenities: 1,2,9,10,11,12
Breakfast: Full

Dbl. Oc.: $48.64
Sgl. Oc.: $37.83
Third Person: $10.00

Bellevue Bed And Breakfast—Hilltop mountain & city views. Private suite or single rooms. Full breakfast, gourmet coffee; reasonable rates. Listed in Seattle's Best Places.

Bellevue

Svendsen, Ruth
803-92 Ave., N.E., 98004
(206) 455-1018

Amenities: 1,2,4,5,6,7,8,9,10
Breakfast: Continental

Dbl. Oc.: $49.00
Sgl. Oc.: $43.24
Third Person: $10.00

The Lions Bed & Breakfast—Serene, quiet, yet in the heart of the city. Private quarters with kitchen (two bedrooms), also large room with private bath in main house. Scandinavian hostess; executive style home; one acre grounds.

Bellingham

DeFreytas, M/M Frank
1014 N. Garden, 98225
(206) 671-7828

Amenities: 1,9,10
Breakfast: Continental

Dbl. Oc.: $44.00-$49.00
Sgl. Oc.: $39.00-$44.00
Third Person: $5.00

North Garden Inn has 10 luxurious guest rooms with a view of Bellingham Bay. Located near W.W.U., shopping & fine dining. This 1897 Queen Anne Victorian boasts 2 grand pianos & maple grand staircase.

Bellingham

Harriman, Gloria & Larry
1103 15th St., Old Fairhaven, 98225
(206) 676-0974

Amenities: 1,2,3,5,6,7,8,9
Breakfast: Full
Dbl. Oc.: $59.30-$80.85
Sgl. Oc.: $37.75-$48.50
Third Person: $11.00

The Castle Bed & Breakfast—N.W. Washington's extraordinary bed & breakfast. Excellent views of B'ham Bay, San Juan Islands, & historic district. Lavish honeymoon suite. Old world grandeur; private bathroom; shops & restaurants close-by.

AMENITIES

1. No Smoking
2. No Pets
3. No Children
4. Senior Citizen Rates
5. Tennis Available
6. Golf Available
7. Swimming Available
8. Skiing Available
9. Credit Cards Accepted
10. Personal Check Accepted
11. Off Season Rates
12. Dinner Available (w/sufficient notice)

Washington

Bellingham

Hudson, Barbara & Van
2610 Eldridge Ave., 98225
(206) 734-9172

Amenities: 1,2,5,10
Breakfast: Full

Dbl. Oc.: $47.00-$52.00
Sgl. Oc.: $38.00-$43.00

Bellingham's DeCann House Bed And Breakfast—Friendly hosts offer Victorian rooms overlooking San Juan Islands, full of treasures with tales attached. Private baths, plus a special breakfast to send you on your way with a smile northwest style!!

Bellingham

McAllister, Mrs. Donna
4421 Lakeway Dr., 98226
(206) 733-0055

Amenities: 1,5,7,9,10
Breakfast: Full

Dbl. Oc.: $65.00-$97.00
Third Person: $11.00

Schnauzer Crossing Bed & Breakfast—Quiet elegance set amidst tall evergreens overlooking Lake Whatcom. King bedroom suite with fireplace, TV, & jacuzzi tub. Lake view, country quiet. Tennis, swimming, bicycling. Gourmet breakfast.

Cathlamet

Feasey, Mrs. Carolyn
4 Little Cape Horn, 98612
(206) 425-7395

Amenities: 1,6,7,9,10
Breakfast: Continental/Full

Dbl. Oc.: $53.50-$64.90
Sgl. Oc.: Negotiable

The Gallery Bed & Breakfast At Little Cape Horn—Beautiful natural tree & floral surroundings overlooking Columbia River and great fishing beach. Bald Eagles, Hummingbirds abound; hot tub on deck; elegant antiques, silver & china; art & gifts to buy.

Clinton

Drew, Sharon
2388 E. Sunlight Beach Rd.
98236
(206) 221-2964

Amenities: 1,2,3,4,9,10
Breakfast: Full

Dbl. Oc.: $86.63
Sgl. Oc.: $80.00

Home By The Sea—Seaside setting on a fjord-like bay offers scenes of boats on the sound, the Olympic Mtns., and Mt. Ranier. International flavor prevails from world travels. Private country cottages with kitchens, fireplace.

AMENITIES

1. No Smoking
2. No Pets
3. No Children
4. Senior Citizen Rates
5. Tennis Available
6. Golf Available
7. Swimming Available
8. Skiing Available
9. Credit Cards Accepted
10. Personal Check Accepted
11. Off Season Rates
12. Dinner Available (w/sufficient notice)

Washington

Concrete-Birdsview

Meyer, Ingrid & Gerhard
3840 Pionee Lane, 98237
(800) 826-0015, (206) 826-4333

Amenities: 1,2,3,9,10
Breakfast: Full
Dbl. Oc.: $66.65
Sgl. Oc.: $52.75
Third Person: $10.75

Cascade Mountain Inn—Halfway between Seattle and Vancouver, BC. off scenic Hwy. 20 in pastoral setting. Near North Cascades Nat'l. Park/Baker Lake. Enjoy hiking, fishing, bicycling, river rafting, hunting.

Ferndale

Anderson, Kelly & David
2140 Main St., Box 1547, 98248
(206) 384-3450

Amenities: 1,2,3,6,8,9,10
Breakfast: Full
Dbl. Oc.: $37.63-$69.87
Sgl. Oc.: $37.63-$69.87
Third Person: $10.00

Anderson House Bed & Breakfast Inn

Anderson House Bed & Breakfast—Welcome home! This internationally known inn is nestled in the past. Wake to a full northwest meal; walk to 6 ethnic restaurants; enjoy the sea or skiing. Just 15 miles to Canada—plan a 2 nation vacation.

Ferndale

Matz, Mrs. Doris E.
5832 Church Rd., 98248
(206) 384-3619

Amenities: 1,4,9,10
Breakfast: Continental

Dbl. Oc.: $34.00-$39.00
Sgl. Oc.: $29.00
Third Person: $10.00

Hill Top Bed And Breakfast—"A quilt lover's delight." Large comfortable rooms, 1 with fireplace. Beds & walls warmed with an array of quilts made by your hostess. Private entry & patio. Children ok. Deposit required.

Forks

Miller, Prue & Ted
E. Division St., Box 953, 98331
(206) 374-6806

Amenities: 4,9,10,11
Breakfast: Full

Dbl. Oc.: $50.00
Sgl. Oc.: $40.00
Third Person: $7.50

Miller Tree Inn—A comfy country homestead on 3 acres in Olympic Peninsula's finest fishing & hiking area. Close to beach and Hoh Rain Forest. 6 bedrooms, reasonable rates, relaxed atmosphere.

AMENITIES

1. No Smoking
2. No Pets
3. No Children
4. Senior Citizen Rates
5. Tennis Available
6. Golf Available
7. Swimming Available
8. Skiing Available
9. Credit Cards Accepted
10. Personal Check Accepted
11. Off Season Rates
12. Dinner Available (w/sufficient notice)

Washington

Freeland

Jordan, M/M Walker
1367 E. Bayview Ave., 98249
(206) 221-7738

Amenities: 5,9,10
Breakfast: Full

Dbl. Oc.: $60.00-$70.00

Turn-of-the-century with three bedrooms each with queen size bed and private bath. Breakfast is served with great view of historical Holmes Harbor. Bicycles available. Good beach walking. Quiet and serene.

Freeland

Moore, Peggy
5440 Windmill Rd., 98249
(206) 321-1566

Amenities: 1,2,3,6,10
Breakfast: Continental

Dbl. Oc.: $177.87

Cliff House on Whidbey Island, a stunning luxurious home for just one couple. Breathtaking views, miles of driftwood beach, fireplace, kitchen, spa. A truly romantic retreat for two on this beautiful island.

Friday Harbor
(San Juan Island)

Tuller, Evelyn & Charles
3021 Beaverton Valley Rd.
98250
(206) 378-4138

Amenities: 1,2,10,11
Breakfast: Full

Dbl. Oc.: $54.00-$81.00
Sgl. Oc.: $43.00-$70.00

Moon & Sixpence—3 rooms in 1906 farmhouse, a 1-room cabin & water tower suite on 16 acres at center of San Juan Island. Resident weaver & weaving studio. On ferry route from Anacortes to Victoria, B.C.

Granger

Stear, JoAnn
530 Gurley Rd., 98932
(509) 854-2508

Amenities: 9,10
Breakfast: Full

Dbl. Oc.: $55.00
Sgl. Oc.: $45.00
Third Person: $10.00

Rinehold Cannery Homestead—1905 Farmhouse, country charm. 14 wineries nearby for tasting. Children under 12 or pets by advance arrangement. Reservations necesssary. Enjoy the beautiful Yakima Valley.

Issaquah

Caldwell, Mrs. Laureita
25237 S.E. Issaquah,
Fall City Rd., 98027
(206) 392-1196

Amenities: 1,2,3,4,10
Breakfast: Full

Dbl. Oc.: $50.00
Sgl. Oc.: $45.00
Third Person: $15.00

The Wildflower—In a small delightful suburb of Seattle, here is quiet country charm. A 2-story log home in tall trees welcomes you to spacious rooms, country atmosphere, and home-cooked breakfasts. Rest and relax!

AMENITIES

1. No Smoking
2. No Pets
3. No Children
4. Senior Citizen Rates
5. Tennis Available
6. Golf Available
7. Swimming Available
8. Skiing Available
9. Credit Cards Accepted
10. Personal Check Accepted
11. Off Season Rates
12. Dinner Available (w/sufficient notice)

Washington

Kirkland

Harris, Salli & Richard
11410 99th Pl., N.E., 98033
(206) 823-2303

Amenities: 1,2,3,5,6,7,8,9,10
Breakfast: Full
Dbl. Oc.: $67.50
Sgl. Oc.: $67.50

Shumway Mansion—Award-winning 1909 B&B; 7 rooms all with private baths, queen size beds, & lake views. Close to all amenities, beaches, parks, easy downtown Seattle access. Children over 12 welcome; smoking public room only.

La Conner

Everton, Mr. Wayne
505 Maple, Box 237, 98257
(206) 466-4675

Amenities: 2,3,6,7,9,10
Breakfast: Continental

Dbl. Oc.: $43.00-$70.00
Sgl. Oc.: $43.00-$70.00

Heather House is a 3 bedroom 2 bath Cape Cod overlooking farms, mountains & fabulous Skagit Valley. Easy walk to outstanding restaurants and shopping. Bridal suite with fireplace and sofa. Queen beds.

Langley

Martin, Trudy & Whitey
215 6th St., Box 459, 98260
(206) 221-8709

Amenities: 1,2,3,4,6,9,10,11
Breakfast: Full

Dbl. Oc.: $80.00
Sgl. Oc.: $70.00

Country Cottage—Casual elegance on Whidbey Island. 3 acres with sweeping view of Cascades and Saratoga Passage; within short walk of art filled village. Park-like garden with hot tub. 5 suites with baths.

Langley

Metcalf, Mrs. Norma & Senator Jack
3273 E. Saratoga Rd., 98260
(206) 321-5483

Amenities: 1,2,3,7,9,10
Breakfast: Full
Dbl. Oc.: $60.00-$80.00
Sgl. Oc.: $60.00-$80.00
Third Person: $12.50

Log Castle Bed & Breakfast—On Whidbey Island, 40 minutes north of Seattle. Log lodge on secluded beach. Turret bedrooms, private baths; rustic elegance; homemade cinnamon rolls & breads included in full breakfast.

AMENITIES

1. No Smoking
2. No Pets
3. No Children
4. Senior Citizen Rates
5. Tennis Available
6. Golf Available
7. Swimming Available
8. Skiing Available
9. Credit Cards Accepted
10. Personal Check Accepted
11. Off Season Rates
12. Dinner Available (w/sufficient notice)

Washington

Leavenworth

Harrild, Kathryn & Bob
12882 Ranger Rd., 98826
(509) 548-7024

Amenities: 1,2,5,6,7,8,9,10
Breakfast: Full

Dbl. Oc.: $70.00-$86.00
Sgl. Oc.: $54.00-$76.00
Third Person: $11.00

Haus Rohrbach Pension—A cheery European country inn, a bit of the Austrian Alps in Washington's Cascade Mountains. Warm hospitality, charm, spectacular view. Pool, hot tub.

Leavenworth

Krieg, Mrs. Wendi
11150 Hwy. 209, 98826
(509) 548-7863

Amenities: 2,9,10
Breakfast: Full

Dbl. Oc.: $55.00-$70.00
Sgl. Oc.: $45.00-$60.00
Third Person: $10.00

Brown's Farm Bed & Breakfast—Hug Barney, our loving Australian shepherd, gather fresh eggs, snuggle under a down comforter. Experience year-round country delight.

Leavenworth

Riley, Judy & Bob
11097 Eagle Creek Rd., 98826
(509) 548-4449

Amenities: 1,2,3,5,6,8,9,10
Breakfast: Full
Dbl. Oc.: $85.00
Sgl. Oc.: $55.00-$65.00
Third Person: $15.00

Bavarian Meadows—European country theme, 3 miles from Bavarian Village. Cascade Mts. & forest view; near rivers for fishing, rafting, hiking. Hot tub, covered decks, laundry facilities. Enjoy forest wildlife & peacefulness.

Lopez

Bergstrom, M/M Michael D.
Rt. 1, Box 1940, 98261
(206) 468-2253

Amenities: 1,2,3,6,9,10,12
Breakfast: Full

Dbl. Oc.: $63.43-$74.18
Sgl. Oc.: $52.68-$63.43
Third Person: $16.13

Mackaye Harbor Inn—The ideal beachfront getaway! This recently restored Victorian home is filled with warmth, nostalgia, & charm. Waterfront dining on fresh seafoods & steak. Biking, beachcombing, & rowing. Prolific wildlife.

AMENITIES

1. No Smoking
2. No Pets
3. No Children
4. Senior Citizen Rates
5. Tennis Available
6. Golf Available
7. Swimming Available
8. Skiing Available
9. Credit Cards Accepted
10. Personal Check Accepted
11. Off Season Rates
12. Dinner Available (w/sufficient notice)

Washington

Lumni Island

Flynn, Victoria Taft
2579 West Shore Dr., 98262
(206) 758-2620

Amenities: 1,2,3,7,8,9,10,12
Breakfast: Full

Dbl. Oc.: $70.00
Sgl. Oc.: $70.00

The Willows Inn, B&B—On the sunset side of the island. Hourly car ferry from Bellingham area. 4 rooms, 2 with private baths, honeymoon cottage. Beach access, eagle watching. Wine & dine at this romantic inn.

Lumni Island

Hanson, Polly & Carl
2781 West Shore Dr., 98262
(206) 758-2600

Amenities: 1,2,9,10,12
Breakfast: Full
Dbl. Oc.: $53.75
Sgl. Oc.: $43.00
Third Person: $16.13

West Shore Farm Bed & Breakfast—Memorable escape. Farm fresh bountiful meals. Quiet beach, 180 degree view of eagles, islands, sunsets, Canadian Mountains. Hosts: librarian & homebuilt pilot who plays bagpipes. 2 rooms, octagonal home. Brochure.

Montesano

Murphy, JoAnne & Mike
417 Wilder Hill, Box 416, 98563
(206) 249-3453

Amenities: 1,2,3,4,7,9,10
Breakfast: Full

Dbl. Oc.: $45.78
Sgl. Oc.: $35.78

Sylvan Haus Hilltop Country Home—2 bedrooms, private bath, gourmet breakfast, decks. 5 minutes to Sylvan Lake, 30 minutes to the ocean, 1 hour to Seattle; secluded.

Mt. Vernon

Goldfarb, Peter
1388 Moore Rd., 98273
(206) 445-6805

Amenities: 1,2,9,10
Breakfast: Continental

Dbl. Oc.: $55.90
Sgl. Oc.: $53.75

The White Swan Guest House—One hour north of Seattle, 6 miles to La Conner. Country setting; Victorian home with three cozy guest rooms. Bird watching; bike paths; like grandma's house; great antique shops & restaurants nearby.

AMENITIES

1. No Smoking
2. No Pets
3. No Children
4. Senior Citizen Rates
5. Tennis Available
6. Golf Available
7. Swimming Available
8. Skiing Available
9. Credit Cards Accepted
10. Personal Check Accepted
11. Off Season Rates
12. Dinner Available (w/sufficient notice)

Washington

Olympia

Yunker, Barbara & Dick
7924 61st Ave. N.E., 98506
(206) 459-1676

Amenities: 4,7,9,10,11
Breakfast: Continental

Dbl. Oc.: $55.00 & up

Puget View Guesthouse—Classic Puget Sound—charming waterfront guest cottage suite next to host's log home. Peaceful, picturesque, panoramic. One of "N.W. Best Places." 5 minutes off I-5. Boat outings, cook-outs during summer.

Port Angeles

Shannon-Moore, Gaye
139 W. 14th., 98362
(206) 457-3424

Amenities: 1,5,6,7,10
Breakfast: Full

Dbl. Oc.: $48.51
Sgl. Oc.: $43.12
Third Person: $10.00

Harbour House Bed & Breakfast—Enjoy a warm and elegant atmosphere in our Cape Cod style home located near downtown Port Angeles and the Victoria Ferry. Visit Olympic National Park.

Port Orchard

Ogle, M/M Quentin J.
1307 Dogwood Hill S.W., 98366
(206) 876-9170

Amenities: 1,2,3,5,6,7,8,10
Breakfast: Full

Dbl. Oc.: $43.00
Sgl. Oc.: $35.00

Ogle's Bed & Breakfast—View ships, water & mountains on Puget Sound West. Comfortable & gracious hillside home will make you glad you came. Restaurants, shops, marina closeby. Off #160, 25 miles north of Tacoma.

Port Townsend

Michael (Your Innkeeper)
1891 S. Jacob Miller, 98368
(206) 385-5245

Amenities: 1,2,3,9,10
Breakfast: Continental

Dbl. Oc.: $44.50-$70.00
Sgl. Oc.: $44.50-$70.00

Arcadia Country Inn—70 quiet country acres one mile from the main street of our Victorian town. All rooms feature antiques, private baths, handmade quilts. Views of pasture; orchard; mountains. Hot tub. Wickered porch.

AMENITIES

1. No Smoking
2. No Pets
3. No Children
4. Senior Citizen Rates
5. Tennis Available
6. Golf Available
7. Swimming Available
8. Skiing Available
9. Credit Cards Accepted
10. Personal Check Accepted
11. Off Season Rates
12. Dinner Available (w/sufficient notice)

Washington

Port Townsend

Sokol, Edel & Bob
744 Clay St., 98368
(206) 385-3205

Amenities: 1,2,3,5,6,7,8,9,10,11
Breakfast: Continental
Dbl. Oc.: $47.00-$90.00
Third Person: $12.00

Starrett House Inn—Most photographed house in Washington. Located on a bluff above downtown with views of the Cascade & Olympic Mtns., Puget Sound, and Port Townsend Bay. 1889 historic landmark. Scrumptious breakfast.

Port Townsend

Wickline, Pattie & Bill
731 Pierce St., 98368
(206) 385-4168

Amenities: 3,5,6,9,10,11
Breakfast: Continental

Dbl. Oc.: $46.00-$85.00
Sgl. Oc.: $40.00-$79.00

Lizzie's Italianate Victorian Mansion—In historic seacoast town. Near hiking, biking, beaches, sailing, & Olympic Nat'l. Park. 7 guest rooms some with private baths. No children under 10. "Quite simply, the finest."

Redmond

Brown, Mary Ellen & Walt
1011-240th Ave., N.E. 98053
(206) 868-4159

Amenities: 1,2,3,5,6,7,8,9,10
Breakfast: Full
Dbl. Oc.: $44.00
Sgl. Oc.: $38.00

Cedarym, A Colonial Bed & Breakfast, offers adult guests a step back to another era when the pace was slower & life simpler. Stroll the woods path, relax in the gazebo covered spa. A few minutes & a couple centuries away from Seattle!

Seattle

Conway, Rita
18821 2nd Ave., SW, 98166
(206) 248-2240

Amenities: 1,2,6,8,10
Breakfast: Continental

Dbl. Oc.: $38.00
Sgl. Oc.: $32.00

Sunset House—Quiet residential area convenient to Sea-Tac Airport. Lovely view of Puget Sound and Olympic Mts. from room and adjacent deck. Private bath, queen bed, color TV. Fine dining nearby. Beautiful sunsets.

AMENITIES

1. No Smoking
2. No Pets
3. No Children
4. Senior Citizen Rates
5. Tennis Available
6. Golf Available
7. Swimming Available
8. Skiing Available
9. Credit Cards Accepted
10. Personal Check Accepted
11. Off Season Rates
12. Dinner Available (w/sufficient notice)

Washington

Seattle

Giles, Chris & Terry
318 W. Galer, 98119
(206) 282-5339

Amenities: 4,8,9,10,11
Breakfast: Full

Dbl. Oc.: $55.00-$80.00
Sgl. Oc.: $50.00-$75.00
Third Person: $15.00

Gater Place Bed & Breakfast—1906 private home; four guest rooms, 2 with private baths. Generous full breakfast, tea & cookies available at all times; hot tub in garden; friendly cozy atmosphere with personal service.

Seattle

Jones, M/M Dick
4915 Linden Ave., N. 98103
(206) 547-6077

Amenities: 1,2,3,5,6,7,9,10,11
Breakfast: Full

Dbl. Oc.: $64.00
Sgl. Oc.: $59.00
Third Person: $11.00

Chelsea Station Bed & Breakfast Inn lies nestled in a quiet, wooded setting within a 5 minute drive to Seattle's activities. Across the street, Woodland Park's Zoo and peaceful rose garden await your arrival.

Seattle

Lucero, Virginia
1405 Queen Anne Ave., North
98109
(206) 281-7037

Amenities: 1,4,9,10
Breakfast: Full

Dbl. Oc.: $55.00-$65.00
Sgl. Oc.: $50.00-$55.00
Third Person: $15.00

Beech Tree Manor—Wood panelling, English wallpaper & matching fabrics create the ambiance of an English country home. Decorated with original art & antique beds. Antique linen shop on premises. Minutes to Seattle center downtown.

Seattle

Sarver, Mrs. Mildred J.
1202 15th Ave., East, 98112
(206) 325-6072

Amenities: 5,6,7,10
Breakfast: Full
Dbl. Oc.: $48.00-$70.00
Sgl. Oc.: $38.00
Third Person: $10.00

Mildred's Bed & Breakfast—Step back in time at this 1890 Victorian home. Old fashioned hospitality; 3 guest rooms & private suite for 2-4. Park & art museum across street. City bus at door—minutes to freeway.

AMENITIES

1. No Smoking
2. No Pets
3. No Children
4. Senior Citizen Rates
5. Tennis Available
6. Golf Available
7. Swimming Available
8. Skiing Available
9. Credit Cards Accepted
10. Personal Check Accepted
11. Off Season Rates
12. Dinner Available (w/sufficient notice)

Washington

Seattle

Sweet, Deborah; McDill, Kate
5005 22nd Ave., N.E., 98105
(206) 522-2536

Amenities: 1,2,9,10
Breakfast: Full
Dbl. Oc.: $50.00-$80.00
Sgl. Oc.: $48.00-$72.00
Third Person: $10.00

Chambered Nautilus Bed & Breakfast Inn, classic 1915 Georgian mansion comfortably furnished with antiques & persians. Quiet location with excellent access to downtown & Univ. of Wash. Some rooms have porches & views. Exquisite breakfast!

Seattle

Vennes, Lee
907 14th Ave., E., 98112
(206) 329-4628

Amenities: 1,2,3,10
Breakfast: Continental

Dbl. Oc.: $65.00
Sgl. Oc.: $55.00
Third Person: $20.00

The Shafer Mansion is ideally located in Seattle's prestigious Capitol Hill area. The second floor suites have old world charm and comfort featuring many antiques.

Seattle

Weaver, Ms. Jody
1526 Palm Ave., SW, 98116
(206) 937-4157

Amenities: 1,3,5,6,7,8,9,10
Breakfast: Continental

Dbl. Oc.: $75.67
Sgl. Oc.: $75.67

Hanson House Bed And Breakfast—This award-winning home has the best view of Seattle in Seattle. Chosen 1 of 100 best B&B in No. America by Frommer's Guide. Private guest solarium with outside deck. 2 Siamese cats in residence. Reserve early

Seattle

Williams, Susan & Doug
1505 4th Ave., N., 98109
(206) 285-0810

Amenities: 1,2,5,9,10
Breakfast: Full

Dbl. Oc.: $50.00-$75.00
Sgl. Oc.: $45.00-$65.00
Third Person: $10.00

Williams House Bed & Breakfast—In turn-of-the-century elegance guests enjoy historic neighborhood & city activities close by. 5 rooms, 3 1/2 baths; views of Puget Sound, mountains, lake & downtown. Children welcomed.

AMENITIES

1. No Smoking
2. No Pets
3. No Children
4. Senior Citizen Rates
5. Tennis Available
6. Golf Available
7. Swimming Available
8. Skiing Available
9. Credit Cards Accepted
10. Personal Check Accepted
11. Off Season Rates
12. Dinner Available (w/sufficient notice)

Washington

Seattle

Wolf, Mrs. Mary A.
2215 E. Prospect, 98112
(206) 322-1752

Amenities: 2,5,6,7,8,9,10
Breakfast: Continental

Dbl. Oc.: $40.00
Sgl. Oc.: $30.00

Capitol Hill House—Near city center and University of Washington. Open all year. Built in 1932, lovely old brick home on tree lined street in a quiet, exclusive neighborhood. Your host is retired from the University, loves to travel.

Seaview

Anderson, Laurie
P.O. Box 250, 98644
(206) 642-2442

Amenities: 1,9,10,11,12
Breakfast: Full

Dbl. Oc.: $85.00
Sgl. Oc.: $79.00
Third Person: $10.00

The Shelburne Inn And Shoalwater Restaurant is surrounded by some of the most stunning scenery on the West Coast. The Shoalwater Restaurant is one of the most widely heralded restaurants in the region. Elegant antique furnishings.

Sequin

Vorhies, Mrs. Margie
120 Forrest Rd., 98382
(206) 683-7011

Amenities: 1,2,3,5,6,7,8,9,10
Breakfast: Full

Dbl. Oc.: $50.00-$79.25
Sgl. Oc.: $45.00-$74.25
Third Person: $15.00

Margie's Bed & Breakfast—A modern ranch-style home. Sequim's only water front B&B near the new John Wayne Marina. Total country comfort, like walking into Mom's. Breathtaking Olympic Peninsula's only sunny spot. Friendly.

Snoqualmie Falls

Potter, Dr./Mrs. Conrad H.
8910A-384th Ave., S.E., 98065
(206) 888-1637

Amenities: 1,2,3,6,8,9
Breakfast: Continental

Dbl. Oc.: $49.00
Sgl. Oc.: $39.00

The Old Honey Farm located on one of Snoqualmie Valley's most beautiful pastoral settings with full view of Mt. Si and Cascades. Easy walk to famous Snoqualmie Falls, Salis Lodge, winery, historic railroad. Skiing & golf.

AMENITIES

1. No Smoking
2. No Pets
3. No Children
4. Senior Citizen Rates
5. Tennis Available
6. Golf Available
7. Swimming Available
8. Skiing Available
9. Credit Cards Accepted
10. Personal Check Accepted
11. Off Season Rates
12. Dinner Available (w/sufficient notice)

Washington

So. Cle Elum

Moore, Monty
Box 2861, 526 Marie, 98943
(509) 674-5939

Amenities: 2,6,8,9,10,12
Breakfast: Full
Dbl. Oc.: $37.63-$84.93
Sgl. Oc.: $32.25-$79.55
Third Person: $10.75

The Moore House Bed & Breakfast—historic railroad hotel nestled in Cascade Foothills, center of recreational wonderland. Bicycle, golf, fish, river raft, X-C ski, sleigh rides. Caboose unit available. Adjacent to Ironhorse State Park.

Spokane

Dunton, Sister
W. 4000 Randolph Rd., 99204
(509) 325-4739

Amenities: 1,2,9,10,12
Breakfast: Continental

Dbl. Oc.: $40.00
Sgl. Oc.: $35.00

Durocher House Bed And Breakfast is located at historic Fort Wright. This Victorian house is surrounded by grace and beauty from the past. Only 4 miles from downtown Spokane. Public transportation.

Vashon Island

Bradley, M/M Jerry
Rt. 1, Box 950, 98070
(206) 567-4832

Amenities: 1,5,6,7,10,11
Breakfast: Continental

Dbl. Oc.: $64.68
Sgl. Oc.: $59.25
Third Person: $5.39

The Island Inn—A lovely Victorian farmhouse set among five acres. Breakfast is served in your room or on the veranda overlooking our gardens, Puget Sound and the Olympic Mountains.

Vashon Island

Keller, Robert
Rte. 3, Box 221, 98070
(206) 463-2646

Amenities: 1,5,6,7,9,10
Breakfast: Continental

Dbl. Oc.: $48.55 & up
Sgl. Oc.: $48.56 & up
Third Person: $5.00

The Swallows Nest Cottages—High on a bluff overlooking Puget Sound & Mt. Ranier, are a brief ferry boat ride from Seattle or Tacoma. Birding, fishing, sailing, & antiquing await you on rural Vashon Island.

AMENITIES

1. No Smoking
2. No Pets
3. No Children
4. Senior Citizen Rates
5. Tennis Available
6. Golf Available
7. Swimming Available
8. Skiing Available
9. Credit Cards Accepted
10. Personal Check Accepted
11. Off Season Rates
12. Dinner Available (w/sufficient notice)

Washington

White Salmon

Stone, Rebeka & Jerry
1980 Hwy. 141, 98672
(509) 395-2786

Amenities: 1,6,8,9,10,11
Breakfast: Continental

Dbl. Oc.: $48.15
Sgl. Oc.: $42.80

Llama Ranch Bed & Breakfast—Five guest rooms with panoramic view of two mountains! Free llama walks! Llamas provide a relaxing atmosphere of serenity, dignity, and beauty. Please come & enjoy yourself as our very special guest. Wind surfing nearby.

AMENITIES

1. No Smoking
2. No Pets
3. No Children
4. Senior Citizen Rates
5. Tennis Available
6. Golf Available
7. Swimming Available
8. Skiing Available
9. Credit Cards Accepted
10. Personal Check Accepted
11. Off Season Rates
12. Dinner Available (w/sufficient notice)

West Virginia

The Mountain State

Capital: Charleston
Statehood: June 20, 1863, the 35th state
State Motto: Mountaineers Are Always Free
State Song: "The West Virginia Hills" and
"West Virginia, My Home Sweet Home"
State Bird: Cardinal
State Flower: Rhododendron
State Tree: Sugar Maple

The state of West Virginia is an outgrowth of the Civil War. Unable to reconcile themselves to the southern philosophy, these western Virginians separated from Virginia at the height of the War and became allied with the union states, and subsequently called this area West Virginia.

West Virginia has some of the same beautiful scenery that Virginia has, along with mineral springs and plenty of hunting and fishing that brings delight to the many fishermen and hunters who come here every year.

The land is very mountainous and rugged, and has extensive bituminous coal beds. The major industry here has been and is coal mining.

Its pleasant climate, hunting, fishing and mineral springs has made it a most attractive state for tourists.

West Virginia

Berkeley Springs

Perry, Peg
201 Independence St.
(304) 258-2021 or 5915

Amenities: 5,6,7,9,10,12
Breakfast: Full

Dbl. Oc.: $45.00-$55.00
Sgl. Oc.: $35.00-$45.00
Third Person: $10.00

Maria's Garden & Inn—Nestled in the heart of town just one block from the famed mineral water and baths and the castle. Maria's Garden offers 10 rooms each individaully decorated and named. Just 5 minutes off I-70.

Charles Town

Heiler, Mrs. Jean Reid
Box 1104, 25414
(304) 725-0637

Amenities: 2,3,6,9,10,12
Breakfast: Full

Dbl. Oc.: $81.00-$135.00
Sgl. Oc.: $81.00-$118.80
Third Person: $21.60

Gilbert House (Middleway)—Magnificent historic home, circa 1760, near Harpers Ferry & I-81. 2 large rooms, 1 deluxe suite, private baths, antiques, oriental rugs, house hospitality. Special celebrations welcome. 5% service charge for credit cards.

Charles Town

Kaetzel, Virginia & Bob
417 E. Washington St., 25414
(304) 728-8003

Amenities: 2,5,6,7,9,10,12
Breakfast: Full

Dbl. Oc.: $71.00-$92.00
Sgl. Oc.: $71.00-$92.00
Third Person: $15.00

The Carriage Inn—Large Colonial home in historical district. All rooms have private baths, fireplaces, queen-sized canopy beds and central air; large yard, front porch with rockers, and private parking facilities.

Charles Town

Santucci, Mrs. Katherine
201 E. Washington St., 25414
(304) 725-8052

Amenities: 2,3,10
Breakfast: Full

Dbl. Oc.: $95.00

Magnus Tate's Kitchen is a short trip from Washington D.C. Stay in your own historic 1796 dwelling with 2 fireplaces, canopy bed, private bath & courtyard entrance. Enjoy shopping, touring, & sports in the historic area.

Gerrardstown

Hucock, Hazel
P.O. Box 135, 25420
(304) 229-3346

Amenities: 2,5,6,7,9,10
Breakfast: Full

Dbl. Oc.: $78.75-$89.25

Prospect Hill Bed & Breakfast—18th century Georgian mansion located 3 miles from I-81 on 225 acres. Furnished in period furniture and antiques. Two large elegant rooms and separate guest cottage, fireplaces, A/C.

AMENITIES

1. No Smoking
2. No Pets
3. No Children
4. Senior Citizen Rates
5. Tennis Available
6. Golf Available
7. Swimming Available
8. Skiing Available
9. Credit Cards Accepted
10. Personal Check Accepted
11. Off Season Rates
12. Dinner Available (w/sufficient notice)

West Virginia

Martinsburg

Sullivan, Owen
601 S. queen St., 25401
(304) 263-1448

Amenities: 1,2,3,6,9,10,12
Breakfast: Full

Dbl. Oc.: $70.00-$95.00

Boydville, The Inn At Martinsburg—Romantic 1812 stone manor house on 10 acres, near Civil War sites, outlet shopping, & recreation. A stately home with all its original details: wallpaper, woodwork, high ceilings.

Mathias

Shipe, Edna & Ernest
Rt. 1, Box 467, 26812
(304) 897-5229

Amenities: 5,7,8,10,12
Breakfast: Full

Dbl. Oc.: $30.00
Sgl. Oc.: $15.00
Third Person: $8.00

Valley View Farm—Lodging by day or night in Lost River Valley. Guest rooms for 6 to 8. Children welcome. Country hospitality and home cooking. Inviting country lanes and backroads, Lost River State park nearby. Infants free.

Morgantown

Bonasso, Nancy & Sam
1000 Stewartstown Rd., 26505
(304) 598-2262

Amenities: 1,2,10
Breakfast: Continental

Dbl. Oc.: $61.04
Sgl. Oc.: $50.14
Porta Crib: $6.00

Chestnut Ridge School B&B is a former elementary school surrounded by scenic attractions and recreation areas. Four tastefully decorated rooms have queen size beds and private marble baths.

Summit Point

Hileman, Mrs. Lisa
P.O. Box 57, 25446
(304) 725-2614

Amenities: 1,2,3,9,10
Breakfast: Continental

Dbl. Oc.: $52.50
Sgl. Oc.: $52.50

Countryside—Enjoy country lodging in quaint village near Harper's Ferry, West Virginia. Old-fashioned hospitality welcomes the traveler with a cheerful rooms, bath, and breakfast amidst rural quiet.

AMENITIES

1. No Smoking
2. No Pets
3. No Children
4. Senior Citizen Rates
5. Tennis Available
6. Golf Available
7. Swimming Available
8. Skiing Available
9. Credit Cards Accepted
10. Personal Check Accepted
11. Off Season Rates
12. Dinner Available (w/sufficient notice)

Wisconsin

The Badger State

Capital: Madison
Statehood: May 29, 1848; the 30th state
State Motto: Forward
State Song: "On Wisconsin"
State Bird: Robin
State Flower: Wood Violet
State Tree: Sugar Maple

Wisconsin means gathering of the waters. Water is everywhere in this state and water means fun. There is much boating and swimming and general all-around recreational activities. The cold and snow of winter brings downhill and cross-country skiing, with great ice-skating on the many ponds and lakes.

Dairy products and farming are the major industries here. Wisconsin is famous for its cheese. The early settlers from Switzerland and Germany brought their knowledge of how to make cheese with them, and it has been something Wisconsin has been famous for since those early times. The farms here also produce wonderful apples and berries.

The people of Wisconsin are proud of their state and are most hospitable and eager that you come and enjoy all their state has to offer.

Wisconsin

Appleton

Riley, Bonnie
402 E. North St., 54911
(414) 733-0200

Amenities: 5,6,7,10
Breakfast: Full
Dbl. Oc.: $61.80
Sgl. Oc.: $51.50

The Parkside is a 1906 Romanesque-styled home located a short walk from Lawrence University and downtown Appleton. 3rd floor suite with private bath, sitting room & balcony, overlooks park. Gourmet breakfast.

Bayfield

Phillips, Mary & Jerry
31 Rittenhouse Ave., Box 584, 54814
(715) 779-5111

Amenities: 1,5,6,7,8,9,10,11,12
Breakfast: Continental
Dbl. Oc.: $79.00-$109.00
Sgl. Oc.: $79.00-$109.00
Third Person: $15.00

Old Rittenhouse Inn—Elegant Victorian dining and lodging in Bayfield's historic district. Guest rooms furnished with antiques & working fireplaces. Open all seasons; by reservation.

Cedarburg

Drefahl, Judith
W62N573 Washington Ave., 53012
(414) 375-3550

Amenities: 2,4,5,6,7,8,9,10
Breakfast: Continental
Dbl. Oc.: $59.99-$129.00
Sgl. Oc.: $59.00-$129.00
Third Person: $10.00

The Washington House Inn—A country Victorian inn located in the Cedarburg historic district. Walking distance to shops & restaurants. Rooms feature antiques, whirlpool baths, TVs. fireplaces & phones.

AMENITIES

1. No Smoking
2. No Pets
3. No Children
4. Senior Citizen Rates
5. Tennis Available
6. Golf Available
7. Swimming Available
8. Skiing Available
9. Credit Cards Accepted
10. Personal Check Accepted
11. Off Season Rates
12. Dinner Available (w/sufficient notice)

Wisconsin

Clintonville

Jansen, Joan & Norman
21 N. Main St., 54929
(715) 823-5734

Amenities: 2,3,6,7,9,10
Breakfast: Full

Dbl. Oc.: $47.25
Sgl. Oc.: $35.70

The Tudor House is a lovley English Tudor within walking distance of churches, shopping, recreation, and restaurants. The house is air conditioned and a private pool is available for guests.

Hartford

Jones, Mary & Art
81 S. Main St., 53027
(414) 673-5643

Amenities: 2,5,6,7,8,10
Breakfast: Full

Dbl. Oc.: $42.00-$52.50
Sgl. Oc.: $36.75-$47.25
Third Person: $5.25

Jordan House—Lovely Victorian home close to shops, restaurants. Drive to golf, tennis, swimming. Near majestic Holy Hill Shrine, Horicon Marsh Flyway, state's largest antique auto museum. Antique shop in home.

Janesville

Sessler, Mrs. Ilah
210 S. Jackson St., 53545
(608) 754-7250

Amenities: 2,4,5,6,7,8,9,10,11
Breakfast: Full

Dbl. Oc.: $49.05
Sgl. Oc.: $38.15
Third Person: $10.90

Jackson Street Inn, near I-90 on Highway 11. Ideally located, 1899 home has oak paneled coffered ceilings, air conditioning, bay windows, bevel glass windows giving rainbow prism effect. Putting green, shuffleboard, brochure.

La Farge

Boyett, Ms. Rosanne
Rt. 2, Box 121, 54639
(608) 625-4492

Amenities: 2,7,8,10,11
Breakfast: Full

Dbl. Oc.: $63.00
Sgl. Oc.: $52.50
Third Person: $10.50

Trillium—A cozy private country cottage plus farm breakfast. Bike; canoe; hike; ski. Completely furnished, plus stone fireplace & large porch overlooking woods & fields. Nearby lakes, rivers & state parks. Open year round.

Madison

Elder, Mrs. Polly
424 N. Pinckney St., 53703
(608) 255-3999

Amenities: 2,3,9,10,12
Breakfast: Continental

Dbl. Oc.: $112.00-$258.00
Sgl. Oc.: $90.00-$236.00
Third Person: $20.00

Mansion Hill Inn—Victorian elegance in eleven exquisite rooms. Fireplaces, private baths with whirlpools, valet service. In town near capitol and university. Whether a soujourn of business or pleasure, we await your arrival.

AMENITIES

1. No Smoking
2. No Pets
3. No Children
4. Senior Citizen Rates
5. Tennis Available
6. Golf Available
7. Swimming Available
8. Skiing Available
9. Credit Cards Accepted
10. Personal Check Accepted
11. Off Season Rates
12. Dinner Available (w/sufficient notice)

Wisconsin

Manitowoc

Mahloch, M/M Allen
2104 Madson Rd., 54220
(414) 775-4404

Amenities: 5,6,7,8
Breakfast: Continental

Dbl. Oc.: $25.00
Sgl. Oc.: $22.00
Third Person: $30.00

Mahloch's Cozy B&B—125 year old remodelled log house. Beverage, cheese & crackers in evening, full bath with shower, two rooms—1 has 2 single beds. 45 acres to hike, ski, ride, bike. 7 miles west of city. Chilren welcome.

Menomonie

Dahl, Kari & John
2013 Wilson St., 54751
(715) 235-1792

Amenities: 5,6,7,8,10
Breakfast: Full

Dbl. Oc.: $44.00
Sgl. Oc.: $37.00
Third Person: $10.00

The Katy May House—1½ acres of heaven located 1 hour east of the Twin Cities on I-94. Enjoy bike trails, museums, theatre, fine restaurants, or relaxing on the beautiful veranda. 4 rooms share 2 baths.

Newton

Stuntz, Judie & Pete
8825 Willever Lane, 53063
(414) 726-4388

Amenities: 7,8,10
Breakfast: Full
Dbl. Oc.: $36.75
Sgl. Oc.: $26.25
Third Person: $10.50

Rambling Hills Tree Farm—Modern country home on 50 acres with scenic view of pond nestled among rolling hills. Located in popular lakeshore area 71 miles north of Milwaukee, 3 miles off I-43. Call for reservations, directions.

Sparta

Justin, Donna & Don
Rt. 1, Box 263, 54656
(608) 269-4522

Amenities: 1,2,8,9,10
Breakfast: Full
Dbl. Oc.: $63.00
Sgl. Oc.: $47.25
Third Person: $10.50

Just - N - Trails
Bed & Breakfast

Just-N-Trails Bed & Breakfast—Four Laura Ashley rooms, shared bath, charming "country" farmhouse, new handcrafted log cabin, hearty breakfast. Dairy farm near Elroy-Sparta and Lacrosse River. Bike trails, Amish community, 20 K. X/C ski & hike.

AMENITIES

1. No Smoking
2. No Pets
3. No Children
4. Senior Citizen Rates
5. Tennis Available
6. Golf Available
7. Swimming Available
8. Skiing Available
9. Credit Cards Accepted
10. Personal Check Accepted
11. Off Season Rates
12. Dinner Available (w/sufficient notice)

Wyoming

The Equality State

Capital: Cheyenne
Statehood: July 10, 1890; the 44th state
State Motto: Equal Rights
State Song: "Wyoming"
State Bird: Meadow Lark
State Flower: Indian Paintbrush
State Tree: Cottonwood

This is a very beautiful and scenic state. Its climate is dry and sunny with cold and snowy winters and warm summers. The majestic Rocky Mountain peaks tower over much of this land. The oldest national park, Yellowstone, was founded here by John Colter in 1807. The first national monument, Devil's Tower, was dedicated by President Teddy Roosevelt. The beautiful Teton Park and Fort Laramie, established in 1840 to protect the white man from Indians as he crossed this state in covered wagons, contribute to the fascination of this state for tourists.

Women won the right to vote here in 1869 and in 1870, Esther Morris became the first Justice of the Peace in the U.S. In 1925, Nellie Tayloe Ross became the first woman to become Governor.

Wyoming

Big Horn

Spahn, Bobbie & Ron
Box 579, 82833
(307) 674-8150

Amenities: 9,10,12
Breakfast: Continental

Dbl. Oc.: $46.35
Sgl. Oc.: $36.05
Third Person: $10.30

Spann's Big Horn Mountain B&B—Owner built log lodge nestled in pines high on the mountain overlooking Sheridan, Wyoming. Hiking trails, with deer and moose, lead to over a million acres of national forest. Close to I-90.

Bondurant

Warburton, Denise & Brad
Box 33, 82922
(307) 733-1184

Amenities: 8,9,10,12
Breakfast: Full

Dbl. Oc.: $46.35
Sgl. Oc.: $36.05
Third Person: $10.30

Fall River Ranch & Outfitters—For those who want a taste of the "Old West." Log cabins surrounded by forest with the Hoback River running by; horses and fishing. 40 miles south of Jackson, Hwy. 189, turn at 139 mile marker, 8 miles.

Casper

McInroy, Mrs. Opal
5120 Alcova, Rt., Box 40, 82604
(307) 265-6819

Amenities: 1,2,10,12
Breakfast: Full

Dbl. Oc.: $40.00
Sgl. Oc.: $35.00
Third Person: $5.00

Bessemer Bend Bed And Breakfast—Large home in scenic area 10 miles southwest of Casper on North Platte River. 2 miles from fish hatchery. Historic area; wildlife; tours arranged; free transportation to Casper air and bus lines; fishing.

Cody

Baldwin, Cindy & Mark
109 W. Yellowstone, 82414
(307) 587-6074

Amenities: 1,2,5,6,7,8,9,10,11
Breakfast: Full

Dbl. Oc.: $63.00
Sgl. Oc.: $63.00
Third Person: $8.00

The Lockhart Bed & Breakfast Inn—Historic author's home, restored & furnished with antiques, private baths. AAA rated; 50 miles east of Yellowstone National Park. Parlor for visiting, complimentary hot beverages & brandy, warm friendly western hospitality.

Devils Tower

Robinson, Gisele & Pete
R-Place. 82714
(307) 467-5938

Amenities: 1,2,3,4,10,11
Breakfast: Continental

Dbl. Oc.: $45.00
Sgl. Oc.: $45.00
Third Person: $7.00

R-Place—Luxury/modest country home at the foot of Devils Tower Nat'l. Monument. Unique kingsize room with terrific view. Private deck entrance, shower. Swedish & German spoken. Host former park supt.

AMENITIES

1. No Smoking
2. No Pets
3. No Children
4. Senior Citizen Rates
5. Tennis Available
6. Golf Available
7. Swimming Available
8. Skiing Available
9. Credit Cards Accepted
10. Personal Check Accepted
11. Off Season Rates
12. Dinner Available (w/sufficient notice)

Wyoming

Douglas

Akers, Dr. Lucy
81 Inez Rd., 82633
(307) 358-3741

Amenities: 2,9,10,11,12
Breakfast: Full

Dbl. Oc.: $46.80
Sgl. Oc.: $41.60
Third Person: $15.60

Akers Ranch Bed & Breakfast—Located in east-central Wyoming, 1 mile off I-25. This working cattle ranch offers scenic vistas & wide open spaces. 5 guest rooms separate from the main house. Evening desserts & snacks complimentary. 10% off Nov.-March.

Douglas

Pellatz, Betty & Don
1031 Steinle Rd., Rt. 2, 82633
(307) 358-2380

Amenities: 1,2,7,10,12
Breakfast: Full

Dbl. Oc.: $25.00-$55.00
Sgl. Oc.: $25.00-$55.00

Pellatz Ranch—Experience real ranch life—50 miles north of Douglas, on Hwy. 59 to Billings, 11 miles N.E. on Co. Rd. 40. Daily chores, riding, trail rides, rock hunting, cook-outs. Discover western hospitality.

Jackson Hole

McGinnis, Laury
Box 7453,
Winchester Station, 83001
(307) 733-1981

Amenities: 1,2,5,6,7,8,9,10,11
Breakfast: Full

Dbl. Oc.: $85.00-$135.00
Sgl. Oc.: $85.00-$135.00
Third Person: $15.00

Big Mountain Inn—Secluded quiet inn located on 7 wooded acres, decorated with antiques, private bath, full breakfast, color TV, close to skiing, golf, tennis, & swimming. 9 miles from Grand Teton National Park.

Savery

Saer, J.B.
Box 24, 82332
(307) 383-7840

Amenities: 4,5,6,7,8,9,10,11,12
Breakfast: Full

Dbl. Oc.: $55.00-$85.00
Sgl. Oc.: $30.00-$45.00
Third Person: $20.00

YL Hideaway Holiday - Working Ranch—Delightful & untouristy. Historic rambling ranch house & cabins with fireplaces & private baths. Superb horseback riding, fly fishing & meals. 9 miles of Savery at end of dirt road. Child under 4 free.

Wilson

Hardeman, Lois & Howard
Box 22, 83014
(307) 733-2462

Amenities: 2,10
Breakfast: Full

Dbl. Oc.: $58.85
Sgl. Oc.: $42.80
Third Person: $10.00

Eagle's Nest Bed & Breakfast—A cozy ranch home located in the quiet village of Wilson just 8 miles from downtown Jackson in Jackson Hole country. Gateway to Grand Teton and Yellowstone National Parks.

AMENITIES

1. No Smoking
2. No Pets
3. No Children
4. Senior Citizen Rates
5. Tennis Available
6. Golf Available
7. Swimming Available
8. Skiing Available
9. Credit Cards Accepted
10. Personal Check Accepted
11. Off Season Rates
12. Dinner Available (w/sufficient notice)

Bed & Breakfast Homes & Inns in the Provinces of Canada, Bermuda, Puerto Rico & U.S. Virgin Islands

Alberta

The Westernmost Prairie Province of Canada

Capital: Edmonton
Entered The Dominion: September 1, 1905; the 8th province
The Floral Emblem: Wild Rose

Alberta is the largest of the prairie provinces. Because of the oil boom in 1947, it is one of the wealthiest provinces as well.

Some of the most attractive scenery to be found is in this area are the majestic snow-capped Canadian Rockies, and Banff and Jasper National Parks. Tourists can ride horseback through these areas, as well as enjoy boating, golfing and swimming.

Alberta

Canmore

Doucette, Ms. Patricia
P.O. Box 1162
(403) 678-4751

Amenities: 1,2,5,6,7,8,11,12
Breakfast: Full

Dbl. Oc.: $40.00-$50.00
Sgl. Oc.: $25.00-$35.00
Third Person: $10.00-$15.00

Cougar Creek Inn—Quaint, quiet mountain home. Rugged mountain scenery. All types of summer/winter outdoor activities available. Guests have their own private entrance, sitting room, fireplace, bath, dining room. Meals are hearty.

Gwynne

Glaser, Mrs. Mable
Gwynalta Farms, T0C 1L0
(403) 352-3587

Amenities:
Breakfast: Full

Dbl. Oc.: $25.00
Sgl. Oc.: $20.00

Gwynalta Farms—Working dairy farm close to Alberta's capital of Edmonton. A quite average farm with plenty of complimentary coffee and fellowship.

Nanton

Squire, Rosemary & Sam
RR #1, T0L 1R0
(403) 646-5789, 646-2736

Amenities: 4,5,6,7,8,12
Breakfast: Full

Dbl. Oc.: $40.00 (Can.)
Sgl. Oc.: $25.00 (Can.)

Squire Ranch—Situated in the foothills of the Rockies, our Christian ranch offers a serene setting close to areas of interest; enroute to Calgary, Banff, Kanaskis, & Waterton. Riding, playground, indoor games.

Okotoks

Samek, Mrs. Jennifer
Box 8, Site 1, RR 2, T0L 1T0
(403) 938-5755

Amenities: 1,2,3
Breakfast: Full

Dbl. Oc.: $45.00
Sgl. Oc.: $30.00

Wildflower country House Bed And Breakfast—20 minutes south of Calgary. 2 cozy bedrooms, peace and quiet on 20 acres. Convenient to Canadian Rockies, Banff Park, Tyrrell Museum, winter ski resorts.

Rocky Mountain House

Kennedy, Claire & Larry
Box 1636, T0M 1T0
(403) 845-6786

Amenities: 2,8,10,12
Breakfast: Full

Dbl. Oc.: $70.00
Sgl. Oc.: $70.00
Third Person: $35.00

Terratima Lodge—A small warm hospitable family-run year round lodge with antiques. Fishing, hiking, X-crossing; minimum 2 nights; brochure available. 16 miles southwest of Rocky Mountain House.

AMENITIES

1. No Smoking
2. No Pets
3. No Children
4. Senior Citizen Rates
5. Tennis Available
6. Golf Available
7. Swimming Available
8. Skiing Available
9. Credit Cards Accepted
10. Personal Check Accepted
11. Off Season Rates
12. Dinner Available (w/sufficient notice)

Alberta

Turner Valley

Lyon, Doris & Douglas
656 Royalite Way, S.E.,
Box 771, T0L 2A0
(403) 933-4714

Amenities: 5,6,7,8,12
Breakfast: Full

Dbl. Oc.: $38.00
Sgl. Oc.: $20.00
Third Person: $8.00

Bighorn Pension Bed And Breakfast—Situated in the center of the Turner Valley Golf and Country Club, within minutes of the Kananaskis Country, the Alberta Rockies, the Foothills Country, & its abundance of sports & outdoor recreation. Close to the Olympic City of Calgary. Four season accommodations.

British Columbia

Canada's Third Largest Province

Capital: Victoria
Entered The Dominion: July 20, 1871; the 6th province
Motto: Unfailing Splendor
The Floral Emblem: Flowering Dogwood

British Columbia is the westernmost province of Canada. It is a powerful province with great potential. It possesses great lands that can be used to grow crops, large mineral deposits, and enormous tracts of forest.

Victoria is the capitol of this province and has an excellent harbor. Visitors come from all over to purchase imported goods that come into this harbor as well as Vancouver's harbor on this southwestern coast.

The temperature is pleasant. Because of the mild winds from the Pacific Ocean, British Columbia's coast in the winter is fairly warm and cool in the summer. This king of moderate climate makes for a wide range of recreational advantages.

British Columbia

Brentwood Bay
(Vancouver Island)

Turner, Marion & Donald
7212 Peden Ln.,
Box 88, V0S 1A0
(604) 652-9828

Amenities: 1,2,5,6,7,9
Breakfast: Full

Dbl. Oc.: $39.00-$49.00 (Can.)
Sgl. Oc.: $29.00 (Can.)

Bobbing Boats—Sunny waterfront home with Salmon fishing marina, near Butchart Gardens, on bus route to Victoria. Modern village shopping centre; newly renovated guest facilities. Friendly Dalmation lives here!

Campbell River

Arbour, Ted
1760 Island Highway, V9W 2E7
(604) 287-7446

Amenities: 1,4,5,6,7,8,9,11,12
Breakfast: Continental
Dbl. Oc.: $63.72 (Can.)
Sgl. Oc.: $52.92 (Can.)
Third Person: $7.00 (Can.)

Campbell River Lodge—Built in 1948, this lodge contains: sauna, whirlpool, pub, dining room, entertainment, satellite TV, & childrens' playground. Small pets allowed. Boat & experienced guides available for famous salt water Salmon fishing.

Mayne Island

Somerville, Karen & Ken
Campbell Bay Rd., V0N 2J0
(604) 539-3133

Amenities: 1,2,3,4,5,7,9,12
Breakfast: Full

Dbl. Oc.: $54.00-$85.00 (Can.)
Sgl. Oc.: $49.00-$80.00 (Can.)
Third Person: $20.00 (Can.)

Gingerbread House—A fully restored heritage home, circa 1900. Each color coordinated guest room emphasises comfort & elegance. Most rooms with water views. Located in the heart of Canadian Gulf Islands, renowned for Salmon fishing.

East Kelowna

Karius, Dianne & Elroy
3950 Borland Rd.,
Box 158, V0H 1G0
(604) 763-9333

Amenities: 1,2,5,6,7,8,10,11
Breakfast: Full

Dbl. Oc.: $40.00
Sgl. Oc.: $30.00
Third Person: $10.00

Kalkar Acres—Quiet country home with fabulous view of orchards, lake, canyon, minutes away from city. Large rooms, separate guest bath, full breakfast. R.V. and horse trailers accommodated. A pleasant stay awaits you.

AMENITIES

1. No Smoking
2. No Pets
3. No Children
4. Senior Citizen Rates
5. Tennis Available
6. Golf Available
7. Swimming Available
8. Skiing Available
9. Credit Cards Accepted
10. Personal Check Accepted
11. Off Season Rates
12. Dinner Available (w/sufficient notice)

British Columbia

Mill Bay

Clarke, Barbara & Cliff
3191 Mutter Rd., V0R 2P0
(604) 743-4083

Amenities: 1,2,9,10
Breakfast: Full
Dbl. Oc.: $70.20
Sgl. Oc.: $37.80
Third Person: $16.20

Pinelodge Farm Bed And Breakfast—Charming Pine lodge built on a hillside overlooking the ocean with breathtaking views of sea & islands. Walking trails, fields & farm animals add to the paradise-like setting, 25 miles north of Victoria, B.C.

New Westminster

Van Kessel, Alice & Gerry **Amenities:** 5,7,10 **Dbl. Oc.:** $40.00
325 Pine St., V3L 2T1 **Breakfast:** Full **Sgl. Oc.:** $25.00
(604) 526-0978

Welcome! We invite you to share our turn-of-the-century home remodeled for your comfort. Enjoy true Dutch hospitality. Close to stores, parks, restaurants & 20 minutes north of Skytrain ride into downtown Vancouver.

North Vancouver

Chalmers, Donna & Guy
1617 Grand Blvd., V7L 3Y2
(604) 988-6719

Amenities: 2
Breakfast: Full
Dbl. Oc.: $55.00-$85.00
Sgl. Oc.: $40.00-$60.00
Third Person: $10.00-$20.00

Grand Manor Bed & Breakfast—Heritage house built in 1914 in the heart of North Vancouver. Public transportation across the street, 20 min. from downtown. Rooms are newly renovated in the charm & character of days gone by. Breakfast in dining room; $5.00 more for 1 night stays.

AMENITIES

1. No Smoking
2. No Pets
3. No Children
4. Senior Citizen Rates
5. Tennis Available
6. Golf Available
7. Swimming Available
8. Skiing Available
9. Credit Cards Accepted
10. Personal Check Accepted
11. Off Season Rates
12. Dinner Available (w/sufficient notice)

British Columbia

North Vancouver

Evers, Dorothy & Allan
4388 Prospect Rd., V7N 3L7
(604) 980-5800

Amenities: 2,3,5,6,7,8,11
Breakfast: Full

Dbl. Oc.: $55.00 (Can.)
Sgl. Oc.: $50.00 (Can.)

Prospect B&B—In modern home; quiet area; view overlooking Vancouver. Full breakfast includes homemade bread & jam. Double bed, private bath ensuite. Color TV, phone. 8 minutes to bus. Shops & pub 1 mile.

Tofino

Mae, Ms. Olivia A.
Box 188, V0R 2Z0
(604) 725-3998

Amenities: 5,6,9
Breakfast: Continental

Dbl. Oc.: $75.60
Sgl. Oc.: $75.60
Third Person: $48.60

"Silver Cloud"—Wooded, quiet & very private. 2 wings with kitchen. "Silver Cloud" is as unique & delightfully surprising as the sea itself. Do book well ahead.

Ucluelet

Burley, Ron
1078 Helen Rd., V0R 3A0
(604) 726-4444

Amenities: 1,2,3,5,6,7,9
Breakfast: Continental

Dbl. Oc.: $48.60
Sgl. Oc.: $43.20
Third Person: $16.20

Burley's Lodge—Waterfront, guest lounge, recreation room, pool table, rowboat, horseshoes, close to beach & lighthouse, hiking trails, twin, double and water beds, color TV, decks, lawn, shorebirds, Eagles, Herons, Pacific Rim Park.

Vernon

Pringle, Colleen & Rod
Site 10, Comp. 16,
R.R. #4, V1T 6L7
(604) 542-8293

Amenities: 1,5,6,7,10
Breakfast: Full

Dbl. Oc.: $50.00
Sgl. Oc.: $45.00
Third Person: $15.00

Twin Willows By The Lake—Beautiful lakefront home in Canada's sunbelt. Private suite, bath, fridge, TV, patio, entrance, queen bed, 2 sofa beds; enjoy wharf, rowboat, hammock, & giant willows; homemade jam, farm eggs, wholewheat pancakes, fresh fruit in season.

AMENITIES

1. No Smoking
2. No Pets
3. No Children
4. Senior Citizen Rates
5. Tennis Available
6. Golf Available
7. Swimming Available
8. Skiing Available
9. Credit Cards Accepted
10. Personal Check Accepted
11. Off Season Rates
12. Dinner Available (w/sufficient notice)

British Columbia

Victoria

Flavelle, Sharon & Bill
10858 Madrona Dr., R.R. #1, V8L 3R9
(604) 656-9549

Amenities: 4,5,6,7,10,11
Breakfast: Full
Dbl. Oc.: $50.00-$95.00

Great Snoring On Sea—Let us pamper you at our luxurious antique-furnished villa on a cliff overlooking the sea. 2 ensuites, pool, towreing forests, quaint Empress Hotel, Butchart Gardens, San Juan Island. Ferries nearby.

Victoria

MacDonald, Michele & Ian
5373 Pat Bay Hwy. (17), V8Y 1S9
(604) 658-8404, 658-5531

Amenities: 2,7,9,10,11
Breakfast: Full

Dbl. Oc.: $41.92 (Can.)
Sgl. Oc.: $36.68 (Can.)
Third Person: $10.36 (Can.)

Tucker's Bed & Breakfast—A delightful lakeside B&B offering hearty home cooking, character rooms, all the charm of the country but convenient to downtown Victoria. Butchart Gardens & ferries. Hobby farm.

Victoria

Hicks, Mrs. Brenda
5259 Patricia Bay,
Hwy. (17), V8Y 1S8
(604) 658-8879

Amenities: 9,10,11
Breakfast: Full

Dbl. Oc.: $54.00-$60.48
Sgl. Oc.: $41.00-$45.36
Third Person: $15.00

Elk Lake Lodge—Built in 1910 as a chapel, Elk Lake Lodge has been beautifully restored. Four individually decorated guest rooms, a magnificent lounge & an outdoor hot tub. Fifteen minutes from the ferry and Victoria.

Victoria

Lydon, Mrs.
747 Helvetia Cr., V8Y 1M1
(604) 658-5519

Amenities: 1,2,5,6,7,10
Breakfast: Full

Dbl. Oc.: $35.00
Sgl. Oc.: $20.00

Hibernia Bed And Breakfast—15 min. from Victoria, close to Butchart Gardens, beaches, restaurants, 5 min. off Hwy. I-7, 8N. Cul-de sac with lawns, trees & vines, no traffic noise. Antique furnishings, full homemade Irish breakfast, TV room.

AMENITIES

1. No Smoking
2. No Pets
3. No Children
4. Senior Citizen Rates
5. Tennis Available
6. Golf Available
7. Swimming Available
8. Skiing Available
9. Credit Cards Accepted
10. Personal Check Accepted
11. Off Season Rates
12. Dinner Available (w/sufficient notice)

British Columbia

Victoria

Gordon, Pat
1144 Dallas Rd., V8V 1C1
(604) 383-7098

Amenities: 1,2,3,11
Breakfast: Full

Dbl. Oc.: $60.00
Sgl. Oc.: $40.00

Seaviews Bed & Breakfast—Beautiful views of the Olympic Mts. from our seafront home beside Beacon Hill Park. A quote in the San Francisco Examiner Sept. 7, 1986, "Of interest to tourists is the Seaview B&B only 5 mins. from the City Center."

Victoria

McKechnie, Bill
998 Humbolt St., V8V 2Z8
(604) 384-4044

Amenities: 2,9
Breakfast: Full
Dbl. Oc.: $84.24-$170.64
Third Person: $24.30

Beaconfield Inn is an award-winning restoration of an English mansion. Walk downtown; antiques throughout; rich textures: velvets, leather, warm woods; delicious breakfast and pampering service.

Victoria

Verduyn, Mrs. Pamela
670 Battery St., V8V 1E5
(604) 385-4632

Amenities: 1,2,10
Breakfast: Full

Dbl. Oc.: $40.00-$60.00
Sgl. Oc.: $25.00-$40.00
Third Person: $10.00-$15.00

Battery Street Guest House—Comfortable guesthouse (1898) in downtown Victoria. Centrally located, within walking distance to town & sites. Park & ocean one block away. Hostess speaks Dutch as well as English.

Whistler

Morel, Ursula & Jacques
7162 Nancy Green Dr.
V0N 1B0
(604) 932-3641

Amenities: 1,2,3,4,5,6,7,8,9,10,11,12
Breakfast: Full

Dbl. Oc.: $49.00 & Up (Can.)
Sgl. Oc.: $39.00 & Up (Can.)
Third Person: $20.00 (Can.)

Edlelweiss Pension—Traditional European hospitality in walking distance to lifts, village & Lost Lake & Park. View rooms with balconies, down comforters, priv. bathrooms, sauna, guest lounge. Full gourmet breakfast.

AMENITIES

1. No Smoking
2. No Pets
3. No Children
4. Senior Citizen Rates
5. Tennis Available
6. Golf Available
7. Swimming Available
8. Skiing Available
9. Credit Cards Accepted
10. Personal Check Accepted
11. Off Season Rates
12. Dinner Available (w/sufficient notice)

New Brunswick

One of Canada's Four Atlantic Provinces

Capital: Fredericton
Entered The Dominion: July 1, 1867
Provincial Motto: Hope Restored
Floral Emblem: Purple Violet

New Brunswick is one of the original provinces of Canada. It has great natural beauty. Forest covers about 90% of the land yet in the St. John River Valley area there is rich farmland where potatoes are grown in great abundance.

More than one half of the people of this province live in the cities and towns. St. John is the largest city and chief industrial and shipping center. Most of the people are French descent, some are decendents from the United Empire Loyalists who left the U.S. after the Revolutionary War. This event of 1783 is still celebrated every year on May 18th in St. John.

New Brunswick has one of the best fishing grounds in North America. Thousands of visitors come here yearly to enjoy fishing, boating and swimming off the Banks of the Bay of Fundy and the Gulf of St. Lawrence.

New Brunswick

Sackville

Hanrahan, Georgette & Richard
146 West Main, E0A 3C0
(506) 536-1291

Amenities: 5,6,7,9
Breakfast: Continental

Dbl. Oc.: $47.00
Sgl. Oc.: $38.00
Third Person: $7.00

The Different Drummer—Spacious Victorian house 10 minute walk from restaurants and shops. 8 bedrooms with private baths and furnished with antiques. 15 minutes to Nova Scotia border, 45 minutes to PEI ferry.

St. Andrews

Lazare, M/M Michael
59 Carleton St., E0G 2X0
(506) 529-3834

Amenities: 2,3,5,6,7,9,10,12
Breakfast: Full

Dbl. Oc.: $65.00 (Can.)
Sgl. Oc.: $55.00 (Can.)
Third Person: $12.50

Pansy Patch's deck overlooks the Bay of Fundy. It is a unique turreted house with antique-filled guest rooms. Breakfasts consist of a different fresh fruit & waffles, pancakes or eggs or French toast.

St. Andrews

Parke, Eleanor & Bob
208 Prince of Wales St.
P.O. Box 318, E0G 2X0
(506) 529-3445

Amenities: 1,2,3,5,6
Breakfast: Continental

Dbl. Oc.: $55.00-$65.00

Pippincott—First class all the way! Gracious hosts welcome you to their quiet 1860 home in the historic resort town. Private baths, homebaked treats. Short walk to restaurants, shops, waterfront.

AMENITIES

1. No Smoking
2. No Pets
3. No Children
4. Senior Citizen Rates
5. Tennis Available
6. Golf Available
7. Swimming Available
8. Skiing Available
9. Credit Cards Accepted
10. Personal Check Accepted
11. Off Season Rates
12. Dinner Available (w/sufficient notice)

Nova Scotia

One Of The Four Atlantic Provinces Of Canada

Capital: Halifax
Entered The Dominion: July 1, 1867;
                        one of the four original provinces
Provincial Motto: One Offends and The Other Conquers
The Floral Emblem: Trailing Arbutus

    Halifax is the capital of Nova Scotia and was founded in 1749 by an English Governor named Cornwallis. He made this city the capital, and to this day it has remained very pro English and proud of its British connection.
    Halifax is an extremely busy and large shipping port, perhaps one of the busiest in the world.
    The beaches and resorts of Nova Scotia are beautiful, and visitors travel from all over to see and enjoy them. There is great hunting and fishing in this area as well. The climate is conducive to many sports; it never gets too hot nor too cold.
    One can read more about Nova Scotia and its early times in Henry Wadsworth Longfellow's poem, Evangeline.

Nova Scotia

Annapolis Royal N.S.

Williams, Iris Mrs.
124 Victoria St.,
Box, 277, B0S 1A0
(902) 532-7936

Amenities: 1,2
Breakfast: Continental

Dbl. Oc.: $49.50
Sgl. Oc.: $47.30
Third Person: $8.80

The Poplars Bed & Breakfast is one block east of main traffic light on Hwy. #1. 2 blocks to all amenities and attractions. Victorian heritage home with 6 rooms in attached carriage house each with full bath. Complimentary evening coffee.

Collingwood

Beattie, Bernice & Joe
B0M 1E0
(902) 686-3381

Amenities: 1,2,6,8,11,12
Breakfast: Full

Dbl. Oc.: $30.00-$32.00
Sgl. Oc.: $25.00
Third Person: $7.50

Cobequid Hills Country Inn—15 minutes from Hwy. 104, exit 6, to village, left 1/2 mile. Tour scenic Glooscap & Sunrise trails from here. Cozy home nestled in hills, lawns, gardens, river in back, Relaxed comfort.

Halifax

McKeever, William
5184 Morris St., B3J 1B3
(902) 420-0658

Amenities: 2,9,12
Breakfast: Continental
Dbl. Oc.: $77.00-$88.00
Sgl. Oc.: $88.00-$98.00
Third Person: $10.00

The Halliburton House Inn—An elegant inn in the heart of historic downtown Halifax. Gracious 1820 heritage home furnished in antiques. Convenient waterfront location. Sightseeing, gardens, dining, shops in walking distance.

N.E. Margaree

Hart, Mary & Laird
B0E 2H0
(902) 248-2765

Amenities: 6,7,10
Breakfast: Full

Dbl. Oc.: $44.00
Sgl. Oc.: $27.50

Heart of Harts Tourist Home—100 year old country home. 5 double rooms, 4 cottages, 3 mobile homes. Restaurants, museums, & gift shops close by. Trout & Salmon fishing on property. Hiking in area.

AMENITIES

1. No Smoking
2. No Pets
3. No Children
4. Senior Citizen Rates
5. Tennis Available
6. Golf Available
7. Swimming Available
8. Skiing Available
9. Credit Cards Accepted
10. Personal Check Accepted
11. Off Season Rates
12. Dinner Available (w/sufficient notice)

Nova Scotia

Parrsboro

Boles, Kathy & Bruce
17 Western Ave., Box 247, B0M 1S0
(902) 254-3735

Amenities: 1,2,5,6,8,9,12
Breakfast: Full
Dbl. Oc.: $41.80-$71.50
Sgl. Oc.: $41.80-$71.50
Third Person: $8.80

The Maple Inn—Century old house, private & shared baths, 3 room suite with whirlpool. One block from live summer theatre, dining room specializing in local fare—seafood, maple syrup delights & produce. Licensed.

Pugwash

Bond, Bonnie
Box 405, B0K 1L0
(902) 243-2900

Amenities: 2,5,6,9,10
Breakfast: Continental

Dbl. Oc.: $38.00-$44.00
Sgl. Oc.: $36.00-$40.00
Third Person: $7.00

The Blue Heron Inn—A charming renovated inn in the village of Pugwash. Tennis, swimming, boating and golf close by. Off season phone number (902) 243-2516.

AMENITIES

1. No Smoking
2. No Pets
3. No Children
4. Senior Citizen Rates
5. Tennis Available
6. Golf Available
7. Swimming Available
8. Skiing Available
9. Credit Cards Accepted
10. Personal Check Accepted
11. Off Season Rates
12. Dinner Available (w/sufficient notice)

Ontario

Canada's Second Largest Province

Capital: Toronto
Entered The Dominion: July 1, 1867;
 one of the four original provinces
Motto: Loyal She Began, Loyal She Remains
The Floral Emblem: White Trillium

Ontario is most properous in agriculture and industry. There are still large farms in this province, even though more than half of its population is urbanized.

Ottawa, the capital of Canada, is situated in this province, and here most of the population is employed by the government. Toronto, the capital of Ontario, is large and modern, and gradually becoming the metropolis and center for all English Canada.

The history of this province is interesting. It was first settled by British loyalists who left the American colonies after the Revolutionary War ended in defeat for the English. As a result, they set the pattern for social behavior, architecture and style of living, which gives it a stong American bond.

There are many lakes which offer a variety of vacation attractions in Ontario. The southern areas along Lake Erie and Ontario are sunny and make for enjoyable vacationing.

The Dionne quintuplets were born here in Callander in 1934, and insulin was discovered here by Frederick Banting and Charles Best in 1921.

Ontario

Alma

Grose, Mrs. Sharon
R.R. #2, N0B 1A0
(519) 846-9788

Amenities: 1,8,10,12
Breakfast: Full

Dbl. Oc.: $60.00 (Can.)
Sgl. Oc.: $40.00 (Can.)
Third Person: $20.00 (Can.)

Washa Farms—1877 home mixes past & present: air-conditioning, jacuzzi & antiques. Enjoy quiet rest away from hustle & bustle. 200 acres to stroll, cattle, horses & hens. Visit Elora Gorge, farmers' market, Menonite area crafts.

Alton

Hough, Jennifer & Rodney
R.R. #2, L0N 1A0
(519) 927-5779

Amenities: 2,5,6,8,9,12
Breakfast: Continental

Dbl. Oc.: $58.85
Sgl. Oc.: $37.45
Third Person: $21.40

Caratact Inn—An historical country inn completely renovated. With overnight rooms, two shared baths, and a sixty seat dining room. South of Hwy. 136 and 24 in Caledon (Cataract) one hour from Toronto.

Ancaster

Morin, Marcy & George
1034 Hwy. 53 W., L9G 3K9
(416) 648-5225

Amenities: 6,8,9,10,12
Breakfast: Full

Dbl. Oc.: $100.00
Sgl. Oc.: $90.00
Third Person: $30.00

The Philip Shaver House Country Inn is situated in a one-acre country setting on the outskirts of Ancaster. This Georgian mansion was built in 1835 by Philip Shaver whose ancestors settled in the area in 1789.

Bancroft

Montgomery, Mrs. R.
RR 2, K0L 1C0
(613) 332-4369

Amenities: 1,2,5,6,7,10,12
Breakfast: Continental

Dbl. Oc.: $35.00
Sgl. Oc.: $25.00

Grant's General Store & Country Inn—Baptiste Village built in the early 1900's. Rooms and coffee shop maintained in that era. Shared bathroom; verandah overlooks lake. Hwy. 62 or 28 north to Bancroft turn left at Birds Creek, go 4 miles.

AMENITIES

1. No Smoking
2. No Pets
3. No Children
4. Senior Citizen Rates
5. Tennis Available
6. Golf Available
7. Swimming Available
8. Skiing Available
9. Credit Cards Accepted
10. Personal Check Accepted
11. Off Season Rates
12. Dinner Available (w/sufficient notice)

Ontario

Bracerbridge

Rickard, Janet & Peter
17 Dominion St., P0B 1C0
(705) 645-2245

Amenities: 2,5,6,7,8,9,10,11,12
Breakfast: Full
Dbl. Oc.: $81.90
Sgl. Oc.: $71.80
Third Person: $12.60

Inn At The Falls—A 125 year old inn set on a wooded hill overlooking falls & river. Full dining room & pub open year round. Children under 18 no charge. Dinner from $12.00 per person. In the heart of Muskoka.

Braeside

McGregor, Noreen & Steve
RR #1, K0A 1G0
(613) 432-6248 or 432-9726

Amenities: 6
Breakfast: Full

Dbl. Oc.: $35.00
Sgl. Oc.: $25.00
Third Person: $5.00

100 Year Old Stone House in quiet countryside. Working farm, 50 miles from Ottawa, Canada's capitol. Our home is situated close to the Ottawa River on Cty. Rd. #6 in the heart of the Ottawa Valley, 10 miles from Renfrew & Arnprior. Dinner $10.00 per person.

Cobourg

Thiele, Mike
RR 5, K9A 4J8
(416) 372-7500, 372-3712

Amenities: 2,7,8,9,10,12
Breakfast: Full

Dbl. Oc.: $60.00
Sgl. Oc.: $54.00
Third Person: $8.00

Northumberland Heights Country Inn—Fine dining, indoor pool, sauna, hot tub, total relaxation, walking trails. East Hwy. 2, Coburg to Brookside follow signs.

Collingwood

Szelestowski, Diane & Steve
Box 254, L9Y 3Z9
(705) 445-7598

Amenities: 1,2,6,7,8,9,11
Breakfast: Continental

Dbl. Oc.: $55.00 (Can.)
Sgl. Oc.: $47.50 (Can.)
Third Person: $10.00 (Can.)

Pretty River Valley Farm—Log home nestled in Blue Mts. Pine furnished rooms with private bath & fireplaces; spa, pond, 120 acres. Near skiing, beaches & hiking trails. 5 miles S. of Collingwood Hwy. 24 to SR 30131, 5 miles W. to farm.

AMENITIES

1. No Smoking
2. No Pets
3. No Children
4. Senior Citizen Rates
5. Tennis Available
6. Golf Available
7. Swimming Available
8. Skiing Available
9. Credit Cards Accepted
10. Personal Check Accepted
11. Off Season Rates
12. Dinner Available (w/sufficient notice)

Ontario

Lakeside

Ball M/M Willis
RR #2, N0M 2G0
(519) 283-6244

Amenities: 2,5,6,7,8,10,11,12
Breakfast: Full
Dbl. Oc.: $35.00
Sgl. Oc.: $18.00
Third Person: $10.00

Blamoral Vacation Farm—"Country living at its best." Dairy farm; fresh homecooked meals; Thanksgiving & Christmas specials; brochure available; close to Stratford Shakespearean Festival and London.

New Hamburg

Elkeer, W. Gordon
17 Huron St., N0B 2G0
(519) 662-2020

Amenities: 1,2,3,5,6,7,8,9,10,12
Breakfast: Continental
Dbl. Oc.: $60.00
Sgl. Oc.: $60.00
Third Person: $40.00

The Waterlot Restaurant & Inn—1840 house on Nith River, above award-winning French country restaurant. 2 rms., shared bath/bidet. One suite with double bed & queen size sleeper. Rooms have king size single. Near Stratford's Shakespeare.

Niagara-On-The-Lake

Hiebert, Marlene & Otto
275 John St.,
Box 1371, L0S 1J0
(416) 468-3687

Amenities: 1,2,5,6,7,8,10,11
Breakfast: Full
Dbl. Oc.: $50.00
Sgl. Oc.: $45.00
Third Person: $20.00

Heibert's Guest House—We offer warm Mennonite hospitality. Our quaint, historic town is located 10 miles from Niagara Falls and USA border. Enjoy theatre, boutiques, scenery, and locally grown fruit. Reservations please!

Ottawa

Chiarelli, Ron
172 O'Connor St., K2P 1T5
(613) 236-4221

Amenities: 2,9,10
Breakfast: Full
Dbl. Oc.: $46.00 (Can.)
Sgl. Oc.: $42.00 (Can.)
Third Person: $10.00 (Can.)

O'Connor House Bed & Breakfast—Built in 1907, is located in downtown Ottawa. It is a short walk to the Parliament Buildings, Rideau Canal, downtown business core, Chinatown and major downtown shopping & eating areas.

AMENITIES

1. No Smoking
2. No Pets
3. No Children
4. Senior Citizen Rates
5. Tennis Available
6. Golf Available
7. Swimming Available
8. Skiing Available
9. Credit Cards Accepted
10. Personal Check Accepted
11. Off Season Rates
12. Dinner Available (w/sufficient notice)

Ontario

Ottawa

Delroy, Cathy & John
478 Albert St., K1R 5B5
(613) 236-4479

Amenities: 9
Breakfast: Full
Dbl. Oc.: $48.00-$58.00
Sgl. Oc.: $45.00-$53.00
Third Person: $10.00

Albert House—Fine Victorian home built in 1875. Located in the heart of downtown. All rooms are air-conditioned with private baths, telephone and television. Parking on premises. Famous Albert House breakfast.

Ottawa

Haydon, Mary & Andrew
18 K2P 1C6
(613) 230-2697

Amenities: 2,5,6,7,8,10
Breakfast: Continental

Dbl. Oc.: $50.00
Sgl. Oc.: $40.00
Third Person: $10.00

Haydon House is a gracious Victorian home nestled beside the historic Rideau Canal & scenic Parkway within downtown core. It has air-conditioned comfort & modern facilities, with Canadian Pine decor.

Ottawa

Leclerec, J-J & Clemence
253 McLeod, K2P 1A1
(613) 234-7577

Amenities: 1,2,3,5,6,7,8
Breakfast: Full

Dbl. Oc.: $50.00-$55.00
Sgl. Oc.: $45.00-$50.00
Third Person: $20.00

Al-Leclerc's Residence is an elegant centre town Victorian home close to museums, Parliment buildings, canal, restaurants, & shops. Free parking, TV, sitting room, breakfast in lovely dining room. French speaking.

Ottawa

Lyon, Mrs. Beatrice
479 Slater St., K1R 5C2
(613) 236-3904

Amenities: 10,11
Breakfast: Full

Dbl. Oc.: $35.00
Sgl. Oc.: $30.00
Third Person: $10.00

Beatrice Lyon Guest Home—An old fashioned family home within walking distance to Parliament buildings, National Archives Museum of Man, Byward Market, Rideau Canal. We enjoy children. Leave Hwy. 417 at Bronson Exit north to Slater St.

AMENITIES

1. No Smoking
2. No Pets
3. No Children
4. Senior Citizen Rates
5. Tennis Available
6. Golf Available
7. Swimming Available
8. Skiing Available
9. Credit Cards Accepted
10. Personal Check Accepted
11. Off Season Rates
12. Dinner Available (w/sufficient notice)

Ontario

Ottawa

Peterson, Esther
62 Sweetland Ave., K1N 7T6
(613) 235-8888

Amenities: 1,9
Breakfast: Full

Dbl. Oc.: $56.70
Sgl. Oc.: $50.40
Third Person: $5.00

Constance House—An award-winning Victorian home near downtown Ottawa activities. Air-conditioned. From Hwy. 417 take Nicholas St. exit to Laurier Ave., turn right to Sweetland Ave.

Ottawa

Schutte, Mrs. Anne; Unger, Mrs. Mary
185 Daly Ave., Sandy Hill, K1N 6E8
(613) 237-6089

Amenities: 1,2,9
Breakfast: Full
Dbl. Oc.: $50.40-$102.90
Sgl. Oc.: $44.10-$96.10
Third Person: $15.75

Auberge McGee's Inn—Welcome to a by-gone era of Victorian elegance. 14 guest rooms, private baths, jacuzzi ensuite & fireplaces. Recommended by Country Inns, CAA/AAA. Downtown location. Reservations recommended.

Ottawa

Waters, Mrs. Carol
35 Marlborough Ave., K1N 8E6
(613) 235-8461

Amenities: 2
Breakfast: Full

Dbl. Oc.: $45.00
Sgl. Oc.: $35.00
Third Person: $10.00

Australis Guest House—Our 60 year old home is a classic residence with fireplaces & leaded windows in a lovely part of downtown Ottawa in an area of parks, embassies & the river. Our breakfasts are hearty & friendly.

Picton

Whitney, Mrs. Jean
RR #2, K0K 2T0
(613) 476-3513

Amenities: 2,6,7,9,10,12
Breakfast: Full

Dbl. Oc.: $35.00-$45.00
Sgl. Oc.: $25.00
Third Person: $10.00

The Poplars—A comfortable century home on the Bay of Quinte, just 6 minutes from exit 566 off Highway 401. Near Belleville, Picton & Kingston. Good fishing; swim at Sandbanks; Provincial Park.

AMENITIES

1. No Smoking
2. No Pets
3. No Children
4. Senior Citizen Rates
5. Tennis Available
6. Golf Available
7. Swimming Available
8. Skiing Available
9. Credit Cards Accepted
10. Personal Check Accepted
11. Off Season Rates
12. Dinner Available (w/sufficient notice)

Ontario

Port Elgin

Levere, M/M Terry
611 Ruby St.,
Box, 1233, N0H 2C0
(519) 832-5520

Amenities: 1,2,5,6,7,10
Breakfast: Full

Dbl. Oc.: $35.00
Sgl. Oc.: $25.00

Levere's Guest Home—Experience warm hospitality in quiet area. We feature a private floor with 3 double rooms, 1 1/2 bathrooms, large family room, sandy beach sunsets, flea market, tea & muffins in the evening.

Portland-on-the-Rideau

Dickey, Eleanor & Patrick
West Water St., K0G 1V0
(613) 272-3132

Amenities: 6,7,8,9,11,12
Breakfast: Full

Dbl. Oc.: $42.50-$84.00
Sgl. Oc.: $37.50-$79.00
Third Person: $8.00

Gallagher House Lakeside Country Inn—Nestled on the shore of big Rideau lake. Country inn style meals, fully licensed. Old fashion charm. Accessible to disabled. Spa overlooks public docks. Relaxed Rideau hospitality with country inn ambiance.

Priceville

Hutchinsen, Jean & Bill
RR #3, N0C 1K0
(519) 924-2506

Amenities: 1,2,8
Breakfast: Full

Dbl. Oc.: $40.00-$45.00
Sgl. Oc.: $30.00

Lakeside Farm—Turn-of-the-century house on 300 acre farm in quiet picturesque area. 10 minutes from Flesherton, Beaver Valley, Bruce Trail, Eugenia Falls, skiing, golf, and unique towns with antique and collectable shops..

Rodney

Van Aston, Dorothy & Theo
RR 2, N0L 2C0
(519) 785-0218

Amenities: 4,7,11
Breakfast: Full
Dbl. Oc.: $38.00
Sgl. Oc.: $28.00
Third Person: $12.00

Serene Acres Vacation Farm—80 miles east of Detroit between Highway 401 & north shore of Lake Erie. 4 minutes from Interchange 129. Our separate renovated farmhouse accommodates 9 people. Daily-weekly rates. Rustic atmosphere.

AMENITIES

1. No Smoking
2. No Pets
3. No Children
4. Senior Citizen Rates
5. Tennis Available
6. Golf Available
7. Swimming Available
8. Skiing Available
9. Credit Cards Accepted
10. Personal Check Accepted
11. Off Season Rates
12. Dinner Available (w/sufficient notice)

Ontario

Rossport

Basher, Shelagh & Ned
6 Bowman St., P0T 2R0
(807) 824-3213

Amenities: 9,11,12
Breakfast: Full
Dbl. Oc.: $63.00 (Can.)
Sgl. Oc.: $53.00 (Can.)

The Rossport Inn—Built in 1884, this charming family-run railway inn overlooks Rossport Harbour on Lake Superior, 110 miles east of Thunder Bay. 6 rooms; open May-Oct.; fresh local fish; log sauna; kayaking & fishing.

Toronto

Bosher, Kenneth
322 Palmerston Blvd., M6G 2N6
(416) 920-7842

Amenities: 9
Breakfast: Continental

Dbl. Oc.: $50.00-$55.00
Sgl. Oc.: $40.00-$50.00
Third Person: $15.00

Burken Guest House—Convenient, central location on quiet residential boulevard. Clean, beautifully furnished rooms. Continental breakfast included. Reservations recommended. Limited free parking.

Toronto

Enid, Ms. Evans
17 Waverley Rd., M4L 3T3
(416) 699-0818

Amenities: 1,4,5,7,10,11
Breakfast: Continental

Dbl. Oc.: $42.00
Sgl. Oc.: $32.00
Third Person: $12.00

Beaches Bed And Breakfast—Located in a distinctive part of the city known for its famous boardwalk boutiques, cafes and lovely parks. Cat and dog ready for petting.

Toronto

Oppenheim, Ms. Susan
153 Huron St., M5T 2B6
(416) 598-4562

Amenities: 1,5,7,10
Breakfast: Full

Dbl. Oc.: $50.00 (Can.)
Sgl. Oc.:: $40.00 (Can.)
Third Person: $20.00 (Can.)

Oppenheim's in its 7th year. The house boasts Victorian and 4 pianos. Breakfast fresh daily and features international cuisine from Kensington Market. Parking. 4 double rooms, 1 single. Book early. Susan is a singer.

AMENITIES

1. No Smoking
2. No Pets
3. No Children
4. Senior Citizen Rates
5. Tennis Available
6. Golf Available
7. Swimming Available
8. Skiing Available
9. Credit Cards Accepted
10. Personal Check Accepted
11. Off Season Rates
12. Dinner Available (w/sufficient notice)

Prince Edward Island

Capital: Charlottetown
Entered The Dominion: July 1, 1873; the 7th province
Provincial Motto: The Small Under The Protection
                     Of The Great
The Floral Emblem: Lady's Slipper

    P.E.I., as it is often referred to, is the smallest yet the most densely populated province of the Canadian provinces. It is the only one of the provinces that is separated from the main land of North America.

    The people of this island depend greatly upon its green meadows and rich red soil for the agriculture which brings them their yearly income.

    Tourism helps the economy, too. Over 600,000 vacationers visit Prince Edward Island each year. The climate is mild during the summer, and the beaches are beautiful.

    The biggest event of the year takes place in August in the capitol of Charlottetown. It is called Old Home Week. People come from all over to enjoy this happy event.

Prince Edward Island

Brackley Beach

Huck, Jean & John
Rte. 6, C0A 2H0
(902) 672-2874

Amenities: 1,2,3,10
Breakfast: Full

Dbl. Oc.: $22.00-$60.50

Windsong Farm—Quiet, peaceful retreat centrally located. 2 miles form National Park beaches; short drive to Charlottetown. 1860 renovated farmhouse on 7 acres surrounded by fields. Warm hospitality, wholesome food. Open June-Sept.

Kensington

Hickey, Erma & James
R.R. 1, C0B 1M0
(902) 836-5430

Amenities: 7,10,11
Breakfast: Continental

Dbl. Oc.: $40.00
Sgl. Oc.: $30.00
Third Person: $5.00

Sherwood Acres Guest Home—Rte. 20, 14 KM. north of Kensington. 500 acre potato & grain farm. 8 well appointed rooms: TV, piano, & living area available. BBQ & picnic tables, private entrance, homemade breads & jams.

O'Leary

Smallman, Eileen & Arnold
Knutsford, RR #1, C0B 1V0
(902) 859-3469

Amenities: 1,5,6,7,8,11,12
Breakfast: Full

Dbl. Oc.: $27.50-$33.00
Sgl. Oc.: $16.50
Third Person: $5.50

Smallman's Bed & Breakfast—Just off Hwy. 142. 4 miles west of O'Leary. Comfortable split level home in the country. Homebaked breakfast specialty. Beaches, musuems, woolen mill, grain mills. Fresh lobster & shell fish.

Panmure Island

Partridge, Gertrude
R.R. 2, Montague, C0A 1R0
(902) 838-4687

Amenities: 1,6,7,8,9,10,11
Breakfast: Full

Dbl. Oc.: $38.50
Sgl. Oc.: $28.60
Third Person: $6.00

Partridge's Bed And Breakfast—3 bedrooms, private bath, 2 bedrooms, shared bath, 2 rooms w/wheelchair accessible. 5 minute walk to sandy beach. Warm hospitable home. Children welcome.

Vernon River

Lea, Dora
Vernon P.O. C0A 2E0
(902) 651-2501

Amenities: 1,2,3,5,6,7,8,10
Breakfast: Full

Dbl. Oc.: $24.00
Sgl. Oc.: $20.00
Third Person: $5.00

Hobby Farm has small animals and birds on 25 acres of land. Quiet location. Bedrooms with double beds & two double housekeeping units. Homemade cinnamon rolls, 3 bathrooms in all.

AMENITIES

1. No Smoking
2. No Pets
3. No Children
4. Senior Citizen Rates
5. Tennis Available
6. Golf Available
7. Swimming Available
8. Skiing Available
9. Credit Cards Accepted
10. Personal Check Accepted
11. Off Season Rates
12. Dinner Available (w/sufficient notice)

Quebec

The Largest Province Of Canada

Capital: Quebec
Entered The Dominion: July 1, 1867
Provincial Motto: I Remember
The Floral Emblem: White Garden Lily
Provincial Tree: Sugar Maple

The province of Quebec is quite different from all the other provinces. Most of its people speak French and adhere to French customs. Old Quebec is a site of much history, and visitors come here and enjoy the charm of this city and its 300-year-old winding and cobblestone streets.

Montreal is the largest city in this province and it is a beautiful city. It has lovely parks and shops and a large community of business from around the world. It has a metropolitan air about it.

In Montreal, the University of McGill is located. This particular university is English speaking.

Quebec is known for its great religious faith. There are many Catholic and Protestant churches available for the people. Tourists love Quebec, and return here by the thousands every day.

Quebec

Georgeville

Morissette, Monique & Jacques
Rte. 247, Box 17, J0B 1T0
(819) 843-8683

Amenities: 2,5,6,7,8,9,12
Breakfast: Full
Dbl. Oc.: $76.00-$88.00 (Can.)
Sgl. Oc.: $45.00-$54.00 (Can.)
Third Person: $28.00-$34.00 (Can.)

Auberge Georgeville—12 room Victorian home in a quiet little village on the east shore of Memphremagog. We offer past era and homey atmosphere, refined regional cuisine in peaceful and scenic area. Welcome.

Knowlton

Seebohm, Irsula Mrs.
RR 2, Stage Coach Road,
J0E 1V0
(514) 243-6604

Amenities: 2,7,8,10
Breakfast: Full

Dbl. Oc.: $35.00
Sgl. Oc.: $35.00
Third Person: $35.00

Laketree Inn (Auberge)—Beautiful lake & mountain view. Quiet, swimming, boats, rafts, canoes, marked trails, hiking skiing & bicycling. Large artistic house with antiques, arts, books, plants, grand piano. European atmosphere, hospitality. Children up to 12 years—$20.00.

Montreal

Kahn, Marina
4912 Victoria Ave., H3W 2N1
(514) 738-9410

Amenities: 1,2,5,6,7,8,9,11
Breakfast: Full

Dbl. Oc.: $60.00-$75.00 (Can.)
Sgl. Oc.: $35.00-$45.00 (Can.)
Third Person: $10.00 (Can.)

Marian Extends A Warm Welcome to her large Georgian-style home centrally located near St. Joseph's Oratory, the University of Montreal, the Metro, fine international restaurants. 1 double, 1 triple. 1 single. Common sitting room.

Montreal

Seguin, Lucie
3422 Stanely, H3A 1R8
(514) 288-6922

Amenities: 9
Breakfast: Continental

Dbl. Oc.: $60.00
Sgl. Oc.: $50.00
Third Person: $10.00

Manoir Ambrose—Gracious 19th century Victorian home. Situated on the quiet and restful slope of Mount Royal right in the middle of city restaurants, theaters, shopping and business center.

AMENITIES

1. No Smoking
2. No Pets
3. No Children
4. Senior Citizen Rates
5. Tennis Available
6. Golf Available
7. Swimming Available
8. Skiing Available
9. Credit Cards Accepted
10. Personal Check Accepted
11. Off Season Rates
12. Dinner Available (w/sufficient notice)

Quebec

Mt. Tremblant

Ridell, M/M Alex
Box 138, J0T 1Z0
(819) 425-7275

Amenities: 2,5,6,7,8,10,11
Breakfast: Full

Dbl. Oc.: $54.00
Sgl. Oc.: $27.00

Chateau Beauvallon offers a quiet relaxing country inn with a delicious breakfast. Situated on four acres of wooded property with private beach & two miles from skiing.

Quebec City

Corriveau, Marguerite
13, Avenue Ste. Genevieve,
G1R 4A7
(418) 694-1666

Amenities: 1,3,4,5,6,7,8,11
Breakfast: Continental

Dbl. Oc.: $65.00-$90.00
Sgl. Oc.: $60.00-$75.00
Third Person: $8.00

Au Manor Ste Genevieve—Antique manor with modern facilities. Private bath & color TV in all rooms. English & French spoken. Drive through entrance of Chateau Frontenac Hotel past park, turn right, first block on Ste. Genevieve Ave. to #13.

Quebec City

Couturier, Lily
17 Ave. St. Genevieve,
G1R 4A8
(418) 694-0429

Amenities: 2,10,11
Breakfast: Continental

Dbl. Oc.: $72.00
Sgl. Oc.: $82.00
Third Person: $8.00

An Old English Colonial mansion located in the heart of Old Quebec. Well appointed units, garage parking. One of the nicest spots of Quebec City near historical sites & shopping area.

Quebec City

Desjardins, Richard
61 St. Denis, C.P. 1229,
St. Sauveur Des Monts, J0R 1R0
(514) 227-4602

Amenities: 2-5,6-12
Breakfast: Full

Dbl. Oc.: $132.00
Sgl. Oc.: $120.00
Third Person: $20.00

Auberge St. Denis—Heart of the Laurentians; a Victorian style house with warm personnel. Shops and art galleries within walking distance. Quiet area. Fine dining. Member of Romantic Inns. 45 minutes from airport.

AMENITIES

1. No Smoking
2. No Pets
3. No Children
4. Senior Citizen Rates
5. Tennis Available
6. Golf Available
7. Swimming Available
8. Skiing Available
9. Credit Cards Accepted
10. Personal Check Accepted
11. Off Season Rates
12. Dinner Available (w/sufficient notice)

Quebec

St. Jean Ile d'Orleans

Godolphin, Mrs. Lorraine
170 Chemin des Ormes,
G0A 3W0
(418) 829-2613

Amenities: 1,6,7,10
Breakfast: Full

Dbl. Oc.: $50.00 (Can.)
Sgl. Oc.: $40.00 (Can.)

La Vigie Du Pilote (The Pilot's Look-Out) on beautiful Orleans Island, only 35 minutes from Quebec City. A "Yankee Barn" luxury home on a 4 acre cliff-top site with magnificent views over the Saint Lawrence River.

Sur Richelieu

Handfield, Conrad
555 Chemin du Prince St Marc,
J0L 2E0
(514) 584-2226

Amenities: 2,5,6,7,9,12
Breakfast: Continental

Dbl. Oc.: $53.00
Sgl. Oc.: $44.00
Third Person: $8.00

The Auberge Handfield is a great many things: it is a venerable mansion that has seen a century and a half of history with French & Canadian cuisine. This country inn is about 25 miles from Montreal, Different plans available.

AMENITIES

1. No Smoking
2. No Pets
3. No Children
4. Senior Citizen Rates
5. Tennis Available
6. Golf Available
7. Swimming Available
8. Skiing Available
9. Credit Cards Accepted
10. Personal Check Accepted
11. Off Season Rates
12. Dinner Available (w/sufficient notice)

Saskatchewan

One of the Prairie Provinces of Canada

Capital: Regina
Entered The Dominion: September 1, 1905
Motto: From Many People Strength
The Floral Emblem: The Prairie Lilly

    Saskatchewan is the greatest wheat growing region in North America, producing half of Canada's wheat. The world's largest Grain Handling Cooperative is located in Regina. Saskatchewan has 2/5th of the farmland in all of Canada. More than any of the other Provinces.
    The Province got its name from the Sashat River, named by the Cree Indians. It ranks 6th among the Canadian Provinces, and from 1883 to 1905 was the capital of the Northwest Territories. The Royal Canadian Mounted Police have their training center in Regina.

Saskatchewan

Ile-a-la Crosse

Cornett, M/M Ken
Box 59, S0M 1C0
(306) 833-2590

Amenities: 7,8,9,10,12
Breakfast: Full

Dbl. Oc.: $60.00
Sgl. Oc.: $40.00
Third Person: $10.00

Rainbow Ridge is located on a beautiful 14 acre peninsula. Nature surrounds this luxury home. Large rooms, food, hospital, auto and air charter accessible. An excellent setting for burnout and stressout persons.

Qu'Appelle

Mader, Jo & Ken
P.O. 173, S0G 4A0
(306) 699-7192

Amenities: 6,7,9,12
Breakfast: Full
Dbl. Oc.: $38.00 (Can.)
Sgl. Oc.: $28.00 (Can.)
Third Person: $20.00 (Can.)

Bluenose—2 miles north of Qu'Appelle on Highway 35 or 3 miles north of junction Highway 35 & Trans-Canada. Large farm; animals, fowl, indoor pool, play area. Large fieldstone home. Meals on request. Fresh air & hospitality.

Traux

Demerse, Mrs. Linda
Box 51, S0H 4A0
(306) 868-4614

Amenities: 2,6,7,10,12
Breakfast: Full

Dbl. Oc.: $20.00
Sgl. Oc.: $15.00

45 miles southeast of Regina along a creek. Working farm with in-house accommodations. Share the farm animals, wagon riding, hiking, canoeing, berry picking in season with our children aged 10-14.

AMENITIES

1. No Smoking
2. No Pets
3. No Children
4. Senior Citizen Rates
5. Tennis Available
6. Golf Available
7. Swimming Available
8. Skiing Available
9. Credit Cards Accepted
10. Personal Check Accepted
11. Off Season Rates
12. Dinner Available (w/sufficient notice)

Bermuda

Hamilton

Smith, Mrs. James
P.O. Box 374
(809) 295-0503

Amenities: 5,6,7,11
Breakfast: Continental

Dbl. Oc.: $96.28
Sgl. Oc.: on request
Third Person: $24.36

Oxford Guest House—Closest guest house to Hamilton. Easy walk to bus, ferry, restaurants. All bathrooms en suite with air conditioning, TV, telephone. Sightseeing & sports activities easily arranged. Twelve rooms.

Warwick

Ashton, Carol & Michael
One Longford Rd., Box 533WK, WKBX
(809) 236-1805

Amenities: 7,9,10,11
Breakfast: Continental
Dbl. Oc.: $106.00-$120.00
Sgl. Oc.: $90.00
Third Person: $30.00

"Granaway"—A gracious Bermuda home built in 1734. Delightful waterviews with a private terrace for swimming. Come and relax in the elegant English garden. Golf, tennis, ferry, bus all within walking distance.

AMENITIES

1. No Smoking
2. No Pets
3. No Children
4. Senior Citizen Rates
5. Tennis Available
6. Golf Available
7. Swimming Available
8. Skiing Available
9. Credit Cards Accepted
10. Personal Check Accepted
11. Off Season Rates
12. Dinner Available (w/sufficient notice)

Puerto Rico

Condado (San Juan)

Rodriques, Mr. Eduardo
1350 Calle Luchetti, 00907
(809) 728-5925, 5526, 5134

Amenities: 4,7,9,10,11
Breakfast: Continental

Dbl. Oc.: $63.25
Sgl. Oc.: $74.75
Third Person: $10.00

El Prado Inn—Elegant Spanish inn located in Condado section of San Juan only steps from famous hotels, casinos, bars and a three minute walk to a beautiful beach.

San Juan

Larsen, Mr. & Mrs.
3 Guerrero Noble, 00913
(809) 727-0033

Amenities: 1,2,3,7,11
Breakfast: Continental

Dbl. Oc.: $35.00-$45.00
Sgl. Oc.: $35.00-$45.00
Third Person: $10.00

Larsen's Bed And Breakfast is centrally located next to San Juan's finest beach. Breakfast includes tropical fruit and homemade bread served on the patio. Smoking outside. Two and a half miles from the airport.

AMENITIES

1. No Smoking
2. No Pets
3. No Children
4. Senior Citizen Rates
5. Tennis Available
6. Golf Available
7. Swimming Available
8. Skiing Available
9. Credit Cards Accepted
10. Personal Check Accepted
11. Off Season Rates
12. Dinner Available (w/sufficient notice)

United States Virgin Islands

St. Thomas

Cooper, Barbara
P.O. Box 1903, 00803-1903
(800) 524-2023

Amenities: 2,3,5,6,7,11
Breakfast: Continental

Dbl. Oc.: $80.00
Sgl. Oc.: $74.00
Third Person: $18.50

Island View Guest House is located midway between the town & airport, on Crown Mt., 545 feet in elevation overlooking the town & harbor pool. Free beach towels, pool lounges, kitchens available upon request. 27th year.

St. Thomas

Hart, Mrs. Bobbe
P.O. Box 7158
(809) 775-6651

Amenities: 2,3,6,7,10,11
Breakfast: Full

Dbl. Oc.: $75.00
Sgl. Oc.: $75.00
Third Person: $15.00

The Cottage On The Rocks—Studio cottage with kitchenette overlooking private pool and deck. Comfortable twin Murphy beds. Spacious screened porch. Close to Secret Harbor Beach & Red Hook. Quiet residential area. Brochure.

St. Thomas

Palmer, John
Box 8373, 00801
(809) 775-2100

Amenities: 5,6,7,11,12
Breakfast: Continental

Dbl. Oc.: $65.00
Sgl. Oc.: $65.00
Third Person: $10.00

Inn At Mandahl Beach—8 ocean facing units with large private terraces with chaise lounges, view of 14 islands, pool, beach and sailing at inn. King size four poster beds, frig. in room. 15 acres of land; ultimate privacy & relaxation.

St. Thomas

Slone, Donna & John
P.O. Box 6577, 00804
(800) 524-2052, (809) 774-6952

Amenities: 7,9,11
Breakfast: Continental

Dbl. Oc.: $60.00 & up
Sgl. Oc.: $55.00 & up
Third Person: $15.00

Galleon House Guest Hause—Guest house with historic flavor one block from town with major shopping & restaurants. Warm hospitable place with home cooked breakfasts and helpful service. Fresh water pool. Beaches nearby. Fourteen rooms.

AMENITIES

1. No Smoking
2. No Pets
3. No Children
4. Senior Citizen Rates
5. Tennis Available
6. Golf Available
7. Swimming Available
8. Skiing Available
9. Credit Cards Accepted
10. Personal Check Accepted
11. Off Season Rates
12. Dinner Available (w/sufficient notice)

United Statesd Virgin Islands

Water Island (St. Thomas)

Murray, Joan & Paul
00802
(809) 774-2148, (800) 872-8784,
(201) 329-6309 (NJ)

Amenities: 2,7,9,10,11
Breakfast: Continental
Dbl. Oc.: $110.00-$148.00
Sgl. Oc.: $95.00-$134.00
Third Person: $21.00-$41.00

Limestone Reef Terraces—Studio apartment on Water Island in St. Thomas harbor. Ferry takes 7 minutes 7 a.m.-12 a.m. Panoramic view, near palm-lined beach & restaurant. Free use of snorkel & mask transportation on Water Island.

Reservation Services

Alabama

Millbrook

Maier, Mrs. Helen
P.O. Box 886, 36054
(205) 285-5421

Amenities: 6

Dbl. Oc.: $56.00
Sgl. Oc.: $36.00

Areas covered: Montgomery

Bed & Breakfast Montgomery—History buffs will love Montgomery, cradle of the Confederacy: also home of the nationally acclaimed Shakespeare Festival. Accommodations range from antebellum to contemporary with a typical farmhouse in between.

Alaska

Anchorage

Reardon, Mary
1236 W. 10th Avenue, 99501
(907) 258-1717

Amenities: 3,5

Dbl. Oc.: $40.00-$75.00
Sgl. Oc.: $35.00-$60.00

Areas covered: State of Alaska: Seward, Kenai River, Homer, Denali Park area & Fairbanks.

Carefully selected homes in many Alaska communities.—Guest rooms & suites in private homes. Let Alaska help you enjoy your vacation. Write for free brochure and Host Home Directory. Experience Alaska by staying in the homes of Alaskans.

Juneau

Hamilton, Stephen
3/6500 Ste. 169, 99802
(809) 586-2959

Amenities: 1,3,4,5,6

Dbl. Oc.: $44.00-$77.00
Sgl. Oc.: $35.00-$77.00

Areas covered: Juneau, Sitka, Skagway, Haines, Ketchikan, Petersburg, Gustavus & Angoon.

Alaska Bed & Breakfast Assoc.—Enjoy Alaskan hospitality in a B&B home or inn throughout the southwest. All towns convenient to ferry system and airports. Most locations open year-round. Full or continental breakfast served daily.

Arizona

Prescott

Thomson, George
Box 3999, 86302-3999
(602) 776-1102, 998-7044

Amenities: 4,6

Dbl. Oc.: $40.00-$150.00
Sgl. Oc.: $35.00-$150.00

Areas covered: Scottsdale, Phoenix, Arizona, California, Colorado, New Mexico.

B&B Scottsdale & The West—Guest rooms, suites, cottages and villas in a variety of exceptional western settings. Several locations have been used as movie and ad sets. Many spectacular homes at modest to luxury rates.

AMENITIES

1. American Express
2. Senior Citizen Rates Available
3. VISA
4. Personal Check Accepted
5. MasterCard
6. Brochure Available

Arizona

Scottsdale

Thomas, Thomas
P.O. Box 8628, 85252
(602) 995-2831

Amenities: 1,3,5,6

Dbl. Oc.: $45.00-$150.00
Sgl. Oc.: $35.00-$90.00

Areas covered: State of Arizona.

Bed & Breakfast In Arizona—Great breakfasts, new friends, and western hospitality at homes, inns, ranches. Personally inspected for friendliness and cleanliness. Take a B&B tour in magnificent Arizona! Free brochure.

Tempe

Yound, Mrs. Ruth
603 Saquaro Dr.,
P.O. Box 950 NB, 85281
(602) 990-0682

Amenities: 6

Dbl. Oc.: $35.00-$110.00
Sgl. Oc.: $25.00-$90.00

Areas covered: Phoenix, Scottsdale, Tempe, Mesa, Fountain Hills, Sun City, Tucson, Yuma, Flagstaff, Sedona, Prescott, Cottonwood, Ajo etc.

Mi Casa Su Casa—Modest to luxurious homestays, cottages, ranches. Most near golf, tennis, pools, national and state parks, canyons, mountains, lakes, birds, Indians, art, sports.

Tucson

Nelson, Dorna; Kiekebusch, Rena
Box 13603, 85732
(602) 790-2399

Amenities: 4,6

Dbl. Oc.: $35.00-$80.00
Sgl. Oc.: $25.00-$65.00

Areas covered: Tucson.

Old Pueblo Homestays—Wide variety of homes in Tucson proper, the foothills and surrounding areas. All are inspected. Hosts carefully chosen. Truly friendly people who enjoy offering that personal touch. For brochure S.A.S.E.

California

Altadena

Judkins, Ruth
P.O. Box 694, 91001
(213) 684-4428

Amenities: 3,4,5,6

Dbl. Oc.: $35.00-$200.00 & up
Sgl. Oc.: $30.00-$180.00 & up

Areas covered: All of California.

Eye Openers Bed & Breakfast Reservations—For a new experience in lodging in the European tradition, Eye Openers B&B Reservations has selected bed & breakfast accommodations throughout California.

AMENITIES

1. American Express
2. Senior Citizen Rates Available
3. VISA
4. Personal Check Accepted
5. MasterCard
6. Brochure Available

California

Dana Point

Sakach, Deborah
P.O. Box 336, 92629
(714) 496-7050

Amenities: 4

Dbl. Oc.: $25.00-$85.00
Sgl. Oc.: $20.00-$85.00

Areas covered: All of California, San Francisco, San Diego, L.A., all coastal cities & Yosemite.

Hospitality Plus—Inns & homes in every nook & cranny of California. Try a coastal tour! Oceanfront and ocean views are our specialty.

Fullerton

Garrison, Ms. Joyce
1943 Sunny Crest Dr.,
Ste. 304, 92635
(714) 738-8361

Amenities: 4,6

Dbl. Oc.: $40.00-$70.00
Sgl. Oc.: $30.00-$50.00

Areas covered: Southern California.

Bed & Breakfast Of Southern California—Mainly Orange County/southern California. Joyce Garrison & Lois Tait provide personalized service to their clients. Thier homes are charming and intimate. The hosts are warm and friendly.

Garden Grove

MacLachlan, Esther
11531 Varna St., 92640
(714) 638-1406

Amenities: 6

Dbl. Oc.: $30.00-$50.00
Sgl. Oc.: $25.00-$40.00

Areas covered: Southern California between Los Angeles and San Diego, Pacific coast.

Rent A Room—Attractive, private homes with hosts eager to make your visit pleasant in every way. Heart of tourist country; Los Angeles, Palos Verdes, Laguna, Anaheim, Disneyland, La Jolla, San Diego.

San Diego

Schubert, Barbara
416 Third Ave., #25, 92010
(619) 422-7009

Amenities: 6

Dbl. Oc.: $45.00-$100.00
Sgl. Oc.: $30.00-$90.00

Areas covered: San Diego County, California.

Carolyn's Bed & Breakfast Homes Of San Diego—Over 45 hosts in beautiful San Diego and adjacent vacation areas. Near beaches, Old Mexico, Sea World, San Diego Zoo, San Diego Harbor, Balboa Park, Old Town, San Diego and the famous Wild Animal Park.

AMENITIES

1. American Express
2. Senior Citizen Rates Available
3. VISA
4. Personal Check Accepted
5. MasterCard
6. Brochure Available

California

San Francisco

Brown, Mrs. Jean
1181-B Solano, Albany, 94706
(415) 525-4569

Amenities: 1,2,3,5,6

Dbl. Oc.: $40.00-$125.00
Sgl. Oc.: $32.00 & up

Areas covered: San Francisco, Los Angeles, San Diego & throughout California. Las Vegas, Seattle, New York City, Hawaii.

Bed & Breakfast International—We are celebrating 10 years of experience placing travelers in fine private homes—Victorians, houseboats, studios. Economy to luxury lodgings, average $50.00. Send for brochure or phone M-F 9-5, 9-12 Sat.

San Francisco

Kreibich, Susan
Box 349, 94101
(415) 931-3083

Amenities: 1,3,4,5,6

Dbl. Oc.: $55.00-$125.00
Sgl. Oc.: $45.00-$125.00

Areas covered: San Francisco Bay area, Wine Country & Monterey/Carmel.

American Family Inn/Bed & Breakfast San Francisco—The real hospitality of San Franciscans! Bed & Breakfast in better homes, mansions and small inns. Full breakfast served.

San Luis Obispo

Segor, Joyce & Robert
1776 Royal Way, 93401
(805) 544-4406

Amenities: 4

Dbl. Oc.: $40.00-$75.00
Sgl. Oc.: $30.00-$75.00
Fee to Traveler: $10.00

Areas covered: San Luis Obispo County, Santa Barbara County, California central coast.

Meagan's Bed & Breakfast Reservation Service—Private membership for non-smokers. Exclusive listings—host homes by the ocean, bay, hillside. Ideal for honeymoons & anniversaries. Near golf courses, walking trails, beaches, shops, visit Hearst Castle.

Tarzana

Alexy, Trudi
6051 Lindley Ave. #6, 91356
(818) 344-7878

Amenities: 4,6

Dbl. Oc.: $45.00-$250.00
Sgl. Oc.: $25.00-$85.00

Areas covered: California, USA, many foreign countries.

California Houseguests, Int'l., Inc.—Charming guest rooms in homes, condos, apts., elegant Victorians, rustic chalets, beach pads, mountain cabins. Some unhosted, 2 nite min. Weekly, monthly rates. Free brochure with S.A.S.E. Phone calls returned promptly!

AMENITIES

1. American Express
2. Senior Citizen Rates Available
3. VISA
4. Personal Check Accepted
5. MasterCard
6. Brochure Available

California

Westlakes Village

Kobabe, Mrs. Angie
32074 Waterside Lane, 91361
(818) 889-7325, 889-8870

Amenities: 3,4,5,6

Dbl. Oc.: $35.00-$200.00
Sgl. Oc.: $30.00-$125.00
Fee to Traveler: $10.00

Areas covered: Greater Los Angeles, Calif. coastline from San Diego to San Francisco.

Bed And Breakfast Of Los Angeles—For a memorable experience try a home stay or small inn. All homes are inspected to assure comfort and hospitality. For directory send $2.00

Whittier

Davis, Coleen
11715 South Circle Dr., 90601
(213) 699-8427

Amenities: 2,4,6

Dbl. Oc.: $40.00-$85.00
Sgl. Oc.: $35.00-$67.00

Areas covered: All of California, & selected establishments throughout the U.S.

Cohost, America's Bed & Breakfast—Cohosts enjoy guests, full breakfast, clean bath, good bed, help with planning, and some extras such as baby sitting, dinner & tour guiding. Wine & cheese at homes up and down the coast & inland.

Connecticut

New Haven

Argenio, Jack
Box 216, 06513
(203) 469-3260 (Academic year: PM,
anytime weekends. Summer anytime.)

Amenities: 6

Dbl. Oc.: $45.00—65.00
Sgl. Oc.: $35.00-$45.00

Areas covered: All of CT with selected listings in Mass. & Rhode Island.

Bed And Breakfast, Ltd. offers over 125 gracious & affordable accommodations from simply elegant to elegantly simple. For wonderful variety, warm hospitality & affordable prices. Wake up to B&B Ltd.! Tops in So. CT!

Norfolk

Tremblay, Mrs. Diane
Maple Ave., Box 447, 06058
(203) 542-5944

Amenities: 1,3,4,5

Dbl. Oc.: $45.00-$150.00
Sgl. Oc.: $40.00-$120.00

Areas covered: Shore line & northwestern Connecticut, Hudson Valley New York, Berkshires, Massachusetts, Southern Vermont.

Covered Bridge—Historic Colonial Victorian estates and working farms. Guestrooms, many with fireplaces and furnished with antiques. Our goal is to provide guests with a memorable B&B stay at homes of distinction.

AMENITIES

1. American Express
2. Senior Citizen Rates Available
3. VISA
4. Personal Check Accepted
5. MasterCard
6. Brochure Available

Colorado

Vail

Fagan, Ms. Kathy
P.O. Box 491, 81658
(303) 949-1212

Amenities: 2,3,4,5,6

Dbl. Oc.: $45.00-$100.00
Sgl. Oc.: $30.00-$75.00
Fee to Traveler: $10.00-$15.00

Areas covered: Ski areas; Vail, Summit County, Aspen, Breckenridge, Steamboat, Telluride.

B&B Vail Valley—A reservation service offering downtown or secluded mountain homes. Private lock-offs available. Homemade breakfast offered. Properties inspected. Wide range of homes & hosts make for a memorable vacation.

Delaware

Wilmington

Alford, Mrs. Millie
3650 Silverside Rd.,
Box 177, 19810
(302) 479-9500

Amenities: 4

Dbl. Oc.: $55.00-$75.00
Sgl. Oc.: $45.00-$55.00

Areas covered: New Castle, Rehoboth, Wilmington, Odessa, Dover, Laurel in Delaware, Elkton, Maryland and Landenberg, PA.

Bed & Breakfast Of Delaware is a reservation service that arranges accommodations for tourist, business persons, and other visitors in private homes in the historic Brandywine Valley area. Modern to historic, near scenic museums, beaches and country for biking.

District of Columbia

Washington, D.C.

Stofan, Lisa
Box 12011, 20005
(202) 328-3510

Amenities: 1,3,5,6

Dbl. Oc.: $50.50-$94.50
Sgl. Oc.: $34.00-$78.00

Areas covered: Washington, D.C. & nearby Maryland & Virginia.

Bed 'N' Breakfast, Ltd. of Washington, D.C.—Accommodations in private home B&B's. Several large historic homes convenient to tourist attractions & public transportation. Apartments also available for families or longer stays. Budget-luxury. $15.00 fee to traveler for cancellation.

AMENITIES

1. American Express
2. Senior Citizen Rates Available
3. VISA
4. Personal Check Accepted
5. MasterCard
6. Brochure Available

Florida

Palm Beach

Maxwell, Peggy
Box 3025, 33480
(407) 842-5190

Amenities: 6

Dbl. Oc.: $45.00-$65.00
Sgl. Oc.: $35.00-$55.00

Areas covered: Florida's Gold Coast, Jupiter, Juno, Palm Beach Gardens, Boca Raton, W. Palm Beach, Lake Worth, Lantana, Singer Island, Palm Beach.

Open House Bed And Breakfast Registry—Choose a luxurious pied-a-terre near the ocean or try a galley equipped houseboat, safely anchored. Many low budget accommodations boast swimming pools. Efficiencies and guest rooms are in private homes.

Georgia

Savannah

Fort, Alan P., Jr.
417 E. Charlton St., 31401
(912) 232-7787

Amenities: 1,3,4,5

Dbl. Oc.: $65.00-$185.00
Sgl. Oc.: $55.00-$75.00

Areas covered: Savannah & St. Simons, GA.; Beaufort, S.C.

R.S.V.P. Savannah, B&B Reservation Service—Choice accommodations in historic inns, guest houses, private homes. Special events/tours; group tour & convention planning. For the best in the coastal empire. Mon.-Fri. 10-5 p.m.

Savannah

Hill, Mrs. Caroline
147 Bull St., 31401
(800) 262-4667

Amenities: 1,3,4,5,6

Dbl. Oc.: $38.00-$135.00
Sgl. Oc.: $30.00-$65.00

Areas covered: Savannah, GA.

Savannah Historic Inns & Guest Houses—Reach Savannah's finest inns and guest houses with one phone call. Rooms with semi-private bath, rooms with private bath, garden apts., and carriage houses. Continental breakfast included.

Hawaii

Honolulu

Lee, Mrs. Mary
3242 Keohinani Dr., 96817
(808) 595-7533

Amenities: 4,6

Dbl. Oc.: $38.50-$120.00
Sgl. Oc.: $22.00-$100.00
Fee to Traveler: $5.00

Areas covered: All the islands in Hawaii.

Bed & Breakfast Honolulu (statewide) offers over 200 inspected homestays & studios. On all islands. Free brochure. Toll free reservation/information.

AMENITIES

1. American Express
2. Senior Citizen Rates Available
3. VISA
4. Personal Check Accepted
5. MasterCard
6. Brochure Available

Hawaii

Kapa

Warner, Evie; Davis, Al
Box 449, 96746
(808) 822-7771

Amenities: 4,6

Dbl. Oc.: $38.15-$87.20
Sgl. Oc.: $27.25-$43.60

Areas covered: All islands in the state of Hawaii.

Bed & Breakfast Hawaii—Private homes, beach or mountain in tropical settings. Most homes have private baths & continental breakfast. Resident hosts are knowledgable about beaches, special events, etc. Affordable paradise.

Illinois

Chicago

Shaw, Mary
Box 14088, 60614-0088
(312) 951-0085

Amenities: 1,3,4,5,6

Dbl. Oc.: $53.00-$116.60
Sgl. Oc.: $42.40-$106.00

Areas covered: Downtown Chicago and North Shore suburbs.

Bed & Breakfast Chicago Inc.—Our reservation service provides comfortable, reasonably-priced lodging in either private homes or furnished "self-catering" apartments. Most of our accommodations are in the center of Chicago.

Indiana

Nappanee

Harman, Sonya L.
1600 W. Market, 46550
(219) 773-4188

Amenities: 1,3,4,5,6

Dbl. Oc.: $40.00
Sgl. Oc.: $30.00
Deposit: $15.00

Areas covered: Elkhart County, Indiana.

Indiana Amish Country Bed & Breakfast—Accommodations are in large farm homes located in Elkhart County area. Hosts are members of the Amish, Mennonite, or German Baptist faith with plenty of friendly conversation and Hoosier hospitality.

Kansas

Lenexa

Monroe, Mrs. Edwina
Box 14781, 66215
(913) 888-3636

Amenities: 6

Dbl. Oc.: $35.00-$65.00
Sgl. Oc.: $30.00-$55.00

Areas covered: Metro area Kansas City, St. Joseph, Parkville, Liberty, Independence, Lee's Summit, Grandview; In Kansas, Lenexa, Topeka, Carthage, Warrensburg, Louisiana, Mo.

Bed & Breakfast Kansas City, Missouri & Kansas—28 Victorian, turn-of-the-century & contemporary homes. Hot tubs, pools, riding, fishing, tennis, golf. Two inns. Call anytime.

AMENITIES

1. American Express
2. Senior Citizen Rates Available
3. VISA
4. Personal Check Accepted
5. MasterCard
6. Brochure Available

Louisiana

New Orleans

Brown, Sarah Margaret
Box 8128, 70182
(504) 822-5038

Amenities: 1,3,4,5,6

Dbl. Oc.: $35.00-$150.00
Sgl. Oc.: $30.00-$100.00

Areas covered: New Orleans, Louisiana.

New Orleans Bed & Breakfast—Accommodations for one or a bunch; French Quarter, Garden district, uptown—almost any area. Most places are on direct public transportation to French Quarter. All inspected for your comfort. Hosts knowledgable about the area.

Maine

Falmouth

Tierney, Peg
32 Colonial Village, 04105
(207) 781-4528

Amenities: 3,4,5,6

Dbl. Oc.: $45.00-$95.00
Sgl. Oc.: $35.00-$65.00

Areas covered: State of Maine.

Bed & Breakfast Of Maine—This service offers legendary Maine hospitality in select private homes and small inns with complimentary breakfast. Send $1.00 for descriptive list of a variety of locations from the coast to the mountains.

Maryland

Baltimore

Grater, Betsy
1428 Park Ave., 21217
(301) 225-0001

Amenities: 1,3,5,6

Dbl. Oc.: over $100.00
Sgl. Oc.: $47.25

Areas covered: Baltimore, Annapolis, the Eastern shore of MD. & VA. Other neighborhoods in & around Baltimore, MD. Towns in PA., W.V., D.C., & DE.

Amanda's Bed & Breakfast Reservation Service—Private homes, small inns, & yachts. Water settings, docks, pools, beaches, antiques, intown or country.

Massachusetts

Bedford

Phillips, Phyllis
48 Springs Rd., 01730
(617) 275-9025

Amenities: 4

Dbl. Oc.: $50.00
Sgl. Oc.: $40.00

Areas covered: Acton, Bedford, Billerica, Burlington, Boxborough, Carlisle, Concord, Groton, Dunstable, Pepperell, Chelmsford, Lowell, Westford, Tyngsborough.

Bed & Breakfast Folks offers homey lodgings within an easy ride to Boston & southern New Hampshire. Monthly rates available.

AMENITIES

1. American Express
2. Senior Citizen Rates Available
3. VISA
4. Personal Check Accepted
5. MasterCard
6. Brochure Available

Massachusetts

Beverly

Champion, Helena
Box 172, 01915
(508) 921-1336

Amenities: 1,3,4,5,6

Dbl. Oc.: $45.00-$85.00
Sgl. Oc.: $36.00-$50.00
Fee to traveler: $15.00-$25.00

Areas covered: Marblehead, Swampscott, Salem, Danvers, Gloucester, Rockport, Newburg, Newburyport, also New Hampshire, Maine, Vermont, & Cape Cod.

Bed & Breakfast Marblehead & North Shore—Just 30 minutes north & northwest of Boston. Selected Colonials & Victorians in towns dating to the 1600's. Apartments for business travel, witch museums, whale watches, fascinating museums, bicycling, canoeing.

Brookline

Simonelli, Mrs. Lauren
Box 1142, 02146
(617) 277-5430

Amenities: 2,3,4,5,6

Dbl. Oc.: $42.00-$145.00
Sgl. Oc.: $35.00-$100.00

Areas covered: Boston, Charlestown, Dorchester, Brookline, Newton, Wellesley, Needham, Cambridge, Arlington, Danvers, Marblehead, Gloucester, Lexington, Concord and Lowell.

Greater Boston Hospitality offers a wide selection of affordable accommodations in comfortable and spacious homes, inns, condos; short term rentals, many near universities, hospitals, waterfront.

Boston (Waban Branch)

Whittington, Marcia
Box 117, 02168
(617) 244-1308

Amenities: 1,3,4,5,6

Dbl. Oc.: $45.00-$94.00
Sgl. Oc.: $40.00-$94.00

Areas covered: Boston, Cambridge, Brookline, Newton, Chestnut Hill, Needham, Wellesley, Framingham, Westwood, Bedford, Reading, Lexington, Marblehead, Quincy, Weymouth, Sandwich.

Host Homes Of Boston—Marcia has culled a variety of select private homes in excellent areas in and around Boston near colleges, museums and cultural life. 2 night minimum stay. Send for her free directory of the lovely homes.

Cambridge

Carruthers, Pamela
Box 665, 02140
(617) 576-1492

Amenities: 1,2,3,4,5,6

Dbl. Oc.: $52.00-$90.00
Sgl. Oc.: $39.00-$75.00

Areas covered: Boston, Cambridge, Lexington, Bedford, Concord, Greater Boston & Route 128 belt.

Bed & Breakfast Cambridge & Greater Boston/Minuteman Country—Welcoming homes; clean, comfortable rooms, good people and great places. Inspected regularly. Most on public transit. Call 9-6, M-F & 2-6, Sat. For the best in Bed & Breakfast, come home to us!

AMENITIES

1. American Express
2. Senior Citizen Rates Available
3. VISA
4. Personal Check Accepted
5. MasterCard
6. Brochure Available

Massachusetts

New Bedford

Mulford, Judy
47 N. Second, Ste. 3A, 02740
(617) 990-1696

Amenities: 1,3,4,5,6

Dbl. Oc.: $50.00-$165.00
Sgl. Oc.: $40.00-$95.00

Areas covered: Connecticut, Rhode Island, Massachusetts, New Hampshire, Maine, Vermont.

Pineapple Hospitality Bed & Breakfast Reservation Service—New England coverage. Stay in a cozy Cape, rustic farmhouse, summer cottage on the Maine coast, or whaling era mansion. Write for 150 descriptive listings or call M-F, 9-7.

Orleans

Griffin, Richard
Box 1881, 02653
(508) 896-7053

Amenities: 1,2,3,4,5,6

Dbl. Oc.: $40.00-$200.00
Sgl. Oc.: $32.00-$90.00
Fee to Traveler: $15.00

Areas covered: Everytown on Cape Cod, Nantucket & Martha's Vineyard!

B&B Accommodations House Guest Cape Cod And The Island—The charm & natural beauty of Cape Cod & the islands is expressed in our listings of 125 historic homes, estates & inns, some cottages & condos too! Every accommodation is inspected annually.

Plymouth

Gillis, Diane & Dave
Box 1333, 02360
(617) 837-9867

Amenities: 1,3,4,5,6

Dbl. Oc.: $45.00-$65.00
Sgl. Oc.: $32.00-$45.00

Areas covered: Plymouth, Boston, Cape Cod, Scituate, Hanover, Kingston, Duxbury.

Be Our Guest Bed & Breakfast, Ltd. is a personal reservation service offered to travelers. We offer the opportunity to be welcomed into local private homes in America's hometown of Plymouth.

Springfield

Hall, Barbara L.;
Carpenter, Mary Hill
Box 4616, 01101

Amenities: 6

Dbl. Oc.: $35.00-$150.00
Sgl. Oc.: $35.00-$150.00

Areas covered: Entire United States.

Bed & Breakfast/The National Network—Selected independent reservation services, "each rooted in the region it represents." Arranging customized accommodations in quality, inspected B&B homes & inns. Send S.A.S.E.

AMENITIES

1. American Express
2. Senior Citizen Rates Available
3. VISA
4. Personal Check Accepted
5. MasterCard
6. Brochure Available

Massachusetts

West Hyannisport

Diehl, Clark
Box 341, 02672
(508) 775-2772

Amenities: 1,3,4,5,6

Dbl. Oc.: $45.00-$195.00
Sgl. Oc.: $32.00-$55.00
Fee to traveler: 5.00

Areas covered: Cape Cod, Nantucket & Martha's Vineyard Islands, Cape Ann, Boston suburbs.

Bed & Breakfast Cape Cod—Historic country inns, sea captains houses or host homes await your holiday vacation. Deluxe or modest rates, pvt. or shared baths, some with water views, fireplaces, beaches. Choose from Cape Cod's best B&B's.

Michigan

Dearborn

Shields, Diane
Box 1731, 48121
(313) 561-6041

Amenities: 3,4,5,6

Dbl. Oc.: $35.00-$75.00
Sgl. Oc.: $35.00-$70.00

Areas covered: State of Michigan.

Betsey Ross Bed & Breakfast In Michigan—From metro Detroit to college towns to Michigan's beach and ski areas, a fine assortment of homes and small inns has been assembled for vacationers and business travelers. SASE for listing.

Mississippi

Meridian

Lincoln Hall, Barbara
Box 3479, 39303
(601) 482-5483

Amenities: 3,4,5,6

Dbl. Oc.: $45.00-$150.00
Sgl. Oc.: $45.00-$135.00

Areas covered: Mississippi, Natchez, Vicksburg, Meridian, Jackson, Port Gibson, Aberdeen, Greenville, Oxford, Indianola, Holly Springs, Brookhaven, Houston, Como, Corinth, Columbus, The MS Gulf coast.

Lincoln, Ltd. Bed & Breakfast Reservation Service—Elegant accommodations in selected historic inns & private homes. Experience pilgrimages, festivals, Civil Ear memoribilia, southern hospitality! Representing 40 inspected homes statewide. Come see us!

Natchez

Natchez Pilgrimage Tours
Canal at State St., 39120
(800) 647-6742

Amenities: 1,3,4,5,6

Dbl. Oc.: $60.00-$150.00
Sgl. Oc.: $60.00-$150.00

Areas covered: Natchez, MS area.

Natchez Pilgrimage Tours—Experinece true southern hospitality in one of our magnificent antebellum listings offering accommodations in main houses, servants' quarters and guest cottages. All furnished in period antiques.

AMENITIES

1. American Express
2. Senior Citizen Rates Available
3. VISA
4. Personal Check Accepted
5. MasterCard
6. Brochure Available

Missouri

Branson

Cameron, Kay
Box 295, 65616
(417) 334-4720

Amenities: 3,4,5,6

Dbl. Oc.: $30.00-$79.00
Sgl. Oc.: $25.00-$73.00

Areas covered: S.W. Missouri, N.W. Arkansas & N.E. Oklahoma.

Ozark Mountain Country Bed & Breakfast Service—Choose from 30+ carefully selected homes & inns where guests are specail! Our homes are in/near Branson, Springfield, Camdenton, Carthage, Marionville in MO, Eureka Springs, AK. Tulsa, OK. Ozark breakfast included.

Montana

Billings

Deigert, Paula
Box #20972
806 Poly Dr., 59102
(406) 259-7993

Amenities: 3,4,5,6

Dbl. Oc.: $29.00-$135.00
Sgl. Oc.: $25.00-$87.00
Fee to Traveler: $4.00-$6.00

Areas covered: Montana & Wyoming.

Bed & Breakfast Western Adventure—B&B's in Wyoming & Montana: homes, ranches, cabins, in cities, ski areas, mountains & on fishing rivers. For reservations call or write. Directory available.

New Jersey

Denville

Bergins, Alex
11 Sunset Trail, 07834
(201) 625-5129

Amenities: 4,6

Dbl. Oc.: $40.00-$66.00
Sgl. Oc.: $30.00-$66.00

Areas covered: Northern & Central New Jersey.

Northern New Jersey Bed & Breakfast provides accommodations in private homes & inns near urban centers and rural settings, several are on lakes. Lodgings for corporate personnel at reduced weekly rates.

Midland

Mould, Aster
103 Godwin Ave., S., 132, 07432
(201) 444-7409

Amenities: 1,2,3,4,5,6

Dbl. Oc.: $35.00-$135.00
Sgl. Oc.: $30.00-$65.00
Fee to traveler: $10.00
$15.00 on occasion.

Areas covered: State of New Jersey.

Bed & Breakfast Of New Jersey, Inc.—Interesting & unusual inspected accommodations throughout N.J., many certified. Mountain, seashore, country, Atlantic City, Cape May, urban & rural. Call for free brochure/information M-F, 9-3.

AMENITIES

1. American Express
2. Senior Citizen Rates Available
3. VISA
4. Personal Check Accepted
5. MasterCard
6. Brochure Available

New Jersey

Princeton

Hurley, John
Box 571, 08540
(609) 924-3189

Amenities:

Dbl. Oc.: $40.00-$65.00+
Sgl. Oc.: $30.00-$55.00+

Areas covered: Princeton, N.J.

Bed & Breakfast Of Princeton provides a pleasant alternative to local hotel lodging. These private homes are all within a few miles radius of the town center and university; some within walking distance.

New York

Buffalo

Brannan, Georgia
758 Richmond Ave., 14222
(716) 283-4794

Amenities:

Dbl. Oc.: $35.00-$65.00
Sgl. Oc.: $25.00-$45.00

Areas covered: Buffalo, Chautauqua, Lewiston, Niagara Falls, Olcott, Youngstown.

Rainbow Hospitality Bed & Breakfast Reservation Service—The scenic splendor of Niagara Falls, fishing & antiquing are just the beginning of the attractions in this area. The best part—the hosts who open their homes to extend the hand of friendship.

Frankfort

McCraith, Floranne
389 Brockway Rd., 13340
(315) 733-0040

Amenities: 2,3,4,5,6

Dbl. Oc.: $31.80-$74.20
Sgl. Oc.: $26.50-$47.20
Fee to Traveler: $3.00

Areas covered: Central New York State.

Bed & Break Leatherstocking provides complete reservation services, routing and travel assistance. Each B&B offers comfort, safety and hospitality to make your stay special with just one call.

New York City

Leifer, Ms. Shelli
Box 20022, 10028
(212) 472-2000

Amenities: 1,3,6

Dbl. Oc.: $50.00-$100.00
Sgl. Oc.: $45.00-$80.00

Areas covered: New York City & Brooklyn Heights, New York.

Abode Bed & Breakfast, Ltd.—Hosted B&B's & unhosted fully equipped apartments available at choice NYS locations; all personally inspected. From Soho Village to the upper East/West side. Apartments, townhouses & suites, all tastes & budgets.

AMENITIES

1. American Express
2. Senior Citizen Rates Available
3. VISA
4. Personal Check Accepted
5. MasterCard
6. Brochure Available

New York

New York City

Mensch, Ruth & Elyn
266 West 71st., 10023
(212) 580-4437

Amenities: 1,3,5,6

Dbl. Oc.: $90.00-$200.00
Sgl. Oc.: $65.00-$150.00

Areas covered: Manhattan, with special emphasis on the Lincoln Center area.

A Lincoln Center Bed & Breakfast—We strive to seek a unique blend of hosts/lodgings...from a sleek cont. high-rise apt. to a handsome Victorian townhouse. Hosts are required to maintain a very high level of hospitality. Hosted/unhosted.

New York

Salisbury, William
Box 200, 10108
(212) 246-4000

Amenities: 1

Dbl. Oc.: $50.00-$90.00
Sgl. Oc.: $45.00-$70.00

Areas covered: New York City, New York; London, England; Paris, France.

AAAH! Bed & Breakfast #1—New York City, London, Paris, hosted & unhosted reservations agency, in N.Y.C. Will make sure your accommodations make you feel warm & welcome. Beat big city prices. Book early!

New York City

Tilden, Ms. Laura
150 Fifth Ave., 10011
(212) 675-5600 or (800) 443-3800

Amenities: 1,3,4,5,6

Dbl. Oc.: $60.00-$90.00
Sgl. Oc.: $50.00-$70.00

Areas covered: (N.Y.C.).

New World B&B offers clean, safe and convenient guest accommodations in the homes of New Yorkers. Both tourist & business people appreciate saving half the cost of Manhattan hotel rates by using B&B.

Rochester

Kinsman, Beth
Box 444, Fairport, 14450
(716) 223-8877

Amenities: 4,6

Dbl. Oc.: $42.50-$80.00
Sgl. Oc.: $37.50-$48.00

Areas covered: FingerLakes & Lake Ontario.

Bed & Breakfast Rochester—Friendly host homes in city & suburbs, and lakeside locations in Finger Lakes. Easy access to museums, art galleries, colleges. Full breakfast included. Advanced reservations required. Brochure available.

AMENITIES

1. American Express
2. Senior Citizen Rates Available
3. VISA
4. Personal Check Accepted
5. MasterCard
6. Brochure Available

North Dakota

Regent

Prince, Mrs. Marlys　　**Amenities:**　　Dbl. Oc.: $25.00-$50.00
Box 211, 58650　　　　　　　　　　　　　Sgl. Oc.: $20.00-$40.00
(701) 563-4542

Areas covered: North Dakota.

Old West Bed & Breakfast, a new service listing about 13 B&B's offers a wide range of homes throughout the state.

Ohio

Cleveland

McCarroll, Ms. Jane　　**Amenities:** 4,6　　Dbl. Oc.: $85.00
Box 18590, 44118　　　　　　　　　　　　　Sgl. Oc.: $35.00
(216) 321-3213

Areas covered: Greater Cleveland area.

Private Lodgings, Inc.—Many unique and historic homes located close to Cleveland's cultural and business centers, as well as country and recreational areas. Daily, weekly and monthly stays. Houses and apts. also available.

Oregon

Ashland

Spalding, Sandy　　**Amenities:** 3,4,5　　Dbl. Oc.: $45.00-$150.00
Box 1376, 97520　　　　　　　　　　　　　Sgl. Oc.: $45.00-$150.00
(503) 488-0338

Areas covered: Northern California; Crescent City, Brookings, Yveka, Orland, Redding & Southern Oregon; Ashland, Medford, Jacksonville, Grants Pass.

Roomservice Reservations will find the perfect place for you & reserve it instantly for free! We've seen all the rooms & know what's available. Try us—you'll like us! Call 9-9 PST daily except Sunday.

Pennsylvania

Chester Springs (Philadelphia)

Mullen, Louise　　**Amenities:** 3,4,5,6　　Dbl. Oc.: $35.00-$120.00
Box 630, 19425　　　　　　　　　　　　　Sgl. Oc.: $30.00-$75.00
(215) 827-9650

Areas covered: City of Philadelphia; surrounding counties.

Bed & Breakfast Of Philadelphia—Pennsylvania's original bed and breakfast service with houses in: Center City historic areas, Valley Forge, New Hope & Brandywine Valley.

AMENITIES

1. American Express　　3. VISA　　5. MasterCard
2. Senior Citizen Rates Available　　4. Personal Check Accepted　　6. Brochure Available

Pennsylvania

Devon

Goodman, Ann, Gregg, Peggy   **Amenities:** 1,3,4,5,6   **Dbl. Oc.:** $37.10-$90.10
Box 21, 19333   **Sgl. Oc.:** $26.50-$90.10
(215) 687-3565   **Fee to Traveler:** $5.00

Areas covered: Philadelphia, Historic Center City, Main Line, Germantown, Valley Forge, & other suburbs.

Bed & Breakfast Connections—Gracious hosts welcome you to pre-Revolutionary Colonials, quaint 1800's townhouses & farmhouses, turn-of-the-century mansions & contemporary homes. Cont. gourmet breakfasts. Reservations: M-Sat., 9-9, Sun. noon-9.

Hershey

Deutel, Renee   **Amenities:** 3,4,5,6   **Dbl. Oc.:** $42.50-$95.40
Box 208, 17033   **Sgl. Oc.:** $31.80-$58.30
(717) 533-2928

Areas covered: Hershey, Middletown, Harrisburg, Hanover, Lebanon, Lancaster County (Southeastern PA).

Hershey Bed & Breakfast Reservation Service—Experience country living in a warm friendly atmosphere with easy access to many recreational facilities. Be it a private home; farm; country inn, our hosts are pleased to extend their hospitality.

Montville

Reno, Pat   **Amenities:** 3,5   **Dbl. Oc.:** $55.00-$75.00
407 East Main St.,   **Sgl. Oc.:** $45.00-$55.00
Box 19, 17554
(717) 285-7200

Areas covered: Lancaster county, Gettysburg, Harrisburg, Hershey, York & Reading.

Bed & Breakfast Of Lancaster County—Enjoy the flavor of true country living & old-fashioned hospitality. Comfortable lodgings in gracious homes, hospitable farms, & quaint inns. Hosts anxious to extend the warm hospitality of Pennsylvania Dutch country.

Valley Forge

Williams, Carolyn   **Amenities:** 1,2,3,4,5,6   **Dbl. Oc.:** $53.00-$90.10
Box 562, 19481-0562   **Sgl. Oc.:** $26.50-$74.20
(215) 783-7838

Areas covered: Philadelphia, the Main Line to West Chester, Valley Forge, King of Prussia north to Reading.

Bed & Breakfast Of Valley Forge—Vacationers, visitors, business travelers welcome. 200 locations near town, country, historic, ski, universities, horse shows, corporate centers, conventions. Call/write for nightly, weekly, monthly rates.

AMENITIES

1. American Express
2. Senior Citizen Rates Available
3. VISA
4. Personal Check Accepted
5. MasterCard
6. Brochure Available

Pennsylvania

West Chester

Archbold, Janice, K.
Box 2137, 19380
(215) 692-4575

Amenities: 1,3,4,5,6

Dbl. Oc.: $45.00-$200.00+
Sgl. Oc.: $40.00-$195.00+

Areas covered: Pennsylvania, Delaware, Maryland, New Jersey & the Chesapeake Bay.

Guesthouses—Specilaizing in historic private & public Landmark & National Register sites. Special packages are available from $198.000 per couple! 3 days/2 nights. Call Monday-Friday: 12-4 P.M. for reservations.

Rhode Island

Newport

Meiser, Joy
Box 3291, Bellevue, 02840
(401) 849-1298

Amenities: 1,3,4,5,6

Dbl. Oc.: $55.00-$135.00
Sgl. Oc.: $45.00-$125.00

Areas covered: State of RI; Mystic, CT; Seekonk, Attleboro, Rehoboth, MA.

Bed & Breakfast Of Rhode Island—We have personally inspected all the B&B's listed with our service to be sure they meet our high standards. We are happy to answer any questions or send our directory to you for $2.00

South Carolina

Charleston

Fairey, Charlotte
43 Legare St., 29401
(803) 722-6606

Amenities: 1,3,4,5,6

Dbl. Oc.: $50.00-$115.00
Sgl. Oc.: $50.00-$115.00

Areas covered: Charleston & Summerville.

Historic Charleston Bed & Breakfast—Historic homes & private carriage houses with lovely walled gardens, sitting rooms, fireplaces, stocked kitchens or served breakfasts are available within walking distance of historic sites, specialty shops & restaurants.

Charleston

Rogers, Eleanor
84 Murray Blvd., 29401
(803) 723-4948

Amenities: 4

Dbl. Oc.: $100.00
Sgl. Oc.: $60.00

Areas covered: Historic Charleston.

Charleston Society Bed And Breakfast—Lovely and charming accommodations in historic homes and carriage houses. All within walking distance of points of interest. Call for reservations.

AMENITIES

1. American Express
2. Senior Citizen Rates Available
3. VISA
4. Personal Check Accepted
5. MasterCard
6. Brochure Available

Tennessee

Memphis

Denton, Helen V.
Box 41621, 38174-1621
(901) 726-5920

Amenities: 3,4,5,6

Dbl. Oc.: $36.08-$62.01+
Sgl. Oc.: $29.32-$62.01+

Areas covered: Memphis, the mid-south, London, New York City, etc.

Bed & Breakfast In Memphis—European-style, private home. Also furnished apartments, condos & carriage houses for relocating corporate executives. Weekly and monthly rates available, S.A.S.E.

Texas

Dallas

Wilson, P. Ruth
4224 W. Red Bind Ln., 75237
(214) 298-8586

Amenities: 3,4,5,6

Dbl. Oc.: $40.00-$85.00
Sgl. Oc.: $30.00-$60.00

Areas covered: Texas.

Bed & Breakfast Texas Style—Lakeside getaways, romantic guesthouses, Victorian mansions, new condos are available for guests lodging pleasure. Stay at a ranch or farm. Reservations can be made by phone or mail. We're the best!

Houston

Thomas, Pat
8880-B2 Bellaire, #296,
77036-4900
(713) 771-3919

Amenities: 3,4,5,6

Dbl. Oc.: $96.90-$142.50
Sgl. Oc.: $28.50-$85.50

Areas covered: Texas.

Bed & Breakfast Society Of Texas—A true "Texas hospitality" with locations throughout Texas. Lovely private homes, cozy bungalows, townhomes, waterfront cottages and cabins, Victorian mansions & inns.

San Antonio

Campbell, Lavern
166 Rockhill, 78209
(512) 824-8036

Amenities: 3,4,5,6

Dbl. Oc.: $31.64-$94.10
Sgl. Oc.: $24.86-$86.00
Fee to Traveler: $7.50
per person per day

Areas covered: San Antonio, outlying areas.

Bed & Breakfast Hosts Of San Antonio—Unique private homes, guest houses, river and ranch cottages near the famous River Walk and historic King William district. Fantastic Terrell Castle, ideal for wedding receptions. Sea World locations. Latin charm!

AMENITIES

1. American Express
2. Senior Citizen Rates Available
3. VISA
4. Personal Check Accepted
5. MasterCard
6. Brochure Available

Vermont

East Fairfield

Zurn, Jane Torbert
Box 1, 05448
(802) 827-3827

Amenities: 3,4,5,6

Dbl. Oc.: $40.00-$150.00
Sgl. Oc.: $35.00-$90.00
Fee to Traveler: $15.00-$25.00

Areas covered: State of Vermont.

Vermont Bed & Breakfast Reservation Service—Locations throughout VT; from a houseboat on Lake Champlain to a log cabin on a mountain top; village Victorian to rural farmhouse. Come enjoy the state of mind that is Vermont.

St. Albans

Zurn, Jane Torbert
Box 983, 05478
(802) 827-3827

Amenities: 3,4,5,6

Dbl. Oc.: $40.00-$150.00
Sgl. Oc.: $30.00-$90.00
Fee to traveler: 15.00-$25.00

Areas covered: United States.

American Bed & Breakfast—Locations throughout the United States. Great variety. Convenient locations. Cheerful service. Save yourself the exasperating search process, we do it for you.

Virginia

Alexandria

Mansmann, Mr. E.J.
819 Prince St., 22314
(703) 683-2159

Amenities: 4

Dbl. Oc.: $73.15-$78.38

Areas covered: Alexandria, VA.

Princely Bed & Breakfast, Ltd.—Deluxe program, historic homes (1750-1830), many with museum-quality antiques. Closest area to Washington, D.C. New metro subway is fast, frequent, immaculate—15 minutes to D.C./Virginia history; easily travelled in 1 day.

Berryville

Duncan, Rita Mrs.
Rt. 2, Box 3895, 22611
(703) 955-1246

Amenities: 2,3,4,5,6

Dbl. Oc.: $40.00-$135.00
Sgl. Oc.: $35.00-$100.00

Areas covered: West VA, Pennsylvania, Maryland, Virginia.

Blue Ridge Bed & Breakfast—Reservation service in 4 states. Includes gracious homes, historic farms and quaint country inns. Facilities include hiking, biking, canoeing, fishing, horseback riding, swimming, outstanding cuisine & antiquing.

AMENITIES

1. American Express
2. Senior Citizen Rates Available
3. VISA
4. Personal Check Accepted
5. MasterCard
6. Brochure Available

Virginia

Charlottesville

Caperton, Mary Hill Mrs. **Amenities:** 1,3,4,5,6 **Dbl. Oc.:** $46.00-$150.00
Box 5737, 22905 **Sgl. Oc.:** $38.00-$80.00
(804) 979-7264 (weekdays 12-5 p.m.)

Areas covered: Charlottesville, Albermarle Co., & Luray, VA.

Guesthouses—Offering refined accommodations in private homes and guest cottages throughout historic Thomas Jefferson's country. Monticello, Ash Lawn, the University of Virginia. Adjacent to the Blue Ridge Mountains.

Norfolk

Willcox, Ms. Ashby & **Amenities:** 4,5 **Dbl. Oc.:** $35.00-$65.00
Hubbard, Ms. Susan **Sgl. Oc.:** $30.00-$50.00
Box 3343, 23514
(804) 627-1983

Areas covered: Eastern Virginia (coastal) including Norfolk, Virginia Beach, the Eastern shore, Northern Neck & Mathews County.

Bed & Breakfast Of Tidewater Virginia—A variety of homes located in colorful Ghent in Norfolk, in the beautiful restored area of Virginia Beach on the Atlantic Ocean, and on the picturesque Eastern shore overlooking the Chesapeake Bay.

Richmond

Benson, Lyn **Amenities:** 1,3,4,5,6 **Dbl. Oc.:** $55.00-$125.00
2036 Monument Ave., 23220 **Sgl. Oc.:** $48.00-$105.00
(804) 648-7560

Areas covered: Fredericksburg, The Northern Neck, Orange, Petersburg, Richmond, Williamsburg.

Benson House Of Richmond And Williamsburg—Lovely homes & inns are represented; many are in historic districts and include a 1750 house used as a Civil War hospital; an 1870 Victorian near Richmond and a reproduction of a 17th century tavern in Williamsburg.

Woodstock

Kollar, Patricia **Amenities:** 3,4,5,6 **Dbl. Oc.:** $40.00-$110.00
Lee Rt. 1, Box 217A1, 22664 **Sgl. Oc.:** $35.00-$60.00
(703) 459-8241 **Fee:** Deposit-1/4 rate of visit

Areas covered: Stephens City, Front Royal, Woodstock, Maurestown, New Market, Harrisburg, McGaheysville, Rawley Springs, Staunton, Roanoake, Dublin & Luray.

Shenandoah Valley Bed & Breakfast Reservation—Our inns/residences offer exclusive cultural experiences and variety. Historic homes, mansions, and farms, cozy cabins and lodges all offer the traveler the comforts of home in an exciting place.

AMENITIES

1. American Express
2. Senior Citizen Rates Available
3. VISA
4. Personal Check Accepted
5. MasterCard
6. Brochure Available

Wisconsin

Milwaukee

Gardner, Barbara
320 E. Buffalo St., 53202
(414) 271-2337

Amenities: 3,4,5,6

Dbl. Oc.: $35.00-$100.00
Sgl. Oc.: $30.00-$75.00

Areas covered: Milwaukee metro area.

Bed & Breakfast Of Milaukee, Inc.—A free reservation service for Milwaukee area private homes. Modest to luxurious accommodations. City, suburban, or country settings. Annual inspections assure cleanliness, comfort and congenial hosts.

British Columbia

Burnaby

McCurrach, Norma
4390 Frances St., V5C 2R3
(604) 298-8815

Amenities: 1,2,3,5,6

Dbl. Oc.: $45.00-$60.00
Sgl. Oc.: $30.00-$40.00

Areas covered: Vancouver, Victoria & other areas in B.C.

A B C Bed & Breakfast—Clean comfortable homes from modest to luxurious. Meet the friendly British Columbians in our super natural province. Tours & car rentals can be arranged. member of West Coast Bed & Breakfast Assoc.

North Vancouver

Massey, Mrs. Ellison
Box 86607, V7L 4L2
(604) 987-9338

Amenities: 3,4,5,6

Dbl. Oc.: $50.00-$60.00 (Can.)
Sgl. Oc.: $40.00 (Can.)

Areas covered: British Columbia: Vancouver, Victoria, Kelowna, Quesnel.

Canada-West Accommodations B&B Registry—Quality homes. Friendly host families welcome you to British Columbia. Vancouver (604) 987-9338, Victoria 388-4620, Kelowna 769-4028, Quesnel 747-2020. Full breakfast. Efficient reservation system.

North Vancouver

Tyndall, Vicki
Box 86818, V7L 4L3
(604) 986-5069

Amenities: 3,4,5,6

Dbl. Oc.: $50.00-$60.00 (Can.)
Sgl. Oc.: $35.00-$45.00 (Can.)

Areas covered: Vancouver, North Vancouver, West Vancouver, & Victoria on Vancouver Island.

Old English Bed & Breakfast Registry—At Old English we are dedicated to the traditional values of traveler accommodation. Our guest homes provide a friendly, hospitable environment plus valued knowledge about the area you will be visiting.

AMENITIES

1. American Express
2. Senior Citizen Rates Available
3. VISA
4. Personal Check Accepted
5. MasterCard
6. Brochure Available

Canada

Vancouver

Burich, Helen
1733 Waterloo St., V6R 4G6
(604) 731-5942

Amenities: 4,6

Dbl. Oc.: $45.00-$150.00
Sgl. Oc.: $35.00-$45.00

Areas covered: Most area of British Columbia. Most areas in Vancouver & Victoria.

Town & Country Bed & Breakfast In B.C.—We offer varied and select accommodations in over 180 homes throughout B.C., including Vancouver & Victoria. Also some guest houses and "special places." We have been established since 1980.

Victoria

Gordon, Pat
Box 421, Station "E", V8W 2N8
(604) 385-1962

Amenities: 3,5

Dbl. Oc.: $50.00-$90.00 (Can.)
Sgl. Oc.: $30.00-$40.00 (Can.)

Areas covered: Victoria, Vancouver Island, Vancouver.

City & Sea B&B Homes Agency—A group of homes offering queen size and twin accommodations, some with ensuite or private bath; most on or near seafront & city center. All inspected by tourism Victoria. Some self contained suites.

Victoria

Vesey, Maureen
Box 5511, Ste. B., V8R 5A9
(604) 595-2337

Amenities: 3,4,5,6

Dbl. Oc.: $50.00-$150.00 (Can.)
Sgl. Oc.: $40.00-$75.00 (Can.)
Fee to Traveler: $12.00 (Can.)

Areas covered: Victoria, Vancouver Island, & the Gulf Islands.

All Season Bed And Breakfast Agency—Come and stay in our island paradise. B&B in homes, inns, farms, cottages and suites. Come for fishing, skiing, sailing or sightseeing. In All The Best of Bed & Breakfast Guide—$4.95 U.S., $5.95 CDN. Free brochure. Come on.

Victoria

Wensley, M. Doreen
660 Jones Terrace, V8Z 2L7
(604) 479-9999

Amenities: 1,3,5,6

Dbl. Oc.: $35.00-$125.00
Sgl. Oc.: $25.00-$45.00

Areas covered: Victoria, Vancouver Island, Gulf Islands.

Garden City Bed & Breakfast Reservation Service—A complete reservation service for Victoria, Vancouver Island and the Gulf Islands. A home for every taste and requirement. Together we can plan an exciting itinerary for a holiday you won't forget.

AMENITIES

1. American Express
2. Senior Citizen Rates Available
3. VISA
4. Personal Check Accepted
5. MasterCard
6. Brochure Available

Manitoba

Winnipeg

Loewen, Len
93 Healy Cres., R2N 2S2
(204) 256-6151

Amenities: 6

Dbl. Oc.: $28.00-$40.00
Sgl. Oc.: $22.00-$30.00

Areas covered: Manitoba

B&B Of Manitoba—Come and enjoy Manitoba hosts—experience multi-culturalism at its best! We have homes ranging from Victorian style to contemporary. Join us for events like Folklorama, folk music festival, etc.

Ontario

Lakefield

Wilkins, Mrs. Wallace
R.R. #3, K0L 2H0
(705) 652-6290

Amenities: 4,6

Dbl. Oc.: $40.00-$50.00
Sgl. Oc.: $29.00-$36.00

Areas covered: Peterborough, Lakefield, Buckhorn, Bridgenworth, Norwood.

Bed & Breakfast Registry Of Peterborough Area—You choose your style of accommodation—a period home in the country, a modern lakeside bungalow or a restful home on a quiet street in town. All offer homestyle comfort and a full breakfast.

Niagara Falls

Wetherup, Monique
2631 Dorchester Rd., L2J 2Y9
(416) 358-8988

Amenities: 1,3,5,6

Dbl. Oc.: $50.00-$75.00
Sgl. Oc.: $45.00-$75.00

Areas covered: Niagara Peninsula, Niagara Falls, Welland, St. Catherines, Niagara-on-the-Lake.

Niagara Region Bed & Breakfast Service—A selection of private homes throughout the area: some within walking distance to the falls or the Shaw Theatre; others are in the country on fruit farms.

Ottawa

Rivoire, Robert
Box 4848, St. E, K1S 5J1
(613) 563-0161

Amenities: 4,6

Dbl. Oc.: $40.00-$44.00 (Can.)
Sgl. Oc.: $30.00-$34.00 (Can.)

Areas covered: Ottawa, Ontario, Hull, Quebec.

Ottawa Area Bed & Breakfast—Welcome to friendly affordable accommodations in Canada's capital. Our hosts are residents of Ottawa who are anxious to meet you, show you their homes and provide you with much advice about our city.

AMENITIES

1. American Express
2. Senior Citizen Rates Available
3. VISA
4. Personal Check Accepted
5. MasterCard
6. Brochure Available

Ontario

Port Credit

Ricciuto, William
31 Lake Shore Rd., E.,
Box 353, L5G 4L8
(416) 363-6362

Amenities: 1,3,5,6

Dbl. Oc.: $40.00-$60.00
Sgl. Oc.: $35.00-$40.00

Areas covered: Toronto.

B&B Homes Of Toronto—20 comfortable carefully selected independent homes from nearby countryside to the very heart of cosmopolitan Toronto. Friendly informed hosts & hostesses, interesting guests from all over the world.

St. Catherine

Worth, M/M Murray
489 Carlton St., L2M 4W9
(416) 937-2422

Amenities: 1,2,3,6

Dbl. Oc.: $35.00
Sgl. Oc.: $30.00

Areas covered: St. Catherines, Lincoln, Jordan, Vineland, Grimsby, Niagara-on-the-Lake.

St. Catherine Bed & Breakfast Association offers quality lodging in private homes & inns throughout the city & vicinity. Located in the heart of wine country, 10 min. from Niagara Falls. Our Garden city offers variety & hospitality for everyone.

Toronto

Friedrichkeit, Burke
253 College St.
Box 269, M5T 1R5
(416) 961-3676

Amenities: 3,5,6

Dbl. Oc.: $55.00-$85.00
Sgl. Oc.: $45.00-$85.00

Areas covered: Toronto.

Toronto Bed & Breakfast (1987) Inc.—A professional reservation for quality B&B accommodations throughout metropolitan Toronto. Brochure on request; advance reservations recommended. Hours: Mon.-Fri., 9-6.

Toronto

Oppenheim, Susan
153 Huron St., M5T 2B6
(416) 598-4562

Amenities: 4,6

Dbl. Oc.: $50.00-$65.00 (Can.)
Sgl. Oc.: $40.00-$50.00 (Can.)

Areas covered: Centre North Toronto.

Downtown Tour Group of B&B Guest Houses—9th year of operation, an alternative company. Non-smokers, special diets, interesting hosts in refurbished Victorian houses. Singers, actors, sculptors, writers; full and gourmet breakfasts. Free brochure. Phone 9-2 daily.

AMENITIES

1. American Express
2. Senior Citizen Rates Available
3. VISA
4. Personal Check Accepted
5. MasterCard
6. Brochure Available

Ontario

Welland

Donohue, Rita
102 Aqueduct St., L3C 1C1
(416) 788-9054

Amenities: 3,5,6

Dbl. Oc.: $40.00
Sgl. Oc.: $30.00

Areas covered: Welland, Port Colborne, Fonthill, Fenwick, Wainfleet.

Rose City Bed & Breakfast Association offers a variety of accommodations in friendly pleasant well situated homes along the Welland Ship Canal between Lakes Ontario & Erie. A home away from home among the roses & waterways.

Quebec

Montreal

Finkelstein, Bob
3458 Laval Ave., H2X 3C8
(514) 289-9749

Amenities: 1,3,4,5

Dbl. Oc.: $35.00-$50.00
Sgl. Oc.: $25.00-$40.00

Areas covered: Montreal, Westmount, Outremount & Quebec City.

Downtown Bed And Breakfast Network—We are a network of fine private homes in the downtown core. We offer a complete breakfast at prices you can well afford. "One of Canada's oldest bed and breakfast." Brochure available just phone or write.

Montreal

Kahn, Marian
4912 Victoria Ave., H3W 2N1
(514) 738-9410

Amenities: 1,3,5,6

Dbl. Oc.: $45.00-$75.00 (Can.)
Sgl. Oc.: $30.00-$45.00 (Can.)

Areas covered: Montreal, Westmount & Outremont; Laurentian Mountains resort area.

Bed & Breakfast Montreal—Since 1980. Montreal's original B&B network has received rave reviews from guests for its top quality homes and hosts. Downtown locations and nearby. Accurate rates shown. Gray Line discounts for guests.

AMENITIES

1. American Express
2. Senior Citizen Rates Available
3. VISA
4. Personal Check Accepted
5. MasterCard
6. Brochure Available

THE NATIONAL BED & BREAKFAST GUIDE • (Comments)

Help us serve you better!
Aidez-nous à vous mieux servir!
¡Ayúdennos servirles mejor!

Name of B. & B. _____
Address _____

_____

I found this B. & B. to be	Excellent _____	Good _____	Poor _____
J'ai trouvé cette pension	Excellente _____	Bonne _____	Mauvaise _____
Encontré esta pensión	Excelente _____	Bueno _____	Malo _____

Signature _____
Address _____

_____

Comments _____
Remarques _____
Comentos _____

THE NATIONAL BED & BREAKFAST GUIDE • (Comments)

Help us serve you better!
Aidez-nous à vous mieux servir!
¡Ayúdennos servirles mejor!

Name of B. & B. _____
Address _____

_____

I found this B. & B. to be	Excellent _____	Good _____	Poor _____
J'ai trouvé cette pension	Excellente _____	Bonne _____	Mauvaise _____
Encontré esta pensión	Excelente _____	Bueno _____	Malo _____

Signature _____
Address _____

_____

Comments _____
Remarques _____
Comentos _____

NATIONAL B. & B. ASSOCIATION
P.O. Box 332
Norwalk, CT 06852

NATIONAL B. & B. ASSOCIATION
P.O. Box 332
Norwalk, CT 06852

MEMBERSHIP CARD

Please send me at the address below, an application for membership in The National Bed & Breakfast Assoc. which will entitle me to a listing in your Bed & Breakfast Guide for the U.S. & Canada.

_____

_____

_____

_____ Zip Code

Thank you,
Phyllis Featherston, President
Barbara F. Ostler, Vice President

MEMBERSHIP CARD

Please send me at the address below, an application for membership in The National Bed & Breakfast Assoc. which will entitle me to a listing in your Bed & Breakfast Guide for the U.S. & Canada.

_____

_____

_____

_____ Zip Code

Thank you,
Phyllis Featherston, President
Barbara F. Ostler, Vice President

NATIONAL B. & B. ASSOCIATION
P.O. Box 332
Norwalk, CT 06852

NATIONAL B. & B. ASSOCIATION
P.O. Box 332
Norwalk, CT 06852

Traveler's Notes

Traveler's Notes

Traveler's Notes

Traveler's Notes

Traveler's Notes

Traveler's Notes